Drugs, Society, and Behavior

Twenty-Third Edition

08/09

EDITOR

Hugh T. Wilson

California State University—Sacramento

Professor Hugh Wilson received his Bachelor of Arts degree from California State University, Sacramento, and a Master of Arts degree in Justice Administration and a Doctorate in Public Administration from Golden Gate University in San Francisco. Dr. Wilson is currently a Professor within the Criminal Justice Division at California State University, Sacramento, one of the largest such programs in the United States. He has taught drug abuse recognition, enforcement, and policy to students, educators, and police officers for 30 years. Dr. Wilson interacts regularly with primary and secondary educators in the interests of drug-related youth at risk. His primary professional and academic interest lies in the study and reduction of Fetal Alcohol Syndrome within Native American populations.

 **Higher Education**

Boston   Burr Ridge, IL   Dubuque, IA   New York   San Francisco   St. Louis
Bangkok   Bogotá   Caracas   Kuala Lumpur   Lisbon   London   Madrid   Mexico City
Milan   Montreal   New Delhi   Santiago   Seoul   Singapore   Sydney   Taipei   Toronto

ANNUAL EDITIONS: DRUGS, SOCIETY, AND BEHAVIOR, TWENTY-THIRD EDITION

1 2 3 4 5 6 7 8 9 0 QPD/QPD 0 9 8

ISBN 978–0–07–339773–3
MHID 0–07–339773–3
ISSN 1091–9945

Managing Editor: *Larry Loeppke*
Senior Managing Editor: *Faye Schilling*
Developmental Editor: *Dave Welsh*
Editorial Assistant: *Nancy Meissner*
Production Service Assistant: *Rita Hingtgen*
Permissions Coordinator: *Lenny Behnke*
Senior Marketing Manager: *Julie Keck*
Marketing Communications Specialist: *Mary Klein*
Marketing Coordinator: *Alice Link*
Project Manager: *Sandy Wille*
Design Specialist: *Tara McDermott*
Senior Administrative Assistant: *DeAnna Dausener*
Senior Production Supervisor: *Laura Fuller*
Cover Graphics: *Kristine Jubeck*

Compositor: Laserwords Private Limited
Cover Images: Brand X Pictures and Lawrence Lawry/Getty Images

Library in Congress Cataloging-in-Publication Data
Main entry under title: Annual Editions: Drugs, Society, and Behavior 2008/2009
1. Drugs, Society, and Behavior—Periodicals. I. Wilson, Hugh, *comp.* II. Title: Drugs, Society, and Behavior.
658'.05

www.mhhe.com

Editors/Advisory Board

Members of the Advisory Board are instrumental in the final selection of articles for each edition of ANNUAL EDITIONS. Their review of articles for content, level, currentness, and appropriateness provides critical direction to the editor and staff. We think that you will find their careful consideration well reflected in this volume.

EDITOR

Hugh T. Wilson
California State University—Sacramento

ADVISORY BOARD

Preface

In publishing ANNUAL EDITIONS we recognize the enormous role played by the magazines, newspapers, and journals of the public press in providing current, first-rate educational information in a broad spectrum of interest areas. Many of these articles are appropriate for students, researchers, and professionals seeking accurate, current material to help bridge the gap between principles and theories and the real world. These articles, however, become more useful for study when those of lasting value are carefully collected, organized, indexed, and reproduced in a low-cost format, which provides easy and permanent access when the material is needed. That is the role played by ANNUAL EDITIONS.

It is difficult to define the framework by which Americans make decisions and develop perspectives on the use of drugs. There is no predictable expression of ideology. A wide range of individual and collective experience defines our national will toward drugs.

Despite drug prevention efforts, millions of Americans use illegal drugs on a monthly basis and over 22 million are estimated to need drug treatment. Social costs from drugs are measured in the billions. Drugs impact almost every aspect of public and private life. Drugs are the subjects of presidential elections, congressional appointments, and military interventions. Financial transactions from smuggling help sustain terrorist organizations. Drugs impact families, schools, health care systems, and governments in more places and in more ways than many believe imaginable.

Although it takes little effort to expose social costs manifested by the abuse of drugs, there are tiny victories through which harm from drug abuse can be reduced. Scientific discovery relative to creating a new understanding of the processes of addiction is one. New treatment modalities, the successful use of drug courts and the political support to expand these concepts has reduced drug-related impacts. **In 2008 the federal government refunded a $98 million grant to states and local communities** for the Access to Recovery program which assists individuals and provides them options in obtaining treatment and recovery services. Although good evidence suggests that many of the most egregious forms of drug abuse have leveled off or been reduced, other disturbing trends, such as the non-medical use of prescription drugs and the manufacture, abuse, and trafficking of methamphetamine are worsening. Drug abuse is a multifaceted problem requiring a multifaceted response. Complacency, encouraged by positive trends, has finally been recognized as a fatal mistake.

The articles contained in *Annual Editions: Drugs, Society, and Behavior 08/09* are a collection of facts, issues, and perspectives designed to provide the reader with a framework for examining current drug-related issues. The book is designed to offer students something to think about and something with which to think. It is a unique collection of materials of interest to the casual as well as the serious student of drug-related social phenomena. Unit 1 addresses the significance that drugs have in affecting diverse aspects of American life. It emphasizes the often-overlooked reality that drugs—legal and illegal—have remained a pervasive dimension of past as well as present American history. The unit begins with an emphasis on the continuing ways that so many lives are affected by illegal drugs, crime, and violence and continues through diverse discussions about drugs and ordinary life. Unit 2 examines the ways that drugs affect the mind and body that result in dependence and addiction. Unit 3 examines the major drugs of use and abuse, along with issues relative to understanding the individual impacts of these drugs on society. It addresses the impacts produced by the use of legal and illegal drugs and emphasizes the alarming nature of widespread methamphetamine abuse and prescription drug abuse. Unit 4 reviews the dynamic nature of drugs as it relates to changing patterns and trends of use. **It gives special attention this year to drug trends among youth, particularly those related to prescription drug abuse.** Unit 5 focuses on the social costs of drug abuse and why the costs overwhelm many American institutions. **Significant emphasis is given to Fetal Alcohol Syndrome. Unit 6 illustrates the complexity in creating and implementing drug policy, such as that associated with providing legalized injection sites for addicts, and addressing the needs of children displaced by methamphetamine abuse.** Unit 7 concludes the book with discussions of current strategies for preventing and treating drug abuse. Can we deter people from harming themselves with drugs, and can we cure people addicted to drugs? What does work and what does not? Special attention is given to programs that address at-risk youth and programs that reduce criminal offender rehabilitation and recidivism.

Annual Editions: Drugs, Society, and Behavior 08/09 contains a number of features that are designed to make the volume "user friendly." These include a *table of contents* with abstracts that summarize each article and key concepts in boldface, a *topic guide* to help locate articles on specific individuals or subjects, *Internet References* that can be used to further explore the topics, and a comprehensive *Index*.

We encourage your comments and criticisms on the articles provided and kindly ask for your review on the postage-paid rating form at the end of the book.

Hugh T. Wilson

Hugh T. Wilson
Editor

Contents

Preface   *iv*

Topic Guide   *xiii*

Internet References   *xv*

UNIT 1
Living with Drugs

Unit Overview   xviii

1. **Over the Limit,** Nancy Shute, *U.S. News & World Report,* April 23, 2007
   From triple-shot lattes to Red Bull to Ritalin, Americans are more wired than ever. ***Here's why it may be harmful to your health.***   **3**

2. **Smoking, Drugs, Obesity Top Health Concerns for Kids,** *Medical News Today,* May 6, 2007
   Concern about kids' health, on the roads, at school, and even on line is a given. This article discusses ***some of today's biggest worries*** relative to kids and drugs.   **7**

3. **Living the High Life,** Karenza Moore and Steven Miles, *Drugs and Alcohol Today,* August 2005
   The vast majority of ***young drug users*** see drug use as a positive experience. Read this article and discover the views the authors hold regarding the social roles of drug use.   **9**

4. **Methamphetamine Abuse: A Perfect Storm of Complications,** Timothy W. Lineberry and J. Michael Bostwick, *Mayo Clinic Proceedings,* January 2006
   In this article, physicians Lineberry and Bostwick provide a detailed summation of the ***medical impacts of methamphetamine*** use across America.   **13**

5. **HIV Apathy,** Zach Patton, *Governing,* February 2007
   New drugs have changed HIV from a terminal to a chronic illness. To counter complacency, health officials ***are pushing to make testing more widespread.***   **22**

6. **Not Invented Here,** Tinker Ready, *Fast Company,* April 2007
   Drug companies must aggressively compete for ***the best and the brightest scientists to*** pioneer new drug discoveries. This article provides an inside look into the billion dollar industry of pharmaceutical recruiting.   **25**

7. **Did Prohibition Really Work?** Jack S. Blocker, Jr., *American Journal of Public Health,* February 2006
   This article discusses the ***legacies of Prohibition*** from diverse historical perspectives. Is failure the correct word to associate with this complex social process?   **27**

8. **Vice Vaccines,** Christen Brownlee, *Science News,* February 10, 2007
   How scientists give a shot in the arm to the fight against smoking, drug abuse, and obesity.   **36**

9. **Pass the Weed, Dad,** Marni Jackson, *Maclean's,* November 7, 2005
   Parents smoking dope with their kids—what are they thinking? Marni Jackson discusses the reality of children whose parents used marijuana and the effects this has on them.   **39**

The concepts in bold italics are developed in the article. For further expansion, please refer to the Topic Guide.

UNIT 2
Understanding How Drugs Work—Use, Dependency, and Addiction

Unit Overview   **44**

10. **Reducing the Risk of Addiction to Prescribed Medications,** Brian
    Johnson et al., *Psychiatric Times,* April 15, 2007
    Mistreating pain, particularly that complicated by insomnia, anxiety, and stress can
    lead to drug addiction. This article discusses the detailed considerations for ***treating
    a patient's pain*** and reducing the risk of addiction.   **47**

11. **Predicting Addiction,** Lisa N. Legrand, William G. Iacono, and Matt
    McGue, *American Scientist,* March-April 2005
    The science of behavioral genetics has used twins and time to decipher the ***origins of
    addiction*** to help learn who is most vulnerable. Some markers of risk are analyzed.   **51**

12. **Better Ways to Target Pain,** Gary Stix, *Scientific American,*
    January 2007
    Improved understanding of the chemical pathway on which drugs like aspirin and vioxx
    work may lead to the development of ***pain killing drugs with fewer side effects.***   **56**

13. **The Effects of Alcohol on Physiological Processes and Biological
    Development,** *Alcohol Research and Health,* vol. 28, no. 3, 2004/2005
    This article summarizes the physiological ***effects of alcohol on adolescents.*** To what
    degree is early drinking related to biological changes that influence one's later liability
    for addiction?   **58**

14. **A Small Part of the Brain, and Its Profound Effects,** Sandra Blakeslee,
    The New York Times, February 6, 2007
    In a startling discovery, some people who had sustained injury to a small portion of the
    brain were able to give up smoking instantly. According to neuroscientists, the insula
    is a long over-looked region of the brain that may prove critical to ***understanding the
    chemistry of addiction.***   **65**

15. **The Changing Science of Pain,** Mary Carmichael, *Newsweek,*
    June 4, 2007
    Millions of aging Boomers and the latest generation of wounded soldiers hope that the
    secrets of the ***most enduring human foe can be unlocked.*** What are the implications
    of this new science for understanding addiction?   **67**

16. **The Toxicity of Recreational Drugs,** Robert S. Gable, *American Scientist,*
    May/June 2006
    "***All things are poisons,*** for there is nothing without poisonous qualities. It is only the
    dose which makes a thing a poison." Paracelsus (1493–1541). To what degree does
    a scientific understanding of a drug's pharmacology influence a person's decision to
    use it?   **71**

17. **Stress and Drug Abuse,** *Science World,* March 12, 2007
    How your mind and your body respond to stress is believed to be one of the impor-
    tant influences on becoming addicted to drugs. This article briefly discusses some of the
    latest research, and provides some advice about handling stress.   **74**

The concepts in bold italics are developed in the article. For further expansion, please refer to the Topic Guide.

18. **Does Cannabis Cause Psychosis or Schizophrenia?,** *Drugs and Alcohol Today,* August 2005

While most agree that there are links between **cannabis use and psychosis and cannabis use and schizophrenia,** the verdict is not in. This article discusses some recent findings.   **76**

UNIT 3
The Major Drugs of Use and Abuse

Unit Overview   **78**

19. **Methamphetamine Abuse,** Teena McGuinness, *American Journal of Nursing,* December 2006

Meth, Speed, Crank, Biker Dope, Hillbilly Crack: No matter what you call it, there is no question that methamphetamine has changed the nature of drug use in America.   **81**

20. **Mexico Drug Cartels Reap Big Profits from Meth,** Laurence Iliff, *Knight Ridder/Tribune News Service,* April 29, 2007

The FBI says that Mexican drug cartels are responsible for producing over 80 percent of the methamphetamine consumed in the United States. While Mexican authorities argue with American law enforcement agents about who's mostly responsible for production, a steady pipeline of drugs continues to flow north.   **87**

21. **The Taliban's Opium War,** Jon Lee Anderson, *The New Yorker,* July 9 & 16, 2007

As the Taliban continues to reap financial support from some of the most aggressive opium producing regions in the world, **U.S. officials express frustration** at the complexities of eradicating a target in plain sight.   **89**

22. **The Opposite Result,** Karen DeYoung, *The Washington Post National Weekly Edition,* December 11–17, 2006

In spite of U.S. efforts to eradicate Afghanistan's opium fields, a bumper crop pours through. According to CIA Director, Michael Hayden, "It's almost the devil's own problem."   **98**

23. **The Teen Drinking Dilemma,** Barbara Kantrowitz and Anne Underwood, *Newsweek,* June 25, 2007

While some parents let their kids drink alcohol at home, others argue that it simply sets the stage for **perpetuating a culture of alcohol abuse.**   **100**

24. **An Update on the Effects of Marijuana and Its Potential Medical Use,** Sherwood O. Cole, *Forensic Examiner,* Fall 2005

While the public continues to be bombarded with information about **the effects and usefulness of marijuana,** author Sherman Cole attempts to clarify some of the reasons fueling these debates.   **102**

UNIT 4
Other Trends in Drug Use

Unit Overview   **110**

25. **Fentanyl-Laced Street Drugs "Kill Hundreds",** David Boddiger, *The Lancet,* August 12, 2006

With street names such as Drop-Dead, Flatline, and Lethal Injection, **Fentanyl-laced heroin and cocaine** are pushed by dealers as the ultimate high. This article discusses how hundreds have been killed by the new mix.   **113**

The concepts in bold italics are developed in the article. For further expansion, please refer to the Topic Guide.

26. **A Nation Without Drunk Driving,** Janet Dewey-Kollen, *Law & Order,*
April 2007

Rather than continuing to allow bad decisions made by people with alcohol-soaked brains to **cause almost 40% of all U.S. traffic fatalities,** representatives from MADD discuss the use of technology to eliminate driving under the influence.　　　**115**

27. **Some Cold Medicines Move Behind the Counter,** Linda Bren, *FDA
Consumer,* July/August 2006

Some **over-the-counter** cold and allergy medicines are being locked up as pharmacies nationwide are asked to join the fight against illegal drug production.　　　**117**

28. **Drug Addiction,** Ezekiel J. Emanuel, *The New Republic,* July 3, 2006

The relationship between toxic drugs and cancer is inextricable and often painful. This article discusses some of the difficult dilemmas faced by doctors, cancer victims, and families.　　　**119**

29. **The Right to a Trial,** Jerome Groopman, *The New Yorker,*
December 18, 2006

In a companion article, author Jerome Groopman presents the **complications of using experimental drugs to save lives.**　　　**122**

30. **New Study Shows 1.8 Million Youth Use Inhalants,** Teddi Dineley
Johnson, *The Nation's Health,* May 2006

While overall drug use among young people has gone down the last four years, rates of **children abusing inhalants** rose sharply. The reasons for this are discussed.　　　**128**

31. **Teens and Prescription Drugs,** *Office of the National Drug Control Policy,
Executive Office of the President,* February 2007

Among young people, prescription drugs have become the second most abused illegal drug. This publication provides some of the most recent survey data to describe this **significant new drug trend.**　　　**130**

32. **Studies Identify Factors Surrounding Rise in Abuse of Prescription
Drugs by College Students,** Lori Whitten, *National Institute on Drug
Abuse,* March 2006

This study's findings suggest that students enrolled in the most selective colleges have high levels of past-year **stimulant abuse.** What variables are contributing to this trend?　　　**135**

UNIT 5
Measuring the Social Costs of Drugs

Unit Overview　　　**138**

33. **The Role of Substance Abuse in U.S. Juvenile Justice Systems and
Populations,** Heather Horowitz, Hung-En Sung, and Susan E. Foster,
Corrections Compendium, January/February 2006

Nearly 89 percent of juvenile arrests involve children and teens who are under the influence of drugs and/or alcohol. This article includes some discussion of the variables that influence this.　　　**141**

34. **Sobering Thoughts,** Doreen Major Ryan, Doreen M. Bonnett, and Callie
B. Gass, *American Journal of Public Health,* December 2006

In an attempt to refuel public awareness of this dangerous condition, one organization outlines an agenda for **reducing the number of children born with FASD.**　　　**148**

The concepts in bold italics are developed in the article. For further expansion, please refer to the Topic Guide.

35. **Students with Fetal Alcohol Syndrome,** Darcy Miller, *Teaching Exceptional Children,* March/April 2006

In this third article about fetal alcohol syndrome, author Darcy Miller provides a guide for educators to update knowledge and improve school programs that must address the host of issues **expressed by children who suffer from FASD.** 153

36. **Keep Your Older Patients Out of Medication Trouble,** Sherrill A. Shepler, Tracy A. Grogan, and Karen Steinmetz Pater, *Nursing,* 2006, Volume 36, Number 9

This article discusses why aging puts people at **greater risk for adverse drug reactions** and what clinicians can do to lessen that risk. 160

37. **My Spirit Lives,** Roxanne Chinook, *Social Justice,* Vol. 31, No. 4, 2004

This personal narrative reflects the reality of life for many contemporary Native American women: **violence, addiction, and fear.** 164

38. **The Problem With Drinking,** Cheryl Harris Sharman, *Perspectives in Health,* vol. 10, no. 1, 2005

The **abuse of alcohol is an international issue.** The wider problem of alcohol in the Americas is discussed in this article. Is this a good example of a world-wide epidemic of alcohol abuse? 170

39. **High on the Job,** Michael A. Gips, *Security Management,* February 2006

Drug dealers in the workplace are becoming increasingly common and difficult to identify. This article discusses the impact of drugs in the American workplace. 173

UNIT 6
Creating and Sustaining Effective Drug Control Policy

Unit Overview 178

40. **Reorienting U.S. Drug Policy,** Jonathan P. Caulkins and Peter Reuter, *Issues in Science and Technology,* Fall 2006

Authors Jonathan Caulkins and Peter Reuter argue that the nature and extent of the illegal drug problems in the United States have changed during the past two decades, and that **U.S. drug policy needs to adjust to these changes.** Do you agree? 181

41. **Is Drug Testing of Athletes Necessary?,** Matthew J. Mitten, *USA Today,* November 2005

Matthew Mitten argues that imposing **drug-testing programs on sports organizations** is wrong. The federal government disagrees. Who should police performance enhancing drug use by professional athletes? 186

42. **Medical Marijuana, Compassionate Use, and Public Policy,** Peter J. Cohen, *Hastings Center Report,* May/June 2006

Although cannabis has been used as a therapeutic agent throughout history, it has never been submitted to the FDA for approval. **Would it pass the test?** 190

43. **Researchers Explore New Visions for Hallucinogens,** Susan Brown, *The Chronicle of Higher Education,* December 8, 2006

After a long hiatus, medical investigators return to studying the benefits of **once banned compounds.** Does this conflict with current federal drug policy? 193

The concepts in bold italics are developed in the article. For further expansion, please refer to the Topic Guide.

44. **State's Evidence,** Will Baude, *The New Republic,* June 7, 2005

In response to California's ***medical use of marijuana,*** the Supreme Court lays down the law relative to **federal authority** over state marijuana laws.   **197**

45. **Durbin, Grassley Introduce Bipartisan Bill to Combat Meth,** *Capitol Hill Press Release,* May 3, 2007

As methamphetamine abuse spreads across the country exceeding even crack epidemic proportions, many in government say that federal ***government officials have had*** their heads in the sand. This is a proposal of some new legislation.   **199**

46. **How to Stand Up to Big Tobacco,** Noreena Hertz, *New Statesman,* June 12, 2006

Five hundred million people will die of smoking-related diseases in the next fifty years. Poor households in Morocco spend more on tobacco than on health and education combined. Can ***taxation of tobacco*** products derail this?   **201**

UNIT 7
Prevention, Treatment, and Education

Unit Overview   **202**

47. **Keeping Drug Prevention for Kids 'Real',** Michael L. Hecht and Amber Johnson, *Behavioral Health Management,* November/December 2005

This article explains how a ***culturally grounded substance abuse prevention*** curriculum can help make kids an integral part of a successful program.   **205**

48. **An Update on Adolescent Drug Use,** Scott Hiromoto et al., *Professional School Counseling,* December 1, 2006

School counselors need accurate and age appropriate education information in order ***to counsel teens about drug abuse.*** This article presents information about some of the most pressing drug issues.   **208**

49. **Combination Treatment for One Year Doubles Smokers' Quit Rate,** Patrick Zickler, *National Institute on Drug Abuse,* March 2006

Nearly 80 percent of ***smokers trying to quit*** relapse within one year. A new program, however, is making progress with this powerful and deadly addiction. Why is treating nicotine addiction so difficult?   **215**

50. **Parent Power,** Joseph A. Califano, Jr., *America,* October 31, 2005

Author Joseph Califano argues that the price for parental pessimism and ***ambivalence toward drugs*** is high. This discussion centers on the importance of talking to kids about drugs.   **217**

51. **Nonconventional and Integrative Treatments of Alcohol and Substance Abuse,** James Lake, *Psychiatric Times,* May 1, 2007

The relationship between ***alcohol and drug abuse and psychiatric disorders has long been established. This article discusses a combination of treatments,*** such as exercise and acupuncture that can be successfully used to treat these disorders.   **219**

52. **Exercise and Drug Detoxification,** Simon Oddie, *Prison Service Journal,* November 2004

It has long been recognized in the physical education community that physical ***exercise can play a major role in detoxification and rehabilitation.*** This article describes a British correctional program proving successful in helping prisoners recover from drug abuse.   **223**

The concepts in bold italics are developed in the article. For further expansion, please refer to the Topic Guide.

53. **Rehab Reality Check,** Jerry Adler, *Newsweek,* February 19, 2007

As the traditional treatment centers do battle with glitzy newcomers, everyone is ***debating what works.***   **227**

54. **No Longer Theory: Correctional Practices That Work,** Harvey Shrum, *Journal of Correctional Education,* September 2004

Harvey Shrum asserts that America has become so focused on prisons as the answer to social ills that today, one in thirty-seven Americans is or has been incarcerated. Over eighty percent of those incarcerated committed their offense while under the influence of drugs. This article discusses two new ways to ***prevent drug-related recidivism.***   **230**

Test-Your-Knowledge Form   **236**

Article Rating Form   **237**

The concepts in bold italics are developed in the article. For further expansion, please refer to the Topic Guide.

Correlation Guide

The *Annual Editions* series provides students with convenient, inexpensive access to current, carefully selected articles from the public press. **Annual Editions: Drugs, Society, and Behavior 08/09** is an easy-to-use reader that presents articles on important topics such as *drug lifestyle, drug types, drug-use trends, drug policy,* and many more. For more information on *Annual Editions* and other *McGraw-Hill Contemporary Learning Series* titles, visit www.mhcls.com.

This convenient guide matches the units in **Annual Editions: Drugs, Society, and Behavior 08/09** with the corresponding chapters in one of our best-selling McGraw-Hill Criminal Justice textbooks by Goode.

Annual Editions: Drugs, Society, and Behavior 08/09	Drugs in American Society, 7/e by Goode
Unit 1: Living with Drugs	**Chapter 1:** Drugs: A Sociological Perspective
	Chapter 2: Drugs: A Pharmacological Perspective
	Chapter 3: Theories of Drug Use
	Chapter 8: Legal Drugs: Alcohol, Tobacco, and Psychotherapeutic Drugs
	Chapter 9: Marijuana, LSD, and Club Drugs
Unit 2: Understanding How Drugs Work—Use, Dependency, and Addiction	**Chapter 2:** Drugs: A Pharmacological Perspective
	Chapter 8: Legal Drugs: Alcohol, Tobacco, and Psychotherapeutic Drugs
	Chapter 9: Marijuana, LSD, and Club Drugs
	Chapter 10: Stimulants: Amphetamines, Methamphetamine, Cocaine, and Crack
	Chapter 11: Heroin and the Narcotics
Unit 3: The Major Drugs of Use and Abuse	**Chapter 7:** Historical Trends in Drug Consumption: From Past to Current Use
	Chapter 8: Legal Drugs: Alcohol, Tobacco, and Psychotherapeutic Drugs
	Chapter 9: Marijuana, LSD, and Club Drugs
	Chapter 10: Stimulants: Amphetamines, Methamphetamine, Cocaine, and Crack
	Chapter 11: Heroin and the Narcotics
Unit 4: Other Trends in Drug Use	**Chapter 5:** Drugs in the News
	Chapter 6: How Do We Know It's True: Methods of Research
	Chapter 7: Historical Trends in Drug Consumption: From Past to Current Use
Unit 5: Measuring the Social Costs of Drugs	**Chapter 1:** Drugs: A Sociological Perspective
	Chapter 4: Controlling Drugs: The Historical Context
	Chapter 5: Drugs in the News
	Chapter 8: Legal Drugs: Alcohol, Tobacco, and Psychotherapeutic Drugs
	Chapter 13: The Illicit Drug Industry
Unit 6: Creating and Sustaining Effective Drug Control Policy	**Chapter 12:** Drugs and Crime: What's the Connection?
	Chapter 13: The Illicit Drug Industry
	Chapter 14: Drug Control: Law Enforcement, Drug Courts, and Drug Treatment
	Chapter 15: Legalization, Decriminalization, and Harm Reduction
Unit 7: Prevention, Treatment, and Education	**Chapter 2:** Drugs: A Pharmacological Perspective
	Chapter 3: Theories of Drug Use
	Chapter 4: Controlling Drugs: The Historical Context
	Chapter 12: Drugs and Crime: What's the Connection?
	Chapter 13: The Illicit Drug Industry
	Chapter 14: Drug Control: Law Enforcement, Drug Courts, and Drug Treatment
	Chapter 15: Legalization, Decriminalization, and Harm Reduction

Topic Guide

This topic guide suggests how the selections in this book relate to the subjects covered in your course. You may want to use the topics listed on these pages to search the Web more easily.

On the following pages a number of Web sites have been gathered specifically for this book. They are arranged to reflect the units of this *Annual Edition*. You can link to these sites by going to the student online support site at *http://www.mhcls.com/online/*.

ALL THE ARTICLES THAT RELATE TO EACH TOPIC ARE LISTED BELOW THE BOLD-FACED TERM.

Addiction
4. Methamphetamine Abuse: A Perfect Storm of Complications
5. HIV Apathy
7. Did Prohibition Really Work?
10. Reducing the Risk of Addiction to Prescribed Medications
12. Better Ways to Target Pain
15. The Changing Science of Pain
19. Methamphetamine Abuse
28. Drug Addiction
36. Keep Your Older Patients Out of Medication Trouble

Alcohol
7. Did Prohibition Really Work?
23. The Teen Drinking Dilemma
26. A Nation Without Drunk Driving
31. Teens and Prescription Drugs
34. Sobering Thoughts
35. Students with Fetal Alcohol Syndrome

Amphetamines
4. Methamphetamine Abuse: A Perfect Storm of Complications
5. HIV Apathy
19. Methamphetamine Abuse
20. Mexico Drug Cartels Reap Big Profits from Meth
45. Durbin, Grassley Introduce Bipartisan Bill to Combat Meth

Cocaine
7. Did Prohibition Really Work?
20. Mexico Drug Cartels Reap Big Profits from Meth

College
23. The Teen Drinking Dilemma

Depression
6. Not Invented Here
17. Stress and Drug Abuse

Designer drugs
25. Fentanyl-Laced Street Drugs "Kill Hundreds"
30. New Study Shows 1.8 Million Youth Use Inhalants
43. Researchers Explore New Visions for Hallucinogens

Drug economy
2. Smoking, Drugs, Obesity Top Health Concerns for Kids
6. Not Invented Here
7. Did Prohibition Really Work?
19. Methamphetamine Abuse
21. The Taliban's Opium War
23. The Teen Drinking Dilemma

Epidemiology
2. Smoking, Drugs, Obesity Top Health Concerns for Kids
4. Methamphetamine Abuse: A Perfect Storm of Complications
5. HIV Apathy
19. Methamphetamine Abuse
23. The Teen Drinking Dilemma
30. New Study Shows 1.8 Million Youth Use Inhalants

31. Teens and Prescription Drugs
34. Sobering Thoughts
35. Students with Fetal Alcohol Syndrome
36. Keep Your Older Patients Out of Medication Trouble
45. Durbin, Grassley Introduce Bipartisan Bill to Combat Meth

Gender
23. The Teen Drinking Dilemma
34. Sobering Thoughts

Heroin
21. The Taliban's Opium War
22. The Opposite Result

Law enforcement
7. Did Prohibition Really Work?
19. Methamphetamine Abuse
20. Mexico Drug Cartels Reap Big Profits from Meth
21. The Taliban's Opium War
22. The Opposite Result
24. An Update on the Effects of Marijuana and Its Potential Medical Use
26. A Nation Without Drunk Driving
54. No Longer Theory: Correctional Practices That Work

Legalization
7. Did Prohibition Really Work?
24. An Update on the Effects of Marijuana and Its Potential Medical Use

Marijuana
24. An Update on the Effects of Marijuana and Its Potential Medical Use

Nicotine
2. Smoking, Drugs, Obesity Top Health Concerns for Kids
46. How to Stand Up to Big Tobacco

Over-the-counter-drugs
2. Smoking, Drugs, Obesity Top Health Concerns for Kids
10. Reducing the Risk of Addiction to Prescribed Medications
31. Teens and Prescription Drugs

Policy
7. Did Prohibition Really Work?
10. Reducing the Risk of Addiction to Prescribed Medications
19. Methamphetamine Abuse
20. Mexico Drug Cartels Reap Big Profits from Meth
21. The Taliban's Opium War
22. The Opposite Result
24. An Update on the Effects of Marijuana and Its Potential Medical Use
26. A Nation Without Drunk Driving
29. The Right to a Trial
40. Reorienting U.S. Drug Policy
43. Researchers Explore New Visions for Hallucinogens
45. Durbin, Grassley Introduce Bipartisan Bill to Combat Meth
46. How to Stand Up to Big Tobacco

Prescription drugs

10. Reducing the Risk of Addiction to Prescribed Medications
28. Drug Addiction
29. The Right to a Trial
31. Teens and Prescription Drugs
36. Keep Your Older Patients Out of Medication Trouble

Prevention

4. Methamphetamine Abuse: A Perfect Storm of Complications
5. HIV Apathy
23. The Teen Drinking Dilemma
34. Sobering Thoughts
35. Students with Fetal Alcohol Syndrome
36. Keep Your Older Patients Out of Medication Trouble
51. Nonconventional and Integrative Treatments of Alcohol and Substance Abuse

Prison

4. Methamphetamine Abuse: A Perfect Storm of Complications
20. Mexico Drug Cartels Reap Big Profits from Meth
21. The Taliban's Opium War
26. A Nation Without Drunk Driving
54. No Longer Theory: Correctional Practices That Work

Race

4. Methamphetamine Abuse: A Perfect Storm of Complications
20. Mexico Drug Cartels Reap Big Profits from Meth
21. The Taliban's Opium War
22. The Opposite Result

Research

2. Smoking, Drugs, Obesity Top Health Concerns for Kids
4. Methamphetamine Abuse: A Perfect Storm of Complications
5. HIV Apathy
8. Vice Vaccines
12. Better Ways to Target Pain
14. A Small Part of the Brain, and Its Profound Effects
15. The Changing Science of Pain
24. An Update on the Effects of Marijuana and Its Potential Medical Use
28. Drug Addiction
29. The Right to a Trial
34. Sobering Thoughts
51. Nonconventional and Integrative Treatments of Alcohol and Substance Abuse

Treatment

4. Methamphetamine Abuse: A Perfect Storm of Complications
5. HIV Apathy
19. Methamphetamine Abuse
51. Nonconventional and Integrative Treatments of Alcohol and Substance Abuse

Youth and drugs

2. Smoking, Drugs, Obesity Top Health Concerns for Kids
4. Methamphetamine Abuse: A Perfect Storm of Complications
8. Vice Vaccines
23. The Teen Drinking Dilemma
30. New Study Shows 1.8 Million Youth Use Inhalants
31. Teens and Prescription Drugs
34. Sobering Thoughts
35. Students with Fetal Alcohol Syndrome

Internet References

The following Internet sites have been carefully researched and selected to support the articles found in this reader. The easiest way to access these selected sites is to go to our student online support site at *http://www.mhcls.com/online/*.

AE: Drugs, Society, and Behavior 08/09

The following sites were available at the time of publication. Visit our Web site—we update our student online support site regularly to reflect any changes.

General Sources

Higher Education Center for Alcohol and Other Drug Prevention
http://www.edc.org/hec

The U.S. Department of Education established the Higher Education Center for Alcohol and Other Drug Prevention to provide nationwide support for campus alcohol and other drug prevention efforts. The Center is working with colleges, universities, and preparatory schools throughout the country to develop strategies for changing campus culture, to foster environments that promote healthy lifestyles, and to prevent illegal alcohol and other drug use among students.

Narconon
http://www.youthaddiction.com

This site contains drug information, information on addiction, rehab information, online consultations, and other related resources.

National Clearinghouse for Alcohol and Drug Information
http://ncadi.samhsa.gov

This site provides information to teens about the problems and ramifications of drug use and abuse. There are numerous links to drug-related informational sites.

NSW Office of Drug Policy Home Page
http://www.druginfo.nsw.gov.au

This is an Australia government based website with a great deal of drug related information. The site includes information about: illicit drugs (Amphetamines, Pseudoephedrine, GHB, Heroin, Ketamine, Rohypnol, Marijuana, Paramethoxyamphetamines [PMA], Steroids, Cocaine, Hallucinogens, Inhalants, Ecstasy, Ritalin, and Psychostimulants), Information and resources, Treatment services, Law and Justice, Illicit Drug Diversion, and Medical Cannabis. It also includes statistics on drug use in Australia.

ONDCP (National of Drug Control Policy)
http://www.whitehousedrugpolicy.gov

This site contains a vast amount of drug related information, resources and links. Included is information about drug policy, drug facts, publications, related links, prevention, treatment, science and technology, enforcement, state and local along with international facts, and policies, and programs. The site is easy to use and understand.

US Department of Health and Human Services
http://ncadi.samhsa.gov/research

This site contains links, and resources on various topics that include, but are not limited to: Substance Abuse and Mental Health Data Archive, OAS Short Reports (on such drugs as marijuana, crack cocaine, inhalants, club drugs, heroin, alcohol, and tobacco). Also included are government studies and an online library and databases.

UNIT 1: Living With Drugs

Freevibe Drug Facts
http://www.freevibe.com/Drug_Facts/why_drugs.asp#1

This website contains information on Drug Facts with links on: drug information, why people take drugs, the physical effects and drug related behavior, drug recognition, and discussions of addiction. The site also includes personal accounts by addicts.

National Council on Alcoholism and Drug Dependence, Inc.
http://www.ncadd.org

According to its Web site, The National Council on Alcoholism and Drug Dependence provides education, information, help, and hope in the fight against the chronic, and sometimes fatal, disease of alcoholism and other drug addictions.

Parents. The Anti-Drug
http://www.theantidrug.com

Tips and links for helping children avoid drugs can be found at this site. Also provided is help in parenting with drug related issues such as how to advise young persons about the drug related influences of peer pressure.

UNIT 2: Understanding How Drugs Work— Use, Dependency, and Addiction

AddictionSearch.com
www.addictionsearch.com

Check this site out for information on addiction and rehabilitation. Some of the other features of this site are the use of statistics, identifies social issues, provides resources for treatment, facility listings for the United States, and analyzes types of addictions by race, sex and age of human populations.

Addiction Treatment Forum
www.atforum.com

News on addiction research and reports on substance abuse are available here.

APA Help Center from the American Psychological Association
http://www.apahelpcenter.org/articles/article.php?id=45

This site is a good resource with several articles and information mostly on alcohol.

British Broadcasting Company Understanding Drugs
http://www.bbc.co.uk/health/conditions/mental_health/drugs_use.shtml

This is a good reference for information about drug use, addiction, and dependence. Includes links.

Centre for Addiction and Mental Health (CAMH)
http://www.camh.net

One of the largest addictions facilities in Canada, CAMH advances an understanding of addiction and translates this knowledge into resources that can be used to prevent problems and to provide effective treatments.

Dealing with Addictions

http://kidshealth.org/teen/your_mind/problems/addictions.html

This site contains information on addictions, and includes a quiz on substance abuse. There are categories for: Your Mind, Your Body, Sexual Health, Food and Fitness, Drugs and Alcohol, Diseases and Conditions, Infections, School and Jobs, Staying Safe, and questions and answers. Much of this site is available in Spanish.

Drugs and the Body: How Drugs Work

http://www.doitnow.org/pdfs/223.pdf

This site pinpoints some basic but critical points in a straightforward manner. It explains how drugs can be administered, the processes through the body, effects, changes over time. Included are drug related information resources and links.

The National Center on Addiction and Substance Abuse at Columbia University

http://www.casacolumbia.org

The National Center on Addiction and Substance Abuse at Columbia University is a unique think/action tank that brings together all of the professional disciplines (health policy, medicine and nursing, communications, economics, sociology and anthropology, law and law enforcement, business, religion, and education) needed to study and combat all forms of substance abuse—illegal drugs, pills, alcohol, and tobacco—as they affect all aspects of society.

National Institute on Drug Abuse (NIDA)

http://www.nida.nih.gov

NIDA's mission is to lead the nation in bringing the power of science to bear on drug abuse and addiction.

Public Agenda

http://www.publicagenda.org

A guide on illegal drugs has links that include: understanding the issues, public opinions, and additional resources. Includes several links for each of these groups.

Understanding Addiction-Regret, Addiction and Death

http://teenadvice.about.com/library/weekly/aa011501a.htm

This site has several resources and articles related to drug use by young persons.

UNIT 3: The Major Drugs of Use and Abuse

National Institute on Drug Abuse

www.drugabuse.gov

This is the National Institute on Drug Abuse web site that identifies the major drugs of use and abuse. It provides resources and information for students, parents, and teachers, as well as reports on drug trends.

Office of Applied Studies

www.oas.samhsa.gov

Data and statistics on the major drugs of use and abuse along with reports on the effects of these drugs focusing on the emotional, social, psychological and physical aspects are contained at this site. Also available are extensive survey findings on drug use related to evolving patterns of drug abuse.

QuitNet

http://www.quitnet.org

The QuitNet helps smokers control their nicotine addiction. This site operates in association with the Boston University School of Public Health.

The American Journal of Psychiatry

http://ajp.psychiatryonline.org/cgi/content/abstract/155/8/1016

This site contains a study on female twins and cannabis.

UNIT 4: Other Trends in Drug Use

Drug Story.org

http://www.drugstory.org/drug_stats/druguse_stats.asp

This site contains lots of information—"Hard Facts, Real Stories, Informed Experts"; information on drugs and their effects. Also covered are prevention and treatment, drugs and crime, drug trafficking, drug use statistics, costs of drugs, and subtopics including: healthcare costs, loss of productivity in the workplace, and crime statistics.

Marijuana as a Medicine

http://mojo.calyx.net/~olsen

This site promotes the concept of marijuana as medicine. This is a controversial issue that has been in the news quite a bit over the past few years. At this site, you will find numerous links to other sites that support this idea, as well as information developed specifically for this site.

Monitoring the Future

www.monitoringthefuture.org

Located at this site is a collaboration of drug trend data tables from 2005 focusing on students in the eighth, tenth, and twelfth grades; also described are trends in the availability of drugs, the attitudes of users, and the use of major drugs.

Prescriptions Drug Use and Abuse

http://www.fda.gov/fdac/features/2001/501_drug.htm

This site contains lots of resources and links related to prescription drug use and abuse.

SAMHSA

http://www.samhsa.gov/

This link is to the office of applied studies, where you can link to numerous drug related resources. It includes the latest and most comprehensive drug survey information in the U.S.

United States Drug Trends

www.usdrugtrends.com

Provided at this site are drug trends for each state in the United States, such as information where each drug is most likely to be used in each state, cost of the drug, and where the drug supply is coming from.

UNIT 5: Measuring the Social Costs of Drugs

Drug Enforcement Administration

http://www.usdoj.gov/dea

The mission of the Drug Enforcement Administration is to enforce the controlled substances laws and regulations of the United States.

Drug Use Cost to the Economy

www.ccm-drugtest.com/ntl_effcts1.htm

This site identifies the economic and social costs associated with drug use and abuse in the United States.

Drug Policy Alliance

http://www.drugpolicy.org/about/

News about drug policies and articles critiquing the real social and economic costs associated with drug abuse versus the cost of the drug war policies can be found here.

National Drug Control Policy

http://www.ncjrs.org/ondcppubs/publications/policy/ndcs00/chap2_10.html

This site contains information about the consequences of illegal drug use including: economic loss, drug related death, drug related medical emergencies, spreading of infectious diseases, homelessness, and drug use in the workplace.

The November Coalition

http://www.november.org

The November Coalition is a growing body of citizens whose lives have been gravely affected by the present drug policy. This group represents convicted prisoners, their loved ones, and others who believe that U.S. drug policies are unfair and unjust.

TRAC DEA Site

http://trac.syr.edu/tracdea/index.html

The Transactional Records Access Clearinghouse (TRAC) is a data gathering, data research, and data distribution organization associated with Syracuse University. According to its Web site, the purpose of TRAC is to provide the American people—and institutions of oversight such as Congress, news organizations, public interest groups, businesses, scholars, and lawyers—with comprehensive information about the activities of federal enforcement and regulatory agencies and the communities in which they take place.

United Nations Chronicle—online edition

http://www.un.org/Pubs/chronicle/1998/issue2/0298p7.html

This site contains information about the global nature of drugs.

UNIT 6: Creating and Sustaining Effective Drug Control Policy

Drug Policy Alliance

www.drugpolicy.org

This site explores and evaluates drug policy in the United States and around the world.

DrugText

http://www.drugtext.org

The DrugText library consists of individual drug-related libraries with independent search capabilities.

Effective Drug Policy: Why Journey's End is Legalisations

http://www.drugscope.org.uk/wip/23/pdfs/journey.pdf

This site contains the Drug scope policy and public affairs in the United Kingdom.

The Higher Education Center for Alcohol and Other Drug Prevention

http://www.edc.org/hec/pubs/policy.htm

"Setting and Improving Policies for Reducing Alcohol and Other Drug Problems on Campus: A Guide for School Administrators."

The National Organization on Fetal Alcohol Syndrome (NOFAS)

http://www.nofas.org

NOFAS is a nonprofit organization founded in 1990 dedicated to eliminating birth defects caused by alcohol consumption during pregnancy and improving the quality of life for those individuals and families affected. NOFAS is the only national organization focusing solely on fetal alcohol syndrome (FAS), the leading known cause of mental retardation.

National NORML Homepage

http://www.norml.org

This is the home page for the National Organization for the Reform of Marijuana Laws.

UNIT 7: Prevention, Education and Treatment

American Council for Drug Education

www.acde.org

This site educates employers, parents, teachers, and health professionals about drugs and includes information on recognizing the signs and symptoms of drug use.

D.A.R.E.

http://www.dare-america.com

This year 33 million schoolchildren around the world—25 million in the United States—will benefit from D.A.R.E. (Drug Abuse Resistance Education), the highly acclaimed program that gives kids the skills they need to avoid involvement in drugs, gangs, or violence. D.A.R.E. was founded in 1983 in Los Angeles.

Drug Watch International

http://www.drugwatch.org

Drug Watch International is a volunteer nonprofit information network and advocacy organization that promotes the creation of healthy drug-free cultures in the world and opposes the legalization of drugs. The organization upholds a comprehensive approach to drug issues involving prevention, education, intervention/treatment, and law enforcement/interdiction.

Join Together

www.jointogether.org

Contained here are multiple types of resources and web links regarding youth drug prevention for parents, teachers, community members, public officials and faith leaders.

Marijuana Policy Project

http://www.mpp.org

The purpose of the Marijuana Policy Project is to develop and promote policies to minimize the harm associated with marijuana.

National Institute on Drug Abuse

http://www.nida.nih.gov/Infofacts/TreatMeth.html

Information on effective drug treatment approaches, costs for treating drug addiction, and the different treatment options (inpatient, outpatient, group, etc) can all be found at this site.

Office of National Drug Control Policy (ONDCP)

http://www.whitehousedrugpolicy.gov

The principal purpose of ONDCP is to establish policies, priorities, and objectives for the nation's drug control program, the goals of which are to reduce illicit drug use, manufacturing, and trafficking; drug-related crime and violence; and drug-related health consequences.

Hazelden

http://www.hazelden.org

Hazelden is a nonprofit organization providing high quality, affordable rehabilitation, education, prevention, and professional services and publications in chemical dependency and related disorders.

KCI (Koch Crime Institute) The Anit-Meth Site

http://www.kci.org/meth_info/faq_meth.htm

This site contains Frequently Asked Questions on Methamphetamine. Very interesting.

The Drug Reform Coordination Network (DRC)

http://www.drcnet.org

According to its home page, the DRC Network is committed to reforming current drug laws in the United States.

United Nations International Drug Control Program (UNDCP)

http://www.undcp.org

The mission of UNDCP is to work with the nations and the people of the world to tackle the global drug problem and its consequences.

We highly recommend that you review our Web site for expanded information and our other product lines. We are continually updating and adding links to our Web site in order to offer you the most usable and useful information that will support and expand the value of your Annual Editions. You can reach us at: *http://www.mhcls.com/annualeditions/.*

UNIT 1
Living with Drugs

Unit Selections

1. **Over the Limit,** Nancy Shute
2. **Smoking, Drugs, Obesity Top Health Concerns for Kids,** *Medical News Today*
3. **Living the High Life,** Karenza Moore and Steven Miles
4. **Methamphetamine Abuse: A Perfect Storm of Complications,** Timothy W. Lineberry and J. Michael Bostwick
5. **HIV Apathy,** Zach Patton
6. **Not Invented Here,** Tinker Ready
7. **Did Prohibition Really Work,** Jack S. Blocker, Jr.
8. **Vice Vaccines,** Christen Brownlee.
9. **Pass the Weed, Dad,** Marni Jackson

Key Points to Consider

- Why is history important when attempting to understand contemporary drug-related events?

- How does the American response to drug-related issues compare to that which occurs in other countries?

- What role do the media play in American society's perception of drug-related events?

- How have national crises such as the war in Iraq and shootings in high schools influenced thinking about drugs?

- What important drug-related issues do you believe the American public is uninformed about?

Student Web Site
www.mhcls.com/online

Internet References
Further information regarding these websites may be found in this book's preface or online.

Freevibe Drug Facts
http://www.freevibe.com/Drug_Facts/why_drugs.asp#1
National Council on Alcoholism and Drug Dependence, Inc.
http://www.ncadd.org
Parents. The Anti-Drug
http://www.theantidrug.com/

When attempting to define the American drug experience, one must examine the past as well as the present. Too often drug use and its associated phenomena are viewed through a contemporary looking glass relative to our personal views, biases, and perspectives. Although today's drug scene is definitely a product of the counterculture of the 1960s and 1970s, the crack trade of the 1980s, and the current escalating methamphetamine problem, it is also a product of the more distant past. This past and the lessons it has generated, although largely unknown, forgotten, or ignored, provide one important perspective from which to assess our current status and to guide our future in terms of optimizing our efforts to manage the benefits and control the harm from legal and illegal drugs.

The American drug experience is often defined in terms of a million individual realities, all meaningful and all different. In fact, these realities often originated as pieces of our national, cultural, racial, religious, and personal past that combine to influence present-day drug-related phenomena significantly. The contemporary American drug experience is the product of centuries of human attempts to alter or sustain consciousness through the use of mind-altering drugs. Early American history is replete with accounts of the exorbitant use of alcohol, opium, morphine, and cocaine.

Further review of this history clearly suggests the precedents for Americans' continuing pursuit of a vast variety of stimulant, depressant, and hallucinogenic drugs. Drug wars, drug epidemics, drug prohibitions, and escalating trends of alarming drug use patterns were present throughout the early history of the United States. During this period the addictive properties of most drugs were largely unknown. Today, the addictive properties of almost all drugs are known. So why is it that so many drug-related lessons of the past repeat themselves in the face of such powerful new knowledge? Why does Fetal Alcohol Syndrome remain as the leading cause of mental retardation in infants? How is it that the abuse of drugs continues to defy the lessons of history? How big is the American drug problem and how is it measured?

One important way of answering questions about drug abuse is by conducting research and analyzing data recovered through numerous reporting instruments. These data are in turn used to assess historical trends and make policy decisions in response to what has been learned. For example: one leading source of information about drug use in America is the annual federal Substance Abuse and Mental Health Services Administration's National Survey on Drug Use and Health. Released again in September of 2007, it reports that there continues to be about 20.4 million Americans over 12 years of age who are current users of illicit drugs. The most widely used illicit drug is marijuana with 14.8 million users—a figure that has remained constant for the past 4 years. Approximately 51 percent of Americans over 12 are drinkers of alcohol; over 40 percent of full-time enrolled college students are binge drinkers (defined as consuming 5 or more drinks during a single drinking occasion). Approximately 30 percent of Americans over 12 use tobacco. Almost 23 million people are believed to be drug-dependent on alcohol or illicit drugs—a slight increase from the figures reported in last year's survey. This year's survey identified a steadily increasing 5.2 million persons using prescription painkillers for non-medical reasons, an alarming trend. The size of the economy associated with drug use is staggering; Americans continued to spend more than $70 billion last year on illegal drugs alone.

Drugs impact our most powerful public institutions on many fronts. Drugs are *the* business of our criminal justice system, and drugs compete with terrorism, war, and other major national security concerns as demanding military issues. Over 3.4 billion dollars was committed this year to The Department of Homeland Security to strengthen drug-related land and maritime border interdictions. The multi-agency apprehension last year of four Colombian nationals piloting a submarine loaded with 5.5 tons of cocaine bound for the U.S. is one example of these efforts. Only terrorism and war distract the continuing military emphasis on drug fighting. And as the war in Iraq, Afghanistan, and Pakistan continues, American drug agents in those countries struggle to contain the expanding heroin trade, a major source of funding for the Taliban. As you read through the pages of this book, the pervasive nature of drug-related influences will become more apparent.

The lessons of our drug legacy are harsh, whether they are the subjects of public health or public policy. Methamphetamine is now recognized as having surpassed crack as the drug associated with the most serious consequences. The entire dynamic of illicit drug use is changing. Once quiet rural towns, counties, and states are now reporting epidemics of methamphetamine abuse that suggest comparisons to the inner-urban crack epidemics of the 1980s—only worse. The non-medical use of prescription drugs, particularly pain relievers such as oxycodone, has surged the past three years. This issue is competing for the most widely cited emerging drug problem. Families, schools, and workplaces continue to be impacted by the many facets of drug abuse. One in three Americans has a close relationship to someone who abuses drugs. It is only because of war and terrorism that more public attention toward drug problems has been diverted.

The articles and graphics contained in this unit illustrate the evolving nature of issues influenced by the historical evolution of legal and illegal drug use in America. The changing historical evolution of drug-related phenomena is reflected within the character of all issues and controversies addressed by this book. Unit 1 presents examples of the contemporary and diverse nature of current problems, issues, and concerns about drugs and how they continue to impact all aspects of public and private life. The drug related events of today continue to forecast the drug related events of tomorrow. The areas of public health, public policy, controlling crime, and education exist as good examples for discussion. As you read this and other literature on drug-related events, the dynamics of past and present drug-related linkages will become apparent.

Over the Limit?

Americans young and old crave high-octane fuel, and doctors are jittery.

NANCY SHUTE

Linleigh Hawk starts the day at 5:30 A.M. by downing her first cup of coffee. She then stops at Starbucks for a grande vanilla skim latte on the way to Winston Churchill High School in Potomac, Md., where she's a senior. At 3 P.M., it's time for a jumbo iced tea to power her through hip-hop dance rehearsals and yearbook meetings. Homework, which often keeps her up past 1 A.M., requires more coffee. "I've got so much to do," she says. "I've got to have the caffeine." The java-fired schedule has paid off, says Hawk: She's been accepted by 15 of her 16 college choices, including first pick Wake Forest.

Hawk may sound like an anomaly, but she isn't. Overworked and sleep-deprived Americans young and old so crave a buzz these days that even alcoholic drinks come loaded with caffeine, and doctors are getting worried. In the past three years alone, the number of 18-to-24-year-olds who drink coffee daily has doubled, from 16 percent to 31 percent—and some of them go on to pop prescription stimulants such as Adderall or Ritalin for late-night study sessions. Energy drinks like Red Bull and Cocaine, with several times the buzz of a can of Coke, have mushroomed into a $3.5 billion-a-year industry.

"I can't go out and keep up with these 20-year-olds without it," says Jeremy Freer, a 29-year-old music teacher from Virginia Beach, Va., of his Saturday-night beverage of choice: vodka with Red Bull. (Partyers can opt instead for the new double espresso-double caffeinated Van Gogh vodka or a Bud Extra, a caffeinated beer.)

Wired. Health experts understand all too well why Americans gotta get wired. People of all ages are chronically sleep deprived, from teens who catch the bus before sunrise to working mothers who report they spend less than six hours a night in bed, according to a poll released in March by the National Sleep Foundation. But we may be pushing the limits of self-medication. Poison control centers and emergency room doctors report increasing numbers of people suffering from the rapid heartbeat and nausea of a caffeine overdose—like the 14-year-old boy who earlier this year showed up at a Minneapolis emergency room in respiratory distress after washing down caffeine pills with energy drinks so he could play video games all night.

Instead, he spent the night in the pediatric intensive care unit, intubated, until the caffeine exited his system. They're also seeing more teens and young adults in distress after having bought or "borrowed" stimulant drugs from friends.

And, in the extreme, there are tragedies like that of James Stone, a 19-year-old from Wallingford, Conn., who died last November of cardiac arrest after taking nearly two dozen caffeine pills. His parents say he had been putting in long hours on a job search.

Doctors are particularly troubled to see youngsters forming the caffeine habit, even as toddlers. Children's consumption of soft drinks has doubled in the past 35 years, with sodas supplanting milk. A 2003 study of Columbus, Ohio, middle schoolers found some taking in 800 milligrams of caffeine a day—more than twice the recommended maximum for adults of 300 milligrams. "Their body weight is low," says Wahida Karmally, director of nutrition for the Irving Center for Clinical Research at Columbia University Medical Center. "They can't tolerate as much caffeine as adults."

Since scientists have never studied how caffeine affects growing bodies and brains, children who go through the day guzzling soda after iced tea after energy drink are serving as tiny guinea pigs. "This is something that nobody is looking at carefully," says Nora Volkow, a psychiatrist who directs the National Institute on Drug Abuse. "We really have no idea how it affects development long term."

Teenagers need at least nine hours of sleep; grade schoolers, 10 to 12. Few come close.

The appeal to kids of high-octane energy drinks has some officials concerned enough to act. Just last week, the Food and Drug Administration announced it had sent a warning letter to the manufacturer of Cocaine Energy Drink, Redux Beverages LLC of Las Vegas, for marketing the beverage "as an alternative to an illicit street drug." Until last week, the manufacturer's website boasted "Cocaine—instant rush." Hyping the performance enhancements caffeine offers at the time you're introducing the drug to children "is a terrible message. It has implications for drug use in the future," says Roland Griffiths, a professor of behavioral biology at Johns Hopkins University Medical Center who has studied caffeine's effects for more than 30 years.

And last month, Doherty High School in Colorado Springs, Colo., banned a drink called Spike Shooter. Two students were taken to the hospital complaining of nausea, vomiting, and heart palpitations after drinking an 8-ounce can, which packs 300 mg of caffeine—the same as almost four Red Bulls.

For adults, and in reasonable doses—the equivalent of three 8-ounce cups of coffee, six Excedrin Migraine, or a half-dozen 12-ounce colas a day—caffeine has much to recommend it. As the world's most popular habit-forming drug, it fights fatigue, brightens mood, and eases pain while it's forestalling sleep. Test subjects dosed with the amount found in a cup of coffee come out ahead on problem-solving tasks. And by triggering the release of adrenaline to help muscles work harder and longer, caffeine so clearly enhances athletic performance that until 2004 it was considered a controlled substance by the International Olympic Committee. Supercaffeinated energy drinks like Redline RTD are marketed to bodybuilders.

Elixir of Life. The latest findings on coffee suggest that it even staves off disease. Caffeine reduces the risk of Parkinson's disease, for example, by blocking receptors for adenosine, a neurotransmitter that plays a role in motor function. It is now being tested as a Parkinson's treatment. Caffeine also heads off migraines by contracting blood vessels in the brain.

And probably because coffee, like blueberries and broccoli, contains potent antioxidants, it appears to reduce the risk of colon cancer, gallstones, and liver cancer, among other illnesses. In 2005, Harvard researchers found that drinking six cups of coffee or more daily cut the risk of getting type 2 diabetes by half in men and 30 percent in women. One study of 80,000 women showed that those who drank more than two or three cups of coffee daily reduced their risk of suicide over 10 years by a third.

Alas, that glorious rush of energy isn't entirely benign. Numerous studies have found no link between caffeine and cardiovascular disease. But it can cause anxiety, jitters, and heart palpitations, particularly in people who are sensitive to it. It also can cause stomach pain and gastrointestinal reflux, may make it harder for a woman to get pregnant, and may increase the risk of miscarriage or a low-birth-weight baby. Doctors advise pregnant women to give up caffeine, or keep consumption down to a cup or two of coffee daily.

Sleeplessness, not surprisingly, is a notorious side effect of caffeine. In recent years, as the number of people taking prescription sleeping pills has soared, more than a few doctors have wondered if people should reconsider their use of caffeine before downing an Ambien or Lunesta. According to Medco Health Solutions of Franklin Lakes, N.J., use of such medications by adults ages 20 to 44 increased 114 percent from 2000 to 2005.

In kids, lack of sleep is both a worrisome cause and effect of the caffeine craze. Wilkie Wilson, a professor of pharmacology at Duke University Medical Center and coauthor of *Buzzed*, a guide to commonly used drugs, says he's stunned by how little sleep kids get these days. Teenagers, he says, need at least nine hours of sleep a night; grade schoolers, 10 to 12 hours. Very few get close to that much—either, as in Linleigh Hawk's case, because they're actively fighting sleep, or because they're so jazzed from caffeine that they can't settle down at bedtime. The downside: "I'm exhausted. I can't remember simple things," Hawk says. But she gets the work done.

Indeed, lack of sleep interferes with concentration, says William Kohler, medical director of the Florida Sleep Institute in Spring Hill. It also can make kids fidgety. Since inattention and restlessness are signs of attention deficit hyperactivity disorder as well, sleep researchers increasingly believe that some kids diagnosed with ADHD are actually sleep deprived.

The caffeine itself makes kids fidgety, too, of course. Just ask Maya Thompson, a Sacramento, Calif., mother. "It's like two totally different extremes," she says of how much more aggressive her son Jordan, 12, becomes with even a sip of a caffeinated drink. Jordan, for his part, says that lots of kids in his sixth-grade class pull Monster or Rock Star energy drinks out of their backpacks and drink them before PE class. "Oh my gosh!" says Maya, 30. "I'm shocked by that—that is crazy!"

The young adult crowd who favor caffeine with their alcohol appear to be putting themselves at some risk, too. The stimulant does mitigate the effects of alcohol by improving response time, according to Mark Fillmore, a psychologist at the University of Kentucky who has been testing the combination on student volunteers. But it fails to reduce the number of errors that a person under the influence makes. "Caffeine seems to restore the speed of your behavior but not the accuracy," Fillmore says.

Until the advent of caffeine pills and highly caffeinated energy drinks, caffeine overdoses were exceedingly rare, because people became anxious, shaky, and nauseated before they could imbibe enough. Now, people are sometimes shocked to find out how few servings equal too much. "I'm a strong, 47-year-old man, and I tell you what, that stuff put me on my knees," says Scott Silliman, a construction worker from Citrus Heights, Calif., who recently grabbed two cans of Redline RTD energy drink at 7-Eleven when he picked up lunch for the crew.

Silliman pounded down the drinks, then ate a burrito. Twenty minutes later, "I was sweating, I was shaking, I was freezing cold. I never felt anything like that in my life." Silliman thought he was having a heart attack. Actually, he had drunk 500 mg of caffeine in a few minutes, the equivalent of five cups of coffee. "The government should put some kind of regulations on this, or at least warning labels."

Consumer watchdog groups think so, too. The government puts caffeine in its category of "generally recognized as safe" and so doesn't require food and drink manufacturers to list caffeine content. For more than a decade, the American Medical Association and the Center for Science in the Public Interest have been lobbying the Food and Drug Administration to require caffeine content labels, as well as the words "not appropriate for children." Meantime, soft drink manufacturers, seeing growing concern in Congress and among local politicians about children's access to energy drinks, announced in February that they'll now list caffeine content on drinks. The Coca-Cola Co.

has already relabeled Full Throttle energy drink (141 mg per 16 ounces) and its new Enviga sparkling green tea (100 mg in 12 ounces); classic Coke will reveal its 34 milligrams in May. PepsiCo will have caffeine content on Pepsi and other drinks this summer.

Even as they're upping their dosage of caffeine, many high schoolers and college students are seeking a stronger boost than it can give. Prescription stimulants such as Ritalin, Concerta, and Adderall, widely prescribed to treat the inattention of ADHD, have become a source of alertness and energy for studying, and for late-night parties. About 3 percent of college students say they've used prescription stimulants illegally, according to a March 2007 study by the National Center on Addiction and Substance Abuse at Columbia University. The number is small compared with students' use of alcohol, marijuana, and tobacco, but stimulant abuse is increasing faster, almost doubling between 1993 and 2005, according to Susan Foster, vice president and director of policy research and analysis.

The drugs are "universal performance enhancers," says Lawrence Diller, a pediatrician in Walnut Creek, Calif., and author of *The Last Normal Child*. He thinks doctors, including himself, overprescribe drugs for mild ADHD. About 1.5 million adults and 2.5 million children—some 10 percent of all 10-year-old boys—now have prescriptions.

That means just about everybody under age 20 knows someone with a potential source of Adderall or Ritalin. (Most nonmedical users prefer Adderall to the slower-acting Ritalin.) On college campuses, prices rise as exams approach, from $7 to $15 for a 10-mg pill.

Marshall Dines, 23, a senior at the University of Michigan, even had strangers E-mailing him to sell them medicine after he joined a Facebook group about Adderall. (He refused and later left the group.)

Caffeine was considered a controlled substance by the olympic committee until 2004.

Prescription stimulants can be big trouble when used to excess; that's been apparent since World War II, when both Axis and Allies gave troops amphetamines like Dexedrine to keep them alert on the front lines and many soldiers came home addicted (Adolf Hitler was reportedly a fan). More recently, stimulants have been popular with truck drivers and dieters. In 1971, the federal government added amphetamines (Adderall and other brands) and methylphenidates (Ritalin, Concerta, and other brands) to its Schedule II list of controlled substances—drugs with legitimate medical uses that also have a high potential for abuse. Stimulants account for just 1 percent of drug-related emergency room visits. But the number of people showing up with symptoms like confusion and convulsions after nonmedical use rose 33 percent from 2004 to 2005, according to a Substance Abuse and Mental Health Services Administration survey. Visits due to Ritalin and other methylphenidates more than doubled.

All stimulant medications work by increasing the amount of dopamine in the brain, a neurotransmitter that's a major player in the pleasure response to food, say, or sex. Cocaine and methamphetamine, a powerful (and illegal) cousin of the amphetamine in Adderall, create sharp upward spikes in dopamine, causing an intensely pleasurable rush. The equally quick crash, and the memory of the euphoric high, are powerful spurs to addiction. Prescription amphetamines raise dopamine levels slowly and lose their effect gradually. Thus, they're less likely to prompt a high and crash and be addictive.

But the reality is that people can become addicted to prescription stimulants, and repeated overuse can lead to hostility, paranoia, confusion, hallucinations, psychotic episodes, depression, and seizures. "There's an optimal level of dopamine in your brain," says NIDA's Volkow, who studies how drugs of abuse remodel the brain. Go beyond that level, and the brain, in effect, gets stuck.

These days, the impetus on campus is often less the urge for a high than the desire to get more done. "I saw no point in sleeping," says Derek Simeone, now 22, who was prescribed stimulant medication while in high school—and took it more often as a freshman at Syracuse University. "Adderall allows me to do more with my life in a certain amount of time." Beyond studying, the medication helped him stay up and play video games, party, and hang out. He finally cut back after a week without sleep left him hot, pale, and sweaty, and he eventually gave up Adderall altogether. Now a programmer in New Jersey, Simeone relies on coffee.

Heart Risks. Stimulant drugs also increase the chance of heart attacks and strokes, a risk that's well documented in abuse of drugs like cocaine and methamphetamine. In February 2006, after studies revealed 25 cases of fatal strokes or heart attacks in children and adults taking stimulant medication for ADHD, the FDA ordered manufacturers to put warnings on all prescription stimulants, including Ritalin, Adderall, and Concerta. Those complications are rare. But Steven Nissen, chairman of the department of cardiovascular medicine at the Cleveland Clinic, thinks the agency should go further, particularly since so many people are taking stimulants to treat only mild symptoms of ADHD.

"Can it possibly be that 10 percent of all the sixth-grade boys in America have a disease that requires amphetamines?" Nissen asks. "I'm unwilling to accept that that's an appropriate use of a psychotropic agent, particularly one that has well-known cardiovascular risks." He also worries about the rapidly increasing use of ADHD drugs by adults. "Ten percent of them are over age 55," Nissen says. "That's a potential disaster."

The popularity of stimulants on campus has not escaped the notice of university health officials. Although they are far more concerned about the dangers of binge drinking—a much more widespread problem—schools are becoming considerably more cautious about handing out stimulant medications. Two years ago, Indiana University initiated a screening process for students claiming to need stimulants that includes standardized tests, evaluation of a student's records as far back as elementary school, and a survey sent to parents, according to Hugh Jessop, director of the IU Health Center. Of the 283 students who scheduled appointments to get medication at Indiana in the past couple years, only 47 completed the process. The University of Wisconsin no longer even fills prescriptions from family doctors back home.

More than two or three coffees a day cut women's suicide risk over 10 years by a third.

The lure of prescription stimulants may well fade, as it has in decades past, when the ugly effects of abuse and addiction become clear. (Hippies in the late 1960s graffitied the walls of San Francisco's Haight-Ashbury district with "Speed kills," a testament to the fact that overuse was no summer of love.) But the $4 minivacation from the stresses of daily life appears to be a destination with real staying power. "Coffee culture" has become so much a part of American culture that 36-year-old Starbucks, once considered a gourmet's treat, now boasts 9,401 stores nationwide and has focused growth on economically struggling neighborhoods far from the yuppified precincts of its early success.

Even McDonald's hawks a premium blend; Dunkin' Donuts sells lattes. "It's like a miniature splurge," says Tracy Allen, vice president for Zoka Coffee Roaster and Tea Co. in Seattle, which markets a barista-brewed cup of organic Ethiopian Yirgacheffe as if it were a fine wine. "The coffee shop is the 21st-century version of the 1950s malt shop," says Joseph DeRupo, director of communications for the National Coffee Association. "It's where kids go to meet friends and socialize."

What's next? Richard Holschen, a police officer in Kaktovik, Alaska, couldn't tote around coffee in the subzero temperatures above the Arctic Circle, so he invented caffeinated SpazzStick lip balm. "I needed to stay awake if I was on duty three days straight," Holschen, 34, says. "Caffeine and lip balm were a logical conclusion for me." Internet sales have been brisk, he says.

Robert Bohannon's phone started ringing off the hook in January, when the Durham, N.C.-based inventor announced that he'd perfected a recipe for caffeinated doughnuts and bagels. "I feel completely overwhelmed," he says. He hasn't yet produced the pastry on a commercial scale but plans to license his invention this year.

With Justin Ewers, Alison Go, David LaGesse, and Adam Voiland

Smoking, Drugs, Obesity Top Health Concerns for Kids

I t's only natural to for adults to worry about children's health and well-being at school, on the roads and even online.

But adults' No. 1 health concern for children and adolescents in the United States? It's smoking, according to new results from the University of Michigan C.S. Mott Children's Hospital National Poll on Children's Health. Drug abuse ranked No. 2.

The poll, which asked adults to rate 17 different health problems for children living in their communities, also found that childhood obesity now ranks among the public's top three concerns for children's health, ahead of alcohol abuse and teen pregnancy.

Also making the public's overall list of top 10 health concerns for kids: Driving accidents, Internet safety, school violence, sexually transmitted infections, and abuse and neglect. The child health issues that didn't make the top 10 list, but were still rated as "big problems" by 6 to 18 percent of adults: Psychological stress, depression, eating disorders, suicide, autism, childhood cancer and food contamination.

"We found that major race/ethnicity groups differ when it comes to the top three health concerns for children as well. While white adults list smoking, drug abuse and alcohol abuse at their top three concerns, black adults rate teen pregnancy, smoking and drug abuse, and Hispanic adults rank smoking, drug abuse and childhood obesity as the three major health problems for children," says Matthew M. Davis, M.D., M.A.P.P., director of the National Poll on Children's Health, part of the U-M Department of Pediatrics and Communicable Diseases and the Child Health Evaluation and Research (CHEAR) Unit in the U-M Division of General Pediatrics.

To rank the public's top health concerns for children, the National Poll on Children's Health, in collaboration with Knowledge Networks, Inc., conducted a national online survey in March 2007. The survey, administered to a random sample of 2,076 adults who are a part of Knowledge Network's online KnowledgePanelSM, revealed the top 10 out of 17 health concerns for children in the U.S.

Top 10 Overall Health Concerns for Children in the U.S.

1. Smoking. Forty percent of adults rate smoking as their top health concern for children. Among black adults, smoking ranks No. 2. Forty-five percent of black adults, however, rate smoking as a big problem.

2. Drug abuse. Adults are more likely to rate drug abuse as a concern based on their children's emotional health. Those who report their child's emotional health as "good," "fair" or "poor" are more likely to view drug abuse as a major health problem for children compared with parents who rate their child's emotional health as "excellent" or "very good."

3. Childhood obesity. According to poll results, adults with higher education are more likely to rate childhood obesity as their No. 1 health issue for children than adults with high school education or less. In fact, 40 percent of adults with a college degree view obesity as a top concern, while those with less than a high school education rate it as their No. 10 concern, with 25 percent reporting it as a top concern. The National Poll on Children's Health also found Hispanic adults are more likely to report obesity as a problem, with 42 percent viewing it as a major problem, compared with only 31 percent of white adults and 36 percent of black adults. "These differences somewhat reflect the higher prevalence of obesity among black and Hispanic youth compared with white youth," notes Davis.

4. Alcohol abuse. "Households with lower incomes less than $30,000 per year are significantly more likely to rate alcohol abuse as a problem than families with higher annual incomes," says Davis. "We also found that alcohol abuse by teens was a bigger concern in households with a single or divorced parent, compared with households with married parents."

5. Motor vehicle accidents. Driving accidents involving teenagers are a universal concern across all socio-economic groups studied, says Davis.

6. Teen pregnancy. Black adults rate teen pregnancy as the No. 1 health problem for youth, with 51 percent reporting it's a major health concern compared with only 25 percent of white adults. "This difference echoes differences in rates of teen pregnancy by race/ethnicity, which have declined among all teens over the past decade, but remain two times higher among blacks than whites," says Davis.

7. Internet safety. "Internet safety is a relatively new health concern in relation to other health issues," says Davis. "Women and black adults are more likely to report it as a major concern." Thirty-two percent of women and

21 percent of men report they are concerned about Internet safety, while 37 percent of black adults and 25 percent of white adults say it is a big problem.

8. School violence. "School violence didn't rate as high as driving accidents and alcohol use. Yet it still is in the top 10, and that speaks to the current level of concern in the U.S. about this problem," says Davis. "We measured school violence concerns before the recent tragedy at Virginia Tech, so it is likely that it may rank higher today than it did just a few weeks ago." Davis also notes that black adults are more than twice as likely as white adults to report school violence as a big problem, ranking it their No. 4 health concern. It also was viewed as a bigger health problem among lower income households.

9. Sexually transmitted infections. Sexually transmitted infections among youth are considered to be a bigger problem by black adults and Hispanics, with 40 percent of black adults and 34 percent of Hispanics adults viewing it as a big problem, compared with only 20 percent of white adults. Households with lower incomes also rate sexually transmitted infections as a greater health concern for children.

10. Abuse and neglect. About 22 percent of survey respondents view abuse and neglect as a health concern for children. "Similar to other health issues in the poll, more black respondents feel abuse and neglect is a big health concern than among Hispanic and white respondents," says Davis.

Ratings for the top 10 list did not differ between adults who have children in their households, and those who do not. Overall, higher proportions of blacks and Hispanic adults rated all 17 concerns as "big problems" compared with white adults.

"This poll provides us with a detailed picture of what the public views as some of the biggest health concerns for children and adolescents today," says Davis, associate professor of general pediatrics and internal medicine at the U-M Medical School, and associate professor of public policy at the Gerald R. Ford School of Public Policy. "It also suggests that the government may want to target more investment toward issues such as teen smoking, drug abuse and childhood obesity, in a way that reflects the fact that the public is currently prioritizing these problems as even bigger than other issues on the list."

About the National Poll on Children's Health

The C.S. Mott Children's Hospital National Poll on Children's Health is funded by the Department of Pediatrics and Communicable Diseases at the U-M Health System. As part of the U-M Division of General Pediatric Child Health Evaluation and Research (CHEAR) Unit, the National Poll on Children's Health is designed to measure major health care issues and trends for U.S. children. For a copy of the reports from National Poll on Children's Health, visit http://www.chear.umich.edu. For regular podcasts of polling results, go to http://www.med.umich.edu/podcast.

About Knowledge Networks

Knowledge Networks delivers quality and service to guide leaders in business, government and academia uniquely bringing scientifically valid research to the online space through its probability-based, online KnowledgePanelSM. The company delivers unique study design, science, analysis, and panel maintenance, along with a commitment to close collaboration at every stage of the research process. KN leverages its expertise in brands, media, advertising, and public policy issues to provide insights that speak directly to clients' most important concerns. For more information about Knowledge Networks, visit http://www.knowledgenetworks.com.

From *Medical News Today,* May 6, 2007. Copyright © 2007 by Medical News Today. Reprinted by permission. www.medicalnewstoday.com

Living the High Life
The Role of Drug Taking in Young People's Lives

The vast majority of young drug users see substance use as a positive experience. Why else would they continue to take them? Most research on the other hand pathologises drug use by looking solely at the negative consequences, contributing to the misunderstanding that young people are increasingly self-indulgent and, in a meaningless world, hell-bent on self-destruction. In this refreshing new article Karenza Moore and Steven Miles try to understand the social roles of drug use in the everchanging lives of young people and come up with an alternative view. Rather than seeing drugs as a destructive force, Moore and Miles portray drug-taking as a stabilising factor in the volatile world of growing up.

KARENZA MOORE AND STEVEN MILES

Clubbing is a leisure pursuit enjoyed by millions of young people. So-called 'dance drugs', predominately ecstasy, amphetamines, cocaine and 'new' substances such as GHB and ketamine, are an integral part of localised and globalised club cultures.

There is a considerable danger that in the midst of media and academic conjecture the impact of drugs upon young people's lives and the role that drugs partake in the active construction of young people's lifestyles is neglected in favour of a melodramatic vision of young people as risk-takers, and of young clubbers as being at the forefront of such 'risk behaviour'.

We argue that much like other forms of consumption, young people's use of drugs in clubbing settings (pre-club bars, in-club spaces, dance music festivals, after-parties) is less about exploring the unpredictability of risk or about the corruption of innocence, and more about young people actively maintaining a sense of stability in their everyday lives.

Exploring the Nature of Drug Use

To explore this alternative view of young people's drug consumption we draw on our small-scale survey of young clubbers in Manchester and Sheffield and two years of observation in various clubbing settings within these two cities.

Many commentators have noted that young people's lives are perhaps increasingly precarious, not least in light of the apparently vast number of choices and hurdles that lie between them and their futures. In order to understand the role of drugs in young people's lives it is important to have some comprehension of the broader nature of their social experience.

Young people do not consume drugs in isolation. The consumption of drugs represents an active expression of how young people cope with the demands of the social structures within which they operate. Drug consumption, and most particularly that found in club settings, is one such way that young people can actually impart some control over their everyday lives.

Drug Use Has Meaning for Young People

The apparently mundane contexts in which young people consume drugs are particularly useful in understanding what drug consumption actually *means*. The fact that young people's cultural lives are not always deemed to be of significant policy interest has a dangerous side-effect insofar as it serves to magnify the problematisation of young people—a phenomenon already encountered among services that deal with drug use among young people.

Clubbing can offer young people a sense of identity that goes beyond the antics of the weekend. It can have an impact upon a person's sense of self, their identifications with others and their sense of 'belonging' in sometimes confusing and menacing urban spaces.

Clubbing may provide some young people with a sense of stability in their lives, opening up a space in which they can depend on something, in a world in which arguably at least they can depend on very little.

Such aspects of young people's drug use, notably within club settings, are often overlooked in moralistic prescriptions of zero tolerance and the dominant 'war on drugs' discourse.

Dedication to Clubbing and Drugs

To 'be a clubber' is hard work. Young people who regularly go clubbing invest considerable time and effort ensuring that their nights out, and dancing till the early hours of the morning, will be fun, and to a certain extent trouble-free. Clubbers demonstrate considerable local (and wider) knowledge about clubs, DJs, music and musical genres.

Preparation for some nights out clubbing starts weeks or even months in advance, while at other times a more spontaneous decision to go clubbing is made. In terms of preparation, procuring desired substances sometimes takes place days in advance and can be a source of considerable anxiety.

The Routine

Due to the very familiarity of the practices that have to be undertaken in order for the night out to run smoothly, these preparations act as basis for the expectations that clubbers build up around a night. When clubbers have 'sorted' themselves out in terms of deciding where to go and obtaining substances, this adds to the excitement and anticipation.

Events, such as being caught in-club with drugs, undermine the 'flow' of a night out, and the possibility that such events may occur contributes to the anxiety that some clubbers experience. Of course mundane clubbing practices such as obtaining, hiding and consuming 'dance drugs' form the basis for the more spectacular aspects of clubbing, such as when a crowd is 'brought up' by the DJs with a popular record.

Broadening Social Encounters

There are other mundane and possibly routine practices on which the spectacular aspects of clubbing rest. Many young dance drug users for example see interacting with strangers in-club as a 'natural' part of clubbing.

'Normally I'm quite shy but when I'm out clubbing I just chat to anyone and hug and dance with everyone. That's the best thing about it. If I like someone's hair or what they're wearing, or they just look friendly, I'll go right up and tell them' (Male, age 26).[1]

'It makes you feel special, like you're out clubbing with the whole club' (Male, age 20).

Sociability, Indicators and Rules

Mundane practices undertaken pre-club and in-club play a part in the more spectacular feeling of 'clubbing with the whole club'. Young clubbers share water, chewing gum and 'poppers' with friends and strangers, and use physical contact as a 'marker' for the friendliness and togetherness of a crowd, and an indication of a good night out.

'You can tell it's a good one if the crowd are there with their hands in the air, jumping up and down with each other and hugging random people!' (Female, age 19, Sat 12 July 2003: Manchester).

Many of the young people we spoke to said they would help a fellow clubber who appeared to be in trouble, by calling security or a paramedic for example. Such practices relate to the social etiquette that surrounds the consumption of substances in the clubbing space.

Extravagant displays of 'self-expression' in settings where it may be presumed that 'anything goes' rest on the nuances of behaviours that are deemed socially, culturally and contextually acceptable or unacceptable.

Some young people for example thought that ketamine users in clubs can somehow break the 'rules', describing users as *'like zombies roaming around the club'* (Male, age 20).

Drugs of Choice

The northwest of England is similar to many areas of the UK in providing a huge range of club nights, all playing a wide variety of dance music genres, often under the same roof. On a single night out clubbers may consume alcohol, ecstasy, GHB, amyl nitrate (poppers), ketamine and cannabis (Saturday 13 September 2003: Sheffield).

Many young clubbers take a range of drugs, although ecstasy remains the drug of choice for many. This seems to be related to the perception that ecstasy makes people friendlier than any other 'clubbing drug', especially alcohol.

'People are all very nice on pills' (Female, age 21)

Musical genre affects what drugs people take and how: Our respondents said they are more likely to take ecstasy (and for some ketamine) at hard house, trance, and hard trance nights. Those that attend funky/soulful house nights say they are more likely to take alcohol at such events than at other nights (such as hard trance).

'You will rarely find clubbers taking Ket in a trance club. It's not that type of scene. You would also rarely find people taking cocaine in a hard house/trance environment, because it makes you more arrogant and unsociable' (Male, age 20).

'Funky house: people are more likely to take cocaine due to the pretensions associated with it. Hard house and trance: Ecstasy is more commonly used' (Male, age 20).

Here we see a process occurring in which clubbers distinguish between the friendliness of a crowd depending on the genre of music being played and the related substance use. There may not actually be any substantive differences in the types of substances being consumed according to musical genre in the club setting but clubbers perceive there to be a difference.

Young clubbers also report experiencing what are ostensibly the 'same' substances differently according to musical genre and (club) setting. Some clubbers indicated that they consume less, if any, alcohol at hard house nights than they do at funky/soulful house nights.

'I drink alcohol at funky house nights, don't know why just seems like the thing to do. Also I always end up feeling more f**ked at hard house nights and the comedowns are worse' (Female, age 27).

Knowing the Score and Feeling in Control

Many young clubbers perceive that they are well informed about drug harm and risk-reduction techniques.

'Have a nice bath when I get in, sleep! Drink plenty of water, orange juice, take 5-HTP (to aid replenishment of Serotonin) and Echinacea (to boost immune system). Eat healthily, ie, lots of vegetables, fruit etc. Be around people/friends for comedown company!' (Male, age 20).

In addition to clubbers' perceptions that they know 'what pills do to you', young people deployed the notion of

'balance' between clubbing and 'real-life' as itself a harm-reduction technique.

'I make sure I still do other things I love like playing football, and I take a break every couple of weekends. I know one really smart guy that went to Imperial in London and basically fucked up his life from too many pills and too much clubbing' (Male, age 21, Saturday 25 October 2003: Manchester).

Clubbing Folklore and Setting Boundaries

Clubbers tell anecdotes about people who had 'overdone' clubbing, or become too 'hardcore', letting their weekend activities interfere with 'normal' life. While the use of ecstasy in club culture may be becoming 'normalised', this does not necessarily entail the existence of a 'reckless' chemical generation.

Clubbers engage with discourses surrounding drug 'abuse' and distance themselves from the notion of abuse by referring to the ways in which they 'manage' their 'recreational' drug use so that it does not interfere with their everyday lives.

The general feeling among many young clubbers is that 'recreational' drug consumption in club settings is a temporary pursuit and that at some point in the future they will stop.

'When I get older, I suppose I'll grow out of it. If I carried on, I'd look out of place. I believe it's a phase people go through. Eventually I'll stop taking them. I've cut down a lot of the stuff I used to do already. I never have to take drugs when I'm out' (Male, age 20).

However, from our participant observation in dubs in the northwest of England, it is dear that there are substantial numbers of older people who continue to enjoy dance–drug dubbing.

The Social Benefits of Clubbing

However this view appears not to detract from the symbolic importance that many young clubbers attribute to dubbing, particularly in terms of the friendship groups they had built up around dubbing activities.

'The music, dancing, the feeling/energy doing pills gives you, enjoying myself and seeing other people I know and care about enjoying themselves, sense of community and feeling "special"!' (Male, age 20).

This again suggests that young clubbers' drug consumption is strategic in nature. Strategic in the sense that it provides young people with something very tangible in the short-term: the feeling that they belong to something that has its own structure and language that takes them away from their broader life-concerns while simultaneously being formed by, and forming, those concerns.

Importance of a Non-pathological View

If we resist the temptation to pigeonhole and demonise young people, we may begin to comprehend the pragmatic and at times rational ways with which they cope with social change. Involvement in club culture may be one way in which young people are negotiating such changes.

Note

1. These responses are taken from the aforementioned questionnaire on young 'clubbers' in Manchester and Sheffield.

KARENZA MOORE and **STEVEN MILES** (2004) Young people, dance and the sub-cultural consumption of drugs. *Addiction, Research and Theory 12* (6) 507–523 k.moore@salford.ac.uk

Acknowledgement—An extended version of this paper is available in *Addiction, Research and Theory*.

Methamphetamine Abuse:
A Perfect Storm of Complications

TIMOTHY W. LINEBERRY, MD AND J. MICHAEL BOSTWICK, MD

Previously restricted primarily to Hawaii and California, methamphetamine abuse has reached epidemic proportions throughout the United States during the past decade, specifically in rural and semirural areas. Particular characteristics of methamphetamine production and use create conditions for a "perfect storm" of medical and social complications. Unlike imported recreational drugs such as heroin and cocaine, methamphetamine can be manufactured locally from commonly available household ingredients according to simple recipes readily available on the Internet. Methamphetamine users and producers are frequently one and the same, resulting in both physical and environmental consequences. Users experience emergent, acute, subacute, and chronic injuries to neurologic, cardiac, pulmonary, dental, and other systems. Producers can sustain life-threatening injuries in the frequent fires and explosions that result when volatile chemicals are combined. Partners and children of producers, as well as unsuspecting first responders to a crisis, are exposed to toxic by-products of methamphetamine manufacture that contaminate the places that serve simultaneously as "lab" and home. From the vantage point of a local emergency department, this article reviews the range of medical and social consequences that radiate from a single hypothetical methamphetamine-associated incident.

Mayo Clin Proc. 2006;81(1):77–84

ED = emergency department; EMS = emergency medical services; STD = sexually transmitted disease; HIV = human immunodeficiency virus

Methamphetamine production and abuse have increased dramatically during the past decade in the United States.[1,2] US admissions, primarily for treatment of methamphetamine/amphetamine abuse

and dependence, increased more than 500% from 1992 to 2002, from 10 to 52 per 100,000 people aged 12 years or older.[3] Of these admissions in 2002, more than 90% were methamphetamine related.

In 2002, 13 states had admission rates greater than 100 per 100,000 members of the general population; all but 1 of those states (Arkansas) was west of the Mississippi River. Oregon, Hawaii, and California reported rates greater than 200 per 100,000 people (Table 1). The criminal justice system referred more than half of these admissions.

Methamphetamine, a stimulant, was synthesized first in Japan in 1893.[4] German, English, American, and Japanese military personnel, as well as civilian Japanese factory workers, used the drug during World War II for its energy-promoting and performance-enhancing properties.[5] After World War II, the Japanese military dumped large supplies of methamphetamine on the civilian market, precipitating Japan's "first epidemic" of methamphetamine abuse.[6]

Methamphetamine is a highly addictive street drug with a variety of forms and street names (Table 2). The drug gives users a "rush" that includes feelings of enhanced well-being, heightened libido, increased energy, and appetite suppression.[7] Psychological effects observed with methamphetamine use include euphoria, paranoia, agitation, mood disturbances, violent behavior, anxiety, depression, and psychosis. Cheaper than cocaine, its stimulant effects are also longer lasting.[8] As the mood- and energy-enhancing effects of binging methamphetamine begin to wear off, users begin "tweaking,"[5] a term describing a dangerous combination of restless anxiety, irritability, fatigue, and dysphoria. Further use of methamphetamine temporarily improves the symptoms and further reinforces the addiction. Eventually, after days of sleeplessness, users "crash" into a nonrestful sleep.

From Hawaii and California, critical geographic stepping stones between Japan and the rest of the United States, methamphetamine use radiated eastward via its original primary mainland users, truckers and biker gangs.[1] Although "super labs" in California and northern Mexico still make

Table 1   Methamphetamine/Amphetamine Admission Rates*

	1992	2002		1992	2002
United States	10.4	52.1			
Northeast			Midwest		
Connecticut	1.0	3.8	Illinois	2.0	13.4
Maine	1.5	3.5	Indiana	1.6	22.8
Massachusetts	1.1	1.3	Iowa	9.2	*198.1*
New Hampshire	0.3	7.0	Kansas	9.8	*61.3*
New Jersey	2.6	1.9	Michigan	2.1	5.1
New York	1.8	3.4	Minnesota	4.6	*77.6*
Pennsylvania	2.5	2.3	Missouri	5.2	*86.2*
Rhode Island	2.1	2.4	Nebraska	6.8	*102.2*
Vermont	4.7	4.3	North Dakota	2.3	*65.4*
South			Ohio	5.3	1.9
Alabama	1.3	35.9	South Dakota	4.0	*68.9*
Arkansas	7.2	*124.9*	Wisconsin	0.4	3.5
Delaware	2.1	1.8	West		
District of Columbia	†	3.6	Alaska	4.5	15.0
Florida	1.5	5.3	Arizona	†	27.7
Georgia	1.9	22.2	California	48.6	*200.1*
Kentucky	†	13.3	Colorado	*14.0*	*67.7*
Louisiana	3.9	18.4	Hawaii	32.8	*217.2*
Maryland	1.5	2.3	Idaho	9.7	*116.2*
Mississippi	†	7.5	Montana	33.5	*118.6*
North Carolina	1.1	3.2	Nevada	34.6	*156.8*
Oklahoma	*15.5*	*118.8*	New Mexico	4.9	4.5
South Carolina	1.3	6.7	Oregon	*72.4*	*323.6*
Tennessee	0.1	9.3	Utah	10.0	*115.2*
Texas	7.2	13.0	Washington	*11.4*	*150.4*
Virginia	0.9	3.2	Wyoming	*15.2*	*166.9*
West Virginia	1.4	0.5			

* Per 100,000, aged ≥12 years, for 1992 and 2002. Italics indicate rates above the national rate for that year.
† Incomplete data.

most methamphetamine used in the United States, readily available ingredients and ease of production have encouraged the exponential growth[9] of makeshift labs operated by "do-it-yourselfers" throughout the country, particularly in rural areas (Figure 1). Despite methamphetamine's illegality, "recipes" for making the drug are found easily on the Internet and passed from user to user.

Using methods reminiscent of a college chemistry class, methamphetamine "cookers" brew methamphetamine from ingredients readily available in farm implement, hardware, and convenience stores.[10] The most common recipes include steps that extract ephedrine from over-the-counter pseudoephedrine-containing cold preparations, create hydroiodic acid from water and iodine, and mix both products with red phosphorus. The resulting series of chemical reactions replace a hydroxyl group on the ephedrine with a hydrogen atom to yield methamphetamine. If red phosphorus is unavailable and hypophosphoric acid must be used as a phosphorus source instead, the process is especially dangerous because of the production of highly toxic phosphine gas. A farm country variation of the phosphorus-hydroiodic acid step uses lithium found in batteries and anhydrous ammonia from fertilizer tanks.

All the basic elements of a "meth lab" can fit into a suitcase, closet, or car trunk. Although methamphetamine is produced in cities, the isolation of rural settings decreases

Table 2   Methamphetamine Forms, Time to Effect, and Street Names

	Intravenous	Smoked	Snorted	Ingested
Time to effect	15-30 s	Immediate	3-5 min	15-20 min
Peak concentration (h)	2-4	2-4	2-4	2-4
Elimination half-life (h)	10-12	10-12	10-12	10-12

Street terms for methamphetamine

Blue meth	Granulated orange	Speed
Chalk	Hillbilly crack	Spoosh
Chicken feed	Hot ice	Stove top
Cinnamon	Ice	Super ice
Crank	Kaksonjae	Tick tick
Crink	L.A. glass	Trash
Crystal	Lemon drop	Wash
Crystal meth	Meth	Working man's cocaine
Desocsins	OZs	Yaba
Geep	Peanut butter	Yellow barn
Glass	Sketch	Yellow powder

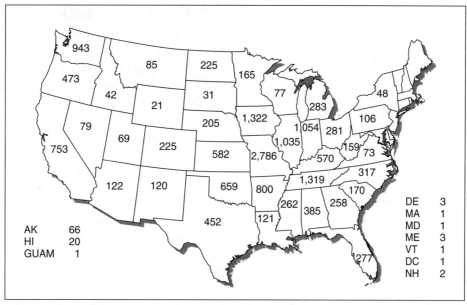

Figure 1 Number of US methamphetamine lab incidents in 2004 from the National Clandestine Laboratory Database. Total number was 17,033.

the likelihood that the potent chemical smells from cooking "meth" (ammonia, ether, or acetone) will be noticed by neighbors or law enforcement.

Each pound of methamphetamine produced yields an estimated 6 pounds of toxic waste,[11] including acid, lye, and phosphorus dumped into ditches, rivers, yards, and drains, and a fine particulate methamphetamine residue settles on exposed surfaces in household interiors.[12] Such flammable ingredients as acetone, red phosphorus, ethyl alcohol, and lithium metal, combined with the poor judgment of methamphetamine-intoxicated "cookers," result in fires and explosions. Accidents in home labs are one of the most common reasons that labs are discovered by law enforcement officials.

Medical and Social Consequences

Between 1999 and 2002, emergency department (ED) visits resulting from medical and psychiatric complications of methamphetamine abuse increased nearly 75%.[13] The Drug Abuse and Warning Network database recorded 17,696 ED visits nationwide in 2002, up from 10,447 in 1999.[13] Exponential increases in admissions for primary methamphetamine inpatient treatment[3] and the medical complications associated with methamphetamine abuse directly affect the operations of medical and surgical units throughout the medical center.

To describe the extent and effect of methamphetamine abuse on the network of individuals around a user as well as the user himself or herself, we illustrate a series of ED encounters that flow from a hypothetical methamphetamine-fueled accident. We outline the types of presenting symptoms, physical findings, and medical and psychosocial concerns that result from methamphetamine abuse. Users face certain physical consequences particular to methamphetamine that require immediate medical attention. However, methamphetamine use has longer lasting consequences for users, their families, and their communities that also must be addressed in the initial ED evaluation.

Incident

After a neighbor calls 911 to report hearing an explosion and seeing a neighbor's house engulfed in flames, police and other emergency medical services (EMS) personnel respond to the scene of the house fire. Police had already been investigating the tenants for possible involvement in methamphetamine manufacture. Without protective gear available, a police officer races into the burning structure and rescues an occupant from certain immolation.

Emergent Presentation

A 25-year-old man is pulled from the fire and has multiple penetrating wounds and second- and third-degree burns on 50% of his body surface. He is dyspneic and in shock.

A worst case contemporary ED scenario involves EMS personnel transporting a methamphetamine-intoxicated patient with burns, wounds, and cardiorespiratory compromise. "Meth cookers" sustain burns from chemicals used in production, including acids and anhydrous ammonia, and/or from the explosions that result when volatile chemicals are combined. If the patient is able to give a medical history, it may not match the physical findings because the patient may try to disguise the illegal nature of the injurious activities.[14]

15

Patients with methamphetamine-related burns require more aggressive fluid resuscitation[15,16] and airway management and have a higher mortality rate[16] than matched-age controls not exposed to methamphetamine. In a sample of 668 patients admitted to a burn center over a 2-year period,[16] 15 patients were methamphetamine users, 11 of whom required tracheal intubation as a result of inhalation injury or combativeness. Among the methamphetamine users, 6 had burns on more than 40% of their body areas and died, compared with 60% who survived in a comparable age group at the burn center. Compared with controls, patients who were methamphetamine users also required more invasive cardiac monitoring, pressor support, and procedures.

Exposure to phosphine, a by-product of methamphetamine cooking, can damage multiple organ systems.[17–19] An agricultural pesticide, phosphine gas is colorless and has a fishy or garlicky odor. Although its exact mechanism of injury is uncertain, it is known to inhibit cytochrome C oxidase, with subsequent generation of damaging oxygen free radicals.[19] Phosphine exposure can cause ocular and respiratory irritation, shortness of breath, headache, nausea, fatigue, and stomach pain. Its most devastating effects are pulmonary and cardiac damage, including acute, potentially fatal respiratory and hemodynamic failure.

Severe methamphetamine abuse may complicate the management of shock. Methamphetamine-induced sympathetic vasoconstriction exacerbates the acidosis typically expected from comparable trauma.[20,21] Thus, the additive effects of methamphetamine on already-present metabolic abnormalities should be considered in the emergency treatment of patients in shock, among whom methamphetamine use may be a factor. Either vasoconstriction-induced acute renal failure or methamphetamine-induced rhabdomyolysis[22] can present alone or in conjunction with any cardiorespiratory or vascular condition.

Cardiovascular problems can be acute or chronic. As with cocaine users, new-onset chest pain secondary to coronary vasoconstriction may herald myocardial infarctions or potentially lethal arrhythmias.[23] Emergent vascular presentations can include aortic dissections, ruptured berry aneurysms,[24] or spontaneous intracerebral[25] and retinal[26] hemorrhages. Acute pulmonary edema may occur[27] and complicate management. Long-term methamphetamine abuse with its associated catecholamine-related toxicity may cause dilated cardiomyopathy.[28]

If antisocial behavior or the psychosis or agitation stemming from intoxication interferes with initial ED stabilization, in patients who are not critically ill, aggressive intervention with benzodiazepines may be required. The use of antipsychotics according to standard psychiatric protocols may be needed to sedate or immobilize the motorically labile patient.

Acute Presentation

The girlfriend of the burned patient, a disheveled and emaciated 23-year-old woman, appears with her 6-year-old son. She tells the triage nurse that she was not at the house during the explosion but had earlier taken her son to a nearby pharmacy to pick up some pseudoephedrine "for his cold." She admits to having smoked "crystal" intermittently during the past week and says she has slept little during that time.

Extremely agitated about whether her boyfriend will die or go to jail, the woman threatens staff loudly about his care and says she has no reason to live and wants to die. She demands to be seen by a physician immediately. Pressured in speech and hyperkinetic, she describes recent physical altercations with her boyfriend and his sister. Recently discharged from a psychiatric inpatient unit after a suicide attempt, she states that she is again suicidal. She feels restless and believes she is infested by "bugs." She did not follow through with previously recommended sexually transmitted disease (STD) testing from her earlier hospitalization.

Agitation and psychosis from methamphetamine use may be difficult to distinguish from primary mania or schizophrenia. A primary psychotic disorder can be comorbid with methamphetamine abuse, which may itself be one among many drugs that methamphetamine users abuse.[15,29] The agitation directly relates to the severity of intoxication.[30] Although serum and urine toxicology screens are of little use in initial treatment in the ED, obtaining these screens early is critical for later treatment.

Patients commonly deny the role of illegal drug use in their behavior. However, an ED drug screen with positive results for methamphetamine can be critical for psychiatrists who later try to differentiate primary psychotic illness from psychosis resulting from mania/schizophrenia or methamphetamine abuse. Positive screening results serve as objective data to confront denial and deceit in hospital-based addiction interventions. Positive test results also assist in planning for further treatment by medical and surgical services.

However, because of the short half-life of methamphetamine and relative unreliability of detection, negative test results do not rule out methamphetamine intoxication or abuse. Collateral medical history from family and friends regarding a history of possible methamphetamine use and the patient's presentation and response over time may be enough to definitively establish diagnosis.

Patients suspected of methamphetamine intoxication should be placed in a calm and quiet environment, and benzodiazepines and/or antipsychotics should be administered to control agitated behavior. Violence-prevention protocols in the ED should include security searches of intoxicated patients and their belongings for weapons and a high level of vigilance for potential violent behavior directed against staff. Zweben et al,[31] in a sample of 1016 previous methamphetamine users, found that 40% of men and 46% of women had difficulty controlling their violent behavior when taking methamphetamine. The 239 subjects in the sample who used intravenous methamphetamine collectively had lifetime totals of 146 assault charges and 72 weapons violations.

Sympathetic stimulation from recent methamphetamine use results in appetite loss, tachycardia, mydriasis, coronary and peripheral vasospasm, headache, hyperreflexia, agitation, irritability, hypertension, hyperthermia, tachypnea, hypervigilance, and paranoia (Figure 2). Although patients such as the young woman described here do not come to the ED strictly for medical reasons, detecting the emerging cardiovascular and respiratory complications described earlier should be attempted at the physical examination. Long-term users typically appear cachectic and older than their chronological age. Oral examination may reveal "meth mouth," damaged and discolored teeth resulting from dry mouth, heavy sugar intake, and tooth-grinding associated with sympathetic nervous system overstimulation combined with poor dental hygiene.[32–34] Skin lesions may include excoriations and ulcers from the users compulsive picking at "meth bugs," the result of methamphetamine-induced delusional parasitosis,[35]

needle marks from injections, or chemical burns sustained while "cooking" methamphetamine. Cellulitis from poor wound care may require treatment.

Methamphetamine both increases libido and reduces inhibition, a synergy that increases the risk of STD for users and their partners. This fueling of risky sexual behaviors has had particular ramifications for homosexual and bisexual men.[36] Men who are human immunodeficiency virus (HIV)-positive and engage in methamphetamine-driven homosexual activity report high rates of unprotected anal sex and low rates of condom use.[37] They are more likely to have multiple sex partners, participate in sexual marathons, and engage in anonymous sex. Increased seroconversion rates in certain subpopulations reflect the relaxation of HIV transmission–prevention practices encouraged since the emergence of the HIV epidemic in the 1980s. Public health efforts to prevent HIV must contend with methamphetamine's capacities to instill a sense of relief from the negative affects associated with being HIV-positive and to enhance sexual pleasure.

Men having sex with men are not alone in being endangered by methamphetamine use. In a sample of 98 heterosexual women, methamphetamine use was associated with a positive subjective experience of sex.[38] Heterosexual male and female users also are more likely to engage in risky sexual behaviors that include multiple sexual partners, anonymous partners, or unprotected sex.[38,39] Thus, the non–methamphetamine-abusing sexual partners of both male and female users have an elevated risk of STD themselves. Clinicians should have a low threshold for ordering STD screening for methamphetamine abusers and their partners.

Pediatric Presentation

The on-call social worker has been summoned to evaluate the 6-year-old son. She learns that the boy not only has had irregular school attendance but also has been experiencing academic difficulties and behavioral outbursts.

During the past 5 years, according to the US Drug Enforcement Administration, more than 15,000 children were affected at sites where methamphetamine was being made.[40] Unlike adults who can choose to walk away from methamphetamine labs, children are captives of their caregivers and homes. Infants and toddlers naturally crawl on the floors and put things into their mouths. Analogous to those exposed to second-hand cigarette smoke, children living in methamphetamine-tainted environments are at high risk of passively absorbing, ingesting, or inhaling methamphetamine dust or toxic gases.[12] Easy access to ingredients such as acids and red phosphorus used in methamphetamine production and equipment for "shooting up" such as syringes and needles places children at further risk.

Dermatologic
- Infection and injury from
  Picking at "meth bugs"
  Chemical burn
  Injection injury
  Fire

Dental
- Darkened teeth
- Canies
- Broken teeth
- Periodontal disease

Cardiac
- Hypertension
- Tachycardia
- Dilated cardiomyopathy
- Dysrhythmia
- Myocardial Infarction
- Aneurysm
- Aortic dissection
- Acute coronary syndrome

Infectious
- HIV risk
- Hepatitis B and C risk
- Sexually transmitted diseases
- Depressed immune function

Pulmonary
- Acute pulmonary edema
- Pulmonary hypertension
- Inhalation injury
- Dyspnea
- Tachypnea

Psychiatric
- Depression
- Violence
- Impulsivity
- Obsessive behavior
- Compulsive behavior
- Irritability
- Mania
- Anxiety
- Paranoia
- Hallucinations
  Auditory
  Visual
  Formication ("meth bugs")

Metabolic
- Increased creatinine kinase
- Hyperthermia
- Metabolic acidosis

Renal
- Rhabdomyolysis
- Acute renal failure
- Dehydration
- Vasoconstriction

Neurologic
- Stroke
- Hyperreflexia
- Seizure

Figure 2 Systemic effects of methamphetamine. HIV = human immunodeficiency virus.

Some states are beginning to address pediatric issues stemming from methamphetamine-contaminated physical and social environments. California, Idaho, and Washington have policies ordaining intervention with methamphetamine-exposed children by teams consisting of medical personnel, law enforcement, child protective services, and local prosecutors. These policies require comprehensive physical examination of all affected children. The increased number of children taken from parental custody has caused difficulties in finding crisis foster care placement in heavily affected states.[41] The recent media focus on the effects of methamphetamine on families and children may have led to changes in many local hospital and community regulations. We recommend consultation with hospital social workers or child protective services to ensure that appropriate community contacts are made and that policies are followed for physical and psychological examinations. The decision to admit a child to the hospital or to place a child in foster care is made in consultation with child protective services, the evaluating physician, the admitting physician, and the extended family and depends on local laws.

On arrival at the ED, a child found at a methamphetamine lab will require decontamination, including removal of methamphetamine-impregnated clothing and careful washing of skin and hair, if not already performed. Anecdotally, adult methamphetamine users may drug children with antihistamines or benzodiazepines to keep them asleep and "safe" while they crash after their high.[42] Full toxicology screens for methamphetamine and other suspected drug exposures should be ordered to aid in understanding physiologic and behavioral symptoms and in planning treatment. A child living with methamphetamine users is at increased risk of physical, emotional, and sexual abuse.[41,43] Child protective services should thus be involved to develop a systematic plan to address these potential sources of pediatric comorbidity along with the child's basic needs.

Children in methamphetamine labs frequently live in squalor and neglect. The associated lack of stimulation, poor nutrition, and medical problems resulting from prenatal and postnatal exposure frequently leads to developmental delay, particularly in speech and language skills.[43] Children may not meet developmental milestones and may lack basic socialization skills.

Long-term physiologic effects of methamphetamine exposure, interacting with the toxic psychosocial environments within which these children grow up, can produce cognitive and behavioral symptoms such as those described in the 6-year-old boy in our case. Of 18 children in a study by Kolecki,[44] 9 were agitated, and 6 were irritable or inconsolable. Objective findings in children with prenatal methamphetamine exposure include smaller subcortical volumes with associated neurocognitive deficits.[45]

In laboratory animals, the heart was a particular target for arrested development with changes in messenger RNA expression.[46] All 18 pediatric patients, inadvertently poisoned with methamphetamine in the study by Kolecki,[44] had tachycardia. The same sympathetic hyperstimulation associated with methamphetamine abuse in adults can occur in children and may be even more pronounced.

First Responder

The police officer without personal protective equipment who rescued the young man from the burning house comes to the ED with progressive shortness of breath.

First responders—police and fire rescue teams rushing to disaster scenes—often are injured by toxic exposures at clandestine methamphetamine labs.[47] In 2003, 255 police officers reported sustaining injuries while responding to incidents in methamphetamine labs, up from 129 in 2002.[1] Respiratory injuries have been reported most commonly.[47] The phosphine gas that injures the methamphetamine user causes similar pulmonary and cardiac injuries in first responders. Police, firefighters, and other EMS personnel may experience respiratory distress, headache, dizziness, fatigue, or nausea associated with breathing fumes without respiratory protection in a methamphetamine lab. First responders inadvertently may contaminate skin or clothing or sustain injuries by contact with "cooking" ingredients or by-products. They risk injury from both explosions and violent users. Use of protective gear is essential. Supportive management of respiratory injury is recommended.

Subacute and Chronic Symptoms

The girlfriend's 26-year-old sister arrives in the ED as part of the child protective services evaluation. She stopped using methamphetamine 3 months ago and is currently in an outpatient substance abuse treatment program. After an interview with child protective services, she asks to be examined for "problems with depression."

It is the rule rather than the exception that psychiatric disorders accompany methamphetamine abuse. Preexisting psychiatric symptoms, including poor impulse control and a history of childhood trauma, may predispose to methamphetamine use.[39,48,49] A neurotoxin, methamphetamine induces psychiatric symptoms on its own. It can damage dopaminergic neurons in the striatum and serotonergic neurons in the hippocampus, striatum, and frontal lobes.[50] Damage to the former is associated with Parkinson disease and to the latter with depression, anxiety, and impulsive behavior. Ongoing methamphetamine abuse atop a preexisting psychiatric disorder alters the natural history of the disorder and increases treatment resistance.

Methamphetamine users in treatment are more likely than cocaine users to have psychiatric diagnoses and take psychotropic agents.[51] In a sample of 1073 methamphetamine-abusing patients from California treatment programs,[49] divided approximately evenly between the sexes, 39% of women and 30% of men reported severe depression. Anxiety was even more common, with 43% of women and 37% of men experiencing severe anxiety; 36% of men and 27% of women described problems with concentration and memory. In their sample of 1016 previous methamphetamine users, Zweben et al[31] emphasized a high level of distress manifested in a broad constellation of overlapping symptomatology, including elevated rates of attempted suicide, depression, anxiety, violent behavior, paranoid ideation, and frank psychosis. Residual psychotic symptoms, difficult to distinguish from chronic schizophrenia, can linger for years after methamphetamine abuse ceases and reappear with stressors.[52]

Summary

Like the "great imitators" tuberculosis and syphilis, the multitude of clinical presentations associated with methamphetamine mimic many other illnesses (Figure 2). It is vital for clinicians of all specialties to become aware of medical and social considerations in treating patients affected by methamphetamine abuse. The severe and wide-ranging effects of methamphetamine have whipped up a "perfect storm" in rural Middle America, with direct damage to users, their children, and first responders and collateral damage to the legal, social, and health care systems. Efforts to turn the tide have begun in legislative bodies, law enforcement agencies, and drug abuse prevention efforts, but the methamphetamine-driven storm surge is nowhere near to being stemmed.

Questions about Methamphetamine Abuse

1. Selective damage in which *one* of the following is associated with methamphetamine psychosis?

   a. Locus coeruleus
   b. Pons
   c. Mammillary bodies
   d. Striatum
   e. Cerebellum

5. Which *one* of the following is a reported motivation for HIV-positive men who abuse methamphetamine?

   a. Self-medication for the negative affects associated with HIV positivity
   b. Enhanced immune response
   c. Pain control
   d. Suicidal ideation
   e. Denial

3. Which *one* of the following gases is a harmful by-product of the illicit manufacture of methamphetamine?

   a. Phosgene
   b. Phosphine
   c. Carbon monoxide
   d. Carbon dioxide
   e. Methane

4. Which *one* of the following is *accurate* regarding the percentage of women methamphetamine users who reported problems with controlling violent behavior in a sample studied by Zweben et al?[31]

   a. 17%
   b. 26%
   c. 33%
   d. 46%
   e. 58%

5. Which *one* of the following states had the highest admission rates per 100,000 for methamphetamine/ amphetamine substance abuse treatment in 1992 and 2002?

   a. Massachusetts
   b. Oregon
   c. Hawaii
   d. Missouri
   e. California

Correct answers: 1. *d*, 2. *a*, 3. *b*, 4. *d*, 5. *b*

References

1. US Dept of Justice. *National Drug Threat Assessment 2005.* Johnstown, Pa: National Drug Intelligence Center; February 2005. Available at: www.usdoj.gov/ndic/pubs11/12620/. Accessibility verified November 17, 2005.

2. Substance Abuse and Mental Health Services Administration, Office of Applied Studies. *Drug Abuse Warning Network, 2003: Interim National Estimates of Drug-Related Emergency Department Visits.* DAWN Series D26, DHHS Publication No. (SMA) 04-3972. Rockville, Md; 2004.

3. Substance Abuse and Mental Health Services Administration, Office of Applied Studies. *The DASIS Report: Primary Methamphetamine/Amphetamine Treatment Admissions: 1992–2002.* September 17, 2004. Available at: http://oas. samhsa.gov/2k4/methTX/methTX.pdf. Accessibility verified November 17, 2005.

4. Suwaki H, Fukui S, Konuma K. Methamphetamine abuse in Japan: its 45 year history and the current situations. In: Klee H, ed. *Amphetamine Misuse: International Perspectives on Current Trends.* Amsterdam, Netherlands: Harwood Academic Publishers; 1997.

5. Logan BK. Methamphetamine-effects on human performance and behavior. *Forens Sci Rev.* 2002;14:133–151.

6. Matsumoto T, Kamijo A, Miyakawa T, et al. Methamphetamine in Japan: the consequences of methamphetamine abuse as a function of route of administration. *Addiction.* 2002;97:809–817.

7. National Institute on Drug Abuse. *Research Report Series: Methamphetamine Abuse and Addiction.* Bethesda, Md: National Institutes of Health; January 2002. NIH Publication No. 02–4210.

8. Anglin MD, Burke C, Perrochet B, Stamper E, Dawud-Noursi D. History of the methamphetamine problem. *J Psychoactive Drugs.* 2000;32:137–141.

9. US Drug Enforcement Administration. Maps of methamphetamine lab seizures: 1999–2004. Available at: www. usdoj.gov/dea/concern/map_lab _seizures.html. Accessibility verified November 17, 2005.

10. New Mexico Sentencing Commission. *Research Overview: Methamphetamine Production, Precursor Chemicals, and Child Endangerment.* January 2004. Available at: www.nmsc. state.nm.us/download/MethLabReport2004.pdf. Accessibility verified November 17, 2005.

11. Holton WC. Unlawful lab leftovers. *Environ Health Perspect.* 2001;109: A576.

12. Martyny JW, Arbuckle SL, McCammon CS Jr, Esswein EJ, Erb N. Chemical exposures associated with clandestine methamphetamine laboratories. Available at: www.njc.org/pdf/chemical_exposures. pdf. Accessibility verified November 22, 2005.

13. Substance Abuse and Mental Health Services Administration, Office of Applied Studies. *Emergency Department Trends From Drug Abuse Warning Network, Final Estimates 1995–2002,* DAWN series: D-24, DHHS Publication No. (SMA) 03–3780. Rockville, Md; 2003.

14. Danks RR, Wibbenmeyer LA, Faucher LD, et al. Methamphetamine-associated burn injuries: a retrospective analysis. *J Burn Care Rehabil.* 2004; 25:425–429.

15. Santos AP, Wilson AK, Hornung CA, Polk HC Jr, Rodriguez JL, Franklin GA. Methamphetamine laboratory explosions: a new and emerging burn injury. *J Burn Care Rehabil.* 2005;26: 228–232.

16. Warner P, Connolly JP, Gibran NS, Heimbach DM, Engrav LH. The methamphetamine burn patient. *J Burn Care Rehabil.* 2003;24:275–278.

17. Burgess JL. Phosphine exposure from a methamphetamine laboratory investigation. *J Toxicol Clin Toxocol.* 2001;39:165–168.

18. Willers-Russo LJ. Three fatalities involving phosphine gas, produced as a result of methamphetamine manufacturing. *J Forensic Sci.* 1999;44:647–652.

19. Sudakin DL. Occupational exposure to aluminium phosphide and phosphine gas? a suspected case report and review of the literature. *Hum Exp Toxicol.* 2005;24:27–33.

20. Burchell SA, Ho HC, Yu M, Margulies DR. Effects of methamphetamine on trauma patients: a cause of severe metabolic acidosis? *Crit Care Med.* 2000;28:2112–2115.

21. Horiguchi T, Hori S, Shinozawa Y, et al. A case of traumatic shock complicated by methamphetamine intoxication. *Intensive Care Med.* 1999;25: 758–760.

22. Richards JR, Johnson EB, Stark RW, Derlet RW. Methamphetamine abuse and rhabdomyolysis in the ED: a 5-year study. *Am J Emerg Med.* 1999; 17:681–685.

23. Turnipseed SD, Richards JR, Kirk JD, Diercks DB, Amsterdam EA. Frequency of acute coronary syndrome in patients presenting to the emergency department with chest pain after methamphetamine use. *J Emerg Med.* 2003; 24:369–373.

24. Davis GG, Swalwell CI. Acute aortic dissections and ruptured berry aneurysms associated with methamphetamine abuse. *J Forensic Sci.* 1994;39: 1481–1485.

25. McGee SM, McGee DN, McGee MB. Spontaneous intracerebral hemorrhage related to methamphetamine abuse:

autopsy findings and clinical correlation. *Am J Forensic Med Pathol.* 2004;25:334–337.

26. Wallace RT, Brown GC, Benson W, Sivalingham A. Sudden retinal manifestations of intranasal cocaine and methamphetamine abuse. *Am J Ophthalmol.* 1992;114:158–160.

27. Nestor TA, Tamamoto WI, Kam TH, Schultz T. Acute pulmonary oedema caused by crystalline methamphetamine [letter]. *Lancet.* 1989;25:1277–1278.

28. Wijetunga M, Seto T, Lindsay J, Schatz I. Crystal methamphetamine-associated cardiomyopathy: tip of the iceberg? *J Toxicol Clin Toxicol.* 2003;41:981–986.

29. Drug Abuse Warning Network. *The DAWN Report: Amphetamine and Methamphetamine Emergency Department Visits, 1995–2002.* July 2004. Available at http://dawninfo. samhsa.gov/old_dawn/pubs_94_02/shortreports/ files/DAWN_ tdr_amphetamine.pdf. Accessibility verified November 23, 2005.

30. Batki SL, Harris DS. Quantitative drug levels in stimulant psychosis: relationship to symptom severity, catecholamines and hyperkinesia. *Am J Addict.* 2004;13:461–470.

31. Zweben JE, Cohen JB, Christian D, et al, Methamphetamine Treatment Project. Psychiatric symptoms in methamphetamine users. *Am J Addict.* 2004; 13:181–190.

32. Richards JR, Brofeldt BT. Patterns of tooth wear associated with methamphetamine use. *J Periodontol.* 2000;71:1371–1374.

33. Venker D. Crystal methamphetamine and the dental patient. *Iowa Dent J.* 1999;85:34.

34. Shaner JW. Caries associated with methamphetamine abuse. *J Mich Dent Assoc.* 2002;84:42–47.

35. Ellinwood EH Jr. Amphetamine psychosis, I: description of the individuals and the process. *J Nerv Mental Dis.* 1967;144:273–283.

36. Halkitis PN, Parsons JT, Stirratt MJ. A double epidemic: crystal methamphetamine drug use in relation to HIV transmission among gay men. *J Homosex.* 2001;41:17–35.

37. Semple SJ, Patterson TL, Grants I. Motivations associated with methamphetamine use among HIV+ men who have sex with men. *J Subst Abuse Treat.* 2002;22:149–156.

38. Semple SJ, Grant I, Patterson TL. Female methamphetamine users: social characteristics and sexual risk behavior. *Women Health.* 2004;40:35–50.

39. Semple SJ, Patterson TL, Grant I. The context of sexual risk behavior among heterosexual methamphetamine users. *Addict Behav.* 2004;29:807–810.

40. Avergun JL. Defending America's most vulnerable: safe access to drug treatment and Child Protection Act of 2005—H.R. 1528. Testimony before the House Judiciary Committee Subcommittee on Crime, Terrorism and Homeland Security. April 12, 2005. Available at: www.usdoj.gov/dea/pubs/cngrtest/ ct041205p.html Accessibility verified November 23, 2005.

41. Swetlow K. Children in clandestine methamphetamine labs: helping meth's youngest victims *OVC Bulletin.* June 2003. Available at: www.ojp.usdoj.gov/ovc/publications/bulletins/ children/197590.pdf. Accessibility verified November 23, 2005.

42. Mecham N, Melini J. Unintentional victims: development of a protocol for the care of children exposed to chemicals at methamphetamine laboratories. *Pediatr Emerg Care.* 2002;18:327–332.

43. Hohman M, Oliver R, Wright W. Methamphetamine abuse and manufacture: the child welfare response. *Soc Work.* 2004;49:373–381.

44. Kolecki P. Inadvertent methamphetamine poisoning in pediatric patients. *Pediatr Emerg Care.* 1998;14:385–387.

45. Chang L, Smith LM, LoPresti C, et al. Smaller subcortical volumes and cognitive deficits in children with prenatal methamphetamine exposure. *Psychiatry Res.* 2004;132:95–106.

46. Inoue H, Nakatome M, Terada M, et al. Maternal methamphetamine administration during pregnancy influences

on fetal rat heart development [published correction appears in *Life Sci.* 2004;74:3053]. *Life Sci.* 2004;74: 1529–1540.

47. Centers for Disease Control and Prevention. Public health consequences among first responders to emergency events associated with illicit methamphetamine laboratories—selected states, 1996–1999. *MMWR Morb Mortal Wkly Rep.* 2000;49:1021–1024.

48. Dube SR, Felitti VJ, Dong M, Chapman DP, Giles WH, Anda RF. Childhood abuse, neglect, and household dysfunction and the risk of illicit drug use: the adverse childhood experiences study. *Pediatrics.* 2003;111:564–572.

49. Hser YI, Evans E, Huang YC. Treatment outcomes among women and men methamphetamine abusers in California. *J Subst Abuse Treat.* 2005;28: 77–85.

50. Hanson GR, Rau KS, Fleckenstein AE. The methamphetamine experience: a NIDA partnership. *Neuropharmacology.* 2004;47(suppl 1):92–100.

51. Copeland AL, Sorensen JL. Differences between methamphetamine users and cocaine users in treatment. *Drug Alcohol Depend.* 2001;62:91–95.

52. Yui K, Ikemoto S, Ishiguro T, Goto K. Studies of amphetamine or methamphetamine psychosis in Japan: relation of methamphetamine psychosis to schizophrenia. *Ann N Y Acad Sci.* 2000;914:1–12.

From the Department of Psychiatry and Psychology, Mayo Clinic College of Medicine, Rochester, Minn.

Individual reprints of this article are not available. Address correspondence to Timothy W. Lineberry, MD, Department of Psychiatry and Psychology, Mayo Clinic College of Medicine, 200 First St SW, Rochester, MN 55905 (e-mail: lineberry.timothy@mayo.edu).

HIV Apathy

New drugs have changed HIV from a terminal to a chronic illness. To counter complacency, health officials are pushing to make testing more widespread.

ZACH PATTON

On a rainy day last June, local officials in Washington, D.C., gathered under tents erected on a public plaza to be tested for HIV. The District of Columbia's health department was kicking off a sweeping new effort to encourage city residents to take action against the disease. With banners, music and mobile-testing units, officials hoped the launch event and the campaign would help raise local awareness about HIV—and help the city address its most pressing health concern.

Washington has the nation's highest rate of new AIDS cases, and the city's goal—HIV testing for every resident between the ages of 14 and 84, totaling over 400,000 people—was unprecedented in its scope. City officials said the campaign, which also included distributing an initial 80,000 HIV tests to doctors' offices, hospitals and health clinics, would enable them to get a better idea of how many residents are infected with HIV. And making such screenings routine, they hoped, would help erase the stigma against getting tested for the disease.

Six months later, though, the effort was faltering. Fewer than 20,000 people had been tested. Many of the HIV test kits expired before they were distributed, forcing the city to throw them away. Others were donated to the Maryland health department to use before they went bad. And the city still lacked a comprehensive plan for ensuring effective treatment for those residents who test positive for the disease.

It's not all bad news. The District nearly tripled the number of sites offering free HIV screenings, and the Department of Corrections began screening all inmates for HIV. And the city improved its disease-surveillance technique, recording information on behaviors and lifestyles, in addition to counting the number of new HIV cases.

But D.C.'s struggle to meet its goals underscores a challenge common to local health officials across the country. More than a million U.S. residents are infected with HIV, and one-quarter of them don't know it, experts estimate. Diagnosis rates of HIV have stabilized in recent years, but large cities continue to grapple with much higher rates. They're dealing with higher incidents of the risky behaviors—drug use and unprotected sex, particularly gay sex—that tend to spread the disease. But they're also trying to battle something less tangible: complacency. Antiretroviral drugs have largely changed HIV from a terminal illness into a chronic one. And the fears associated with AIDS have faded over the past 20 years. As health officials work to combat HIV, they're finding that their hardest fight is the one against apathy.

Testing Laws

The first test for the human immunodeficiency virus was licensed by the FDA in March 1985. It was quickly put into use by blood banks, health departments and clinics across the country. But HIV testing at that time faced some major obstacles, which would continue to thwart HIV policies for much of the following two decades. For one, it usually took two weeks to obtain lab results, requiring multiple visits for patients waiting to see if they had HIV. Many patients—in some places, as many as half—never returned for the second visit. Another barrier was that, at the time, a diagnosis of the disease was a death sentence. With no reliable drugs to slow the progression of HIV into AIDS, and with an attendant stigma that could decimate a person's life, many people just didn't want to know if they were HIV-positive. "The impact of disclosure of someone's HIV-positive status could cost them their job, their apartment and their social circle," says Dr. Adam Karpati, assistant commissioner for HIV/AIDS Prevention & Control for the New York City health department. "In a basic calculus, the value to the patient was questionable. Knowing their status could only maybe help them, but it could definitely hurt them."

Because of that stigma and the seriousness of a positive diagnosis, many cities and states developed rigorous measures to ensure that testing was voluntary and confidential, and that it included a full discussion of the risks associated with the disease. That meant requiring written consent in order to perform tests, and mandatory pre- and post-test counseling. "A lot of the laws were, appropriately, concerned with confidentiality and protecting people's rights," Karpati says.

Two major developments have since changed the method—and the purpose—of HIV testing. First, the development of antiretroviral drugs in the mid-1990s has lessened the impact of HIV as a fatal disease. And in the past two or three years, advancements in testing technology have effectively eliminated the wait time for receiving results. Rapid tests using a finger-prick or an oral swab can be completed in 20 minutes, meaning nearly everyone can receive results within a single visit.

Those changes, along with aggressive counseling and education about risk-prevention measures, helped stabilize the rate of HIV diagnosis. After peaking in 1992, rates of AIDS cases leveled off by 1998. Today, about 40,000 AIDS cases are diagnosed every year. Data on non-AIDS HIV infection rates are much harder to come by, but they seem to have stabilized as well.

The problem, however, remains especially acute in urban areas. While health experts take pains to stress that HIV/AIDS is no longer just a "big city" problem, the fact is that 85 percent of the nation's HIV infections have been in metropolitan areas with more than half a million people. "Urban areas have always been the most heavily impacted by the HIV epidemic, and they continue to be," says Jennifer Ruth of the Centers for Disease Control and Prevention. Intravenous drug use, risky sexual behavior and homosexual sex all contribute to higher HIV rates, and they are all more prevalent in urban areas. But cities face other complicating factors as well, including high poverty rates and residents with a lack of access to medical care, which exacerbate the challenges of HIV care.

Prevention Fatigue

Nowhere is that more evident than in Washington, D.C., where an estimated one in every 20 residents is HIV-positive. That's 10 times the national average. But that figure is only a rough guess. The truth is that health officials don't even know what the city's HIV rate is. Last year's campaign was supposed to change that. By setting a goal to test nearly all city residents, District health officials hoped to make HIV screening a routine part of medical care. In the process, the health department hoped it could finally get a handle on just how bad the crisis was. "We've had problems in the past, I'll be the first to say," says D.C. health department director Dr. Gregg A. Pane. "But we have galvanized interest and action, and we've highlighted the problem in a way it hasn't been before."

The effort stumbled, though. The Appleseed Center for Law and Justice, a local public advocacy group, has issued periodic report cards grading the District's progress on HIV.

The most recent assessment, published six months into last year's testing push, found mismanagement and a lack of coordination with the medical community. The District was testing substantially more people than it had been, but the number was still falling far short of officials' goal. "D.C. took a great step forward, but it takes more than just a report announcing it," says Walter Smith, executive director for the Appleseed Center. "You have to make sure there's a plan."

What D.C. did achieve, however, was a fundamental shift in the way health officials perceive the HIV epidemic. "This is a disease that affects everyone," says Pane. "It's our No. 1 public health threat, and treating it like a public health threat is the exact right thing to do."

That paradigm change has been happening in health departments across the country. Last year, the CDC made waves when it announced new recommendations for treating HIV as an issue of public health. That means testing as many people as possible, making HIV testing a routine part of medical care, and removing the barriers to getting tested. Washington was the first city to adopt the CDC's recommendations for comprehensive testing, but other cities have also moved to make testing more routine. San Francisco health officials dropped their written-consent and mandatory-counseling requirements for those about to be tested. New York City has been moving in a similar direction, although removing the written-consent rule there will require changing state law. Many health officials think that since testing has become so easy and social attitudes about the disease have shifted, the strict testing regulations adopted in the 1980s are now cumbersome. The protections have become barriers.

Officials also are moving away from "risk-assessment testing," in which doctors first try to identify whether a patient falls into a predetermined high-risk category. "What has evolved is that, with an epidemic, risk-based testing is not sufficient," says New York City's Karpati. "Now there's a general move toward comprehensive testing." Privacy advocates and many AIDS activists oppose the shift away from individual protections. Yes, the stigma isn't what it used to be, they say, but it still exists. HIV isn't like tuberculosis or the measles, so they believe health officials shouldn't treat it like it is.

But even if officials could strike the perfect balance between public health and private protection, there's another factor that everyone agrees is thwarting cities' efforts to combat HIV. Call it burnout or complacency or "prevention fatigue." In an age when testing consists of an oral swab and a 20-minute wait, and an HIV-positive diagnosis means taking a few pills a day, health officials are battling a growing sense of apathy toward the disease. "The very successes we've made in the past 20 years have hurt us, in a sense," Karpati says. "We don't have hospital wards full of HIV patients. We don't have people dying as much. There's a whole new generation of folks growing up who don't remember the fear of the crisis in the 1980s."

That casual attitude toward the disease can lead to riskier behavior and, in turn, more infections. With HIV and AIDS disproportionately affecting low-income residents, any increase in infections places an additional burden on governments. And while prescription drugs have made the disease more manageable, the fact is that 40 percent of the new HIV diagnoses in the nation are still made within a year of the infection's progressing to AIDS—which is usually too late for medicine to do much good. As cities try to fight HIV complacency through refined testing policies and a focus on comprehensive testing, residents will have increasingly widespread access to tests for the disease. But for health officials, the greatest challenge will be getting the right people to care.

ZACH PATTON can be reached at zpatton@governing.com

Not Invented Here

There's a "scout" stationed in a new Boston research tower just blocks from Fenway Park.

Tinker Ready

But he's no Bill James disciple, and he's not looking for the next Red Sox pitching phenom. Reid Leonard is a neurobiologist, with 10 years' experience as a bench scientist. His job is to find Merck & Co. a blockbuster drug.

He's one of 12 drug scouts Merck employs in seven countries. Last year, the scouts and their scientific teams scoped out 5,000 biotech companies and medical schools—and their finds led to 53 licensing deals, winning Merck rights to discoveries that could lead to new vaccines and antibiotics, as well as treatments for blindness, Alzheimer's, and AIDS.

Those products, of course, would share one notable characteristic: They weren't born in Merck's own labs. That itself represents a defining discovery for the giant drugmaker. It can no longer claim all the best scientific brains, or all the answers. With in-house research failing to produce enough new drugs to fill its pipeline and a wave of older products coming off patent, Merck has to go outside for help.

That's the emerging reality across the industry. While pharma companies still stock their annual reports with images of scientists in lab coats, many now employ teams like Merck's—market-minded scientists assigned to find new drugs from someone else's labs. About 25% of the drugs moved into human testing by the 10 biggest drugmakers from 2003 to 2005 were discovered by outside researchers, according to a Tufts University study. That was up from about 15% in the mid-1990s.

The shift didn't come easily to Merck. Historically, word in the scientific community was Merck folks were condescending and difficult to work with, says Heather Brilliant, an analyst with the Chicago investment-research company Morningstar. "Merck used to have an attitude of, if it wasn't created inside Merck, it wasn't worth spending time on," she says.

More recently, though, the company has tried hard to play nice. "Merck's Got A New Attitude!" was the title of an October meeting of New Jersey drug-licensing executives. Leonard describes the change as a "cultural transformation. . . . It was a very deliberate process."

Three years ago, the company created a team devoted to prospecting for new leads, placing seasoned scientists at the front of the licensing effort. Many, like Leonard, spent a decade or more in Merck's own labs. Neuroscientist Margaret Beer, who scouts Israel and southern Europe, helped develop the migraine drug Maxalt during her 23 years as a Merck scientist.

Reps need a keen eye for both scientific and commercial potential. "It's all about strategy and risk," says former Merck scout Robert Gould. "How does the opportunity fit with your strategy and how much risk are you willing to accept?" They monitor journals and network ceaselessly with industry contacts. In addition to endless private meetings, they prowl the aisles at scientific gatherings and sit in on analyst's meetings. "It's really a matter of how many hours a day can you work and how much travel you are willing to tolerate," says Leonard, who spent much of last year shuttling among 40 medical schools.

Merck's defining discovery: It can no longer claim all the top scientific talent, or all the answers.

Idera Pharmaceuticals, a small biotech in Cambridge, Massachusetts, was one find. Its scientific team, led by Sudhir Agrawal, had struggled for years to find a drug using antisense technology, which aims to prevent the cell's genetic machinery from making harmful proteins. But it had little luck until switching to a different strategy focused on cell proteins called "toll-like receptors" (TLR).

Last summer, that research was going well enough for Idera to approach several drugmakers about using the findings to develop vaccines. But Merck scientists had already taken notice. By December, a deal was done—in part, from Idera's perspective, because Merck already made vaccines. But also, Agrawal says, Merck was simply . . . nicer. "During the negotiating process . . . they were very clear," Agrawal says. "They were driven by the science and the data—not, 'Let's squeeze this company. They're 30 people, and they're running out of cash.'" Merck agreed to pay $30 million up front and $165 million in "milestone payments."

The partnership, of course, is rooted in mutual need. For as much as Idera wants access to Merck's capacity for testing, manufacturing, and selling drugs on a mass scale, Merck needs know-how in areas such as nucleic-acid chemistry and RNA interference, an approach that shuts down selective genes. Indeed, with biotechnology poised to produce more potential drugs these days than traditional research, Big Pharma is racing to tap that expertise. Merck, for one, had just 4 licensed products in its pipeline in 2004; now it has 12.

Which is why, last summer, the scouts were all over Robert Rando. The Harvard biochemist had discovered a molecule that could possibly stave off macular degeneration, a major cause of blindness in the elderly; he needed someone to turn it into a drug. Rando says he spoke to a couple of venture capitalists, but the idea of starting a new company didn't excite him. A deal with Merck would skirt much of that hassle—and besides, company reps also understood the science in a way that some of the venture capitalists didn't, Rando says. After Rando's collaborators at Columbia University confirmed the effectiveness of his molecule, Merck offered Harvard and Rando $3 million for rights to the research. If all goes well, Rando's research could produce a blockbuster.

If not, of course, the work could sit on a shelf forever. That's the downside of these deals. "If it works, it's perfect," Rando says. But "when something goes into someone else's hopper, lots of things can change. . . . Projects get scotched for a variety of reasons—including when they don't work."

But like Merck, he's willing to take a chance.

TINKER READY writes on science and health care from Cambridge, Massachusetts.

Did Prohibition Really Work?

Alcohol prohibition as a public health innovation.

The conventional view that National Prohibition failed rests upon an historically flimsy base. The successful campaign to enact National Prohibition was the fruit of a century-long temperance campaign, experience of which led prohibitionists to conclude that a nationwide ban on alcohol was the most promising of the many strategies tried thus far. A sharp rise in consumption during the early 20th century seemed to confirm the bankruptcy of alternative alcohol control programs.

 The stringent prohibition imposed by the Volstead Act however, represented a more drastic action than many Americans expected. Nevertheless, National Prohibition succeeded both in lowering consumption and in retaining political support until the onset of the Great Depression altered voters' priorities. Repeal resulted more from this contextual shift than from characteristics of the innovation itself.

JACK S. BLOCKER JR. PHD

Probably few gaps between scholarly knowledge and popular conventional wisdom are as wide as the one regarding National Prohibition. "Everyone knows" that Prohibition failed because Americans did not stop drinking following ratification of the Eighteenth Amendment and passage of its enforcement legislation, the Volstead Act. If the question arises why Americans adopted such a futile measure in the first place, the unnatural atmosphere of wartime is cited. Liquor's illegal status furnished the soil in which organized crime flourished. The conclusive proof of Prohibition's failure is, of course, the fact that the Eighteenth Amendment became the only constitutional amendment to be repealed.

Historians have shown, however, that National Prohibition was no fluke, but rather the fruit of a century-long series of temperance movements springing from deep roots in the American reform tradition. Furthermore, Americans were not alone during the first quarter of the 20th century in adopting prohibition on a large scale: other jurisdictions enacting similar measures included Iceland, Finland, Norway, both czarist Russia and the Soviet Union, Canadian provinces, and Canada's federal government.[1] A majority of New Zealand voters twice approved national prohibition but never got it. As a result of 100 years of temperance agitation, the American cultural climate at the time Prohibition went into effect was deeply hostile to alcohol, and this antagonism manifested itself clearly through a wave of successful referenda on statewide prohibition.

Although organized crime flourished under its sway, Prohibition was not responsible for its appearance, as organized crime's post-Repeal persistence has demonstrated. Drinking habits underwent a drastic change during the Prohibition Era, and Prohibition's flattening effect on per capita consumption continued long after Repeal, as did a substantial hard core of popular support for Prohibition's return. Repeal itself became possible in 1933 primarily because of a radically altered economic context—the Great Depression. Nevertheless, the failure of National Prohibition continues to be cited without contradiction in debates over matters ranging from the proper scope of government action to specific issues such as control of other consciousness-altering drugs, smoking, and guns.

We historians collectively are partly to blame for this gap. We simply have not synthesized from disparate studies a compelling alternative to popular perception.[2] Nevertheless, historians are not entirely culpable for prevalent misunderstanding; also responsible are changed cultural attitudes toward drinking, which, ironically. Prohibition itself helped to shape. Thinking of Prohibition as a public health innovation offers a potentially fruitful path toward comprehending both the story of the dry era and the reasons why it continues to be misunderstood.

Temperance Thought Before National Prohibition

Although many prohibitionists were motivated by religious faith, American temperance reformers learned from an early point in their movement's history to present their message in ways that would appeal widely to citizens of a society characterized by divergent and clashing scriptural interpretations. Temperance, its advocates promised, would energize political reform, promote community welfare, and improve public health. Prohibitionism, which was inherently political, required even more urgent pressing of such claims for societal improvement.[3] Through local contests in communities across the nation, liquor control in general and Prohibition In particular became the principal stage on which Americans confronted public health issues, long before public health became a field of professional endeavor.

By the beginning of the 20th century, prohibitionists agreed that a powerful liquor industry posed the greatest threat to American society and that only Prohibition could prevent Americans from falling victim to its seductive wiles. These conclusions were neither willful nor arbitrary, as they had been reached after three quarters of a century of experience. Goals short of total abstinence from all that could intoxicate and less coercive means—such as self-help, mutual support, medical treatment, and sober recreation—had been tried and, prohibitionists agreed, had been found wanting.[4]

For prohibitionists, as for other progressives, the only battleground where a meaningful victory might be won was the collective: the community, the state, or the nation. The Anti-Saloon League (ASL), which won leadership of the movement after 1905, was so focused on Prohibition that it did not even require of its members a pledge of personal abstinence. Battles fought on public ground certainly heightened popular awareness of the dangers of alcohol. In the mass media before 1920, John Barleycorn found few friends. Popular fiction, theater, and the new movies rarely represented drinking in positive terms and consistently portrayed drinkers as flawed characters. Most family magazines, and even many daily newspapers, rejected liquor ads.[5] New physiological and epidemiological studies published around the turn of the century portrayed alcohol as a depressant and plausibly associated its use with crime, mental illness, and disease. The American Medical Association went on record in opposition to the use of alcohol for either beverage or therapeutic purposes.[6] But most public discourse on alcohol centered on its social, not individual, effects.[7]

The only significant exception was temperance education in the schools. By 1901, every state required that its schools incorporate "Scientific Temperance Instruction" into the curriculum, and one half of the nation's school districts further mandated use of a textbook that portrayed liquor as invariably an addictive poison. But even as it swept through legislative chambers, the movement to indoctrinate children in temperance ideology failed to carry with it the educators on whose cooperation its success in the classrooms depended; teachers tended to regard Scientific Temperance Instruction as neither scientific nor temperate. After 1906, temperance instruction became subsumed within more general lessons on hygiene, and hygiene classes taught that the greatest threats to health were environmental and the proper responses were correspondingly social, not individual.[8]

By the time large numbers of voters were confronted with a choice whether or not to support a prohibitionist measure or candidate for office, public discourse over alcohol had produced a number of prohibitionist supporters who were not themselves abstainers. That is, they believed that it was a good idea to control someone else's drinking (perhaps everyone else's), but not

their own. A new study of cookbooks and etiquette manuals suggests that this was likely the case for middle-class women, the most eager recruits to the prohibition cause, who were gaining the vote in states where prohibition referenda were boosting the case for National Prohibition. In addition to the considerable alcoholic content of patent medicines, which women and men (and children) were unknowingly ingesting, women were apparently serving liquor in their recipes and with meals. In doing so, they were forging a model of domestic consumption in contrast to the mode of public drinking adopted by men in saloons and clubs.[9]

Self-control lay at the heart of the middle-class self-image, and middle-class prohibitionists simply acted on the prejudices of their class when they voted to close saloons while allowing drinking to continue in settings they considered to be respectable. Some state prohibition laws catered to such sentiments when they prohibited the manufacture and sale of alcoholic beverages, but allowed importation and consumption.[10] A brisk mail-order trade flourished in many dry communities. Before 1913, federal law and judicial decisions in fact prevented states from interfering with the flow of liquor across their borders. When Congress acted in 1913, the Webb–Kenyon Act only forbade importation of liquor into a dry state when such commerce was banned by the law of that state.[11]

Why National Prohibition?

At the beginning of the 20th century, wet and dry forces had reached a stalemate. Only a handful of states maintained statewide prohibition, and enforcement of prohibitory law was lax in some of those. Dry territory expanded through local option, especially in the South, but this did not mean that drinking came to a halt in towns or counties that adopted local prohibition; such laws aimed to stop manufacture or sale (or both), not consumption.[12] During the previous half-century, beer's popularity had soared, surpassing spirits as the principal source of alcohol in American beverages, but, because of beer's lower alcohol content, ethanol consumption per capita had changed hardly at all.[13] Both drinking behavior and the politics of drink, however, changed significantly after the turn of the century when the ASL assumed leadership of the prohibition movement.

Between 1900 and 1913, Americans began to drink more and more. Beer production jumped from 1.2 billion to 2 billion gallons (4.6 billion to 7.6 billion liters), and the volume of tax-paid spirits grew from 97 million to 147 million gallons (367 million to 556 million liters). Per capita consumption of ethanol increased by nearly a third, a significant spike over such a short period of time.[14]

Meanwhile, the area under prohibition steadily expanded as a result of local-option and statewide prohibition campaigns. Between 1907 and 1909, 6 states entered the dry column. By 1912, however, prohibitionist momentum on these fronts slowed, as the liquor industry began a political counteroffensive. In the following year, the ASL, encouraged by congressional submission to its demands in passing the Webb–Kenyon Act. launched a campaign for a prohibition constitutional amendment.

The best explanation for this decision is simply that National Prohibition had long been the movement's goal. The process of constitutional amendment in the same year the ASL launched its campaign both opened the way to a federal income tax and mandated direct election of US senators (the Sixteenth and Seventeenth Amendments), seemed to be the most direct path to that goal.[15] Its supporters expected that the campaign for and amendment would be long and that the interval between achievement of the amendment and their eventual object would also be lengthy. Ultimately, drinkers with entrenched habits would die off, while a new generation would grow up abstinent under the salubrious influence of prohibition.[16] ASL leaders also needed to demonstrate their militance to ward off challenges from intramovement rivals, and the route to a constitutional amendment lay through state and national legislatures, where their method of pressuring candidates promised better results than seeking popular approval through a referendum in every state.[17]

Once the prohibition movement decided to push for a constitutional amendment it had to negotiate the tortuous path to ratification. The fundamental requirement was sufficient popular support to convince federal and state legislators that voting for the amendment would help rather than hurt their electoral chances.

"Between 1900 and 1913, Americans began to drink more and more. Beer production jumped from 1.2 billion to 2 billion gallons, and the volume of tax-paid spirits grew from 97 million to 147 million gallons."

The historical context of the Progressive Era provided 4 levers with which that support might be engineered, and prohibitionists manipulated them effectively. First the rise in annual ethanol consumption to 2.6 US gallons (9.8 liters) per capita of the drinking-age population, the highest level since the Civil War, did create a real public health problem.[18] Rates of death diagnosed as caused by liver cirrhosis (15 per 100,000 total population) and chronic alcoholism (10 per 100,000 adult population) were high during the early years of the 20th century.[19]

Second, the political turbulence of the period—a growing socialist movement and bitter struggles between capitalists and workers—made prohibition seem less radical by contrast.[20] Third, popular belief in moral law and material progress, trust in science, support for humanitarian causes and for "uplift" of the disadvantaged, and opposition to "plutocracy" offered opportunities to align prohibitionism with progressivism.[21] Concern for public health formed a central strand of the progressive ethos, and, as one historian notes, "the temperance and prohibition movements can . . . be understood as part of a larger public health and welfare movement active at that time that viewed environmental interventions as an important means of promoting the public health and safety."[22] Finally, after a fleeting moment of unity, the alliance between brewers and distillers

to repel prohibitionist attacks fell apart.[23] The widespread local battles fought over the previous 20 years brought new support to the cause, and the ASL's nonpartisan, balance-of-power method worked effectively.[24]

The wartime atmosphere during the relatively brief period of American participation in World War I played a minor role in bringing on National Prohibition. Anti-German sentiment shamelessly whipped up and exploited by the federal government to rally support for the war effort discredited a key and prohibitionist organization, the German-American Alliance. A federal ban on distilling, adopted to conserve grain, sapped the strength of another major wet player, the spirits Industry.[25] But most prohibition victories at the state level and in congressional elections were won before the United States entered the war, and the crucial ratification votes occurred after the war's end.[26]

In sum, although the temperance movement was a century old when the Eighteenth Amendment was adopted, and National Prohibition had been a goal for many prohibitionists for half that long, its achievement came about as a product of a specific milieu. Few reform movements manage to win a constitutional amendment. Nevertheless, that achievement, which seemed at the time so permanent—no constitutional amendment had ever before been repealed—was vulnerable to shifts in the context on which it depended.

Public Health Consequences of Prohibition

We forget too easily that Prohibition wiped out an industry. In 1916, there were 1300 breweries producing full-strength beer in the United States; 10 years later there were none. Over the same period, the number of distilleries was cut by 85%, and most of the survivors produced little but industrial alcohol. Legal production of near beer used less than one tenth the amount of malt, one twelfth the rice and hops, and one thirtieth the corn used to make full-strength beer before National Prohibition. The 318 wineries of 1914 became the 27 of 1925.[27] The number of liquor wholesalers was cut by 96% and the number of legal retailers by 90%. From 1919 to 1929, federal tax revenues from distilled spirits dropped from $365 million to less than $13 million, and revenue from fermented liquors from $117 million to virtually nothing.[28]

The Coors Brewing Company turned to making near beer, porcelain products, and malted milk. Miller and Anheuser-Busch took a similar route.[29] Most breweries, wineries, and distilleries, however, closed their doors forever. Historically, the federal government has played a key role in creating new industries, such as chemicals and aerospace, but very rarely has it acted decisively to shut down an industry.[30] The dosing of so many large commercial operations left liquor production, if it were to continue, in the hands of small-scale domestic producers, a dramatic reversal of the normal course of industrialization.

Such industrial and economic devastation was unexpected before the introduction of the Volstead Act, which followed adoption of the Eighteenth Amendment The amendment forbade the manufacture, transportation, sale, importation, and exportation of "intoxicating" beverages, but without defining the term. The Volstead Act defined "intoxicating" as containing 0.5% or more alcohol by volume, thereby prohibiting virtually all alcoholic drinks. The brewers, who had expected beer of moderate strength to remain legal, were stunned, but their efforts to overturn the definition were unavailing.[31] The act also forbade possession of intoxicating beverages, but included a significant exemption for custody in one's private dwelling for the sole use of the owner, his or her family, and guests. In addition to private consumption, sacramental wine and medicinal liquor were also permitted.

The brewers were probably not the only Americans to be surprised at the severity of the regime thus created. Voters who considered their own drinking habits blameless, but who supported prohibition to discipline others, also received a rude shock. That shock came with the realization that federal prohibition went much farther in the direction of banning personal consumption than all local prohibition ordinances and many state prohibition statutes. National Prohibition turned out to be quite a different beast than its local and state cousins.

Nevertheless, once Prohibition became the law of the land, many citizens decided to obey it. Referendum results in the immediate post-Volstead period showed widespread support, and the Supreme Court quickly fended off challenges to the new law. Death rates from cirrhosis and alcoholism, alcoholic psychosis hospital admissions, and drunkenness arrests all declined steeply during the latter years of the 1910s, when both the cultural and the legal climate were increasingly inhospitable to drink, and in the early years after National Prohibition went into effect. They rose after that, but generally did not reach the peaks recorded during the period 1900 to 1915. After Repeal, when tax data permit better-founded consumption estimates than we have for the Prohibition Era, per capita annual consumption stood at 1.2 US gallons (4.5 liters), less than half the level of the pre-Prohibition period.[32]

Prohibition affected alcoholic beverages differently. Beer consumption dropped precipitously. Distilled spirits made a dramatic comeback in American drinking patterns, reversing a three-quarters-of-a-century decline, although in volume spirits did not reach its pre-Prohibition level. Small-scale domestic producers gave wine its first noticeable, though small, contribution to overall alcohol intake, as wine-grape growers discovered that the Volstead Act failed to ban the production and sale of grape concentrate (sugary pulp that could be rehydrated and fermented to make wine).[33]

Unintended and Unexpected Consequences

Unexpected prosperity for wine-grape growers was not the only unintended consequence of National Prohibition. Before reviewing other unexpected outcomes, however, it is important to list the ways in which National Prohibition did fulfill prohibitionists' expectations. The liquor industry was virtually destroyed, and this created an historic opportunity to socialize rising generations in a lifestyle in which alcohol had no place.

To some degree, such socialization did take place, and the lessened consumption of the Prohibition Era reflects that. Although other forces contributed to its decline, Prohibition finished off the old-time saloon, with its macho culture and links to urban machine politics.[34] To wipe out a long-established and well-entrenched industry, to change drinking habits on a large scale, and to sweep away such a central urban and rural social institution as the saloon are no small achievements.

Nevertheless, prohibitionists did not fully capitalize on their opportunity to bring up a new generation in abstemious habits. Inspired and led by the talented writers of the Lost Generation, the shapers of mass culture—first in novels, then in films, and finally in newspapers and magazines—altered the popular media's, previously negative attitude toward drink. In the eyes of many young people, especially the increasing numbers who populated colleges and universities, Prohibition was transformed from progressive reform to an emblem of a suffocating status quo.[35] The intransigence of the dominant wing of the ASL, which insisted on zero tolerance in law enforcement, gave substance to this perception and, in addition, aligned the league with the Ku Klux Klan and other forces promoting intolerance.[36] Thus, the work of attracting new drinkers to alcohol, which had been laid down by the dying liquor industry, was taken up by new hands.

One group of new drinkers—or newly public drinkers—whose emergence in that role was particularly surprising to contemporary observers was women. Such surprise, however, was a product of the prior invisibility of women's domestic consumption: women had in fact never been as abstemious as the Woman's Christian Temperance Union's activism had made them appear.[37] Women's new willingness to drink in public—or at least in the semipublic atmosphere of the speakeasy—owed much to Prohibition's achievement the death of the saloon, whose masculine culture no longer governed norms of public drinking. The saloon's demise also made it possible for women to band together to oppose Prohibition, as hundreds of thousands did in the Women's Organization for National Prohibition Reform (WONPR).[38]

Public drinking by women and college youth and wet attitudes disseminated by cultural media pushed along a process that social scientists call the "normalization of drinking"—that is, the breakdown of cultural proscriptions against liquor. Normalization, part of the long history of decay in Victorian social mores, began before the Prohibition Era and did not fully bear fruit until long afterward, but the process gained impetus from both the achievements and the failures of National Prohibition.[39]

Other unintended and unexpected consequences of Prohibition included flourishing criminal activity centered on smuggling and bootlegging and the consequent clogging of the courts with drink-related prosecutions.[40] Prohibition also forced federal courts to take on the role of overseer of government regulatory agencies, and the zeal of government agents stimulated new concern for individual rights as opposed to the power of the state.[41] The bans on liquor importation and exportation crippled American ocean liners in the competition for transatlantic passenger service, thus contributing to the ongoing decline of the US merchant marine, and created an irritant in diplomatic relations with Great Britain and Canada.[42] Contrary to politicians' hopes that the Eighteenth Amendment would finally take the liquor issue out of politics, Prohibition continued to boil the political waters even in the presidential seas, helping to carry Herbert Hoover first across the finish line in 1928 and to sink him 4 years later.[43]

Why Repeal?

All prohibitions are coercive, but their effects can vary across populations and banned articles. We have no estimates of the size of the drinking population on the eve of National Prohibition (or on the eve of wartime prohibition, which preceded it by several months), but because of the phenomenon of "drinking drys" it was probably larger than the total of votes cast in referenda against state prohibition measures, and many of the larger states did not even hold such referenda. So Prohibition's implicit goal of teetotalism meant changing the drinking behavior of a substantial number of Americans, possibly a majority.

Because the Volstead Act was drafted only after ratification of the Eighteenth Amendment was completed, neither the congressmen and state legislators who approved submission and ratification, nor the voters who elected them, knew what kind of prohibition they were voting for.[44] The absolutism of the act's definition of intoxicating liquors made national alcohol prohibition a stringent ban, and the gap between what voters thought they were voting for and what they got made this sweeping interdict appear undemocratic. Nevertheless, support for prohibition in post-ratification state referenda and the boost given to Herbert Hoover's 1928 campaign by his dry stance indicate continued electoral approval of Prohibition before the stock-market crash of 1929.

Historians agree that enforcement of the Volstead Act constituted National Prohibition's Achilles' heel. A fatal flaw resided in the amendment's second clause, which mandated "concurrent power" to enforce Prohibition by the federal government and the states. ASL strategists expected that the states' existing criminal-justice machinery would carry out the lion's share of the work of enforcement. Consequently, the league did not insist on creating adequate forces or funding for federal enforcement, thereby avoiding conflict with Southern officials determined to protect states' rights. The concurrent-power provision, however, allowed states to minimize their often politically divisive enforcement activity, and the state prohibition statutes gave wets an obvious target, because repeal of a state law was easier than repeal of a federal law or constitutional amendment, and repeal's success would leave enforcement in the crippled hands of the federal government.[45] Even if enforcement is regarded as a failure, however, it does not follow that such a lapse undermined political support for Prohibition. Depending on the number of drinking drys, the failure of enforcement could have produced the opposite effect, by allowing voters to gain access to alcohol themselves while voting to deny it to others.

Two other possible reasons also fall short of explaining Repeal. The leading antiprohibitionist organization throughout the 1920s was the Association Against the Prohibition Amendment (AAPA), which drew its support mainly from conservative businessmen, who objected to the increased power given to the federal government by National Prohibition. Their well-funded arguments, however, fell on deaf ears among the voters throughout the era, most tellingly in the presidential election of 1928. Both the AAPA and the more widely supported WONPR also focused attention on the lawlessness that Prohibition allegedly fostered. This argument, too, gained little traction in the electoral politics of the 1920s. When American voters changed their minds about Prohibition, the AAPA and WONPR, together with other repeal organizations, played a key role in focusing and channeling sentiment through an innovative path to Repeal, the use of specially elected state conventions.[46] But they did not create that sentiment.

> **"Thus, the arguments for Repeal that seemed to have greatest resonance with voters in 1932 and 1933 centered not on indulgence but on economic recovery. Repeal, it was argued, would replace the tax revenues foregone under Prohibition, thereby allowing governments to provide relief to suffering families."**

Finally, historians are fond of invoking widespread cultural change to explain the failure of National Prohibition. Decaying Victorian social mores allowed the normalization of drinking, which was given a significant boost by the cultural trendsetters of the Jazz Age. In such an atmosphere, Prohibition could not survive.[47] But it did. At the height of the Jazz Age, American voters in a hard-fought contest elected a staunch upholder of Prohibition in Herbert Hoover over Al Smith, an avowed foe of the Eighteenth Amendment. Repeal took place, not in the free-flowing good times of the Jazz Age, but rather in the austere gloom 4 years into America's worst economic depression.

Thus, the arguments for Repeal that seemed to have greatest resonance with voters in 1932 and 1933 centered not on indulgence but on economic recovery. Repeal, it was argued, would replace the tax revenues foregone under Prohibition, thereby allowing governments to provide relief to suffering families.[48] It would put unemployed workers back to work. Prohibitionists had long encouraged voters to believe in a link between Prohibition and prosperity, and after the onset of the Depression they abundantly reaped what they had sown.[49] Voters who had ignored claims that Prohibition excessively centralized power, failed to stop drinking, and fostered crime when they elected the dry Hoover now voted for the wet Franklin Roosevelt. They then turned out to elect delegates pledged to Repeal in the whirlwind series of state conventions that ratified the Twenty-First Amendment, Thus, it was not the stringent nature of National Prohibition, which set a goal that was probably impossible to reach and that thereby foredoomed enforcement, that played the leading role in discrediting alcohol prohibition. Instead, an abrupt and radical shift in context killed Prohibition.

Legacies of Prohibition

The legacies of National Prohibition are too numerous to discuss in detail; besides, so many of them live on today and continue to affect Americans' everyday lives that it is even difficult to realize that they are Prohibition's byproducts. I will briefly mention the principal ones, in ascending order from shortest-lived to longest. The shortest-lived child of Prohibition actually survived to adulthood. This was the change in drinking patterns that depressed the level of consumption compared with the pre-Prohibition years. Straitened family finances during the Depression of course kept the annual per capita consumption rate low, hovering around 1.5 US gallons. The true results of Prohibition's success in socializing Americans in temperate habits became apparent during World War II, when the federal government turned a more cordial face toward the liquor industry than it had during World War I, and they became even more evident during the prosperous years that followed.[50] Although annual consumption rose, to about 2 gallons per capita in the 1950s and 2.4 gallons in the 1960s, it did not surpass the pre-Prohibition peak until the early 1970s.[51]

The death rate from liver cirrhosis followed a corresponding pattern.[52] In 1939, 42% of respondents told pollsters that they did not use alcohol at all. If that figure reflected stability in the proportionate size of the non-drinking population since the pre-Prohibition years, and if new cohorts—youths and women—had begun drinking during Prohibition, then the numbers of new drinkers had been offset by Prohibition's socializing effect. By 1960, the proportion of abstainers had fallen only to 38%.[53]

The Prohibition Era was unkind to habitual drunkards, not because their supply was cut off, but because it was not. Those who wanted liquor badly enough could still find it. But those who recognized their drinking as destructive were not so lucky in finding help. The inebriety asylums had closed, and the self-help societies had withered away. In 1935, these conditions gave birth to a new self-help group, Alcoholics Anonymous (AA), and the approach taken by these innovative reformers, while drawing from the old self-help tradition, was profoundly influenced by the experience of Prohibition.

AA rejected the prohibitionists' claim that anyone could become a slave to alcohol, the fundamental assumption behind the sweeping approach of the Volstead Act. There were several reasons for this decision, but one of the primary ones was a perception that Prohibition had failed and a belief that battles already lost should not be refought. Instead, AA drew a rigid line between normal drinkers, who could keep their consumption within the limits of moderation, and compulsive drinkers, who could not. Thus was born the disease concept of alcoholism. Although the concept's principal aim was to encourage sympathy for alcoholics, its result was to open the door to drinking by everyone else.[54] Influenced by Repeal to reject temperance ideology, medical researchers held the door open by denying previously accepted links between drinking and disease.[55]

Another force energized by Prohibition also promoted drinking: the liquor industry's fear that Prohibition might return. Those fears were not unjustified, because during the late 1930s two fifths of Americans surveyed still supported national Prohibition.[56] Brewers and distillers trod carefully, to be sure, attempting to surround liquor with an aura of "glamour, wealth, and sophistication," rather than evoke the rough culture of the saloon. To target women, whom the industry perceived as the largest group of abstainers, liquor ads customarily placed drinking in a domestic context giving hostesses a central role in dispensing their products.[57] Too much can easily be made of the "cocktail culture" of the 1940s and 1950s, because the drinking population grew only slightly and per capita consumption rose only gradually during those years. The most significant result of the industry's campaign was to lay the foundation for a substantial increase in drinking during the 1960s and 1970s.

By the end of the 20th century, two thirds of the alcohol consumed by Americans was drunk in the home or at private parties.[58] In other words, the model of drinking within a framework of domestic sociability, which had been shaped by women, had largely superseded the style of public drinking men had created in their saloons and clubs.[59] Prohibition helped to bring about this major change in American drinking patterns by killing the saloon, but it also had an indirect influence in the same direction, by way of the state. When Prohibition ended, and experiments in economic regulation—including regulation of alcohol—under the National Recovery Administration were declared unconstitutional, the federal government banished public health concerns from its alcohol policy, which thereafter revolved around economic considerations.[60]

Some states retained their prohibition laws—the last repeal occurring only in 1966—but most created pervasive systems of liquor control that affected drinking in every aspect.[61] Licensing was generally taken out of the hands of localities and put under the control of state administrative bodies, in an attempt to replace the impassioned struggles that had heated local politics since the 19th century with the cool, impersonal processes of bureaucracy. Licensing policy favored outlets selling for off-premise consumption, a category that eventually included grocery stores. With the invention of the aluminum beer can and the spread of home refrigeration after the 1930s, the way was cleared for the home to become the prime drinking site.

Lessons for Other Drug Prohibitions

Perhaps the most powerful legacy of National Prohibition is the widely held belief that it did not work. I agree with other historians who have argued that this belief is false: Prohibition did work in lowering per capita consumption. The lowered level of consumption during the quarter century following Repeal, together with the large minority of abstainers, suggests that Prohibition did socialize or maintain a significant portion of the population in temperate or abstemious habits.[62] That is, it was partly successful as a public health innovation. Its political failure is attributable more to a changing context than to characteristics of the innovation itself.

Today, it is easy to say that the goal of total prohibition was impossible and the means therefore were unnecessarily severe—that, for example, National Prohibition could have survived had the drys been willing to compromise by permitting beer and light wine[63]—but from the perspective of 1913 the rejection of alternate modes of liquor control makes more sense. Furthermore, American voters continued to support Prohibition politically even in its stringent form, at least in national politics, until their economy crashed and forcefully turned their concerns in other directions. Nevertheless, the possibility remains that in 1933 a less restrictive form of Prohibition could have satisfied the economic concerns that drove Repeal while still controlling the use of alcohol in its most dangerous forms.

Scholars have readied no consensus on the implications of National Prohibition for other forms of prohibition, and public discourse in the United States mirrors our collective ambivalence.[64] Arguments that assume that Prohibition was a failure have been deployed most effectively against laws prohibiting tobacco and guns, but they have been ignored by those waging the war on other drugs since the 1980s, which is directed toward the same teetotal goal as National Prohibition.[65] Simplistic assumptions about government's ability to legislate morals, whether pro or con, find no support in the historical record. As historian Ian Tyrell writes, "each drug subject to restrictions needs to be carefully investigated in terms of its conditions of production, its value to an illicit trade, the ability to conceal the substance, and its effects on both the individual and society at large."[66] From a historical perspective, no prediction is certain, and no path is forever barred—not even the return of alcohol prohibition in some form. Historical context matters.

References

1. Esa Österberg, "Finland," in *Alcohol and Temperance in Modern History: An International Encyclopedia*, vol 1, ed. Jack S. Blocker Jr, David M. Fahey, and Ian R. Tyrrell (Santa Barbara, Calif: ABC-Clio, 2003). 240–243: Sturla Nordlund, "Norway," in *Alcohol and Temperance in Modern History*, vol 2, 458–463: William Lahey, "Provincial Prohibition (Canada), in *Alcohol and Temperance in Modern History*, vol 2, 496–499: Daniel J. Malleck, "Federal Prohibition (Canada)," in *Alcohol and Temperance in Modern History*, vol 1, 229: Laura L. Phillips, *Bolsheviks and the Bottle: Drink and Worker Culture in St. Petersburg. 1900–1920* (Dekalb: Northern Illinois University Press, 2000).

2. Thomas R. Pegram, *Battling Demon Rum: The Struggle for a Dry America. 1800–1933* (Chicago: Ivan R. Dee, 1998): Jack S. Blocker Jr, *American Temperance Movements: Cycles of Reform* (Boston: Twayne, 1989), 106–129: W. J. Rorabaugh, "Reexamining the Prohibition Amendment," *Yale Journal of Law and the Humanities* 8 (1996): 285–294; Ian Tyrrell, "The US Prohibition Experiment: Myths, History and Implications," *Addiction* 92 (1997): 1405–1409.

3. Ian R. Tyrrell, *Sobering Up: From Temperance to Prohibition in Antebellum America. 1800–1860* (Westport, Conn: Greenwood Press, 1979), 89–90 and passim: Jack S. Blocker Jr, *Retreat From Reform The Prohibition Movement in the United States, 1890–1913* (Westport, Conn: Greenwood Press, 1976), 83; Blocker, *American Temperance Movements*, 24–25; Edward J. Wheeler, *Prohibition: The Principle, the Policy, and the Party* (New York: Funk & Wagnalls, 1889), 39–49, 57–66.

4. Blocker, *American Temperance Movements*, 21–27, 69–70; Tyrrell, *Sobering Up*, 135–145, 227–245; K. Austin Kerr, *Organized for Prohibition: A New History of the Anti-Saloon League* (New Haven, Conn: Yale University Press, 1985), 35–138; Anne-Marie E. Szymanski, *Pathways to Prohibition: Radicals, Moderates, and Social Movement Outcomes* (Durham, NC: Duke University Press, 2003); Sarah W. Tracy, *Alcoholism in America: From Reconstruction to Prohibition* (Baltimore, Md: Johns Hopkins University Press, 2005).

5. Joan L. Silverman, "I'll Never Touch Another Drop": *Images of Alcohol and Temperance in American Popular Culture, 1874–1919* [PhD dissertation] (New York: New York University, 1979), 338–340, and "The Birth of a Nation: Prohibition Propaganda," *Southern Quarterly* 19 (1981): 23–30.

6. James H. Timberlake, *Prohibition and the Progressive Movement, 1900–1920* (Cambridge. Mass: Harvard University Press, 1963). 39–66, Denise Herd, "Ideology, History and Changing Models of Liver Cirrhosis Epidemiology," *British Journal of Addiction* 87 (1992): 1113–1126; Brian S. Katcher, "The Post-Repeal Eclipse in Knowledge About the Harmful Effects of Alcohol," *Addiction* 88 (June 1993): 729–744.

7. Harry Gene Levine, "The Discovery of Addiction: Changing Conceptions of Habitual Drunkenness in America," *Journal of Studies on Alcohol* 39 (January 1978): 161–162.

8. Jonathan Zimmerman, *Distilling Democracy: Alcohol Education in America's Public Schools, 1880–1925* (Lawrence: University Press of Kansas, 1999).

9. Catherine Gilbert Murdock, *Domesticating Drink: Women, Men, and Alcohol in America, 1870–1940* (Baltimore: Johns Hopkins University Press, 1998). For studies of saloon culture, see Madelon Powers, *Faces Along the Bar: Lore and Order in the Workingman's Saloon, 1870–1920* (Chicago: University of Chicago Press, 1998); Craig Heron, *Booze: A Distilled History* (Toronto: Between the Lines, 2003), 105–121; Perry Duis, *The Saloon: Public Drinking in Chicago and Boston, 1880–1920* (Urbana: University of Illinois Press, 1983), 172–197; Elaine Frantz Parsons, *Manhood Lost: Fallen Drunkards and Redeeming Women in the 19th-century United States* (Baltimore: Johns Hopkins University Press, 2003).

10. Local option, through which many areas in states lacking prohibition statutes were rendered "dry," of course affected only the sale of liquor within the local jurisdiction; it could not, nor did it attempt to, prevent local drinkers from importing alcohol from wet areas, either by bringing it themselves or through mail order. Pegram, *Battling Demon Rum*, 141–142.

11. Richard F. Hamm, *Shaping the Eighteenth Amendment: Temperance Reform, Legal Culture, and the Polity, 1880–1920* (Chapel Hill: University of North Carolina Press, 1995), 56–91, 212–226.

12. Szymanski, *Pathways to Prohibition*, 100–121, 131–140.

13. Jack S. Blocker Jr, "Consumption and Availability of Alcoholic Beverages in the United States, 1863–1920," *Contemporary Drug Problems* 21(1994): 631–666.

14. Ibid.

15. David E. Kyvig, *Explicit and Authentic Acts: Amending the US Constitution, 1776–1995* (Lawrence: University Press of Kansas, 1996), 216–218. Creation of a national income tax also provided an alternative source of revenue for the federal government, thereby freeing Congress from reliance on liquor excise taxes. Donald J. Boudreaux and A. C. Pritchard, "The Price of Prohibition," *Arizona Law Review* 10 (1994): 1–10.

16. Kerr, *Organized for Prohibition*, 139–147.

17. Blocker, *Retreat From Reform*, 228; Kerr, *Organized for Prohibition*, 140–141; Thomas R. Pegram, "Prohibition," in *The American Congress: The Building of Democracy*, ed. Julian E. Zelizer (Boston: Houghton Mifflin, 2004), 411–427.

18. National Institute for Alcohol Abuse and Alcoholism (NIAAA), "Apparent per Capita Ethanol Consumption for the United States, 1850–2000," available at http://www.niaaa.nih.gov/databases/consum01.htm, accessed August 2004; Blocker, "Consumption and Availability," 652. All statistics given in this article for per capita consumption are for US gallons of ethanol per capita of population 15 years of age and older prior to 1970 and population 14 years of age and older thereafter.

19. Angela K. Dills and Jeffrey A. Miron, "Alcohol Prohibition and Cirrhosis," *American Law and Economics Review* 6 (2004): 285–318, esp. Figure 3; E. M. Jellinek, "Recent Trends in Alcoholism and in Alcohol Consumption," *Quarterly Journal of Studies on Alcohol*, 8 (1947): 40.

20. Blocker, *American Temperance Movements*, 117.

21. Timberlake, *Prohibition and the Progressive Movement*.

22. Robert G. LaForge, *Misplaced Priorities: A History of Federal Alcohol Regulation and Public Health Policy* [PhD dissertation] (Baltimore: Johns Hopkins University, 1987), 56.

23. Kerr, *Organized for Prohibition*, 181–184.

24. Szymanski, *Pathways to Prohibition*, LaForge, *Misplaced Priorities*; Kerr, *Organized for Prohibition*, 181–184.

25. Pegram, *Battling Demon Rum*, 144–147.

26. Blocker, *American Temperance Movements*, 118; Kyvig, *Explicit and Authentic Acts*, 224.

27. *Statistical Abstract of the United States: 1928* (Washington, DC: US Bureau of the Census, 1928), 767.

28. *Statistics Concerning Intoxicating Liquors* (Washington, DC: Bureau of Industrial Alcohol, US Treasury Department, 1930), 3, 60, 64, 72.

29. William H. Mulligan Jr, "Coors, Adolph, Brewing Company," in *Alcohol and Temperance in Modern History*, vol 1, 174; Mulligan, "Miller Brewing Company," in *Alcohol and Temperance in Modern History*, vol 2. 418; Amy Mittelman, "Anheuser-Busch," in *Alcohol and Temperance in Modern History*, vol 1, 43–45.

30. Even the death of slavery, although it put an end to the domestic slave trade, did not hinder cotton culture.

31. Pegram, *Battling Demon Rum*, 149.

32. Jeffrey A. Miron and Jeffrey Zwiebel, "Alcohol Consumption During Prohibition," *American Economic Review* 81 (1991): 242–247; Dills and Miron, "Alcohol Prohibition and Cirrhosis"; NIAAA, "Apparent per Capita Ethanol Consumption." The figure is for 1935.

33. John R. Meers, "The California Wine and Grape Industry and Prohibition," *California Historical Society Quarterly* 46 (1967): 19–32.

34. Norman H. Clark, *Deliver Us From Evil: An Interpretation of American Prohibition* (New York: W. W. Norton, 1976), 143–146; Powers, *Faces Along the Bar*, 234–236; Duis, *The Saloon* 274–303; Pegram, *Battling Demon Rum*, 163.

35. Robin Room, "'A Reverence for Strong Drink': The Lost Generation and the Elevation of Alcohol in American Culture," *Journal of Studies on Alcohol* 45 (1984): 540–546; John C. Burnham, *Bad Habits: Drinking, Smoking, Taking Drugs, Gambling, Sexual Misbehavior, and Swearing in American History* (New York: New York University Press, 1993), 34–38; Paula Fass, *The Damned and the Beautiful: American Youth in the 1920's* (New York: Oxford University Press, 1977); Murdock, *Domesticating Drink*, 93–94.

36. Thomas R. Pegram, "Kluxing the Eighteenth Amendment: The Anti-Saloon League, the Ku Klux Klan, and the Fate of Prohibition in the 1920s," in *American Public Life and the Historical Imagination*, ed. Wendy Gamber, Michael Grossberg, and Hendrik Hartog (Notre Dame, Ind: University of Notre Dame Press, 2003), 240–261.

37. Murdock, *Domesticating Drink*.

38. Ibid, 134–158; Kenneth D. Rose, *American Women and the Repeal of Prohibition* (New York: New York University Press, 1996).

39. Burnham, *Bad Habits*, 34–49; Room, "A Reverence for Strong Drink": Room, The Movies and the Wettening of America: The Media as Amplifiers of Cultural Change," *British Journal of Addiction* 83 (1988): 11–18; David E. Kyvig, *Repealing National Prohibition* (Chicago: University of Chicago Press, 1979), 28–29.

40. Andrew Sinclair, *Prohibition: The Era of Excess* (New York: Harper & Row, 1962), 211–212, 220–230; Kyvig, *Repealing National Inhibition*, 30.

41. Paul L. Murphy, "Societal Morality and Individual Freedom," in *Law, Alcohol, and Order: Perspectives on National Prohibition*, ed. David E. Kyvig (Westport, Conn: Greenwood Press, 1985), 67–80; Rayman L. Solomon, "Regulating the Regulators: Prohibition Enforcement in the Seventh Circuit," in *Law, Alcohol, and Order*, 81–96.

42. Lawrence Spinelli, *Dry Diplomacy: The United States, Great Britain, and Prohibition* (Wilmington, Del: Scholarly Resources, 1989).

43. Kyvig, *Repealing National Prohibition*, 147–168; Alan P. Grimes, *Democracy and the Amendments to the Constitution* (Lexington, Mass: Lexington Books, 1978), 109–112.

44. Kerr, *Organized for Prohibition*, 222.

45. Hamm, *Shaping the Eighteenth Amendment*, 266–269; Pegram, *Battling Demon Rum*, 156–160.

46. Kyvig, *Repealing National Prohibition*.

47. Kerr, *Organized for Prohibition*, 279; Hamm, *Shaping the Eighteenth Amendment*, 269; Pegram, *Battling Demon Rum*, 175–176.

48. Boudreaux and Pritchard, "Price of Prohibition," 5–10.

49. Sinclair, *Prohibition*, 387–399.

50. Jay L. Rubin, "The Wet War: American Liquor Control, 1941–1945," in *Alcohol, Reform and Society: The Liquor Issue in Social Context*, ed. Jack S. Blocker Jr (Westport, Conn: Greenwood Press, 1979), 235–258.

51. NIAAA, "Apparent per Capita Ethanol Consumption."

52. Dills and Miron, "Alcohol Prohibition and Cirrhosis," Figure 3.

53. Blocker, *American Temperance Movements*, 138. The United States continues to be distinguished among societies where temperance ideology was once influential by its high proportion

of abstainers. Michael H. Hilton, "Trends in US Drinking Patterns: Further Evidence From the Past 20 Years," *British Journal of Addiction* 83 (1988): 269–278; Klaus Mäkelä, Robin Room, Eric Single, Pekka Sulkunen, and Brendan Walsh, *A Comparative Study of Alcohol Control*, vol 1 of Alcohol, Society, and the State (Toronto: Addiction Research Foundation, 1981), 21–24.

54. Ernest Kurtz, *Not-God: A History of Alcoholics Anonymous,* rev ed (Center City, Minn: Hazelden, 1991); Bruce H. Johnson, *The Alcoholism Movement in America: A Study in Cultural Innovation* [PhD dissertation] (University of Illinois at Urbana-Champaign, 1973); Blocker, *American Temperance Movements,* 139–154.

55. Herd, "Ideology, History and Changing Models of Liver Cirrhosis Epidemiology"; Katcher, "Post-Repeal Eclipse in Knowledge"; Philip J. Pauly, "How Did the Effects of Alcohol on Reproduction Become Scientifically Uninteresting?" *Journal of the History of Biology* 29 (1996): 1–28.

56. Blocker, *American Temperance Movements*, 136.

57. Cheryl Krasnick Warsh, "Smoke and Mirrors: Gender Representation in North American Tobacco and Alcohol Advertisements Before 1950," *Histoire sociale/Social History* 31 (1998): 183–222 (quote from p. 220); Lori Rotskoff, *Love on the Rocks: Men, Women, and Alcohol in Post-World War II America* (Chapel Hill: University of North Carolina Press, 2002), 194–210; Burnham, *Bad Habits*, 47.

58. Stephen R Byers, "Home, as Drinking Site," in *Alcohol and Temperance in Modern History*, vol 1, 296.

59. Murdock, *Domesticating Drink.*

60. LaForge, *Misplaced Priorities.*

61. Harry Gene Levine, "The Birth of American Alcohol Control: Prohibition, the Power Elite, and the Problem of Lawlessness," *Contemporary Drug Problems* 12 (1985): 63–115; David Fogarty. "From Saloon to Supermarket: Packaged Beer and the Reshaping of the US Brewing Industry," *Contemporary Drug Problems* 12 (1985): 541–592.

62. John C. Burnham, "New Perspectives on the Prohibition 'Experiment' of the 1920's," *Journal of Social History* 2 (1968): 51–68; Clark, *Deliver Us From Evil*, 145–158; Kerr, *Organizing for Prohibition.* 276–277; Tyrrell, "US Prohibition Experiment," 1406.

63. Murdock, *Domesticating Drink*, 170.

64. Burnham, *Bad Habits*, 293–297; Jeffrey A. Miron, "An Economic Analysis of Alcohol Prohibition," *Journal of Drug Issues* 28 (1998): 741–762; Harry G. Levine and Craig Reinarman, "From Prohibition to Regulation: Lessons From Alcohol Policy to Drug Policy," *Milbank Quarterly* 69 (1991): 461–494.

65. James A. Morone, *Hellfire Nation: The Politics of Sin in American History* (New Haven, Conn: Yale University Press, 2003), 343.

66. Tyrrell, "US Prohibition Experiment" 1407; Robin Room, "Alcohol Control and Public Health," *Annual Review of Public Health* 5 (1984): 293–317.

The author is with the Department of History, Huron University College, University of Western Ontario, London, Ontario.

Requests for reprints should be sent to Jack S. Blocker Jr, PhD, Huron University College, 1349 Western Road, London. Ontario N6G 1H3 Canada (e–mail: jblocker@uwo.ca).

Acknowledgments—Tom Pegram and Ted Brown provided helpful comments on an earlier version of the article.

Vice Vaccines

Scientists give a shot in the arm to the fight against smoking, drug abuse, and obesity.

CHRISTEN BROWNLEE

When Rachel Harrison was 16 years old, she took a drag from her first cigarette. She remembers loving it right away—the taste, the warmth, and especially the lightheaded rush that smoking gave her. Like a bad character in an after-school special, she chain-smoked an entire pack that first time while hanging out with other smokers from the popular crowd.

"I know it sounds cliché, but I started smoking because all the cool kids were doing it," says Harrison, now 32.

From high school through college, and now in her job as a public relations professional in New York, Harrison has kept up the habit. Nowadays, she paces her smoking to three or four cigarettes each workday. The weekends are a "free-for-all," she says, when she goes through often more than a pack a day.

But even though some part of her still loves each smoke as much as her first one, Harrison says, she longs to escape cigarettes' fiery grip. In her quest to avoid the bad breath, wrinkles, and cancer that smoking can bring, she guesses that she's tried to quit about 30 times in the past 15 years. But no matter which method she's used—nicotine gum, the patch, or just quitting cold turkey—she's never succeeded.

"I come back to it usually because a friend will be smoking and I'll ask for a drag," Harrison says. "That first drag will taste so disgusting, but for some reason, literally an hour later I'm asking for a full cigarette, then buying a new pack."

Soon, Harrison and other people plagued by some of Western societies' hardest-to-kick habits may literally get a shot in the arm: vaccines to help them quit. Vaccinations have long had a starring role in preventing a variety of diseases. But now, researchers are aiming the needle at a new set of targets—smoking, obesity, and illicit drugs. These vaccines, currently in development, could give people a novel way to boost their health and vanquish their vices.

Smoke Out

Vaccines have been doing their part to eradicate disease since the 18th century, typically by jump-starting the immune system to fight infectious bacteria and viruses such as those that cause the flu, cholera, or tetanus. But in 1974, narcotics researcher C. Robert Schuster, then at the University of Chicago, and his colleagues published the first evidence that vaccines could rev up the immune system against a different type of target—heroin. In a twist on their typical preventive role, these vaccines stop substances from satisfying an already-addicted user's cravings.

Normally, the immune system doesn't recognize heroin and other drugs as foes worthy of attack. That's because drug molecules are significantly smaller than the foreign proteins on bacteria and viruses that trigger the body to defend itself, says immunologist Michael Owens of the University of Arkansas for Medical Sciences in Little Rock.

"In general, the cutoff in size for the immune system to recognize something as foreign will be about 10,000 daltons in weight. Most drugs of abuse are less than 500 [daltons]," he says. One dalton is about the weight of a single hydrogen atom.

To get the immune system fired up to fight heroin, Schuster and his team decided to make a vaccine by attaching heroin molecules to something that reliably triggers a response in healthy people and other animals. They used a protein from cows' blood. When the immune system senses the large, foreign protein with drug molecules piggybacked onto them, it pumps out a variety of antibodies, explains Owen. Some antibodies recognize pieces of the protein, but others home in on the drug.

> **"People can still smoke, but they don't get the rush, they don't feel good, and they don't keep the addiction. You take away the reason they smoke,"**
>
> —Henrik Rasmussen,
> Nabi Biopharmaceuticals

"The small drug molecules are just along for the ride," adds vaccine researcher Kim Janda of the Scripps Research Institute in La Jolla, Calif., but the immune system generates antibodies against them nonetheless.

After Schuster's team gave the vaccine to heroin-addicted rhesus monkeys that could self-administer the drug by pushing a lever, the animals did so significantly less often than they had previously. The researchers hypothesized that the vaccine somehow prevented the monkeys from getting high, taking away their incentive to keep using the drug.

However, notes Owens, the idea of vaccinating against illegal drugs didn't immediately catch on. Methadone, a drug that satisfies heroin's cravings without causing a high, was already in use in the 1970s for treating heroin addiction, and Schuster's team wasn't seeing as strong an effect with its vaccine.

Over the next few decades, however, researchers began to see the value of Schuster's approach for treating other types of addiction. For example, vaccines to help smokers such as Harrison quit are now advancing through clinical trials.

One of these vaccines, called NicVax and manufactured by Nabi Biopharmaceuticals in Boca Raton, Fla., works by attaching multiple nicotine molecules to a protein taken from *Pseudomonas aeruginosa,* a species of bacteria that occasionally infects people.

When a smoker lights up and draws the addictive drug into his or her bloodstream, antibodies glom on to individual nicotine molecules, explains Nabi scientist Henrik Rasmussen. As a result, the formerly tiny molecules morph into clumps made of nicotine and antibodies. Those clusters are far too big to cross the blood-brain barrier and stimulate the brain's feel-good centers, an action that normally cements nicotine's addictive power.

Smokers still experience the typical array of withdrawal symptoms, including cravings for cigarettes. But after learning that cigarettes are no longer satisfying, Rasmussen notes, people find that their cravings quickly decline.

"People can still smoke, but they don't get the rush, they don't feel good, and they don't keep the addiction. You take away the reason they smoke," he says.

After the promising results in animals, Nabi scientists began a series of clinical trials 4 years ago to test whether NicVax is safe and effective in people. In 2005, the company released its latest results. Sixty-four smokers who were all interested in quitting participated in that trial. Some of them received various doses of the vaccine, delivered in a series of injections over 6 weeks. Others got a series of placebo shots.

Only 9 percent of the placebo group successfully laid off cigarettes for 30 days—a standard criterion that the U. S. Food and Drug Administration uses to define smoking cessation. However, of those smokers who got the highest vaccine dose, 33 percent passed the 30-day test of success. Moreover, even smokers who got the vaccine but didn't quit smoking, lit up significantly fewer cigarettes after the trial than smokers who got the placebo did.

Nabi is currently performing a similar trial with 300 smokers at nine sites across the country. The company expects to announce the results of this larger study in April or May, says spokesperson Tom Rathjen.

With the market hot for new smoking-cessation products, Nabi has some competition. Two other companies—Cytos Biotechnology of Zurich and Celtic Pharma of Hamilton, Bermuda—are developing their own versions of nicotine vaccines. Celtic is also working toward a vaccine based on similar technology to fight cocaine addiction. All these vaccines are currently going through clinical trials.

Weighing In

If these vaccines eventually head to the market, they'll be welcomed by addicted people, who currently have few effective treatment options, says vaccine researcher Janda. He and his team saw a similar possibility for people struggling against obesity.

"Success has been limited with obesity, [the] same as with treating addiction to drugs of abuse. We thought we could take a similar tack" by developing an antiobesity vaccine, Janda says. In the Aug. 29, 2006 *Proceedings of the National Academy of Sciences,* Janda and his colleagues published a proof-of-principle study showing that a vaccine they'd developed can prevent weight gain in rats.

To produce their antiobesity vaccine, the researchers needed a molecule on which to focus the immune system's antibodies, like the nicotine or cocaine molecules targeted by vaccines against those addictions. But obesity is a complex phenomenon spurred by hundreds of different molecules in the body. Eventually, Janda's team settled on ghrelin, a hormone that spikes hunger, slows metabolism, encourages fat storage, and shifts food preferences toward diets rich in fat.

The scientists created molecules that mimic the structure of different forms of ghrelin. By attaching each one to a larger carrier protein, the team created three different vaccines. The researchers then vaccinated groups of rats with one of the vaccines or a placebo.

Janda's group found that rats vaccinated against either of two forms of the hormone called ghrelin 1 and ghrelin 3 gained significantly less weight and had less body fat over the next several months than did rats vaccinated with the placebo, even though all the animals ate the same amount of chow.

Nevertheless, the vaccine has far to go before it is shown to be effective in people, Janda says. For example, lab rats that received the vaccine ate healthy, low-fat diets. Now, Janda and his team plan on testing whether immunizing against ghrelin is still effective for animals that eat high-fat food more typical of a Western diet.

"I'm not saying this is a magic bullet, but this could eventually be used as a crutch" to help people lose weight, says Janda. He notes that a combination of vaccines against ghrelin and other weight-loss drugs currently on the market might someday be used to boost people's chances of success.

Passive Aggression

Vaccines such as those in the works for nicotine and obesity take advantage of a natural tendency of the immune system: the antibodies that it pumps out when stimulated can linger in the body and work a long time.

However, these vaccines also have their disadvantages, says Owens. It can take weeks or months for an antibody to reach an effective concentration in the blood, so a patient's response to these treatments would be delayed. Furthermore, long-lasting antibodies aren't always desirable. For example, in the case of the antiobesity vaccine, doctors would need to end patients' treatments once they reached their target weight, rather than have patients continue to drop pounds.

With that in mind, Owens, Janda, and other researchers are crafting vaccines that work in a different way. Rather than prompting the body to create its own antibodies, these passive vaccines consist of custom-made antibodies to be pumped directly into a patient's bloodstream. They'd go to work right away against a habit-driving substance but then degrade and be cleared from the circulation in a few weeks, says Owens.

Janda's team is planning to develop a passive version of its antighrelin vaccine, while Owens and his colleagues have such vaccines in the works against a variety of addictive drugs, such as phencyclidine (PCP), methamphetamine, and cocaine. Each of these vaccines has had some success in limiting the amounts of drugs that addicted lab animals choose to self-administer.

Such vaccines could be expensive in quantities suited to people, notes Janda. The versions being tested are monoclonal antibodies, which are crafted to recognize a single target, such as one type of drug molecule. Until recently, researchers assumed that at least one antibody molecule was needed to neutralize each drug molecule. With some drug addicts using many grams of a drug at a time, Owens estimates that such an approach could cost tens of thousands of dollars for a month of treatment.

In 2003, however, he and his team discovered that a heavy dose isn't always necessary. After tweaking the molecular structure of a PCP vaccine that they'd developed, the researchers reported success with an amount of antibodies less than 1/100th the molecular equivalent of the amount of PCP that rats were receiving. The animals given that vaccine dose avoided the extreme weight loss and death that befell about 25 percent of rats given sham vaccines, the researchers reported.

"We don't need huge amounts to offer a tremendous effect," says Owens. "If cost is on the left hand and effectiveness is on the right hand, we're finally moving those to the point of merging."

Owens and his colleagues are currently planning a clinical trial of their PCP vaccine, which they hope to start this year.

The Old Standby

Although vaccines against smoking, obesity, and drugs would offer new ways of fighting these conditions, Frank Vocci, director of the division of treatment and research at the National Institute on Drug Abuse in Baltimore, says that such vaccines probably wouldn't be foolproof. Theoretically, smokers and drug addicts could override the vaccines by taking an amount of nicotine or another drug that overwhelms their capacities. And none of the vaccines addresses the behavioral components of addiction that often lead people to relapse. Those include being around the people and places that lead smokers to light up or food addicts to overeat.

"This isn't something you can give to someone who doesn't want to have treatment," says Vocci. "They're going to have to want to stop their addictive behaviors."

Thomas Kosten, of the Yale University School of Medicine, who is developing both active and passive vaccines against cocaine, proposes that the vaccines' best use would be in combination with other treatments or as supports to get people through times when they're likely to relapse. For example, although cocaine addicts on the vaccine might still get high by taking four to five times the normal amount of drug, "if nothing else, that's expensive," says Kosten. Inability to buy the massive amounts of a drug needed to get high after getting a vaccine may be just the trick to help addicts overcome the urge to use, he speculates.

Even though vaccines might be something an addict could lean on, says Nabi Biopharmaceuticals spokesperson Rathjen, people will still need to rely on an old standby for quitting any addictive behavior: willpower.

Harrison, the reluctant smoker, says that she "would love to get on the [nicotine] vaccine." But since she's not in any nicotine vaccine clinical trial, she's still relying on simple willpower. With a New Year's resolution to quit smoking, she's now halved the number of cigarettes that she was smoking last year.

From *Science News,* February 10, 2007, pp. 90–92. Copyright © 2007 by Science Service Inc. Reprinted by permission via the Copyright Clearance Center.

Pass the Weed, Dad

Parents are smoking dope with their kids. What are they thinking? Marni Jackson investigates.

MARNI JACKSON

"It was a little weird, seeing my parents stoned," Tom confesses. The Toronto high school student was describing the first time he'd smoked marijuana—at home last spring, just after turning 17, when he shared a joint with his hard-working, middle-class parents. "But I had an amazing, fantastic connection with my dad, and it was a good experience for all of us. They showed me how to take the seeds and stems out of the pot. Then, basically, we ate. My mom ordered sushi, and we made a mountain of nachos. It kind of felt like a rite of passage."

After his family initiation, Tom bought six or seven joints of his own for a camping trip, "and that was cool too." But his new girlfriend didn't approve of pot, or him on it. "She said there was this separation thing that happened whenever I smoked." So Tom gave it up, even though his older sister had just given him a nice handmade pipe for his birthday. "But my other sister could care less about pot. Lots of kids try it and don't like it. I think it's totally individual."

Nicole, who maintained a scholarship throughout university and has now graduated, grew up in a household where pot smoking was as casually present as wine with dinner. "Marijuana was so integrated into our social life that it didn't seem to make sense to hide it," says her father, a lawyer. "So we didn't. She began smoking pot when she was around 16. This was in the nineties, when the police were pretty aggressive about it, so we thought that it was safer for her to smoke at home than in the streets. And then when she was in college, there were definitely times when she and I would smoke a joint together. Or I might buy some dope and give her some."

"But lately, we've made some new rules. No smoking dope together. No tobacco in the house. We are rethinking things in general."

He pauses. "Yes, we were open about smoking pot around her. But was it a good idea? I don't know."

Nicole, now 24, says she's "always believed it was a good thing that it wasn't hidden or taboo. I've seen a lot of shel-

tered kids who got into it at 12 or 13, as rebellion. I wasn't interested till later. I tried it and thought, 'Hey, this is good!' It was relaxing, and fun, and it numbs you out, which can be a good thing."

Most parents, of course, aren't sitting around the family bong with their kids. They go along with the authorities who view marijuana as a drug with addictive potential that turns kids into over-snacking, under-motivated, learning-impaired couch potatoes. But the 1.5 million Canadian adults who, according to the Canadian Medical Association, smoke marijuana recreationally might not agree. In fact, a recent Canadian Addiction Survey found that 630,000 of us aged 15 and older smoke cannabis every day. And among middle-aged Canadians, dope use in the past year has increased from 1.4 per cent in 1994 to 8.4 per cent in 2004.

Perhaps as a consequence of this ongoing boomer buzz, some parents feel a zero-tolerance policy with teenagers simply doesn't work and may only increase the allure of pot. They would rather keep the lines of communication open, talk to their children about the genuine risks of individual drugs, and help them develop their own good judgment about drug use—whether it's tobacco, alcohol or marijuana.

'When she was in college, there were definitely times when she and I would smoke a joint together.'

Sharing a joint with your 16- or 17-year-old may be pushing it. Nevertheless, parents who talk about "drugs" as if they're all the same, equating pot with more lethal substances like cocaine or crystal meth—a popular form of amphetamine that is wildly addictive and blatantly destructive—run the risk of not being listened to at all. When we demonize drugs, ironically we tend to empower the drugs, rather than our kids.

Families have changed since the days of *Father Knows Best* (the equivalent show today would be "Father Tokes Best"). Many parents are veterans of the counterculture who did a lot more than inhale in the sixties. For some, marijuana was just an ambient phase, like black-light posters. Others have grown up into successful, civilized, recreational pot smokers who don't want to lie to their kids. They consider the moderate use of pot to be a relatively benign activity—and certainly better than drinking eight beers and getting behind the wheel of a car. Binge drinking, which has become epidemic among college students, can also be fatal, but no one has ever died from a marijuana overdose (although it carries its own health risks, affects driving ability, and has certainly caused repeated screenings of bad movies).

One thing is clear, though: regardless of whether their parents are strict or permissive, most kids will try cannabis sooner or later. By the time they exit their teen years, the Canadian Addiction Survey reports, 70 per cent of them will have smoked a joint at some point—if not in the past hour. Among everyone who's tried it, 18 per cent smoke daily.

Tom and Nicole waited longer than most teenagers to experiment with marijuana. The average age of first use has gone down, from 14.5 years in 1995 to 13.7 in 2003. In fact, Toronto's Centre for Addiction and Mental Health (CAMH) reports that five per cent of school kids have tried pot before the end of Grade 6. (Can the preschool doobie be far behind? Hemp soothers?) Twenty-eight per cent of students who've finished Grade 9 will have smoked pot in the past year. Roughly the same percentage, it's worth noting, have never tried any drugs, including alcohol or tobacco, and—before we get too hysterical—47 per cent of Canadian high school students "strongly disapprove of regular marijuana smoking."

Nevertheless, cannabis remains the No. 1 illicit drug in North America. And its reputation may be shifting, as science uncovers new medical potential for the cannabinoids that are the active ingredients in marijuana. Last month, a Saskatchewan study reported that a cannabis-like substance injected into rats caused new nerve-cell growth in the hippocampus, suggesting the possibility that marijuana might actually improve certain brain functions—contrary to its reputation as a memory-shredder. (It should be added that the rats were getting a drug 100 times more powerful than THC, the compound that gives marijuana its high.) A study published in a recent issue of the journal *Nature* also suggested that marijuana may "more closely resemble an antidepressant than a drug of abuse." And, of course, the much-debated medical benefits of cannabis for people suffering with chronic pain, AIDS or multiple sclerosis are already well known.

Marijuana is also firmly embedded in popular culture, from the slim green leaves featured on the cover of Willie Nelson's recent CD (reggae, of course), to the phenomenon of "bud porn" (coffee-table books featuring photos of dewy, resin-oozing exotic strains of cannabis), to *Weeds*, the new series currently airing on Showcase. It stars Mary-Louise Parker as a freshly widowed mother who supports her family by dealing pot in her upscale Californian suburb. ("But not to kids," she explains, setting the moral high bar of the show.)

'We call them Jell-O-heads. Boys who can't really think. My son and his friends just seem sedated.'

The series traffics in lame stereotypes (her suppliers are a trash-talkin' black family whose mother cleans and bags her product at the kitchen table). But it flies in the face of George W. Bush's $35-billion War on Drugs, which focuses many of its public awareness programs on the evils of smoking pot while largely ignoring the scourge of crystal meth use in North America. And it's one more sign that marijuana is not about to be weeded out of the culture any time soon.

If this is the case, what sort of limits should parents offer, when their 13-year-old comes home from a party to announce—because they encourage the kid to be open—that he has just smoked his first joint? Of course, they turn off David Letterman, pour a glass of wine, sit down and say, "We don't want you smoking marijuana, sweetheart. You're too young." Then he says, with a red-eyed glare, "Why not? You do."

How does a parent respond to that? With a lecture on how dope impairs concentration and learning, and may not be the best thing for the lungs? Or with a mini-joint and some Neil Young on the CD player?

The Pot (Smoker) Calling the Kettle Black

"When it comes to my own son, I'm totally protective—I veer right into *Reefer Madness* territory," says Ray, a Toronto father and regular grass smoker who was introduced to hash at the age of 15 by his own, scientist father. (Note: not even the most nonchalant pot smoker would agree to be named here. Apparently no one, 15 or 55, wants to be known as a pothead—or arrested. So the names and some identifying details in these stories have been changed.)

"When my son asked if I smoked dope, I simply lied and said no," Ray continues. "But his older sister was with us. She knew that I smoked, and said, 'What are you talking about, dad? Of course you do!" But Ray's double standard is just fine with his son; kids don't necessarily want their parents to be cool. The writer and film director Nora Ephron once observed that if children are given the choice between a happy, gratified parent off boogie-boarding in Hawaii, or a suicidal parent in the next room, they'll pick the miserable, available one every time. The baby boomer pursuit of pleasure and openness may have produced parents who resemble party-hearty older siblings rather than helpful, boring authority figures. "Even though in the real world, marijuana may occupy an unclear, grey zone," says Bob Glossop, a spokesman for the Vanier Institute for the Family, "one of the roles of the parent is to simplify their kids' world, and offer limits."

Some parents are open about their dope smoking while drawing firm lines about drug use for their kids. Patrick is a Toronto writer, poet, parent and cannabis fan. He finds a joint in the late afternoon helps him write. "When my son confronted me and said, 'But you do it,' I said, 'Yes, I smoke pot, but I also earn a living. You are 12 and in Grade 8 and you shouldn't smoke marijuana." Patrick mostly confines his habit to his workspace, but he has always smoked in the house. "My line with my two sons was clear. I told them, 'If you want to finish your education, don't smoke weed.' It tends to de-motivate kids regarding school. I know it brought out my own rebellion, and made me want to quit school and fight the system."

Patrick's relationship to marijuana goes back 27 years, when his stepson, then six, entered his life. "The vibe around pot smoking was different then; it was a more legitimate activity. I smoked in the house, but I explained to my stepson that it was an herb—coltsfoot—that I had to smoke, for my lungs." He sounds a bit sheepish here. "So, yeah, it was a lie, but not entirely; it was an herbal supplement."

His stepson grew up to become a very conservative adult, and a non-smoker, but "surprisingly tolerant" of marijuana. "Coltsfoot has become a kind of joke between us," says Patrick.

When he had his own sons, they both ignored his advice and took up dope smoking around 13. His eldest, Richard, then started dealing; he encountered some violence, got robbed, and finally decided that the dope life was not a good one. "Although I do think he honed his business skills when he was selling," Patrick muses. "He was making good money." Gradually, Richard gave up dope. "He saw that all his friends were dropping out of school, and he didn't want to. He's now in university, studying philosophy, doing well, and he rarely smokes pot. He'd rather argue about philosophy now, which drives me crazy, because . . ."—and here the truly committed pot smoker can be detected—"it's so damn rational."

But Patrick remembers his sons' drug years as a "worrying time. I was really concerned." And he's not alone. Parents worry about the dangers associated with the criminal aspect of marijuana—which is, after all, still an illegal substance, carrying a maximum fine of $1,000 and/or six months in jail for simple possession. The government may be pondering the wisdom of spending millions on imprisoning cannabis offenders when gunshot deaths seem to be everywhere, and white collar crime flies under the radar. With 69 per cent of Canadians favouring decriminalization of pot posses-

sion, according to a February 2003 poll, the feds have taken a step to acknowledging the country's dope use. Last year, they introduced a bill that would decriminalize possession of small amounts of cannabis. But it's currently sitting with a Commons committee and is unlikely to become law before the next federal election.

As they step out onto their back decks to have a quick after-dinner toke, noticing that thick feeling in their lungs again, parents also worry about the long-term effects of marijuana on a 13-year-old's developing mind and body. (Many experts believe regular pot smoking damages the lungs, though there's debate over whether it's more or less harmful than tobacco.) And then there's the school issue: chronic use is linked to declining school work and dropping out.

One Toke Too Many Over the Line

Young people who have already smoked marijuana for a decade are discovering what some of their parents know—it is more habit-forming than its reputation suggests. Eric, who works as a fly-fishing guide near Vancouver, is 19 and has been smoking pot daily—except for the brief periods when he's tried to stop—for about seven years. He lives in a province where more than half the population has tried pot and many are regular users.

Eric's parents were both involved in the political upheaval of the sixties. His mother once spent a night in jail for possession of pot, and, Eric says, "my father told me that he tried everything once, which I tend to believe." Eric's dad, Dmitri, is now a criminal psychologist who is in favour of the legalization of marijuana—although he no longer smokes it himself, and dearly wishes his son would stop too. Despite his liberal perspective, Dmitri views the heavy pot smoking among his son's circle as "insidiously costly." Eric—whom his father proudly describes as a "beautiful, athletic, creative, sensitive young man"—couldn't agree more.

"I would like to quit, a lot," Eric says. "And every single friend I know who smokes heavily wants to stop too. Dope is okay in moderation, but when your life starts to revolve around it every day, it becomes like any other addiction. You lose your motivation. Your senses get numbed. And you don't get out of life what you could if you weren't stoned all the time. It was fun to party at 14. But the older you get, the more you kind of want to pull up your socks and get your life going. I've quit a few times, but it's hard. I don't even have to go out and buy it—it's all around me."

'Yes we were open about smoking pot around her. But was it a good idea? I don't know.'

41

Bestselling American health and wellness author Dr. Andrew Weil could not be called anti-pot by any stretch. And the 2004 edition of his book, *From Chocolate to Morphine*, is an unhysterical guide to a wide spectrum of mind-altering drugs. But Weil is very clear about the risks of habitual use. "Marijuana dependence can be sneaky in its development," he writes. "It doesn't appear overnight like cigarette addiction . . . but rather builds up over a long time. The main danger of smoking marijuana is simply that it will get away from you, becoming more and more of a repetitive habit and less and less of a useful way of changing consciousness."

Elizabeth Ridgely is a Toronto therapist and executive director of the George Hull Centre for Children and Families, which has a substance-abuse program open to heavy pot smokers. "The most important thing for parents to know is that marijuana is stronger than it used to be in the Woodstock days," she says. "People who use it habitually use it to soothe themselves, and when they stop, they can feel agitated and anxious. It can really mess up a kid. But kids are surprised to hear this—families aren't having those kinds of conversations about drugs."

Dreams Gone Up in Smoke

"We call them Jell-O-heads," says Tanya, a 52-year-old photo-archivist who lives in Toronto. "Boys who can't really think." She is referring to her 19-year-old son and his friends, who regularly smoke dope on the third floor of her house. "When they come in the door and go up the stairs, it's like having large cedar trees in the house. Everything shakes and rattles. Then they go up to my son's room, and the music starts, and the laughing."

Tanya is a former pot smoker who now considers dope a "real time-waster. I wasted so many years as a hippie, smoking. But it was part of the language back then. It was social, it was anti-authority, it was very sensual. I don't see that with my son's crowd. They just seem sedated. They use a bong, and the drug is really clean and refined and incredibly potent—it's not the ditch weed we used to smoke. It doesn't give you the big fuzzy body stone we used to get from dope. They just get high. I think it dumbs my kid down. The thing that bothers me is that he doesn't seem present when he's stoned.

"My son gave me some of his dope once," says Tanya. "I thought it would be a good way to, you know, talk about it. I didn't want to smoke, so I ate it, and suddenly my eyelids had no function—I mean, I would close my eyes and it would just go on forever. When will this be over, I thought."

After some ineffective drug counseling, her son eventually cut down on his own. "Now he says he only smokes it to get to sleep, as a sedative." She laughs. "Remember when we thought smoking marijuana made us more aware?"

A friend of Tanya's, a Gestalt therapist, has a theory about the downside of heavy pot smoking for teenagers. She considers it a "dream-stealer. At the age when they should be generating their own fantasies and dreams, a drug can usurp that. The visions belong to the drug, not to them."

Smokescreen for Other Problems

Mario, a handsome, athletic 23-year-old, went the whole nine yards with drugs and teen rebellion. He started smoking dope, taking acid and staying out till 4 A.M. when he was 12 and 13. He and his friends would get stoned and go chase skunks through the park in the middle of the night, until somebody called the cops. "If there was a rule, he would break it," remembers his father. He had separated from the boy's mother and was living with his new partner. The separation was civil, and Mario and his younger brother, Paul, were welcome in both households.

"My mother didn't hide the fact that she would smoke around the house occasionally," Mario says. "But she didn't glamorize it. If you're going to have a parent who smokes pot, she went about it the right way. Kids are supersensitive to anything that's hypocritical, especially in their parents. It breaks trust." But his parents worried about the effect Mario's behaviour was having on Paul. They asked him to honour one final rule—no smoking pot in the house, or around his younger brother. When Mario broke that one, his father asked him to move out.

So at the age of 15, for almost two years, Mario was out on the street, couch-surfing at friends' houses and living for a time in a hostel for street kids. He quit school after three weeks of Grade 9. "We gave him money to buy toiletries, which he probably spent on dope," his father says. They stayed in touch, though, and finally his mother said, "That's enough," and let him move in with her. He went back to high school and graduated. He reconnected with the rest of his family, was accepted at Queen's and got a degree in anthropology, and by his late teens had lost interest in pot.

Mario now looks back on those years with hard-earned intelligence and insight. "As far as our family problems go, I think dope was more of a flashpoint than the real issue. My pot smoking was an abrasive thing, and my parents concentrated on that. And it did have tangible fallout—in terms of punctuality and procrastination and school. You know, if a kid isn't getting his work done, and he's smoking dope, it's an easy equation to make. But there's usually more than dope going on."

Poor parents—they always seem to miss the point. And what has become the ultimate parental sin now that pot is out of the closet? Smoking cigarettes. Mario also has a sister, Lucy. At the age of 11, she came home one night to find a dinner party in progress, and her non-smoking mother sitting back with a lit cigarette in hand. "She went ballistic," recalls the mother, "and after everyone left, Lucy came down and sprayed the room with perfume. It was a big deal—kids hate it when their parents do anything self-destructive."

So, a memo to all you law-breaking, pot smoking parents: if you want your kids not to worry, just say no—to tobacco.

From *Maclean's*, November 7, 2005, pp. 27–31. Copyright © 2005 by Marni Jackson. Reprinted by permission of the author.

UNIT 2

Understanding How Drugs Work—Use, Dependency, and Addiction

Unit Selections

10. **Reducing the Risk of Addiction to Prescribed Medications,** Brian Johnson et al.
11. **Predicting Addiction,** Lisa N. Legrand, William G. Iacono, and Matt McGue
12. **Better Ways to Target Pain,** Gary Stix
13. **The Effects of Alcohol on Physiological Processes and Biological Development,** *Alcohol Research and Health*
14. **A Small Part of the Brain, and Its Profound Effects,** Sandra Blakeslee
15. **The Changing Science of Pain,** Mary Carmichael
16. **The Toxicity of Recreational Drugs,** Robert S. Gable
17. **Stress and Drug Abuse,** *Science World*
18. **Does Cannabis Cause Psychosis or Schizophrenia?,** *Drugs and Alcohol Today*

Key Points to Consider

- Why do some people become dependent on certain drugs far sooner than other people?

- How is it possible to predict one's own liability for becoming drug dependent?

- Is it possible for a person to say that he or she intends to be only a recreational user of drugs like cocaine or methamphetamine?

- Of all of the influences that combine to create one's liability for addiction, which ones do you believe to be the most significant?

Student Web Site
www.mhcls.com/online

Internet References
Further information regarding these websites may be found in this book's preface or online.

AddictionSearch.com
www.addictionsearch.com

Addiction Treatment Forum
www.atforum.com

APA Help Center from the American Psychological Association
http://www.apahelpcenter.org/articles/article.php?id=45

British Broadcasting Company Understanding Drugs
http://www.bbc.co.uk/health/conditions/mental_health/drugs_use.shtml

Centre for Addiction and Mental Health (CAMH)
http://www.camh.net

Dealing with Addictions
http://kidshealth.org/teen/your_mind/problems/addictions.html

Drugs and the Body: How Drugs Work
http://www.doitnow.org/pdfs/223.pdf

The National Center on Addiction and Substance Abuse at Columbia University
http://www.casacolumbia.org

National Institute on Drug Abuse (NIDA)
http://www.nida.nih.gov

Public Agenda
http://www.publicagenda.org/issues/frontdoor.cfm?issue_type=illegal_drugs

Understanding Addiction-Regret, Addiction and Death
http://teenadvice.about.com/library/weekly/aa011501a.htm

Understanding how drugs act upon the human mind and body is a critical component to the resolution of issues concerning drug use and abuse. An understanding of basic pharmacology is requisite for informed discussion on practically every drug-related issue and controversy. One does not have to look far to find misinformed debate, much of which surrounds the basic lack of knowledge of how drugs work.

Different drugs produce different bodily effects and consequences. All psychoactive drugs influence the central nervous system, which, in turn, sits at the center of how we physiologically and psychologically interpret and react to the world around us. Some drugs, such as methamphetamine and LSD, have great immediate influence on the nervous system, while others, such as tobacco and marijuana, elicit less-pronounced reactions. Almost all psychoactive drugs have their effects on the body mitigated by the dosage level of the drug taken, the manner in which it is ingested, and the physiological and emotional state of the user. Cocaine smoked in the form of crack versus snorted as powder produces profoundly different physical and emotional effects on the user. However, even though illegal drugs often provide the most sensational perspective from which to view these relationships, the abuse of prescription drugs is being reported as an exploding new component of the addiction problem. Currently, the non-medical use of pain-relievers such as oxycodone and hydrocodone is continuing at alarming rates. This trend has been increasing steadily since 1994, and it currently competes with methamphetamine abuse as the most alarming national trend of drug abuse. Currently, 5.2 million Americans use prescription pain medications for non-medical reasons.

Molecular properties of certain drugs allow them to imitate and artificially reproduce certain naturally-occurring brain chemicals that provide the basis for the drug's influence. The continued use of certain drugs and their repeated alteration of the body's biochemical structure provide one explanation for the physiological consequences of drug use. The human brain is the quintessential master pharmacist and repeatedly altering its chemical functions by drug use is risky. Doing such may produce profound implications for becoming addicted. For example, heroin use replicates the natural brain chemical endorphin, which supports the body's biochemical defense to pain and stress. The continued use of heroin is believed to deplete natural endorphins, causing the nervous system to produce a painful physical and emotional reaction when heroin is withdrawn. Subsequently, one significant motivation for continued use is realized.

A word of caution is in order, however, when proceeding through the various explanations for what drugs do and why they do it. Many people, because of an emotional and/or political relationship to the world of drugs, assert a subjective predisposition when interpreting certain drugs' effects and consequences. One person's alcoholic is another's social drinker. People often argue, rationalize, and explain the perceived nature of

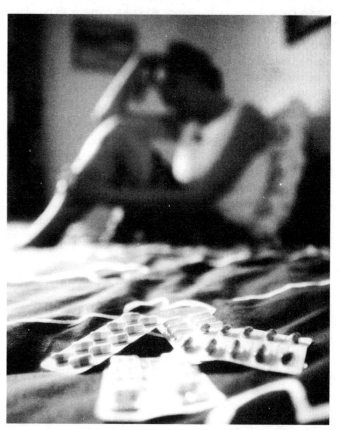

Laurant Hamels/PhotoAlto/Picture Quest

drugs' effects based upon an extremely superficial understanding of diverse pharmacological properties of different drugs. A detached and scientifically sophisticated awareness of drug pharmacology may help strengthen the platform from which to interpret the various consequences of drug use.

Drug addiction results as a continuum comprised of experimentation, recreational use, regular use, and abuse. The process is influenced by a plethora of physiological, psychological, and environmental factors. Although some still argue that drug dependence is largely a matter of individual behavior—something to be chosen or rejected—most experts agree that new scientific discoveries clearly define the roots of addiction to live within molecular levels of the brain. Powerful drugs, upon repeated administration, easily compromise the brain's ability to make decisions about its best interests.

Largely, drugs are described as more addictive or less addictive due to a process described as "reinforcement." Simply explained, reinforcement results from a drug's physiological and psychological influence on a person's behavior to such a degree that it causes that person to repeatedly introduce the drug to the body. Cocaine and the amphetamines are known as drugs with rapidly occurring reinforcement potential. Persons addicted to drugs known to be strongly reinforcing typically report that they care more about getting the drug than about anything else. Reinforcement does not, however, provide "the" basis for understanding addiction.

Drug addiction and the rate at which it occurs must compete with certain physiological and psychological, as well as environmental variables that are unique to individuals. A drug user with a greater number of biological markers known to be associated with drug addiction, such as mental illness, alcoholism, and poor physical health, may encourage drug dependency sooner than a person with fewer biological markers. Similarly, a person's positive environmental associations, or 'natural reinforcers,' such as a strong family structure, and healthy personal and professional relationships may not only make experimentation unappealing, it may delay a user's developing drug addiction. Subsequently, one's liability for drug addiction is closely associated with genetics, environment, and the use of psychoactive drugs. Understanding the concept of addiction requires an awareness of these factors. For many people, drug addiction and the reasons that contribute to it are murky concepts.

The articles in Unit 2 illustrate some of the current research and viewpoints on the ways that drugs act upon the human body. New science is suggesting that a new era has begun relative to understanding drugs and their pharmacological influence on the human body. This new science is critical to understanding the assorted consequences of drug use and abuse. Science has taken us closer to understanding that acute drug use changes brain function profoundly, and that these changes may remain with the user long after the drug has left the system. Subsequently, many new issues have emerged for drug and health-related public policy. Increasingly, drug abuse competes with other social maladies as public enemy number one. Further, the need for a combined biological, behavioral, and social response to this problem becomes more evident. Many health care professionals and health care educators, in addition to those from other diverse backgrounds, argue that research dollars spent on drug abuse and addiction should approach that spent on heart disease, cancer, and AIDS. The articles in Unit 2 provide examples of how some new discoveries have influenced our thinking about addiction. They also provide examples of how, even in light of new knowledge, breaking addictions is so very hard to do.

Reducing the Risk of Addiction to Prescribed Medications

BRIAN JOHNSON, ET AL.

Physicians are often conflicted regarding prescription medications for pain, especially pain complicated by insomnia and anxiety. Concerns that patients may become addicted to medications, exacerbated by limited time available to get to know patients, can lead to underprescribing of needed medications, patient suffering, and needless surgery. At the other extreme, pressure to alleviate patients' distress can lead to overprescribing, needless side effects, and even addiction. These risks can be substantially reduced by forming a therapeutic alliance through careful interviews that are directed toward understanding a patient's potential for addiction. In a trusting alliance, supported by specialized consultation on an as-needed basis, the physician and patient can develop an individualized treatment plan.[1] Furthermore, patients who are empowered to take responsibility for their choices will be more likely to avoid addiction, minimize side-effect impairments, and avoid unnecessary surgery regardless of whether medications are prescribed.

Reducing the Risk of Addiction to Prescribed Medication

Pain is a key sign of illness and is more likely than any other complaint to bring a patient to the doctor.[2] Yet studies show that patients' concerns about pain are all too often at odds with those of their treating physicians.[3,4] Patients describe how their pain affects them functionally and spiritually. In response, physicians use biomedical models to "solve" the pain. However, physicians sometimes worry that the patient may become addicted to prescription medications.

From 1992 to 2002, the number of prescriptions for controlled drugs increased by 150%. The number of Americans who abused controlled prescription drugs nearly doubled from 7.8 million to 15.1 million from 1992 to 2003; more Americans abuse prescribed drugs than abuse cocaine, hallucinogens, inhalants, and heroin combined. A 2004 survey of physicians showed that 59% blamed patients for prescription drug abuse. Patients can manipulate the system to obtain controlled prescription drugs by faking symptoms that are commonly treated with opioids, depressants,

and stimulants; by visiting and obtaining prescriptions from many doctors; and by altering prescriptions.[5]

Much is at stake in this relationship. If patients cannot trust their physicians, their pain may be compounded by feelings of isolation and fear.[1] Furthermore, if these differences cannot be negotiated, there is a greater chance that attempted treatment could lead to a poor result—both in terms of medical outcome and liability.

This article presents strategies that help physicians overcome misunderstandings with their patients and provides support to physicians in their journeys through the shoals of clinical uncertainty and medical liability.[6] Instead of a formula, the goal is to provide a framework to help clinicians focus on structuring a beneficial relationship with their patients by integrating good care with complementary rather than unduly burdensome risk management.

Addiction: Defining without Disempowering

What is addiction? Its meaning has varied over time and in different settings (eg, clinical vs social). The adopted definition guides clinicians' and patients' treatment choices. For potentially addictive prescribed medications, a useful definition would state that addiction is the overuse of a drug leading to impairment in social function and judgment.

This definition does not disempower or stigmatize the patient; rather, it acknowledges that the patient has legitimate pain. This definition also allows physicians to broaden their thinking while they consider prescribing potentially addictive medication: first, do no harm; then, improve functioning; and finally, relieve suffering.

According to study data, empowering patients with choice when prescribing potentially addictive substances appears to limit the use of such drugs immediately following surgery. Compared with patients who were given as-needed doses by nursing staff, patients who were allowed to self-administer pain medication took the same amount or less of the drug.[7,8]

Fixed-schedule administration to avoid pain breakthrough can be the most appropriate manner of pain treatment. However, on an outpatient basis, it requires mutual trust between physician and patient, as well as the ability for the patient to follow a fixed schedule. Thus, assessment of patient competency to form and maintain a therapeutic alliance and follow a fixed-dosage schedule is essential in pain management on an outpatient basis.

What types of medications raise the specter of addiction among prescribing physicians? Opiates, such as oxycodone and hydrocodone, as well as sedatives and antianxiety drugs, such as benzodiazepines and barbiturates, cause concern. These medications are prescribed for pain and for the sleep and anxiety problems that may accompany pain.[9]

How can legitimately prescribed medications get a patient into trouble? Functional MRI shows addiction as a change in the brain's reward pathway, which involves the ventral tegmental neurons that secrete dopamine in the nucleus accumbens, leading to compulsive drug seeking.[10] However, addiction cannot be reduced simply to the notion of repetitive stimulation of a reward pathway.

A helpful model addresses a triad of factors in understanding addiction. The first includes a patient's biology (brain chemistry and genetics). The second involves "self-medicating," in which patients use medications in response to feeling helpless about emotions generated in interpersonal situations or to treat a psychiatric disorder. The third aspect notes that addictive drugs may serve as a "companion," substituting for meaningful relationships with other people.[11] A physician may feel trapped by this combination of factors when the patient behaves in a subtly complex way and attempts to get his or her feeling of helplessness understood by the physician. As a result, the physician may feel compelled to issue a prescription as the only way to immediately disengage from an uncomfortable encounter. Unfortunately, this same process is likely to recur at the next visit.[12]

This point of view can initially seem to complicate our task: We would aim to treat all patients for pain, even those with histories of addictive behaviors. But this view gives us more tools, too. Helping a patient understand his individual history and what drug use means to him may allow the physician to form a trusting relationship with the patient, thereby helping him find the personal strength to work through vulnerabilities and disorders in a healthy way.[13,14]

Existing studies leave gaps in our ability to predict future addiction potential—data cannot predict which group of patients with no addictive or substance abuse history will become addicted or abuse opioids. Nonetheless, in some instances, addiction by prescription is both clinically foreseeable and preventable. This underscores the need for a thorough therapeutic alliance and a comprehensive assessment of patient competency before opioid prescription.

How to Make the Most of Limited Patient Time

Even with limited time, a physician can make it a priority to take a thorough health and social history of a new patient who seeks or apparently needs a potentially addictive drug. Physicians must also be aware that the reliability of this history may be undermined by the lack of time allowed for the development of trust, as well as by the pain and possible stigma experienced by the patient. Therefore, the physician may need to use a variety of methods to obtain information and build trust, from the use of previsit questionnaires to developing indirect interview methods that support a patient's self-esteem and self-control, even in the presence of painful self-disclosure.[15]

In some cases, a history will not be reliable because a patient is malingering or being deliberately deceptive. In such circumstances, physicians should look for consistencies and inconsistencies in reports and the reporting of symptoms that do not fit into any meaningful diagnostic category; they should also attempt to understand where a patient is getting all of his medical treatment.

Table 1 presents the factors that are associated with an increased risk of addiction. Situations in which complaints of chronic pain are motivated by primary gain (eg, staged automobile accidents) or secondary gain (eg, cases of complex family psychodynamics, where a lack of visible suffering leads to a lack of attention) should raise concerns.[16] Other factors that should signal concern include a current addictive disorder,[17,18] a current anxiety or mood disorder,[19] a family history of addiction,[16] and childhood physical or sexual abuse.[20]

Chronic pain is often a presenting complaint of unremitting depression.[19] The Hamilton Rating Scale for Depression (HAM-D) or Beck Depression Inventory can help uncover mood disorders that may present as somatization, conversion, or part of the patient's baseline personality. These depression-scale instruments need to be used with caution and are not substitutes for a thorough clinical interview. Some of these instruments, especially the HAM-D, contain questions on somatic complaints, so patients with pain and medical illness can receive scores indicating marked depression just by endorsing these items. On the other hand, unrecognized and untreated depression-compounding pain symptoms may drive patients both to overuse prescribed pain medication and to seek unnecessary surgery and grow impatient with conservative measures.

Elements of the best patient care overlap with our recommendations for physician self-protection. There are some patients who present with no risk factors but nevertheless become addicted to appropriately prescribed pain medications. Thus, a comprehensive initial interview, an ongoing therapeutic alliance, and nonjudgmental but careful monitoring of medication

Table 1 Risk Factors for Addiction to Medication

- History of addiction to alcohol or drugs
- Family history of addiction
- Situational stressors and helplessness
- Failure to take personal responsibility
- Childhood physical or sexual abuse
- Current mood or anxiety disorder (presenting as pain)
- Complaints motivated by primary gain (eg, workers' compensation)
- Complaints motivated by secondary gain (eg, suffering leads to gratification of dependency needs)

use are essential. The patient should have the opportunity to make an informed choice of treatment options, and the process leading to this choice should be documented. The potential adverse outcomes stemming from medication abuse should be discussed with the patient.

The physician should note the conversation on the patient's chart and offer the patient a written summary of their joint decision. Pain and its accompanying anxiety can lead to dissociative states, which may prevent the patient from accurately remembering conversations with a provider. Patients may have trouble concentrating because of their pain and anxiety; occasionally, the level of impairment can rise to clinical dissociation and even frank amnesia.

In the course of developing a relationship with a patient, other issues may arise. Some physicians may feel compelled to prescribe benzodiazepines, for instance, without adequate knowledge of the patient, and may even use drugs as substitutes for listening to and talking with the patient. Physicians should do their best to monitor their feelings toward difficult patients[9,21]; they can improve their ability to treat patients by seeking further training in addictive disorders. It may also prove helpful to consult with clinicians who have such specialized training or experience, including addiction or pain specialists, or to refer patients for consultation with such experts.

Physicians can ease the potential misunderstanding that patients may have about referrals by educating patients about the complex nature of the problem and by reassuring them that the treating physician will continue to be involved in their care.[22] However, the physician must also retain the right to refuse indefinite treatment to a patient who will not accept this process as deemed necessary for proper prescribing.[12] An implicit benefit of consultation is that it provides a healthy model for seeking help and shows how a primary treating clinician can seek help without humiliation.

Alternatives to Potentially Addictive Drugs

There are a number of alternatives to benzodiazepines for the treatment of anxiety[23] as well as medications other than opiates for the treatment of chronic pain (Table 2).[24–26] This is not to say that benzodiazepines and opiates are the most effective treatment options; for example, there are many common pain conditions for which nonopioids may be more effective. Moreover, benzodiazepines are generally contraindicated for patients with chronic pain since their extended use can lower pain threshold. But if a physician decides that a potentially addictive drug is the best choice, the physician needs to explore alternatives with the patient and document that other nonaddictive therapies are less likely to be effective or have greater risks than the potentially addictive drug.

Informed consent and assessment of a patient's capacity to engage in an informed-consent process need to be implemented in tandem. This is true regardless of the intervention, whether medication is being prescribed or surgery is being recommended. Pro forma informed consent is no substitute for the informed-consent process.

Table 2 Nonaddictive Treatments for Chronic Pain[23–26]

• NSAIDs	• Family therapy
• Acetaminophen	• Group psychotherapy
• Physical therapy/exercise	• Hot yoga
• Antidepressants	• Hypnosis
• Low-dose tricyclics	• Massage
• Anticonvulsants	• Meditation
• Topical aromatics	• Chiropractic
• Nerve block	• Naltrexone
• Transdermal electrical nerve stimulation	• Inpatient or outpatient detoxification
• Psychotherapy	

Table 3 Summary Points: Physician Protection

- Screen for history of addiction; if present, share anticipation of risk with patient
- Screen for depression and anxiety disorders[19]
- Include nonaddictive alternatives in the discussion[23–29]
- Monitor your mood (eg, anger, anxiety)[12]
- If in doubt, consult with a specialist, even before any potentially addictive medications are prescribed[6,7]
- Document the informed-consent process in the patient record[6,7]

In addition, physicians need to be careful that they do not withhold conservative yet comprehensive pain management from patients; and physicians should not make patients vulnerable to the promises of the quick fixes of surgical solutions before conservative alternatives have been implemented (see Table 2).[27–29]

Concluding Thoughts

Those of us willing to treat patients who have pain need to find the time to explore the patient's history and provide options, to listen carefully to patients, and to help patients individualize their treatment plans (Table 3). By attending to the therapeutic alliance with the patient, clinicians will not fall into the trap of automatic prescription or automatic medication avoidance and patients will not be subjected to needless suffering, heightened risk of addiction, or the complications of unnecessary surgery.[30]

Evidence-based Medicine

- Leo RJ. *Pain Management for Psychiatrists.* Washington, DC: American Psychiatric Publishing; 2003.
- Mantyselka P, Kumpusalo E, Ahonen R, et al. Pain as a reason to visit the doctor: a study in Finnish primary health care. Pain. 2001;89:175–180.

Therapeutic Agents Mentioned in This Article

Hydrocodone (Vicodin, others)
Naltrexone (Depade)
Oxycodone (OxyContin, others)

Brand names are listed in parentheses only if a drug is not available generically and is marketed as no more than two trademarked or registered products. More familiar alternative generic designations may also be included parenthetically.

References

1. Bursztajn HJ, Feinbloom RI, Hamm RM, Brodsky A. *Medical Choices, Medical Chances: How Patients, Families, and Physicians Can Cope With Uncertainty.* New York: Routledge; 1990.
2. Mantyselka P, Kumpusalo E, Ahonen R, et al. Pain as a reason to visit the doctor: a study in Finnish primary health care. *Pain.* 2001;89:175–180.
3. Merrill JO, Rhodes LA, Deyo RA, et al. Mutual mistrust in the medical care of drug users: the key to the "narc" cabinet. *J Gen Intern Med.* 2002;17:327–333.
4. Dunbar SA, Katz NP. Chronic opioid therapy for nonmalignant pain in patients with a history of substance abuse: report of 20 cases. *J Pain Symptom Manage.* 1996;11:163–171.
5. New CASA report: controlled prescription drug abuse at epidemic level. New York: Columbia University Center for Addiction and Substance Abuse; July 7, 2005. Press release.
6. Gutheil TG, Bursztajn HJ, Brodsky A. Malpractice prevention through the sharing of uncertainty: informed consent and the therapeutic alliance. *N Engl J Med.* 1984; 311:49–51.
7. Lange MP, Dahn MS, Jacobs LA. Patient-controlled analgesia versus intermittent analgesic dosing. *Heart Lung.* 1988; 17:495–498.
8. Colwell CW Jr, Morris BA. Patient-controlled analgesia compared with intramuscular injection of analgesics for the management of pain after an orthopaedic procedure. *J Bone Joint Surg.* 1995;77:726–733.
9. Bursztajn HJ, Brodsky A. Managed health care complications, liability risks, and clinical remedies. *Prim Psychiatry.* 2002;4:37–41.
10. Breiter HC, Gollub RL, Weisskoff RM, et al. Acute effects of cocaine on human brain activity and emotion. *Neuron.* 1997;19:591–611.
11. Johnson B. Three perspectives on addiction. *J Am Psychoanal Assoc.* 1999;47:791–815.
12. Johnson B. The mechanism of codependence in the prescription of benzodiazepines to patients with addiction. *Psychiatr Ann.* 1998;28:166–171.
13. Rollnick S, Mason P, Butler C. *Health Behavior Change: A Guide for Practitioners.* Edinburgh: Churchill Livingstone; 2000.
14. Berk WA, Bernstein E, Bernstein J, et al. Substance and alcohol abuse. In: Tintinalli JE, ed. *Emergency Medicine: A Comprehensive Study Guide.* 6th ed. New York: McGraw Hill; 2004.
15. Bursztajn HJ. Physicians indicated the need to frame questions and develop indirect approaches that foster patient trust in evaluating victims of domestic violence. *Evid Based Ment Health.* 2002;3:63.
16. Compton P, Darakjian J, Miotto K. Screening for addiction in patients with chronic pain and "problematic" substance use: evaluation of a pilot assessment tool. *J Pain Symptom Manage.* 1998;16:355–363.
17. Miller NS, Greenfield A. Patient characteristics and risk factors for development of dependence on hydrocodone and oxycodone. *Am J Ther.* 2004;11:26–32.
18. Sproule BA, Busto UE, Somer G, et al. Characteristics of dependent and nondependent regular users of codeine. *J Clin Psychopharmacol.* 1999;19:367–372.
19. Fava M. Depression with physical symptoms: treating to remission. *J Clin Psychiatry.* 2003;7:24–28.
20. Goldberg RT, Pachas WN, Keith D. Relationship between traumatic events in childhood and chronic pain. *Disabil Rehabil.* 1999;21:23–30.
21. Johnson B, Longo LP. Considerations in the physician's decision to prescribe benzodiazepines to patients with addiction. *Psychiatr Ann.* 1998;28:160–165.
22. Bursztajn HJ, Barsky AJ. Facilitating patient acceptance of a psychiatric referral. *Arch Intern Med.* 1985; 145: 73–75.
23. Longo LP. Non-benzodiazepine pharmacotherapy of anxiety and panic in substance abusing patients. *Psychiatr Ann.* 1998;28:142–153.
24. Streltzer J. Pain management in the opioid-dependent patient. *Curr Psychiatry Rep.* 2001;3:489–496.
25. Marcus DA. Treatment of nonmalignant chronic pain. *Am Fam Physician.* 2000;61:1331–1338, 1345–1346.
26. Maizels M, McCarberg B. Antidepressants and antiepileptic drugs for chronic non-cancer pain. *Am Fam Physician.* 2005;71:483–490.
27. Groopman J. A knife in the back. *The New Yorker.* April 8, 2002.
28. Carragee EJ. Persistent low back pain. *N Engl J Med.* 2005;352:1891–1898.
29. Leo RJ. *Pain Management for Psychiatrists.* Washington, DC: American Psychiatric Publishing; 2003.
30. King SA. Treatment of low back pain. *Psychiatr Times.* 2007;24:53.

Predicting Addiction

Behavioral genetics uses twins and time to decipher the origins of addiction and learn who is most vulnerable.

LISA N. LEGRAND, WILLIAM G. IACONO AND MATT McGUE

In 1994, the 45-year-old daughter of Senator and former presidential nominee George McGovern froze to death outside a bar in Madison, Wisconsin. Terry McGovern's death followed a night of heavy drinking and a lifetime of battling alcohol addiction. The Senator's middle child had been talented and charismatic, but also rebellious. She started drinking at 13, became pregnant at 15 and experimented with marijuana and LSD in high school. She was sober during much of her 30s but eventually relapsed. By the time she died, Terry had been through many treatment programs and more than 60 detoxifications.

Her story is not unique. Even with strong family support, failure to overcome an addiction is common. Success rates vary by treatment type, severity of the condition and the criteria for success. But typically, fewer than a third of alcoholics are recovered a year or two after treatment. Thus, addiction may be thought of as a chronic, relapsing illness. Like other serious psychiatric conditions, it can cause a lifetime of recurrent episodes and treatments.

Given these somber prospects, the best strategy for fighting addiction may be to prevent it in the first place. But warning young people about the dangers of addiction carries little force when many adults drink openly without apparent consequences. Would specific warnings for individuals with a strong genetic vulnerability to alcoholism be more effective? Senator McGovern became convinced that his daughter possessed such a vulnerability, as other family members also struggled with dependency. Perhaps Terry would have taken a different approach to alcohol, or avoided it altogether, if she had known that something about her biology made drinking particularly dangerous for her.

How can we identify people—at a young enough age to intervene—who have a high, inherent risk of becoming addicted? Does unusual susceptibility arise from differences at the biochemical level? And what social or environmental factors might tip the scales for kids at greatest risk? That is, what kind of parenting, or peer group, or neighborhood conditions might encourage—or inhibit—the expression of "addiction" genes? These questions are the focus of our research.

Minnesota Twins

We have been able to answer some of these questions by examining the life histories of almost 1,400 pairs of twins. Our study of addictive behavior is part of a larger project, the Minnesota Center for Twin Family Research (MCTFR), which has studied the health and development of twins from their pre-teen years through adolescence and into adulthood. Beginning at age 11 (or 17 for a second group), the participants and their parents cooperated with a barrage of questionnaires, interviews, brainwave analyses and blood tests every three years. The twin cohorts are now 23 and 29, respectively, so we have been able to observe them as children before exposure to addictive substances, as teenagers who were often experimenting and as young adults who had passed through the stage of greatest risk for addiction.

Studies of twins are particularly useful for analyzing the origins of a behavior like addiction. Our twin pairs have grown up in the same family environment but have different degrees of genetic similarity. Monozygotic or identical twins have identical genes, but dizygotic or fraternal twins share on average only half of their segregating genes. If the two types of twins are equally similar for a trait, we know that genes are unimportant for that trait. But when monozygotic twins are more similar than dizygotic twins, we conclude that genes have an effect.

This article reviews some of what we know about the development of addiction, including some recent findings from the MCTFR about early substance abuse. Several established markers can predict later addiction and, together with recent research, suggest a provocative conclusion: that addiction may be only one of many related behaviors that stem from the same genetic root. In other words, much of the heritable risk may be nonspecific. Instead, what is passed from parent to child is a tendency toward a group of behaviors, of which addiction is only one of several possible outcomes.

Markers of Risk

Personality. Psychologists can distinguish at-risk youth by their personality, family history, brainwave patterns and behavior. For example, certain personality traits do not distribute equally among addicts and nonaddicts: The addiction vulnerable tend to be more impulsive, unruly and easily bored. They're generally outgoing, sociable, expressive and rebellious, and they enjoy taking risks. They are more likely to question authority and challenge tradition.

Some addicts defy these categories, and having a certain personality type doesn't doom one to addiction. But such traits do place individuals at elevated risk. For reasons not completely understood, they accompany addiction much more frequently than the traits of being shy, cautious and conventional.

Although these characteristics do not directly cause addiction, neither are they simply the consequences of addiction. In fact, teachers' impressions of their 11-year-old students predicted alcohol problems 16 years later, according to a Swedish study led by C. Robert Cloninger (now at Washington University in St. Louis). Boys low in "harm avoidance" (ones who lacked fear and inhibition) and high in "novelty seeking" (in other words, impulsive, disorderly, easily bored and distracted) were almost 20 times more likely to have future alcohol problems than boys without these traits. Other studies of children in separate countries at different ages confirm that personality is predictive.

Family Background. Having a parent with a substance-abuse disorder is another established predictor of a child's future addiction. One recent and intriguing discovery from the MCTFR is that assessing this risk can be surprisingly straightforward, particularly for alcoholism. The father's answer to "What is the largest amount of alcohol you ever consumed in a 24-hour period?" is highly informative: The greater the amount, the greater his children's risk. More than 24 drinks in 24 hours places his children in an especially risky category.

How can one simple question be so predictive? Its answer is laden with information, including tolerance—the ability, typically developed over many drinking episodes, to consume larger quantities of alcohol before becoming intoxicated—and the loss of control that mark problematic drinking. It is also possible that a father who equivocates on other questions that can formally diagnose alcoholism—such as whether he has been unsuccessful at cutting down on his drinking or whether his drinking has affected family and work—may give a frank answer to this question. In our society, episodes of binge drinking, of being able to "hold your liquor," are sometimes a source of male pride.

Brainwaves. A third predictor comes directly from the brain itself. By using scalp electrodes to detect the electrical signals of groups of neurons, we can record characteristic patterns of brain activity generated by specific visual stimuli. In the complex squiggle of evoked brainwaves, the relative size of one peak, called P300, indicates addiction risk. Having a smaller P300 at age 17 predicts the development of an alcohol or drug problem by age 20. Prior differences in consumption don't explain this observation, as the reduced-amplitude P300 (P3-AR) is not a consequence of alcohol or drug ingestion. Rather, genes strongly influence this trait: P3-AR is often detectable in the children of fathers with substance-use disorders even before these problems emerge in the offspring. The physiological nature of P300 makes it an especially interesting marker, as

it may originate from "addiction" genes more directly than any behavior.

Precocious Experimentation. Lastly, at-risk youth are distinguished by the young age at which they first try alcohol without parental permission. Although the vast majority of people try alcohol at some point during their life, it's relatively unusual to try alcohol *before* the age of 15. In the MCTFR sample of over 2,600 parents who had tried alcohol, only 12 percent of the mothers and 22 percent of the fathers did so before the age of 15. In this subset, 52 percent of the men and 25 percent of the women were alcoholics. For parents who first tried alcohol after age 19, the comparable rates were 13 percent and 2 percent, respectively. So, what distinguishes alcoholism risk is not *whether* a person tries alcohol during their teen years, but *when* they try it.

In light of these data, we cannot regard very early experimentation with alcohol as simply a normal rite of passage. Moreover, drinking at a young age often co-occurs with sex, the use of tobacco and illicit drugs, and rulebreaking behaviors. This precocious experimentation could indicate that the individual has inherited the type of freewheeling, impulsive personality that elevates the risk of addiction. But early experimentation may be a problem all by itself. It, and the behaviors that tend to co-occur with it, decrease the likelihood of sobriety-encouraging experiences and increase the chances of mixing with troubled peers and clashing with authority figures.

A General, Inherited Risk

Some of these hallmarks of risk are unsurprising. Most people know that addiction runs in families, and they may intuit that certain brain functions could differ in addiction-prone individuals. But how can people's gregariousness or their loathing of dull tasks or the age at which they first had sex show a vulnerability to addiction? The answer seems to be that although addiction risk is strongly heritable, the inheritance is fairly nonspecific. The inherited risk corresponds to a certain temperament or disposition that goes along with so-called *externalizing* tendencies. Addiction is only one of several ways this disposition may be expressed.

Externalizing behaviors include substance abuse, but also "acting out" and other indicators of behavioral under control or disinhibition. In childhood, externalizing traits include hyperactivity, "oppositionality" (negative and defiant behavior) and antisocial behavior, which breaks institutional and social rules. An antisocial child may lie, get in fights, steal, vandalize or skip school. In adulthood, externalizing tendencies may lead to a personality marked by low constraint, drug or alcohol abuse, and antisocial behaviors, including irresponsibility, dishonesty, impulsivity, lawlessness and aggression. Antisociality, like most traits, falls on a continuum. A moderately antisocial person may never intentionally hurt someone, but he might make impulsive decisions, take physical and financial risks or shirk responsibility.

It's worth reiterating that an externalizing disposition simply increases the risk of demonstrating problematic behavior. An individual with such tendencies could express them in ways that are not harmful to themselves and actually help society: Fire fighters, rescue workers, test pilots, surgeons and entrepreneurs are often gregarious, relatively uninhibited sensation-seekers—that is, moderate externalizers.

So a genetic inclination for externalizing can lead to addiction, hyperactivity, acting-out behavior, criminality, a sensation-seeking personality or *all* of these things. Although the contents of this list may seem haphazard, psychologists combine them into a single group because they all stem from the same *latent factor*. Latent factors are hypothesized constructs that help explain the observed correlations between various traits or behaviors.

For example, grades in school generally correlate with one another. People who do well in English tend to get good marks in art history, algebra and geology. Why? Because academic ability affects grades, regardless of the subject matter. In statistical lingo, academic ability is the "general, latent factor" and the course grades are the "observed indicators" of that factor. Academic ability is latent because it is not directly measured; rather, the statistician concludes that it exists and causes the grades to vary systematically between people.

Statistical analyses consistently show that externalizing is a general, latent factor—a common denominator—for a suite of behaviors that includes addiction. Furthermore, the various markers of risk support this conclusion: Childhood characteristics that indicate later problems with alcohol also point to the full spectrum of externalizing behaviors and traits. Thus, drinking alcohol before 15 doesn't just predict future alcohol and drug problems, but also future antisocial behavior. A parent with a history of excessive binge drinking is apt to have children not only with substance-use problems, but with behavioral problems as well. And a reduced-amplitude P300 not only appears in children with a familial risk for alcoholism, but in kids with a familial risk for hyperactivity, antisocial behavior or illicit drug disorders.

The associations between externalizing behaviors aren't surprising to clinicians. Comorbidity—the increased chance of having other disorders if you have one of them—is the norm, not the exception, for individuals and families. A father with a cocaine habit is more likely to find that his daughter is getting into trouble for stealing or breaking school rules. At first glance, the child's behavioral problems look like products of the stress, conflict and dysfunction that go with having an addict in the family. These are certainly aggravating factors. However, the familial and genetically informative MCTFR data have allowed us to piece together a more precise explanation.

Environment has a strong influence on a child's behavior—living with an addict is rife with challenges—but genes also play a substantial role. Estimates of the genetic effect on externalizing behaviors vary by indicator and age, but among older adolescents and adults, well over half of the differences between people's externalizing tendencies result from inheriting different genes.

Our analysis of the MCTFR data indicates that children inherit the general, latent factor of externalizing rather than specific behavioral factors. Thus, an antisocial mother does not pass on genes that code simply for antisocial behavior, but they do confer vulnerability to a range of adolescent disorders and behaviors. Instead of encounters with the law, her adolescent son may have problems with alcohol or drugs. The outcomes are different, but the same genes—expressed differently under different environmental conditions—predispose them both.

The Role of the Environment

Even traits with a strong genetic component may be influenced by environmental factors. Monozygotic twins exemplify this principle. Despite their matching DNA, their height, need for glasses, disease susceptibility or personality (just to name a few) may differ.

When one member of a monozygotic pair is alcoholic, the likelihood of alcoholism in the other is only about 50 percent. The high heritability of externalizing behaviors suggests that the second twin, if not alcoholic, may be antisocial or dependent on another substance. But sometimes the second twin is problem free. DNA is never destiny.

Behavioral geneticists have worked to quantify the role of the environment in addiction, but as a group we have done much less to specify it. Although we know that 50 percent of the variance in alcohol dependence comes from the environment, we are still in the early stages of determining what those environmental factors are. This ignorance may seem surprising, as scientists have spent decades identifying the environmental precursors to addiction and antisocial behavior. But only a small percentage of that research incorporated genetic controls.

Instead, many studies simply related environmental variation to children's eventual problems or accomplishments. A classic example of this failure to consider genetic influence is the repeated observation that children who grow up with lots of books in their home tend to do better in school. But concluding that books create an academic child assumes (falsely) that children are born randomly into families—that parent-child resemblance is purely social. Of course, parents actually contribute to their children's environment *and* their genes. Moreover, parents tend to provide environments that complement their children's genotypes: Smart parents often deliver both "smart" genes and an enriched environment. Athletic parents usually provide "athletic" genes and many opportunities to express them. And, unfortunately, parents with addiction problems tend to provide a genetic vulnerability coupled with a home in which alcohol or drugs are available and abusing them is normal.

To understand the true experiential origins of a behavior, one must first disentangle the influence of genes. By using genetically informative samples, we can subtract genetic influences and conclude with greater confidence that a particular environmental factor affects behavior. Using this approach, our data suggest that deviant peers and poor parent-child relationships exert true environmental influences that promote substance use and externalizing behaviors during early adolescence.

When considering the effect of environment on behavior, or any complex trait, it's helpful to imagine a continuum of liability. Inherited vulnerability determines where a person begins on the continuum (high versus low risk). From that point, psychosocial or environmental stressors such as peer pressure or excessive conflict with parents can push an individual along the continuum and over a disease threshold.

However, sometimes the environment actually modifies gene expression. In other words, the relative influence of genes on a behavior can vary by setting. We see this context-dependent gene expression in recent, unpublished work comparing study participants from rural areas (population less than 10,000) with those from more urban settings. Within cities of 10,000 or more, genes substantially influence which adolescents use illicit substances or show other aspects of the externalizing continuum—just as earlier research indicated. But in very rural areas, environmental (rather than genetic) factors overwhelmingly account for differences in externalizing behavior.

One way to interpret this finding is that urban environments, with their wider variety of social niches, allow for a more complete expression of genetically influenced traits. Whether a person's genes nudge her to substance use and rule-breaking, or abstinence and obedience, the city may offer more opportunities to follow those urges. At the same time, finite social prospects in the country may allow more rural parents to monitor and control their adolescents' activities and peer-group selection, thereby minimizing the impact of genes. This rural-urban difference is especially interesting because it represents a gene-by-environment interaction. The genes that are important determinants of behavior in one group of people are just not as important in another.

The Future of Addiction Research

This complex interplay of genes and environments makes progress slow. But investigators have the data and statistical tools to answer many important addiction-related questions. Moreover, the tempo of discovery will increase with advances in molecular genetics.

In the last fifteen years, geneticists have identified a handful of specific genes related to alcohol metabolism and synapse function that occur more often in alcoholics. But the task of accumulating the entire list of contributing genes is daunting. Many genes influence behavior, and the relative importance of a single gene may differ across ethnic or racial populations. As a result, alcoholism-associated genes in one population may not exert a measurable influence in a different group, even in well-controlled studies. There are also different pathways to addiction, and some people's alcoholism may be more environmental than genetic in origin. Consequently, not only is any one gene apt to have small effects on behavior, but that gene may be absent in a substantial number of addicts.

Nonetheless, some day scientists should be able to estimate risk by reading the sequence of a person's DNA. Setting aside the possibility of a futuristic dystopia, this advance will usher in a new type of psychology. Investigators will be able to observe those individuals with especially high (or low) genetic risks for externalizing as they respond, over a lifetime, to different types of environmental stressors.

This type of research is already beginning. Avshalom Caspi, now at the University of Wisconsin, and his colleagues divided a large group of males from New Zealand based on the expression level of a gene that encodes a neurotransmitter-metabolizing enzyme, monoamine oxidase A or MAOA. In combination with the life histories of these men, the investigators demonstrated that the consequences of an abusive home varied by genotype. The gene associated with high levels of MAOA was protective—those men were less likely to show antisocial behaviors after childhood maltreatment than the low-MAOA group.

Further advances in molecular genetics will bring opportunities for more studies of this type. When investigators can accurately rank experimental participants by their genetic liability to externalizing, they will gain insight into the complexities of gene-environment interplay and answer several intriguing questions: What type of family environments are most at-risk children born into? When children with different genetic risks grow up in the same family, do they create unique environments by seeking distinct friends and experiences? Do they elicit different parenting styles from the same parents? Could a low-risk sibling keep a high-risk child from trouble if they share a close friendship? Is one type of psychosocial stressor more apt to lead to substance use while another leads to antisocial behavior?

Molecular genetics will eventually deepen our understanding of the biochemistry and biosocial genesis of addiction. In the interim, quantitative geneticists such as ourselves continue to characterize the development of behavior in ways that will assist molecular geneticists in their work. For example, if there is genetic overlap between alcoholism, drug dependence and antisocial behavior—as the MCTFR data suggest—then it may help to examine extreme externalizers, rather than simply alcoholics, when searching for the genes that produce alcoholism vulnerability.

Much Left to Learn

Although the MCTFR data have resolved some addiction-related questions, many others remain, and our team has just begun to scratch the surface of possible research. Our work with teenagers indicates that externalizing is a key factor in early-onset substance-use problems, but the path to later-life addiction may be distinct. Some evidence suggests that genes play a lesser role in later-onset addiction. Moreover, the markers of risk may vary. Being prone to worry, becoming upset easily and tending toward negative moods may, with age, become more important indicators. We don't yet know. However, the MCTFR continues to gather information about its participants as they approach their 30s, and we hope to keep following this group into their 40s and beyond.

Meanwhile, the evidence suggests that for early-onset addiction, most relevant genes are not specific to alcoholism or drug dependence. Instead, the same genes predispose an overlapping set of disorders within the externalizing spectrum. This conclusion has significant implications for prevention: Some impulsive risk-takers, frequent rule-breakers and oppositional children may be just as much at risk as early users.

At the same time, many kids with a genetic risk for externalizing don't seem to require any sort of special intervention; as it is, they turn out just fine. DNA may nudge someone in a certain direction, but it doesn't force them to go there.

Bibliography

Burt, S. A., M. McGue, R. F. Krueger and W. G. Iacono. 2005. How are parent-child conflict and childhood externalizing symptoms related over time? Results from a genetically informative cross-tagged study. *Development and Psychopathology* 17:1–21.

Caspi, A., J. McClay, T. E. Moffitt, J. Mill, J. Martin, I. W. Craig, A. Taylor and R. Poulton. 2002. Role of genotype in the cycle of violence in maltreated children. *Science* 297:851–854.

Cloninger, C. R., S. Sigvardsson and M. Bohman. 1988. Childhood personality predicts alcohol abuse in young adults. *Alcoholism: Clinical and Experimental Research* 12:494–505.

Hicks, B. M., R. F. Krueger, W. G. Iacono, M. McGue and C. J. Patrick. 2004. Family transmission and heritability of externalizing disorders: A twin-family study. *Archives of General Psychiatry* 61:922–928.

Iacono, W. G., S. M. Malone and M. McGue. 2003. Substance use disorders, externalizing psychopathology, and P300 event-related potential amplitude. *International Journal of Psychophysiology* 48:147–178.

Krueger, R. F., B. M. Hicks, C. J. Patrick, S. R. Carlson, W. G. Iacono and M. McGue. 2002. Etiologic connections among substance dependence, antisocial behavior, and personality: Modeling the externalizing spectrum. *Journal of Abnormal Psychology* 111:411–424.

Malone, S. M., W. G. Iacono and M. McGue. 2002. Drinks of the father: Father's maximum number of drinks consumed predicts externalizing disorders, substance use, and substance use disorders in preadolescent and adolescent offspring. *Alcoholism: Clinical and Experimental Research* 26:1823–1832.

McGovern, G. 1996. *Terry: My Daughter's Life-and-Death Struggle With Alcoholism.* New York: Random House.

McGue, M., W. G. Iacono, L. N. Legrand, S. Malone and I. Elkins. 2001. The origins and consequences of age at first drink. I. Associations with substance-abuse disorders, disinhibitory behavior and psychopathology, and P3 amplitude. *Alcoholism: Clinical and Experimental Research* 25:1156–1165.

Porjesz, B., and H. Begleiter. 2003. Alcoholism and human electrophysiology. *Alcohol Research & Health* 27:153–160.

Turkheimer, E., H. H. Goldsmith and I. I. Gottesman. 1995. Some conceptual deficiencies in "developmental" behavioral genetics: Comment. *Human Development* 38:142–153.

Walden, B., M. McGue, W. G. Iacono, S. A. Burt and I. Elkins. 2004. Identifying shared environmental contributions to early substance use: The respective roles of peers and parents. *Journal of Abnormal Psychology* 113:440–450.

Lisa N. Legrand received her PhD in behavioral genetics and clinical psychology from the University of Minnesota in 2003 and is currently a research associate at the Minnesota Center for Twin and Family Research (MCTFR). **William G. Iacono** is a Distinguished McKnight University Professor at the University of Minnesota and a past president of the Society for Psychophysiological Research. **Matt McGue** is a professor of psychology at the University of Minnesota and a past president of the Behavior Genetics Association. He and William Iacono have co-directed the MCTFR for the last dozen years. Address for Legrand: MCTFR, 75 East River Road, Minneapolis, MN 55455-0344. Internet: legra002@umn.edu

Better Ways to Target Pain

Improved understanding of the chemical pathway on which aspirin and Vioxx act may lead to analgesics with fewer side effects

GARY STIX

Bengt Samuelsson won the Nobel Prize in Physiology or Medicine in 1982 for his work on providing an exacting picture of how the body generates prostaglandins. These hormonelike substances play a role in regulating various biological processes, including the pain induction, fever and inflammation that are blocked by aspirin, ibuprofen and related drugs. Samuelsson did his research, along with Sune Bergström, another of that year's co-winners, on the red-brick campus of Sweden's Karolinska Institute, which also selects the annual Nobel medicine prize.

Karolinska has a long history with prostaglandins, one that dates back to the discovery of these fatty acid derivatives in 1935 and extends up to the present day. In recent years Samuelsson and his collaborators have further elucidated prostaglandin biochemistry—research that is now being exploited in an attempt to develop painkillers and anti-inflammatory drugs that are safer than existing agents, including the now tarnished group known as COX-2 inhibitors. "There's an enormous demand for anti-inflammatory drugs," Samuelsson notes. "And if we can develop a drug that's as effective as previous drugs with fewer side effects, that's very important."

The Tree and Its Branches

The karolinska's 1982 press release applauding Samuelsson's Nobel credits the scientist for "our present knowledge of the prostaglandin tree with all its branches." Samuelsson had shown that prostaglandins are manufactured when arachidonic acid in the cell membrane is processed by enzymes through a series of steps. These steps eventually result in compounds that supply a variety of regulatory functions within the body—ensuring, for instance, that the kidneys receive sufficient blood flow, controlling the contraction of the uterus during birth and menstruation, or invoking inflammation (marked by redness and swelling) as a protective response to infection and injury.

Aspirin and other nonsteroidal anti-inflammatory drugs, such as ibuprofen, function by blocking the action of two enzymes that act early in the prostaglandin-making pathway: cyclooxygenase 1 and 2 (COX-1 and COX-2). By inhibiting the COX enzymes, the medicines shut down production of the full suite of prostaglandins.

By hitting the off switch so hard, however, aspirin and its relatives sometimes cause problems of their own. When aspirin damps production of prostaglandins responsible for inflammation, it also does the same for one or more of the arachidonic acid derivatives that protect the stomach lining from the hydrochloric acid in digestive juices. Drug companies came up with a fix in the 1990s when they developed Vioxx, Celebrex and other drugs that specifically block COX-2, a move that leaves intact some of the stomach-protective prostaglandins produced in response to COX-1 activity.

Interrupting COX-2, however, soon turned out to have its own drawbacks. The disruption apparently upsets a series of complex interactions among prostaglandins. Although blocking the enzyme decreases manufacture of prostaglandin E_2 (PGE_2), thought to play a major role in inducing pain and inflammation, it also reduces synthesis of prostacyclin (PGI_2), a heart-protective prostaglandin that dilates blood vessels and prevents blood platelets from aggregating. And that diminution has potentially dangerous consequences.

In 1999 Garrett A. FitzGerald of the University of Pennsylvania Medical Center reported in the *Proceedings of the National Academy of Sciences USA* on a small clinical trial that demonstrated the PGI_2 inhibition. FitzGerald also showed that when PGI_2 diminishes after ingestion of a COX-2 inhibitor, thromboxane, another prostaglandin produced in the arachidonic acid pathway still functions, exerting vessel-constricting and platelet-clumping properties normally opposed by PGI_2. The imbalance, the report observed, could encourage formation of clotting (thrombosis) that could provoke heart attacks and strokes, a conclusion lawyers for plaintiffs in much publicized suits against makers of COX-2 inhibitors have duly noted in recent years. FitzGerald had begun reporting his findings at conferences in 1997, a year before approval of the first COX-2 inhibitor, Celebrex.

When FitzGerald's group was uncovering the early-warning sign of dangers to come, Samuelsson's research group was laboring away on putting a new leaf on one of the branches of the prostaglandin tree. A postdoctoral fellow in the lab, Per-Johan Jakobsson, led a project that discovered the human version of an enzyme that produces PGE_2. The abstract of a 1999 paper co-authored by Jakobsson, Samuelsson and two collaborators ends on an upbeat note, saying that the enzyme "is a potential novel target for drug development."

A small company started by two Karolinska scientists took notice of both publications. Biolipox opened its doors in 2000 to develop anti-inflammatory drugs for respiratory diseases by tweaking a newly discovered class of biochemicals, called eoxins, that are also generated from arachidonic acid. A year later the company decided to diversify. It licensed from Karolinska the intellectual property for the enzyme, called microsomal prostaglandin E synthase (mPGES-1). A drug that could selectively block the enzyme's making of PGE_2 might quell pain and inflammation without gastrointestinal or cardiovascular side effects because it would not diminish PGI_2 levels. "We realized that this might be interesting as a third-generation nonsteroidal anti-inflammatory," says Charlotte Edenius, Biolipox's chief scientific officer.

Unleashing Inhibitors

Biolipox is now installed in a nondescript building that also houses the scientific library and the bioinformatics and teaching departments on the Karolinska campus. Samuelsson has signed on as a scientific adviser and member of the board of directors. And Boehringer Ingelheim, the manufacturer of the COX-2 inhibitor Mobic, inked an agreement with Biolipox in 2005 to fund research on mPGES-1 and then license inhibitors for final development and marketing.

The more than \$10-billion annual U.S. market for nonnarcotic painkillers—combined with the COX-2 debacle—has meant that other companies have also devoted keen attention to the enzyme. Merck has published a study on inhibitors of mPGES-1. Pfizer has filed for a patent for a mouse with the gene for mPGES-1 eliminated so that the effects of blocking the enzyme can be examined. Other major drug firms have also filed for mPGES-1-related patents. "Tectonic plates are shifting," FitzGerald remarks. "It's currently a huge market with a lot of insecurity around the current repertoire of drugs." He adds that one company, whose name he is unable to disclose, plans to enter clinical trials with an mPGES-1 inhibitor in 2007. (Separately, other makers are trying to develop drugs that would bind to PGE_2 receptors and directly block them from functioning.)

More to Explore

Identification of Human Prostaglandin E Synthase: A Microsomal, Glutathione-Dependent, Inducible Enzyme, Constituting a Potential Novel Drug Target. Per-Johan Jakobsson, Staffan Thorén, Ralf Morgenstern and Bengt Samuelsson in *Proceedings of the National Academy of Sciences USA*, Vol. 96, No. 13, pages 7220–7225; June 22, 1999.
Is mPGES-1 a Promising Target for Pain Therapy? Klaus Scholich and Gerd Geisslinger in *Trends in Pharmacologicol Sciences*, Vol. 27, No. 8, pages 399–401; August 2006.
Deletion of Microsomal Prostaglandin E Synthase-1 Augments Prostacyclin and Retards Atherogenesis. Miao Wang, Alicia M. Zukas, Yiqun Hui, Emanuela Ricciotti, Ellen Puré and Garret A. FitzGerald in *Proceedings of the National Academy of Sciences USA*, Vol. 103, No. 39, pages 14507–14512; September 26, 2006.

The Vioxx trials may deter any new anti-inflammatory drug from being rushed to market. The doubters, in fact, have already come forward. An article published in 2006 in *Trends in Pharmacological Sciences* entitled "Is mPGES-1 a Promising Target for Pain Therapy?" raises the issue of whether the complexity of prostaglandin metabolism will foil prospects for a new drug. Turning off mPGES-1 may result in less production of PGE_2 but more of another prostaglandin, with unknown physiological consequences, the article observes. Moreover, most other prostaglandins, not just PGE_2, play some role in triggering pain.

Only clinical trials for safety and effectiveness in humans will resolve any disputes. But early studies in knockout mice with mPGES-1 removed lend some hope. In one report from FitzGerald's group in 2006, mPGES-1 knockouts had increased levels of the heart-sparing PGI_2, while the detrimental thromboxane remained stable. At the same time, both clotting and blood pressure remained normal. A subsequent study by FitzGerald's team demonstrated that an mPGES-1 knockout experienced certain cardiovascular benefits, perhaps from elevated PGI_2.

The search continues for compounds that can replicate the effects of silencing mPGES-1. And preparations have begun to take the delicate next step of moving from mouse to human.

The Effects of Alcohol on Physiological Processes and Biological Development

Adolescence is a period of rapid growth and physical change; a central question is whether consuming alcohol during this stage can disrupt development in ways that have long-term consequences. In general, the existing evidence suggests that adolescents rarely exhibit the more severe chronic disorders associated with alcohol dependence such as liver cirrhosis, hepatitis, gastritis, and pancreatitis. Adolescents who drink heavily, however, may experience some adverse effects on the liver, bone, growth, and endocrine development. Evidence also is mounting, at least in animal models, that early alcohol use may have detrimental effects on the developing brain, perhaps leading to problems with cognition later in life. This article summarizes the physiological effects of alcohol on adolescents, including a look at the long-term behavioral and physiological consequences of early drinking.

Overview

The damage that long-term heavy alcohol consumption can do to the health of adults is well documented. Some research suggests that, even over the shorter time frame of adolescence, drinking alcohol can harm the liver, bones, endocrine system, and brain, and interfere with growth. Adolescence is a period of rapid growth and physical change; a central question is whether consuming alcohol during this stage can disrupt development in ways that have long-term consequences.

Liver disease is a common consequence of heavy drinking. More severe alcohol-related liver disease typically reflects years of heavy alcohol use. However, elevated liver enzymes that are markers of harm have been found in adolescents with alcohol use disorders and in overweight adolescents who consume more modest amounts of alcohol.

During puberty, accelerating cascades of growth factors and sex hormones set off sexual maturation, growth in stature and muscle mass, and bone development. Studies in humans have found that alcohol can lower the levels of growth and sex hormones in both adolescent boys and girls. In animals, alcohol has been found to disrupt the interaction between the brain, the pituitary gland (which regulates secretion of sex hormones), and the ovaries, as well as systems within the ovaries that are involved in regulating sex hormones. In adolescent male animals, both short- and long-term alcohol administration suppresses testosterone; alcohol use also alters growth hormone levels, the effects of which differ with age.

Studies on alcohol and adolescent bone development are limited. In studies of male and female rats, chronic alcohol consumption (an alcohol diet) for the length of adolescence was to stunt limb growth. One study found that feeding female rats alcohol in a way that mimics binge drinking resulted in either increases in bone length and density or in no change with more frequent bingeing. In human adolescent males but not females, studies have found that alcohol consumption decreases bone density.

The brain also is changing during adolescence. Adolescents tend to drink larger quantities on each drinking occasion than adults; this may in part be because adolescents are less sensitive to some of the unpleasant effects of intoxication. However, research suggests that adolescents may be more sensitive to some of alcohol's harmful effects on brain function. Studies in rats found that alcohol impairs the ability of adolescent animals more than adult animals to learn a task that requires spatial memory. Research also suggests a mechanism for this effect; in adolescents more than adults, alcohol inhibits the process in which, with repeated experience, nerve impulses travel more easily across the gap between nerve cells (i.e., neurons) involved in the task being learned. The reasons for these differences in sensitivity to alcohol remain unclear.

Research also has found differences in the effects of binge-like drinking in adolescents compared with adults. Normally, as people age from adolescence to adulthood, they become more sensitive to alcohol's effects on motor coordination. In one study, however, adolescent rats exposed to intermittent alcohol never developed this increased sensitivity. Other studies in both human subjects and animals suggest that the adolescent brain may be more vulnerable than the adult brain to chronic alcohol abuse.

Young people who reported beginning to drink at age 14 or younger also were four times more likely to report meeting the criteria for alcohol dependence at some point in their lives than were those who began drinking after age 21. Although it is possible that early alcohol use may be a marker for those who are at risk for alcohol disorders, an important question is whether early alcohol exposure may alter neurodevelopment in a way that increases risk of later abuse. Research in rats has found that prenatal or early postnatal exposure to alcohol results in a greater preference for the odor and consumption of alcohol later in life. Social experiences associated with youthful drinking also may influence drinking later in life. Additional research is needed to resolve the question of whether and how early alcohol exposure might contribute to drinking problems years down the road.

Alcohol's Effects on the Liver, the Neuroendocrine System, and Bone

The medical consequences of chronic alcohol abuse and dependence have been well documented in adults. They include liver disease, lung disease, compromised immune function, endocrine disorders, and brain changes. Investigations of the health problems associated with adolescent alcohol abuse are sparse and rely mainly on self-report (see Clark et al. 2001; Aarons et al. 1999; Brown and Tapert 2004). In general, the existing evidence suggests that adolescents rarely exhibit the more severe chronic disorders associated with alcohol dependence, such as liver cirrhosis, hepatitis, gastritis, and pancreatitis. However, more research is needed to determine whether severe alcohol-induced organ damage is strictly a cumulative process that begins in adolescence and culminates in adulthood as a result of long-term chronic heavy drinking or whether serious alcohol-related health problems can emerge during the teenage years. The few studies available indicate that adolescents who drink heavily experience adverse effects on the liver, bones, growth, and endocrine development, as summarized below. The effects of chronic alcohol consumption on the adolescent brain are discussed in the section "Long-Term Behavioral and Physiological Consequences of Early Drinking."

Liver Effects

Elevated liver enzymes have been found in some adolescents who drink alcohol. Clark and colleagues (2001) found that adolescent alcohol use disorders were associated with higher gamma-glutamyl transpeptidase (GGT) and alanine amino transferase (ALT). Moreover, young drinkers who also are overweight or obese exhibit elevated levels of serum ALT with even modest amounts of alcohol intake (Strauss et al. 2000).

Growth and Endocrine Effects

In general, there has been a gradual decline in the onset of female puberty over the last century, at least when puberty is defined by age at menarche (Tanner 1989). Whether initiation of female puberty is continuing to decline and at what rate are the subjects of some debate (Lee et al. 2001; Herman-Giddens et al. 1997). Much less information exists on pubertal development in males because of the greater difficulty in assessing developmental milestones. However, a recent study comparing data from two national surveys, one conducted between 1988 and 1994 and the other between 1963 and 1970, found that American boys from the later generation had earlier onset of some pubertal stages as measured by standard Tanner staging (Herman-Giddens et al. 2001; Karpati et al. 2002). Perhaps not surprisingly, early puberty—especially among girls—is associated with early use of alcohol, tobacco, and other drugs (Wilson et al. 1994; Dick et al. 2000). In addition, alcohol use in early maturing adolescents has implications for normal growth and neuroendocrine development.

In both males and females, puberty is a period of activation of the hypothalamic-pituitary-gonadal (HPG) axis. Pulsatile secretion of gonadotrophin-releasing hormone (GnRH) from the hypothalamus stimulates pituitary secretion of follicle-stimulating hormone (FSH) and luteinizing hormone (LH) pulses, followed by marked increases in gonadal sex steroid output (estrogen and testosterone), which in turn increases growth hormone (GH) and insulin-like growth factor-1 (IGF-1) production (see Mauras et al. 1996). Data from several studies suggest that both androgens and estrogens stimulate GH production, but that estrogen controls the feedback mechanism of GH production during puberty even in males (Mauras et al. 1996; Dees et al. 2001). The increase in these hormones not only promotes maturation of the gonads but also affects growth, muscle mass, and mineralization of the skeleton. Thus, alcohol consumed during rapid development (i.e., prior to or during puberty) has the potential to disrupt normal growth and endocrine development through its effects on the hypothalamus, the pituitary gland, and the various target organs such as the ovaries and testes.

Most human and animal research on alcohol and endocrine development has been conducted in females, but the limited data on both genders suggest that alcohol can have substantial effects on neuroendocrine function (see Dees et al. 2001; Emanuele et al. 1998; Emanuele et al. 2002a,b). Human studies have found that alcohol ingestion can lower estrogen levels in adolescent girls (Block et al. 1993) and lower both LH and testosterone levels in midpubertal boys (Diamond et al. 1986; Frias et al. 2000a). In both genders, acute alcohol intoxication produces a decrease in GH levels without significant change in either IGF-1 or insulin-like growth factor binding protein-3 (IGFBP3) (Frias et al. 2000*b*).

In female rats, alcohol has been shown to suppress the secretion of specific female reproductive hormones, thereby delaying the onset of puberty (see Dees et al. 2001 and Emanuele et al). Dees and colleagues (2000) found that immature female rhesus macaques exposed daily to alcohol (2 g/kg via nasogastric tube) exhibit lower levels of GH, FSH, LH, estradiol (E_2), and IGF-1 (but not FSH or Leptin) compared with control subjects. Moreover, even though there was no effect on age of menarche in these animals, the interval between subsequent menstruations was lengthened, thereby interfering with the development of regular monthly cycles. Additional studies in rats have found that alcohol interferes with intraovarian systems, including IGF-1 and IGF-1 receptors; the nitric oxide (NO) system (Dees et al. 2001; Srivastava et al. 2001*a*), and the steroidogenic acute regulatory protein (StAR) (Srivastava et al. 2001*b*), all of which combine to decrease estradiol secretion. Thus, alcohol not only disrupts the interaction between the brain, pituitary gland, and ovaries, it also directly impairs the regulatory systems within the ovaries (see Dees et al. 2001 for review).

Alcohol exposure during adolescence actually may alter neurodevelopmental processes in such a way that the likelihood of later abuse is increased.

In male rats, both acute and chronic alcohol exposure during adolescence results in a reversible suppression of serum testosterone (Little et al. 1992; Cicero et al. 1990; Tentler et al. 1997; Emanuele et al. 1998, 1999a,b; Steiner et al. 1997). Evidence exists for involvement at the hypothalamic, pituitary, and gonadal levels, although the testes appear to be the prime target of alcohol's actions (Emanuele et al. 1999a). Furthermore, GH levels are affected by acute and chronic alcohol exposure in male adolescent rats, whereas IGF-1, growth hormone releasing factor (GRF), and GRF mRNA content are variable, depending on the type of administration (Steiner et al. 1997; Tentler et al. 1997).

Thus, the data so far indicate that females who consume alcohol during early adolescence may be at risk for adverse effects on maturation of the reproductive system. Although in males the long-term effects of alcohol on reproductive function are unclear, the fact that GH as well as testosterone and/or estrogen levels are altered by alcohol in both genders may have serious implications for normal development because these hormones play a critical role in organ maturation during this stage of development.

Bone Density and Growth Effects

Only a handful of studies have examined the effects of adolescent drinking on bone development, with the most informative data thus far coming from animal research. Male rats chronically fed an alcohol liquid diet for 60 days encompassing the adolescent period (postnatal days 35 to 90) display limb length reduction and reduced metaphyseal and cortical bone growth in the limbs (Wezeman et al. 1999). These skeletal effects may be mediated through a reduction in osteoblast formation, which is associated with a decline in testosterone but not IGF-1. In addition, with abstinence, normal bone metabolism is not completely restored. Similarly, in female rats, Sampson and colleagues (Sampson et al. 1996; Sampson and Spears 1999) found that chronic alcohol consumption (4 weeks on an ethanol liquid diet) produces decreased limb length and reductions in cortical and cancellous bone, which are not fully reversed following cessation of drinking. Interestingly, female adolescent animals administered a binge model of drinking (i.e., 5 percent alcohol by gavage for either 2 or 5 consecutive days per week) show increased bone length, weight, and density, or no change, respectively (Sampson et al. 1999). Human studies indicate an inverse relationship between alcohol consumption and bone mineral density in adolescent males, but not females (Fehily et al. 1992; Neville et al. 2002; Elgan et al.

2002; Fujita et al. 1999). However, more studies are needed in humans and animals to get a clearer picture of alcohol's effects on bone growth in adolescents, particularly with respect to dose and pattern of consumption.

Long-Term Behavioral and Physiological Consequences of Early Drinking

Although increased tolerance to alcohol's sedative effects may enable greater intake in adolescents, repeated exposure to alcohol may produce increased sensitivity to alcohol's harmful effects. Studies in rats show that ethanol-induced inhibition of synaptic potentials mediated by N-methyl-D-aspartate (NMDA) and long-term potentiation (LTP) is greater in adolescents than in adults (Swartzwelder et al. 1995a,b; see White and Swartzwelder 2005 for review). Initially, the developmental sensitivity of NMDA currents to alcohol was observed in the hippocampus, but more recently this effect was found outside the hippocampus in pyramidal cells in the posterior cingulate cortex (Li et al. 2002). Behaviorally, adolescent rats show greater impairment than adults in acquisition of a spatial memory task after acute ethanol exposure (Markwiese et al. 1998) in support of greater LTP sensitivity to alcohol in adolescents. Behavioral and neurobiological mechanisms for the ontogenetic differences in alcohol tolerance and sensitivity are unclear, as is the relationship between differential sensitivity to ethanol and onset of alcohol abuse and alcoholism.

Binge alcohol exposure (i.e., chronic intermittent exposure to high alcohol doses) in rats during adolescence produces long-lasting changes in memory function (White et al. 2000) and interferes with the normal development of sensitivity to alcohol-induced motor impairments (White et al. 2002). In addition, prolonged alcohol exposure during adolescence, but not adulthood, produces alterations in neurophysiological response to ethanol challenge, tolerance to the sedative effects of ethanol, enhanced expression of withdrawal-related behavior, and long-lasting neurophysiological changes in the cortex and hippocampus in rats (Slawecki et al. 2001; Slawecki 2002; Slawecki and Roth 2004). Furthermore, chronic ethanol treatment in rats may lead to increased NMDA-mediated neurotoxicity, which could be exacerbated by repeated withdrawals (Hunt 1993). Consistent with this hypothesis is the finding that severity of alcohol and drug withdrawal symptoms may be a powerful marker of neuropsychological impairments in detoxified older human adolescents and young adults (Brown et al. 2000; Tapert and Brown 1999; Tapert et al. 2002). Moreover, one recent study found reduced hippocampal volumes in human adolescents with a history of alcohol abuse/dependence disorder (De Bellis et al. 2000), and another preliminary investigation of alcohol-abusing teenagers observed subtle white-matter microstructure abnormalities in the corpus callosum (Tapert et al. 2003), which may be a precursor of more severe damage produced by long-term chronic drinking (Pfefferbaum and Sullivan 2002). Juvenile rats exposed to heavy bingelike episodes of ethanol have

Table 1 A Snapshot of Findings on Alcohol's Physiological Effects in Adolescent Humans and Animals

	Findings	Study
On the Liver		
In humans	Levels of enzymes that indicate liver damage are higher in adolescents with alcohol use disorders	Clark et al. 2001
	And in obese adolescents who drink more moderate amounts.	Strauss et al. 2000
On the Endocrine System		
In humans	Drinking alcohol can lower estrogen levels in adolescent girls.	Block et al. 1993
	Drinking alcohol can lower luteinizing hormone and testosterone levels in adolescent boys.	Diamond et al. 1986; Frias et al. 2000a
	In both sexes, acute intoxication reduces levels of growth hormones.	Frias et al. 2000b
In rats	In female rats, ingesting alcohol during adolescence is associated with adverse effects on maturation of the reproductive system.	Dees et al. 2001
	Alcohol suppresses the secretion of certain female reproductive hormones, delaying the start of puberty.	Emanuelle et al. 2002a,b
	Alcohol not only disrupts the interaction between the brain, pituitary gland, and ovaries, but also impairs regulatory systems within the ovaries.	Dees et al. 2001
	In male rats, alcohol consumption alters growth hormone and testosterone levels, which may have serious consequences for normal development.	Little et al. 1992; Cicero et al. 1990; Tentler et al. 1997; Emanuelle et al. 1998, 1999a, 1999b; Steiner et al. 1997
In rhesus macaques	In immature female monkeys, daily exposure to alcohol lowered levels of female hormones and affected the development of regular monthly cycles.	Dees et al. 2000
On Bone Density		
In humans	Increased alcohol consumption is associated with lowered bone mineral density in adolescent males but not females.	Fehily et al. 1992; Neville et al. 2002; Elgan et al. 2002; Fujita et al. 1999
In rats	In adolescent female rats, chronic alcohol consumption produced shorter limb lengths and reductions in bone growth, neither of which was fully reversed with abstinence.	Sampson et al. 1996; Sampson and Spears 1999
	In adolescent male rats, chronic alcohol ingestion was associated with shorter limb length and reduced bone growth, which are not fully reversed with abstinence.	Wezeman et al. 1999
On the Brain		
In humans	A history of alcohol abuse or dependence in adolescents was associated with reduced hippocampal volumes	De Bellis et al. 2000
	And with subtle white-matter microstructure abnormalities in the corpus callosum.	Tapert et al. 2003
In rats	Chronic intermittent exposure to high alcohol doses (i.e., bingeing) results in long-lasting changes in memory in adolescent rats	White et al. 2000
	And to more damage to the frontal-anterior cortical regions of the brain than are produced in adult rats.	Crews et al. 2000
	Prolonged alcohol exposure during adolescence produces: • Neurophysiological changes in the response to alcohol challenge and in the tolerance to alcohol's sedative effects; • Enhanced expression of withdrawal behaviors; and • Long-lasting neurophysiological effects in the cortex and hippocampus.	Slawecki et al. 2001; Slawecki 2002; Slawecki and Roth 2004

greater damage than adults in frontal-anterior cortical regions, including the olfactory frontal cortex, anterior perirhinal, and piriform cortex (Crews et al. 2000). Thus, the immature brain may be more susceptible to binge ethanol-induced neurotoxicity, although the mechanisms are unknown.

Because teenagers are likely to engage in binge drinking, it is important to study the effects of chronic binge patterns of ethanol exposure on brain structure, neurochemistry, and cognitive functioning. Care must be taken in extrapolating from the described animal studies to the binge-drinking adolescent. Because binge drinking does not usually entail withdrawal, it is important to distinguish between damage caused by the alcohol itself and that caused by repeated withdrawals. In addition, primate models may be a better choice for studying the long-term consequences of alcohol exposure because of primates' prolonged adolescent period, which allows extensive manipulation of different types and lengths of exposure. These models, coupled with new neuroanatomical and neuroimaging techniques, offer a unique opportunity to study the brain changes associated with adolescent drinking and determine whether adolescent brains are able to recover more easily because of greater plasticity.

Early Exposure as a Predictor of Later Alcohol Abuse

Early exposure to alcohol—at or before age 14—is strongly associated with later alcohol abuse and dependence (Grant and Dawson 1998). Two possible explanations for this effect are obvious. First, early alcohol use may simply be a marker for later alcohol abuse rather than a causative factor. A good deal of evidence indicates that at least one behavioral factor, behavioral undercontrol, is measurable very early in life and is a consistently robust predictor of earlier alcohol use as well as of elevated risk for later alcohol use disorder (NIAAA 2000; Zucker and Wong 2005; Caspi et al. 1996).

Second, it is possible that alcohol exposure during adolescence actually may alter neurodevelopmental processes in such a way that the likelihood of later abuse is increased. For example, alcohol use could promote rewiring or alter normal maturation and pruning within the nervous system. Ample evidence exists that exposing rats to low or moderate doses of alcohol during the prenatal or early postnatal period yields a greater preference for ethanol's odor and its consumption later in life (Abate et al. 2000; Honey and Galef 2003; see Molina et al. 1999 and Spear and Molina 2001 for reviews). The young rat's response to alcohol also is mediated by social factors such as maternal interactions and/or nursing from an intoxicated dam (e.g., Hunt et al. 2001; Pepino et al. 2001, 2002; Spear and Molina 2001). Recent evidence shows that prior nursing experience from an ethanol-intoxicated dam heightens ethanol consumption in infant and adolescent rats (Ponce et al. 2004; Pepino et al. 2004). In contrast, relatively few reports using animal models to study the effects of adolescent alcohol exposure on later alcohol consumption exist, and the results are conflicting (see Spear and Varlinskaya 2005). Yet, as is the case with younger animals, social experiences associated with adolescent drinking may influence future drinking behaviors (Hunt et al. 2001; Varlinskaya and Spear 2002). More studies are needed, however,

to explore whether a causal relationship between early chronic exposure to alcohol and later alcohol problems exists, as well as to discover the underlying mechanisms for this effect. Non-human primates, because of their extended adolescent period, offer a good opportunity to study the effects of early exposure to alcohol.

References

Aarons, G.A.; Brown, S.A.; Coe, M.T.; et al. Adolescent alcohol and drug abuse and health. *Journal of Adolescent Health* 24:412–421, 1999. PMID: 10401969

Abate, P.; Pepino, M.Y.; Dominguez, H.D.; et al. Fetal associative learning mediated through maternal alcohol intoxication. *Alcoholism: Clinical and Experimental Research* 24:39–47, 2000. PMID: 10656191

Block, G.D.; Yamamoto, M.E.; Mallick, E.; and Styche, A. Effects on pubertal hormones by ethanol abuse in adolescents. *Alcoholism: Clinical and Experimental Research* 17:505, 1993.

Brown, S.A., and Tapert, S.F. Health consequences of adolescent alcohol involvement. In: NRC and IOM. Bonnie, R.J., and O'Connell, M.E., eds. *Reducing Underage Drinking: A Collective Responsibility*. Washington, DC: National Academies Press, 2004. pp. 383–401. Available online at: http://www.nap.edu/books/0309089352/html.

Brown, S.A.; Tapert, S.F.; Granholm, E.; and Dellis, D.C. Neurocognitive functioning of adolescents: Effects of protracted alcohol use. *Alcoholism: Clinical and Experimental Research* 24:164–171, 2000. PMID: 10698367

Caspi, A.; Moffitt, T.E.; Newman, D.L.; and Silva, E.P.A. Behavioral observations at age 3 years predict adult psychiatric disorders: Longitudinal evidence from a birth cohort. *Archives of General Psychiatry* 53:1033–1039, 1996. PMID: 8911226

Cicero, T.J.; Adams, M.L.; O'Connor, L.; et al. Influence of chronic alcohol administration on representative indices of puberty and sexual maturation in male rats and the development of their progeny. *Journal of Pharmacology and Experimental Therapeutics* 255:707–715, 1990. PMID: 2243349

Clark, D.B.; Lynch, K.G.; Donovan, J.E.; and Block, G.D. Health problems in adolescents with alcohol use disorders: Self-report, liver injury, and physical examination findings and correlates. *Alcoholism: Clinical and Experimental Research* 25:1350–1359, 2001. PMID: 11584156

Crews, F.T.; Braun, C.J.; Hoplight, B.; et al. Binge ethanol consumption causes differential brain damage in young adolescent rats compared with adult rats. *Alcoholism: Clinical and Experimental Research* 24:1712–1723, 2000. PMID: 11104119

De Bellis, M.D.; Clark, D.B.; Beers, S.R.; et al. Hippocampal volume in adolescent-onset alcohol use disorders. *American Journal of Psychiatry* 157:737–744, 2000. PMID: 10784466

Dees, W.L.; Dissen, G.A.; Hiney, J.K.; et al. Alcohol ingestion inhibits the increased secretion of puberty-related hormones in the developing female rhesus monkey. *Endocrinology* 141:1325–1331, 2000. PMID: 10746635

Dees, W.L.; Srivastava, V.K.; and Hiney, J.K. Alcohol and female puberty: The role of intraovarian systems. *Alcohol Research & Health* 25(4):271–275, 2001. PMID: 11910704

Diamond, F., Jr.; Ringenberg, L.; MacDonald, D.; et al. Effects of drug and alcohol abuse upon pituitary-testicular function in adolescent males. *Journal of Adolescent Health Care* 7:28–33, 1986. PMID: 2935515

Dick, D.M.; Rose, R.J.; Viken, R.J.; and Kaprio, J. Pubertal timing and substance use: Associations between and within families across late adolescence. *Developmental Psychology* 36:180–189, 2000. PMID: 10749075

Elgan, C.; Dykes, A.K.; and Samsioe, G. Bone mineral density and lifestyle among female students aged 16–24 years. *Gynecological Endocrinology* 16:91–98, 2002. PMID: 12012629

Emanuele, M.A.; LaPaglia, N.; Steiner, J.; et al. Reversal of ethanol-induced testosterone suppression in peripubertal male rats by opiate blockade. *Alcoholism: Clinical and Experimental Research* 22:1199–1204, 1998. PMID: 9756033

Emanuele, M.A.; Wezeman, F.; and Emanuele, N.V. Alcohol's effects on female reproductive function. *Alcohol Research & Health* 26(4):274–281, 2002a. PMID: 12875037

Emanuele, N.; Ren, J.; LaPaglia, N.; et al. EtOH disrupts female mammalian puberty: Age and opiate dependence. *Endocrine* 18:247–254, 2002b. PMID: 12450316

Emanuele, N.V.; LaPaglia, N.; Vogl, W.; et al. Impact and reversibility of chronic ethanol feeding on the reproductive axis in the peripubertal male rat. *Endocrine* 11:277–284, 1999a. PMID: 10786824

Emanuele, N.V.; Lapaglia, N.; Steiner, J.; et al. Reversal of chronic ethanol-induced testosterone suppression in peripubertal male rats by opiate blockade. *Alcoholism: Clinical and Experimental Research* 23:60–66, 1999b. PMID: 10029204

Fehily, A.M.; Coles, R.J.; Evans, W.D.; and Elwood, P.C. Factors affecting bone density in young adults. *American Journal of Clinical Nutrition* 56:579–586, 1992. PMID: 1503072

Frias, J.; Rodriguez, R.; Torres, J.M.; et al. Effects of acute alcohol intoxication on pituitary-gonadal axis hormones, pituitary-adrenal axis hormones, β-endorphin and prolactin in human adolescents of both sexes. *Life Sciences* 67:1081–1086, 2000a. PMID: 10954041

Frias, J.; Torres, J.M.; Rodriguez, R.; et al. Effects of acute alcohol intoxication on growth axis in human adolescents of both sexes. *Life Sciences* 67:2691–2697, 2000b. PMID: 11105985

Fujita, Y.; Katsumata, K.; Unno, A.; et al. Factors affecting peak bone density in Japanese women. *Calcified Tissue International* 64:107–111, 1999. PMID: 9914316

Grant, B.F., and Dawson, D.A. Age at onset of alcohol use and its association with DSM–IV alcohol abuse and dependence: Results from the National Longitudinal Alcohol Epidemiologic Survey. *Journal of Substance Abuse* 9:103–110, 1998. PMID: 9494942

Herman-Giddens, M.E.; Slora, E.J.; Wasserman, R.C.; et al. Secondary sexual characteristics and menses in young girls seen in office practice: A study from the Pediatric Research in Office Settings Network. *Pediatrics* 99:505–512, 1997. PMID: 9093289

Herman-Giddens, M.E.; Wang, L.; and Koch, G. Secondary sexual characteristics in boys: Estimates from the National Health and Nutrition Examination Survey III, 1988–1994. *Archives of Pediatric & Adolescent Medicine* 155:1022–1028, 2001. PMID: 11529804

Honey, P.L., and Galef, B.G., Jr. Ethanol consumption by rat dams during gestation, lactation and weaning increases ethanol consumption by their adolescent young. *Developmental Psychobiology* 42:252–260, 2003. PMID: 12621651

Hunt, W.A. Are binge drinkers more at risk of developing brain damage? *Alcohol* 10:559–561, 1993. PMID: 8123218

Hunt, P.S.; Holloway, J.L.; and Scordalakes, E.M. Social interaction with an intoxicated sibling can result in increased intake of ethanol by periadolescent rats. *Developmental Psychobiology* 38:101–109, 2001. PMID: 11223802

Karpati, A.M.; Rubin, C.H.; Kieszak, S.M.; et al. Stature and pubertal stage assessment in American boys: The 1988–1994 Third National Health and Nutrition Examination Survey. *Journal of Adolescent Health* 30:205–212, 2002. PMID: 11869928

Lee, P.A.; Guo, S.S.; and Kulin, H.E. Age of puberty: Data from the United States of America. *APMIS (Acta Pathologica, Microbiologica, et Immunologica Scandinavica)* 109:81–88, 2001. PMID: 11398998

Li, Q.; Wilson, W.A.; and Swartzwelder, H.S. Differential effect of ethanol on NMDA EPSCs in pyramidal cells in the posterior cingulate cortex of juvenile and adult rats. *Journal of Neurophysiology* 87:705–711, 2002. PMID: 11826039

Little, P.J.; Adams, M.L.; and Cicero, T.J. Effects of alcohol on the hypothalamic-pituitary-gonadal axis in the developing male rat. *Journal of Pharmacology and Experimental Therapeutics* 263:1056–1061, 1992. PMID: 1469619

Markwiese, B.J.; Acheson, S.K.; Levin, E.D.; et al. Differential effects of ethanol on memory in adolescent and adult rats. *Alcoholism: Clinical and Experimental Research* 22:416–421, 1998. PMID: 9581648

Mauras, N.; Rogol, A.D.; Haymond, M.W.; and Veldhuis, J.D. Sex steroids, growth hormone, insulin-like growth factor-1: Neuroendocrine and metabolic regulation in puberty. *Hormone Research* 45:74–80, 1996. PMID: 8742123

Molina, J.C.; Dominguez, H.D.; Lopez, M.F.; et al. The role of fetal and infantile experience with alcohol in later recognition and acceptance patterns of the drug. In: Hannigan, J.; Goodlett, C.; Spear, L.; Spear, N., eds. *Alcohol and Alcoholism: Brain and Development.* Hillsdale, NJ: Erlbaum, 1999, pp. 199–227.

National Institute on Alcohol Abuse and Alcoholism (NIAAA). Alcohol involvement over the life course. In: *Tenth Special Report to the U.S. Congress on Alcohol and Health: Highlights from Current Research.* Bethesda, MD: Dept. of Health and Human Services, NIAAA, 2000. pp. 28–53. Available online at: http://pubs.niaaa.nih.gov/publications/10report/intro.pdf.

Neville, C.E.; Murray, L.J.; Boreham, C.A.G.; et al. Relationship between physical activity and bone mineral status in young adults: The Northern Ireland Young Hearts Project. *Bone* 30:792–798, 2002. PMID: 11996922

Pepino, M.Y.; Spear, N.E.; and Molina, J.C. Nursing experiences with an alcohol-intoxicated rat dam counteract appetitive conditioned responses toward alcohol. *Alcoholism: Clinical and Experimental Research* 25:18–24, 2001. PMID: 11198710

Pepino, M.Y.; Abate, P.; Spear, N.E.; and Molina, J.C. Disruption of maternal behavior by alcohol intoxication in the lactating rat: A behavioral and metabolic analysis. *Alcoholism: Clinical and Experimental Research* 26:1205–1214, 2002. PMID: 12198395

Pepino, M.Y.; Abate, P.; Spear, N.E.; and Molina, J.C. Heightened ethanol intake in infant and adolescent rats after nursing experiences with an ethanol-intoxicated dam. *Alcoholism: Clinical and Experimental Research* 28:895–905, 2004. PMID: 15201632

Pfefferbaum, A., and Sullivan, E.V. Micro structural but not macrostructural disruption of white matter in women with chronic alcoholism. *Neuroimage* 15:708–718, 2002. PMID: 11848714

Ponce, L.F.; Pautassi, R.M.; Spear, N.E.; and Molina, J.C. Nursing from an ethanol-intoxicated dam induces short- and long-term disruptions in motor performance and enhances later self-administration of the drug. *Alcoholism: Clinical and Experimental Research* 28:1039–1050, 2004. PMID: 15252290

Sampson, H.W., and Spears, H. Osteopenia due to chronic alcohol consumption by young actively growing rats is not completely reversible. *Alcoholism: Clinical and Experimental Research* 23:324–327, 1999. PMID: 10069563

Sampson, H.W.; Perks, N.; Champney, T.H.; and Defee, B., 2nd. Alcohol consumption inhibits bone growth and development in young actively growing rats. *Alcoholism: Clinical and Experimental Research* 20:1375–1384, 1996. PMID: 8947313

Sampson, H.W.; Gallager, S.; Lange, J.; et al. Binge drinking and bone metabolism in a young actively growing rat model. *Alcoholism: Clinical and Experimental Research* 23:1228–1231, 1999. PMID: 10443990

Slawecki, C.J. Altered EEG responses to ethanol in adult rats exposed to ethanol during adolescence. *Alcoholism: Clinical and Experimental Research* 26:246–254, 2002. PMID: 11964565

Slawecki, C.J., and Roth, J. Comparison of the onset of hypoactivity and anxiety-like behavior during alcohol withdrawal in adolescent and adult rats. *Alcoholism: Clinical and Experimental Research* 28:598–607, 2004. PMID: 15100611

Slawecki, C.J.; Betancourt, M.; Cole, M.; and Ehlers, C.L. Periadolescent alcohol exposure has lasting effects on adult neurophysiological function in rats. *Developmental Brain Research* 128:63–72, 2001. PMID: 11356263

Spear, L.P., and Varlinskaya, E.I. Adolescence: Alcohol sensitivity, tolerance, and intake. In: Galanter, M., ed. *Recent Developments in Alcoholism, Vol. 17: Alcohol Problems in Adolescents and Young Adults: Epidemiology, Neurobiology, Prevention, Treatment.* New York: Springer, 2005. pp. 143–159. PMID: 15789864

Spear, N.E., and Molina, J.C. Consequences of early exposure to alcohol: How animal studies reveal later patterns of use and abuse in humans. In: Carroll, M.E., and Overmier, J.B., eds. *Animal Research and Human Health: Advancing Human Welfare through Behavioral Science.* Washington, DC: American Psychological Association, 2001. pp. 85–99.

Srivastava, V.K.; Hiney, J.K.; Dearth, R.K.; and Dees, W.L. Effects of alcohol on intraovarian insulin-like growth factor-1 and nitric oxide systems in prepubertal female rats. *Recent Research Developments in Endocrinology* 2(part 1):213–221, 2001*a*.

Srivastava, V.K.; Hiney, J.K.; Dearth, R.K.; and Dees, W.L. Acute effects of ethanol on steroidogenic acute regulatory protein (StAR) in the prepubertal rat ovary. *Alcoholism: Clinical and Experimental Research* 25:1500–1505, 2001*b*. PMID: 11696671

Steiner, J.C.; LaPaglia, N.; Hansen, M.; et al. Effect of chronic ethanol on reproductive and growth hormones in the peripubertal male rat. *Journal of Endocrinology* 154:363–370, 1997. PMID: 9291847

Strauss, R.S.; Barlow, S.E.; and Dietz, W.H. Prevalence of abnormal serum aminotransferase values in overweight and obese adolescents. *Journal of Pediatrics* 136:727–733, 2000. PMID: 10839867

Swartzwelder, H.S.; Wilson, W.A.; and Tayyeb, M.I. Age-dependent inhibition of long-term potentiation by ethanol in immature versus mature hippocampus. *Alcoholism: Clinical and Experimental Research* 19:1480–1485, 1995*a*. PMID: 8749814

Swartzwelder, H.S.; Wilson, W.A.; and Tayyeb, M.I. Differential sensitivity of NMDA receptor-mediated synaptic potentials to ethanol in immature versus mature hippocampus. *Alcoholism: Clinical and Experimental Research* 19:320–323, 1995*b*. PMID: 7625564

Tanner, J.M. *Foetus into Man: Physical Growth From Conception to Maturity.* Ware, Great Britain: Castlemead Publications, 1989.

Tapert, S.F., and Brown, S.A. Neuropsychological correlates of adolescent substance abuse: Four-year outcomes. *Journal of the International Neuropsychological Society* 5:481–493, 1999. PMID: 10561928

Tapert, S.F.; Granholm, E.; Leedy, N.G.; and Brown, S.A. Substance use and withdrawal: Neuropsychological functioning over 8 years in youth. *Journal of the International Neuropsychological Society* 8:873–883, 2002. PMID: 12405538

Tapert, S.F.; Theilmann, R.J.; Schweinsburg, A.D.; et al. Reduced fractional anisotropy in the splenium of adolescents with alcohol use disorder. *Proceedings of the International Society for Magnetic Resonance in Medicine* 11:8217, 2003.

Tentler, J.J.; LaPaglia, N.; Steiner, J.; et al. Ethanol, growth hormone and testosterone in peripubertal rats. *Journal of Endocrinology* 152:477–487, 1997. PMID: 9071969

Varlinskaya, E.I., and Spear, L.P. Acute effects of ethanol on social behavior of adolescent and adult rats: Role of familiarity of the test situation. *Alcoholism: Clinical and Experimental Research* 26:1502–1511, 2002. PMID: 12394283

Wezeman, F.H.; Emanuele, M.A.; Emanuele, N.V.; et al. Chronic alcohol consumption during male rat adolescence impairs skeletal development through effects on osteoblast gene expression, bone mineral density, and bone strength. *Alcoholism: Clinical and Experimental Research* 23: 1534–1542, 1999. PMID: 10512321

White, A.M., and Swartzwelder, H.S. Age-related effects of alcohol on memory and memory-related brain function in adolescents and adults. In: Galanter, M., ed. *Recent Developments in Alcoholism, Vol. 17: Alcohol Problems in Adolescents and Young Adults: Epidemiology, Neurobiology, Prevention, Treatment.* New York: Springer, 2005. pp. 161–176. PMID: 15789865

White, A.M.; Ghia, A.J.; Levin, E.D.; and Swartzwelder, H.S. Binge pattern ethanol exposure in adolescent and adult rats: Differential impact on subsequent responsiveness to ethanol. *Alcoholism: Clinical and Experimental Research* 24: 1251–1256, 2000. PMID: 10968665

White, A.M.; Truesdale, M.C.; Bae, J.G.; et al. Differential effects of ethanol on motor coordination in adolescent and adult rats. *Pharmacology, Biochemistry, and Behavior* 73:673–677, 2002. PMID: 12151043

Wilson, D.M.; Killen, J.D.; Hayward, C.; et al. Timing and rate of sexual maturation and the onset of cigarette and alcohol use among teenage girls. *Archives of Pediatrics and Adolescent Medicine* 148:789–795, 1994. PMID: 8044254

Zucker, R.A., and Wong, M.M. Prevention for children of alcoholics and other high risk groups. In: Galanter, M., ed. *Recent Developments in Alcoholism, Vol. 17: Alcohol Problems in Adolescents and Young Adults: Epidemiology, Neurobiology, Prevention, Treatment.* New York: Springer, 2005. pp. 299– 320. PMID: 15789872

From *Alcohol Research and Health*, vol. 28, no. 3, 2004/2005, pp. 125–131. Published by National Institute on Alcohol Abuse and Alcoholism (NIAAA).

A Small Part of the Brain, and Its Profound Effects

SANDRA BLAKESLEE

The recent news about smoking was sensational: some people with damage to a prune-size slab of brain tissue called the insula were able to give up cigarettes instantly.

Suppose scientists could figure out how to tweak the insula without damaging it. They might be able to create that famed and elusive free lunch—an effortless way to kick the cigarette habit.

That dream, which may not be too far off, puts the insula in the spotlight. What is the insula and how could it possibly exert such profound effects on human behavior?

According to neuroscientists who study it, the insula is a long-neglected brain region that has emerged as crucial to understanding what it feels like to be human.

They say it is the wellspring of social emotions, things like lust and disgust, pride and humiliation, guilt and atonement. It helps give rise to moral intuition, empathy and the capacity to respond emotionally to music.

Its anatomy and evolution shed light on the profound differences between humans and other animals.

The insula also reads body states like hunger and craving and helps push people into reaching for the next sandwich, cigarette or line of cocaine. So insula researchd offers new ways to think about treating drug addiction, alcoholism, anxiety and eating disorders.

Of course, so much about the brain remains to be discovered that the insula's role may be a minor character in the play of the human mind. It is just now coming on stage.

The activity of the insula in so many areas is something of a puzzle. "People have had a hard time conceptualizing what the insula does," said Dr. Martin Paulus, a psychiatrist at the University of California, San Diego.

If it does everything, what exactly is it that it does?

An interpreter that helps put the human in human experience.

For example, the insula "lights up" in brain scans when people crave drugs, feel pain, anticipate pain, empathize with others, listen to jokes, see disgust on someone's face, are shunned in a social settings, listen to music, decide not to buy an item, see someone cheat and decide to punish them, and determine degrees of preference while eating chocolate.

Damage to the insula can lead to apathy, loss of libido and an inability to tell fresh food from rotten.

The bottom line, according to Dr. Paulus and others, is that mind and body are integrated in the insula. It provides unprecedented insight into the anatomy of human emotions.

Of course, like every important brain structure, the insula—there are actually two, one on each side of the brain—does not act alone. It is part of multiple circuits.

The insula itself is a sort of receiving zone that reads the physiological state of the entire body and then generates subjective feelings that can bring about actions, like eating, that keep the body in a state of internal balance. Information from the insula is relayed to other brain structures that appear to be involved in decision making, especially the anterior cingulate and prefrontal cortices.

The insula was long ignored for two reasons, researchers said. First, because it is folded and tucked deep within the brain, scientists could not probe it with shallow electrodes. It took the invention of brain imaging techniques, such as functional magnetic resonance imaging, or fMRI, to watch it in action.

Second, the insula was "assigned to the brain's netherworld," said John Allman, a neuroscientist at the California Institute of Technology. It was mistakenly defined as a primitive part of the brain involved only in functions like eating and sex. Ambitious scientists studied higher, more rational parts of the brain, he said.

The insula emerged from darkness a decade ago when Antonio Damasio, a neuroscientist now at the University of Southern California, developed the so-called somatic marker hypothesis, the idea that rational thinking cannot be separated from feelings and emotions. The insula, he said, plays a starring role.

Another neuroscientist, Arthur D. Craig at the Barrow Neurological Institute in Phoenix, went on to describe exactly the circuitry that connects the body to the insula.

According to Dr. Craig, the insula receives information from receptors in the skin and internal organs. Such receptors are nerve cells that specialize in different senses. Thus there are receptors that detect heat, cold, itch, pain, taste, hunger, thirst, muscle ache, visceral sensations and so-called air hunger, the need to breathe. The sense of touch and the sense of the body's position in space are routed to different brain regions, he said.

All mammals have insulas that read their body condition, Dr. Craig said. Information about the status of the body's tissues and organs is carried from the receptors along distinct spinal pathways, into the brain stem and up to the posterior insula in the higher brain or cortex.

As such, all mammals have emotions, defined as sensations that provoke motivations. If an animal is hot, it seeks shade. If hungry, it looks for food. If hurt, it licks the wound.

But animals are not thought to have subjective feelings in the way that humans do, Dr. Craig said. Humans, and to a lesser degree the great apes, have evolved two innovations to their insulas that take this system of reading body states to a new level.

One involves circuitry, the other a brand new type of brain cell.

In humans, information about the body's state takes a slightly different route inside the brain, picking up even more signals from the gut, the heart, the lungs and other internal organs. Then the human brain takes an extra step, Dr. Craig said. The information on bodily sensations is further routed to the front part of the insula, especially on the right side, which has undergone a huge expansion in humans and apes.

It is in the frontal insula, Dr. Craig said, that simple body states or sensations are recast as social emotions. A bad taste or smell is sensed in the frontal insula as disgust. A sensual touch from a loved one is transformed into delight.

The frontal insula is where people sense love and hate, gratitude and resentment, self-confidence and embarrassment, trust and distrust, empathy and contempt, approval and disdain, pride and humiliation, truthfulness and deception, atonement and guilt.

A new focus on the insula after a report linked it to the desire to smoke.

People who are better at reading these sensations—a quickened heart beat, a flushed face, slow breathing—score higher on psychological tests of empathy, researchers have found. The second major modification to the insula is a type of cell found in only humans, great apes, whales and possibly elephants, Dr. Allman said. Humans have by far the greatest number of these cells, which are called VENs, short for Von Economo neurons, named for the scientist who first described them in 1925. VENs are large cigar-shaped cells tapered at each end, and they are found exclusively in the frontal insula and anterior cingulate cortex.

Exactly what VENs are doing within this critical circuit is not yet known, Dr. Allman said. But they are in the catbird seat for turning feelings and emotions into actions and intentions.

The human insula, with its souped-up anatomy, is also important for processing events that have yet to happen, Dr. Paulus said. "When you decide to go outside on a cold day, your body gets ready before you hit the cold air," he said. "It starts pumping blood to where you need it and adjusts your metabolism. Your insula tells you what it will feel like before you step outside."

The same goes for drug addicts. When an addict is confronted with sights, sounds, smells, situations or other stimuli associated with drug use, the insula is activated before using the drug.

"If you give cocaine to an addict, you are affecting their brain's reward system, but this is not what drives the person to keep using cocaine," Dr. Paulus said. The craving is what gets people to use.

For example, smokers enjoy whole-body effects, said Nasir Naqvi, a student at the University of Iowa Medical Scientist Training Program, who was the lead author of the recent article on smoking. It is not just nicotine binding to parts of the brain, he said, but sensations—heart rate, blood pressure, a tickle in the lungs, a taste in the mouth, the position of the hands, all the rituals.

The insula's importance makes it an ideal target for many kinds of treatment, Dr. Paulus said, including drugs and sophisticated biofeedback. But methods to quell insular activity must be approached carefully, he said. People might lose the craving to smoke, drink alcohol or take other drugs, but they could simultaneously lose interest in sex, food and work.

As clinicians explore the possibilities, Dr. Craig is thinking about the insula in grander terms.

For example, lesions in the frontal insula can wipe out the ability to appreciate the emotional content of music. It may also be involved in the human sense of the progress of time, since it can create an anticipatory signal of how people may feel as opposed to how they feel now. Intensely emotional moments can affect our sense of time. It may stand still, and that may be happening in the insula, a crossroads of time and desire.

Archieved articles on the brain, and a podcast interview with **SANDRA BLAKESLEE.**

The Changing Science of Pain

Millions of aging boomers and the latest generation of wounded soldiers hope the secrets of our most enduring medical foe can finally be unlocked.

MARY CARMICHAEL

Late into the night of May 2, 1863, a few hours after Thomas (Stonewall) Jackson took two bullets in his left arm at the Battle of Chancellorsville, surgeon Hunter Holmes McGuire sawed off the bleeding limb, trying to save the general's life. With the knife came another medical tool, one fairly new to the battlefield—a rag soaked in chloroform. As he awaited amputation, Jackson, who would die a week later, was as stoic as his nickname suggested. But as he slipped into unconsciousness, it's said, he betrayed his vulnerability in the face of pain just once, mumbling that the anesthesia was "an infinite blessing."

For most of the 144 years since then, the military has stuck with similarly crude techniques for treating its soldiers' pain. Morphine, also given to Jackson and many others in the Civil War, is still the Army's most commonly used painkilling drug. It works, but compared with more-modern options, it's one step above chloroform and two above biting the bullet. Now, though, with casualties mounting in Iraq and Afghanistan, the military is being forced to change its strategy. More than 90 percent of wounded soldiers have made it off the battlefield—the highest survival rate in American history—only to overwhelm chronic-pain clinics when they come home. "We're seeing the tip of a tidal wave of pain," says Lt. Col. Chester (Trip) Buckenmaier, an anesthesiologist at Walter Reed Army Medical Center, who has emerged as a sort of pain czar for the Army. After decades of "sucking it up," the military has finally started to respond in new and innovative ways to this escalating pain crisis. Even as the VA hospital system has come under fire for poor care, Army doctors haven't just joined up in medicine's larger war against pain—they're leading the charge.

Winning this medical war is crucial, and not just for the sake of the soldiers, who are far from the only burgeoning new group of pain sufferers. Chronic pain is one of the most pervasive and intractable medical conditions in the United States, with one in five Americans afflicted. Aging baby boomers have reported in surveys more aches and pains than any previous generation. Cancer patients have more treatments to choose from than ever, but more pain, too. Even retired NFL players—a suck-it-up group if ever there was one—have started speaking out about the wear and tear on their bodies. Civilian chronic pain already costs the country $61 billion in lost productivity and many more in medical fees. Treating the soldiers in the coming years will add at least $340 billion to the toll.

As the number of patients has grown, though, so has medicine's understanding of what pain is. Scientists once viewed it as merely a symptom of injury, an intuitive idea that resonated with laymen. "The public understanding of pain has been that it's a stubbed toe or a broken bone," says Will Rowe, executive director of the American Pain Foundation. "But that's just one aspect of it. Now there's a growing awareness that pain is a disease of its own."

This is far more than a semantic change, Rowe adds: it's "tectonic." Docs now know that the brain and spinal cord rewire themselves in response to injuries, forming "pain pathways" that can become pathologically overactive years later. They are trying to sever this maladaptive mind-body connection with a host of new drugs and approaches. Some focus on recently discovered chemical receptors in the brain and muscles. Others pack all the punch of narcotics with less of the specter of addiction. (Patients can still become dependent on a new form of the morphine derivative called Kadian, for instance, but if they crush one of the pills for snorting, its center explodes, releasing a substance that blocks the euphoric high.) New types of electrical stimulators targeting the brain, the spine and the muscles hit the market almost every year. Fentanyl skin patches, first introduced in 1990, have evolved into a patient-controlled, push-button device called IONSYS, available by the end of this year. And complementary and alternative medicine offer a parallel universe of treatments: herbs, yoga, acupuncture, chiropractic, massage and "prolotherapy," which injects various solutions, including cod-liver oil, into ligaments and tendons near the area of pain.

The military is pioneering its own new approaches. Since 2003, a small but growing number of soldiers in Iraq have been treated at the front with high-tech nerve-blocking devices that are effective but not addictive. They are common in civilian life, but their use on the battlefield is unprecedented. Back at home, many VA clinics are offering extensive and elaborate pain treatments, and they're learning how to get tough guys and girls to soften up and admit they need help. At Walter Reed, Bucken-maier's team is conducting groundbreaking research on the link between acute and chronic pain; his findings, due in the next few years, could revolutionize treatment. "The military needs people to be functioning out on the field," says Rollin (Mac) Gallagher, chief of pain medicine at the Philadelphia VA hospital. "What we're now starting to recognize is that if you control people's pain, they're not liabilities—they're assets."

That's not to say pain is all bad. It's unpleasant, of course, but in an evolutionary sense, it has its uses. Acute pain begins in the peripheries of the body, where sensory neurons are constantly on patrol for signs of damage. They are the mechanisms that alert us to one injury so we can avoid a second one. Touch a hot stove for the first time and you won't be happy, but you'll ultimately be better off—because you'll certainly never want to do it again.

By the time it has become a chronic condition, however, pain is no longer useful. It is, as Rowe says, a disease—specifically, an overactivity of the nervous system. The brain keeps a diary of the injuries the body receives, writing each entry by reconfiguring certain neurons into new, interconnected patterns. In healthy people, these neurons stop firing once the initial damage is fixed. But in chronic pain, they keep going long after the injury has healed. "The circuits get turned up, and they stay up. They get stuck," says Gallagher. "Most diseases are physiology gone wrong. Pain is one of them."

Scientists don't know why some people develop chronic problems after injuries while others continue on with no pain. It is nearly impossible to answer the question on a wide scale; pain simply has too many causes. Some patients fully recover from massive trauma. Others, like most of the boomers with aching backs and knees, find themselves debilitated by nothing more than the accumulated, mundane strains put on joints, bones and muscles every day. Even soldiers can fall into this second category—if the bullets don't get them, the back pain brought on by months of jumping out of trucks, burdened with heavy equipment, well may.

Complicating the issue even further is pain's inherently subjective nature—we may say we "feel each other's pain," but really, we can't. Doctors don't have any good way of measuring pain from one person to the next. The best they can do is ask patients to rate it for themselves on a scale of 1 to 10, with 10 being the greatest agony of their lives. This is absurdly imprecise. Patients are usually honest (and fakery is fairly easy to spot), but they can exaggerate. A person feeling a 4 may claim a 7 to get aggressive treatment, and a person feeling a 7 may downplay it as a 4 in hopes of looking tough. Robyn Walker, a psychologist at the Tampa (Fla.) VA, says she's seen the latter dynamic in her clinic. "These patients know what a 10 feels like," she says. "But they are active-duty soldiers, and they minimize their problems. Unless you really ask them about their pain, they may be very hesitant to tell you." Doctors are trying to develop new methods of measuring pain, but their most advanced idea so far is to study facial expressions—which aren't much more standardized than the 10-point scale.

On top of that, one patient's 7 may be another's 4. "Our bodies are not one-size-fits-all," notes Rowe, "and doctors are finding that this is far more true with pain than they ever imagined." Genes may vastly influence how intensely people feel pain and how much they can withstand—although genetic testing for pain susceptibility is probably decades away. Gender matters, too. Women have up to twice as many nerve fibers in the skin as men do, so they feel some types of pain more intensely. (This doesn't mean they're weaker; it means that, all other factors being equal, their 10 is off a man's chart.) Even traits that seem unrelated to pain, like vitamin D deficiency, may increase it for reasons no one fully understands. Trying to untangle all these factors is a scientific nightmare.

Regardless of their injuries, their genes, their gender or their background, though, nearly all chronic-pain patients agree on one thing: the hyperactive neurons can make life near unbearable. The cascade of changes in the nervous system can lead to an equally painful cascade of events in a patient's life: memory loss, job loss, marital strife, depression, suicide. And through it all the body hurts like hell. "Imagine somebody holding a knife in your back and twisting it against your nerves continually, never stopping. That's what chronic pain is," says Dan O'Neal, a contractor who herniated two vertebrae in 2003 while cleaning up a job site. "At first you just shut off totally. It's terrible living like that."

Among chronic-pain patients, O'Neal is actually one of the lucky ones. He, at least, knows why his pain started; some patients are denied even that knowledge. Chronic regional pain syndrome, for instance, is a rare disorder that can begin with something as trivial as a skinned knee. The scrape heals, but the nervous system does not. Within a few years the knee that was skinned feels like it is on fire, even though nothing is outwardly wrong. Similarly, fibromyalgia assails the bones, muscles and joints, but has no obvious bodily causes and doesn't show up on X-rays. Growing evidence now suggests that it is in part a brain disorder that sets the pain pathways afire, responding to imaginary wounds—as if the brain's diary of injuries has suddenly filled up with wild, untrue stories. The pain itself is not imaginary. But because it is hard to pinpoint and even harder to treat, for years many doctors used to write it off as such. Andrea Cooper says that's all doctors did when she first developed fibromyalgia, which afflicts 6 million Americans. "There was a bunch of 'We can't figure out what's wrong with you, therefore there's nothing wrong with you,'" she says. "People don't like to hear about symptoms that they can't do anything about."

Chronic pain is one of the most pervasive and intractable medical conditions in the U.S., with one in five Americans afflicted.

Some fibromyalgia patients may be helped by standard pain treatments. Others aren't. In that, at least, fibromyalgia patients are just like all other pain patients: relief can come for them, but it is often hard-won. Cooper, who is now on fentanyl and Kadian, compares her current pain to "the roar of the faraway interstate, as opposed to being in traffic." But to get to her current regimen she had to go through nearly everything else—antidepressants, anticonvulsants, muscle relaxers, acupuncture and six operations that probably made the pain worse.

Some of the most promising pain treatments of the past decade have turned out to be disappointments. Studies of some radio-frequency therapies show they work no better than placebos. Spinal-fusion surgery, a recent review found, has "no acceptable evidence" to support it. And if a treatment does work, says Edward Covington, a pain specialist at the Cleveland Clinic, "for most people, the effect is temporary." There is no cure for chronic pain, period.

There's not even any "single drug or technology alone" that can treat all the types of pain, says Eugene Viscusi, director of acute-pain management at Thomas Jefferson University Hospital in Philadelphia. Most people need two or three therapies in combination. Scientists' new understanding of pain's broad effects on many levels of the nervous system explains why: a multipart syndrome requires multipart therapy. Viscusi notes that patients under anesthesia still have elevated levels of the pain enzyme COX-2 in their spinal fluid following surgery. They may not feel pain, but some parts of their brains still think they're in it. For any treatment to work long term, it will have to address not just the immediate sensation of pain but the other, subtler aspects—and there are surely some of those that scientists don't know about yet.

At the American Pain Society's annual meeting in May, a panel drew attention to what seems like the best option pain medicine currently has to offer: "multidisciplinary pain centers," essentially rehab clinics that employ doctors, nurses and therapists from a variety of fields. They prescribe a tough-love regimen of physical therapy (as well as the psychological kind), and many also make a point of cutting down on drug use. Pain specialists have been singing their praises for the past three decades. Data show why: they help many debilitated patients get back to work. But multidisciplinary clinics are on the wane. There are no statistics, but Covington says he suspects their numbers have dwindled by about 90 percent in the past 30 years. The problem is that a lot of patients just don't like them. "Americans love deep brain stimulation, replacement discs, things that are sexy and magical and frequently hyped," Covington notes. Multidisciplinary clinics are a much harder sell. They're not a quick fix, and their emphasis on exercise strikes fear in some people who are already worried about injuring themselves.

Insurance companies also sometimes balk at multidisciplinary clinics, which are costly. They'll cover them, Covington says, but usually "only enough so they lose just a little bit of money on them every year." Insurers say they sometimes have trouble determining how legitimate the clinics are or how much of a service they'll provide, since there are no national guidelines for what the clinics should encompass.

Insurers usually prefer to pay for single therapies, like opioids, the narcotics that block messages in the brain and make patients care less about their pain. The drugs are hugely widespread; almost 200 million opioid prescriptions get written in America each year, most of them for Vicodin, OxyContin and various forms of fentanyl. But "widespread" doesn't mean "effective," nor does it mean "popular." In opioid trials, fewer than a third of patients on average report relief, and more than a third drop out of the same trials rather than deal with the side effects, which include nausea, constipation and trouble breathing. "Most of the soldiers I treat say they don't want to take these strong medications," says Walker, the Tampa VA psychologist. "They say, 'These things make me groggy. I want to get back to my life.'"

Opioid users also run two parallel risks: that they will become addicted, and that they will suffer the stigma of addiction even if they're not abusing the drugs. Steven Passik, a pain specialist at Memorial Sloan-Kettering Cancer Center, notes that "the issue of addiction doesn't lie in the drugs," but in a complex interaction between the chemicals and biological predispositions. Still, many patients struggle. Brooks Bono, 28, was born with a tumor on his spine and has spent his whole life in pain. At one point he was on so much OxyContin that "the dosages would have killed someone else," says his mother, Kadie Dempsey. He sees Passik now for counseling, and a few months ago he switched to methadone. It's not as addictive, says Bono, but it does little to dull the pain and it brings its own problems. "I went to about 20 different pharmacies," he says, "and they told me, 'We don't treat drug addicts here.'"

No one wants to avoid an epidemic of drug abuse more than the military. Addicted Vietnam vets still wander into VAs, and as Gallagher notes, "if our soldiers can't get pain relief in the medical system, they'll turn to other ways." Many VA clinics make a point of cutting down on soldiers' use of opioids and other drugs. At a congressional hearing on pain in December 2005, Capt. John Pruden said he'd talked with one of his old buddies, who had been wounded in Iraq. "As we were talking, he bragged how he was not using his pain meds," Pruden told the audience. "But unfortunately it turns out he was self-medicating with alcohol to cope with the pain."

After injuries, the brain and spinal cord rewire themselves, forming pain pathways that can become overactive years later.

The military is now pursuing a new pain strategy: stop the trouble before it starts. Historically, wars have led to medical advances, and this one is no different; the notion of a kind of pre-emption has captured the interest and excitement of the entire pain-medicine community. Treat acute pain early, the thinking goes, and you stop the brain from responding to it. You might just wipe out chronic pain in the process.

This is where Buckenmaier's research comes in. His team is responsible for bringing those high-tech nerve blocks to the battlefield. Since 2003, hundreds of injured soldiers have received anesthetic pumps within hours of their injuries. Buckenmaier and Gallagher are jointly tracking these soldiers over the next year and beyond. If the ones who got pumps quickly have less chronic pain—and animal studies suggest they will—the research will not only point the way to new treatments, says Gallagher: for civilians and soldiers alike, "it will be a revolution." It may mean that injuries will be treated much more aggressively. That sprained ankle that only registered a 4 on the pain scale? If you want to avoid chronic pain later, you might need serious therapy, and right away.

It's too soon to say what will ultimately become of the Walter Reed study, though the hospital believes in Buckenmaier's work: despite being short-staffed and underfunded, it decided two weeks ago to fully finance his vision for a new acute-pain-management service, one that may remain in place after the war is over. There is much else left to do. Buckenmaier's nerve-block program needs to be expanded; thousands of soldiers injured in Iraq still don't get the advanced treatment. And, he says, on the battlefield there's usually "no one in charge" of pain in any given unit. The VA system, like the rest of the country, needs more pain specialists, not to mention mental-health professionals. Indeed, there's call for change at every level of a lumbering bureaucracy that, as has been amply documented in NEWSWEEK and elsewhere, lets too many soldiers fall through the cracks.

But Will Castillo, a 27-year-old Army sergeant, is not one of these soldiers. Like Stonewall Jackson, he is an amputee. Iraqi insurgents shot him in the head—twice—and as he lay on the ground, an IED blew his leg off. It is a horrible story, but sitting in his hospital bed with his leg covered, Castillo shows no sign that it even happened. He is one of the soldiers who have nerve-blocking pain pumps. He feels good, he says, and once he gets a prosthetic leg, he might even consider going back to Iraq for another round. It's hard to believe it, but yes: this is a man who feels infinitely blessed.

With Samantha Henig, Dan Ephron, and Julie Scelfo

The Toxicity of Recreational Drugs

Alcohol is more lethal than many other commonly abused substances

ROBERT S. GABLE

The Shuar tribes in Ecuador have for centuries used native plants to induce religious intoxication and to discipline recalcitrant children. By comparison, most North Americans know little about the mood-altering potential of the wild vegetation around them. And those who think they know something on this subject are often dangerously ignorant. Over a three-week period in 1983, for example, 22 Marines wanting to get high were hospitalized because they ate too many seeds of the jimsonweed plant (*Datura stramonium*), which they found growing wild near their base, Camp Pendleton in southern California.

A dozen seeds of jimsonweed contain about 1 gram of atropine, 10 grams of which can cause nausea, severe agitation, dilation of pupils, hallucinations, headache and delirium. Tribal groups in South America refer to datura plants as the "evil eagles." Of approximately 150 hallucinogenic plants that are routinely consumed around the world, those with atropine have the most pernicious reputation—something these Marines discovered the hard way.

Toxicity Profiles

The easier way to learn about the relation between the quantity of a substance taken and the resulting level of physiological impairment is through careful laboratory study. The first example of such an exercise, in 1927, used rodents. Research toxicologist John Trevan published an influential paper that reported the use of more than 900 mice to assess the lethality of, among other things, cocaine. As he and others have since found, a substance that is tolerated or even beneficial in small quantities often has harmful effects at higher levels. The amount of a substance that produces a beneficial effect in 50 percent of a group of animals is called the *median effective dose*. The quantity that produces mortality in 50 percent of a group of animals is termed the *median lethal dose*.

Laboratory tests with animals can give a general picture of the potency of a substance, but generalizing experimental results from, say, mice to humans is always suspect. Thus toxicologists also use two other sources of information. The first is survey data collected from poison-control centers, hospital emergency departments and coroners' offices. Another consists of published clinical and forensic reports of fatalities or near-fatalities.

But these sources, like animal studies, have their limitations. Simply tallying the number of people who die or who show up at emergency rooms is, by itself, meaningless because the number of such incidents will be influenced by the total number of people using a particular substance, something that is impossible to know. For example, atropine is more toxic than alcohol, but more deaths will be reported for alcohol than for atropine because so many more people get drunk than ingest jimsonweed. Furthermore, most overdose fatalities involve the use of two or more substances (usually including alcohol), situations for which the overall toxicity is largely unknown. In short: When psychoactive substances are combined, all bets are off.

How then does one gauge the relative risks of different recreational drugs? One way is to consider the ratio of effective dose to lethal dose. For example, a normally healthy 70-kilogram (154-pound) adult can achieve a relaxed affability from approximately 33 grams of ethyl alcohol. This effective dose can come from two 12-ounce beers, two 5-ounce glasses of wine or two 1.5-ounce shots of 80-proof vodka. The median lethal dose for such an adult is approximately 330 grams, the quantity contained in about 20 shots of vodka. A person who consumes that much (10 times the median effective dose), taken within a few minutes on an empty stomach, risks a lethal reaction. And plenty of people have died this way.

As far as toxicity goes, such deaths are quite telling. Indeed, autopsy reports from cases of fatal overdose (whether from alcohol or some other substance) provide key information linking death and drug consumption. But coroners are generally hard-pressed to determine the size of the dose because significant redistribution of a drug often occurs after death, typically from tissues of solid organs (such as the liver) into associated blood vessels. As a result, blood samples may show different concentrations at different times after death. Even if investigators had a valid way to measure the concentration of a lethal drug in a decedent's blood, they would still need to work backward to make a retrospective estimate of the quantity of the drug consumed. Although the approximate time of death is often known, the time the drug was taken and the rate at which it was metabolized are not so easily established. Lots of guesswork is typically involved. Obviously, people who want clean answers should not seek information from corpses.

Safety Comparison

Despite these difficulties, it is evident that there are striking differences among psychoactive substances with respect to the lethality of a given quantity The way a substance is absorbed is also a critical factor. The common routes of consumption, from the least toxic to the most toxic (in general), are eating or drinking a substance, depositing it inside the nostril, breathing or smoking it, and injecting it into a vein with a hypodermic syringe. So, for example, smoking methamphetamine (as is done with the increasingly popular illicit drug "crystal meth") is more dangerous than ingesting it.

Once a drag enters the body, physiological reactions are determined by many factors, such as absorption into various tissues and the rates of elimination and metabolism. Individuals vary enormously in how they metabolize different substances. One person's sedative can be another person's poison. This variability alone introduces unavoidable ambiguities in estimating effective and lethal doses. Still, the wide range between different substances suggests that they can be rank-ordered with reasonable confidence. One can be quite certain, for example, that the risk of death from ingesting psilocybin mushrooms is less than from injecting heroin.

The most toxic recreational drugs, such as GHB (gamma-hydroxybutyrate) and heroin, have a lethal dose less than 10 times their typical effective dose. The largest cluster of substances has a lethal dose that is 10 to 20 times the effective dose: These include cocaine, MDMA (methylenedioxymeth-amphetamine, often called "ecstasy") and alcohol. A less toxic group of substances, requiring 20 to 80 times the effective dose to cause death, include Rohypnol (flunitrazepam or "roofies") and mescaline (peyote cactus). The least physiologically toxic substances, those requiring 100 to 1,000 times the effective dose to cause death, include psilocybin mushrooms and marijuana, when ingested. I've found no published cases in the English language that document deaths from *smoked* marijuana, so the actual lethal dose is a mystery. My surmise is that smoking marijuana is more risky than eating it but still safer than getting drunk.

Alcohol thus ranks at the dangerous end of the toxicity spectrum. So despite the fact that about 75 percent of all adults in the United States enjoy an occasional drink, it must be remembered that alcohol is quite toxic. Indeed, if alcohol were a newly formulated beverage, its high toxicity and addiction potential would surely prevent it from being marketed as a food or drug. This conclusion runs counter to the common view that one's own use of alcohol is harmless. That mistaken impression arises for several reasons.

First, the more frequently we experience an event without a negative outcome, the lower our level of perceived danger. For

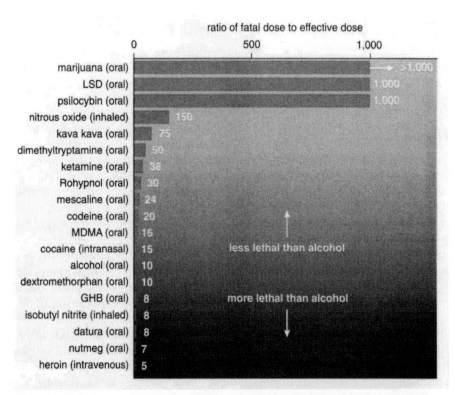

Figure 1 Ranking psychoactive substances by their ratios of lethal dose to effective dose gives a general picture of how likely each is to precipitate an acute fatal reaction. By this measure, many illicit drugs are considerably safer than alcohol.

example, most of us have not had a life-threatening traffic accident; thus, we feel safer in a car than in an airplane, although we are 10 to 15 times more likely to die in an automobile accident than in a plane crash. Similarly, most of us have not had a life-threatening experience with alcohol, yet statistics show that every year about 300 people die in the United States from an alcohol overdose, and for at least twice that number of overdose deaths, alcohol is considered a contributing cause.

Second, having a sense of control over a risky situation reduces fear. People drinking alcoholic beverages believe that they have reasonably good control of the quantity they intend to consume. Control of the dose of alcohol is indeed easier than with many natural or illicit substances where the active ingredients are not commercially standardized. Furthermore, alcohol is often consumed in a beverage that dilutes the alcohol to a known degree.

Consider the following: The stomach capacity of an average adult is about 1 liter; therefore, a person is unlikely to overdose after drinking beer containing 5 percent alcohol. Compare this situation to GHB (a depressant originally marketed in health food stores as a sleep aid), where stomach capacity does not place much of a limit on consumption because the effective dose is only one or two teaspoonfuls. No wonder that more than 50 percent of novice users of GHB have experienced an overdose that included involuntary loss of consciousness.

Another reason that alcohol is often thought to be safe is that popular media do not routinely report fatalities from alcohol overdoses. Deaths are usually considered newsworthy when they involve a degree of novelty. Thus a fatality caused by LSD or MDMA is thought to be more interesting than one caused by alcohol.

Other Ways to Invite Death

A simpleminded look at the ratio of effective to lethal doses ignores many complications, some of which are well recognized, some rather subtle. Take, for example, the fact that danger generally increases with repetitive consumption. High blood levels of a drug, without rest periods between use, tend to heighten risk, because the affected organs do not have sufficient time to recover. Studies of MDMA use, for example, show that relatively small repeated doses result in disproportionately large increases of MDMA in blood plasma. Cocaine is the substance that induces the highest rate of repetitive consumption as a result of mood change. Heroin and alcohol come in second and

third. Also, the tendency of a user to take a "booster" dose prematurely is greater with substances that require an hour or more to provide the full psychological effect—during the interim the user often assumes that the original dose was not sufficiently potent. This phenomenon routinely occurs with dextromethorphan (found in cough medicines), GHB and MDMA.

Overdose quantities that are based on acute toxicity also do not take into account the probability that an individual will become addicted. This probability can be cast as a drug's capture ratio: Of the people who sample a particular substance, what portion will become physiologically or psychologically dependent on the drug for some period of time? Heroin and methamphetamine are the most addictive by this measure. Cocaine, pentobarbital (a fast-acting sedative), nicotine and alcohol are next, followed by marijuana and possibly caffeine. Some hallucinogens—notably LSD, mescaline and psilocybin—have little or no potential for creating dependence.

Finally, a comparison of overdose fatalities does not take into account cognitive impairments and risky or aggressive behaviors that sometimes follow drug use. And as most people are well aware, a substantial proportion of violent confrontations, rapes, suicides, automobile accidents and AIDS-related illnesses are linked to alcohol intoxication.

Despite the health risks and social costs, consciousness-altering chemicals have been used for centuries in almost all cultures. So it would be unrealistic to expect that all types of recreational drug use will suddenly cease. Self-management of these substances is extremely difficult, yet modern Western societies have not, in general, developed positive, socially sanctioned rituals as a means of regulating the use of some of the less hazardous recreational drugs. I would argue that we need to do that. The science of toxicology may provide one step in that direction, by helping to teach members of our society what a lot of tribal people already know.

ROBERT S. GABLE is an emeritus professor of psychology at Claremont Graduate University. He receipted both a doctorate in education from Harvard and a doctorate in experimental psychology from Brandeis in 1964. Much of his professional work has centered on developing behavioral therapy for juvenile delinquents, including remote radio-frequency monitoring of physiological responses. Address: Department of Psychology, Claremont Graduate University, 150 E. 10th St., Claremont, CA 91711. Internet: **Robert.Gable@cgu.edu**

Stress and Drug Abuse

The Brain Connection

You are about to take a test. The coach is announcing who made the team. Your best friend is mad at you. Most people find such situations stressful. *Stress* can be defined as an emotional or physical demand or strain (a "stressor") that causes your body to release powerful neurochemicals and hormones. These changes help your body gear up to respond to the stressor. Your blood-sugar levels and blood pressure rise; your heart beats faster; your muscles tense.

There are different levels of stress: *Short-term stress* can cause uncomfortable physical reactions, but can also help you to focus. *Long-term stress*—such as stress caused by illness, divorce, or the death of a loved one—can lead to serious health problems. Traumatic events—such as natural disasters, violence, and terrorism—can cause *post-traumatic stress disorder* (PTSD), a serious illness.

Brain research now indicates that people exposed to stress are more likely to abuse alcohol or other drugs, or to relapse to drug addiction.

Read on to get important facts about this connection.

How Your Body Responds to Stress

Your body's central nervous, endocrine, immune, and cardiovascular systems are involved in responding to stress.

The physical responses can vary: Short-term responses can cause a racing heart, sweaty palms, and a pounding head. Long-term responses can cause back pain, high blood pressure, sleeplessness, and an inability to make decisions. Constant stress floods the body with stress hormones, which can increase the risk of serious health problems.

The hormone that initiates the body's response to stress, CRF, is found throughout the brain. Drugs of abuse also stimulate release of CRF.

Managing Stress

Anyone can learn to manage stress, but it does take practice. Here are some practical tips:

- **Take care of yourself** Healthy foods, exercise, and enough sleep really do make you feel better and better able to cope!

Myth vs. Reality

Myth 1: Drug abuse is harmful, but it does relieve stress.
Reality: Some drugs of abuse affect your brain the same way stress does. Long-term abuse of drugs makes users more sensitive to everyday stress than non-users.

Myth 2: All stress is bad for you.
Reality: Stress can help you deal with tough situations. It can also be associated with positive changes, such as a new job. However, long-term stress can lead to physical and emotional health problems.

Myth 3: Everyone deals with stress in the same way.
Reality: People deal with stress in different ways. How you deal with stress determines how it affects your body.

The Stress Hormone Cycle and Drugs

Under stress, the brain releases CRF, a hormone, into the bloodstream. Some drugs of abuse also stimulate the release of CRF. Through blood vessels, CRF travels to the pituitary gland.

Here CRF causes the release of ACTH, another hormone. ACTH travels to the adrenal glands and triggers the release of still more hormones, the most important of which is cortisol.

Cortisol helps you cope with stress. If stress is mild, cortisol prevents further release of CRF and ACTH. If stress is intense, the cycle continues.

- **Focus** To keep from feeling overwhelmed, concentrate on challenges one at a time.
- **Keep calm** Step away from an argument or confrontation by taking a deep breath. Go for a walk or do some other physical activity.

Latest Research

NIDA researchers have found the following connections between stress and drug abuse;

- Stress can cause changes in the brain like those caused by addictive drugs. This suggests that some people who experience stress may be more vulnerable to drug addiction or drug relapse.
- Those who become addicted to drugs may already be hypersensitive to stress.
- Long-term potentiation (LTP) is a key brain mechanism involved in memory and learning. Researchers have shown that LTP is involved in how both drug exposure and stress affect the brain.
- Stress can put people at risk for substance abuse.
- Scientists have uncovered a rise in substance abuse among people in New York City neighborhoods affected by 9/11, which raises new questions about the public health effects of traumatic events such as disasters.

For more information, visit: www.scholastic.com/headsup and http://teens.drugabuse.gov.

Stressing Out?

Read what some teens have said causes them stress:

Being Successful:

"Between my job, homework, responsibilities at home, and studying for my SATs, it's easy to feel stressed out and overwhelmed."

—*Female, Los Angeles*

Being "Perfect":

"Having struggled with eating disorders for many years, I finally realize that I make comparisons and let the appearance/discussions of my peers sometimes alter my own body image."

—*Female, Chicago*

Physical Appearance:

"Television and movies influence the physical appearance and style of most teens … the most important influence comes from the opposite sex."

Male, Los Angeles

- **Move on** If you don't achieve something you were trying for, practice and prepare for the next time. Or check out some other activity.
- **Talk about it** Talking to an understanding listener who remains calm can be very helpful.

From scholastic and the scientists of the National Institute on Drug Abuse, National Institutes of Health, U.S. Department of Health and Human Services.

"We all must develop healthy ways to manage stress, and avoid turning to drugs or other substances to escape stressful realities."

Nora D. Volkow, M.D., Director,
National Institute on Drug Abuses

Does Cannabis Cause Psychosis or Schizophrenia?

There is no shortage of studies on cannabis and its links with psychosis and schizophrenia. While most agree there is a link, causality is not clear-cut. Here we examine recent studies and invite two UK experts to comment on their findings.

Dutch Studies
Cannabis Linked to Early Onset of Schizophrenia

This Dutch study speculates that cannabis use brings on schizophrenic episodes at an earlier age. They looked at schizophrenia in 133 patients in The Hague. Following assessment and interviews they found that those who smoked cannabis encountered schizophrenic episodes on average 6.9 years earlier than non-users.

They looked at three milestones in the early development of schizophrenia: 1) first social and/or occupational dysfunction; 2) first psychotic episode and 3) first negative symptoms.

Male patients were significantly younger than female patients at first social and/or occupational dysfunction, first psychotic episode and first negative symptoms. Cannabis-using patients were significantly younger at these milestones than were patients who did not use cannabis.

They conclude that there is a strong association between use of cannabis and earlier age at first psychotic episode in male schizophrenia patients.[1]

Cannabis and Psychosis Reciprocally Linked

Cannabis use and psychosis are shown to be inextricably linked with one preceding the other and vise versa. This Dutch study followed 1,580 young people (4 to 16-year-olds) for 14 years.

They found that people who initially did not have psychotic symptoms were more likely to develop them if they started using cannabis. Similarly, they found that those who did not take cannabis but later developed psychotic symptoms were more likely to subsequently take cannabis—suggesting cannabis is used to self-medicate.

The results imply either a common vulnerability with cannabis and psychosis or a two-way causal relationship between the two.[2]

New Zealand Study
Cannabis Almost Doubles Risk of Psychosis

New Zealand research forms much of present-day thinking on cannabis and psychosis. This one goes that step further by concluding that not only does heavy cannabis cause psychosis, but that this is one-way and not down to confounding factors.

The study is impressive, using a 25-year longitudinal study of 1,265 children. Using the usual regression analysis, they found that daily cannabis users are 1.6 to 1.8 times more likely to develop psychotic symptoms.

They suggest that these associations reflected the effects of cannabis use on symptom levels rather than the effects of symptom levels on cannabis use. In other words, cannabis is the trigger for psychosis, and not, as other studies suggest, psychosis the trigger for people to start using cannabis.[3]

Statistical Reviews
Increase in Cannabis Use Not Matched by Increase in Psychosis

This study refutes a causal link between cannabis use and psychosis on the grounds that recent increase in cannabis use are not matched by increases in the number of people developing cannabis psychosis.

Newcombe asserts that for a causal link to exist, trends in cannabis use and cannabis psychosis should be positively correlated.

The annual rate of cannabis psychosis among English cannabis users is typically one in 10,000. However, although recent cannabis use (used in past year) climbed from 2.55 million in 1994 to 3.36 million in 2002/03, there are no clear trends in either schizophrenia. (36,000–38,500 cases annually) or cannabis psychosis cases (280–380).

Interestingly, when incidences of acute cannabis intoxication and harmful cannabis use are taken into account, there does seem to be a correlation.

The study concludes therefore that there is not support for the claim that cannabis use can cause psychosis, nor for a 'true' cannabis psychosis. Instead, cannabis psychosis cases are arguable misdiagnoses of extreme cases of acute cannabis intoxication and harmful cannabis use, and/or mental and behavioral disorders arising from other/multiple drug use.[4]

Review Confirms Link but Not Causation

This extensive review of success studies concludes that almost all research shows that frequent use of cannabis increases the risk of subsequent psychotic symptoms. According to their figures regular cannabis use doubles the relative risk for later schizophrenia. They speculate that if cannabis use were eradicated the incidence of schizophrenia would fall by approximately 8%, assuming of course a causal relationship.

Though importantly, they rule out direct causality by saying *"cannabis use appears to be neither a sufficient nor a necessary cause for psychosis. It is a component cause, part of a complex constellation of factors lead to psychosis."*

The authors call for the identification of "vulnerable youths" and efforts to discourage use among this group.[5]

US study on general health
Age of Onset Predicts Physical and Mental Health Problems

This US study predicts that the younger you are when you start using cannabis the more likely you are to develop physical and mental health problems and other "unhealthy" behaviors such as using other drugs.

However, once frequency of recent marijuana use was included in the calculations, age of initiation was only associated with other illicit drug use.

This is another longitudinal study starting in 1984 with 2,079 school-age children from various ethnical groups, such as white, African-American, Hispanic, Asian and others.[6]

Notes

1. Veen N, Selten SP, van der Tweel I, Feller WG, Hock HW & Kahn RS (2004) Cannabis use and age at onset of Schizophrenia. *American Journal of Psychiatry* 161 501–506.

2. Ferdinand RF, Sondeikjer F, van der Ende J, Selten J-P, Huizink A & Verhulst FC (2005) Cannabis use predicts future psychotic symptoms, and vice versa. *Addiction* 100 (5) 612–618.

3. Fergusson DM, Horwood LJ & Ridder EM (2005) Tests of casual linkages between cannabis use and psychotic symptoms. *Addiction* 100 (3) 354–366.

4. RD Newcombe (2004) Does cannabis use cause psychosis? A study of trends in cannabis use and psychosis in England, 1995–2003. *Adiktologie* 4 (4) 492–507.

5. Arsenealut L, Cannon M, Witton J & Murray RM (2004) Causal association between cannabis and psychosis: examination of the evidence. British Journal of Psychiatry 104 (2) 110–117.

6. Ellickson PI, D'Anico EJ, Collins R & Klein DJ (2005) Marijuana use and later problems when frequency of recent use explains age of initiation effects (and when it does not). *Substance Use & Misuse* 40 (3) 343–359.

UNIT 3

The Major Drugs of Use and Abuse

Unit Selections

19. **Methamphetamine Abuse,** Teena McGuinness
20. **Mexico Drug Cartels Reap Big Profits from Meth,** Laurence Iliff
21. **The Taliban's Opium War,** Jon Lee Anderson
22. **The Opposite Result,** Karen DeYoung
23. **The Teen Drinking Dilemma,** Barbara Kantrowitz and Anne Underwood
24. **An Update on the Effects of Marijuana and Its Potential Medical Use,** Sherwood O. Cole

Key Points to Consider

- Why is it that some drugs have remained popular throughout history while others have not?

- How does the manner in which a drug is consumed change or influence the effects on the user?

- What influences help perpetuate the problem of binge drinking on college campuses?

- In what ways do the United States and its allies intend to disrupt heroin production in Afghanistan and Colombia?

- What are the distinct features associated with the spread of methamphetamine use across the United States?

Student Web Site
www.mhcls.com/online

Internet References
Further information regarding these websites may be found in this book's preface or online.

National Institute on Drug Abuse
www.drugabuse.gov
Office of Applied Studies
www.oas.samhsa.gov
QuitNet
http://www.quitnet.org
The American Journal of Psychiatry
http://ajp.psychiatryonline.org/cgi/content/abstract/155/8/1016

Mikael Karlsson

The following articles discuss those drugs that have evolved historically to become the most popular drugs of choice. Although pharmacological modifications emerge periodically to enhance or alter the effects produced by certain drugs or the manner in which various drugs are used, basic pharmacological properties of the drugs remain unchanged. Crack is still cocaine, ice is still methamphetamine, and black tar is still heroin. In addition, tobacco products all supply the drug nicotine, coffee and a plethora of energy drinks provide caffeine, and alcoholic beverages provide the drug ethyl alcohol. These drugs all influence how we act, think, and feel about ourselves and the world around us. They also produce markedly different effects within the body and within the mind.

To understand why certain drugs remain popular over time, and why new drugs become popular, one must be knowledgeable about the effects produced by individual drugs. Why people use drugs is a bigger question than why people use tobacco. However, understanding why certain people use tobacco, or cocaine, or marijuana, or alcohol is one way to construct a framework from which to tackle the larger question of why people use drugs in general. One of the most complex relationships is the one between Americans and their use of alcohol. More than 76 million Americans have experienced alcoholism in their families.

The most recent surveys of alcohol use estimate that 125 million Americans currently use alcohol. The use of alcohol is a powerful influence that serves to shape our national consciousness about drugs. The relationship between the use of alcohol and the use of tobacco, and the use of alcohol and illicit drugs provide long-standing statistical relationships. The majority of Americans, however, believe that alcohol is used responsibly by most people who use it, even though approximately 10 percent of users are believed to be suffering from various stages of alcoholism.

Understanding why people initially turn to the non-medical use of drugs is a huge question that is debated and discussed in a voluminous body of literature. One important reason why the major drugs of use and abuse, such as alcohol, nicotine, cocaine, heroin, marijuana, amphetamines, and a variety of prescription, designer, over-the-counter, and herbal drugs retain their popularity is because they produce certain physical and psychological effects that humans crave. They temporarily restrain our inhibitions; reduce our fears; alleviate mental and physical suffering; produce energy, confidence, and exhilaration; and allow us to relax. Tired, take a pill; have a headache, take a pill; need to lose weight, take a pill; need to increase athletic performance, the options seem almost limitless. There is a drug for everything. Some drugs even, albeit artificially, suggest a greater capacity to transcend, redefine, and seek out new levels of consciousness. And they do it upon demand. People initially use a specific drug, or class of drugs, to obtain the desirable effects historically associated with the use of that drug. Heroin and opiate-related drugs such as Oxycontin and Vicodin produce, in most people, a euphoric, dreamy state of well-being. The abuse of these prescription painkillers is one of the fastest growing (and alarming) drug trends. Methamphetamine and related stimulant drugs produce euphoria, energy, confidence, and exhilaration. Alcohol produces a loss of inhibitions and a state of well-being. Nicotine and marijuana typically serve as relaxants. Ecstasy and other "club drugs" produce stimulant as well as relaxant effects. Various over-the-counter and herbal drugs all attempt to replicate the effects of more potent and often prohibited or prescribed drugs. Although effects and side effects may vary from user to user, a general pattern of effects is predictable from most major drugs of use and their analogs. Varying the dosage and altering the manner of ingestion is one way to alter the drug's effects. Some drugs, such as LSD and certain types of designer drugs, produce effects on the user that are less predictable and more sensitive to variations in dosage level and to the user's physical and psychological makeup.

Although all major drugs of use and abuse have specific reinforcing properties perpetuating their continued use, they also produce undesirable side effects that regular drug users attempt to mitigate. Most often, users attempt to mitigate these effects with the use of other drugs. Cocaine, methamphetamine, heroin, and alcohol have long been used to mitigate each other's side effects. A good example is the classic "speedball" of heroin and cocaine. When they are combined, cocaine accelerates and intensifies the euphoric state of the heroin, while the heroin softens the comedown from cocaine.

Additionally, other powerful influences on drug taking such as advertising for alcohol, tobacco, and certain prescription drugs, significantly impact the public's drug related consciousness. The alcohol industry, for example, dissects numerous layers of society to specifically market alcoholic beverages to subpopulations of Americans, including youth. The same influences exist with tobacco advertising. What is the message in Philip Morris's advertisements about its attempts to mitigate smoking by youth? Approximately 500 thousand Americans die each year from tobacco related illness. Add to the mix advertising by prescription drug companies for innumerable human maladies and one soon realizes the enormity of the association between business and drug taking. Subsequently, any discussion of major drugs could begin and end with alcohol, tobacco, and prescription drugs.

Methamphetamine Abuse

Meth, speed, crank, biker dope, hillbilly crack: no matter what users call it, there's no question that methamphetamine is a powerful and dangerous drug.

TEENA MCGUINNESS

Rodney Sterling, a 34-year-old white man, was brought by emergency medical services to the ED of a rural community hospital. (This case is a composite based on the author's experience.) Upon arrival, his pupils were dilated and his temperature was 103.2°F. Mr. Sterling's heart rate was 160 beats per minute; his blood pressure was 180/120 mmHg. He vomited and shortly thereafter had a generalized clonic–tonic seizure. The physician injected pancuronium (Pavulon), a neuromuscular blocking agent, and inserted an endotracheal tube. Although the seizure then subsided, Mr. Sterling's high blood pressure persisted. A nurse administered metoprolol (Toprol and others) 5 mg IV, but the blood pressure continued to increase. Mr. Sterling was transferred by helicopter to a university medical center.

During the flight, he remained hypertensive and tachycardic. Cardiac monitoring showed ST depression, indicating possible myocardial ischemia. Tachycardia, hypertension, and hyperthermia persisted after arrival at the medical center's ED. Initial electrocardiography showed ST elevation in all of the anterior leads. Intravenous nitroglycerin (Nitro-Bid IV, Tridil) was given, but the hypertension worsened and within a few minutes, Mr. Sterling went into cardiac arrest. Despite vigorous cardiopulmonary resuscitation, he died. Toxicology results showed that he had taken methamphetamine.

Mr. Sterling's altered vital signs illustrate methamphetamine's effects on the sympathetic nervous system. Amphetamines, a drug class that includes methamphetamine, stimulate the release of endogenous catecholamines, particularly norepinephrine and dopamine.[1] The initial signs of abuse reflect an overstimulated sympathetic nervous system (hypertension, agitation, and tachycardia). Severe consequences can include myocardial infarction, rhabdomyolysis, liver damage, and acute renal failure.[1, 2] A methamphetamine-associated hypertensive crisis ultimately results in significant organ damage.[3]

Two serious errors occurred during the course of Mr. Sterling's care. The first was the assumption that the neuromuscular blocking agent had stopped the seizure. Pancuronium, a muscle relaxant, blocked the outward signs of seizure and, in this case, permitted intubation. It also paralyzed the muscles of respira-tion and the diaphragm but did not lessen the brain's need for oxygen, which is increased by methamphetamine. As a result, hypoxia rapidly developed. It would have been more appropriate to use a benzodiazepine, such as diazepam (Valium and others), to control the seizure and aid in intubation.[4]

The second error involved the use of metoprolol, a β-blocker. Central nervous system (CNS) stimulants like methamphetamine cause hypertension by stimulating both α- and β-adrenergic receptors. Metoprolol prevented β-adrenergic receptors from stimulating vasodilation in the peripheral vascular system, but the increased vasoconstriction induced by the α-adrenergic receptor stimulation continued unopposed, worsening the hypertension. Abuse of stimulants, such as cocaine and amphetamines, is a common cause of hypertensive crises.

Like cocaine, methamphetamine is a powerful CNS stimulant. The drug produces euphoria and increases alertness while reducing fatigue and appetite. Methamphetamine is less expensive than cocaine and has become widely available in recent years with the advent of "superlabs" in Mexico and the American Southwest that may produce as much as 10 lbs. of methamphetamine in each manufacturing cycle.[5] Methamphetamine has a 12-hour half-life, compared with 90 minutes for cocaine.[6] In short, methamphetamine offers a relatively cheap and prolonged "high." The drug can be manufactured in an impure powdered form (often known as *speed* or *crank*) that can be injected, snorted, or pressed into pills taken orally.[7] It can also be dissolved and injected intravenously or rectally with a syringe without a needle. Higher quality methamphetamine (nicknamed *ice* or *crystal* because of its crystalline appearance) has had most of its impurities removed and yields a longer-lasting effect. This form can be smoked in glass pipes and other devices or injected.[8]

Consequences

Methamphetamine users may fit no particular profile. Some abusers begin in their teens, and younger users constitute a greater proportion of methamphetamine treatment admissions.[9] However, according to the U.S. Substance Abuse and Mental

A Short History of Methamphetamine

Amphetamine was first synthesized in 1887, and experimental medical use began in the 1920s. In 1932, Smith, Kline, and French first marketed the Benzedrine (racemic amphetamine) inhaler, and by the late 1930s, amphetamine became available in tablet form. In 1940 Burroughs Wellcome marketed methamphetamine, a related compound, under the trade name Methedrine. In 1943 the U.S. Food and Drug Administration (FDA) approved desoxyephedrine (Desoxyn), a pharmaceutical form of methamphetamine hydrochloride manufactured by Abbott Laboratories, for the treatment of narcolepsy, mild depression, postencephalitic Parkinson syndrome, chronic alcoholism, cerebral arteriosclerosis, and hay fever.[1] The next year, approval was given to Endo Products to manufacture Hydrin, another desoxyephedrine compound, for similar indications as well as for the treatment of obesity. However, this use was still considered controversial. It would be three more years before the FDA approved Desoxyn and Hydrin "as adjuncts to the dietary management of obesity." By 1960 five more amphetamine-derived anorectic drugs had entered the marketplace for the treatment of obesity.

These stimulants were used and abused by people in many walks of life, including truck drivers, students, housewives, and entertainers. Around 1950 Pan American World Airways was giving away Benzedrine inhalers—along with more innocuous items such as toothbrushes, chewing gum, and tissues—to help ease passengers' nasal discomfort. (To see an image of a flight menu offering "Beverages and Diversions," including Benzedrine, go to http://wings.buffalo.edu/aru/preprohibition.htm.)

During World War II, soldiers and pilots on both sides used amphetamine to enhance endurance and alertness and ward off fatigue. The U.S. military continues to dispense amphetamines today. In a 2002 "friendly fire" incident in Afghanistan, for example, four Canadian soldiers were killed and eight more wounded by U.S. pilots who bombed them; U.S. military lawyers argued in the pilots' defense that their use of amphetamines, sanctioned by the Air Force, had affected the pilots' judgment.[2]

By the 1960s, amphetamines were available only by prescription but were widely used and abused recreationally.

In 1971 all forms of amphetamine and methamphetamine were classified as Drug Enforcement Agency Schedule II drugs (those that carry a high potential for abuse but are considered to have some medical uses).

Home manufacture. In recent years, the dozens of recipes available online for methamphetamine have stimulated its manufacture. These recipes call for easy-to-obtain ingredients: drain cleaner, over-the-counter medications that contain pseudoephedrine, fertilizer, and starter fluid. Four federal regulations enacted between 1989 and 1996 have restricted access to the chemicals needed to manufacture the drug.[3] Most of these efforts have focused on ephedrine and pseudoephedrine, the main ingredients in home manufacture. The 1996 Methamphetamine Control Act tightened controls on the drug's ingredients and imposed stiffer penalties for its possession, distribution, and manufacture. The Combat Methamphetamine Epidemic Act of 2005 required nonprescription products containing pseudoephedrine to be placed behind store counters.[4] Purchasers of these products may buy only in limited amounts and must show identification and sign a logbook, but Internet sale of these products bypass the law. Profit margins for manufacturing methamphetamine can be high, returning as much as $1,000 in sales for about $100 worth of materials.[5] —*James M. Stubenrauch, senior editor, and Teena McGuinness, PhD, APRN,BC*

References

1. Colman E. Anorectics on trial: a half century of federal regulation of prescription appetite suppressants. *Ann Intern Med* 2005;143(5): 380–5.
2. Halbfinger D. Threats and responses: military; hearing starts in bombing error that killed 4. *The New York Times* 2003 Jan 15.
3. Cunningham JK, Liu LM. Impacts of federal precursor chemical regulations on methamphetamine arrests. *Addiction* 2005;100(4):479–88.
4. Mitka M. Methamphetamine bill. *JAMA* 2006;295(18):2130.
5. Chamberlain J, et al. Methamphetamine: tools and partnerships to fight the threat. *J Law Med Ethics* 2004;32(4 Suppl):104–5.

Health Services Administration, the mean age at admission increased from 28.7 years in 1993 to 30.6 years in 2003. Fifty-five percent of patients admitted for primary methamphetamine or amphetamine treatment in 2003 were male; this figure was 53% in 1993. During the same period, the proportion who were white decreased from 83% to 73% while the proportion who were Latino increased from 9% to 16%, with the biggest increase being seen among people of Mexican origin or ancestry (rising from 7% in 1993 to more than 12% in 2003). In both years, blacks represented 3% of those admitted for methamphetamine or amphetamine treatment.[10]

Women who use methamphetamine are relatively understudied. According to one study of current female users, their reasons for using the drug—aside from "getting high"—were to get more energy, lose weight, feel more attractive, and cope with their moods.[11] Though few said they used the drug to enhance sexual pleasure, its use was associated with frequent high-risk sexual behavior, as well as with a variety of medical and social problems.

Much more extensively studied is the connection between methamphetamine use and high-risk sexual behavior among homosexual men. Primary motivations for its use in this population

How Big Is the Meth Problem?

No matter what users call it, there is no question that methamphetamine is a powerful drug. But it has been difficult to sift good information about all aspects of the drug and its manufacture from the exaggerated accounts that have appeared in government reports and the popular press. According to Ryan S. King, author of *The Next Big Thing? Methamphetamine in the United States,* a report issued by the Sentencing Project (a nonprofit organization "engaged in research and advocacy on criminal justice policy issues"), "Mischaracterizing the impact of methamphetamine by exaggerating its prevalence and consequences while downplaying its receptivity to treatment succeeds neither as a tool of prevention nor a vehicle of education."[1] The report provides reliable information on trends in methamphetamine use and treatment and also critiques the idea often put forth in the media that methamphetamine abuse is "epidemic" in scope. Here are some highlights of the report. (To see the report, go to http://sentencingproject.org/pdfs/ methamphetamine_report.pdf.)

Prevalence. Reports that frame the methamphetamine problem as an "epidemic" frequently emphasize the lifetime prevalence rate, but as King points out, this is not a precise measure of how many are currently using the drug.[1] In 2004 only about 0.2% of Americans older than 12 years—roughly 583,000 people—were "regular users" of methamphetamine (meaning they had used it at least once in the past month), putting methamphetamine use on a par with crack cocaine use and among the least commonly used illegal drugs. By comparison, four times as many Americans used cocaine, 30 times as many used marijuana, and 90 times as many reported binge drinking in the previous month. In 2004, 1.4 million Americans had used the drug in the previous year, but this number (and 1.3 million) has been cited as the number of regular users and even as the number of those addicted to the drug. The Substance Abuse and Mental Health Services Administration began systematically collecting data on methamphetamine use in 1999, and it seems safe to say that since then, monthly use rates have remained fairly steady at approximately 0.2% to 0.3% of the total population.

Since 2002 the number of "new initiates"—those who used the drug for the first time during the preceding year—has hovered around 300,000 per year.[1] This rate is double that in the mid-1990s but is lower than that extending from the mid-1970s through the early 1980s. In 1975 there were 400,000 new methamphetamine users.

While the lifetime prevalence rate of U.S. methamphetamine use nearly doubled (to 9.4 million) from 1994 to 1999 and had grown to 12 million by 2004, as a percentage of the total population, this rate *decreased* between 2002 (5.3%) and 2005 (4.3%).[2]

Regional variations. King reports that, nationally, "5% of adult male arrestees tested positive for methamphetamine, compared with 30% for cocaine and 44% for marijuana."[1] But "in some west coast cities—Los Angeles, Portland (OR), San Diego, San Jose—positive responses for methamphetamine use among arrestees" was between 25% and 37%. Also, "in those cities, the *overall* rate of drug use did not rise between 1998 and 2003, suggesting that the increased use of methamphetamine *replaced* other drugs, particularly cocaine."

Treatment. "Studies in 15 states have demonstrated significant effects of treatment in the areas of abstention, reduced arrests, employment, and other measures. Methamphetamine abuse has generally been shown to be as receptive to treatment as other addictive drugs."[1]

Many have expressed concern over the rate of admissions to treatment programs for methamphetamine abuse—data show that among the population age 12 years or older, admissions increased from 13 per 100,000 in 1993 to 56 per 100,000 in 2003[3]—but such measures often reflect factors other than the prevalence of drug use. King cites changes in the criminal justice system, such as the expansion of drug courts and new alternative sentencing programs, as heavy influences on the number of people being referred for treatment.[1] Treatment for methamphetamine abuse remains a small percentage (6.3% in 2003) of treatment admissions for substance abuse.

Likewise, data on ED admissions may not be very reliable indicators of the prevalence of drug use.[1] In the past, the Drug Abuse Warning Network (DAWN) of the Substance Abuse and Mental Health Administration has collected "mentions" of illicit drugs in ED admissions without specifying whether the drug's use was the primary reason for the ED visit. The latest DAWN report, for 2004, uses a redesigned sample of hospitals and states that the new data shouldn't be compared with data from previous years but should be considered a new baseline for future comparisons. According to that report, of the estimated 106 million ED visits in the United States in 2004, about 1% were related to drug misuse or abuse. (The report can be found online at http://dawninfo.samhsa.gov/files/DAWN2k4ED. pdf. For more press coverage of methamphetamine, see the series of articles by Jack Shafer online at *Slate* [www.slate. com].)—*James M. Stubenrauch, senior editor, and Teena McGuinness, PhD, APRN,BC*

References

1. King R. *The next big thing? Methamphetamine in the United States.* The Sentencing Project. 2006. http://sentencingproject.org/pdfs/methamphetamine_report.pdf.

2. Substance Abuse and Mental Health Services Administration. Table H.2: types of illicit drug use in lifetime, past year, and past month among persons aged 12 or older: percentages, 2002–2004. In: *Results from the 2004 National Survey on Drug Use and Health: national findings.* Rockville, MD: U.S. Department of Health and Human Services; 2005. p. 233.

3. Substance Abuse and Mental Health Services Administration. Trends in methamphetamine/amphetamine admissions to treatment: 1993–2003. DASIS Report 2006(9). http:// drugabusestatistics.samhsa.gov/2k6/ methTx/methTX.htm.

include the enhancement of sexual performance and pleasure, and the drug is often used in environments where the focus is on sexual contact, such as sex clubs and "circuit" parties.[12] Its use is also associated with the use of other drugs, which can lead to impaired judgment and riskier sexual behaviors, such as engaging in unprotected sex with partners of unknown HIV status.[13] Use of the drug is also associated with decreased use of condoms and increased rates of sexually transmitted infections, including HIV.[14]

Psychiatric symptoms resulting from methamphetamine use can include paranoia, auditory and visual hallucination, compulsive behavior, labile mood, rage, and depression.[9,15] These symptoms result from neuronal damage caused by inadequate perfusion in and ischemic lesions of the brain. In addition, methamphetamine affects behavior by influencing the monoamine neurotransmitters dopamine, norepinephrine, and serotonin, which affect appetite, alertness, and mood. Methamphetamine blocks their reuptake from the synaptic cleft and inhibits their breakdown[16]; the resultant euphoria lasts for 12 to 14 hours.

Methamphetamine may change the structure of gray matter in the brain[17] and affect the metabolism of the corpus striatum, which is responsible for sensorimotor functions, cognitive control of movement sequences, and motor aspects of emotion.[18] Methamphetamine also morphologically changes the corpus callosum, which connects the right and left hemispheres of the brain.[19] These changes are particularly apparent in the frontal and parietal cortices, areas of the brain associated with judgment and cognitive functioning. It's not yet clear whether the psychiatric effects of methamphetamine use are reversible with time. Several clinical trials are under way to determine whether drug therapy is helpful.[20–22]

Skin manifestations of methamphetamine toxicity may look like scabies; however, the lesions don't get better, despite treatment.[25] Picking at the skin causes polymicrobial infections, which are slow to resolve because of repeated scratching. Antibiotics are often indicated.

Drug-endangered children. Shortly after Mr. Sterling died, a 30-year-old pregnant woman named Stephanie Quill was admitted with psychosis and hypertension. (This case is also a composite.) Belligerent and paranoid, she reported that although her contractions had begun a short time before, her due date was still weeks away. Ms. Quill appeared cachectic and looked much older than 30. During admission, she picked at deep excoriations on her chest. Shortly thereafter, Ms. Quill delivered a boy who appeared small for his gestational age. The infant was quickly transferred to the neonatal ICU.

Infants exposed in utero to methamphetamine are likely to be smaller for their gestational age and born earlier than those not exposed.[23] Other perinatal complications include small head circumference, cerebral infarction, cardiac defect, cleft palate, and biliary atresia. The children of methamphetamine users may

also be exposed to the drug environmentally. Children exposed to methamphetamine manufacture—who have been called "drug-endangered children"[24]—are subjected to both exposure to chemical toxins created by the manufacture of methamphetamine and parental abuse and neglect.

Implications for Nurses

Recognize the symptoms of methamphetamine toxicity. The treatment of methamphetamine toxicity is based on the symptoms. Hypertension, can be treated with benzodiazepines.[1] For severe and difficult to control hypertension, nitroglycerin or nitroprusside (Nitropress) may be required in a critical care setting. The use of β-blockers must be avoided to prevent unopposed α-adrenergic receptor activity from producing dramatic and dangerous hypertension. In addition, the patient's temperature must be carefully monitored because CNS agitation, combined with vasoconstriction, can compromise the ability to moderate core temperature and ultimately induce hyperthermia, rhabdomyolysis, and death. Treatment involves continuously monitoring core temperature and employing evaporative cooling methods, beginning with spraying the undressed patient with cool water while directing a large fan toward him.[2] Ice baths are also used.

If patients have not ingested methamphetamine but have recently been exposed to its manufacture, they should change clothes and be bathed. Solvents such as xylene, acetone, trichloroethane, and toluene have been documented in methamphetamine-related incidents; a history of materials found at the site should be taken by either law enforcement officers or child welfare authorities. Red phosphorus, iodine, and sodium metal—also used in methamphetamine manufacturing—may cause the lungs, liver, or kidneys to fail. A complete blood count and renal- and liver-function tests should be performed.[26] Even if a patient shows no signs or symptoms of toxicity, a urine methamphetamine assay should be performed within 24 hours. The Minnesota Department of Health has devised protocols to be applied to children exposed to methamphetamine. To view one example, created for Benton County, Minnesota, go to www. health.state.mn.us/divs/eh/meth/ordinance/bentonchild.pdf.

Consider the needs of children exposed to methamphetamine. Considerable risks are associated with prenatal methamphetamine exposure, including abruptio placentae, intraventricular hemorrhage, and intrauterine growth retardation.[23] Prenatal exposure is also associated with premature birth, low birth weight, small subcortical volumes, and cognitive deficits.[27]

If a government agency is assuming custody of a child who is less than three years of age, referral to early intervention services is appropriate. Young children in foster care are said to have "multiple vulnerabilities and complex service needs,"[28] and those exposed to methamphetamine are at great risk for developmental delay because of neglect and abuse. Don't count on child welfare authorities to make a referral to early intervention. Their priorities are safety, not development. Know what organization is responsible for early intervention in your state and make the referral.

Become a "fetal advocate." Emphasize to women that drug and alcohol use are unsafe during any trimester. If a woman's urine is positive on drug screening for methamphetamine, review for her the changes associated with prenatal exposure: small size for gestational age, reduced head circumference, and learning difficulties such as delays in math and language. Become knowledgeable about treatment options in your locale, listen supportively, and then refer the woman to an appropriate facility.

In patients with symptoms of psychosis, consider a diagnosis of methamphetamine abuse. Take a careful history of patients exhibiting signs of psychosis, noting any substance abuse. Methamphetamine abusers exhibit abnormalities in metabolic activity, emotional processing, and short-term memory.[29] Methamphetamine-induced changes to the structure of the brain can alter cognitive skills and produce psychosis, both sudden and enduring.[30] Methamphetamine's physiologic effects may also affect the physical symptoms of concomitant disorders. During the acute phase of methamphetamine withdrawal (the first week), increases in the need for sleep and in appetite are seen and usually peak at about 24 hours after last methamphetamine use.[31]

If you are caring for a patient who has clearly "crashed," address the physical and mental hazards of methamphetamine use. Listen supportively, and understand that users experiencing withdrawal may be irritable and emotionally labile. If the patient using methamphetamine has children, discuss with him or her the very real possibility that child welfare authorities could gain custody of the children. Loss of child custody can be a powerful motivator for seeking treatment for addiction.

Instill hope. Suggest to methamphetamine users that despite the obstacles, recovery is possible. Refer them to methamphetamine support groups.

References

1. Del Rios M, et al. Drugs of abuse: providing the best in evidence-based care to "self-medicated" patients. *Emergency Medicine Practice* 2005;7(5):1–24.
2. White SR. Amphetamine toxicity. *Semin Respir Crit Care Med* 2002;23(1):27–36.
3. Turnipseed SD, et al. Frequency of acute coronary syndrome in patients presenting to the emergency department with chest pain after methamphetamine use. *J Emerg Med* 2003; 24(4):369–73.
4. Sirven JI, Waterhouse E. Management of status epilepticus. *Am Fam Physician* 2003;68(3):469–76.
5. Meredith CW, et al. Implications of chronic methamphetamine use: a literature review. *Harv Rev Psychiatry* 2005;13(3):141–54.
6. Cho AK, et al. Relevance of pharmacokinetic parameters in animal models of methamphetamine abuse. *Synapse* 2001; 39(2):161–6.
7. Maxwell JC. Emerging research on methamphetamine. *Curr Opin Psychiatry* 2005;18(3):235–42.
8. National Drug Intelligence Center. *National drug threat assessment* 2006. Johnstown, PA: U.S. Department of Justice; 2006 Jan. Product No. 2006-Q0317-001. http://www.dea.gov/concern/18862/18862p.pdf.
9. Cretzmeyer M, et al. Treatment of methamphetamine abuse: research findings and clinical directions. *J Subst Abuse Treat* 2003;24(3):267–77.
10. Substance Abuse and Mental Health Services Administration. Trends in methamphetamine/amphetamine admissions to treatment: 1993–2003. *DASIS Report* 2006(9). http://drugabusestatistics.samhsa.gov/2k6/methTx/methTX.htm.
11. Semple SJ, et al. Female methamphetamine users: social characteristics and sexual risk behavior. *Women Health* 2004;40(3):35–50.
12. Halkitis PN, et al. A double epidemic: crystal methamphetamine drug use in relation to HIV transmission among gay men. *J Homosex* 2001;41(2):17–35.
13. Patterson TL, et al. Methamphetamine-using HIV-positive men who have sex with men: correlates of polydrug use. *J Urban Health* 2005;82(1 Suppl 1):i120–6.
14. Barnett M. Sex, drugs and HIV. *Posit Aware* 2002;13(2):34–5.
15. Srisurapanont M, et al. Psychotic symptoms in methamphetamine psychotic in-patients. *Int J Neuropsychopharmacol* 2003;6(4):347–52.
16. Sekine Y, et al. Methamphetamine-related psychiatric symptoms and reduced brain dopamine transporters studied with PET. *Am J Psychiatry* 2001;158(8):1206–14.
17. Kim SJ, et al. Prefrontal grey-matter changes in short-term and long-term abstinent methamphetamine abusers. *Int J Neuropsychopharmacol* 2006;9(2):221–8.
18. Wang GJ, et al. Partial recovery of brain metabolism in methamphetamine abusers after protracted abstinence. *Am J Psychiatry* 2004;161(2):242–8.
19. Oh JS, et al. Shape changes of the corpus callosum in abstinent methamphetamine users. *Neurosci Lett* 2005;384(1–2):76–81.
20. Brodie JD, et al. Safety and efficacy of gamma-vinyl GABA (GVG) for the treatment of methamphetamine and/or cocaine addiction. *Synapse* 2005;55(2):122–5.
21. Hser YI, et al. Treatment outcomes among women and men methamphetamine abusers in California. *J Subst Abuse Treat* 2005;28(1):77–85.
22. Piasecki MP, et al. An exploratory study: the use of paroxetine for methamphetamine craving. *J Psychoactive Drugs* 2002;34(3):301–4.
23. Smith L, et al. Effects of prenatal methamphetamine exposure on fetal growth and drug withdrawal symptoms in infants born at term. *J Dev Behav Pediatr* 2003;24(1):17–23.
24. Altshuler SJ. Drug-endangered children need a collaborative community response. *Child Welfare* 2005;84(2):171–90.
25. Frieden J. Skin manifestations may signal crystal meth use: think "meth mites" when patients are picking at their skin and think they have insects crawling on them. *Fam Pract News* 2006;36(2):47.
26. Baer DM. Answering your questions: methamphetamine testing in children. *MLO Med Lab Obs* 2005;37(5):40–1.
27. Chang L, et al. Smaller subcortical volumes and cognitive deficits in children with prenatal methamphetamine exposure. *Psychiatry Res* 2004;132(2):95–106.

28. Vig S, et al. Young children in foster care: multiple vulnerabilities and complex service needs. *Infants Young Child* 2005;18(2):147–60.

29. London ED, et al. Cerebral metabolic dysfunction and impaired vigilance in recently abstinent methamphetamine abusers. *Biol Psychiatry* 2005;58(10):770–8.

30. Chen CK, et al. Morbid risk for psychiatric disorder among the relatives of methamphetamine users with and without psychosis. *Am J Med Genet B Neuropsychiatr Genet* 2005; 136(1):87–91.

31. McGregor C, et al. The nature, time course and severity of methamphetamine withdrawal. *Addiction* 2005;100(9): 1320–9.

TEENA MCGUINNESS *is professor of community mental health nursing, University of South Alabama College of Nursing, Mobile, AL. Contact author: teena@adoption-research.org.* Emergency *is coordinated by Polly Gerber Zimmermann, MS, MBA, RN, CEN: pollyzimmermann@ msn.com.*

Mexico Drug Cartels Reap Big Profits from Meth

Laurence Iliff

The anti-drug operation was in the works for months. And the news would be big, officials said. But when Mexican police burst into a plush home in the capital's exclusive Lomas de Chapultepec neighborhood last month, guided in part by the U.S. Drug Enforcement Administration, they were taken aback.

They found stacks and stacks of crisp U.S. $100 bills. In closets, in drawers, and suitcases. The attorney general's office arranged the bills into a huge, bed-shaped platform, with Ben Franklin beaming from a thousand eyes. The first estimate by authorities put the take at $100 million. Then the bill-counting machines came in and the figure topped $200 million. It was the biggest drug cash seizure ever.

There was another surprise. The money did not belong to one of Mexico's powerful drug cartels, nor did it represent profits from the sale of traditional drugs such as Colombian cocaine, Mexican marijuana and black-tar heroin.

Rather, authorities said, it was amassed by a naturalized Mexican from China, Zhenli Ye Gon, who is accused of using his Asian contacts to illegally import the precursor drugs to make the new star of the U.S. and Mexican drug markets: methamphetamine.

As a U.S. crackdown against meth labs and precursor chemicals has been drying up domestic production in recent years, the Mexican cartels are enthusiastically filling the void, U.S. and Mexican officials say. Moreover, officials say, meth has advantages for the cartels over even highly profitable cocaine. It is a highly addictive drug that can be made at home, smuggled easily and reap huge profit margins.

Like the nonamphetamine designer drug "cheese" that is causing deaths in the Dallas area, cheap meth distributed through existing drug channels may be the coming nightmare on both sides of the border.

In September, police in Fort Worth reported a record seizure of methamphetamine: more than 48 pounds, with a street value of $3 million. In March, a convicted methamphetamine dealer was charged with the fatal shooting of a Dallas police officer, Senior Cpl. Mark Nix.

Mexican cartels are not just supplying demand for meth, a Mexican official said, but creating it as well.

"What we are seeing is a manipulation of the drug markets," said Santiago Vasconcelos, deputy director of international and legal matters for Mexico's attorney general's office.

"It is a diabolical plan by these criminal organizations" to increase sales of homemade amphetamines as an alternative to South American cocaine, which must be grown, processed, and transported thousands of miles.

"The lesson we get from this is very painful," said Vasconcelos. "The American people have yet to wake up from the nightmare of synthetic drugs, especially the nightmare that has brought them to methamphetamines."

It costs 20 cents to make a dose of meth that garners $20, he said in an interview.

Amphetamines can be taken as a pill, smoked as "ice," snorted as "crystal," or dissolved in water like the club drug "ecstasy," or MDMA. Some of the varied forms are old, some are new, but together they threaten to create new U.S. addictions and financially strengthen the Mexican cartels and their war against each other and the government.

"Methamphetamine is something we're very concerned about, because we go back to our history in the early '80s when cocaine was not a big deal here," said Steven M. Robertson, DEA special agent for congressional and public affairs.

"Then, all of a sudden, it took off, and we were playing catch-up. DEA has learned from the cocaine flood in the '80s and we're saying, OK, (with) methamphetamine, we don't want to get to the point where they're bringing in thousand-kilo amounts," he said in an interview.

The effects in Dallas, and across the U.S., could be devastating over time. Meth addicts are infamous for their obsessive addictions and failure to care for themselves, which causes their teeth to fall out and leaves their emaciated bodies susceptible to illness. This is especially true among those who inject or smoke the drug.

In contrast, ecstasy, an amphetamine derivative taken as a pill, is best known as a "club drug" that causes hours of energy followed by lethargy.

Use of amphetamines has not exploded in the U.S., but the promise of a drop-off due to the U.S. crackdown on precursor chemicals and drug labs has not materialized—because of increased Mexican supply.

And hard-core addiction seems to be rising quickly.

The U.S. Justice Department's "National Methamphetamine Threat Assessment" found that while the total number of meth users had stayed steady from 2002 to 2004 at about 600,000, the percentage of addicts within that group had increased significantly.

The number of people admitted to programs for treatment of methamphetamine-related drug use rose from about 68,000 in 2000 to nearly 130,000 in 2004, the report said.

One reason, it suggests, is the influx of Mexican ice methamphetamine, similar in its addictive qualities to crack cocaine.

"Smoking methamphetamine may result in more rapid addiction to the drug than snorting or injection, because smoking causes a nearly instantaneous, intense, and longer-lasting high," the report said. Seizures of ice along the Southwest border rose from 260 pounds in fiscal 2003 to nearly 1,500 pounds in 2005.

U.S. and Mexican officials do not agree on Mexico's role in meth production.

A.J. Turner, section chief for the FBI's criminal investigative division, said in an interview that Mexican cartels are the source of 85 percent to 90 percent of the methamphetamine in the U.S., according to the agency's intelligence. "The supply is on the Mexican side; the demand is on the United States side," he said.

Vasconcelos said suggestions that Mexico had become the dominant supplier to the U.S. were false. While U.S. meth lab seizures number in the thousands each year, Mexico raids about 100 labs annually, he said.

He described Mexico as an "incipient" producer that is now cracking down on the illegal import of precursor chemicals, such as ephedrine and pseudoephedrine. Mexico needs about 70 tons a year of pseudoephedrine for legal drugs but has imported as much as 240 tons year. It is now getting a handle on imports, although China remains a problem, he said.

Likewise, all ephedrine and pseudoephedrine coming into Mexico—100 percent—passes through U.S. ports such as Long Beach before arriving in Mexico. Finger-pointing by U.S. officials, Vasconcelos said, only plays into the cartels' hands.

"The challenge here is to see ourselves as the community that we are; to see ourselves as neighbors," he said.

According to the U.S. government's 2007 International Narcotics Control Strategy Report, more methamphetamine labs are turning up on Mexican soil, and increasing amounts of the drug are being seized.

"Seizure statistics for cocaine and methamphetamine during 2006 demonstrate Mexico's significance as a production and transit country," the report says.

The suspect in the huge cash seizure in mid-March, Zhenli Ye Gon, was an important middleman for Mexican cartels because he was importing massive quantities of pseudoephedrine, a common cold medicine that can be easily transformed into amphetamine, Mexican authorities said.

Vasconcelos said the suspect appeared to be a legitimate businessman who found a profitable side business diverting pseudoephedrine to Mexican and U.S. meth producers. The fact that he was unable to launder the $205 million found in his home shows that Mexican bank controls are working.

Zhenli Ye Gon, the attorney general's office said, ran a pharmaceutical company, Unimed Pharm Chem de Mexico, that illegally imported more than 60 tons of pseudoephedrine, which he processed into its purest form. Authorities say he was building a 45,000-square-foot laboratory near Mexico City, which officials have now dismantled.

The suspect got the attention of U.S. and Mexican officials in a big way in December when they seized 19 tons of pseudoephedrine in the port of Lazaro Cardenas, the biggest Mexican seizure ever. The ship carrying it came from China and had passed through the port of Long Beach on its way to Mexico.

The ensuing investigation, "Operation Dragon," led officials not only to the $205 million and the laboratory under construction, but also to seven suspects and additional residences.

Zhenli Ye Gon remains a fugitive while Mexican authorities divide up the confiscated cash, one-third of which is to go toward drug treatment.

Letter from Afghanistan

The Taliban's Opium War
The Difficulties and Dangers of the Eradication Program

Jon Lee Anderson

In the main square in Tirin Kot, the capital of Uruzgan Province, in central Afghanistan, a large billboard shows a human skeleton being hanged. The rope is not a normal gallows rope but the stem of an opium poppy. Aside from this jarring image, Tirin Kot is a bucolic-seeming place, a market town of flat-topped adobe houses and little shops on a low bluff on the eastern shore of the Tirinrud River, in a long valley bounded by open desert and jagged, treeless mountains. About ten thousand people live in the town. The men are bearded and wear traditional robes and tunics and cover their heads with turbans or sequinned skullcaps. There are virtually no women in sight, and when they do appear they wear all-concealing burkas. A few paved streets join at a traffic circle in the center of town, but within a few blocks they peter out to dirt tracks.

Almost everything around Tirin Kot is some shade of brown. The river is a khaki-colored wash of silt and snowmelt that flows out of the mountain range to the north, past mud-walled family compounds. On either side of the river, however, running down the valley, there is a narrow strip of wheat fields and poppy fields, and for several weeks in the spring the poppies bloom: lovely, open-petalled white, pink, red, and magenta blossoms, the darker colors indicating the ones with the most opium.

One afternoon this spring, at the height of the harvest, I drove through the area with Douglas Wankel, a former Drug Enforcement Administration official who was hired by the United States government in 2003 to organize its counter-narcotics effort here. Wankel, who is sixty-one and has piercing blue eyes, was stationed in Kabul as a young D.E.A. official in 1978 and 1979, during the bloody unrest that led up to the Soviet invasion. "I left on a flight to New Delhi a couple of hours before the Soviets rolled in," he said. "People thought it was because I knew it was coming. I didn't; I just happened to be leaving on a trip. But the Soviets branded me a C.I.A. agent, and so I couldn't come back—until now, that is."

Working first with the D.E.A. and then with the State Department, Wankel helped create the Afghan Eradication Force, with troops of the Afghan National Police drawn from the Ministry of the Interior. Last year, an estimated four hundred thousand acres of opium poppies were planted in Afghanistan, a fifty-nine-percent increase over the previous year. Afghanistan now supplies more than ninety-two per cent of the world's opium, the raw ingredient of heroin. More than half the country's annual G.D.P., some $3.1 billion, is believed to come from the drug trade, and narcotics officials believe that part of the money is funding the Taliban insurgency.

Wankel was in Uruzgan to oversee a poppy-eradication campaign—the first major effort to disrupt the harvest in the province. He had brought with him a two-hundred-and-fifty-man A.E.F. contingent, including forty-odd contractors supplied by DynCorp, a Virginia-based private military company, which has a number of large U.S. government contracts in Iraq, Afghanistan, and other parts of the world. In Colombia, DynCorp helps implement the multibillion-dollar Plan Colombia, to eradicate coca. The A.E.F.'s armed convoy had taken three days to drive from Kabul, and had set up a base on a plateau above a deep wadi. With open land all around, it was a good spot to ward off attacks.

Much of Uruzgan is classified by the United Nations as "Extreme Risk / Hostile Environment." The Taliban effectively controls four-fifths of the province, which, like the movement, is primarily Pashtun. Mullah Omar, the fugitive Taliban leader, was born and raised here, as were three other founders of the movement. The Taliban's seizure of Tirin Kot, in the mid-nineties, was a key stepping stone in their march to Kabul, and their loss of the town in 2001 was a decisive moment in their fall. The Taliban have made a concerted comeback in the past two years; they are the de-facto authority in much of the Pashtun south and east, and have recently spread their violence to parts of the north as well. The debilitating and corrupting effects of the opium trade on the government of President Hamid Karzai is a significant factor in the Taliban's revival.

The Taliban instituted a strict Islamist policy against the opium trade during the final years of their regime, and by the time of their overthrow they had virtually eliminated it. But now, Lieutenant General Mohammad Daud-Daud, Afghanistan's deputy minister of the interior for counter-narcotics, told me, "there has been a coalition between the Taliban and the opium smugglers. This year, they have set up a commission to tax the harvest." In return, he said, the Taliban had offered opium farmers protection from the government's eradication efforts. The switch in strategy has an obvious logic: it provides opium money for the Taliban to sustain itself and helps it to win over the farming communities.

Wankel had flown in from Kabul five days earlier to meet with the governor of Uruzgan, Abdul Hakim Munib, about the eradication operation, only to discover that Munib had left for Kabul the day before. Wankel was told that a sister of the governor had died or fallen ill—there were several versions—but nobody believed this was the real reason for his absence. Munib, a former Taliban deputy minister, was suspected of retaining ties to the movement. And, Wankel noted, there were poppy fields within sight of Munib's palace.

"We're not able to destroy all the poppy—that's not the point. What we're trying to do is lend an element of threat and risk to the farmers' calculations, so they won't plant next year," Wankel said later. "It's like robbing a bank. If people see there's more to be had by robbing a bank than by working in one, they're going to rob it, until they learn there's a price to pay."

We came to a wide bend in the river, a stretch of good, flat growing land with broad poppy fields. The fields were neat and well tended, and the swollen bulbs beneath the blossoms on their long green stalks were dripping with dark-brown opium. A heady, acrid odor like stale urine hung in the air. Small groups of men and boys were in the fields, scoring the bulbs to bleed the opium. They stopped and stared at us when we drove past, and then continued their work.

Before Doug Wankel could do anything in Uruzgan, he had to talk to the Dutch. In a bewilderingly complicated arrangement, NATO member states have been put in charge of military operations in different Afghan provinces—the British in Helmand, for instance, and the Canadians in Kandahar. Since August, 2006, the Dutch have been in Uruzgan. A seventeen-hundred-member Dutch force occupies a sprawling walled base southwest of Tirin Kot. Smaller bases within the walls house contingents of Australians, U.S. Special Forces, and the Afghan Army. Military aircraft land at and take off from an airstrip there at all hours. There are small firebases elsewhere in the province, but troops at the main base rarely venture far from Tirin Kot.

Suicide bombings and I.E.D. attacks, major features of the Iraq insurgency, were rare in Afghanistan until 2005, but they have become common, and not just in Uruzgan. On June 17th, a suicide bomber blew up a bus in Kabul, killing dozens of people. Although a threatened Tet-style spring offensive by the Taliban never quite materialized, the level of violence has risen significantly. Some five thousand people were killed in the war last year, including a hundred and ninety-one foreign troops and at least a thousand civilians. By contrast, half that number of people were killed in 2005. As the war gets worse, incidents involving the killing of Afghan civilians by American troops, unintentional or not, have increased, causing widespread discontent. In May, the upper house of the Afghan parliament called for an end to offensive military operations by foreign troops and for dialogue with the Taliban. Karzai has complained publicly about the civilian deaths, but he is dependent on the foreign forces to prop him up. (Thirty-five thousand troops from thirty-seven nations are now in Afghanistan under the NATO umbrella; seventeen thousand are American. Another eight thousand American troops operate under U.S. military command.) Karzai seems isolated and weak, and his authority barely extends beyond the capital.

The effects of the war and the drug boom are evident in Kabul. There are more security barriers and anti-suicide-blast walls in the city, and United Nations personnel and relief workers must adhere to constantly updated safety guidelines and curfews. The rules are even stricter for American diplomats and officials, who live and work within their own new Embassy compound. Meanwhile, in nearby Sherpur, a downtown neighborhood, dozens of gaudy "poppy palaces" have gone up—mansions owned by former warlords and by senior officials in Karzai's government, built on public land that had housed war-displaced families until they were forcibly removed by police.

The official corruption and judicial impunity that have taken root under Karzai are seen as his greatest failings, and feature heavily in Taliban propaganda. Two years ago, his government announced a plan for fighting the opium trade, based on "eight pillars," including building the justice system, eradicating the poppy crop, and funding alternative development programs that would provide seeds for other crops and credits for fertilizer. The plan is backed by a commitment of billions of dollars from the U.S., but so far there has been little to show for it.

A Western official in Kabul told me, "The narcotics issue is an example of the problems this government faces—corruption, tribal politics, and lack of central institutions. Here it's not reconstruction—you're starting from zero on a lot of issues. We're trying to impose all of it at once, and it's hugely frustrating." The official went on, "Right now you've got to work with what you've got, and here you've got people who've figured out how to survive through thirty pretty horrific years. There's a lot of dealmaking. We have to be realistic about whom we're dealing with. And we have to show we're going to be dogged on this."

In Uruzgan, the Dutch have advocated a policy of nonconfrontation and the pursuit of development projects. (The Dutch commander, Hans van Griensven, was quoted in the *Times* in April as telling his officers, "We're not here to fight the Taliban. We're here to make the Taliban irrelevant.") A European official told me that the Dutch had doubts about Wankel's mission; they feared that it might be counterproductive, because it was only about destroying poppies and did not include any of the other seven pillars of the national plan. "There was concern that it might crosscut other activities focussed on security and development," he said.

Wankel was frustrated by the wariness of the Dutch. "Most or all Europeans are opposed to eradication—they're into winning hearts and minds," he said. "But it's our view that it isn't going to work. There has to be a measured, balanced use of force along with hearts and minds." He conceded, however, that the Uruzgan operation fell squarely on the use-of-force side of the scale. Later, he told me, aid, seed, and fertilizer would be offered to the farmers around Tirin Kot, but not yet. Other Americans were frankly contemptuous of the Dutch policy, which they regarded as softheaded.

The Western official told me, "We don't have a lot of time here. If we don't get a handle on this soon, we'll have a situation where you can't get rid of it, like we had in Colombia for a while, where the narcos owned part of the government and controlled significant parts of the economy. And we have a lot of evidence of direct links with the Taliban. These problems, and organized crime, too, are being embedded here while they're talking about 'alternative development.'"

Soona Niloofar, a member of parliament from Uruzgan, found the debate over development versus forceful eradication somewhat abstract; she didn't think much had been accomplished on either front. "Before the Dutch arrived, I told them, 'You must do reconstruction and help the farmers.' And the Ministry of Agriculture also spoke about helping them with alternative livelihoods. But nothing happened," she said. "They have done little reconstruction. There is a big gap between them and the people." The Dutch presence was felt only around Tirin Kot, she said, and, as far as she knew, the only significant things they had done were to repair a damaged bridge and set up a women's sewing coöperative. (A spokesman for the Dutch government said that there had been other projects, including one called Cleaning Up Tirin Kot, which involved painting storefronts and helping with garbage disposal.) At the same time, security had deteriorated. "The Dutch policy is a very weak one, and it makes the enemy stronger," she said.

Niloofar, who is twenty-seven, is a striking woman with a strong face and high cheekbones, and, on the day I met her, at the Parliament, she wore, instead of a burka, a brilliant turquoise shalwar kameez and head scarf—all the more noticeable in the assemblage of drably suited and robed male M.P.s. The Taliban have targeted women in public life, including teachers at girls' schools, and a number have been killed. Niloofar said that she could no longer safely travel to her home in Uruzgan or stay there overnight.

"People are getting very angry with Karzai," Niloofar said. "At the beginning of the year, he promised to sack the governors where opium is grown." She smiled sarcastically. "Nothing has been done."

"There is a fairly strong consensus view here that eradication alone, in the absence of the other seven lines, will not curb poppy cultivation or opium production," Chris Alexander, a Canadian who is one of the top-ranking United Nations officials in Afghanistan, said. "But in Helmand and Uruzgan all of these steps depend on improved security, which must remain the overriding priority. The Taliban have partnered in intimate ways with the drug networks over the past two years. Their alliance deserves to be exposed for the opportunism and criminality it represents." He added, "This Taliban is no fresh-faced Islamist movement. It is a violent, drug-fuelled rabble with a narrow and highly unappealing ideological base. Their defeat—or at least reduced influence—can open the door to a much more effective counter-narcotics policy."

After a meeting with the Dutch, Wankel returned to the A.E.F.'s camp, looking tired and exasperated. He had a map approved by the Dutch, showing a tight quadrant of land within which his team was to confine its work. It was miles away from the Dutch base. "They're as nervous as whores in a church," Wankel said.

The eradication team set off early the next morning for their first day's work. There were nineteen Americans and a hundred Afghans in a convoy made up of twenty-four all-terrain vehicles—similar to small dune buggies—eighteen Ranger pickup trucks carrying Afghan policemen, and four of DynCorp's white Ford F250 pickups. I rode in a truck driven by David Lockyear, an amiable six-foot-seven-inch Tennessean in his thirties, known as Doc Dave. Lockyear, who had a goatee and was covered with tattoos, was a paramedic from Nashville who joined the Marine Corps after September 11th. ("I was just pissed off, like a lot of people, and wanted to do something," he said.) He fought in the first siege of Falluja, and in 2007 he went to work for DynCorp. He smoked a Marlboro and held a cup of coffee in one hand as he drove.

A great dust cloud formed as the A.T.V.s hyperkinetically whizzed past us and the trucks kicked up plumes of swirling yellow powder. Picking up speed, Lockyear exclaimed, "This is redneck heaven. You get to run around the desert on A.T.V.s and pickups, shoot guns, and get paid for it. Man, it's the perfect job!"

When we reached the target area, men on A.T.V.s cut through the fields, dragging metal bars on chains, which knocked down the poppies. Other members of the team whacked at the poppies with shovel handles. Around the edges of the fields and on small hills above them, armed Afghan Interior Ministry policemen stood guard. Wankel had attended a *shura,* or council of local elders, a few days before, to explain the mission, and a small group of local Pashtun policemen were on hand, but the A.E.F. team consisted mostly of men from other areas of the country. Major Khalil, the deputy commander, was an ethnic Tajik, and didn't trust the Pashtuns. (Like many Afghans, Khalil uses only one name.) He came from the same village in the northern province of Panjshir as the mujahideen hero Ahmed Shah Massoud, who was assassinated by Al Qaeda two days before the September 11th attacks. Khalil described the area where we were as "the heart of enemy territory."

Doug Wankel walked up to an angry-looking farmer who was watching his field being destroyed and asked him, through an interpreter named Nazeem, how much he got for his opium. Twenty-one thousand Pakistani rupees for a four-kilo package, the farmer said, and he harvested three to four kilos per jirib (a local land measurement equivalent to about half an acre). He added, "I get only a thousand rupees per jirib of wheat, so I'm obliged to grow poppies." That comes to about thirty-three dollars from an acre of wheat, and between five hundred and seven hundred dollars from an acre of poppies. In Uruzgan, the opium was sold to middlemen who then smuggled it out of Afghanistan to Pakistan or Iran.

"How long have you been growing poppies?" Wankel asked him.

The farmer looked surprised. "When I was born, I saw the poppies," he said.

When we were ready to move on, the farmer said, as if to be polite, "Thank you—but I can't really thank you, because you haven't destroyed just my poppies but my wheat, too." He pointed to where A.T.V.s had driven through a wheat patch. Wankel apologized, then commented that it was only one small section. "But you have also damaged my watermelons," the farmer insisted, pointing to another part of the field. "Now I will have nothing left."

Wankel turned away. As we walked on, the farmer called out, "Are you destroying all the poppies or just my field?"

About a dozen men and boys gathered on a low dirt wall next to another field and watched the proceedings impassively. A young girl wiped away tears with her scarf and yelled angrily at a policeman. Nearby, several Americans were resting in the shade of some mulberry trees, talking to each other. One of the local men, who wore a black turban, said to them, "We're poor—we're not with the Taliban or anything. You've made a big mistake. Now we'll grow more against you." He added, "I have to feed my children."

Nazeem, the translator, spoke to the men in Pashto, and recited passages from the Koran proscribing opium. One of the men retorted, "The Koran also says to fight against *kafirs*"—that is, infidels. His companions stirred and nodded.

A farmer approached Glen Vaughn, one of the DynCorp medics, and told him that he had pains in his back which made it hard to move his legs. He had gone to the Dutch base to be treated at the hospital there, but had been turned away. Vaughn, a stocky former fireman from Denton, Texas, began to examine him. As he did so, another man made a lunge for Vaughn's holstered sidearm. Vaughn jerked backward and the man dodged away, grinning. "I'll shoot you in the head if you try that again," Vaughn said in English.

Nazeem and a couple of Afghan policemen formed a protective circle around Vaughn. The other farmers, seeing Vaughn's alarm as a display of fear, laughed at him. Nazeem spoke to them sharply, saying, "I'm Pashtun, too, like you, and I'm not afraid of you." Staring coldly at him, the oldest farmer, a gray-bearded man, said, "You will be afraid when the time comes."

Back at the base camp, Wankel changed into shorts and a T-shirt decorated with the Stars and Stripes and an eagle, and lay down on the cot in his tent to read Bob Woodward's most recent book, "State of Denial." On balance, he was pleased with how the first day had gone; it had been a good start. "It's not fair to judge the eradication program against the figures for drug cultivation, because it's really just getting off the ground," Wankel said. "Corruption is a huge problem, though, and no doubt some of the guys we're involved with are up to some stuff. But you just have to try and steer them."

On the second day of the operation, the local police, who were supposed to show up at seven, were forty minutes late and, when they finally arrived, there were only a few of them. This was worrisome, because after the previous day's foray there was more potential for trouble; the presence of the police was seen as a guarantee of local coöperation, and therefore of security for the eradication force. Mick Hogan, a tall, muscular man of fifty with a silver beard, who was Wankel's manager in the field, stood silently, watching the convoy get ready. Hogan was a veteran of Special Forces anti-guerrilla operations in Central America during the nineteen-eighties, and of the I.N.L.'s counter-narcotics programs in Colombia, Guatemala, and Bolivia. He remarked evenly that the late arrival of the policemen was "not a good sign."

The convoy moved out anyway. We travelled slowly in a long line of vehicles. I was in a Ford truck with Eric Sherepita, one of two DynCorp commanders of the operation in Uruzgan. Sherepita was a burly man in his thirties with a shaved head and tattoos, a goatee and a Fu Manchu mustache. The other DynCorp commander, Kelly, a former policeman from Arizona, also goateed, was driving another. The remaining DynCorp trucks were packed with guns and men, including two specialists in land-mine and explosives removal: a husky, soft-spoken Samoan named Suani, who often wore a sarong and draped a kaffiyeh over his head, like an Arab sheikh, and Anton, a Croatian from Mostar, who rarely spoke.

As we entered the nearest village, children gathered along the track waving and holding their hands out, and some of the DynCorp men tossed them gray plastic packages. "Halal M.R.E.s," Sherepita explained. "The kids love them." He threw a few, and the children scrambled to retrieve them. Some opened them immediately and began eating the contents, while others threw them under the tires of the trucks to watch them get squashed.

The area chosen for the day's mission had been relayed to Wankel and the DynCorp team by the Dutch only the evening before. The drive, on the opposite bank of the river from the camp, took nearly two hours. We bivouacked on some sloping open ground above a village on a bluff. Below were poppy fields and the river; behind us was a row of bare hills and, a half mile or so farther away, the steep flanks of the mountains.

Two helicopters, called Diablo One and Diablo Two, flew in and landed on the ground near us, disgorging a small group of television journalists, including Dutchmen and a couple of Australians, who were to film that morning's eradication work. They stumbled toward us, clutching plastic water bottles and their gear, and were introduced to Doug Wankel, who led the way down the hill.

Wankel climbed on the back of an A.T.V. driven by Mick Hogan to get across a stream at the base of the bluff, and, at the last minute, one of the Dutch newsmen got on, despite Hogan's warnings that his weight would throw off the balance. The A.T.V. cleared the stream but toppled off the steep embankment on the other side. The Dutchman leaped clear; Wankel and Hogan were pitched into the field as the A.T.V. flipped over.

Wankel was on his back, and both his legs were pinned under the vehicle. Several of us lifted the A.T.V. and saw that his legs had deep, ugly gashes; on one, the white bone of his shin was exposed. Hogan, unhurt, began cursing the Dutchman, who had vanished. Someone brought a stretcher, and Wankel, managing a pained smile, was carefully loaded onto it and carried to one of the choppers, which would fly him to the Tirin Kot base.

Policemen were already busy whacking and crushing poppies, using sticks and A.T.V.s. They were spread out over several hundred metres. Unlike the day before, there were no children or any other civilians in sight.

As I walked along a trail between the poppy fields, gunshots rang out. Men began running, taking cover, and looking up toward the village on the bluff; the firing seemed to be coming from the mud-walled compounds there. Kelly, the ex-cop from Arizona, yelled at me to take cover. I headed toward a stand of trees with Aaron Huey, the photographer who was travelling with me; from there we could no longer see any other Americans. A group of six or seven Interior Ministry policemen—almost all of the local police had disappeared as soon as the shooting started—ran past with their guns drawn, and we followed.

Moments later, we were in an open section of the village, and under fire. There were now twenty or so policemen, in small groups bunched up against mud walls, shooting in various directions. One of them had been shot in the shoulder and was bleeding. I tried, with Huey, to make a run for where I thought the American convoy was, but we were turned back by gunfire.

Some of the policemen began pointing at a distant farm compound. *"Dushman!"*—enemy—one yelled. They fired an R.P.G. at the compound. The grenade exploded, sending up a large black burst of smoke and dust.

Major Khalil appeared, leading a few of the policemen and a prisoner in a brown robe; they had tied his hands behind his back with his own shawl. Huey and I joined them as they made their way down an alley and toward the fields. When we were in the middle of the poppy field, Khalil screamed, "Taliban! Get down!" Then he and his men, firing their guns, advanced, with us among them.

We could see the helicopters flying over the village and the river, seeming to leave the area. Several of the policemen asked me why they weren't firing at our attackers. I didn't know what to tell them. (Later, I learned that they were evacuating the television journalists.)

As we approached a steep hill, from which the Afghan policemen were firing rockets and Kalashnikovs into the village, Khalil told everyone in our group to lift our hands and weapons in the air, and he began calling out loudly, identifying us to the policemen above us, telling them to hold their fire. As they covered us, we climbed the hill to join them.

It had been about ninety minutes since the shooting began. As we looked for cover on the hill, Khalil directed his men to fire into the village. Bullets came cracking at us. The prisoner, his arms still bound, crouched next to me. There was a plume of black smoke; the men said that it was one of our vehicles burning. Khalil, seemingly panicked, ordered everyone to run. (He later told me that he had seen movement below and feared that the Taliban were about to surround us.) We headed for another hill, from which I was finally able to see the convoy, about a half mile away, across a wadi.

A group of men had gathered in a large foxhole at the summit of our hill, and I spotted Mick Hogan, who was looking through his gun's scope at the village below. I crawled up to him. Below us, I saw a man dressed in black move quickly through the village and dodge out of sight behind a wall. The men in the foxhole pounded bullets in his direction.

Hogan told us to get to the convoy; the Americans wanted to pull out right away. As Huey and I headed down, one of the Afghans came running past us, pointing to a hole in his trousers where a bullet had just missed his leg. I congratulated him on his good luck. Then I spotted Kelly driving one of the white pickups and we got in with him.

We had to get back across the river, but the route we had used that morning was too dangerous; some Afghan policemen had just been ambushed in an attempt to head that way. Our way to the river cut between two walled orchards, and the convoy, a long line of slow-moving trucks, was taking fire from both sides. Kelly called the helicopters on his radio, and soon we heard the grinding sound of the helicopters' miniguns—.30-calibre machine guns that fire up to four thousand rounds per minute.

When we reached the river's edge, we saw that one of the white pickups was stranded in the water and some of the A.T.V.s were submerged. Men were clambering about—trying to hold on to vehicles, calling for towropes—and returning fire. Kelly stopped midstream to help them. Two of the A.T.V.s were towed out, but the others, and the pickup, were abandoned. The DynCorp men ripped the radio out of the pickup so that the Taliban wouldn't take it. Kelly managed to get his truck to the other side, where the shooting continued.

Nearby, a DynCorp crew had opened full automatic fire on a group of gunmen who had moved from deeper in the orchard to the treeline on the opposite bank and were shooting at us. Aaron Huey and I took cover behind a truck as Kelly joined the fight. Rockets exploded near the Diablos, and then the choppers disappeared. (They had both been hit several times, but made it back to the base in Tirin Kot, one with a fire on board.) After a few more minutes, the decision was made to retreat.

The road was almost obscured by the dust kicked up by the trucks in front of us. We passed another orchard, and, again, there were gunshots from both sides of the road. In the back of our truck, Bulmaro Vasconcelos, a machine-gunner from Hemet, California, fired into the orchard with a heavy machine gun. I saw a military cap in the road in front of us, and then a man lying face down. We couldn't tell if he was alive or dead, and swerved to avoid running over him. It was one of the Afghan policemen. Kelly yelled for the truck behind us to pick him up.

A few seconds later, the window on Kelly's side exploded and he yelled, "Shit! I've been hit!" He grabbed his leg, but kept driving, feeling the leg with one hand. He looked at the hand: there was no blood. The bullet, evidently slowed by the metal door, had not pierced his skin. "I'm all right," he said. A bullet hit my side of the truck, and another struck the back. A minute or two later, we were out of the orchards and into more open territory, headed toward the camp. For the first time in four hours, there was no shooting.

About ten minutes after we got back to camp, we heard loud explosions coming from the river. The Dutch had dispatched an Apache helicopter to destroy the abandoned pickup with a Hellfire missile.

In addition to the man we had found in the road, who had been shot in the head and was barely alive, four Afghan policemen had been shot, of whom two were critically wounded. One was spouting blood from the femoral artery in his right leg. Another had been shot in the lung and the liver. Sylvester Pocius, known as Sly, another goateed DynCorp contractor, had been grazed on the neck by a bullet that ricocheted off the bolt of his gun. The wounded were rushed into camp for emergency treatment and driven to the Special Forces hospital. (A month later, the policeman who had been shot in the liver died of his wounds.)

Later, Major Khalil said that he had been informed that eleven other Afghans were wounded and eight killed during the attack. There was conflicting information about the identities of the dead, and uncertainty about whether the reports were accurate, but the victims were said to have included an old woman, or possibly an old man, and a twelve-year-old girl.

T he eradication team remained in camp under a tight security lockdown for ten days. The camp was set up like a *kraal,* with thirty-odd trucks parked in tight groups to form a large, fanlike defensive circle. Within this perimeter, the team members pitched their tents, with the DynCorp men in one area and, in another area, the Afghan police, some of whom slept on cots in the backs of trucks. Each group had its own cookhouse tent and its own toilet truck. The Americans also had a shower truck and a laundry truck. Beyond the camp, at each point of the compass, Nepalese Gurkhas hired by Dyn-Corp maintained sentry positions in foxholes and in sandbagged machine-gun nests on the roofs of trucks.

The DynCorp men spent their time swapping stories, watching DVDs, surfing the Web, and catching up on e-mail; the camp, which had its own satellite gear, was wireless. Camp life soon acquired a "Groundhog Day" routine. Every afternoon, Pocius and Vasconcelos lifted weights, and then Pocius sunbathed. Tyrone, a fifty-seven-year-old logistics man, called his wife in North Carolina every evening, using Skype, and talked to her for hours. Kevin, a personable Ohioan, brewed Starbucks coffee that had been sent from home.

Most of the DynCorp men were Southerners or Midwesterners, and all but a couple were ex-military men. Almost all had children, and told me they had become contractors because they were able to earn a great deal more money than in civilian jobs back home. Their contracts obliged them to stay in Afghanistan for six-month periods, after which they received a month of paid vacation. Money was not their only motivation, however. Many spoke about wanting to recapture the camaraderie and adventure of military life. Being in Afghanistan also gave them a sense of purpose: they were patriotic, and saw themselves as participating in the war on terror.

Hook, a former Army man and prison guard, had been hired by DynCorp just the month before. One morning, he said, "The real problem in this war on terror is you guys, the press. Ties our hands. The only way to fight this is to give them back the same medicine, like Operation Phoenix, in Vietnam. My Lai—what Calley did there was probably just on orders."

Tyrone, who was a Vietnam veteran, said he thought that the war could not be won the way it was being waged. "We're really not fighting it," he said. "The Taliban are just right over the ridge there. The Dutch are tolerating it."

By this time, news had circulated that Khalil's prisoner, who had been tied up and kept in a tent for four or five days and interrogated at the U.S. Special Forces base, had talked. Allegedly, the day before the attack, men from another village had brought in weapons and a group of fifteen to twenty Taliban fighters, and had told the village men to evacuate women and children. (The A.E.F. men estimated that there were forty to fifty attackers in all.)

Mick Hogan had debriefed each of the men who had been in the field on the day of the attack, and he was angry at the Dutch. They hadn't sent an ambulance for the critically wounded Afghan policemen, he said, or treated them at their hospital. From the beginning, Hogan said, the Dutch had issued petty rules that had made it harder to accomplish the mission. "They gave us a grid less than nine clicks by two to operate in, and something my time in the S.F. taught me was that unpredictability is the key to survival," Hogan said. "The more people know what you're doing, the more likely something bad can happen to you. They said, 'Oh, you can't go here, you can't cross the river there.' Makes you think that our so-called international allies are not our friends."

One of the senior members of the A.E.F. told me that it appeared that the fields in the target area belonged primarily to the Alkozai tribe, leaving those of the Populzai—Karzai's tribe—relatively untouched. "So the Dutch, wittingly or unwittingly, appear to be favoring the Populzai," he said. "By targeting the Alkozai, it was almost mandated that they would retaliate."

After hearing so many recriminations, I tried to arrange an interview with the Dutch military. They declined to speak to me while I was in Uruzgan. But when I returned to Kabul I spoke to a European official based in Afghanistan, who dismissed the reports that the Dutch had been unwilling to treat the wounded; the problem was that their hospital had been full at the time, and the Special Forces hospital had had space available. (Later, a Dutch government spokesman said that they had never received a formal request for an ambulance. The spokesman also said that the target area was selected in conjunction with the Afghan government and others in the international community, and was meant to be "tribal neutral," although there were other factors at work, including security and the richness of the fields.)

The ambush, the European official said, should not have surprised anyone, especially that late in the season. "You can put the eradication team wherever you want, but it's not really a fighting force," he said. "If you get attacked, you can only retreat."

O ne problem with eradication operations such as the one in Uruzgan is that they tend to set up confrontations between armed men and poor farmers: the only American a farmer ever meets might be the one who is destroying his harvest, rather than someone who is building a school or a clinic. Another problem is that knocking down or plowing under the flowers is time-consuming. "The per-acre cost of forced eradication is also excruciatingly high," Chris Alexander said.

A way around this would be to spray the poppies with chemicals from the air, as coca is eradicated in Colombia. This is a highly controversial approach, however, because of its indiscriminate destruction of crops and the uncertainty about its health effects. As a compromise, the Americans have strongly advocated ground spraying from tractors. The Western official said, "You have to get past manual eradication and discuss chemical spraying. The Europeans are adamantly opposed—just look at the whole genetically-modified-crop debate in Europe. If they decided to spray over the next few months, we would need to have an information campaign on spraying, telling the Afghans they're not going to have two-headed babies but also telling them so in Europe, in The Hague and in Rome."

The official said that last year Karzai had authorized ground spraying, but, under pressure from the Europeans, decided to wait. "Karzai is balancing a lot on this. If the international community goes to him in a united front, he can make the hard decision. But on this issue we weren't united, and he couldn't make the decision."

The narcotics issue, like almost every other piece in the Afghan jigsaw puzzle, poses a conundrum to the Americans. While attempting to pacify Afghanistan, they must stabilize it politically and rebuild it, too; as the eradication issue shows, the actions required for one can undermine the other. Added to this is the absence of a unified international strategy, and the resultant infighting between the U.S. and its allies. There is disunity not only on the opium problem but on how to fight the war. Doug Wankel said, "Americans have this image of being cowboyish and pushy, and we've suffered in this from what's happened in Iraq."

Distracted by Iraq, the U.S. only belatedly began serious counter-narcotics and reconstruction efforts in Afghanistan. In the vacuum, the Taliban returned, and most of the foreign experts and Afghan officials I met with acknowledged that they, not NATO or the Karzai government, held the initiative. No one speaks with any assurance about "winning"—only about the long road ahead. In Chris Alexander's carefully phrased appraisal, "The trend is not monolithically positive."

Karzai, in his efforts to mollify his restive fellow-Pashtuns, has made conciliatory gestures to the Taliban which have alienated Tajiks and Uzbeks who helped him come to power. There is the danger of a broader divide between north and south. A coalition of former warlords and politicians predominantly from the north recently formed an opposition front to challenge Karzai, who is up for reëlection in 2009. A group of retired generals—again, mostly northerners—have called for a more hard-line approach in the war against the Taliban. While in Afghanistan, I travelled several hours north of Kabul to the Panjshir Valley, and met with Ahmed Kushah, a nephew of the assassinated Ahmed Shah Massoud. Kushah was living with a band of armed followers high up in the mountains, to prepare for the new guerrilla war he believes is coming. He told me he felt certain that Karzai's policies, backed by the West, would lead to a Taliban takeover, and he was preparing to defend the north, just as his uncle had once done. He told me that although he had no immediate plans to attack Americans, he would do so if they moved against him. Islam, he told me, was his inspiration.

Among ordinary Afghans, conspiracy theories are rife. Major Khalil asked me one day, "If the Americans can put a man on the moon, why can't they defeat the Taliban?" His implication was that, if the Americans didn't win, it was because they didn't want to badly enough.

I arranged to be escorted to the poppy fields by a local police unit, so that I could speak to farmers freely, without members of the eradication team present. The policemen, who arrived in a pickup, did not inspire confidence. There were six or seven young men, most of them wearing shalwar kameez instead of uniforms, under the command of a tiny hunchbacked man who walked with difficulty, using crutches. He wore a rakish turban and a dirty robe, and he spat constantly. Suppressing my misgivings, I went with them.

At the edge of a wadi, we found several men and a boy at work, harvesting opium. The policemen stood at the edges of the field as I waded into the poppies with a translator, a local young man named Saibullah, who had learned English as a refugee in Pakistan. Once he had explained that I merely wanted to see how they collected the drug, they were friendly enough. The boy showed me how he ran his thumb over the oozing bulbs and then scraped the gooey brown opium into a glass he held in his other hand. When the glass was full, he emptied the contents into a large bowl. It was 8:20 A.M. and the harvesters had been working since 5 A.M. It looked as though they had already collected about two kilos. Nazir Ahmad, a bearded man in a long, opium-stained smock, said that he had twenty people to support and four jiribs of land, from which he expected to harvest twenty-five kilos of opium.

The development projects meant to offset the loss of the poppies didn't benefit people like him, Ahmad said. "The Karzai government doesn't give the money to poor farmers growing poppy. It gives it only to its friends who grow it"—corrupt officials and landowners with political influence. (Many of the farmers were sharecroppers.) "We would be happy to stop growing opium if they would give us some help, and stop giving the money meant for us to thieves." Instead of receiving aid from government officials, Ahmad said, "if they tell us to break the poppies, we must pay them not to."

Ahmad's younger brother said that he had just returned from the harvest in Helmand Province—the source of forty per cent of Afghanistan's opium. The opium farmers there often had to pay bribes, he said. This echoed what the DynCorp men had told me about their experience in Helmand the previous month. There, after *shuras* with elders, the local policemen had guided them to certain fields while leaving others intact. Presumably, the farmers whose poppies were spared were well connected or had paid bribes. Chris Alexander told me, "In Helmand and Uruzgan, eradication has been subject to political manipulation and corruption. It has also proven virtually impossible to conduct in districts where the Taliban are relatively strong, thereby inevitably penalizing farmers in pro-government districts."

Before I left the field, Ahmad looked at me directly and said, "I know the opium is turned into drugs that destroy young people, and I am sorry, but we are twenty people and we have no help. We must grow it to survive. If we get help, we won't grow it next year."

Driving up out of the wadi, we had to wait for a convoy of three armored personnel carriers, with Australian flags, to pass. In Tirin Kot, we parked in the traffic circle at the center of town, where a large group of turbaned and bearded young men had gathered, waiting for opium farmers to come along and hire them as day laborers. The men looked at us with suspicion. Several covered their faces. One of the men was the farmer who had tried to grab Glen Vaughn's pistol on the first day of the mission. Saibullah, the translator, said, "We should go now—there may be suiciders." As we drove on, he said that there were Taliban among the men in the crowd: "They were the ones who covered their faces."

When we returned to the camp, I heard that a suicide bomber on a motorbike had blown himself up next to an Australian convoy, wounding a number of soldiers and civilians. Most likely, this was the convoy that had passed us.

There were doubts about whether the eradication would resume; the Embassy in Kabul was not sure that it was worth the risk. The Americans had always been cagey about the number of acres of poppies they hoped to eradicate in Uruzgan, claiming that it "wasn't about numbers" but about making their presence felt. They had intended to spend at least ten days in the fields, and thus far had managed only one—in which, by their rough calculations, they had destroyed less than two hundred acres. (By contrast, earlier this year, in a month-long operation in Helmand, they had destroyed an estimated seventy-five hundred acres—out of an estimated hundred and seventy-five thousand planted with poppies.)

"We've been and shown we can mess things up," Hogan said. "Sure, we've taken our losses, too, and maybe we lost the battle, but we haven't lost the war."

After a week, the DynCorp men were told that the Uruzgan mission was complete. The Nepalese Gurkhas slaughtered a goat in celebration. That night, however, Hogan reported that the U.S. Ambassador and the Afghan Minister of the Interior had decided that the team should not leave Uruzgan without a final show of force.

Major Khalil came to see Kelly. The local Afghan Army commander, he said, was worried about accompanying the eradication team into the fields—one of his patrols had recently been ambushed.

"So what are you saying?" Kelly asked warily.

Khalil suggested another *shura,* to get the coöperation of the village elders. He also urged that they move quickly, because the harvest was almost over—the fields were already "trash." Kelly said, "It's true, the fields are shit now, but that's not the point. The point is to go back in there and kick some ass."

Kelly told Khalil to set up the *shura.* Rolling his eyes, he said, "This is just the way it was in Helmand, with the *shuras* repeating themselves over and over again, all the same fucking shit. It's a stalling tactic."

Limping, but managing without crutches, Doug Wankel reappeared the next morning. He had flown from Kabul with Gene Trammell, the head of the DynCorp counter-narcotics program. Colonel Marouf, Major Khalil's superior on the A.E.F., met us at the governor's palace with the local police chief, Qassem. The errant governor of Uruzgan, Abdul Hakim Munib, who had finally returned from Kabul, arrived a few moments later.

Munib began talking about his commitment to eradication. "We've tried to do as much as we could, but we're hampered by lack of tools and equipment," he said. "I was happy when I heard you were coming." The Americans listened quietly, their faces neutral. Then Munib announced that he had met with the elders, and they had agreed to eradicate half their poppy fields by themselves—there was no need for the A.E.F. to do it.

Qassem stood up. He said that there were two areas where eradication could still be conducted. Before he could continue, Wankel cut him off, and announced that President Karzai and the Afghan minister of defense had been informed about the attack on the team. "Kabul says it's very important for the government to come back and eradicate for one, two days in the area where it happened, to show that the government has the ability to exercise the rule of law in Tirin Kot," Wankel said.

Qassem said, "We can come and show you where to go."

"You will have to come early. We leave at seven sharp," Wankel said, standing up. "Thank you, that's it."

Qassem arrived on time, along with several jeeploads of his policemen. I rode with David Lockyear, the Tennessean. Overhead, we could hear the whine of a Special Forces drone. We passed a man on a motorbike; Lockyear exclaimed that he had a Kalashnikov, and radioed to the Afghan police truck behind us to pick him up. The poppy fields were on both sides of the road where we had come under fire during our retreat, running toward the river on one side and toward the desert on the other. Several fields were already brown, drying in the sun, but others were still green. The eradication team entered the fields on the desert side and began whacking the stalks with sticks.

Several farmers ran up to Colonel Marouf, yelling furiously, "We are all Muslims! Why are you doing this to us?" Marouf told the policemen to keep them at the edge of the fields. Allen Barnes, one of the DynCorp medics, was standing guard nearby. He was wearing a khaki kilt, claiming relief from the heat and some Celtic ancestry. One of the other contractors called him a "gear queer." Barnes laughed.

Marouf called off the men once they had destroyed two-thirds of the poppies—to leave the farmers with something, he said. The farmers were released. As they left, one of them said to Marouf, "If we had known you were coming to do this, we would have fought you." Calling after them, Marouf retorted, "When you fight, you use your women and children as shields!"

Governor Munib and the intelligence chief arrived with a clutch of elders. They made their way to a shady spot under a mulberry tree at the edge of a field and sat down. I saw the hunchbacked police commander approach Munib and kiss his hand. Wankel went over and told Munib that the plan for the next day was to destroy poppies on the other side of the road, down by the river, where the fields were bigger and richer, in order to be "fair." Munib just nodded.

Afterward, I asked Munib about the links between the Taliban and the opium trade; he had, after all, been a deputy minister in the Taliban regime.

"In the areas where the poppies are cultivated and there are Taliban, it is under their influence. But elsewhere it is not fully so," Munib said. "We know that the Taliban are telling the people to oppose the government's eradication strategy, but, as you also know, the Taliban, when they were in government, eradicated all the poppies."

He added, "When the Taliban imposed their decree, there was followup. They were capturing and punishing people, so the people stopped growing opium. Also, there was no opposition—the Taliban had all the power."

Munib and the elders did not show up the next day. Qassem and his local policemen appeared, however, with a village councillor. They led the eradication force to the same side of the road where we had been the day before. Doug Wankel was furious. After the policemen had spent half an hour whacking one small field with their sticks, he told them to stop. He said again that he wished to eradicate poppies in the fields toward the river. The councillor told Wankel that he would not accompany the men if they went on that side of the road, nor could he guarantee their safety.

Wankel insisted. He ordered Major Khalil and the DynCorp men to set up a good security perimeter. Qassem and his men stayed behind. Wankel and Trammell and a group of men, guns drawn, walked down into the fields below, a checkerboard of green wheat and luxuriant poppies. After a few minutes, Marouf received a call from Qassem on his field radio saying that he and his men were pulling out. Alarm spread among the Americans and the Afghan policemen who were with us.

"Someone powerful obviously controls this area," Wankel told Trammell. "The local authorities' leaving has sent out the message that we're unsafe and can be attacked. We should go."

We climbed back up the bluff. Qassem was standing there with several of his men. Doug Wankel didn't approach him. Marouf went to talk to Qassem, and then came back and told Wankel, "The police say you can eradicate *there*"—he pointed up to the other side of the road.

"Fuck the police," Wankel snarled, and he turned and walked away. He told his men that it was over.

I walked past one of the jeeps where some of Qassem's policemen, dressed in robes and sparkly skullcaps, were laughing and talking with the opium growers. I caught a whiff of something burning as I passed. They were smoking hashish.

Back at camp, everyone was in a bad mood. Hook, the former prison guard, remarked, "We ought to take all those guys and hang them in public, beginning with the governor." He laughed, and added, "Good thing I'm not an idealist—I'm just here for the money."

Newyorker.com An audio interview with **Jon Lee Anderson** and more photographs by Aaron Huey.

The Opposite Result

U.S.-backed efforts to eradicate Afghanistan's opium poppies yield a bumper crop.

KAREN DEYOUNG

Opium production in Afghanistan, which provides more than 90 percent of the world's heroin, broke all records in 2006, reaching a historic high despite ongoing U.S.-sponsored eradication efforts, the Bush administration reported Dec. 1.

Central Asia

In addition to a 26 percent production increase over past year—for a total of 5,644 metric tons—the amount of land under cultivation in opium poppies grew by 61 percent. Cultivation in the two main production provinces, Helmand in the southwest and Oruzgan in central Afghanistan, was up by 132 percent.

White House drug policy chief John Walters called the news "disappointing."

The administration has cited resurgent Taliban forces as the main impediment to stabilization and reconstruction efforts in Afghanistan, and the U.S. military investment has far exceeded anti-narcotic and development programs. But U.S. military and intelligence officials have increasingly described the drug trade as a problem that rivals and in some ways exceeds the Taliban, threatening to derail other aspects of U.S. policy.

"It is truly the Achilles' heel of Afghanistan," Gen. James L. Jones, the supreme allied commander for NATO, said in a recent speech at the Council on Foreign Relations. Afghanistan is NATO's biggest operation, with more than 30,000 troops. Drug cartels with their own armies engage in regular combat with NATO forces deployed in Afghanistan, he said. "It would be wrong to say that this is just the Taliban. I think I need to set that record straight," he added.

"They have their own capability to inflict damage, to make sure that the roads and the passages stay open and they get to where they want to go, whether it's through Pakistan, Iran, up through Russia and all the known trade routes. So this is a very violent cartel." Jones said. "They are buying their protection by funding other organizations, from criminal gangs to tribes, to inciting any kind of resistance to keep the government off of their back."

Any disruption of the drug trade has enormous implications for Afghanistan's economic and political stability. Although its relative strength in the overall economy has diminished as other sectors have expanded in recent years, narcotics is a $2.6 billion-a-year industry that this year provided more than a third of the country's gross domestic product. Farmers who cultivate opium poppies receive only a small percentage of the profits, but U.S. officials estimate the crop provides up to 12 times as much income per acre as conventional farming, and there is violent local resistance to eradication.

"It's almost the devil's own problem." CIA Director Michael V. Hayden told Congress last month. "Right now the issue is stability. . . . Going in there in itself and attacking the drug trade actually feeds the instability that you want to overcome."

"Attacking the problem directly in terms of the drug trade . . . would undermine the attempt to gain popular support in the region," agrees Lt. Gen. Michael D. Maples, director of the Defense Intelligence Agency. "There's a real conflict, I think."

The Afghan government has prohibited the aerial herbicide spraying used by U.S. anti-narcotic programs in Latin America. Instead, opium poppy plants in Afghanistan are destroyed by tractors dragging heavy bars. But only 38,500 of nearly 430,000 acres under cultivation were eradicated this year.

Because of security concerns and local sensibilities, all eradication is done by Afghan police, and corruption is a major problem at every level from cultivation to international trafficking. Although the drug trade is believed to provide some financing to the Taliban, most experts believe it is largely an organized criminal enterprise. According to a major report on the Afghan drug industry jointly released two weeks ago by the World Bank and the U.N. Office on Drugs and Crime, key narcotics traffickers "work closely with sponsors in top government and political positions."

The report drew specific attention to the Afghan Interior Ministry, saying its officials were increasingly involved in providing protection for and facilitating consolidation of the drug industry in the hands of leading traffickers. "At the lower levels," the report said, "payments to police to avoid eradication or arrest reportedly are very widespread. At higher levels, provincial and district police chief appointments appear to be a tool for key traffickers and sponsors to exercise control and favor their proteges at middle levels in the drug industry."

Opium cultivation was outlawed during Taliban rule in the late 1990s and was nearly eliminated by 2001. After the overthrow of the Taliban government by U.S. forces in the fall of that year, the Bush administration said that keeping a lid on production was among its highest priorities. But corruption and alliances formed by Washington and the Afghan government with anti-Taliban tribal chieftains, some of whom are believed to be deeply involved in the trade, undercut the effort.

Afghan President Hamid Karzai recently noted that "once we thought terrorism was Afghanistan's biggest enemy" but said that now "poppy, its cultivation and drugs are Afghanistan's major enemy."

Eradication and alternative development programs have made little discernible headway. Cultivation—measured annually with high-resolution satellite imagery that is then parsed by analysts using specialized computer software—is nearly double its highest pre-Karzai level.

"There is supposed to be a tremendous energy associated with this," Jones says of the counter-narcotics programs, "but it needs a fresh look because . . . we're losing ground.

From *The Washington Post* National Weekly Edition, December 11–17, 2006. Copyright © 2006 by Washington Post Writers Group. Reprinted by permission.

The Teen Drinking Dilemma

Some parents let their kids use alcohol at home. A most spirited debate.

BARBARA KANTROWITZ AND ANNE UNDERWOOD

In 2002, Elisa Kelly made what she thought was a smart parenting decision. Her son Ryan asked her to buy beer and wine for his 16th-birthday party at the family's Virginia home, promising that no one would leave until morning. Kelly agreed, and to further guard against drunken driving, she collected guests' car keys. But neighbors called police, who arrested Kelly and her ex-husband, George Robinson, for what one official told The Washington Post was the worst case of underage drinking he'd seen in years. Kelly maintained that she was just trying to control drinking that would have gone on whether or not she had bought alcohol for the kids. Both got time in jail; Kelly began her 27-month sentence on June 11.

This graduation season, parents around the country will face a similar dilemma. Should they allow teens to drink under their supervision, or should they follow the law—knowing that their kids are likely to imbibe anyway? Many parents believe teens should learn about drinking at home. Cynthia Garcia Coll, professor of education, psychology and pediatrics at Brown University, grew up in Puerto Rico, where, she says, kids drink at family parties. "Instead, in this country, we go from saying 'No, you can't do it'," and then all at once, we say 'Yes, you can' without really giving them any guidance. It's not like age 21 is a magic time when people become responsible drinkers."

The same reasoning prompted New Yorker Sam Hedrick to offer his three daughters drinks at home. "My youngest is going to be 21 this week," Hedrick says. "She and her friends have had alcohol here with meals." His daughter Lizzie, a student at Bowdoin, agrees with her father. "If your parents are so against alcohol from the start when you're younger, you're never exposed and it just becomes this enigmatic, forbidden thing," she says. "I can understand why it seems cool."

But most researchers who study teen substance abuse say that for every family like the Hedricks, there are many more where allowing alcohol causes problems. "The data is quite clear about teen drinking and it has nothing to do with being puritanical," says William Damon, director of the Stanford University Center on Adolescence. "The earlier a kid starts drinking, the more likely they are to have problems with alcohol in their life." The antidrinking message is especially critical in families with a history of alcoholism, which greatly increases the risk.

Even if they don't become alcoholics, teens who drink too much may suffer impaired memory and other learning problems, says Aaron White of Duke University Medical Center, who studies adolescent alcohol use. He says parents should think twice about offering alcohol to teens because their brains are still developing and are more susceptible to damage than adult brains. "If you're going to do that, I suggest you teach them to roll joints, too," he says, "because the science is clear that alcohol is more dangerous than marijuana."

Girls should be particularly careful, says Dr. Mark Willenbring of the National Institute on Alcohol Abuse and Alcoholism. Women generally weigh less than men and have proportionately more fat and less lean body mass. Because blood circulates primarily to lean body mass, the alcohol is distributed to a smaller volume of tissue, which results in higher blood alcohol levels. "We're absolutely seeing more women competing in drinking games," he says. "That's a terribly dangerous thing to do," in part because they become more vulnerable to sexual assault.

It's also widely believed that youngsters in countries with a lower legal age learn to drink responsibly and moderately. There is one problem with that impression: it is not true. "The highest rate of cirrhosis of the liver is in France," where it's legal to drink at 16, says Chuck Hurley, chief executive officer of Mothers Against Drunk Driving. According to a study by the U.S. Department of Justice, fewer American adolescents drink than teens in most other industrialized countries.

Instead of offering teens a beer, parents should present their children with clear rules and expectations. Research shows that involved parents are less likely to raise kids with drinking problems. Give them strategies for avoiding trouble, like telling them to call home for a ride rather than getting into a car with someone who has been drinking. Most important, be a good role model. "Parenting is not supposed to be a popularity contest," says Richard Lerner of the Institute for Applied Research in Youth Development at Tufts University. "If the parent is not modeling honest, safe behavior, it's unlikely the kid will believe that he's supposed to act responsibly. You don't want to be like Tony Soprano, who seemed surprised that his son, A.J., was not a model citizen." Someday, your kids will thank you.

With Pat Wingert, Sarah Kliff and Aisha Eady

From *Newsweek,* June 25, 2007, pp. 36–37. Copyright © 2007 by Newsweek. www.newsweek.com Reprinted by permission via PARS International.

An Update on the Effects of Marijuana and Its Potential Medical Use

Forensic Focus

SHERWOOD O. COLE

Introduction

Marijuana is the most commonly used illicit drug in the United States (National Institute on Drug Abuse [NIDA], n.d.; Compton, Grant, Colliver, Glantz, & Stinson, 2004). The task of offering expert testimony on the clinical or psychological effects of the drug is particularly difficult. This is due to two primary factors: (1) the controversy related to classifying marijuana compared to other psychoactive drugs and (2) the widespread lack of a balanced perspective on the effects of marijuana.

Regarding the first factor, marijuana is not a simple drug (it contains over 200 compounds) and, unlike most psychoactive drugs, is hard to describe from a single perspective. Also, its effects are phase-dependent and, to a large degree, individualistic. Accordingly, rather than classifying marijuana among other psychoactive drugs, most authors prefer to treat it as a separate topic or issue (Ray & Ksir, 2004). Most certainly, marijuana is not a narcotic, as it is often incorrectly referred to by law-enforcement agencies and the legal system.

Regarding the second factor, the public is bombarded with culturally confusing messages about the risks and benefits of marijuana (Alexander, 2003). The public and some professionals view marijuana from two conflicting perspectives, resulting in a lack of a balanced (moderate) view of its action. Some view marijuana as a very dangerous drug while others see it as a harmless drug. Those viewing marijuana as a dangerous drug are supported by the federal government's prohibition of possession and use of the drug and by outdated and unproven horror stories about marijuana-related criminal acts (Ray & Ksir, 2004). Those viewing marijuana as a harmless drug base their opinions primarily on personal experiences with the drug and on the belief that the federal government has been lying and exaggerating the potential danger of marijuana.

In view of the above issues, there seems to be a specific need to provide updated data on marijuana for scientific accuracy and forensic credibility. Forensic science relies upon facts and scientific findings (not speculation or anecdotal information), and the value of forensic testimony is seriously compromised in those instances where such standards are not implemented.

This article attempts to present an updated picture of the effects, potential dangers, and possible beneficial uses of marijuana in hopes that it will provide a valuable database for scientific reporting in the context of expert forensic testimony. In order to assure that the picture of marijuana presented here is current, only recent studies are reviewed. While no attempt has been made to exhaust all available studies, a genuine attempt has been made to be representative and fair in reviewing such findings.

The Nature of Marijuana and Its Action

Marijuana (also referred to as cannabis in the literature) is a preparation of leafy material from the cannabis plant (Cannabis sativa). While herbal cannabis contains over 400 compounds, including over 60 cannabinoids, its most important and primary active ingredient is delta-9-tetrahydrocannabinol (THC) (Ashton, 2001). Cannabinoids are chemicals that are unique to the cannabis plant and are structurally related to THC. The main recreational purpose of marijuana is its euphoric effect or high, although the drug can also produce dysphoric reactions such as panic and anxiety (Ashton). The potency of marijuana varies depending upon the part of the plant used and the amount of resin present. The flowering top of the plant contains the most resin, with the leaves and fibrous stalk containing progressively less. While marijuana of past years may have been relatively harmless, experimentation and crossbreeding have resulted in an increase in the potency of the drug found on the market today (Compton et al., 2004; ElSohly, et al., 2000). Evidence obtained from confiscated marijuana suggests that its increase in potency nearly doubled during the period from the early 90s to the late 90s (ElSohly, et al.). There is also some suggestion that the increase in the potency of marijuana may contribute to the rising rate in abuse (Compton et al.).

The mechanism of action underlying cannabinoids has only recently been clarified (D'Souza & Kosten, 2001) and involves the identification of two receptor subtypes referred to as CB1 and CB2 (Ledent et al., 1999; Watson, Benson, & Joy, 2000). CB1 receptors are distributed throughout the central nervous system including the cerebral cortex, hippocampus, amygdala, basal ganglia, cerebellum, thalamus, and brainstem (Ashton, 2001) as well as some areas of the peripheral nervous system (Ledent et al.). The newly discovered endogenous cannabinoid anandamide is believed to be a critical pre-synaptic component of neurotransmitter systems related to CB1 subtype systems and involved in the central mediation of marijuana effects (Ashton). This conclusion finds support in studies where pretreatment with the CB1 antagonist SR 141716 blocked the effects of smoked marijuana on self-reports of acute intoxication (Huestis et al., 2001) as well as the effects of peripherally administered anandamide on induced overeating (Williams & Kirkham, 1999). In contrast to CB1 receptors, less is known about CB2 receptor types, although they are found mainly in immune cells. However, the role of cannaboids in the immune system is likely to be multifaceted and, at present, remains vague (Watson et al., 2000).

Marijuana Dependence, Withdrawal, and Treatment

While the latest edition of the American Psychiatric Association's Diagnostic and Statistical Manual of Mental Disorders recognizes marijuana dependence (2000), it is less certain about marijuana withdrawal symptoms and their clinical significance. However, evidence clearly suggests that individuals using marijuana can develop both dependence and withdrawal symptoms, although under a narrower range of conditions than with some other drugs (Watson et al., 2000; Johns, 2001). Such withdrawal symptoms include restlessness, insomnia, anxiety, increased aggression, anorexia, muscle tremors, and autonomic effects (Ashton, 2001). In heavy users of marijuana, these symptoms appear to be more pronounced during the initial 10 days of abstinence, but some symptoms may persist as long as 28 days (Kouri & Pope, 2000). The symptoms are similar in type and magnitude to those observed with nicotine withdrawal and less severe than those observed with alcohol or opiate withdrawal (Budney, Hughes, Moore, & Novy, 2001). While the development of tolerance to the drug may lead some marijuana users to escalate dosage, the presence of withdrawal symptoms encourages continued use of the drug.

While the treatment of marijuana dependence is still in its infancy, there appear to be some interesting prospects on the horizon. For one, there is some optimism about the potential therapeutic use of the CB1 antagonist SR 141716A (and possibly other similar antagonists) in the treatment of marijuana dependence, although caution is advised (D'Souza & Kosten, 2001). In contrast to chemical treatment, brief intervention programs that utilize multi-component therapy (motivational, cognitive, behavioral) appear to be more effective than single component therapy in treating cannabis-dependent adults

(Babor, 2004). Additional intervention programs directed at curbing marijuana use/abuse include the use of targeted public service announcements with high-sensation-seeking adolescents (Palmgreen, Donohew, Lorch, Hoyle, & Stevenson, 2001) and family skill training to equip parents with drug information and coping strategies (Spoth, Redmond, & Shin, 2001).

One additional important finding of interest is the evidence from animal studies of an interconnected role of CBI and opiate receptors in brain areas and its potential importance to the mediation of addictive behavior (Ledent et al., 1999). The cross-sensitization observed between delta-9-THC and morphine, which was symmetrical, suggests that common neurobiological substrates may be involved in addiction to marijuana and opiates (Cadoni, Pisanu, Solinas, Acquas, & DiChiara, 2001). These homologies between cannabinoids and opiates, while not providing direct evidence for a causal relationship between cannabis and opiate use, are nonetheless consistent with this possibility (Parolaro & Rubino, 2002). The functional link in the mechanism of addictive action by both types of drugs may be through u-opiate receptor influence on mesolimbic dopamine systems (Manzanares et al., 1999; Rubino, Massi, Vigano, Fuzio, & Parolaro, 2000). While there may also be functional links between cannabinoid properties and other centrally acting drugs, these links are at present less clearly defined (Wiley & Martin, 2003).

Deleterious Effects of Marijuana

The areas reviewed here include (1) the effects of marijuana on cognitive performance; (2) the potential role of marijuana as a stepping-stone to "hard drug" use; and (3) the relationship of marijuana use to the later development of psychotic illness. Following this, comments will be made regarding some additional marijuana effects of continued interest in the literature.

The effects of marijuana on cognitive performance. The impairment of cognitive performance by cannabis is generally well accepted in the literature. In some respects, this impairment is similar to that observed with alcohol and includes slow reaction time, lack of coordination, deficits in concentration, and impairment in performance of complex tasks (Ashton, 2001). However, two specific issues appear to be of primary interest in the context of such impairment: (1) the influence of amount of marijuana on cognitive impairment, and (2) the duration or sustaining power of the cognitive impairment produced by the drug.

Regarding the first of these issues, evidence clearly suggests that there is a direct relationship between the amount of marijuana use and the degree of cognitive impairment. For example, in studies where a large battery of neuropsychological tests were employed, abstaining subjects with a history of heavy marijuana use performed significantly less well than controls or subjects with a history of moderate drug use (Bolla, Brown, Eldreth, Tate, & Cadet, 2002; Solowij et al., 2002). Interestingly, while heavy marijuana users differed from controls on the majority of tests administered in one study, the moderate drug users differed very little from controls (Solowij et al.). In general, while the impairment in cognitive functions resulting from marijuana use is moderate, it would appear to have the potential of impairing driving ability, operation of equipment, task proficiency, and daily functioning.

Regarding the duration or sustaining power of cognitive impairment resulting from marijuana use, results are less consistent. For example, some evidence suggests that the cognitive deficits associated with cannabis use may persist up to only 7 days after subjects last smoked the drug (Pope, Gruber, Hudson, Huestis, & Yurgelun-Todd, 2001), while other evidence suggests that such cognitive deficits may persist up to 28 days after abstinence from marijuana (Bolla et al., 2002). Such a difference in findings raises critical issues related to possible mechanisms by which the drug mediates such discrepancies. In the case of the short-term deficits, the effects may simply be associated with marijuana-induced agitation associated with withdrawal from the drug often lasting this long (Pope et al.). However, in the case of cognitive deficits persisting up to 28 days, such an explanation is inadequate. In this case, the deficits may be due to neurological changes in the previously mentioned cannabinoid receptor systems and the effect of marijuana on such systems over a longer period of time (Solowij et al., 2002). In addition, marijuana-induced hypo-activity in the posterior cerebellum may play an immediate role in such a cognitive deficit, particularly in light of the role of this brain area in the sense of timing (Block et al., 2000a). The effects of marijuana on attention-related regional cerebral blood flow may also play some underlying role in such a cognitive deficit (Block et al., 2000b). However, the relevance of these changes in activity level and blood flow to the issue of duration of cognitive impairment remains unclear.

While the bulk of evidence strongly supports the findings of a cognitive impairment produced by marijuana, one study reported no evidence for cognitive decline between heavy, light, and non-users of cannabis (Lyketsos, Garrett, Liang, & Anthony, 1999). However, the failure to detect cognitive decline in this case may reflect insufficient heavy or chronic use of cannabis or the use of insensitive assessment instruments (Solowij et al., 2002).

The potential role of marijuana as a stepping stone to "hard drugs." Marijuana has long been referred to as a gateway drug, implying that its use serves as a stepping stone to the later use of other "hard drugs" (e.g., heroin, cocaine, hallucinogens, etc.). Such an assumption finds strong support in studies where both national diversity and differences in subsequent "hard drug" use have been investigated.

In one Australian twin study, twin pair members who had used cannabis by age 17 had higher additional drug-use rates than their twin siblings who had not used cannabis by age 17 (Lynskey et al., 2003). It is unlikely such differences were due to environmental factors since the twin pairs were raised in the same household. While the association between early marijuana use and later additional drug use did not differ significantly between monozygotic and dizygotic twins, the age of initiation of cannabis use (before age 17) was influenced by heritable factors (Lynskey et al.).

Additional non-twin studies conducted in New Zealand and the United States generally support the findings of the above study in that early cannabis use preceded the later use of other

illicit drugs (Fergusson & Horwood, 2000; Wagner & Anthony, 2002; Merline, O'Malley, Schulenberg, Bachman, & Johnston, 2004). In one of these studies, subjects previously using cannabis on more than 50 occasions per year demonstrated hazards of subsequent illicit drug use that were 59 times higher than non-users (Fergusson & Hotwood). Another one of these studies also points out the persistence of such subsequent drug use; it was still rather prevalent among adults 35 years of age, although influenced by adult role and experiences (Merline et al.). Not only does marijuana use increase the risk of subsequent illicit drug use, it also increases the risk of problems in general, which limits the individual's adjustment and performance (Brook, Balka, & Whiteman, 1999).

While there is little dispute over the influence of early marijuana use on subsequent "hard drug" use, one of the major focal points of recent studies has been on the possible mechanism mediating such a relationship. One author suggests that the relationship is due to the fact that initial cannabis use may encourage later broader experimentation, reduce perceived risk of using other drugs, and bring users into contact with other drugs (Lynskey et al., 2003). A similar view is the suggestion that the interconnection between early marijuana use and subsequent illicit drug use is due to drug exposure opportunities; i.e., marijuana users will increasingly be exposed to greater opportunities to experiment with other drugs (Wilcox, Wagner, & Anthony, 2002). While both of the above mechanisms have a ring of truth about them, one cannot rule out, in light of previous evidence of cross-sensitization of delta-9-tetrahydrocannabinol and morphine (Cadoni et al., 2001), the potential role of neurobiological substrates in such a relationship. Although such a mechanism may not mediate the relationship between early marijuana use and all types of subsequent "hard drug" use, it may serve some role in the subsequent use of opioids. It is also possible that the relationship between early marijuana use and subsequent illicit drug use is non-causal and reflects factors not yet adequately addressed by studies (Fergusson & Horwood, 2000).

The relationship of marijuana use to later development of psychotic illness. One of the most interesting and important areas of marijuana research in recent years is the relationship between early marijuana use and the subsequent development of mental illness. In general, recent evidence obtained from cross-sectional national studies supports the conclusion that the previous use of marijuana significantly increases the subsequent occurrence of schizophrenia (van Os et al., 2002; Arseneault, Cannon, Witton, & Murray, 2004; Veen et al., 2004) and major depression (Brook, Brook, Zhang, Cohen, & Whiteman, 2002). Overall, cannabis use appears to confer a two-fold risk of the later development of schizophrenia compared to that found in the general population (Arseneault et al.). Further evidence also suggests that, while gender and age may further influence the onset of the first psychotic episode, it is the use of cannabis itself that proves to be a much stronger predictor of the onset of the first psychotic episode (Veen et al., 2004). Parenthetically, it is of further interest to note that comorbidity (presence of additional mental illness) is also present in many adolescent substance users (including marijuana users) (Latimer, Stone, Voight, Winters, & August, 2002; Robbins et al., 2002). Such an overlap in adolescent predictors increases, markedly, the difficulty of defining the association between early marijuana use and subsequent mental illness (McGee, Williams, Poulton, & Moffitt, 2000).

While the evidence for the previous use of marijuana increasing the subsequent development of mental illness is relatively strong, the mechanism underlying this linkage is a controversial and highly debated topic. Although it is fairly clear that the linkage between previous marijuana use and mental illness is not simply a fortuitous or temporal association, suggestions as to the causative factors that may contribute to it are diversified. For example, one author suggests that early cannabis use may trigger or exacerbate symptoms of mental illness in subjects who may already be at genetic risk for developing the mental illness (Veen et al., 2004). This view appears to have some credibility in light of the aforementioned evidence for a co-occurrence of drug use and mental illness in adolescents (Latimer et al., 2002; Robbins et al., 2002). However, the majority of evidence suggests that cannabis use demonstrates temporal priority in relationship to mental illness (precedes it) and can produce psychosis in individuals who have no history of mental illness (Johns, 2001; van Os et al., 2002). More realistically, it may be appropriate to suggest that cannabis use is likely to play a causal role with regard to psychosis, but that it is not a necessary or sufficient condition for schizophrenia (Arseneault et al., 2004). That is to say, cannabis use is a component cause, one part of a constellation of causes that leads to subsequent schizophrenia (Arseneault et al.). Additional evidence suggests that such a "component cause" explanation of the linkage between cannabis use and mental illness may not go far enough (Leweke, Giuffrida, Wurster, Emrich, & Piomelli, 1999). In this case, the level of endogenous cannabinoids in the cerebrospinal fluids of schizophrenics was significantly higher than in controls, suggesting that a type of "hyper-cannabinergic state" in the central nervous system may contribute to the pathogenesis of schizophrenia (Leweke et al.). However, the relatively small sample of subjects in this study (10 schizophrenic patients) somewhat restricts the generalities of the findings. It is quite apparent that the final word on the mechanism underlying the linkage between marijuana use and subsequent mental illness awaits further study.

Additional miscellaneous marijuana effects. The harmful effects of marijuana on the respiratory and cardiovascular systems have long been recognized (National Institute on Drug Abuse, n.d.; Ashton, 2001). Like tobacco, marijuana smoke increases the risk of cancer and lung damage (Watson et al., 2000). This should not be surprising since marijuana contains most of the same chemical components (except nicotine) that are found in tobacco. Also, the smoking of marijuana causes changes in the cardiovascular system that are, in general, characteristic of stress (Ray & Ksir, 2004). Recent studies further emphasize the increased risk of cardiac problems associated with such changes. For example, evidence suggests that chronic abuse of marijuana may increase the risk of stroke in young men aged 18-30 years (Bulletin Board, 2002) and that such an increased risk remains well past the period of withdrawal symptoms caused by abstinence from the drug. Additional evidence suggests that, within 1 hour after smoking marijuana, the risk of myocardial infarction onset was elevated approximately 5 fold (Mittleman, Lewis, Maclure, Sherwood, & Muller, 2001). Fortunately, after 1 hour, the risk of such an effect decreases markedly. While the risk of myocardial infarction significantly increases after smoking marijuana, the risk is much less than that associated with cocaine use (Mittleman et al., 1999).

Another long-standing interest associated with marijuana use is the concept of "amotivational syndrome" (Ray & Ksir, 2004). This syndrome is generally described as a diminished motivation accompanied by a loss of energy and drive to work. Such characteristics can, undoubtedly, have an important impact on one's ability to learn, school performance, and general effectiveness in dealing with everyday problems. However, such a syndrome may represent nothing more than the ongoing intoxication in frequent marijuana users (Johns, 2001). This appears to be particularly plausible in light of the long half-life of marijuana in the body and the fact that daily smokers can be chronically intoxicated (Ray & Ksir, 2004).

Finally, the impairment of short-term memory (ability to easily recall information learned just seconds or minutes before) by marijuana remains one of the most consistent findings in the literature. Since CB 1 receptors are distributed in the hippocampus, interference with their function may play a role in such impairment by marijuana, possibly by disrupting the encoding process (Hampson & Deadwyler, 1999). As to whether such an impairment in short-term memory is more permanent or tends to diminish with the passage of time is debatable (Johns, 2001). In any event, such impairment in short-term memory has the potential for impacting cognitive performance as discussed previously.

The Potential Medical Use of Marijuana

One of the most hotly-debated issues in our society is the legalization of marijuana for medical purposes. In spite of the continued debate, the evidence for the medical benefits of the drug grows and presently includes, by conservative estimate, the following uses (Watson, et al., 2000; Ray & Ksir, 2004):

1. Reduction of the fluid pressure in the eyes of glaucoma patients.
2. Reduction of severe nausea caused by certain drugs in the treatment of cancer.
3. Stimulation of appetite and reduction of pain associated with wasting syndrome in patients with cancer and AIDS.
4. As a possible anticonvulsant in the treatment of epilepsy.

While the potential medical benefits of marijuana are generally recognized, the legalization of the drug for such purposes has, nevertheless, been hampered by three critical issues:

1. Marijuana is labeled a Schedule I drug under the Controlled Substance Act of 1970, which implies it has no accepted medical use and has high abuse potential. Accordingly, it is not available by prescriptions written by physicians.

2. There is general fear by the public that the legalization of marijuana for medical purposes would open the door to a general increased availability and abuse of the drug in our society.

3. There may not be a necessity for legalizing marijuana for medical purposes since there are presently alternative drugs that are equally effective and available for treatment.

Each of these issues will be briefly discussed in order to disclose the nature and potential fallacy of the position. It is hoped that such a discussion will indicate that medical marijuana may have a future, albeit in a slightly different direction than it is presently going.

Regarding the labeling of marijuana as a Schedule I drug by the federal government (FDA) and its lack of availability by prescription, the issue is not black and white. The National Institute on Drug Abuse did provide medical-grade marijuana cigarettes to a few patients with FDA approval of a "compassionate use" protocol (Ray & Ksir, 2004). The labeling of the drug as Schedule I pertains to the plant (botanical product) or to synthetic equivalents of the plant, not to all drugs containing THC (The Science of Medical Marijuana, n.d.). For example, Marinol (dronabinol) is a synthesized drug in capsule form containing THC in sesame oil and is available by prescription under a Schedule II label (The Science of Medical Marijuana, n.d.). The factor limiting the prescribing of Marinol by physicians may simply be the lack of awareness of the drug's efficacy or the fact that a Schedule II label, while making the drug available, is still a restricted category. In any case, the future of Marinol and other potential cannabinoid medications would appear to be found in pure drugs delivered by some means other than smoking (Watson et al., 2000).

The most promising delivery system to date would appear to be some form of inhalation, owing to the rapid onset and potential for better titration by the patient (The Science of Medical Marijuana, n.d.). Ironically, the federal government's handling of the marijuana issue has been so poor that a growing number of states have passed ballot initiatives (e.g., California's Proposition 215) designed to allow individuals to grow their own marijuana (Nofziger, 1998). This has led to additional state and federal legal action that has only further delayed a solution to the medical-marijuana issue (Murphy, 2004; Ray & Ksir, 2004).

Regarding the issue of general fear by the public that the legalization of marijuana for medical purposes would encourage a general increase in the illicit use and abuse of the drug in society, the answer is not immediately clear. However, evidence available suggests that this is not the case. For example, a comparison of marijuana use practices in two cities that are very similar demographically but different in legal availability of marijuana for recreational use (San Francisco, California, and Amsterdam, Netherlands) indicated such practices do not differ in the two locations (Reinarman, Cohen, & Kaal, 2004). Since total removal of criminalization restraints (Amsterdam) does not appear to increase the abuse potential over that observed in the context of such restraints (San Francisco), the partial relaxing of drug-control standards in making medical marijuana available would not appear to exacerbate marijuana abuse problems.

Furthermore, a time-series analysis could be undertaken to determine whether society is consuming marijuana at higher rates or in greater quantities than it was prior to medical legalization (Yacoubian, 2001). Such results could be achieved by monitoring the use of marijuana with national data collection systems (e.g., The National House Survey on Drug Abuse, The Drug Abuse Warning Network, etc.). A further benefit of the relaxing of drug control standards in making medical marijuana available might possibly be the control in the spread of disease by clean needle programs and controlled environments for drug use.

Regarding the fact that the legalization of marijuana may not be necessary because there are alternative drugs that are equally effective and available for treatment, the statement may be partially true and partially false. In the case of some treatment contexts, additional available drugs may be better and safer than marijuana. This appears to be true in the case of the treatment of fluid pressure in the eyes of glaucoma patients with available prescription eye drops. The effect of marijuana, in this case, is short-lived and the doses so high that the modest benefits gained are outweighed by the side effects (Watson et al. 2000). Also, in the case of the possible use of marijuana as an anticonvulsant, the available drug Dilantin (phenytoin) may prove to be equally effective.

In other instances, medical marijuana may not necessarily be better than other legal drugs on the market, but simply an alternative choice in the array of available medications. If marijuana is chosen as an alternative medication to those legally available, it is important to keep in mind that smoked marijuana is a complex mixture of active and inactive ingredients (The Science of Medical Marijuana, n.d.). Accordingly, concerns arise about product consistency, potency of active ingredients, and contamination.

While the debate over medical marijuana continues, cannabinoids are being developed for therapeutic application beyond those previously mentioned here. One of the most important new applications of cannabinoids is their potential role in "neuroprotection," a role associated with their antioxidant action (The Science of Medical Marijuana, n.d.). However, the future of such medications would appear to be found in pure drugs (chemically defined), not with the use of the plant or smoked form of marijuana (Watson et al., 2000).

Summary and Concluding Comments

Marijuana is not a completely benign substance but, rather, is a powerful drug with a variety of effects. Accordingly, it is important to examine these effects in a fair and balanced manner. This article attempts to do this by, first of all, presenting a general review on the nature of marijuana, its mechanisms of action, and evidence for dependence. Following this, the adverse effects of the marijuana on cognitive performance, the drug's role as a "stepping stone" to hard drugs, its potential for contributing to the development of mental illness, and other effects are reviewed for the purpose of demonstrating the cost associated with the drug's use. While these adverse effects are real, they are well within the range of effects tolerated by other medications on the market (Watson et al., 2000). A counterbalance to the adverse effects of marijuana is the fact that the drug clearly has some therapeutic value, albeit in a somewhat different form than the smoked one. Undoubtedly, the future of the growing medical use of cannabinoids depends upon the development of pure drugs, where the consistency of content, purity, and potency of the product can be carefully controlled.

Such a balanced and up-to-date view on the effects of marijuana, as presented here, is particularly important in the context of the forensic need to assure the accuracy and reliability of expert testimony. Such accuracy and reliability of testimony would appear to be particularly critical in light of the United States Supreme Court's ruling in the Daubert decision (Daubert v. Merrell Dow, 1993). While previous evidence was admissible on the basis of its "general acceptance" in the scientific community, the Daubert decision established a new set of criteria for courts to determine the admissibility of evidence. An outline and discussion of these criteria are presented elsewhere (Bloomer & Hurwitz, 2002; Cole, 2003). One of these criteria, "the actual or potential rate of error in the expert's methodology," is particularly relevant to the present discussion. For example, any inaccuracy or deficiency in the assessment of marijuana effects can potentially increase the rate of error in the testimony offered by expert witnesses. Protective measures appear to be particularly relevant in the case of marijuana, where anecdotal information and unscientific assumptions about the drug are still prevalent in the public mindset.

While there has been considerable debate as to whether the Daubert decision has made it easier or more difficult to admit expert testimony (Joseph, Atkins, & Flaks, 2000), there is little doubt that the decision has provided useful and standardized rules for such admission. Contrary to the loose criteria for expert testimony in existence prior to the Daubert decision, testimony that is subjective and controversial is now more likely to be excluded as unreliable (Cole, 2003). Experts in the courtroom are expected to employ the same level of intellectual rigor that characterizes their practices.

Expert witnesses need to become more aware of the scientific basis of their evidence, and up-to-date data is critical to this process. The evidence presented here provides a solid and current database for such witnessing related to marijuana effects. Thorough preparation by a potential witness will increase his or her credibility and will allow the witness to speak with authority and effectiveness.

While serving as an expert witness on the effects of marijuana (or any other psychoactive drug) can be an exciting and challenging role, the changes that have taken place in court procedures suggest the need for better and more thorough preparation. In the final analysis, it is important to remember that the legal game is still an adversarial system of justice.

References

Alexander, D. (2003). A marijuana screening inventory (experimental version): Description and preliminary psychometric properties. The American Journal of Drug and Alcohol Abuse, 29, 619–646.

American Psychiatric Association. (2000). Diagnostic and Statistical Manual of Mental Disorders (text revision). Washington, DC: Author.

Arseneault, L., Cannon, M., Witton, J., & Murray, R. M. (2004). Causal association between cannabis and psychosis: Examination of the evidence. The British Journal of Psychiatry, 184, 110–117.

Ashton, C. H. (2001). Pharmacology and effects of cannabis: A brief review. The British Journal of Psychiatry, 178, 101–106.

Babor, T. F. (2004). Brief treatments for cannabis dependence: Findings from a randomized multisite trial. Journal of Consulting and Clinical Psychology, 72, 455–466.

Block, R. I., O'Leary, D. S., Hichwa, R. D., Augustinack, J. C., Ponto, L. L. B., Ghoneim, M. M., Arndt, S., Ehrhardt, J. C., Hurtig, R. R., Watkins, G. L., Hall, J. A., Nathan, P. E., & Andreasen, N. C. (2000a). Cerebellar hypoactivity in frequent marijuana users. Neuro Report, 11, 749–753.

Block, R. I., O'Leary, D. S., Augustinack, J. C., Ponto, L. L. B., Ghoneim, M. M., Hurtig, R. R., Hall, J. A., & Nathan, P. E. (2000b). Effects of frequent marijuana use on attention-related regional cerebral blood flow. Society for Neuroscience Abstract, 26, 2080.

Bloomer, R. H., & Hurwitz, B. (2002, September). So you're going to testify: What every young neuropsychologist should know about tests and the courts. Paper presented at the American College of Forensic Examiners Conference, Orlando, FL.

Bolla, K. I., Brown, K., Eldreth, D., Tate, K., & Cadet, J. L. (2002). Dose-related neurocognitive effects of marijuana use. Neurology, 59, 1337–1343.

Brook, J. S., Balka, E. B., & Whiteman, M. (1999). The risks for late adolescence of early adolescent marijuana use. American Journal of Public Health, 89, 1549–1554.

Brook, D. W., Brook, J. S., Zhang, C., Cohen, E, & Whiteman, M. (2002). Drug use and the risk of major depressive disorder, alcohol dependence, and substance use disorders. Archives of General Psychiatry, 59, 1039–1044.

Budney, A. J., Hughes, J. R., Moore, B. A., & Novy, P. L. (2001). Marijuana abstinence effects in marijuana smokers maintained in their home environment. Archives of General Psychiatry, 58, 917–924.

Bulletin Board (2002). Chronic marijuana abuse may increase risk of stroke. NIDA Notes, 17, 14–15.

Cadoni, C., Pisanu, A., Solinas, M., Acquas, E., & DiChiara, G. (2001). Behavioral sensitization after repeated exposure to A9-tetrahydrocannabinol and cross-sensitization with morphine. Psychopharmacology, 158, 259–266.

Cole, S. O. (2003). Comorbidity of mental illness and drug treatment requirements: Impact on forensic evidence. The Forensic Examiner, 12 (11 & 12), 28–34.

Compton, W. M., Grant, B. F., Colliver, J. D., Glantz, M. D., & Stinson, F. S. (2004). Prevalence of marijuana use disorders in the United States, 1991–1992 and 2001–2002. Journal of the American Medical Association, 291, 2114–2121.

Daubert v. Merrell Dow Pharmaceuticals, Inc. (1993). 113, S. Ct. 2786.

D'Souza, D. C., & Kosten, T. R. (2001). Cannabinoid antagonists: A treatment in search of an illness. Archives of General Psychiatry, 58, 330–331.

ElSohly, M. A., Ross, S. A., Mehmedic, Z., Arafat, R., Yi, B., & Banahan, B. F. (2000). Potency trends of A9-THC and other cannabinoids in confiscated marijuana from 1980–1997. Journal of Forensic Science, 45, 24–30.

Fergusson, D. M., & Horwood, L. J. (2000). Does cannabis use encourage other forms of illicit drug use? Addiction, 95, 505–520.

Hampson, R. E., & Deadwyler, S. A. (1999). Cannabinoids, hippocampal function and memory. Life Sciences, 65, 715–723.

Huestis, M. A., Gorelick, D. A., Heishman, S. J., Preston, K. L., Nelson, R. A., Moolchan, E. T., & Frank, R. A. (2001). Blockade of effects of smoked marijuana by the CB1-selective cannabinoid receptor antagonist SR 141716. Archives of General Psychiatry, 58, 322–328.

Johns, A. (2001). Psychiatric effects of cannabis. The British Journal of Psychiatry, 178, 116–122.

Joseph, G. W., Atkins, E. L., & Flaks, D. K. (2000). Admissibility of expert psychological testimony in the era of Daubert. The case of hedonic damages. American Journal of Forensic Psychology, 1 & 3–34.

Kouri, E. M., & Pope, H. G., Jr. (2000). Abstinence symptoms during withdrawal from chronic marijuana use. Experimental and Clinical Psychopharmacology, 8, 483–492.

Latimer, W. W., Stone, A. L., Voight, A., Winters, K. C., & August, G. J. (2002). Gender differences in psychiatric comorbidity among adolescents with substance use disorders. Experimental and Clinical Psychopharmacology, 10, 310–315.

Ledent, C., Valverde, O., Cossu, G., Petitet, E, Aubert, J-F, Beslot, E, Bohme, G. A., Imperato, A., Pedrazzini, T., Roques, B. E, Vassart, G., Fratta, W., & Parmentier, M. (1999). Unresponsiveness to cannabinoids and reduced addictive effects of opiates in CB1 receptor knockout mice. Science, 283, 401–404.

Leweke, F. M., Giuffrida, A., Wurster, U., Emrich, H. M., & Piomelli, D. (1999). Elevated endogenous cannabinoids in schizophrenia. NeuroReport, 10, 1665–1669.

Lyketsos, C. G., Garrett, E., Liang, K. Y., & Anthony, J. C. (1999). Cannabis use and cognitive decline in persons under 65 years of age. American Journal of Epidemiology, 149, 794–800.

Lynskey, M. T., Heath, A. C., Bucholz, K. K., Slutske, W. S., Madden, P. A. E, Nelson, E. C., Statham, D. J., & Martin, N. G. (2003). Escalation of drug use in early-onset cannabis users vs. co-twin controls. Journal of the American Medical Association, 289, 427–433.

Manzanares, J., Corchero, J., Romero, J., Fernandez-Ruiz, J. J., Ramos, J. A., & Fuentes, J. A. (1999). Pharmacological and biochemical interactions between opioids and cannabinoids. Trends in Pharmacological Science, 20, 287–294.

McGee, R., Williams, S., Poulton, R., & Moffitt, T. (2000). A longitudinal study of cannabis use and mental health from adolescence to early adulthood. Addiction, 95, 491–503.

Merline, A. C., O'Malley, P. M., Schulenberg, J. E., Bachman, J. G., & Johnston, L. D. (2004). Substance use among adults 35 years of age: Prevalence, adulthood predictors, and impact of adolescent substance use. American Journal of Public Health, 94, 96–102.

Mittleman, M. A., Mintzer, D., Maclure, M., Tofler, G. H., Sherwood, J. B., & Muller, J. E. (1999). Triggering of myocardial infarction by cocaine. Circulation, 99, 2737–2741.

Mittleman, M. A., Lewis, R. A., Maclure, M., Sherwood, J. B., & Muller, J. E. (2001). Triggering myocardial infarction by marijuana. Circulation, 103, 2805–2809.

Murphy, D. E. (2004, February 26). Court allows medical use of marijuana. New York Times.

National Institute on Drug Abuse. (n.d.). Info-Facts-marijuana. Retrieved March, 3, 2004 from http://www.nida.nih.gov

Nofziger, L. (1998). Forward in Marijuana Rx: The patients' fight for medicinal pot. New York: Thunder's Mouth Press.

Palmgreen, P., Donohew, L., Lorch, E. P., Hoyle, R.H., & Stevenson, M. T. (2001). Television campaigns and adolescent marijuana use: Tests of sensation seeking targeting. American Journal of Public Health, 91, 292–296.

Parolaro, D., & Rubino, T. (2002). Is cannabinoid transmission involved in rewarding properties of drugs of abuse? British Journal of Pharmacology, 136, 1083–1084.

Pope, H. G., Jr., Gruber, A. J., Hudson, J. I., Huestis, M. A., & Yurgelun-Todd, D. (2001). Neuropsychological performance in long-term cannabis users. Archives of General Psychiatry, 58, 909–915.

Ray, O., & Ksir, C. (2004). Drugs, society, and human behavior (10th ed.). New York: McGraw-Hill.

Reinarman, C., Cohen, P. D. A., & Kaal, H. L. (2004). The limited relevance of drug policy: Cannabis in Amsterdam and in San Francisco. American Journal of Public Health, 94, 836–842.

Robbins, M. S., Kumar, S., Walker-Barnes, C., Feaster, D. J., Briones, E., & Szapocznik, J. (2002). Ethnic differences in comorbidity among substance-abusing adolescents referred to outpatient therapy. Journal of the American Academy of Child and Adolescent Psychiatry, 41, 394–401.

Rubino, T., Massi, P., Vigano, D., Fuzio, D., & Parolaro, D. (2000). Long-term treatment with SR141716A, the CB1 receptor antagonist, influences morphine withdrawal syndrome. Life Sciences, 66, 2213–2219.

Solowij, N., Stephens, R. S., Roffman, R. A., Babor, T., Kadden, R., Miller, M., Christiansen, K., McRee, B., & Vendetti, J. (2002). Cognitive functioning of long-term heavy cannabis users seeking treatment. Journal of the American Medical Association, 287, 1123–1131.

Spoth, R. L., Redmond, C., & Shin, C. (2001). Randomized trial of brief family interventions for general populations: Adolescent substance use outcomes 4 years following baseline. Journal of Consulting and Clinical Psychology, 69, 627–642.

The Science of Medical Marijuana. (n.d.). Retrieved June 16, 2004, from http://www.medmjscience.org

van Os, J., Bak, M., Hanssen, M., Bijl, R. V., de Graaf, R., & Verdoux, H. (2002). Cannabis use and psychosis: A longitudinal population-based study. American Journal of Epidemiology, 156, 319–327.

Veen, N. D., Selten, J-P, van der Tweel, 1., Feller, W. G., Hock, H. W., & Kahn, R. S. (2004). Cannabis use and age at onset of schizophrenia. American Journal of Psychiatry, 161, 501–506.

Wagner, F. A., & Anthony, J. C. (2002). Into the world of illegal drug use: Exposure opportunity and other mechanisms linking the use of alcohol, tobacco, marijuana, and cocaine. American Journal of Epidemiology, 155, 918–925.

Watson, S. J., Benson, J. A., Jr., & Joy, J. E. (2000). Marijuana and medicine: Assessing the science base. Archives of General Psychiatry, 57, 547–552.

Wilcox, H. C., Wagner, F. A., & Anthony, J. C. (2002). Exposure opportunity as a mechanism linking youth marijuana use to hallucinogen use. Drug and Alcohol Dependence, 66, 127–135.

Wiley, J. L., & Martin, B. R. (2003). Cannabinoid pharmacological properties common to other centrally acting drugs. European Journal of Pharmacology, 471, 185–193.

Williams, C. M., & Kirkham, T. C. (1999). Anandamide induces overeating: Mediation by central cannabinoid (CB1) receptors. Psychopharmacology, 143, 315–317.

Yacoubian, G. S., Jr. (2001). Beyond the theoretical rhetoric: A proposal to study the consequences of drug legalization. Journal of Drug Education, 31, 319–328.

Sherwood O. Cole, PhD, Diplomate of the American Board Psychological Specialties.

UNIT 4

Other Trends in Drug Use

Unit Selections

25. **Fentanyl-Laced Street Drugs "Kill Hundreds",** David Boddiger
26. **A Nation Without Drunk Driving,** Janet Dewey-Kollen
27. **Some Cold Medicines Move Behind the Counter,** Linda Bren
28. **Drug Addiction,** Ezekiel J. Emanuel
29. **The Right to a Trial,** Jerome Groopman
30. **New Study Shows 1.8 Million Youth Use Inhalants,** Teddi Dineley Johnson
31. **Teens and Prescription Drugs,** *Office of the National Drug Control Policy, Executive Office of the President*
32. **Studies Identify Factors Surrounding Rise in Abuse of Prescription Drugs by College Students,** Lori Whitten

Key Points to Consider

• Why are some drug-related trends more specific to certain subpopulations of Americans than others?

• How significant is socioeconomic status in influencing drug trends? Why?

• What influences have contributed to the dramatic spread of prescription drug abuse in the United States?

• What role do advertising and the media play in influencing drug use?

• What factors cause drug-related trends to change?

Student Web Site
www.mhcls.com/online

Internet References
Further information regarding these websites may be found in this book's preface or online.

Drug Story.org
   http://www.drugstory.org/drug_stats/druguse_stats.asp
Marijuana as a Medicine
   http://mojo.calyx.net/ olsen/
Monitoring the Future
   www.monitoringthefuture.org
Prescriptions Drug Use and Abuse
   http://www.fda.gov/fdac/features/2001/501_drug.html
SAMHSA
   http://www.drugabusestatistics.samhsa.gov/trends.htm
United States Drug Trends
   www.usdrugtrends.com

Rarely do drug-related patterns and trends lend themselves to precise definition. Identifying, measuring, and predicting the consequence of these trends is an inexact science, to say the least. It is, nevertheless, a very important process.

Some of the most valuable data produced by drug-related trend analysis is the identification of subpopulations whose vulnerability to certain drug phenomena is greater than that of the wider population. These identifications may forewarn of the implications for the general population. Trend analysis may produce specific information that may otherwise be lost or obscured by general statistical indications. For example, tobacco is probably the most prominent of gateway drugs, with repeated findings pointing to the correlation between the initial use of tobacco and the use of other drugs.

The analysis of specific trends related to drug use is very important, as it provides a threshold from which educators, health care professionals, parents, and policy makers may respond to significant drug-related health threats and issues. Over 20 million Americans report the use of illegal drugs. The current rate of illicit drug use is similar to rates of the past two years. Marijuana remains as the most commonly used illicit drug at 14.8 million current users.

Historically popular depressant and stimulant drugs—such as alcohol, tobacco, heroin, and cocaine—produce statistics that identify the most visible and sometimes the most constant use patterns. Other drugs such as marijuana, LSD, Ecstasy and other "club drugs" often produce patterns widely interpreted to be associated with cultural phenomena such as youth attitudes, popular music trends, and political climate.

Another continuing concern addressed in this unit focuses on mental illness and its relationship to drug abuse. Currently, 25 million Americans are believed to suffer from Serious Psychological Distress, and of those, more than 5.6 million are dependent upon, or abuse illicit drugs or alcohol. Approximately 30.4 million American adults have suffered at least one Major Depressive Episode in their lifetime. Of those who suffered from MDE in the past year, 24.3 percent abused illicit drugs or alcohol. Among youth 12–17, over 2 million were diagnosed as having a MDE in the past year. Of these youth, 34.6 percent abused illicit drugs or alcohol in the past year. Females in both the adult category and the minor category reported higher rates of MDE than males. The rates of their association with illicit drugs were similar to that of males. The relationship between drug use, mental illness, and suicide among youth continues to be a major nationwide health worry.

Two other continuing trends are those that involve the abuse of prescription drugs and those that involve the use of methamphetamine. Americans are abusing prescription drugs more than ever before with the most frequently mentioned offenders being oxycodone and hydrocodone. There are currently 5.2 million

persons who use prescription pain relievers for non-medical reasons. Of those who used pain relievers for non-medical reasons, 60 percent obtained them free from a friend or relative. Secondly, the pandemic spread of methamphetamine through rural cities, counties, and states is suggesting abuse patterns and health issues beyond those related to cocaine. From the West to the Midwest, methamphetamine is reported by local and state officials as the number one illegal drug problem. This is not, however, reflected in the most recent federal government survey data which puts the number of methamphetamine users at less than 1 million. In contrast, the number of Oxycontin users remains in excess of 1.2 million. Although the federal government has modified its survey methods to more accurately identify the number of meth users, many worry that the meth problem is still understated and greatly outweighs those problems associated with other illegal drugs—at least in the West, Southwest, and Midwest.

Information concerning drug use patterns and trends obtained from a number of different investigative methods is available from a variety of sources. On the national level, the more prominent sources are the Substance Abuse and Mental Health Services

Administration, the National Institute on Drug Abuse, the Drug Abuse Warning Network, the National Centers for Disease Control, the Justice Department, the Office of National Drug Control Policy, and the surgeon general. On the state level, various justice departments, including attorney generals' offices, the courts, state departments of social services, state universities and colleges, and public health offices maintain data and conduct research. On local levels, criminal justice agencies, social service departments, public hospitals, and health departments provide information. On a private level, various research institutes and universities, professional organizations such as the American Medical Association and the American Cancer Society, hospitals, and treatment centers, as well as private corporations, are tracking drug-related trends. Surveys abound with no apparent lack of available data. As a result, the need for examination of research methods and findings for reliability and accuracy is self-evident.

The articles in this unit provide information about some drug-related trends occurring within certain subpopulations of Americans. While reading the articles, it is interesting to consider how the trends and patterns described are dispersed through various subpopulations of Americans and specific geographical areas.

Additionally, much information about drugs and drug trends can be located quickly by referring to the list of websites in the front section of this book.

Fentanyl-Laced Street Drugs "Kill Hundreds"

With street names such as drop dead, flatline, and lethal injection, fentanyl-laced heroin and cocaine are marketed by drug dealers as the ultimate high. But these drugs are so dangerous that hundreds have died.

DAVID BODDIGER

Mike Wickster, a bald and tattooed 34-year-old, has been brought back from death's door ten times after overdosing on heroin, most recently on heroin he believes was laced with the powerful synthetic opiate fentanyl. He survived and eventually wound up in jail where he had to go "clean". With help, he has stayed off drugs for 7 months and now works in a harm-reduction programme trying to help drug users. But friends from his drug-using past still call when they have found a source for heroin with fentanyl.

"Just yesterday someone said, 'I know where to get fentanyl.' People want it because it's powerful and extreme. Deaths are like an advertisement—for every 10 people that die, 100 more will go looking for it," he says.

Fentanyl is not new to veteran abusers, but in the past it had been obtained by diverting prescriptions. According to Timothy Ogden, Chicago's top Drug Enforcement Administration (DEA) official, clandestine fentanyl labs were occasionally discovered in the 1980s and 1990s. But those operations were nowhere near the size and scope of today's fentanyl networks controlled by international drug traffickers.

"In 30 years of law enforcement experience, I haven't seen this much of a threat before," Ogden says. "It's like a game of Russian roulette, only you're putting five bullets in the chamber."

Health workers began to notice a spike in opiate overdoses and overdose deaths late last year. When sophisticated toxicology tests of autopsy material revealed the presence of fentanyl, police started testing the heroin from street dealers finding the synthetic opiate.

By May this year, fentanyl overdoses had spread to cities in eight states, including Chicago, Detroit, St Louis, Philadelphia, Pittsburgh, and Camden, New Jersey. Fentanyl has been linked to 130 deaths in Detroit and 100 in Chicago in only a few months. In New Jersey, the drug cocktail killed three and hospitalised 42 in one weekend alone.

"The May numbers are the highest we've seen yet, and we expect that trend to continue," says Edmund Donoghue, medical examiner for Chicago's Cook County. "This is something we haven't seen in Chicago before. We're really stunned by it. We have had problems where ambulances were called for multiple overdoses, entire groups of people in the same place."

Compounding the problem, the demographics of heroin abuse in the USA are starting to shift. While overall demand for heroin has remained stable in recent years, what once used to be considered an urban drug is now showing up in suburban areas and attracting younger users.

In June, a recent high school graduate and son of a suburban Chicago police officer was found dead in his car from a fatal overdose of fentanyl-laced heroin. In a suburb of Detroit, police arrested a dealer and charged him with the fatal overdose of a 17-year-old female student.

"[Heroin] is no longer considered just an inner city drug. It's out in the suburbs, and that's why it's becoming such a big issue," says Wickster.

A 2005 report by the US Justice Department's National Drug Intelligence Center noted an increase in heroin abuse in Chicago suburbs, "resulting in a rise in the consequences of heroin abuse in Chicago, a primary market area." This increase is attributed particularly to an increase in the number of users under the age of 25 years.

Many health-care workers who help treat substance abusers believe the USA's traditional focus on "supply-side" law enforcement, which emphasises the prosecution over treatment, is futile. The supply-side approach, critics charge, fails to address the root of the problem: demand. Money is poured into enforcement, they say, while effective outreach and addiction treatment programmes go under-funded.

Access to methadone programmes is one of the most pressing problems for heroin users who want help, says Sarz Maxwell, medical director for the Chicago Recovery Alliance (CRA), which runs a mobile methadone clinic and needle-exchange programme. The clinic is operated out of a large van that travels around the city distributing methadone for 2 hours a day, 7 days a week.

"Methadone is one of the best researched tools we have. It's incredibly safe and effective, and without it, the relapse rate is 95%. Yet it continues to be unbelievably regulated", she says.

US Congressman Danny Davis, whose Illinois district has been one of the hardest hit by the fentanyl crisis, agrees that regulation of public methadone programmes is far too restrictive. 600 people are on a waiting list for methadone treatment in Chicago's Cook County alone, he says.

According to Jennifer Smith of the John H. Stroger Hospital, Chicago's largest public hospital system, between April, 2004, and June, 2006, 906 patients in three Chicago hospitals were forced to wait an average of 17 days for entry into methadone maintenance programmes. Only 18% actually entered the scheme. When methadone treatment was made available the day after hospital discharge, 67% of patients entered treatment.

In 2003, some 10000 people seeking publicly funded substance-abuse treatment in Illinois were turned away, says Melody Heaps, president of Treatment Alternatives for Safe Communities, an Illinois non-profit group that provides behavioural health services to people with substance abuse and mental-health disorders. Wickster was one of the statistics. "I'm calling around to get on methadone and they said they were full. I said, 'I'm gonna die' and they told me, 'You're not the only one,'" he recalls.

Westley Clark, director of the Center for Substance Abuse Treatment at the Substance Abuse and Mental Health Services Administration (SAMHSA), part of the federal government's Department of Health and Human Services, noted that during the past 3 years, Illinois received $22 million in federal funding for addiction recovery programmes.

"We are trying to enhance the availability of treatment and prevention strategies. We hope by the end of the fiscal year to have 40 states with more money," Clark says.

Clark adds that SAMHSA also encourages doctors to use methadone and provide behavioural treatment, as well as educating them about buprenorphine, which helps decrease heroin craving.

But many heroin users who lack health insurance coverage have had difficulty affording buprenorphine, says the CRA's Maxwell.

The epidemic also points to the need to pursue a much more aggressive harm-reduction strategy, including providing drug users with the opiate-antagonist naloxone so they can administer the drug to their friends on the spot, says Maxwell. Since the recent spike in overdose deaths, most emergency responders now carry naloxone. But distributing it freely to users has met some resistance.

Maxwell believes her organisation's naloxone distribution programme has saved 450 lives through "peer revival" since the initiative was started in 2000. Wickster, whose life was saved more than once by naloxone injections, including once when his wife injected the drug, now helps distribute it along with clean needles and information on the same street corners where he once bought and sold drugs.

"People need to be educated about naloxone, especially now with fentanyl everywhere," Wickster says. "Saving someone's life just may motivate them to say, 'that's enough'. That's what happened to me."

Federal drug authorities, however, currently do not support naloxone distribution to drug users. "I'm not sure that's a rational strategy in and of itself. Local jurisdictions should be permitted to use whatever strategies they believe are important . . . but it is not a federal position," SAMHSA's Clark says.

According to the European Centre for Drugs and Drug Addiction, trafficking of illegally produced fentanyl is on the rise, noting that seizures of the drug has been reported in a number of countries bordering the Baltic Sea and the Russian Federation. In Estonia, for example, fentanyl appeared on the drug market as a heroin substitute in 2001.

US officials warn that where there is heroin abuse and fentanyl, overdose epidemics like those being seen in US cities are likely to follow. "Other countries should know this can happen and they need to have the resources to address it. If it's not recognised, it's costly", says SAMHSA's Clark.

Donoghue, the Chicago medical examiner, agrees. "We need to warn other countries that if you have a market for heroin and cocaine, you may begin to see this happen."

A Nation Without Drunk Driving

Janet Dewey-Kollen

Rather than continuing to allow bad decisions made by people with alcohol-soaked brains to cause almost 40% of all U.S. traffic crash fatalities, a key component of MADD's campaign is to focus on the major role that advanced technology can play in eliminating drunk driving. MADD has secured the commitment of a number of vehicle manufacturers, alcohol ignition interlock companies, the Insurance Institute for Highway Safety and others to work together on this major task.

In November, Mothers Against Drunk Driving (MADD) announced an ambitious new goal: wipe out drunk driving in the United States within a generation. Many people will consider the goals of MADD's Campaign to Eliminate Drunk Driving impossible to achieve and perhaps even a bit audacious. No doubt forces within the alcohol industry will work to discredit MADD and to devalue the effort.

However, MADD is on the right track, and it is time for innocent motorists and pedestrians to hold the life or death advantage over those who choose to drive after drinking too much. Rather than continuing to allow bad decisions made by people with alcohol-soaked brains to cause almost 40% of all U.S. traffic crash fatalities, a key component of MADD's campaign is to focus on the major role that advanced technology can play in eliminating drunk driving.

Can the more than 13,000 people killed annually by drivers with blood alcohol content levels of 0.08 or higher have been avoided? Fast-forward and imagine a scene where a driver gets into a vehicle, grabs the steering wheel or gear shift, and an automatic, non-invasive sensor measures the drivers BAC level.

When this in-vehicle sensor detects an illegal blood alcohol level, an ignition interlock system prevents the drunk driver's vehicle from starting. When the vehicle won't start, there is no drunk driving, no more critical decisions made by an alcohol-soaked brain, no speeding through a downtown street, no running a red light, and no deaths for an innocent family.

Madd's Four Campaign Elements

The MADD campaign has four key elements. First, intensive and high-visibility law enforcement. MADD will support crackdowns twice a year and frequent enforcement efforts that include sobriety checkpoints and saturation patrols in all 50 states. The deterrence effect of frequent, ongoing and highly visible sobriety checkpoints and saturation patrols simply can-

not be underestimated. Research has proved repeatedly that frequent (weekly) high-visibility enforcement of drunk driving laws can decrease the rate of drunk driving in a community.

Results from a 2005 study by the Insurance Institute for Highway Safety entitled "Low-Manpower Checkpoint: Can They Provide Effective DUI Enforcement in Small Communities?" showed nighttime drinking drivers decreased by 64% in two experimental counties in West Virginia after a year of weekly, low-manpower sobriety checkpoints.

Implementation of Interlock Technologies

The second component includes a push to require alcohol ignition interlock devices for all convicted drunk drivers. A key part of this effort will be working with judges, prosecutors and state driver's license officials to stop the revolving door of repeat offenders.

Alcohol ignition interlocks reduce DUI recidivism by an average of 65% in comparison to drivers with suspended or revoked licenses who should not be driving at all, yet they are woefully underused in the U.S. Most states have interlock-enabling laws, but only about 10% of the 1.4 million drivers arrested for DUI receive mandated interlock use as an outcome of sentencing.

Researchers investigating the limited use of this public safety tool find that many courts still hold outdated images of interlock equipment inadequacies of 15 year ago. But like advances in overall computer technology, microprocessors make today's interlock technology amazingly reliable and effective.

New Mexico is currently the only state to mandate alcohol ignition interlocks for first offense DUI. MADD intends to push for more states to pass similar and upgraded legislation as a short-term strategy to reduce drunk driving. "We need to keep in mind that dependent users of alcohol may not simply be defiant law breakers but people with a significant self-control problem," said Paul Marques of Pacific Institute for Research and Evaluation. About one-third of all drivers arrested or convicted of driving under the influence are repeat offenders. These drivers are 40% more likely to be involved in a fatal crash than those without prior DUIs, according to the NHTSA.

Advanced Vehicle Technologies

The third component is the establishment of a Blue Ribbon panel of international safety experts to assess the feasibility of a range of technologies that would prevent drunk driving. MADD has secured the commitment of a number of vehicle manufacturers, alcohol ignition interlock companies, the Insurance Institute for Highway Safety and others to work together on this major task.

Critical objectives for this technology are that it be unobtrusive to the sober driver, moderately priced, absolutely reliable, and set at the legal BAC limit. With many core components already in place, integrating this technology into vehicles will require committed development resources and time.

Sweden has announced a goal of having alcohol ignition interlocks on trucks and school buses by 2010 and on all new cars in 2012. The move came about after a two-year ignition-interlock trial program in Sweden where DUI recidivism rates dropped, crash rates and hospital admissions decreased, and trial participants experienced lasting decreases in repeat DUI arrests.

Mobilization of Grassroots Support

The fourth component is the public demand for safer roadways free of drunk drivers. MADD and more than 400 of its affiliates will work with drunk driving victims, families, community leaders, and policy makers in the fight to eliminate drunk driving. In its 25 years of traffic safety activism, MADD has worked with more than 500,000 victims of drunk driving crashes. Sadly, most people don't take an active role in drank driving prevention until they actually experience the loss of a loved one or they are involved in a crash themselves.

The chance of being in an alcohol-involved crash is a constant threat for every person who drives or rides on roadways in America and even more of a risk for law enforcement. The U.S. Department of Transportation estimates that about three in every 10 Americans will be involved in an alcohol-related crash at some time in their lives. Certainly families will want to help teens survive their high-risk years, given that more than 36% of crash fatalities of young people age 15–20 are alcohol-related.

MADD's Campaign to Eliminate Drunk Driving will require many levels of effort and cooperation, and everyone can find a way to help make this major shift in U.S. traffic safety a reality. Not since the development and integration of the seat belt into all vehicles have we seen such an important traffic safety opportunity. Forty percent fewer crash deaths in the U.S. and hundreds of thousands fewer injuries and victims is not a goal to be taken lightly; it is one that all should rally behind to bring to fulfillment.

JANET DEWEY-KOLLEN is a longtime traffic safety advocate and has worked at the local, state and national levels. She is also a freelance writer and a child passenger safety technician. E-mail Janet with topic requests atprojplan@aol.com.

Some Cold Medicines Move Behind Counter

Some over-the-counter (OTC) cold and allergy medicines are being moved behind the counter at pharmacies nationwide as part of the fight against illegal drug production.

LINDA BREN

Under the Patriot Act signed by President Bush on March 9, 2006, all drug products that contain the ingredient pseudoephedrine must be kept behind the pharmacy counter and must be sold in limited quantities to consumers after they show identification and sign a logbook.

Pseudoephedrine is a drug found in both OTC and prescription products used to relieve nasal or sinus congestion caused by the common cold, sinusitis, hay fever, and other respiratory allergies. The drug is also a key ingredient in making methamphetamine— a powerful, highly addictive stimulant often produced illegally by "meth cooks" in home laboratories.

The new legal provisions for selling and purchasing pseudoephedrine-containing products are part of the Combat Methamphetamine Epidemic Act of 2005, which was incorporated into the Patriot Act. These "anti-meth" provisions introduce safeguards to make certain ingredients used in methamphetamine manufacturing more difficult to obtain in bulk and easier for law enforcement to track.

According to the National Institute on Drug Abuse, methamphetamine use and abuse is associated with serious health conditions including memory loss, aggression, violence, paranoia, hallucinations, and potential heart and brain damage. The Drug Enforcement Administration says there is a direct relationship between methamphetamine abuse and increased incidents of domestic violence and child abuse.

Meth users ingest the substance by swallowing, inhaling, injecting, or smoking it. There are currently no safe and tested medications for treating methamphetamine addiction.

The new law affects several hundred OTC products for children and adults, such as Sudafed Nasal Decongestant Tablets, Advil Allergy Sinus Caplets, TheraFlu Daytime Severe Cold SoftGels, Tylenol Flu NightTime Gelcaps, and Children's Vicks NyQuil Cold/Cough Relief. "There are very few decongestants

on the market that don't contain pseudoephedrine," says Charles Ganley, M.D., director of the Food and Drug Administration's Office of Nonprescription Products.

Ganley says that products containing pseudoephedrine are still available without a prescription and that they are packaged the same way as any OTC drug. "The only difference is that people will have to go to the pharmacist to buy them," he says. "They just need to ask for them and show ID, and know that there's a limit to the amount they can purchase."

Buyers must show a government-issued photo ID, such as a driver's license, and sign a logbook. Stores are required to keep a record about purchases, which includes the product name, quantity sold, name and address of purchaser, and date and time of the sale, for at least two years. Single-dose packages containing 60 milligrams or less of pseudoephedrine are excluded from the recordkeeping requirement, but must still be stored behind the counter.

The federal law limits the amount of pseudoephedrine an individual can purchase to 3.6 grams in a single day and 9 grams in a month at a retail store. For example, a person may buy Advil Allergy Sinus Caplets, which contain pseudoephedrine and other ingredients, in quantities of up to 146 tablets in one day and 366 tablets in one month. The number of pills or amount of liquid medicine allowable will vary depending on the type of product and its strength.

The limits on the amount an individual can purchase became effective April 8, 2006. The requirements to place products behind the counter and to keep a logbook take effect Sept. 30, 2006. Many drug stores are already complying voluntarily or because some state laws require similar controls.

Drug companies are reformulating some of their products to eliminate pseudoephedrine. Pfizer, for example, while still offering Sudafed nasal decongestants, which contain pseudoephedrine, also markets a line called Sudafed PE as an "on the shelf" alternative. Sudafed PE contains the active ingredient phenylephrine, which is not used to make methamphetamine, and so is not under the same restrictions as pseudoephedrine.

"Drugs that contain phenylephrine are also safe and effective," says Ganley. "The dosing is a little different—you have to take them a little more frequently than the pseudoephedrine-containing drugs because their effects are not as long-lasting."

The anti-meth provisions of the Patriot Act restrict the sale of two other drug ingredients, ephedrine and phenylpropanolamine, because of their potential to be used illegally to make methamphetamine. Like pseudoephedrine, drugs containing these ingredients must be placed behind the counter, and buyers must show identification to purchase a limited quantity.

Synthetic ephedrine is used in some topical drugs, such as nose drops, to temporarily relieve congestion due to colds, hay fever, sinusitis, or other upper respiratory allergies. It is also used orally for temporary relief of asthma symptoms.

Phenylpropanolamine was commonly used in OTC decongestants and weight-loss drugs. Today, it is unlikely that consumers will find phenylpropanolamine in their drug stores, says Ganley. In 2000, the FDA asked drug manufacturers to discontinue marketing products containing phenylpropanolamine because of an increased risk of bleeding in the brain (hemorrhagic stroke) associated with the ingredient. The FDA has taken regulatory actions to remove phenylpropanolamine from all drug products.

From *FDA Consumer*, July/August 2006, pp. 18–19. Published 2006 by U.S. Food and Drug Administration. www.fda.gov

Cancer in the Courts

Drug Addiction

EZEKIEL J. EMANUEL

Virginia waddled down the corridor to an examination room. Her ankles were terribly swollen and her eyes were tinged with yellow. Five years earlier, she had been treated for a very small and early-stage breast cancer. For a while, she was fine—teaching third-graders, living with her husband and four children. Then, at age 56, her cancer came back. She began having difficulty breathing, and a CT scan revealed the cancer had metastasized to her lungs and liver. After a year and a half, the conventional drugs stopped working, but Virginia wanted to fight, and she opted for experimental drugs. The day she came to the office, Virginia had just completed a trial of a second experimental agent, but it had failed to halt the growth of the tumor in her liver.

One of the hardest parts of being an oncologist is explaining to a patient that her battle has come to an end. This has been made more difficult by the growing number of experimental drugs and treatments that give dying patients hope. While I began talking to Virginia about palliative care and hospice, all she wanted to know was if there was another experimental drug that she could take. I told her that her liver was not functioning adequately and her performance status—her energy level and the amount of time she spent resting in bed—excluded her from more trials. But, regardless of her eligibility, Virginia still wanted access to experimental drugs. Like many young, desperate patients, Virginia was willing to stake almost anything—hair loss, infections, nerve or lung damage, nausea and vomiting, even a high chance of death—on the unlikely prospect that an unproven drug could extend her life.

Recently, the courts decided that such a gamble is the prerogative of terminally ill patients like Virginia. On May 2, the District of Columbia Circuit Court ruled, in a 2–1 decision, that dying patients have a constitutional right to any experimental drug that has passed the safety phase of human testing—Phase I—even while the drug's effectiveness is still unproven and undergoing research. The case, *Abigail Alliance* v. *von Eschenbach* (for the FDA), was inspired by a 21-year-old with head and neck cancer named Abigail Burroughs.

In 2001, Abigail had exhausted conventional cancer treatments and wanted to get an experimental agent, Erbitux, being developed by ImClone—the biotech company of Martha Stewart fame—or another drug, Iressa, being developed by the phar-

maceutical giant AstraZeneca. But, like Virginia, Abigail was too frail to qualify for the research trials. She died just three months after conventional treatments failed. Shortly after her death, her father, Frank Burroughs, started the Abigail Alliance for Better Access to Developmental Drugs, a nonprofit organization, which fights to ensure that cancer patients, no matter how sick and weak, can have their insurance companies buy any experimental drug that has passed safety testing. To this end, the Alliance sued the FDA.

But, while the D.C. Circuit Court ruling in favor of the Abigail Alliance might seem like a victory for patients like Virginia, it's not. What cancer patients really need are new drugs that are proven to fight and cure cancer, not access to an array of unproven chemicals that provide false hope. Furthermore, drugs with minimal safety testing could actually increase the suffering of patients dying of cancer. If implemented, the Circuit Court's ruling threatens the very research process that gets drugs tested and quickly delivers safe and effective ones to the most patients. This could force us to relive the types of historic tragedies that shaped federal drug policies in the first place.

In the summer of 1937, Harold Cole Watkins, the chief chemist and pharmacist for the S.E. Massengill Company, set out to make a liquid form of sulfanilamide, a popular drug used to treat strep throat. He quickly discovered that sulfanilamide dissolves in diethylene glycol, and, after adding a raspberry flavor to the concoction, the company sent shipments of the new elixir across the country. But, rather than curing patients, the elixir caused severe abdominal pain, vomiting, and convulsions. Within two months, more than 100 people in 15 states, many of them children, had died. The solvent—diethylene glycol—was a form of anti-freeze.

For most of our history, drug manufacturers have had minimal oversight. After the Civil War, various patented remedies and cures—what became known as "snake oils"—were developed and sold to unsuspecting people. Many of the so-called treatments of the late eighteenth and early nineteenth centuries made people vomit or explode with diarrhea. But, despite the need, there was little ability to test and regulate these concoctions. Doctors did not know how to design a real research study to see if a drug worked; even the statistical techniques necessary to evaluate a study were only just being developed for farming and had not migrated to health care.

Around the turn of the twentieth century, clinical research matured sufficiently to begin early drug-testing, although without today's scientific rigor. In 1906, Congress passed the Wiley Act, which gave the government power to recall drugs that were adulterated or misleadingly labeled. This was an attempt to get "cures" for diabetes and other worthless potions off the market. But the sulfanilamide tragedy created a public furor, and, in response, Congress passed the 1938 Federal Food, Drug, and Cosmetic Act, which required manufacturers to prove that drugs are safe before they can be marketed.

It took another tragedy for Congress to increase FDA regulation. In 1960, the Richardson-Merrell pharmaceutical company in Cincinnati submitted an application to the FDA to sell a drug called Kevadon. It was the very first application for Frances Oldham Kelsey, a new medical officer. After reviewing it, she decided that data from early safety trials were inadequate, and she delayed the approval. But other countries did not. European doctors, who had been prescribing the drug to pregnant women under the name Thalidomide, began to report an increase in deformed newborns. By the time the dangers of the drug were understood, thousands of deformed babies had been born. As a result, Congress passed the Kefauver-Harris Amendments, which required proof of efficacy before drugs could be sold.

The Thalidomide tragedy reminds us that even the early trials for safety (the Phase I trials) are not—and are not intended to be—foolproof tests of safety. Something safe enough to be subjected to further research does not imply it is safe enough to be sold to patients. Typically, these early Phase I studies are done on 20 to 80 patients. Many side effects, such as the deformities found with Thalidomide, just don't show up in the early-phase studies. Subsequent trials that typically involve hundreds and thousands of patients—though they focus on the efficacy of the new drugs—are also designed to closely monitor safety.

The Abigail Alliance approach would eliminate this kind of careful monitoring on larger groups of patients before widespread access becomes available. Instead, unproven drugs would be tested for safety in fewer than 80 people and then could be sold to patients. The benefit of a few desperate patients would come at a steep cost for the rest of us, especially the Virginias and Abigails of tomorrow. It would make it much harder to get people to enroll in research studies and get the data necessary to show whether a drug really was effective or not. Why should people enroll in a randomized, controlled study—where they could be put in the group receiving only conventional treatment—when they could just get their insurance to pay for whatever drug they thought was best?

We have had experience with this "expanded access" folly before. In the late '80s and early '90s, there was tremendous excitement about treating metastatic breast cancer with bone-marrow transplants. The procedure was grueling and included risks like organ damage, life-threatening infections, and even death, and there was little scientific evidence it actually worked. But people were convinced it was a cure and persuaded many states to enact laws mandating insurance companies pay for

transplants. Large, government-funded, randomized clinical studies were designed to evaluate its effectiveness, but over 20,000 women got transplants outside the trials. It took years to enroll just 1,000 women to complete the research.

The results: bone-marrow transplantation was not effective compared with regular chemotherapy. Precious time was wasted due to delayed enrollment. Thousands of women were unnecessarily subjected to bone-marrow transplants—and hundreds died in the process, often in isolation rooms separated from their families. Millions, if not billions, of dollars were spent on a substandard treatment.

If, as in the case of bone-marrow transplantation, the Abigail Alliance's "expanded access" delays research, then future patients with cancer will suffer because they will have access to fewer proven treatments. Americans will get access to unproven experimental agents for a few patients at the expense of more, faster research and access to proven treatments for every patient. This is the height of irrationality born of desperation. And it is the major reason why many, if not most, cancer advocacy groups oppose the Abigail Alliance's effort. As the National Breast Cancer Coalition put it: "[A] policy expanding availability of investigational new drugs for individuals outside of clinical trials will weaken the move towards more and better research, expanded clinical trials, and access to care for all Americans."

Expanded access would also rob the rest of us who may never need a cancer treatment. Individuals and society in general are struggling to pay the nation's $150 billion-plus drug bill. And that is for medications proven to work. Now add the requirement that insurance companies pay for drugs we don't know work, and you have a formula for financial disaster. Costs would skyrocket as we pay billions through our insurance premiums and Medicare taxes for worthless drugs.

Given these Problems, why did the D.C. Circuit Court want to go back to the snake-oil days? Citing a physician-assisted suicide case, *Washington* v. *Glucksberg,* the Court argued that a "mentally competent, terminally ill adult patient [has a substantive due process right] to access potentially lifesaving post-Phase I investigational new drugs." Essentially this makes access to unproven drugs a fundamental constitutional right, not just an interest that can be weighed against other interests. This sets an almost impossibly high bar for the FDA to overcome to restrict access to these drugs. More important, the Circuit Court seems to have gotten the assisted-suicide cases wrong. Chief Justice William H. Rehnquist made clear in both *Cruzan* v. *Director* (the 1990 case about terminating life-sustaining treatments) and *Vacco* v. *Quill* (a 1997 assisted-suicide case) that the right is not a right to die but to not have intrusive life-sustaining treatments imposed against one's wishes, based "on well established traditional rights to bodily integrity and freedom from unwanted touching." A right to bodily integrity does not imply a right to demand medical treatments.

The Circuit Court majority disingenuously claimed that the right it is recognizing is narrow, applying to terminally ill patients, but a constitutional right such as this cannot be so restricted. What about people suffering from multiple sclerosis, rheumatoid arthritis, congestive heart failure, diabetes, or any number of illnesses? They too would have the constitutional right to demand access to whatever experimental drugs they wanted, especially if there were no proven treatments for their debilitating condition. This is hardly narrow.

The court also made an argument from history: "[T]he government has not blocked access to new drugs throughout the greater part of our Nation's history. Only in recent years has the government injected itself into consideration of the effectiveness of new drugs." This is pure historical revisionism. The reason the government failed to limit access to new drugs in the nineteenth century was not based on philosophical or legal objections to such regulation but on limits of science and statistics.

Finally, the court all but ignored the fact that the FDA has not been deaf to the concerns of patients like Abigail. For example, in 1987, the FDA established something called a Treatment Investigational New Drug (IND). This has allowed tens of thousands of terminally ill patients to quickly access drugs before they are approved for general sale. The FDA gives Treatment INDs on the condition that the drug has shown some evidence of being effective (not just safe, as the Abigail Alliance would have it) and that giving it to the patient won't inhibit the collection of research data. But the advantage is that the administration of the drug is carefully monitored for safety. Amazingly, the Circuit Court's majority does not even acknowledge the existence of such a process, although, as the dissenting judge makes clear, the majority was well-aware of it.

If we're not protecting a dying patient's right to safe and effective drugs, what exactly are we protecting with rulings like *Abigail Alliance* v. *von Eschenbach?* What the Circuit Court seeks to preserve on behalf of the terminally ill is hope in a hopeless situation. As every oncologist knows, maintaining a dying patient's hope is essential to their quality of life. But maintaining hope should never be confused with delaying the research studies that could give hope to future patients or administering ever-more ineffective and unproven treatments. Often, giving toxic drugs is just an excuse for appearing to do something—no matter how futile, painful, and ultimately hopeless—rather than offering compassion.

Getting Virginia another experimental drug was not going to stop her breast cancer from growing and eventually killing her. I gently explained to her that investing all her energy chasing after another unproven drug was not going to help her and her family. Virginia was disappointed and refused to consider hospice, because she saw it as giving up. Holding her hand, I talked to her about spending time with her husband and daughters and making a videotape for her future grandchildren. We also discussed getting visiting nurses to come to her house. I saw her once more in my office. She was more accepting and found at least some of the activities meaningful. Because of her failing liver, less than three months later, she lapsed into a coma and died with her family present.

EZEKIEL J. EMANUEL, a breast oncologist and bioethicist, is the author of *The Ends of Human Life* and the creator of the Medical Directive living will form.

The Right to a Trial

Should dying patients have access to experimental drugs?

JEROME GROOPMAN

In 2002, Kianna Karnes, a forty-one-year-old nurse and mother of four in Brownsburg, Indiana, was given a diagnosis of kidney cancer. She had surgery to remove the tumor, but a year later the cancer spread to her bones. Karnes's doctors treated her with interleukin-2, a protein that stimulates the immune system and, in its synthetic form, was the only medication approved by the Food and Drug Administration for use against kidney cancer. The drug causes high fevers and the accumulation of fluid in the lungs, and it shrinks tumors in only fifteen per cent of cases. "High-dose interleukin-2 damn near killed her," Karnes's father, John Rowe, recalled recently. "It's a brutal treatment, but her husband pushed her pretty hard, because he didn't want to lose her."

Karnes did not improve on interleukin-2, and Rowe began to look into experimental therapies. Four years earlier, he, too, had received a diagnosis of a life-threatening cancer, chronic myelogenous leukemia, for which there were few effective treatments. He had found the Web site of a man from South Carolina with leukemia, who had enrolled in a clinical trial of an experimental drug, now called Gleevec, and had experienced a remarkable remission. Rowe learned about a trial comparing Gleevec with interferon, then the standard therapy for his illness, and asked his doctor to help him apply. He was the last patient to be admitted. "Luckily, I got the good stuff," he told me, referring to Gleevec. His cancer has been in remission for five years.

While Rowe was recovering, he worked on Capitol Hill, in the office of Dan Burton, a Republican congressman from Indiana, who chaired the House Government Reform Committee. He became friendly with Frank Burroughs, whose daughter Abigail had died of a head-and-neck cancer at the age of twenty-one, after being denied admission to a clinical trial for a drug that might have helped her. After her death, Burroughs founded the Abigail Alliance, an advocacy group that seeks to make experimental drugs—commonly defined as drugs that are being tested by a pharmaceutical company and have yet to be approved or rejected by the F.D.A.—available to people with terminal illnesses. In 2004, Rowe learned from the Abigail Alliance that Pfizer and Bayer had each developed a drug for kidney cancer and were conducting clinical trials. But, while he was trying to enroll Kianna in a trial, she learned that her cancer had spread to her brain. Surgeons removed the tumors, but a history of brain cancer almost always disqualifies a patient from

participating in a trial. Such patients are prone to seizures, and it can be difficult to distinguish symptoms caused by an experimental therapy from those caused by the illness it is supposed to be treating. Rowe tried to obtain one of the drugs through a provision in F.D.A. regulations known as "compassionate use," which allows pharmaceutical companies, with the agency's permission, to release an experimental drug to a patient who is not enrolled in a clinical trial. With the help of the Abigail Alliance he contacted Pfizer and Bayer to discuss compassionate use, but he made little headway.

"By this time, we were way down the road, and Kianna was in dire straits," Rowe said. "So I finally asked Congressman Burton for help." Burton told a staff member to look into Karnes's case, and, in March, 2005, Rowe got a call from Robert Pollock, a journalist on the editorial board of the *Wall Street Journal,* who had been writing about the efforts of politicians in Congress to prevent the husband of Terri Schiavo, the brain-dead Florida woman, from removing her feeding tube. "I think if the Congress can pass a law for Terri Schiavo, a single person, that's O.K.," Pollock told Rowe. "But there are a lot of people like your daughter. And I think Congress should pass a law to help all of them." On March 24th, the *Journal* published an editorial titled "How About a 'Kianna's Law'?," urging Congress to pass legislation requiring the F.D.A. to grant dying patients access to experimental drugs.

That morning, Burton's office contacted Pfizer and Bayer, as well as the F.D.A. In the afternoon, an F.D.A. official called Rowe and told him that if either of the companies submitted an application for compassionate use on Karnes's behalf the agency would approve it. A couple of hours later, Kianna's doctor heard from representatives of Pfizer and Bayer, offering to prepare applications for Karnes. "At nine-forty-one that same night, Kianna died," Rowe told me. "Just like Abigail. Too little, too late."

By January, both experimental drugs had been approved by the F.D.A. for use against advanced kidney cancer. "Here is a case where her old man understood about clinical trials," Rowe said. "I knew about compassionate use; I had a friendship with a powerful member of Congress; I've got the *Wall Street Journal* behind me. But I still couldn't save her life. Now, what about the thousands of people out there who don't have these kinds of resources available to them? I don't know that either of these drugs would have saved Kianna's life. But wouldn't it have been nice to give her a chance?"

Families of seriously ill patients are understandably consumed by a desire to help, and stories about unexpected recoveries inspire hope that an experimental drug might prove to be lifesaving; it's possible that Abigail Burroughs and Kianna Karnes would now be alive had they been able to take one. Yet a similar impulse—to protect patients' lives—lies behind F.D.A. regulations restricting access to such drugs. Guaranteeing drug safety has been part of the agency's mandate since 1938, when Congress passed the Federal Food, Drug, and Cosmetic Act after more than a hundred people died from taking a medicine for strep throat which contained diethylene glycol, an active ingredient in antifreeze. Today, the vast majority of patients with life-threatening diseases are treated with drugs that have been approved by the F.D.A. after a stringent evaluation process designed to insure that they are safe and effective. It typically takes a pharmaceutical company six and a half years from the time it discovers a promising molecule to gather enough data to apply to the F.D.A. for permission to test a drug on patients. Completing the clinical trials requires, on average, another seven years: an initial set (Phase I), usually involving fewer than a hundred patients, to determine the maximum tolerated dose and likely side effects; a second set (Phase II), involving several hundred patients, to identify the diseases—or stages of a disease—that are affected by the experimental therapy; and a final set (Phase III), in which the drug is given to several thousand patients and compared with another drug that has already been approved by the F.D.A., or with a placebo. After the trials, the F.D.A. reviews the results and, usually in consultation with an advisory panel of experts, decides whether to approve an experimental drug. Drug companies pay most of the costs for clinical trials, and by the time a drug reaches the market the manufacturer will have spent nearly a billion dollars on its development.

Nearly ninety per cent of drugs that enter Phase I trials are eventually abandoned because they are shown to be unsafe or ineffective. (Last week, Pfizer announced that it was cancelling its Phase III trial of torcetrapib, an experimental drug for heart disease, after eighty-two patients in the study died. Pfizer had spent almost a billion dollars on torcetrapib, which had shown exceptional promise in earlier trials. "This drug, if it worked, would probably have been the largest-selling pharmaceutical in history," Steven E. Nissen, the chairman of cardiovascular medicine at the Cleveland Clinic, told the *Times*.) In the past decade, the number of new drugs approved by the F.D.A. has fallen sharply. According to a recent article in the *Journal of the American Medical Association,* between 1994 and 1997 the agency approved an average of nearly thirty-six new drugs a year, but between 2001 and 2004 the approval rate averaged just twenty-three a year.

The Bush Administration, seeking to reverse this trend, has appointed new leaders to the F.D.A., including Andrew von Eschenbach, the recently confirmed commissioner, who is a cancer specialist from Houston and a close friend of the Bush family; and Scott Gottlieb, the deputy commissioner for medical and scientific affairs, who, as a fellow at the American Enterprise Institute, published frequent editorials arguing for a more flexible approach to drug approval, particularly for cancer drugs. "The FDA is trying to save patients from the harmful

effects of new medicines that haven't fully proved their mettle," Gottlieb wrote in an Op-Ed piece in the *Oklahoman,* in May, 2005. "In the process, many more patients will die waiting for the good medicines than from using bad ones."

At the same time, the Abigail Alliance, which shares this view, has gained political influence. In November, 2005, Senator Sam Brownback, a Republican from Kansas, who survived melanoma and is the co-chair of the Senate Cancer Caucus, introduced a bill that would compel the F.D.A. to make experimental drugs available to seriously ill patients who have exhausted standard treatments. Brownback, who had met with Frank Burroughs and read about Kianna Karnes in the *Wall Street Journal,* called the bill "Kianna's Law." Six months later, the Abigail Alliance won its first victory in court against the F.D.A., when the United States Court of Appeals for the District of Columbia upheld, in a two-to-one decision, the group's argument, in Abigail Alliance v. Andrew von Eschenbach, that access to experimental drugs is a constitutional right.

The opinion—by Judge Judith Rogers, a Clinton appointee, and Chief Justice Douglas Ginsburg, a Reagan appointee—shocked legal scholars and officials at the F.D.A., which had begun drafting proposals aimed at increasing patients' access to experimental drugs. The agency, determined not to cede control of drug regulation to Congress or the courts, intends to release some of the proposals for public comment this week. According to senior F.D.A. officials, the agency is also developing plans for a program that would encourage drug companies to distribute experimental drugs to thousands of cancer patients through their personal physicians. If adopted, the program would constitute the most ambitious initiative by the agency in two decades.

The F.D.A.'s reforms, the D.C. circuit-court decision, and the Brownback bill present different guidelines for providing access to experimental drugs, and it's not clear which, if any, of the proposed changes will ultimately take effect. Nevertheless, the efforts reflect an unlikely convergence of interests between patient-advocacy groups and the deregulation-minded Bush Administration, and they underscore the F.D.A.'s vulnerability to political pressure. Some critics worry that the current regulations aren't strict enough to protect patients. (In September, the Institute of Medicine, a branch of the National Academy of Sciences, released a report that was sharply critical of the F.D.A., and, in particular, of a rule passed by Congress in 1992 that allows pharmaceutical companies to pay the agency substantial fees to expedite reviews of their drugs. The report castigated Congress for failing to provide the F.D.A. with sufficient funds to monitor drugs after they have been approved. It cited Vioxx, the arthritis drug that was withdrawn in 2004 after it was found to double the risk of heart attack.) The challenge will be to insure that deregulation does not occur at the expense of science and safety. "The common perception is that safety and efficiency in drug development are not compatible," Scott Gottlieb told me. "I don't think that's true."

During the first four decades of the twentieth century, drug companies often tested experimental medications by sending them to doctors to give to their patients. The F.D.A. required little information from drug-makers about side effects and had no standard criteria for determining safety or efficacy. In 1960, Frances Kelsey, a doctor and pharmacologist, joined the F.D.A. as one of seven full-time physician drug reviewers. Assigned to evaluate thalidomide, which had been approved in forty-two countries, including much of Europe, as a sedative and an anti-nausea drug, Kelsey was shocked at how little data the agency had about the drug's safety, and she was concerned about its side effects. Richardson-Merrell, which wanted to market thalidomide in the United States, had already distributed it to twenty thousand patients in this country, but Kelsey refused to approve the drug and ordered the company to conduct additional clinical studies. Later, it was discovered that thousands of mothers—most of them outside the United States—who took thalidomide during pregnancy to combat nausea had delivered babies with severely deformed arms and legs, segmented intestines, and closed ear canals. In 1962, Congress passed the Kefauver-Harris Amendments, which required pharmaceutical companies to show the F.D.A. that their drugs were effective and gave the agency greater control over clinical trials.

However, with the advent of the AIDS epidemic, in the nineteen-eighties, regulations that had been praised for protecting the public's health were attacked as too restrictive. AIDS activists demanded what they called "expanded access," arguing that AIDS patients who were not enrolled in a clinical trial should be allowed to take experimental drugs under the supervision of their personal physicians. (They also requested that the F.D.A. do away with clinical trials of AIDS drugs in which some patients received a placebo.) In 1987, the F.D.A. agreed to allow patients who could not participate in clinical trials—because they were too sick or lived too far from a university hospital, where trials are typically conducted—to obtain experimental drugs from their doctors on a compassionate basis, or as part of a national expanded-access program. In both cases, only experimental drugs that had completed at least Phase II of clinical trials were eligible for distribution.

AIDS activists persuaded the F.D.A. to relax its policy on experimental drugs in part by relying on dramatic protest tactics and sympathetic media coverage; members of ACT-UP and other groups covered themselves with fake blood and staged "die-ins" in front of the White House and the National Institutes of Health. Pharmaceutical companies, under political pressure to provide promising therapies for AIDS patients, who at the time faced certain death, agreed to distribute the drugs, despite considerable legal and financial risks. (Drug companies are typically reluctant to supply experimental drugs outside a clinical trial, fearing that patients who suffer adverse reactions will sue the company or that the F.D.A. will demand more extensive safety testing. Moreover, manufacturing an experimental drug for thousands of patients in an expanded-access program is hugely expensive, and there is no guarantee that the F.D.A. will ultimately approve the drug for sale.)

Doctors, too, got swept up in the campaign to distribute experimental drugs. I began treating patients with AIDS in 1981, and for more than a decade I watched helplessly as they grew sicker and died. In 1994, saquinavir, the first anti-H.I.V. protease inhibitor, was tested in clinical trials. In test-tube experiments, the compounds were remarkably potent in preventing the virus from multiplying, and studies on rodents suggested that they were relatively safe; the only known side effect was liver damage, and then only at very high doses. Word of the inhibitors' promise spread rapidly through the AIDS community, and, like many doctors, I was eager to get the drugs to my patients as quickly as possible, by enrolling them in clinical trials. Hoffman-LaRoche, the company that made saquinavir, invited several physicians at my hospital to run one of the trials, and four slots in the study were reserved for patients from my practice. I agonized about which names to submit. Some of my patients were expected to die within weeks, and yet I thought it was possible that the drug would help them. Others, who appeared healthier, had abnormal blood-test results—including elevated levels of liver enzymes—which were likely to disqualify them, so I repeated the tests in a vain effort to obtain values in the normal range. Heartsick, I eventually submitted the names of twenty patients to the nurse in charge of administering the trial, believing that they were the most likely to be accepted. Most of the rest had no chance of being admitted, because they had serious infections, such as cytomegalovirus and systemic cryptococcus (a fungus).

Tom (a pseudonym), a physician living near Boston, belonged to this group. He had developed a cytomegalovirus infection in his retina and was slowly going blind, but each time he visited the clinic he pressed me for information about saquinavir and asked me to tell him when the clinical trial would begin. His father begged me to persuade Hoffman-LaRoche to bend its rules and admit Tom. I said that I would try but had little hope of succeeding, explaining that the trial was designed to assess the drug's safety, and if Tom's vision got worse while he was taking the protease inhibitor we would have to report it to the drug company as an "adverse event." Although we might suspect the infection of his retina to be the cause, Hoffman-LaRoche would have to list "declining vision"—and the F.D.A. would have to consider it—as a possible side effect of the drug.

Saquinavir proved to be strikingly effective against H.I.V. Within a few months, the immune systems of most patients who had taken the drug improved and the amount of H.I.V. in their bodies decreased. They gained weight, and had fewer infections. Tom, who had been denied admission to the trial, soon lost his sight and, not surprisingly, became clinically depressed. I assured him that I would make every effort to see that he did not suffer. He developed seizures, and a brain scan revealed a large mass with the characteristics of a lymphoma. He refused further treatment, was placed on a morphine drip at home, and died with his family at his bedside.

At the time, newspapers were filled with stories of AIDS patients whose lives had been saved by the protease inhibitors. It was later discovered that the drugs caused significant side effects in some patients, including an increased risk of diabetes and elevated cholesterol, but, when used with other anti-viral drugs, protease inhibitors helped reduce the death rate from AIDS in the United States by at least seventy per cent. It is possible that Tom would still be alive if he had been able to take saquinavir.

In the case of other experimental AIDS drugs, however, doctors' expectations were tragically misplaced. In 1980, I spent ten months on a fellowship at U.C.L.A., collaborating with other researchers on a project to purify gamma interferon, a naturally occurring protein made by immune cells. Many scientists had a near-mystical regard for gamma interferon, believing that it could help the immune system defeat infections, as well as cancer. Our laboratory succeeded in purifying a small amount of gamma interferon—the first step toward developing a drug—and we published our results in *Nature* in 1982. Not long afterward, Genentech, a biotechnology company, announced that it had created a synthetic version of the protein and was planning to conduct clinical trials. In 1984, after I had returned to Boston, I helped run a trial of gamma interferon for AIDS patients who had Kaposi's sarcoma, a cancer that causes large lesions on the skin and, in many cases, respiratory failure and internal bleeding. Gamma interferon appeared to be the ideal treatment for these patients. It had been shown to have powerful anti-viral effects in test-tube studies and to reduce the size of tumors in rodents.

I enthusiastically told my AIDS patients about the trial, including George (also a pseudonym), who had recently moved to Boston to be with his partner. George was in reasonably good health; he had not developed any serious infections, and his Kaposi's-sarcoma lesions were mostly on his chest and arms. The goal of the trial was to test the effects of different doses of gamma interferon, and George belonged to the group that received the largest dose. Like many participants, he experienced unpleasant side effects—fevers, muscle pain, and headaches—but he was determined to finish the trial. After six weeks, however, new lesions appeared on his skin and in his mouth, and a chest X-ray suggested that the cancer had spread to his lungs. George was not the only patient who grew sicker on gamma interferon. None of the patients improved, and in at least four cases we believed that the therapy had hastened the tumors' growth. Ultimately, the trial was judged a failure. (Gamma interferon has since proved effective in treating children with a rare immune-system disorder called chronic granulomatous disease.) George reluctantly agreed to undergo chemotherapy, which had little effect. He returned to California, where his family lived, and died five months later. (Although I continue to conduct basic research, I currently have no consulting relationships with pharmaceutical companies whose drugs are under review for approval by the F.D.A.)

If Congress passes Brownback's bill, or the D.C. circuit court's opinion in Abigail Alliance is upheld, there will doubtless be more cases like George's. Brownback told me that the goal of his bill is to "get more testing of treatments and options available in the system for cancer patients, much as we did during the AIDS crisis." However, AIDS is caused by a virus whose presence in the body can be measured by a simple blood test, and is thus much easier to monitor than cancer. Lung cancer, one of the most common forms of the disease, encompasses a dozen different kinds of tumors; a given drug is likely to help only a small sub-set of patients, and it is often impossible to predict which ones. Nevertheless, Brownback's bill would grant conditional approval of experimental drugs that have completed Phase I or Phase II testing, based on preliminary evidence—from test-tube experiments, animal studies, computer simulations, and individual patients—that they might be beneficial and safe. "If the potential risk to a patient of the condition or disease outweighs the potential risk of the product, and the product may

possibly provide benefit to the patient," the bill asserts, then the F.D.A. is obligated to approve the drug if a physician and a patient request it. (The new law would coexist with the current system: if an experimental drug approved under the scheme did not win F.D.A. approval at the end of Phase III trials, it would no longer be distributed.)

Brownback's bill would grant access to experimental drugs to patients with "serious or life-threatening" illnesses; the decision in Abigail Alliance limits such access to patients who have terminal diseases. In both instances, patients would be taking drugs whose risks and benefits are largely unknown. "We all know that Phase I testing doesn't prove that a drug is safe enough," Sonia Suter, a professor of law at George Washington University and an expert in medical ethics, told me. "There are very small numbers of participants in Phase I, and they are treated for a very limited period of time. So if you believe that there is this constitutional right, that there are risks you are willing to take and not have the government interfere, why have a cutoff at Phase I? Why not just say, 'Any drug I'm willing to take,' because of some anecdotal experience, or some animal study, or the molecular structure, is reason to think the drug might work?"

In June, F.D.A. lawyers, in an attempt to have the decision in Abigail Alliance reversed, asked that the entire panel of judges on the D.C. circuit court hear the case en banc. The request was granted last month; the full court will hear the case next year. Many constitutional-law scholars believe that the opinion is flawed and that the case could eventually go before the Supreme Court. In the opinion, the circuit-court judges cite the case of Nancy Cruzan, a young woman who had suffered brain death after a car accident and whose parents were seeking legal permission to disconnect her from life support. In 1989, the case went before the Supreme Court, which ruled that patients have a right to decline medical treatment. (With regard to Cruzan, however, the Court said that her parents had not demonstrated "clear and convincing evidence" that she would prefer to die than to be sustained on life support. Several of Cruzan's friends later testified about her wishes in a lower court, and Cruzan's feeding tube was eventually removed.) The judges in Abigail Alliance reasoned that the same right of self-determination that allows someone to refuse treatment allows him to "choose to use potentially life-saving investigational new drugs." They pointed out that for "over half of our Nation's history"—until the passage, in 1906, of the Pure Food and Drug Act, which made it a crime to sell mislabelled or adulterated medicines—"a person could obtain access to any new drug without any government interference whatsoever."

"This is the kind of case that you see tugging at people's heartstrings," Ira Lupu, a professor of constitutional law at George Washington University, said. "Everyone has a friend or a sibling or, especially, a child who has a fatal illness. You think they're going to die in three to six months anyway, so giving them a drug is their only hope. You can see that the sympathies attached to this could push a judge who is otherwise quite disciplined over the edge." By relying on the Cruzan decision, Lupu said, the D.C. circuit court "walks away from a long-standing aspect of common law: touching somebody without his consent is a battery. The Supreme Court assumes, in Cruzan, that the right to refuse continued treatment is a constitutional right, because it is based on the long-standing right to be protected from battery. As a matter of philosophy, it may seem to make sense that if you can refuse treatment you can also have access to treatment. But, from the perspective of constitutional law, it is very hard to see what platform this court is standing on."

Even if the D.C. circuit-court decision survives legal challenges or Brownback's bill passes, neither gives pharmaceutical companies any incentive to make experimental drugs widely available. Under the existing regulations, only once a drug is approved does the Center for Medicare and Medicaid Services decide whether it will be covered by Medicare, and private insurance companies usually follow the government's lead in determining which drugs to cover. Brownback's bill could be amended to require the government to reimburse companies for the costs of experimental drugs, but they would still face daunting practical and financial obstacles. Richard Merrill, a professor at the University of Virginia Law School and a prominent expert on drug regulation, said that Brownback's legislation "would require a major investment to scale up production of an experimental drug"—after treating only a few hundred patients in Phase I and Phase II trials—"and it would not be at all clear that the drug had a good chance of ultimately being widely marketed, because its safety and efficacy could prove problematic in more extensive human testing."

Brownback's bill stipulates that drug companies cannot be held liable for a patient's adverse reactions to an experimental medication. But this may not be enough to reassure pharmaceutical companies, and it could inadvertently encourage retailers of alternative therapies that have little or no basis in science. "The bill opens the space for products that are sold by charlatans," said David Parkinson, an oncologist who worked at the National Cancer Institute for many years and is now a senior vice-president at the biotech company Biogen Idec. One of Parkinson's tasks at the N.C.I. was to evaluate herbal remedies and animal extracts, such as shark cartilage, that are sold in health-food stores and on the Internet, accompanied by testimonials from patients about their anti-cancer benefits. Some of these products could pass Phase I trials, Parkinson said, and, under Brownback's bill, the F.D.A. would be compelled to approve them.

In March, the F.D.A. approved the use of a drug called Gemzar, in combination with a standard chemotherapy medicine, as a treatment for recurrent ovarian cancer. The agency's Oncologic Drugs Advisory Committee, a group of cancer doctors and statisticians, had voted, nine to two, against approving the treatment, on the ground that it didn't significantly improve the survival rate of patients. In July, Richard Pazdur, the director of the F.D.A.'s Office of Oncology Drug Products, issued a statement defending the agency's decision to overrule the committee. He cited data from Gemzar's manufacturer, Eli Lilly, showing that patients who were given the drug as part of their chemotherapy regimens had longer periods of remission than patients who did not take the drug. "Although improvement in overall survival remains the gold standard," Pazdur wrote, "delay in disease progression" has been advocated as a "surrogate" for clinical benefit in cancer patients.

Many cancer doctors saw the F.D.A.'s decision as evidence that the agency is willing to adapt to patients' needs. When I spoke to Pazdur, he mentioned this—and the agency's recent approval of similar drugs for kidney cancer (Nexavar), multiple myeloma (Revlimid), and a rare gastrointestinal tumor (Sutent). "We need to be more flexible in how we evaluate drugs for patients like this," Pazdur said. "The provision is that the drug's benefits have to be clinically meaningful—and it doesn't mean delaying the progression of the tumor by two days—so you're not approving iffy drugs."

Pazdur said that the F.D.A. has rarely denied a patient's request to obtain an experimental drug under the compassionate-use provision. (He recalled only one instance in which the agency has done so: in the case of a boy with a brain tumor whose parents had refused to give him radiation therapy, the standard treatment for his condition. "That's not a regulatory issue; that was bad medicine," Pazdur said.) He also cited a recent program—modelled on the expanded-access programs for AIDS patients in the eighties—in which the drug Iressa was given to more than twenty-four thousand lung-cancer patients after a Phase II trial yielded promising results. (Ultimately, Iressa was not approved; few patients in Phase III trials improved on the drug, and its use is now restricted to those patients.) Nevertheless, Pazdur acknowledged that pharmaceutical companies currently have little motivation to comply with requests for experimental drugs. "There are some companies that flat out refuse to even get involved in expanded access," he said. "We are told over and over by the industry that the F.D.A. will find some toxicity in the expanded-access program, and the evil Dr. Pazdur will take out his ruler and slap your hand, and the drug will be killed."

Pazdur is overseeing the F.D.A.'s plans for a new program that will enable pharmaceutical companies to distribute experimental drugs to thousands of cancer patients through large networks of community-based oncologists. To be eligible for the program, drugs would have to be at the end of Phase II trials or partway through Phase III, depending on the kind of drug and cancer involved. The oncologists who administer the drugs would be required to report their patients' progress and any side effects to the F.D.A. and to the pharmaceutical companies. The doctors would also have to answer simple questions about the drug—whether patients did better on a high dose twice a day or on a lower dose three times a day, say, or whether it helped patients with an advanced stage of cancer.

To encourage drug companies to participate, the F.D.A. would allow them to recover some of the program's costs, including a portion of the doctors' fees, from patients or insurance companies. But the data generated by doctors and patients could prove equally lucrative. The knowledge that a drug works just as well taken twice rather than three times a day—information that might not be obtained in a Phase III trial—could make it easier to market. Similarly, knowing that a drug helps patients with advanced cancer—the kind of severely ill patients who are generally excluded from clinical trials—could enable a company to obtain broader approval for the drug from the F.D.A. and increase revenues by hundreds of millions of dollars.

The program could also save pharmaceutical companies equally large sums in marketing costs. It is against the law to promote a drug to physicians before it has been approved by the F.D.A., but it is perfectly legal for pharmaceutical companies to provide information about such a drug to a doctor in an agency-approved expanded-access program. Many oncologists tend to be wary of prescribing new medications, because anti-cancer drugs usually cause serious side effects. The more rapidly a doctor can be educated about a drug's toxicity and proper dosing, the less money the pharmaceutical company will need to spend to promote the therapy and the greater the likelihood that the doctors will continue to use it.

The F.D.A. is also proposing to make clinical trials more efficient by adapting them while they are in progress. In a traditional trial, an experimental cancer drug would be tested in a group of lung-cancer patients with different types of the disease, in the expectation that perhaps fifteen to twenty per cent might benefit. An "adaptive trial" might begin with a heterogeneous group and then add patients with a particular type of the disease, as data from outside the trial emerged suggesting that they would be most likely to benefit. "Whenever it comes to discussions about the F.D.A. using adaptive clinical trials to be more efficient, critics say, "Oh, the F.D.A. is cutting corners,'" Scott Gottlieb, the deputy commissioner, told me. "But it is really about the F.D.A. using better science and better technology." Moreover, he added, "there's a real difference between assessing the safety of drugs like Vioxx, for arthritis, and drugs for patients with life-threatening diseases. What might be considered too risky for an arthritis patient could be an acceptable risk for a cancer patient."

In early November, Frank Burroughs, of the Abigail Alliance, met with Andrew von Eschenbach and seventeen other senior officials at the F.D.A. The officials did not mention the new initiatives, but after the meeting Burroughs told me, "For the first time in five years, I felt we were heard, that Dr. von Eschenbach is forward-thinking about our position." Under the program for cancer patients being developed by the F.D.A., both Abigail Burroughs and Kianna Karnes would have been able to obtain the experimental drugs they sought. Still, the program is unlikely to satisfy those who believe that people with a terminal illness have a right to take any drug under development without government interference. "The Abigail Alliance holds to the position that the decisions about experimental drugs should rest with the patient and his physician," Burroughs said.

At the same time, critics who believe that the F.D.A. needs stricter drug regulations are likely to consider the program too radical, and it may not altogether please pharmaceutical companies, either. If many patients with different kinds of tumors started taking experimental drugs outside controlled clinical trials, doctors could have a hard time discerning which of the drugs were working and for which cancers. "The signal-to-noise ratio would be very low if we allowed experimental drugs to be widely distributed," David Parkinson, of Biogen Idec, said. As a result, he speculated, some drug companies might be inclined to abandon cancer research. "Many people think cancer is a lucrative market, but it really isn't when you factor in the risks, since so many experimental agents fail at the stage of Phase III testing," Parkinson said. "There are only a few real blockbuster drugs in cancer treatment, and a businessman can take a conservative approach and reap considerable revenues from developing another statin for high cholesterol, or another antihypertensive for elevated blood pressure. When I go to upper management, I have to convince them that it's worth investing hundreds of millions of dollars in an experimental cancer agent that may well fail. With a new approval system that would make it difficult to identify effective drugs, the risk rises considerably, and this will shift investment from oncology to other areas where the developmental process is well defined and much less risky."

Moreover, the F.D.A.'s initiatives could make it more difficult to recruit patients for clinical trials. Only three per cent of cancer patients in the United States are enrolled in such trials, which are typically conducted at academic medical centers. (Many American drug companies, unable to recruit sufficient numbers of patients, have begun to conduct Phase III trials in Eastern Europe and Southeast Asia, where such studies may be the only way to receive treatment.) If patients can obtain experimental drugs from physicians in their communities, they would have little reason to leave home to participate in a trial. Enrollments are particularly likely to suffer in the case of trials comparing an experimental drug with a standard therapy: what patient would want to risk receiving the standard treatment in a trial when he could get the experimental drug directly from his doctor? "Trying to make progress in cancer should be done by professionals, not by hoping that through this process somehow wonderful drugs should emerge," Parkinson said of the agency's plan to give experimental drugs to patients through community oncologists. "I would venture to say that responsible pharmaceutical and biotechnology companies will react to this as a terrible idea."

Ultimately, the F.D.A. is proposing a national experiment. The goal—to deliver experimental drugs to seriously ill patients who otherwise would probably not be able to obtain them—is a worthy one, but, as in a clinical trial, it entails considerable risks. If some version of the Brownback bill, the D.C. circuit-court decision, or, more likely, the F.D.A.'s plan is eventually adopted, the agency will need to be more involved in the oversight of drugs early in the approval process. It will have to develop new techniques for evaluating data from Phase I and Phase II trials in order to predict with greater accuracy which medications are likely to benefit which patients and when they should be distributed. In short, deregulation of experimental drugs will require new forms of regulation in order to insure that patients like Abigail Burroughs and Kianna Karnes are helped, not harmed. As Richard Merrill, the University of Virginia law professor, put it, "The agency won't just be calling balls and strikes but will be taking some initiative. It's not necessarily a mistake to go in this direction, but it will require a commitment to intervene that is unprecedented."

New Study Shows 1.8 Million Youth Use Inhalants

Known as 'silent drugs,' inhalant abuse rising significantly.

TEDDI DINELEY JOHNSON

Parents who think their homes are drug-free received a wake-up call in March from the National Inhalant Prevention Coalition: Dozens of children die each year from abusing products that are purchased and brought into the home by their parents.

While overall drug use among young people has declined substantially over the past four years, inhalant abuse has increased, according to a new report from the Substance Abuse and Mental Health Services Administration. Based on data gathered from 2002–2004, approximately 598,000 children ages 12 to 17 initiated, inhalant use in the past 12 months, the report said, which translates to 1.8 million new inhalant users in the past three years.

The report, "Characteristics of Recent Adolescent Inhalant Initiates," said nearly 20 percent of youth ages 12 to 17 used inhalants for 13 or more days during their first year of abuse, even though sudden death from cardiac arrest or suffocation can occur on the first use. Products identified by the report as most often abused are solvent-based glues, shoe polish, gasoline, lighter fluid, nitrous oxide, solvent-based markers, spray paints, correction fluid, degreasers, cleaning fluids, products in aerosol cans, locker room deodorizer and paint solvents.

The term "inhalants" refers to more than 1,400 household and commercial products "that are intentionally misused, either by sniffing them directly from the container or "huffing" them through the mouth, to achieve a high. Inhalant abuse is difficult to control because the abused products are legal, serve useful purposes and are readily, available in homes.

Inhalants can harm the brain, liver, heart, kidneys and lungs and can interfere with brain development, said Nora Volkow, MD, director of the National Institute on Drug Abuse, during a March news conference in Washington, D.C., releasing the report and kicking off the 14th annual National Inhalants and Poisons Awareness Campaign.

"These products are very accessible because they are all over our homes and garages, and for that reason they have become the most frequently abused drugs by young children," Volkow said, noting that inhalants are often referred to as the "silent" drugs because they are so difficult for parents to detect.

Abuse of inhalants increased significantly between 2002 and 2005, the report said, with the largest increase noted among eighth-graders, "who may be unaware of the damage inhalants can cause," Volkow said.

Thirty percent of those initiating inhalant use during the past year were 12 or 13 years old, the report said; 39 percent were 14 or 15 and 31 percent were 16 or 17. The majority of the youth were white and from homes with incomes well above the poverty line, with girls found to be abusing inhalants more frequently than boys.

"Now is the time to marshal our collective efforts to reduce and prevent inhalant experimentation and abuse," said Harvey Weiss, MBA, founder and executive director of the National Inhalant Prevention Coalition. "Our children's future may depend on it."

Between 100 and 125 deaths from inhalant abuse are reported each year to the National Inhalant Prevention Coalition, "but many inhalant deaths go unreported or are underreported," Weiss said, noting that the coalition has developed guidelines to help medical examiners, coroners and pathologists determine inhalant deaths.

"If you don't know the signs, you can't save your children," warned Jeff Williams, a Cleveland police officer whose 14-year-old son, Kyle, died in March 2005 after huffing a can of computer dust cleaner that Williams had purchased several days earlier to clean the family's computer keyboard.

Kyle, who had started abusing inhalants about a month before his death after a friend in the neighborhood showed him how to do it, had been complaining that his tongue hurt, Williams said during the news conference. The parents also noticed that their son had been exhibiting uncharacteristic anger. At the time, however, neither Williams nor his wife, who is a nurse, were aware that the two issues—anger and a sore tongue—are common warning signs of inhalant abuse.

As he fought back tears, Williams shared the story of how his wife, upon attempting to wake their son for school, found him sitting up in bed cross-legged, the can of dust cleaner in his lap and the straw that came with the can still in his mouth. Their son had died around midnight, Williams said.

Later, Williams and his wife learned that computer dust cleaner is inhaled mostly by children ages 9 to 15.

"They even have a name for it," Williams said. "It's called 'dusting.' It gives them a slight high for about 10 seconds."

But dust cleaner is not just compressed air, Williams said. It also contains a propellant—a refrigerant similar to what is used in refrigerators—and there is no way to predict if sudden death will occur.

"It's a heavy gas," Williams said. "It decreases the oxygen to your brain, to your heart . . . the horrible part about this is there is no warning. There is no level that kills you. It's not cumulative. It's not an overdose. It can just go randomly, terribly wrong. It's Russian roulette."

From *The Nation's Health,* May 2006. Copyright © 2006 by American Public Health Association. Reprinted by permission.

Teens and Prescription Drugs

An Analysis of Recent Trends on the Emerging Drug Threat

A number of national studies and published reports indicate that the intentional abuse of prescription drugs, such as pain relievers, tranquilizers, stimulants and sedatives, to get high is a growing concern—particularly among teens—in the United States. In fact, among young people ages 12–17, prescription drugs have become the second most abused illegal drug, behind marijuana.

Though overall teen drug use is down nationwide and the percentage of teens abusing prescription drugs is still relatively low compared to marijuana use, there are troubling signs that teens view abusing prescription drugs as safer than illegal drugs and parents are unaware of the problem. This report examines this emerging threat by seeking to identify trends in the intentional abuse of prescription drugs among teens.

Prevalence and Incidence

Next to marijuana, the most common illegal drugs teens are using to get high are prescription medications. Teens are turning away from street drugs and using prescription drugs to get high. Indeed, new users of prescription drugs have caught up with new users of marijuana.

- For the first time, there are just as many new abusers (12 and older) of prescription drugs as there are for marijuana. (SAMHSA, 2006)
- Among 12–17-year-olds, the gap between new marijuana users and new prescription drug users is shrinking. Between 2003 and 2005, the gap closed by 5.9 percent.

  In 2005, the estimated number of 12–17-year-olds who started using prescription drugs in the 12 months prior to the survey was 850,000, compared with 1,139,000 marijuana initiates. In 2003 the estimates were 913,000 for prescription drugs, compared to 1,219,000 marijuana initiates. (NSDUH, 2004 and 2006)

Executive Summary

Teens are turning away from street drugs and using prescription drugs to get high. New users of prescription drugs have caught up with new users of marijuana.

Next to marijuana, the most common illegal drugs teens are using to get high are prescription medications.

Teens are abusing prescription drugs because they believe the myth that these drugs provide a medically safe high.

The majority of teens get prescription drugs easily and for free, often from friends or relatives.

Girls are more likely than boys to intentionally abuse prescription drugs to get high.

Pain relievers such as OxyContin and Vicodin are the most commonly abused prescription drugs by teens.

Adolescents are more likely than young adults to become dependent on prescription medication.

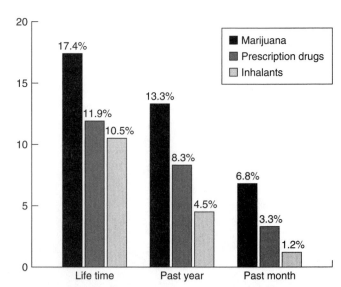

Types of Illicit drug use among teens aged 12–17 (percentage).

Source: 2005 National survey on drug use and health, SAMHSA. 2006

- Three percent, or 840,000 teens ages 12–17, reported current abuse of prescription drugs in 2005, making this illegal drug category the second most abused next to marijuana (7%). (NSDUH, 2006)
- In 2005, 2.1 million teens abused prescription drugs. (NSDUH, 2006)
- Teens ages 12–17 have the second-highest annual rates of prescription drug abuse after young adults (18–25). (SAMHSA, 2006)
- Prescription drugs are the most commonly abused drug among 12–13-year-olds. (NSDUH, 2006)
- Teens (12–17) and young adults (18–25) were more likely than older adults to start abusing prescription drugs in the past year. (SAMHSA, 2006)
- One-third of all new abusers of prescription drugs in 2005 were 12–17-year-olds. (NSDUH, 2006)
- Teens (12–17) in Western and Southeastern states are more likely to abuse prescription pain relievers
  - Arkansas (10.3%), Kentucky (9.8%), Montana (9.6%), Oregon (9.3%), Oklahoma (9.1%), Tennessee (8.9%), and West Virginia (8.9%) lead the country in teen abuse of prescription pain relievers. (SAMHSA, 2007)
- The most recent research on deaths in the U.S. due to poisoning over a five-year period (1999–2004) shows that nearly all poison deaths in the country are attributed to drugs, and most drug poisonings result from the abuse of prescription and illegal drugs. (CDC, 2007)
  - The number of these deaths increased from 12,186 in 1999 to 20,950 in 2004—a 62.5 percent change over five years.

Myth vs. Reality

Teens are abusing prescription drugs because they believe the myth that these drugs provide a medically safe high.

- Nearly one in five teens (19% or 4.5 million) report abusing prescription medications that were not prescribed to them. (PATS, 2006)
- Teens admit to abusing prescription medicine for reasons other than getting high, including to relieve pain or anxiety, to sleep better, to experiment, to help with concentration or to increase alertness. (Boyd, McCabe, Cranford and young, 2006)
- When teens abuse prescription drugs, they often characterize their use of the drugs as "responsible," "controlled" or "safe," with the perception that the drugs are safer than street drugs. (Friedman, 2006)
- More than one-third of teens say they feel some pressure to abuse prescription drugs, and nine percent

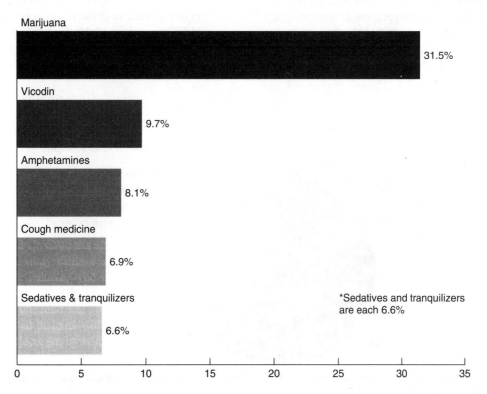

Top five drugs used by 12th graders in the past year.

Source: Monitoring the future study, the University of Michigan. 2006

say using prescription drugs to get high is an important part of fitting in with their friends. (*Seventeen*, 2006)

- Four out of 10 teens agree that prescription medicines are much safer to use than illegal drugs, even if they are not prescribed by a doctor. (PATS, 2006)
- One-third of teens (31% or 7.3 million) believe there's "nothing wrong" with using prescription medicines without a prescription once in a while. (PATS, 2006)
- Nearly three out of 10 teens (29% or 6.8 million) believe prescription pain relievers—even if not prescribed by a doctor—are not addictive. (PATS, 2006)

Availability and Accessibility

The majority of teens get prescription drugs easily and for free, often from friends and relatives.

- Nearly half (47%) of teens who use prescription drugs say they get them for free from a relative or friend. Ten percent say they buy pain relievers from a friend or relative, and another 10 percent say they took the drugs without asking. (NSDUH, 2006)
- More than three in five (62% or 14.6 million) teens say prescription pain relievers are easy to get from parents' medicine cabinets; half of teens (50% or 11.9 million) say they are easy to get through other people's prescriptions; and more than half (52% or 12.3 million) say prescription pain relievers are "available everywhere." (PATS, 2006)

- The majority of teens (56% or 13.4 million) agree that prescription drugs are easier to get than illegal drugs. (PATS, 2006)
- More teens have been offered prescription drugs than other illicit drugs, excluding marijuana. Fourteen percent of 12–17-year-olds have been offered prescription drugs at some point in their lives, compared to 10 percent of teens who have been offered cocaine, ecstasy (9%), methamphetamine (6%) and LSD (5%). (CASA, 2006)
- 14-year-olds are four times more likely than 13-year-olds to be offered prescription drugs. (CASA, 2006)
- Thirty-nine percent of 14–20-year-olds say it is easy to get prescription drugs online or by phone. Of that total, more girls than boys said it was easy (48% vs. 31%). (TRU, 2006)

Gender Differences

Girls are more likely than boys to intentionally abuse prescription drugs to get high.

- Among 12–17-year-olds, girls are more likely than boys to have abused prescription drugs (9.9% of girls vs. 8.2% of boys), pain relievers (8.1% vs. 7.0%), tranquilizers (2.6% vs. 1.9%), and stimulants (2.6% vs. 1.9%) in the past year. (SAMHSA, 2006)
- Among 12–17-year-olds, girls had higher rates of dependence or abuse involving prescription drugs (1.8% for girls and 1.1% for boys), pain relievers (1.4% vs. 0.8%), tranquilizers (0.4% vs. 0.3%) and stimulants (0.5% vs. 0.3%) in the past year. (SAMHSA, 2006)

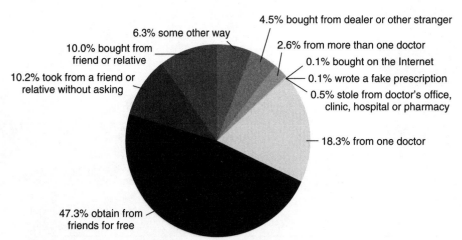

Source where pain relievers were obtained for most recent nonmedical past-year users aged 12–17 (percentage).

Source: 2005 National survey on drug use and health, SAMHSA. 2006

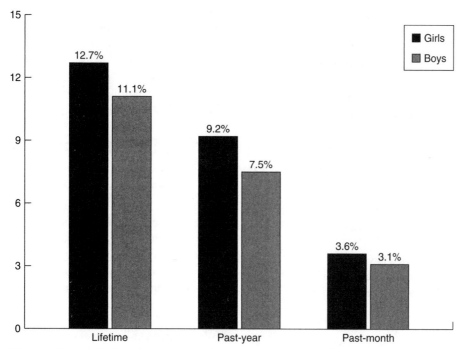

Misuse of prescription drugs among teens aged 12–17 lifetime, past-year, past-month percentage.

Source: 2005 National survey on drug use and health, SAMHSA. 2006

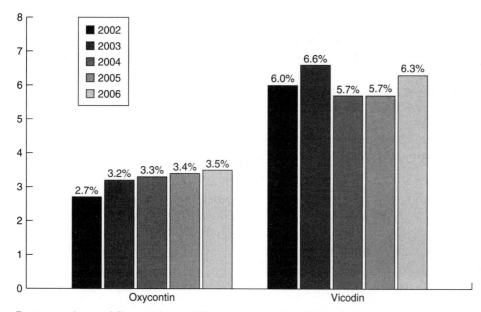

Past-year abuse of Oxycontin and Vicodin among 8th, 10th and 12th graders combined (percentage).

Source: Monitoring the future study, the University of Michigan. 2006

Types of Prescription Drugs Abused by Teens

Pain relievers such as OxyContin and Vicodin are the most commonly abused prescription drugs by teens.

- Pain relievers are currently the most abused type of prescription drugs by 12–17-year-olds, followed by stimulants, tranquilizers and sedatives. (NSDUH, 2006)

- Past-year use of Vicodin is high among 8th, 10th and 12th graders, with nearly one in 10 high school seniors using it in the past year. (MTF, 2006)

- On average, almost four percent (3.5%) of 8th–12th graders reported using OxyContin, and six percent reported using Vicodin in the past year. (MTF, 2006)

- In 2006, past-year abuse of OxyContin among 8th graders exactly doubled—increasing 100 percent over the last four years (from 1.3% in 2002 to 2.6% in 2006). In 10th graders, past-year abuse of OxyContin increased by 26 percent (from 3.0% in 2002, to 3.8% in 2006). (MTF, 2006)

- Five of the top six drugs abused by 12th graders in the past year were prescription drugs or cough and cold medicines. (MTF, 2006)

- Four percent of 8th graders, five percent of 10th graders, and seven percent of 12th graders reported taking medicines with dextromethorphan (DXM) during the past year to get high. (MTF, 2006)

- Almost two out of five teens reported having friends who abused prescription pain relievers and nearly three out of 10 reported having friends who abused prescription stimulants in the past year. (PATS, 2006)

Dependence and Treatment

Adolescents are more likely than young adults to become dependent on prescription medication.

- In 2004, more than 29 percent of teens in treatment were dependent on tranquilizers, sedatives, amphetamines and other stimulants. (TEDS, 2004)

- More 12–17-year-olds than young adults (18–25) (15.9% vs. 12.7%) became dependent on or abused prescription drugs in the past year. (SAMHSA, 2006)

- Abusing prescription drugs for the first time before age 16 leads to a greater risk of dependence later in life. (SAMHSA, 2006)

- In the past year, nearly half (48%) of all emergency department (ED) visits resulting from dextromethorphan abuse were patients 12–20 years old. (DAWN, 2006)

- Prescription drug abuse dramatically increased during the past decade. In the last 10 years, the number of teens going into treatment for addiction to prescription pain relievers has increased by more than 300 percent. (TEDS, 2006)

- Between 2004 and 2005, the proportion of those seeking treatment for prescription pain medication increased nine percent, to more than 64,000 admissions. (TEDS, 2006)

- Emergency room visits involving abuse of prescription or over-the-counter drugs increased 21 percent from 2004-2005. (DAWN, 2007)

Appendix: Definitions

Prescription drugs that are most commonly abused include three classes: opioids, central nervous system (CNS) depressants and stimulants.

- **Opioids** are prescribed to alleviate pain. Examples include oxycodone (OxyContin), propoxyphene (Darvon), hydrocodone (Vicodin), hydromorphone (Dilaudid) and meperidine (Demerol).

- **CNS** depressants slow normal brain function and are used to treat anxiety and sleep disorders. In higher doses, some CNS depressants can become general anesthetics. Tranquilizers and sedatives are examples of CNS depressants and include barbiturates (Amytal, Nembutal, Seconal, Phenobarbital), benzodiazepines (Valium, Xanax) and flunitrazepam (Rohypnol).

- **Stimulants** increase alertness, attention and energy, which are accompanied by increases in blood pressure, heart rate and respiration. Stimulants are prescribed to treat narcolepsy, attention-deficit hyperactivity disorder (ADHD) and depression that has not responded to other treatments. Examples of prescription stimulants include amphetamines (Biphetamine, Dexedrine), cocaine (Cocaine Hydrochloride), methamphetamine (Desoxyn) and methylphenidate (Ritalin).

Dextromethorphan (DXM) is a cough suppressant found in many over-the-counter cough and cold remedies.

Nonmedical use, misuse and abuse of prescription drugs are all defined here as use of prescription medications without medical supervision for the intentional purpose of getting high, or for some reason other than what the medication was intended.

Current use refers to use of prescription drugs during the month prior to the survey interview.

The Office of the National Drug Control Policy, Executive Office of the President, February 2007, pp. 1–11.

Studies Identify Factors Surrounding Rise in Abuse of Prescription Drugs by College Students

Lori Whitten

Prescription drug abuse among students in U.S. colleges and universities has been rising for several years. The 2004 Monitoring the Future (MTF) Survey of College Students and Adults—the most recent data available—estimated that 7.4 percent of college students used the painkiller hydrocodone (Vicodin) without a prescription in that year, up from 6.9 percent in 2002, with similar increases for other opioid medications, stimulants, and sedatives. Three new NIDA-funded studies reveal which students and campuses have the highest rates of abuse and connect such abuse to other unhealthy behaviors. According to the research, rates of collegiate prescription stimulant abuse are highest among men, Whites, fraternity/sorority members, and at schools in the Northeast.

Stimulant Abuse Nationwide

Dr. Sean Esteban McCabe and colleagues at the University of Michigan and Harvard University analyzed the answers from the Harvard School of Public Health College Alcohol Study, which in 2001 surveyed 10,904 randomly selected students enrolled at 119 colleges across the United States. Overall, 4 percent of the respondents reported having taken a stimulant medication without a prescription at least once during the previous year. Men were twice as likely as women (5.8 percent versus 2.9 percent) to have abused methylphenidate (Ritalin), dextroamphetamine (Dexedrine), and amphetamine/dextroamphetamine (Adderall). Stimulant medication abuse was also more prevalent among students who were:

- White (4.9 percent versus 1.6 percent for African-Americans and 1.3 percent for Asians);
- Members of fraternities or sororities (8.6 percent versus 3.5 percent for nonmembers); and
- Earning lower grades (5.2 percent for grade point average of B or lower versus 3.3 percent for B+ or higher).

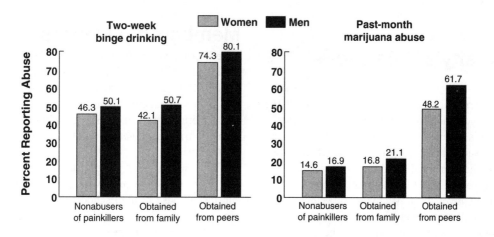

At one university, students who obtained perscription painkillers from peers reported higher levels of binge drinking and marijuana abuse than nonabusers or those who received painkillers from family.

Figure 1   Binge drinking, marijuana abuse are elevated among students who obtain painkillers from peers

Table 1 Stimulant Abuse Varies by Campus Characteristics

Selected Characteristics	Past-year Stimulant Abuse Rates, %
Admission criteria	
More competitive	5.9
Competitive	4.5
Less competitive	1.3
Geographical region	
Northeast	6.3
South	4.6
West	3.2
North Central	2.8
Commuter Status	
Noncommuter school	4.6
Commuter school	1.2

Students enrolled in the most selective colleges reported relatively high levels of past-year stimulant abuse, as did those attending schools in the Northeast. Residential schools reported higher rates than commuter colleges.

Students who abused prescription stimulants reported higher levels of cigarette smoking; heavy drinking; risky driving; and abuse of marijuana, MDMA (Ecstasy), and cocaine. Compared with other survey respondents, for example, they were 20 times as likely to report past-year cocaine abuse and 5 times as likely to report driving after heavy drinking. The campus prevalence of past-year stimulant abuse ranged from 0 percent at 20 colleges—including the three historically African-American institutions included in the survey—to 25 percent. The prevalence was 10 percent or higher at 12 colleges. Students attending colleges in the Northeast, schools with more competitive admission standards, and noncommuter schools reported higher rates of abuse.

One University's Painkiller Picture

At a large Midwestern university, about 9 percent of 9,161 undergraduates surveyed had taken a prescription pain medication without a doctor's order at least once during the past year; 16 percent reported such abuse in their lifetime. Of the latter, 54 percent said they had obtained the drugs from peers, while 17 percent said their source was a family member. Dr. McCabe and colleagues at the University of Michigan Substance Abuse Research Center found that students who obtained medications from peers were more likely to smoke and drink heavily and to have abused other substances—including marijuana, cocaine, and other illegal drugs—than those who obtained them from family members.

The researchers found that exposure to prescription pain medication early in life increased the likelihood of abuse in college. Women who had received prescriptions for pain relievers in elementary school were more than four times as likely as those with no prescribed use to report abuse in the past year. Men with early prescribed use were twice as likely as those without to report such abuse. In addition:

- Women students were more likely to be prescribed pain medication, while men were more likely to be approached to sell or give away prescribed medication.
- More men obtained the drugs from peers while more women obtained them from family members.
- Past-year prescription painkiller abuse was higher among fraternity members than nonmembers (17 percent versus 9 percent) and among sorority members compared with nonmembers (9.6 percent versus 8.6 percent).

"Students abuse prescription drugs to get high, to self-medicate for pain episodes, to help concentrate during exam time, and to try to relieve stress. Regardless of the motivation, people need to know the risks of abuse and the dangers of mixing drugs," says Dr. Lynda Erinoff, formerly of NIDA's Division of Epidemiology, Services and Prevention Research. Most people assume that if a medication is available on the market, it must be safe—even if it has not been prescribed for them, says Dr. Erinoff, "but a drug or dose that a doctor orders for one person is not necessarily appropriate for another, and prescription abusers are potentially taking a serious risk." NIDA continues to work with doctors and pharmacists and to link prevention specialists with researchers focusing on the problem. "Educating the public remains a critical challenge," says Dr. Erinoff.

". . . people need to know the risks of abuse and the dangers of mixing drugs."

Membership Matters

Based on responses from more than 5,000 young people who participated in the MTF when they were high school seniors in 1988 to 1997, and also when they were in college, Dr. McCabe and his Michigan colleagues found that active members of college fraternities or sororities engage in more heavy episodic, or "binge," drinking, cigarette smoking, and marijuana abuse than nonmembers.

The students who joined fraternities or sororities in college were the same ones who reported the highest levels of substance abuse in high school. Moreover, cigarette smoking, binge drinking, and drug abuse increased for all survey participants as they progressed through college. Fraternity and sorority members showed greater elevations in binge drinking and marijuana abuse over time compared with nonmembers. The picture that emerges is of students who are already heavy drinkers when they come to college selecting fraternities and sororities with a reputation for "partying" and then, as members, further increasing their drinking in an environment that supports the behavior.

"It's important for each student to explore, perhaps with counseling, a possible mismatch between his or her college environment and individual needs. Some students benefit from settings that emphasize socialization outside of the party scene; these might include group living arrangements based on shared academic or extracurricular interests," Dr. McCabe says.

Sources

McCabe, S.E., et al. Non-medical use of prescription stimulants among US college students: Prevalence and correlates from a national survey. *Addiction* 100(1): 96–106, 2005.

McCabe, S.E., et al. Selection and socialization effects of fraternities and sororities on US college student substance use: A multi-cohort national longitudinal study. *Addiction* 100(4):512–524, 2005.

McCabe, S.E.; Teter, C.J.; and Boyd, C.J. Illicit use of prescription pain medication among college students. *Drug and Alcohol Dependence* 77(1):37–47, 2005.

From *NIDA Notes,* vol. 20, no. 4. Published by The National Institute on Drug Abuse.

UNIT 5

Measuring the Social Costs of Drugs

Unit Selections

33. **The Role of Substance Abuse in U.S. Juvenile Justice Systems and Populations,** Heather Horowitz, Hung-En Sung, and Susan E. Foster
34. **Sobering Thoughts,** Doreen Major Ryan, Doreen M. Bonnett, and Callie B. Gass
35. **Students with Fetal Alcohol Syndrome,** Darcy Miller
36. **Keep Your Older Patients Out of Medication Trouble,** Sherrill A. Shepler, Tracy A. Grogan, and Karen Steinmetz Pater
37. **My Spirit Lives,** Roxanne Chinook
38. **The Problem with Drinking,** Cheryl Harris Sharman
39. **High on the Job,** Michael A. Gips

Key Points to Consider

- Where does one look to identify the social costs associated with drug abuse?

- Determine what percentage of your class that has been the victim of a crime and determine what percentages of those crimes were related to drugs.

- How has the spread of methamphetamine use and manufacture affected children?

- In which subpopulations of Americans does fetal alcohol syndrome manifest itself differently, and why?

- What do you believe to be the greatest drug-related threat currently facing the United States?

Student Web Site

www.mhcls.com/online

Internet References

Further information regarding these websites may be found in this book's preface or online.

Drug Enforcement Administration
   http://www.usdoj.gov/dea/
Drug Use Cost to the Economy
   www.ccm-drugtest.com/ntl_effcts1.htm
Drug Policy Alliance
   www.drugpolicy.org/database/index.html
National Drug Control Policy
   http://www.ncjrs.org/ondcppubs/publications/policy/ndcs00/chap2_10.html
The November Coalition
   http://www.november.org
TRAC DEA Site
   http://trac.syr.edu/tracdea/index.html
United Nations Chronicle - online edition
   http://www.un.org/Pubs/chronicle/1998/issue2/0298p7.html

The most devastating effect of drug abuse in America is the magnitude with which it affects the way we live. Much of its influence is not measurable. What is the cost of a son or daughter lost, a parent imprisoned, a life lived in a constant state of fear? The emotional costs alone are incomprehensible.

The social legacy of this country's drug crisis could easily be the subject of this entire book. The purpose here, however, can only be a cursory portrayal of drugs' tremendous costs. More than one American president has stated that drug use threatens our national security and personal well-being. The financial costs of maintaining the federal apparatus devoted to drug interdiction, enforcement, and treatment are staggering. Although yearly expenditures vary due to changes in political influence, strategy, and tactics, examples of the tremendous effects of drugs on government and the economy abound. The federal budget for drug control exceeds $12.9 billion and includes almost $1.5 billion dedicated to drug fighting in foreign countries including Mexico, Colombia, Bolivia, Peru, Central America, Afghanistan, and Pakistan. The Department of Justice commits almost $3 billion to antidrug efforts, the Department of Health and Human Services almost $3.5 billion and the Department of Homeland Security over $3.3 billion. Currently, the growing problems associated with methamphetamine use and manufacture are commanding dollars in federal, state, and local budgets. The President has dedicated specific funds to the U.S. Attorney for the high priority prosecution of meth manufacturers. The taking over of large-scale meth production by Mexican criminal syndicates who produce thousands of pounds of methamphetamine in super-labs located in California, the Southwest, and Mexico is a national problem. Over $20 million is committed to state and local authorities to clean up toxic methamphetamine labs, and in 2008 special research funds were again made available to study the harmful effects caused to children exposed to meth labs. Even though much effort is being dedicated to control serious visible problems with methamphetamine, there is great concern that this problem is much worse than numbers indicate. Federal seizures of methamphetamine in the West and Southwest alone number in the thousands of kilos.

Drugs *are* the business of the criminal justice system. Approximately 80 percent of the people behind bars in this country had a problem with drugs or alcohol prior to their arrest. The United States has more violent crime and incarcerates more of its citizens than almost any other comparable society and the financial costs are staggering. Doing drugs and serving time produces an inescapable nexus and it doesn't end with prison. Almost 40 percent of persons on supervised parole or probation are classified with dependence on or abuse of a substance. Some argue that these numbers represent the fact that Americans have come to rely on the criminal justice system as an unprecedented way of responding to social problems. Regardless of the way one chooses to view various relationships, the resulting picture is numbing.

In addition to the highly visible criminal justice-related costs, numerous other institutions are affected. Housing, welfare, education, and health care provide excellent examples of critical institutions struggling to overcome the strain of drug-related impacts. In addition, annual loss of productivity in the workplace exceeds well over a $160 billion per year. Alcoholism alone causes 500 million lost workdays each year. Add to this demographic shifts caused by people fleeing drug-impacted neighborhoods, schools, and businesses and one soon realizes that there is no victimless public or private institution. Last year, almost 4 million Americans received some kind of treatment related to the abuse of alcohol or other drugs. Almost 24 million Americans need treatment for an illicit drug or alcohol problem. Fetal alcohol syndrome is the leading cause of mental retardation in the United States, and still, survey data continues to report over 11 percent of pregnant women drink alcohol; of these, 2.9 percent report binge drinking (down from 4.5 percent last year). Add injured, drug-related accident and crime victims, along with demands produced by a growing population of intravenous-drug users infected with AIDS, and an overwhelmed health care system frighteningly appears. Health care costs from drug-related ills are staggering. Drug abuse continues to cost the economy more than $13 billion annually in health care costs alone.

It should be emphasized that the social costs exacted by drug use infiltrate every aspect of public and private life. The implications for thousands of families struggling with the adverse effects of drug-related woes may prove the greatest and most tragic of social costs. Children who lack emotional support, self-esteem, role models, a safe and secure environment, economic opportunity, and an education because of a parent on drugs suggest costs difficult to comprehend or measure. In some jurisdictions in California and Oregon, as many as 70 percent of child welfare placements are precipitated by methamphetamine abuse.

When reading Unit 5 of this book, consider the diversity of costs associated with the abuse of both legal drugs and illegal drugs. As you read the following articles, consider the historical progressions of social costs produced by drug abuse over the past century. How are the problems of the past replicating themselves and how has science, medicine and social policy changed in an attempt to mitigate these impacts?

Ample evidence informs us that there is no single approach to mitigate the diverse nature of drug related social impacts. Further, some of the most astounding scientific discoveries about how addiction develops remain mysterious when compared to the reality of the lives of millions who find drugs an end in themselves. Some have argued that the roots of drug abuse problems today seem even more elusive, complicated, and desperate. Good progress has been made in treating drug addiction, but only moderate progress has been made in preventing it in the first place. What examples exist of disproportionate ways in which some populations of Americans are harmed by drugs? Are there epidemics within epidemics? How is drug abuse expressed within different populations of Americans? How do the implications for Native American families and culture differ from those implications for other racial and ethnic groups? What are the reasons for these disparities and how should they be addressed?

The Role of Substance Abuse in U.S. Juvenile Justice Systems and Populations

HEATHER HOROWITZ, HUNG-EN SUNG AND SUSAN E. FOSTER

I n 1998, the National Center on Addiction and Substance Abuse (CASA) at Columbia University released a study, *Behind Bars: Substance Abuse and America's Prison Population*, which revealed that substance abuse and addiction is implicated in the felony crimes of 80 percent of the adult prison inmates in America, that few of these inmates receive treatment for their substance abuse problems, and that providing treatment for this adult population would save taxpayers money within a year. CASA (1998) also found that substance-related crime runs in the family. Incarcerated adults are likely to be children of parents who were in prison. Incarcerated adults are themselves the parents of almost 2.5 million children who are more likely than children whose parents have not been incarcerated to end up in prison. About 30 percent of adult inmates admit to being arrested as juveniles.

These revelations led CASA to examine the characteristics and situations of the minors who end up in the juvenile justice population—2.4 million arrests in 2000. The result was the October 2004 report, *Criminal Neglect: Substance Abuse, Juvenile Justice and the Children Left Behind*, the first comprehensive examination of the relationship between substance abuse and juvenile delinquency (CASA, 2004). The findings sketch a bleak portrait of juvenile justice systems overwhelmed by drug and alcohol abuse and addicted adolescents. These substance-involved juveniles slip through the cracks in the nation's health, education and family support systems and exhibit many other health, education and social problems that receive little attention.

America has 51 separate juvenile justice systems with no national standards of practice or accountability. These systems often are part of the problem, not part of the solution. Although they were created to focus on prevention and rehabilitation of juvenile offenders, the trend has been to mimic adult systems of retribution and punishment. By abandoning a commitment to rehabilitation, a more punitive approach renders these juvenile justice systems a dead end for substance-involved youths rather than an opportunity to reshape their lives.

CASA analyzed data from the National Institute of Justice's Arrestee Drug Abuse Monitoring Program, the Office of Juvenile Justice and Delinquency Prevention's Juvenile Court Statistics, and arrest data from OJJDP's *Juvenile Arrests* publications. CASA also examined data from the National Survey on Drug Use and Health, the National Longitudinal Survey of Youth and the National Longitudinal Survey of Adolescent Health. Although more recent statistics are available from many data programs, 2000 data were used to assure comparability. Unless otherwise referenced, all findings reported below are from CASA's analysis of these databases.

Substance Abuse and Juvenile Delinquency

Of the 2.4 million juvenile arrests made in 2000, 78.4 percent (1.9 million) involved children and teens who were under the influence of alcohol or drugs while committing their crime; tested positive for drugs; were arrested for committing an alcohol or drug offense, including drug or liquor law violations, drunkenness or driving under the influence; reported having substance abuse problems such as feeling dependent on alcohol or drugs or needing them at the time of their crime; or shared some combination of these characteristics. More than half of arrested juveniles (53.9 percent) tested positive for drugs at the time of their arrest (see Table 1). The main drugs of abuse among juvenile offenders are alcohol and marijuana. Of the 1.3 million juvenile arrestees who tested positive for drugs at the time of their arrest, 92.2 percent tested positive for marijuana, 14.4 percent for cocaine, 8.8 percent for amphetamines, 7.6 percent for methamphetamines and 2.3 percent for opiates (e.g., heroin, methadone and prescription opioids). Alcohol is not included in the standard drug tests, but of juveniles under the influence of some substance at the time of their crime, 37.8 percent admit being under the influence of alcohol.

Forty-four percent of juveniles arrested during the previous year met the clinical DSM-1V (the fourth edition of the *Diagnostic and Statistical Manual of Mental Disorders*) criteria of substance abuse or dependence, compared with 7.4 percent of nonarrested youths; 27.8 percent met the clinical criteria of substance dependence, compared with 3.4 percent of nonarrested youths.

Table 1 Substance Involvement Among Arrested Juveniles, 2000

	Percentage of All Arrested Juveniles
Positive urinalysis at arrest	53.9
Under the influence during crime	18.2
Arrested for alcohol/drug offense	12.1
Reported substance abuse problems:	62.5
Tried to cut down/quit alcohol/drugs in past year	(58.0)
Felt dependent on alcohol/drugs in past year	(20.3)
Felt they could use treatment for alcohol/drugs	(17.6)
Currently receiving treatment for alcohol/drugs	(8.4)
In need of alcohol/drugs at the time of their crime	(4.6)
Total substance involved*	78.4

*Percentages do not add up to 78.4 percent because many juveniles fall into more than one category.

Source: CASA analysis of 2000 data from the Arrestee Drug Abuse Monitoring Program (ADAM)

Table 2 Substance-Involved Arrested Juveniles by Type of Offense, 2000

Offense	Percentage of all Arrested Juveniles
Violent offenses	69.3
Property offenses	72.0
Other offenses	81.2
Alcohol and drug offenses	100.0
Total arrests	78.4

Source: CASA analysis of 2000 ADAM data

Juvenile substance abuse is implicated in all types of juvenile crime, including violent offenses, property offenses and other offenses such as assaults, vandalism and disorderly conduct (see Table 2). Although juvenile arrest rates overall have declined in recent years, the arrest rate for juvenile drug law violations (637.5 per 100,000 persons ages 10 to 17) is on the rise. From 1991 to 2000, the arrest rate (arrests per 100,000 persons ages 10 to 17) for all juvenile offenses decreased by 12.9 percent, but the arrest rate for drug law violations increased a staggering 105 percent. During this time, the arrest rate for property crimes decreased 38.4 percent and the arrest rate for violent crimes decreased 33.2 percent.

This increase in drug law violation arrests has cascaded through juvenile justice systems, raising the number of drug law violation cases referred to juvenile court, in detention, incarcerated, in other out-of-home placement and on probation. Of the 1.6 million cases referred to juvenile courts in 2000, 40.9 percent were for property offenses, 22.9 percent for person offenses, 22.5 percent for public order offenses and 13.5 percent for drug and liquor law violations. The number of drug law violation cases referred to juvenile courts increased, however, at more than 12.5 times the rate of the total number of cases referred to juvenile courts (196.9 percent vs. 15.6 percent), from 65,400 cases in 1991 to 194,200 cases in 2000.

The Demographics of Juvenile Crime

Age and Gender Disparities. While cases referred to the juvenile courts generally involve youths ages 10 to 17, most cases (57.7 percent) involve those age 15 and younger. Seventy-two percent of the 2.4 million juvenile arrests involve males; however, arrests involving females are on the rise. Between 1991 and 2000, the number of cases referred to juvenile courts involving females increased 51 percent, compared with a 7.3 percent increase for males. The largest percentage growth between 1991 and 2000 for both males and females was in drug law violation cases—these cases grew 311.4 percent for females and 181.2 percent for males.

Racial Disparities. Racial differences are difficult to determine since arrest rates and rates of cases referred to juvenile courts are not reported for Hispanics who may appear in either white or black racial categories. However, given this limitation, in 2000, the total arrest rate for black juveniles (11,094.2) was more than 1.5 times the rate for white juveniles (6,839.8). In 1999, while blacks comprised just 15 percent of the juvenile population (Bilchik, 1999), black juveniles represented 28 percent of all cases referred to juvenile courts and 36 percent of detained cases. Other research Finds that Hispanic juveniles are more likely than white juveniles to be detained, placed in out-of-home residential facilities and incarcerated in adult prisons (Human Rights Watch, 2002; Sickmund, 2004).

Income Disparities. Arrested juveniles are more likely than their nonarrested peers to come from impoverished homes. In 2002, 67.5 percent of teens ages 12 to 17 who had at least one arrest in the previous year reported an annual family income of less than $50,000, compared with 52.8 percent of teens who had not been arrested; 26.1 percent of arrested juveniles reported an annual family income of less than 820,000, compared with 17.4 percent of nonarrested youths.

Drug Involvement Among Juvenile Offenders

Compared with juveniles who have not been arrested, those who have been arrested once in the past year are more than twice as likely to have used alcohol (69.3 percent vs. 32.7 percent), more than 3.5 times more likely to have used marijuana (49.5 percent vs. 14.1 percent), more than three times more likely to have used prescription drugs for nonmedical purposes (26.8 percent vs. 8.1 percent), more than seven times more likely to have used Ecstasy (12.1 percent vs. 1.7 percent), more than nine times

Table 3   Percentage of Arrested Juveniles Who Use Alcohol
and Drugs (ages 12 to 17), 2002

Offense	Ever Arrested		Number of Arrests in Past Year			
	Yes	No	0	1	2	3 or More
Alcohol	60.6	31.9	32.7	69.3	78.1	80.2
Marijuana	43.1	13.1	14.1	49.5	58.1	65.3
Prescription drugs for nonmedical use	24.1	7.7	8.1	26.8	37.0	50.1
Cocaine/crack	11.6	1.1	1.4	13.0	22.5	34.4
Ecstasy	10.4	1.5	1.7	12.1	13.9	32.8
Heroin	1.5	0.1	0.1	2.0	1.7	7.1

Source: CASA analysis of 2000 data from the Arrestee Drug Abuse Monitoring Program (ADAM)

more likely to have used cocaine (13 percent vs. 1.4 percent) and 20 times more likely to have used heroin (2 percent vs. 0.1 percent).

The more often juveniles are arrested, the more likely they are to drink and use drugs. Juveniles with three or more past year arrests are almost twice as likely to abuse prescription drugs, more than 2.5 times more likely to use cocaine, almost three times more likely to use Ecstasy and more than 3.5 times more likely to use heroin than youths with only one past year arrest (see Table 3).

Juveniles who drink and use drugs are more likely than those who do not to be arrested and be arrested multiple times. Each felony conviction a youth receives increases the likelihood of becoming an adult felon by 14 percent; each misdemeanor conviction increases the risk by 7 percent (Washington State Institute for Public Policy, 1997).

Substance-involved juvenile offenders are more likely to be reincarcerated than other juvenile offenders (Dembo et al., 1998) and go on to commit criminal acts as adults. In 2000, compared with nonsubstance-involved juvenile offenders, those who were substance involved were nearly 1.5 times more likely to have at least one previous arrest in the past year (58.1 percent vs. 40.6 percent) and were almost twice as likely to have two or more prior arrests in the past year (31.5 percent vs. 18 percent).

In 2002, almost 1.5 million youths ages 12 to 17 (6 percent) had been incarcerated or held in a juvenile detention center at least once in their lifetime. Compared with those who were never incarcerated or in a detention center, those who have been at least once are 1.5 times more likely to have used alcohol in the past year (49.1 percent vs. 33.7 percent), almost two times more likely to have used inhalants (8.1 percent vs. 4.1 percent), more than twice as likely to have smoked cigarettes (41.4 percent vs. 19 percent), more than twice as likely to have used marijuana (31.7 percent vs. 14.7 percent), 2.5 times more likely to have misused prescription drugs (21.2 percent vs. 8.4 percent), almost four times more likely to have used hallucinogens (12.3 percent vs. 3.3 percent), five times more likely to have used heroin (1 percent vs. 0.2 percent), and more than six times more likely to have used cocaine (9.9 percent vs. 1.6 percent).

The earlier a young adult begins to abuse drugs, the more likely he or she is to be arrested. Juvenile alcohol and drug use also increases the risk of adult substance dependence, which increases the likelihood of criminal involvement (see Table 4).

Missed Opportunities for Prevention

There are often early signs of future trouble. The more these markers are present in a young person's life and the fewer protective influences present, the greater the chances for substance abuse and crime (Lipsey, Wilson and Cothern, 2000; Lipsey, 1999).

Off to a Troubled Start. Children whose parents abuse drugs and alcohol are almost three times more likely to be physically or sexually assaulted and more than four times more likely to be neglected than children of parents who are not substance abusers. Neglected and abused children are more likely to use drugs (43 percent vs. 32 percent) and commit juvenile crimes (42 percent vs. 33 percent) than nonmaltreated children (Kelley, Thornberry and Smith, 1997).

Impoverished and Dangerous Neighborhoods. Being raised in poverty or living in communities plagued by crime, drug selling, gangs, poor housing and firearms contributes to increased involvement in delinquent and violent behavior (Elliot, Huizinga and Menard, 1989; Fingerhut et al., 1991; Hawkins et al., 2000; Thornton et al., 2002).

Disconnected From Schools. Juveniles who test positive for multiple drugs are more than 2.5 times more likely to not be in school than nondrug-using juveniles (40.1 percent vs. 15.3 percent) and they are more likely to be truant, suspended from school and functioning below their grade level. An estimated 50 percent to 80 percent of all juveniles incarcerated in juvenile correctional facilities qualify for services designed to address learning disabilities—three to five times more than the eligible public school population (Leone and Meisel, 1999; Portner, 1996; Stephens and Arnette, 2000).

Table 4 Juvenile Alcohol and Marijuana Use and Young Adult Crime, 2002

Age of First Use	Percentage of 18- to 25-Year-Olds Arrested in Past Year	
	Alcohol	Marijuana
11 or younger	13.7	21.6
12	10.8	13.7
13	9.0	13.7
14	8.3	12.2
15	7.2	9.6
16	6.7	9.7
17	6.6	8.0
18	3.2	5.7
Never used	1.4	2.1

Source: CASA analysis of 2002 National Survey on Drug Use and Health data

Health Problems. Between 50 percent and 75 percent of incarcerated youths have a diagnosable mental health disorder (Coalition for Juvenile Justice, 2000), compared with 20 percent of 9- to 17-year-olds (Office of the Surgeon General, 1999; Coalition for Juvenile Justice, 2000), and at least 80 percent of all young offenders are estimated to have conduct disorders (Cocozza and Skowyra, 2000). Female juvenile offenders have been found three times more likely to have clinical symptoms of depression or anxiety than female adolescents in the general population (Kataoka et al., 2001).

Risky Sexual Behavior. Incarcerated juveniles are more likely to be sexually active, to have initiated sex at an earlier age, to have had more sexual partners and to have less consistent condom use than their nonincarcerated peers (Diclemente et al., 1991). Up to 94 percent of juveniles held in detention facilities are sexually active (Morris et al., 1995), compared with 46 percent of high school students (Grunbaum et al., 2002).

Running With the Wrong Crowd. Children and teens who are involved with juvenile offenders and drug-using peers are more likely to be arrested and use drugs themselves (Brendgen, Vitaro and Bukowski, 2000; Svensson, 2003). Children and teens with marijuana-using peers were 10 times more likely to use marijuana than children and teens with no marijuana-using peers (70 percent vs. 7 percent). Compared with youths who are not gang members, those who are in gangs are more likely to commit assault, robbery, breaking and entering, and felony theft; indulge in binge drinking; use and sell drugs; and be arrested (Hill, Lui and Hawkins, 2001).

Lack of Spiritual Grounding. Teens who do not consider religious beliefs important are almost three times more likely to smoke, drink and binge drink, almost four times more likely to use marijuana and seven times more likely to use illicit drugs than teens who consider religion an important part of their lives (CASA, 2001b). Juveniles who have been arrested one or more times in the past year are almost 1.5 times more likely to never attend religious services than teens who have not been arrested (41.7 percent vs. 31 percent).

Criminal Neglect

By the time juveniles enter juvenile justice systems, the vast majority are troubled and in need of support, health care, education, training and treatment. Limited data are available to document services provided to juveniles in juvenile justice systems. However, available data suggest that youths in custody rarely receive needed services to help them get on the track to responsible adulthood (Pfeiffer, 2004).

Nationwide, only 36.7 percent of juvenile correctional facilities provide on-site substance abuse treatment (SAMHSA, 2002). Only 20,000 (16 percent) of the estimated 122,696 substance-involved juvenile offenders in juvenile correctional facilities receive substance abuse treatment such as detoxification, individual or group counseling, rehabilitation and methadone or other pharmaceutical treatment within these facilities. Another 4,500 juvenile offenders receive substance abuse treatment through drug courts. Together, this adds up to only 24,500 juveniles of the 1.9 million substance-involved arrests for which CASA can document receipt of any form of substance abuse treatment—about 1.3 percent. Even if a full 20 percent of juveniles who received "other sanctions" (community service, restitution, fines, social services) were placed in substance abuse treatment, the percentage of substance-involved arrested juveniles who receive any form of treatment would only be 3.6 percent.

Moreover, mental health services are scarce and many education programs fail to meet even minimum state educational criteria. In 1995, which is when the latest data were available, almost 60 percent of the children admitted to secure detention found themselves in crowded facilities (Annie E. Casey Foundation, 1997). Children in crowded detention centers are more likely to be injured, spend less time in school, participate in fewer constructive programs, receive fewer family visits, have fewer opportunities to participate in religious activities and get sick more often. There are few, if any, programs that provide for the spiritual enrichment of these children and teens.

Instead of providing prevention and remediation, juvenile justice systems compound problems of juvenile offenders, pushing them toward increased substance abuse and crime. At the same time, public policy demands accountability from juvenile offenders. Demanding accountability from children while refusing to be accountable to them is criminal neglect. Because there is no model juvenile justice code or national standards of practice and accountability, states and counties respond to these issues of criminal neglect through federal, state and local investigators, and lawsuits brought by the U.S. Department of Justice under the Civil Rights of Institutionalized Persons Act (U.S. Department of Justice, 2002).

The Cost of Substance Abuse and Delinquency

The cost of substance abuse to juvenile justice programs is at least $14.4 billion annually for law enforcement, courts, detention, residential placement, incarceration, federal formula and block grants to states and substance abuse treatment. Only 1 percent (8139 million) of this cost is for treatment (CASA, 2001a). The costs of probation, physical and mental health services, child welfare and family services, school costs and the costs to victims are impossible to determine. However, together, these costs could more than double this $14.4 billion figure.

On average, a year of incarceration costs taxpayers $43,000 per juvenile (Juvenile Justice FYI, 2004). However, if society were, for example, to invest $5,000 in substance abuse treatment and getting comprehensive services and programs like drug courts just for each of the 123,000 substance-involved juveniles who would otherwise be incarcerated, society would break even on this investment in the first year if only 12 percent of these youths stayed in school and remained drug and crime free. Further, by preventing the crimes and incarceration of just 12 percent of adults now incarcerated who had juvenile arrest records, there would be more than 60,480 fewer inmates, $18 billion in savings from reduced criminal justice and health costs and employment benefits, and at least 5.9 million fewer crimes.

Preventing Substance Abuse and Delinquency

Juvenile crime, violence and substance use are rooted in a host of interrelated social problems, including adult substance abuse, child abuse and neglect, family violence, poor parenting, uneducated and undereducated youths, lack of appropriate health care, lack of community ties and support, increased availability of guns, gangs and poverty (Kumpfer and Alvarado, 1998). Stemming the tide of substance-involved juveniles entering juvenile justice systems will require a concerted effort on the part of parents, child welfare agencies, schools, health care providers, clergy, neighborhoods and local law enforcement officers to look for the signs and signals of risk and intervene early.

Although comprehensive prevention approaches offer the most hope for juveniles at risk for substance abuse and delinquency, few program models exist (SAMHSA, 2001). A comprehensive model would include attention to strengthening families, increasing school engagement, reinforcing positive peer groups, strengthening neighborhood resources, reducing poverty and offering spiritual guidance. The earlier prevention efforts start—whether they focus on the individual child, the family, the school or the community—the more likely they are to succeed in preventing substance abuse and delinquency (Loeber, Farrington and Petechuk, 2003).

Treating Substance-Involved Juvenile Offenders

By the time juveniles enter juvenile justice systems, 44 percent already meet the clinical criteria of substance abuse or dependence and need treatment; up to 80 percent need intervention for learning disabilities, conduct disorders and mental illnesses (Coalition for Juvenile Justice, 2000; Cocozza and Skowyra, 2000; Portner, 1996; Stephens and Arnette, 2000). There are many points in the adjudication process where juveniles can be diagnosed and treated: at arrest, intake, detention, court processing,

probation, incarceration and other out-of-home placement, and aftercare. Juvenile drug courts are a promising venue for intervention. These programs, which provide intensive treatment and monitoring for substance-abusing delinquents, have become increasingly popular in recent years and represent a collaboration among juvenile justice, substance abuse treatment and other health, education, law enforcement and social service agencies. They demonstrate that treatment and accountability are complementary rather than mutually exclusive objectives (Cooper, 2002; National Drug Court Institute, 2003).

Opportunities and Next Steps: Policy Recommendations

A top-to-bottom overhaul of the way the nation treats juvenile offenders is required in order to address the needs of these substance-using juvenile offenders. This overhaul should be designed to achieve two fundamental goals, while assuring that juvenile offenders are held accountable for their actions:

- Ensure that each child entering the systems receives a comprehensive needs assessment; and
- Take advantage of opportunities within juvenile justice systems to divert juveniles from further substance use and crime by providing appropriate treatment and other needed services in custody and detention, during incarceration or other out-of-home placement, while on probation and in aftercare.

To accomplish these goals, the following policy recommendations are essential.

Create a model juvenile justice code, setting forth standards of practice and accountability for states in handling juvenile offenders. This model code should incorporate practice requirements, including staffing and training, screening, assessments, treatment planning, case management, substance abuse, mental health and education services, counseling, access to care and record keeping.

Train all juvenile justice system staff—law enforcement, juvenile court judges and other court personnel, prosecutors and defenders, correctional and probation officers—to recognize substance-involved offenders and know how to respond.

Divert juvenile offenders from deeper involvement with juvenile justice systems through such promising practices as comprehensive in-home services, juvenile drug courts, including reentry courts, and other drug treatment alternatives that assure comprehensive services as well as accountability.

Make available treatment, health care, education and job training programs, including spiritually based programs, to juveniles who are incarcerated.

Develop a state and national data system through which a baseline can be established to judge progress in meeting the many needs of these children.

Expand OJJDP grant programs that provide federal funds to states and localities, conditioning grants under such programs on providing appropriate services to juvenile offenders.

If these recommendations are implemented, billions of citizens' tax dollars can be saved, crime can be reduced and help can be provided to thousands of children—who would otherwise be left behind—to grow up to lead productive, law-abiding lives.

References

Annie E. Casey Foundation. 1997. *Juvenile detention alternatives initiative: A progress report.* Baltimore: Annie E. Casey Foundation.

Bilchik, S. 1999. *Minorities in the juvenile justice system.* Washington, D.C.: Office of Justice Programs, Office of Juvenile Justice and Delinquency Prevention.

Brendgen, M., F. Vitaro and W.M. Bukowski. 2000. Deviant friends and early adolescents' emotional and behavioral adjustment. *Journal of Research on Adolescence*, 10(2): 173–189.

CASA. 1998. *Behind bars: Substance abuse and America's prison population.* New York: Columbia University.

CASA. 2001a. *Shoveling up: The impact of substance abuse an state budgets.* New York: Columbia University.

CASA. 2001b. *So help me God: Substance abuse, religion and spirituality.* New York: Columbia University.

CASA. 2004. *Criminal neglect: Substance abuse, juvenile justice and the children left behind.* New York: Columbia University.

Coalition for Juvenile Justice. 2000. Coalition for Juvenile Justice 2000 annual report. Washington, D.C.: Coalition for Juvenile Justice.

Cocozza, J.J. and K.R. Skowyra. 2000. Youth with mental health disorders: Issues and emerging responses. *Juvenile Justice Journal*, 7(1):3–13.

Cooper, C.S. 2002. Juvenile drug treatment courts in the United States: Initial lessons learned and issues being addressed. *Substance Use and Misuse*, 37(12–13):1689–1722.

Dembo, R., J. Schmeidler, B. Nini-Gough, S.C. Chin, P. Borden and D. Manning. 1998. Predictors of recidivism to a juvenile assessment center: A three year study. *Journal of Child Adolescent Substance Abuse*, 7(3):57–77.

Diclemente, R.J., M.M. Lanier, P.F. Horan and M. Lodico. 1991. Comparison of MDS knowledge, attitudes, and behaviors among incarcerated adolescents and a public school sample in San Francisco. *American Journal Public Health*, 81 (5):628–630.

Elliot, D., D. Huizinga and S. Menard. 1989. *Multiple problem youth: Delinquency, substance use, and mental health problems.* New York: Springer-Verlag.

Fingerhut, L.A., J.C. Kleinman, E. Godfrey and H. Rosenberg. 1991. Firearm mortality among children, youth, and young adults: 1–34 years of age, trends and current status: United States, 1979–88. *Monthly Vital Statistics Report*, 39(11): 1–16.

Grunbaum, J.A., L. Kann, S.A. Kinchen, B. Williams, J.G. Ross, R. Lowry and L. Kolbe. 2002. Youth risk behavior surveillance: United States, 2001. *Morbidity and Mortality Weekly Report*, 51(SS-4): 1–66.

Hawkins, J.D., T.I. Herrenkohl, D.P. Farrington, D. Brewer, R.C. Catalano, T.W. Harachi and L. Cothern. 2000. *Predictors of youth violence.* Washington, D.C.: Office of Juvenile Justice and Delinquency Prevention.

Hill, K.G., C. Lui and J.D. Hawkins. 2001. *Early precursors of gang membership. A study of Seattle youth.* OJJDP juvenile justice bulletin. Washington, D.C.: Office of Juvenile Justice and Delinquency Prevention.

Human Rights Watch. 2002. *Race and incarceration in the United States: Human Rights Watch briefing*, February 27, 2002. New York: Human Rights Watch. Available at www.hrw.org/backgrounder/usa/race.

Juvenile Justice FYI. 2004. Juvenile justice FAQ. Available at www.juvenilejusticefyi.com/juvenile_justice_faqs.html.

Kataoka, S.H., B.T. Zima, D.A. Dupre, K.A. Moreno, X. Yang and J.T. McCracken. 2001. Mental health problems and service use among female juvenile offenders: Their relationship to criminal history. *Journal of the American Academy of Child and Adolescent Psychology*, 40(5):549–555.

Kelley, B.T., T.P. Thornberry and C.A. Smith. 1997. *In the wake of childhood maltreatment.* Washington, D.C.: Office of Juvenile Justice and Delinquency Prevention.

Kumpfer, K.L. and R. Alvarado. 1998. *Effective family strengthening interventions.* Washington, D.C.: Office of Juvenile Justice and Delinquency Prevention.

Leone, P.E. and S.M. Meisel. 1999. *Improving education services for students in detention and confinement facilities.* College Park, Md.: The National Center on Education, Disability and Juvenile Justice. Available at www.edjj.org/Publications/list/leone_meisel-1997.html.

Lipsey, M.W. 1999. Can intervention rehabilitate serious delinquents? *The Annals of the American Academy of Political and Social Sciences*, 564(1): 142–166.

Lipsey, M., D. Wilson and L. Cothern. 2000. *Effective intervention for serious juvenile offenders.* Washington, D.C.: Office of Juvenile Justice and Delinquency Prevention.

Loeber, R., D.P. Farrington and D. Petechuk. 2003. *Child delinquency: Early intervention and prevention.* Child delinquency bulletin series. Washington, D.C.: U.S. Government Printing Office.

Morris, R.E., E.A. Harrison, G.W. Knox, E. Tromanhauser, D.K. Marquis and L.L. Watts. 1995. Health risk behavioral survey from 39 juvenile correctional facilities in the United States. *Journal of Adolescent Health*, 17(6):334–344.

National Drug Court Institute, and National Council of Juvenile and Family Court Judges. 2003. *Juvenile drug courts: Strategies in practice.* Washington, D.C.: Bureau of Justice Assistance.

Office of the Surgeon General. 1999. *Mental health: A report of the surgeon general.* Rockville, Md.: National Institute of Mental Health.

Pfeiffer, M.B. 2004. Juvenile detention system struggles: Use of force a focal point: Boy critically hurt in Lansing. *The Ithaca Journal*, cited 2004 Feb. 17 from www.theithicajournal.com.

Portner, J. 1996. Jailed youths shortchanged on education. *Education Week*, 16(5):1.

Sickmund, M. 2004. *Juveniles in corrections.* Washington, D.C.: Office of Justice Programs, Office of Juvenile Justice and Delinquency Prevention.

Stephens, R.D. and J.L. Arnette. 2000. *From the courthouse to the schoolhouse: Making successful transitions.* OJJDP juvenile justice bulletin. Washington, D.C.: Office of Juvenile Justice and Delinquency Prevention.

Substance Abuse and Mental Health Services Administration (SAMHSA). 2001. *Youth violence: A report of the surgeon general.* Washington, D.C.: U.S. Government Printing Office.

Substance Abuse and Mental Health Services Administration (SAMHSA). 2002. *Drug and alcohol treatment in juvenile correctional facilities: The DASIS report.* Rockville, Md.: Office of Applied Studies.

Svensson R. 2003. Gender differences in adolescent drug use: The impact of parental monitoring and peer deviance. *Youth and Society,* 34(3):300–329.

Thornton, T.N., C.A. Craft, L.L Dahlberg, B.S. Lynch and K. Baer. 2002. *Best practices of youth violence prevention: A sourcebook for community action.* Atlanta: Centers for Disease Control and Prevention.

U.S. Department of Justice. 2002. *Fiscal year 2002 activities under the Civil Rights of Institutionalized Persons Act.* Washington, D.C.: U.S. Department of Justice.

Washington State Institute for Public Policy. 1997. *The class of 1988, seven years later. How a juvenile offender's crime, criminal history, and age affect the chances of becoming an adult felon in Washington State.* Olympia, Wash.: Washington State Institute for Public Policy. Available at www.wsipp.wa.gov.

Authors' Note: The research presented in this article was partially funded by the William T. Grant Foundation, the National Institute on Drug Abuse and the Abercrombie Foundation.

Heather Horowitz, Jd, Mph, is a former research associate, **Hung-En Sung,** Phd, is a research associate, and **Susan E. Foster,** MSW, is vice president and director of policy research and analysis for the National Center on Addiction and Substance Abuse at Columbia University in New York.

Sobering Thoughts

Town Hall Meetings on Fetal Alcohol Spectrum Disorders

Prenatal exposure to alcohol is one of the leading causes of preventable birth defects and developmental disabilities. During the past 30 years, fetal alcohol spectrum disorders (FASD), including fetal alcohol syndrome, have gradually begun to attract attention. However, awareness and understanding of the disorders remain low, and people who are affected are seriously underserved.

The FASD Center for Excellence held a series of town hall meetings in 2002 and 2003 to gauge the issues surrounding FASD nationwide. On the basis of its findings, the center proposed a series of recommendations to begin to remedy some of the deficiencies that were identified. (*Am J Public Health.* 2006;96:2098–2101. doi:10.2105/AJPH.2005.062729)

Doreen Major Ryan, Doreen M. Bonnett, and Callie B. Gass

"All birds have wings. But not all birds can fly."

—*Parent of a child who has fetal alcohol syndrome*

Although the effects of prenatal exposure to alcohol have been studied since the 19th century, the issue has long remained poorly understood and largely overlooked. However, it raises significant concerns for public health. Prenatal exposure to alcohol affects an estimated 40000 newborns annually.[1] It is one of the leading causes of preventable birth defects and developmental disabilities.

After decades of research and a great deal of discussion, in 2004 experts in the field issued a consensus definition for disorders associated with prenatal exposure to alcohol. The term *fetal alcohol spectrum disorders* (FASD) is an umbrella term describing the range of effects that can occur in an individual whose mother drank alcohol during pregnancy. These effects include physical, mental, behavioral, and/or learning disabilities with possible lifelong implications. FASD includes disorders such as fetal alcohol syndrome (FAS), alcohol-related neurodevelopmental disorder, and alcohol-related birth defects.

Behavioral or cognitive deficits associated with FASD include mental retardation, learning disabilities, hyperactivity, attention deficits, and problems with impulse control, social skills, language, and memory. People who have an FASD are vulnerable to numerous problems throughout their lifespan, such as failure in school, substance abuse, mental illness, and involvement in the criminal justice system. The national costs of FAS alone are up to $6 billion per year, including direct costs to the health, social, and justice systems and indirect costs associated with mortality, morbidity, disability, and incarceration.[2] Because of data collection issues, calculating the entire cost of FASD to individuals, families, and society is difficult, but the cost is overwhelming.

An Emerging Public Health Issue

Today, FASD is appropriately viewed as an emerging public health issue, one that may grow with improved diagnosis and surveillance. Recognizing that, Congress established the FASD Center for Excellence in 2001 as part of a federal effort to address FASD. The center is operated by the Substance Abuse and Mental Health Services Administration, which is part of the US Department of Health and Human Services. The center's mandates include studying interventions and strategies for people who have an FASD, identifying communities with exemplary systems of care for FASD, providing technical assistance and training to improve services, and developing techniques for FASD prevention. To help achieve its mandates, the center has sought input from FASD constituency groups through its Steering Committee and a series of town hall meetings.

In 2002 and 2003, the FASD Center for Excellence convened 15 town hall meetings with individuals who have an FASD, their families and caregivers, service providers, researchers, policymakers, and community leaders. The purposes of the meetings were to identify needs and share information about services that prevent and treat FASD. The meetings also were intended to raise awareness, facilitate coordination among service systems, and increase support for services at the state level.

To organize the town hall meetings, the center worked with the FAS Family Resource Institute, the Alaska Office of FAS, and the National Organization on Fetal Alcohol Syndrome.

Table 1 Number of People Who Testified at Town Hall Meetings, by Group: 2002–2003

Category	Approximate No. of Testifiers
Parents and caregivers	216
Adoptive parents	160
Foster parents	19
Grandparents	14
Stepparents	6
Mothers in recovery	12
Birth mothers	5
Individuals who have an FASD	30
Professionals	140
Community leaders	20

Note. FASO = fetal alcohol spectrum disorders.

Table 2 Needs of Individuals, Families, and Communities, Cited in Town Hall Testimony, by Frequency: 2002–2003

Needs Cited in Town Hall Testimony	Approximate No. of Mentions
Appropriate services for individuals who have an FASD and their families overall in every system of care	100
Diagnostic services	75
Adequate training of all providers working with individuals who have an FASD	60
Job support and help managing money for persons who have an FASD	50
Effective prevention strategies	35
Community education about FASD, such as warning signs where alcohol is sold	30
Alcohol treatment for women	20
Recognition of FASD as a disability	20
Physicians' understanding of FASD and their role in prevention	15
Supportive housing options for adults who have an FASD	15
Psychiatric expertise on psychopharmacology for FASD	10
Financial assistance	10
Enactment and enforcement of investigation and disclosure laws on prenatal exposure to alcohol in adoption and foster care	10

Note. FASD = fetal alcohol spectrum disorders.

These advocacy organizations were well positioned to recruit participants through established networks of concerned families, professionals, and organizations, and through traditional social marketing efforts.

More than 800 people participated across the nation, with more than 500 providing testimony in Alaska, Arizona, California, Colorado, the District of Columbia, Florida, Illinois, Maryland, Michigan, Minnesota, Mississippi, New York, South Dakota, Texas, and Washington. Most of the testimony came from foster and adoptive parents of children who have an FASD and service system professionals (Table 1). Their perspectives may have differed from those of groups less represented at the meetings, such as birth parents, persons who have an FASD, and medical professionals. Efforts are under way by the FASD Center for Excellence and others, such as the Centers for Disease Control and Prevention (CDC), to cast a wide net for examining the issue of FASD from all sides. However, the center is confident in the overall validity of the town hall findings. For example, testimony about barriers to obtaining a diagnosis coincides with the known scarcity of professionals who am qualified to make a diagnosis.

Testimony at the town hall meetings focused overwhelmingly on the need for services that treat and prevent FASD. The gaps cut across multiple systems and areas, including health care, education, mental health care, substance abuse treatment, developmental disabilities services, social services, housing, income support, vocational rehabilitation, criminal justice, prevention systems, and adoption laws (Table 2). The issues described in the testimony were consistent geographically, with no notable regional differences. The findings echoed the results of an environmental scan that the center conducted to identify FASD prevention and intervention programs, which revealed a severe shortage of services nationwide.

Each town hall meeting participant who wished to testify was given approximately 5 minutes to provide oral testimony, which was recorded on audiotape and, in some cases, videotape. Those who did not wish to testify onsite were invited to submit written testimony.

On the basis of meeting transcripts, tapes, and written testimony, reviewers noted the general tone of the meeting, the problems and needs that were discussed, and the suggestions and recommendations that were made. Reviewers developed codes for topical categories and subcategories, and they entered a summary of each piece of testimony into a database. To determine how many times an issue was mentioned, reviewers searched the testimony text for key words. Reviewers also used the database to determine the number of persons who testified from particular groups (e.g., parents, professionals).

Understanding the Problem

The concerns raised during the town hall meetings fell into several broad categories: lack of appropriate services for persons who have an FASD, both overall and specifically for adults; lack of access to existing services; lack of effective prevention strategies; and the need for investigation and disclosure of prenatal exposure to alcohol during adoption and foster care placement.

Overall Services

"I don't think my job should be an advocate. . . . My job is to be the Mommy."

—Parent of a child who has an FASD

The town hall meetings revealed a general lack of appropriate FASD-related services. Within the health care system, FASD is often misdiagnosed or inappropriately treated. Obtaining a diagnosis is extremely difficult because of inconsistent diagnostic criteria and terminology combined with a shortage of professionals who are qualified to make a diagnosis. Insufficient knowledge and training about FASD, particularly among pediatricians, social workers, psychologists, and psychiatrists, results in failure to provide necessary services or to make appropriate referrals.

Town hall participants also spoke out repeatedly about the need for respite. Parents and caregivers described the extreme demands of caring for individuals who have an FASD, the resultant toll on families, and the need for relief. However, close supervision is imperative because of behavioral and safety issues, and affordable and appropriate respite care is almost nonexistent.

Finally, the testimony reflected great frustration with the school system, particularly special education, largely because of lack of awareness and understanding about FASD. Many people spoke of their struggles to educate teachers and school administrators about FASD and the negative impact on children of inappropriate educational interventions. Some parents had resorted to quitting their jobs and homeschooling their children, which further isolated their children and created a financial burden. Numerous testifiers portrayed a wrenching educational experience that was fraught with failure.

Services for Adults

"We provide supervised living arrangements for those who have sustained brain damage in accidents, but we cannot extend that understanding to someone who has sustained brain damage prior to birth."

—Parent of an adult child who has an FASD

FASD is often perceived as a children's health issue, but the deficits and functional impairments associated with the disorders last a lifetime. The town hall testimony described the challenges that people who have an FASD face during adulthood. Difficulties with behavior, social skills, impulsivity, and poor judgment translate into problems with life skills, such as maintaining a job and managing money.

A number of people called for recognition of FASD as a disability. Some adults who have an FASD can live independently with proper assistance, such as appropriate homing, vocational rehabilitation, and income support (e.g., Supplemental Security Income, Social Security Disability Insurance). However, services are scarce, and many adults who have an FASD are ineligible. Some have IQs that fall within the normal range, which disqualifies them in some states despite their impairment, and others lack a diagnosis. Many remain at home with their parents or caregivers in the absence of acceptable alternatives. Parents described their fears for their adult children's well-being after they die, highlighting the need for future planning.

Access to Available Services

In addition to expanded services that specifically address FASD, town hall participants asked for increased access to existing services, such as special education, income support, housing, vocational rehabilitation, and developmental disabilities services. Because of low awareness and recognition, people who have an FASD often are not referred to appropriate services or are rejected as ineligible. Those who lack the facial features or low IQ associated with FAS struggle with a hidden disorder. They often are perceived as "normal," although their neurological problems make them function at levels that are far below normal.

Effective Prevention Strategies

"Well, it's okay. My doctor said I could have a little drink. It will help me relax."

—A nurse relaying comments made by pregnant patients

The town hall participants called for effective prevention strategies, particularly in the areas of community education, health care, and substance abuse treatment. Strategies should include all women of childbearing age, including adolescents, because many are potentially at risk for an alcohol-exposed pregnancy. More than half of women of childbearing age drink alcohol, and more than half of all pregnancies are unplanned. Alcohol can cause damage to a fetus during early pregnancy, before a woman knows she is pregnant. Even 1 episode of binge drinking (4 or more drinks on 1 occasion) can harm a fetus.

Many physicians continue to counsel their pregnant patients that it is acceptable to have an occasional drink, yet there is no known safe level of alcohol use during pregnancy. Additionally, some women take such vague advice as a medical green light to drink, leading them down a slippery slope toward heavier drinking. Physicians also fail to screen women who may be at risk and refer them to appropriate services. Their reasons include fear of stigmatizing patients or incurring litigation; lack of screening tools, time, and services; and personal discomfort discussing the issue with patients. Many physicians also have a poor understanding of FASD.[3,4]

Pregnant women and women of childbearing age who are in treatment for substance abuse are at high risk for an alcohol-exposed pregnancy, but many may be in the dark about FASD. During a special town hall meeting for women in recovery, women testified that while in treatment, they had not been told about the dangers of drinking during pregnancy.

The Institute of Medicine classifies prevention programs as universal, selective, or indicated. For FASD, universal prevention includes educating the general public with tools such as alcohol warning labels. Selective prevention efforts target pregnant women or women of childbearing age, often through screening and intervention. Indicated prevention efforts address women at highest risk—such as women who have substance abuse problems or those who have given birth to a child who has an FASD—primarily through treatment. Research shows that selective and indicated prevention strategies can be effective in preventing FASD. Universal strategies help raise awareness but have not been shown to change behavior and prevent FASD.[5,6]

The FASD Center for Excellence has identified and analyzed 639 prevention and intervention programs associated with FASD in the United States and Canada. Few of the programs specifically address FASD, and prevention programs are particularly scarce. It is difficult to discern best practices among the programs, because few have been evaluated to determine their effectiveness. No comprehensive systems of care for the prevention or treatment of FASD have been identified.

The National Registry of Effective Programs, which evaluates promising and best practices for substance abuse prevention and treatment, has approved 2 programs that help reduce rates of FASD. The Nurse-Family Partnership Program in Denver, Colorado, provides home visits by registered nurses to expectant and new mothers and is considered a model program. Although it does not specifically target FASD, the program has been shown to reduce substance use and improve birth outcomes. The Parent-Child Assistance Program in Seattle, Washington, has been recognized as a promising program. It also involves home visits to expectant mothers and has been shown to reduce alcohol use and improve birth outcomes.

Investigation and Disclosure Laws

"Social services denies that kids have problems related to FASD and hides information."

—*Parent of a child who has an FASD*

Many of the town hall attendees who testified were foster or adoptive parents of children who have an FASD. Typically, they had been unaware of their child's health status at the time of placement. In many cases, it took years to unravel the mystery of their child's problems—years in which the children and their families suffered tremendously because of lack of a diagnosis and services. Many parents spoke of their grief upon learning that the adoption agency or social services knew about the birth mother's history of alcoholism. Often, children suffer further from the detrimental effects of multiple foster care placements, which may result in part from a poor understanding of the underlying cause of the children's behavioral problems.

Some states have disclosure laws that require agencies to inform foster or adoptive parents about a child's prenatal exposure to alcohol, but agencies often are unaware of exposure. Only a few states require agencies to investigate whether exposure occurred. Enactment and enforcement of investigation and disclosure laws are insufficient.

Policy Recommendations

The town hall findings paint a vivid picture of the harsh realities that individuals who have an FASD and their families face in America. Meeting the critical needs that were revealed will require a concerted commitment by federal agencies, state governments, and private organizations. The following policy recommendations by the FASD Center for Excellence provide an opportunity for vital change in the prevention and treatment of FASD:

- Foster the development of evidence-based FASD prevention strategies by researchers and funding agencies.
- Ensure FASD training for professionals in various service systems, including health care, mental health care, substance abuse treatment, education, social services, criminal justice, and prevention systems.
- Incorporate information on the prevention and treatment of FASD into the credentialing requirements for teachers, juvenile justice workers, lawmakers, and health care professionals as called for by the National Task Force on Fetal Alcohol Syndrome and Fetal Alcohol Effect.[7]
- Develop a comprehensive system of care for FASD, with cost-effective prevention and treatment programs that increase awareness, build community support, foster legal and judicial reform, and improve diagnosis and services.
- Develop standard diagnostic criteria and terminology across the FASD spectrum and across the lifespan to increase the identification of FASD among all age groups and reduce confusion and misdiagnosis. The CDC recently released diagnostic guidelines that may aid this effort. Working with medical schools, the CDC also has established FAS regional training centers to develop and disseminate curricula on diagnosis and prevention for medical and allied health students and practitioners.[3]
- Ensure that all states adopt the federal definition of developmental disability, which does not set IQ limits. This shift will expand eligibility for benefits and services among individuals who have an FASD, thereby increasing their quality of life and decreasing their risk for poverty, unemployment, homelessness, and incarceration.
- Work with the American Psychiatric Association (APA) and the World Health Organization (WHO) to promote the inclusion of FASD in the APA's *Diagnostic and Statistical Manual of Mental Disorders* and the WHO's *International Classification of Diseases and Related Health Problems.* Inclusion of FASD in standard diagnostic manuals will increase awareness and knowledge among professionals and will support improvements in diagnosis.
- Use the US Surgeon General's 2005 warning to develop a federal consensus statement about abstinence from alcohol during pregnancy, which will form the basis for clear, consistent prevention messages across all agencies that play a role in public health.
- Ensure the enactment and enforcement of state investigation and disclosure laws regarding prenatal exposure to alcohol.

Conclusion

The FASD Center for Excellence's town hall meetings made clear the nation's obligation to address FASD. Of primary concern are the need to close overall gaps in services, improve services for adults who have an FASD, improve access to existing services, implement effective prevention strategies, and enact and enforce state investigation and disclosure laws.

The federal government must improve FASD prevention and treatment by setting policies that will promote change and influence other entities that have a stake in the issue. By taking a leadership role, federal agencies can point the way toward a national strategy for improving the lives of people who have an FASD, preventing new cases of FASD, and reducing the considerable costs to society of prenatal exposure to alcohol.

Contributors

C.B. Gass originated the article and provided quality control and management oversight. D. Major Ryan wrote the article. D.M. Bonnett assisted with data analysis and editorial review.

References

1. May PA, Gossage JP. Estimating the prevalence of fetal alcohol syndrome: A summary. *Alcohol Res Health.* 2001;25:159–167.

2. Lupton C, Burd L, Harwood R. The cost of fetal alcohol spectrum disorders. *Am J Med Genet C Serum Med Genet,* 2004;127:42–50.

3. Sharpe, TT, Alexander M, Hutcherson J, et al. Report from the CDC. Physician and allied health professionals' training and fetal alcohol syndrome. *J Women's Health.* 2004;13:133–139.

4. Logan, TK, Walker R, Nagle L, Lew J, Wiesenhan D. Rural and small-town attitudes about alcohol use during pregnancy: a community and provider sample. *J Rural Health,* 2003;19:497–505.

5. Henkin JR. Fetal alcohol syndrome prevention research. *Alcohol Res Health.* 2002;26:58–65.

6. Murphy-Brennan MG, Oei TPS. Is there evidence to show that fetal alcohol syndrome can be prevented? *J Drug Educ.* 1999;29:5–24.

7. National Task Fame an Fetal Alcohol Syndrome and Fetal Alcohol Effect. Defining the national agenda for fetal alcohol syndrome and other prenatal alcohol-related effects. *MMWR Morb Mortal Wkly Rep.* 2002;51:9–12.

DOREEN MAJOR RYAN and **CALLIE B. GASS** are with the Fetal Alcohol Spectrum Disorders (FASD) Center for Excellence, Substance Abuse and Mental Health Services Administration (SAMHSA), Rockville, Md. **DOREEN M. BONNETT** was with the Center for Excellence when this article was written.

Requests for reprints should be sent to the FASD Center for Excellence, 2101 Gaither Rd, Ste 600, Rockville, MD 20850 (e-mail:fasd-center@samhsa.hhs.gov).

Acknowledgments—The FASD Center for Excellence is operated by Northrop Grumman Information Technology (contract no. 277-01-6068).

This article was developed with the help of staff from the SAMHSA Fetal Alcohol Spectrum Disorders Center for Excellence. Ted Buxton, Dan Dubovsky, Gaff Dym, Chuck Lupton, Sharon Pollack, Crishelle Rivers, and Sharon Williams helped develop the policy recommendations noted in the article. Ammic Bonsu is the government project officer; at the time of the town hall meetings, Deborah Stone was the government project officer.

Note—The views, policies, and opinions expressed are those of the authors and do not reflect those of SAMHSA or the US Department of Health and Human Services.

Students With Fetal Alcohol Syndrome
Updating Our Knowledge, Improving Their Programs

DARCY MILLER

Jack, a 10-year-old fourth-grade student with Fetal Alcohol Syndrome, lives with his adoptive parents, who began as foster parents when he was 3 years old. Jack is a talkative, active, and creative boy who struggles with academics, making friends, and anger management. It is difficult for him to understand the consequences of his behavior, so his decision making doesn't always result in positive outcomes. After negative peer interactions, Jack's teacher uses direct teaching of social skills, modeling, and guided practice. However, Jack tends to repeat the same negative decisions, and therefore has few friends. Jack also has a difficult time understanding social cues and interpreting others' communication, wants, or needs.

Jack receives special education services, as do many other students with Fetal Alcohol Syndrome (FAS; see box, "What is FAS?"). However, since FAS is not a formally recognized category under the Individuals with Disabilities Education Act (IDEA), students with FAS typically receive services by meeting the definition of other disabilities, such as emotional/behavioral disorders, mental retardation, learning disabilities, or health impairments (Gessner, Bischoff, Perham-Hester, Chandler, & Middaugh, 1998). FAS is usually subsumed under other IDEA categories, and is often discussed in texts and resources as a subset of other disabilities, so educators may not have had the opportunity to develop a knowledgeable base about FAS or become familiar with effective instructional strategies. Recent research has provided new information about FAS to consider when designing programs for these students. This article provides an overview of new developments in defining and characterizing FAS, as well as suggestions for effective intervention.

Weaving Student Characteristics and Programming Together

In the past, students with mild characteristics associated with fetal alcohol exposure were designated Fetal Alcohol Effects (FAE; Clarren & Smith, 1978). FAE is no longer considered a useful diagnostic label, as it is too vague to be of much help

What Is FAS?

Fetal Alcohol Syndrome is caused by maternal consumption of alcohol during gestation and currently is viewed as one of a range of alcohol-related outcomes collectively referred to as Fetal Alcohol Spectrum Disorders (FASD; Astley, 2004). The spectrum includes such diagnostic categories as neurobehavioral disorders and static encephalopathy, as well as FAS. The diagnosis of FAS is based on growth deficiencies, facial anomalies, cognitive deficits or abnormalities, and the amount of alcohol exposure during gestation (Astley & Clarren, 2000). The level of impairment or severity across these four areas can range from mild to severe (Roebuck, Mattson, & Riley, 1999). The new four-digit code used to diagnose FAS and the other spectrum disorders rates each of four areas as to the level of impairment or severity, from 1 (no evidence of impairment) to 4 (definite/severe evidence of impairment). A student with severe growth deficiencies (4), moderate facial anomalies (3), mild cognitive deficits (2), and evidence of maternal heavy drinking (4) would receive a diagnostic code of 4324, which is classified as a neurobehavioral disorder—alcohol exposed. Using the four-digit code in diagnosis can result in 256 possible combinations, from 1 to 4 in each category, with each combination resulting in different levels of severity or impact on the student (Astley & Clarren). (See http://depts.washington.edu/fasdpn/ for more information on the diagnosis of FAS, FASD, and the four-digit code.)

to educators or clinicians (Astley, 2004). FASD is now used to denote the full range of fetal alcohol spectrum disorders associated with prenatal alcohol exposure. Students with spectrum disorders may exhibit learning and behavior patterns that are similar to those with Fetal Alcohol Syndrome (FAS), even though they may not meet the specific criteria for a complete FAS diagnosis (see Astley & Clarren, 2000).

The characteristics associated with FAS range from mild to severe, and differentially impact language/communication,

Table 1 Impact of Fetal Alcohol Syndrome Characteristics on Functional Domains

Characteristic	Language/ Communication	Social/Behavioral	Academic/ Cognitive	Adaptive Behavior
Social communication/ language difficulties	Interprets cues incorrectly; difficulty with nonverbal communication	Interpersonal and peer problems; social skills deficits (e.g., lacks skills in sharing, cooperating)		Doesn't follow or understand rules in social games in sports; difficulty communicating needs and wants
Conceptual reasoning/ thinking skills	Doesn't use language to reason and analyze; understands at literal level	Lacks understanding of consequences of behavior; attention difficulties; hyperactive	Difficulty understanding abstract concepts; lack of judgment and reasoning skills; difficulty understanding time and sequence; challenged by meaning of cause and effect	Doesn't understand time-sensitive tasks; difficulty with decision-making skills in home and community; difficulty following directions and problem-solving around functional issues
Emotional/social	May be chatty, talkative, with adequate or above vocabulary	Temper tantrums and angry outbursts; impulsive; unpredictable behavior and/or moods; mood swings; depression; poor self-esteem; aggressive; noncompliant	Unmotivated; unorganized	Immature behavior
Independence/ self-sufficiency	Expressive or receptive language deficits	Difficulty regulating behavior	Deficits in short/ long-term memory	Lacks independent living skills; problems with age-appropriate hygiene tasks

social/behavioral, academic/cognitive, and adaptive functioning (Table 1). Research has reaffirmed many of the characteristics traditionally associated with FAS, but also has clarified some misconceptions (Table 2). This new understanding of FAS, along with well-established research findings, has implications for special education teams as they address the needs of students with FAS. Suggested interventions (Figure 1) should be evaluated in light of the relationship of characteristics across domains. For example, difficulty understanding abstract concepts will affect a student in all areas of functioning, not just the academic/cognitive domain. These suggestions have been synthesized from new research findings on FAS and from clinical practice (Miller, 2003, Miller, 2004, Miller & Emerson, 2004).

FAS Characteristics and Challenges
Language/Communication

New findings regarding the language/communication challenges faced by students with FAS have significantly contributed to our understanding of their communicative functioning. In the past it was assumed that if these students scored within normal limits on standardized speech/language measures, their communications skills were not impaired. But many students with FAS possess strengths in vocabulary and verbal fluency and score within normal limits on standardized measures, yet still experience communication problems (Streissguth, Barr, Kogan, & Bookstein, 1997). Students with FAS often have difficulty using language to solve social problems and understanding the more abstract aspects of verbal and nonverbal language. Language comprehension and pragmatic difficulties contribute to significant social communication problems (Coggins, Friet, & Morgan, 1998; Mattson, Goodman, Caine, Delis, & Riley, 1999).

The characteristics associated with FAS range from mild to severe, and differentially impact language/communication, social/behavioral, academic/cognitive, and adaptive functioning.

As with all effective programming, interventions in the language/communication domain begin with a comprehensive assessment of student strengths and weaknesses. Successful language and communication skills depend on an ability to

Table 2 Misconceptions and Realities Regarding Fetal Alcohol Syndrome

Misconceptions	Realities
Students with alcohol-related disorders have clearly abnormal characteristics	Outcomes of alcohol-related disorders occur along a continuum (spectrum) from mild to severe
Mild FAS is "fetal alcohol effects," or FAE	FAE is not considered a useful term; fetal alcohol spectrum disorders (FASD) more precisely describes FAS and other alcohol-related disorders
Students with FAS are mentally retarded	Many have cognitive profiles that more closely resemble those of students with learning disabilities
If students with FAS have normal intelligence, they can understand abstract concepts	Even those with normal intelligence struggle to understand abstract concepts
Students with FAS who are talkative, chatty and verbal also have good social communication skills	Despite being able to "say a lot," many students with FAS have deficits in social communication; they don't know how to use language to negotiate everyday tasks, demands, and social interactions
You can tell a child has FAS just by looking at his eyes	The diagnosis of FAS is focused on four specific areas: growth patterns, facial features, brain functioning, and alcohol exposure, which are evaluated using standardized, scientifically derived protocol and criteria

understand intangibles such as others' perspectives, gestures, and facial expressions. Special education teams need to look beyond verbal fluency and vocabulary, and assess these students' language comprehension and pragmatics, expressive and receptive understanding, as well as social communication skills. Functional behavior assessments can be used to identify critical skill deficits, as well as to identify settings and interactions for intervention. Direct instruction in social skills and assisting students in understanding language expectations and demands are often pivotal components of intervention plans for students with FAS. Ideally, these interventions should occur across multiple environments.

Social/Behavioral

Social/behavioral functioning presents some of the most difficult challenges for students with FAS (Coggins, Olswang, Carmichael Olson, & Timler, in press; Miller, 2003; Thomas, Kelly, Mattson, & Riley, 1998). Students with FAS frequently have problems controlling their anger, aggression, and impulses, which contribute to other social/behavioral difficulties, such as peer and student-teacher relationships, and school disciplinary actions (Streissguth & Ranter, 1997). These students often demonstrate attention problems and many are diagnosed with attention deficit/hyperactivity disorders (AD/HD; Mattson & Riley, 1998). Students with FAS may be anxious, have mood swings, lie/steal, and act immaturely (Coles et al., 1997). The combination of these difficulties often results in low social competence, with deficits in social skills and interpersonal abilities being quite common.

Using rigorous functional behavior assessments, the special education team can pinpoint areas of concern and design social/behavioral intervention plans. Implementing "positive behavior supports" (Sugai et al., 1999) to respond to social/behavioral challenges shifts the primary focus from *changing the student's behavior to supporting changes in behavior.* Positive behavior

support interventions provide accommodations for behaviors that won't change or that change very slowly, as is the case with some of the social/behavioral challenges of FAS.

> **Many students with FAS possess strengths in vocabulary and verbal fluency and score within normal limits on standardized measures, yet still experience communication problems.**

Effective social/behavioral intervention plans adjust to challenges across settings, and simultaneously provide opportunities for students to learn new behaviors and practice social skills. For example, many students with FAS struggle to understand the consequences of their behavior and actions. This difficulty is usually pervasive (occurs across settings) and is very difficult and slow to change. A positive behavior support plan would include environmental and personnel supports across settings, and at the same time would focus on interventions for specific behaviors. Many strategies implemented for students with emotional/behavioral disorders are also very effective for students with FAS, including social skills instruction, behavioral contracting, differential reinforcement, preferred activities, anger management, self-management, and self-monitoring. Depending on a student's characteristics, mental health counseling may be needed for the student, the family, or both.

Academic/Cognitive

Research has debunked the old assumption that all students with FAS are also mentally retarded (Streissguth et al., 1997). Students with FAS have varied academic and cognitive

Conduct comprehensive assessment of student's use of language; social/communication skills; understanding of abstract concepts and reasoning; and adaptive functioning

	Language/ Communication Domain	Social/ Behavioral Domain	Adaptive Behavior Domain	Academic/ Cognitive Domain
Use assessment to . . .	identify what skills are needed, replace inappropriate communication, and provide tools	develop behavior intervention plan, using positive behavior supports paradigm (Sugai, Horner, & Sprague, 1999)	identify key adaptive behaviors relevant to developmental stage; develop transition planning	establish level of understanding of abstract concepts and reasoning in multiple subjects
Directly teach . . .	social communication skills; practice verbal and nonverbal communication skills	social skills; how to identify emotions, what they "mean," and what to do when feeling a specific emotion; anger and stress management techniques	adaptive behaviors, in appropriate settings; self-determination skills	abstract reasoning using the concrete-semiconcrete-abstract (CSA) model (Mercer & Mercer, 2005); learning strategies (Deshler, Ellis, & Lenz, 1996)
Practice . . .	with peer mentors and models in friendship circles and study groups, in varied settings, to reinforce skills and appropriate social interaction			analyzing complex assignments; using organization tools to work through steps or phases of assignments
Provide . . .	visual prompts, signals, and cues during language interactions	structure, routine, concrete and semi-concrete aids, visual aids, and feedback; explicit instructions, specifying expectations	instruction using mnemonics, concept mapping, visual organizers, diagrams, and other aids when teaching a concept or skill	

Assess student's ability to generalize skills across subjects and in multiple settings; use observation, checklists, rating forms

Figure 1   Interventions for students with FAS

profiles, with strengths and weaknesses that can resemble the cognitive profiles of students with learning disabilities (Kerns, Don, Mateer, & Streissguth, 1997; Weinberg, 1997). Academic/cognitive challenges—such as understanding abstract concepts, reasoning, memory, and organization problems—present barriers to achievement in math, reading, and writing (Streissguth et al., 1997). Students with FAS typically have disrupted school histories, including suspensions and expulsions (Streissguth, 1997).

To design academic/cognitive interventions for students with FAS, special education teams need to begin with comprehensive academic and cognitive assessments. The team should pay particular attention to the extent to which the student can understand abstract concepts, which is an expectation of students across all subject areas and at all grade levels.

The concrete-semiconcrete-abstract (CSA) instructional model (Mercer & Mercer, 2005) can be used across subject areas to facilitate understanding of abstract concepts. The CSA model uses pictures, diagrams, and manipulatives to assist students in understanding increasingly abstract concepts. Direct instruction, with modeling, frequent feedback, and practice with multiple exemplars, also improves student understanding of abstract concepts. Most instructional approaches used with

students who have learning disabilities are also appropriate for students with FAS, including visual aids, organization tools, mnemonics, concept mapping, and learning strategies (Deshler et al., 1996).

Adaptive Behavior

Although we usually associate adaptive behavior deficits with mental retardation, students with FAS who function at or above normal intellectual levels often display deficits in adaptive behavior (Streissguth et al., 2004). Parent reports and clinical research using adaptive behavior measures show that these students have trouble with organization skills, understanding time and sequence (e.g., getting ready for school in the morning), understanding basic safety and routines in the home and community, and everyday decision making, and have difficulty completing tasks independently (Astley, 2000; Olson, Feldman, Streissguth, Sampson, & Bookstein, 1998; Thomas, et al., 1998; Whaley, O'Connor, & Gunderson, 2001). Other adaptive behavior challenges faced by students with FAS include following multistep directions, navigating their own neighborhoods, remembering information, completing simple tasks, and interacting with siblings and friends. Even after graduation or leaving school, these students continue to struggle. Streissguth

IEP Goal: Jack will demonstrate appropriate social skills in a semi-structured peer group setting.

Language/Communication Interventions	Use speech and language therapy sessions to model and role-play appropriate conversation skills with a structured peer group. Teach social skills first on a one-to-one basis using direct instruction and then rehearse prior to group practice.
Social/Behavioral Interventions	Use chart in/on Jack's desk to positively reinforce appropriate social skills in group settings. Groups are structured according to Jack's level of skill and with appropriate peer models. Address social skills instruction in small sets of related behaviors, with visual and concrete reinforcement of progress. Provide adult supervision during recesses to reinforce positive social interactions and prevent inappropriate behavior.
Academic/Cognitive Interventions	Use small, structured group settings to encourage generalization of social skills. Provide concrete directions for group tasks, increasing group time and complexity as Jack progresses. Use visual reminders of expected group behaviors. Use group settings in Jack's strongest areas (math, social studies) so that he has more cognitive energy to devote to learning social skills and is not frustrated with the content. Provide direct problem-solving instruction, focused on content area. Rehearse steps with Jack before group work.
Adaptive Behavior Interventions	Provide practice joining a group during lunch, recess, and physical education class with guidance and prompting from teaching assistant. Teach self-management, including self-monitoring and self-evaluation during resource room time.

IEP Goal: Jack will improve his understanding of cause/effect and consequences.

Language/Communication Interventions	Use language therapy time to reinforce concepts of cause/effect and consequences using role-plays, simulations, and stories. Emphasize verbal explanations from Jack.
Social/Behavioral Interventions	For a set of identified times, settings, and behaviors, design behavioral contracts based on clear expectations and consequences, with short duration and concrete rewards provided or taken away. Use small peer groups for discussion of cause/effect and consequences within the social realm. Facilitate role-playing and simulations in which cause/effect and consequences are the focus.
Academic/Cognitive Interventions	Read stories that clearly focus on cause/effect and consequences. Mediate group discussions of story comprehension, with direct instruction of the concepts. Provide direct instruction in learning strategies, especially those that focus on cause/effect outcomes (e.g., following a mnemonic with a clear message that "If you do these steps, this will be the outcome"). Use Jack's strengths in math to reinforce the strategies.
Adaptive Behavior Interventions	Use the Health/Safety curriculum to teach and reinforce the concepts of cause/effect and consequences. Focus on home and community safety curriculum unit (e.g., using utensils and appliances safely, identifying poisonous and flammable materials, using a fire extinguisher correctly, treating minor wounds appropriately, using selected household tools correctly, etc.). In the resource room using authentic materials, provide direct instruction and demonstration to teach identified adaptive skills, emphasizing the concepts of cause/effect and consequences.

Figure 2   Sample IEP goals and suggested interventions across domains and environments.

(1997) found that many of the challenges faced by students with FAS result in problems with employment, money management, social interactions, relationships, housing, and mental health throughout adulthood.

The adaptive functioning of students with FAS is extremely varied. Some students need assistance learning basic independent living skills, such as laundry, cooking, and safety. Other students with FAS need independent living skills instruction in areas such as budgeting, paying taxes, signing leases, buying cars, obtaining loans, etc. With a detailed adaptive behavior assessment, the special education team can identify critical areas for an individualized education/transition program. Effective

Online Resources on Fetal Alcohol Syndrome

National Organization on Fetal Alcohol Syndrome
http://www.nofas.org/

Fetal Alcohol Syndrome Diagnostic and Prevention Network
http://depts.washington.edu/fasdpn/

FASlink
http://www.acbr.com/fas/

University of Washington Fetal Alcohol and Drug Unit
http://depts.washington.edu/fadu

Fetal Alcohol Syndrome Family Resource Institute
http://www.fetalalcoholsyndrome.org/

Diagnostic and Prevention Network
http://depts.washington.edu/fasdpn/

strategies include direct instruction in the skills needed, and supported practice and generalization activities in the community and vocational settings. Many students with FAS continue to need support from communities and agencies after high school, so connecting these students with community resources is an important part of addressing adaptive and vocational needs.

An Example: Jack's Program

Figure 2 provides a sample of Jack's IEP goals and suggested interventions across domains and environments. Many of the interventions—such as use of concrete language and positive behavior supports—generalize to all environments. The special education team needs to ensure that all the professionals, teaching assistants, and specialists involved in a student's program are knowledgeable about the interventions, so that they can be consistently and comprehensively implemented in each setting (e.g., recess, lunchroom, gymnasium). Special education teams can use the format shown in Figure 2 as a tool to clarify the student's needs, as well as a way to design interventions across domains.

Final Thoughts

We are becoming more knowledgeable about what is, and what is not, FAS (see box, "Online Resources on Fetal Alcohol Syndrome."). In addition, we have a better idea of the characteristics of this syndrome and corresponding strategies for intervention. With this new knowledge, and by working collaboratively with parents and other involved staff, special education teams can design effective programs that meet the needs of students with FAS.

References

Astley, S. J. (2000). *Summary of first 1000 patients evaluated.* (Available from the University of Washington FAS Diagnostic & Prevention Network Core Clinic, Seattle, WA).

Astley, S. J. (2004). *Diagnostic guide for fetal alcohol spectrum disorders: The 4-digit diagnostic code.* Seattle, WA: The University of Washington.

Astley, S. J., & Clarren, S. K. (2000). Diagnosing the full spectrum of fetal alcohol exposed individuals: Introducing the 4-digit code. *Alcohol & Alcoholism, 35,* 400–410.

Clarren, S. K., & Smith, D. W. (1978). Fetal alcohol syndrome. *New England Journal of Medicine, 298,* 1063–1067.

Coggins, T. E., Friet, T., & Morgan, T. (1998). Analysing narrative productions in older school-age children and adolescents with fetal alcohol syndrome: An experimental tool for clinical applications. *Clinical Linguistics and Phonetics, 12,* 221–236.

Coggins, T. E., Olswang, L. B., Carmichael Olson, H., & Timler, G. R. (in press). On becoming socially competent communicators: The challenge for children with fetal alcohol syndrome. In L. M. Glidden (Ed.), *International Review of Research in Mental Retardation.* Burlington, MA: Elsevier/Academic Press.

Coles, C. D., Platzman, K. A., Raskind-Hood, C. L., Brown, R. T., Falek, A., & Smith, I. E. (1997). A comparison of children affected by prenatal alcohol exposure and attention deficit, hyperactivity disorder. *Alcoholism: Clinical and Experimental Research, 21,* 150–161.

Deshler, D., Ellis, E., & Lenz, K. (1996). *Teaching adolescents with learning disabilities* (2nd ed.). Denver, CO: Love.

Gessner, R., Bischoff, H., Perham-Hester, K., Chandler, B., & Middaugh, J. (1998). *The educational attainment of children with fetal alcohol syndrome: Recommendations and reports.* Juneau, AK: Alaska State Department of Health and Social Services, Division of Public Health.

Kerns, J., Don, A., Mateer, C., & Streissguth, A. (1997). Cognitive deficits in nonretarded adults with fetal alcohol syndrome. *Journal of Learning Disabilities, 30,* 685–693.

Mattson, S. N., Goodman, A., Caine, C., Delis, D., & Riley, E. (1999). Executive functioning in children with heavy prenatal alcohol exposure. *Alcoholism: Clinical and Experimental Research, 23,* 1808–1815.

Mattson, S. N., & Riley, E. P. (1998). A review of the neurobehavioral deficits in children with fetal alcohol syndrome or prenatal exposure to alcohol. *Alcoholism: Clinical and Experimental Research, 22,* 279–294.

Mercer, C. D., & Mercer, A. R. (2005). *Teaching students with learning problems* (7th ed). Upper Saddle River, NJ: Pearson, Merrill, Prentice Hall.

Miller, D. (2003, October). *Advances in the diagnosis and understanding of fetal alcohol syndrome: Exploring programming ideas and strategies.* Paper presented at the Washington State Association of School Psychology, Spokane, WA.

Miller, D. (2004, October). *Responding to the needs of students with fetal alcohol syndrome: Strategies and programming ideas.* Paper presented at the meeting of the Washington Association of School Social Workers, Lake Chelan, WA.

Miller, D., & Emerson, R. (2004, June). *Fetal alcohol syndrome: Diagnosis and intervention.* Paper presented at the Fetal Alcohol Syndrome Seminar, Walla Walla Community College, Clarkston, WA.

Olson, H. C., Feldman, J. J., Streissguth, A. P., Sampson, P. D., & Bookstein, F. L. (1998). Neuropsychological deficits in adolescents with fetal alcohol syndrome: Clinical findings. *Alcoholism Clinical and Experimental Research, 22,* 1998–2012.

Roebuck, T., Mattson, S., & Riley, E. (1999). Behavioral and psychosocial profiles of alcohol-exposed children. *Alcoholism: Clinical and Experimental Research, 23,* 1070–1076.

Streissguth, A. P. (1997). *Fetal alcohol syndrome: A guide for families and communities.* Baltimore, MD: Paul. H. Brookes Publishing.

Streissguth, A. P., Barr, J., Kogan, J., & Bookstein, F. (1997). Primary and secondary disabilities in fetal alcohol syndrome. In A. Streissguth, & J. Ranter (Eds.), *The challenge of fetal alcohol syndrome: Overcoming secondary disabilities* (pp. 25–39). Seattle, WA: University of Washington Press.

Streissguth, A. P., Bookstein, F. L., Barr, H.M., Sampson, P. D., O'Malley, K., & Young, J. K. (2004). Risk factors for adverse life outcomes in fetal alcohol syndrome and fetal alcohol effects. *Journal of Developmental and Behavioral Pediatrics, 25,* 228–238.

Streissguth, A. P., & Kanter, J. (Eds.) (1997). *The challenge of fetal alcohol syndrome: Overcoming secondary disabilities.* Seattle, WA: University of Washington Press.

Sugai, G., Horner, R. H., & Sprague, J. R. (1999). Functional assessment-based behavior support planning: Research to practice. *Behavioral Disorders, 24,* 253–257.

Thomas, S., Relly, S., Mattson, S., & Riley, E. (1998). Comparison of social abilities of children with fetal alcohol syndrome to those of children with similar IQ scores and normal controls. *Alcoholism Clinical and Experimental Research, 22,* 528–533.

Weinberg, N. (1997). Cognitive and behavioral deficits associated with prenatal alcohol use. *Journal of the American Academy of Child and Adolescent Psychiatry, 36,* 1177–1186.

Whaley, S. E., O'Connor, M. J., & Gunderson, B. (2001). Comparison of the adaptive functioning of children prenatally exposed to alcohol to a nonexposed clinical sample. *Alcoholism Clinical and Experimental Research, 25,* 1018–1024.

DARCY MILLER (CEC WA Federation), Professor, Department of Teaching and Learning, Washington State University, Pullman. Address correspondence to Darcy Miller, Department of Teaching and Learning, P.O. Box 642132, Pullman, WA 99164-2132 (e-mail: darcymiller@wsu.edu).

From *Teaching Exceptional Children,* March/April 2006, pp. 12–18. Copyright © 2006 by Council for Exceptional Children. Reprinted by permission.

Keep Your Older Patients Out of Medication Trouble

Learn why aging puts your patient at greater risk for adverse drug reactions and what you can do to protect her.

Sherrill A. Shepler, Tracy A. Grogan, and Karen Steinmetz Pater

Older adults are at increased risk for adverse drug events because aging affects their response to drugs and because they're more likely to take multiple medications than younger people. Among women age 65 and older, for example, 12% take 10 prescription drugs and 23% take at least 5 prescription drugs, according to a national survey.

Currently, up to 17% of acute hospital admissions for older adults involve adverse drug reactions. The figure is likely to continue climbing: By 2030, 20% of Americans—over 70 million people—will be over age 65.

In this article, we'll describe how aging changes the way the body processes drugs, why polypharmacy complicates the picture, and what you can do to help protect your older patients from medication-related adverse events.

Age and Pharmacokinetics: Changing the Process

Pharmacokinetics refers to how the body handles drugs and their metabolites via the following four processes.

1. **Absorption** occurs from the time the drug enters the body until it enters the bloodstream. In general, absorption has the smallest clinical impact on the body's ability to handle drugs, but that may change with the increasing use of transdermal medications. Because older adults have thin skin, they may absorb topical medications faster, potentially predisposing them to exaggerated drug effects.

   Other age-related changes affecting drug absorption include changes in gastric pH, slower gastric emptying, decreased cardiac output with a subsequent decrease in gastrointestinal blood flow, and decreased splanchnic blood flow. Also, because the surface area of the small intestine decreases slightly with age, older adults absorb less drug initially. More drug remains in the gut, absorbing and metabolizing slowly, and causing increased drug availability in the systemic circulation of certain drugs, such as propranolol and morphine.

2. **Distribution** refers to the transportation of drug molecules by the circulation and tissue fluids and storage of the drug within the body. Typically with aging, the body's fat content increases and water content and lean muscle mass decrease. These changes tend to lower the serum levels of lipophilic drugs such as diazepam and increase the serum levels of hydrophilic drugs such as alcohol, morphine, and digoxin.

   Altered protein binding, another change that occurs with age, means that for drugs that are protein-bound, higher concentrations of active drug remain in the body. This is an important consideration when interpreting serum drug levels, as these tests usually report only total concentrations (free and bound drug). Plasma albumin decreases slightly with age and can be further reduced by disease. Because albumin binds with salicylates, reduced albumin levels can lead to aspirin toxicity in older patients.

3. **Metabolism** is the means by which drugs are activated or biotransformed by the body. The liver, the body's major site of drug metabolism, shrinks with age, and an age-related decrease in cardiac output reduces liver blood flow. As a result, hepatic metabolism of medications such as imipramine, lidocaine, morphine, and propranolol takes longer. Slower drug metabolism means a longer duration of drug action and a greater likelihood that the drug will accumulate in the body with chronic use.

   Most drugs metabolized in the liver are broken down by enzymes called the cytochrome P450 or microsomalenzymes system, which becomes less efficient as one ages. Severe nutritional deficiencies, which are more common in older adults, may also impair hepatic function.

4. **Excretion** is how the body eliminates a drug and its metabolites. Renal excretion, the primary route of elimination for many drugs, also slows in older adults. Two-thirds of older adults have an age-related decline in creatinine clearance. These changes are fairly predictable, as renal blood flow typically diminishes by 40% by age 75. Renally eliminated medications with narrow therapeutic ranges, such as warfarin, digoxin, cimetidine, and aminoglycosides, are more likely to cause toxicity in older patients.

Because muscle mass and kidney function both decrease with age, serum creatinine is an unreliable predictor of renal function in older adults. Creatinine clearance (rather than serum creatinine) is a more reliable predictor of renal function. Creatinine clearance can be estimated by using the Cockcroft-Gault formula: creatinine clearance (mL/minute/1.73 m^2) for men = (140–age) × body weight in kg/72 × serum creatinine in mg/dL. Multiply the answer by 0.85 to get the value for women. The normal ranges for creatinine clearance are 97 to 137 mL/minute/1.73 m^2 in men and 88 to 128 mL/minute/1.73 m^2 in women. Creatinine clearance also is an estimate of glomerular filtration rate (GFR), which decreases with aging.

Age-related reductions in clearance have been shown for certain medications that are primarily excreted renally, such as acetazolamide, aminoglycosides, atenolol, captopril, cimetidine, digoxin, lithium, and vancomycin.

Pharmacodynamics: The Body Reacts

Pharmacodynamics describes the drug's effects in the body or, more specifically, the relationship between serum drug level and drug effect. In older adults, receptor sensitivity to a drug at a given serum level can decrease or increase. In other words, low levels of some drugs can produce an elevated effect, and high levels of other drugs may produce a diminished effect. For example, older adults are more sensitive to benzodiazepines' central nervous system effects and have a greater response to opioids. Older adults also may have an enhanced response to anticoagulants, but they're less likely to develop the reflex tachycardia usually seen with vasodilator therapy. Older adults may also be less sensitive to beta-agonists, beta-antagonists, furosemide, and calcium channel blockers.

Mixing It Up: Drug Interactions and Adverse Reactions

Besides age-related changes, other factors that make older adults especially vulnerable to adverse drug events include chronic medical conditions, polypharmacy, and failure to adhere to medication regimens. To complicate matters, signs and symptoms of adverse drug reactions—such as falls, anorexia, confusion, urinary retention, and fatigue—may be mistaken for nonspecific signs and symptoms associated with aging.

Polypharmacy is especially risky for older adults. Studies have found that the percentage of patients experiencing adverse drug reactions increases from 10% in those taking 1 drug to nearly 100% in those taking 10 drugs. And some conditions associated with aging, such as Parkinson's disease or Alzheimer's disease, have been found in studies to increase patients' drug sensitivity, in part because of the medications they take for these conditions.

Although any medication can produce untoward effects, some are inherently more troublesome for older adults (be sure to check a drug's prescribing information before administering it). Let's take a closer look at some of those drugs and what you can do to protect your patients.

- **Anticoagulants** such as warfarin, even in routine dosages, can produce excessive anticoagulation and increase an older adult's bleeding risk. Warfarin is metabolized by the cytochrome P450 system in the liver. If the patient is taking other medications that inhibit this system, he needs less warfarin. And because warfarin is highly bound to albumin, an older adult with low albumin levels will have more free warfarin in her bloodstream, producing exaggerated anticoagulant effects.

  Some medications interact with warfarin and raise bleeding risks by increasing the international normalized ratio (INR). These include amiodarone, cimetidine, metronidazole, fluconazole, trimethoprim-sulfamethoxozole (Bactrim), aspirin, cephalosporins, and quinolones.

  Tell patients that foods such as green leafy vegetables, certain legumes, mayonnaise, and vegetable oils are very high in vitamin K, which can interfere with warfarin and other anticoagulants. To maintain consistent anticoagulation, teach them to eat these foods in consistent amounts and to avoid drastic changes in consumption.

- **Cardiac glycosides (digitalis preparations, such as digoxin)** are commonly prescribed to older adults for atrial fibrillation and heart failure. But changes with aging, including decreased GFR, mean that even at recommended dosages, an older person is at higher risk for digoxin toxicity. Interactions between cardiac glycosides and verapamil, quinidine, and diuretics also can increase serum digoxin levels. Digoxin interacts with macrolide antibiotics such as clarithromycin, putting older adults at higher risk for digoxin toxicity.

- **Antihypertensive drugs,** especially thiazide diuretics, can cause hypokalemia, hyperglycemia, and hyperuricemia, which are more dangerous in older adults because they're more likely to have arrhythmias, diabetes, or gout. Diuretics also may cause more pronounced orthostatic hypotension in older adults who take calcium channel blockers or beta-blockers because these drugs prevent the heart rate from increasing to compensate for venous pooling in their legs. And older patients with reduced liver function who are given intravenous nitroprusside to manage hypertensive crisis are at higher risk for toxicity from thiocyanate, a metabolite of nitroprusside.

- **Antimicrobials** that are excreted by the kidneys (such as cephalosporins, aminoglycosides, and fluoroquinolones) have a longer half-life in older adults because of decreased renal clearance. The half-life—the time it takes for serum concentration of the drug to decrease by half—is determined by a drug's rate of metabolism and excretion.

- **Antipsychotics, anxiolytics, antidepressants, and sedatives,** intended to improve the quality of an older patient's life, sometimes have the opposite effect. Selective serotonin reuptake inhibitors were once considered safer than tricyclic antidepressants for patients at risk for falls, but recent studies have found that both drug types increase fall risk. Diphenhydramine, a potent anticholinergic antihistamine, shouldn't be used as a sedative-hypnotic in older patients because it causes oversedation and increases fall risk. When prescribed to treat or prevent allergic reactions, diphenhydramine should be given with extreme caution in the smallest effective dose.

The Pitfalls of OTC Medications

Besides prescription drugs, an older adult may take various over-the-counter (OTC) medications. Many of these products have ingredients and dosages that were prescription-only just a few years ago. As with prescription drugs, the risk of adverse reactions to OTC medication increases with the patient's age. Let's take a closer look at some common OTC drugs an older adult may use.

- **Nonopioid analgesics.** An older adult may take daily aspirin as prophylaxis for myocardial infarction, stroke, or peripheral vascular disease. Because she's more likely to have diminished liver function or low serum albumin levels, she's at higher risk for salicylate toxicity from aspirin or other salicylate-containing medications. Severe salicylate toxicity can cause acid-base imbalances, tachypnea, nausea and vomiting, petechial hemorrhage, delirium, hyperthermia, seizures, coma, and death.

  Teach your patient to read drug labels so she knows what each product contains, to inform her health care provider about all OTC products (including herbal preparations) she uses, and to take medication as directed. Warn her that many OTC products contain aspirin or salicylates. Taking more than the recommended daily allowance of vitamin C (in supplements, foods, or drinks such as cranberry juice) can increase levels of salicylates.

  Also teach her to use nonsteroidal anti-inflammatory drugs (NSAIDs), such as ibuprofen and naproxen, with caution because age increases the risk of developing peptic ulcer disease and gastrointestinal (GI) bleeding.

Four Things Your Older Patient Should Know

1. **Explain** the difference between nonaspirin drugs (such as acetaminophen [Tylenol]) and aspirin-like drugs (aspirin, ibuprofen, and naproxen) and their adverse effects. Tell her to limit her acetaminophen dose to less than 4 grams/day.

2. **She should discuss** over-the-counter (OTC) pain medications with her primary care provider before taking anything. This is especially important if she takes low-dose aspirin, drinks more than three alcoholic drinks per day, or has a chronic condition such as diabetes, cardiovascular disease, liver or kidney disease, asthma, or gout. For example, drinking alcohol while taking acetaminophen increases her risk of liver damage and gastrointestinal bleeding.

3. **Teach her** not to take an OTC pain medication for more than 10 days; if pain is severe or lasts more than 10 days, she should see her primary care provider. If she has chronic pain, she should talk with her primary care provider about nonpharmacologic therapies.

4. **If she takes** warfarin, she should limit her daily acetaminophen dose to six regular-strength tablets, or no more than a total of 2 grams/day. Taking large amounts of acetaminophen with warfarin raises the risk of intracranial hemorrhage.

Long-term NSAID use can increase blood pressure, counteract antihypertensive medications, and cause renal dysfunction.

Acetaminophen is the recommended analgesic of choice in older adults, but it too poses risks. Many OTC products contain acetaminophen, so a patient may inadvertently give herself a dangerous overdose if she takes several products without checking their labels.

- **Antacids,** used chronically, can interfere with other medications and can cause hypercalcemia, renal stones, or renal failure. Tell your patient to take antacids and calcium supplements 2 hours apart from other medications. Warn her that taking calcium supplements or antacids at the same time as enteric-coated medications can cause gastric irritation because the calcium-containing medication dissolves enteric coatings.

  Patients with hypertension, heart failure, or renal failure should avoid antacids containing sodium bicarbonate (such as Alka-Seltzer) because of their sodium content. Rolaids are the antacids of choice for those with chronic renal failure because the aluminum in Rolaids tends to not accumulate in the body, instead binding with phosphate in the GI tract and correcting the hyperphosphatemia seen in chronic renal failure.

- **Laxatives** used chronically can cause diarrhea, nausea, vomiting, and hypokalemia, compromising an older adult's nutritional status. And older patients who take bulk laxatives without drinking enough fluids are at risk for bowel obstruction and fluid volume deficits. A patient with dysphagia is also at risk for life-threatening events such as esophageal obstruction if she takes bulk laxatives and doesn't drink enough fluid.

  Osmotic laxatives such as Epsom salts and milk of magnesia can cause fluid and electrolyte imbalances that lead to arrhythmias, heart failure, renal failure, and colonic ischemia. Stimulant laxatives such as Ex-Lax, Dulcolax, and Senokot shouldn't be used long-term except in patients on opioids because they may impair normal colonic function and lead to bowel dysfunction, laxative dependency, and altered colon anatomy.

What You Can Do

Start your drug reconciliation by obtaining a complete and accurate drug history from your patient. Ask your patient which prescription and OTC drugs she takes, as well as dietary supplements and herbal preparations. (Ask to see the containers if she has them.) Also ask her about alcohol consumption. Be nonjudgmental as you question her; she may hesitate to give you honest answers if she thinks you'll criticize her. Once you have a complete medication list, go over it with the patient at each inpatient and outpatient visit. Teach her about medication hazards (see *Four things your older patient should know*).

Consider the effects of aging and chronic medical conditions when reviewing the patient's drug history and monitor her continually for adverse drug reactions.

Individualize patient education, providing oral and written instructions at the patient's and family caregiver's education level. Make sure the patient knows the generic and brand names of her medications as well as their purpose. If she has multiple health care providers, identify her primary care provider. This person should have a complete and up-to-date account of the patient's condition and therapies. Encourage the patient to use one pharmacy for all her medications. A pharmacist who has the patient's complete medication history can spot potentially dangerous combinations.

Remind the patient to check with her primary care provider before taking OTC medications and herbal products and to tell her provider if she has any adverse reactions.

By teaching your older patient how to take medications safely and when to report problems, you can help keep her healthy and safe.

Selected References

Fick DM, et al. Updating the Beers criteria for potentially inappropriate medication use in older adults: Results of a U.S. consensus panel of experts. *Archives of Internal Medicine.* 163(22):2716–2724, December 8–22, 2003.

Gurwitz JH, et al. Incidence and preventability of adverse drug events among older persons in the ambulatory setting. *JAMA.* 289(9):1107–1116, March 5, 2003.

Kaufman DW, et al. Recent patterns of medication use in ambulatory adult population of the United States: The Slone survey. *JAMA.* 287(3):337–344, January 16, 2002.

Miller CA. The connection between drugs and falls in elders. *Geriatric Nursing.* 23(2):109–110, March–April 2002.

SHERRILL A. SHEPLER is a nurse practitioner in the cardiac cell division at the University of Pittsburgh (Pa.) Medical Center. **TRACY A. GROGAN** is the unit director for the abdominal transplant intensive care unit at the University of Pittsburgh Medical Center Presbyterian-Shadyside. **KAREN STEINMETZ PATER** is a clinical assistant professor at the University of Illinois at Chicago's College of Pharmacy.

My Spirit Lives

ROXANNE CHINOOK

The Nightmare: I close my eyes and lean my head out of the passenger window to feel the warm wind on my face. I do not know who is driving the car, as I travel down a familiar canyon road. It is a highway in Idaho—some road that I may have hitchhiked on my way to visit my mother. The car begins to slow down, and when I open my eyes I notice a row of cars with over a dozen young men standing beside them. As we come closer, I feel an overwhelming sense of fear in every cell of my body. The car moves in slow motion as it goes by the row of cars and men. From the beginning to the end of the long row, I notice their faces and recognize each and every one of them. Yet, I do not understand why I am so scared. Their faces are smug and unsmiling.

I recognize the cars, but can't remember where I've seen their faces before. Suddenly a roaring noise goes off in my head. I hear a loud popping bang and see a white light. My eyes abruptly open and I realize that I am in my bed. I am unable to move because my entire body is frozen in fear; tears emerge as I realize that all these young men were men that raped me.

Before the Relapse: I am a proud tribal member of the Confederated Tribes of the Warm Springs Indian Reservation, a professional artist, and a college graduate. In 1991, I was listed in the Fourteenth Addition of the National Dean's List for receiving a 4.0, while doing postgraduate studies at Boise State University. I am the former Exhibits Coordinator of my tribal museum, and have held several professional positions in the social service field on my reservation. I have three beautiful daughters. My oldest was taken away from me when she was just 14 months old and raised by a very loving and wonderful family in Warm Springs. I was raising my two youngest alone until my illnesses took them away from me in February 1997.

I stand proud today because I am finally healing from my primary illness, post-traumatic stress disorder (PTSD), and secondary illness, substance abuse. My spirit has been broken many times as a result of these illnesses, which are directly related to the incest and multiple rape wounds of my past. The damage caused by these traumas sought to destroy my very being.

Although I did spend a year or two in recovery since 1979, the first time I experienced true long-term recovery began in Boise, Idaho, on August 15, 1987. In 1989, I married a man I had met in the early period of my recovery and we had a child together. However, because he battered me I divorced him. In 1991, I moved back to my reservation to work, raise my two daughters, and live near my family. I had abstained from alcohol and cocaine for almost eight years before I relapsed in April 1995.

The Relapse: Since the early 1980s, I have suffered from muscle tension headaches, extreme anxiety, and depression. However, soon after I moved back to my reservation, I began to experience rape flashbacks, nightmares, insomnia, body numbness, and suicidal thoughts. These symptoms became worse and started to affect all aspects of my life. At times, I felt that I was going crazy. I finally pursued counseling, but I needed something stronger to relieve my anguish. After almost five years of suffering, I went back to my old coping behaviors and took my first drink in April 1995.

It was not long before I started using my new drug of choice, cocaine. I believe it was because the high was more intense than alcohol and I could remain alert. Despite its increased lethality, I was never raped while high on cocaine. I became addicted to cocaine again and found myself on a downhill swirl into darkness. My attempts to recover included everything from counseling, to going to church, to taking different medications.

I started to lose everything that I had gained during my years of abstinence: my self-respect, job, home, car, and my relationship with my family. Most important, my children were losing their mommy, I could not stop the path I was on, and I did not have a clue that all these symptoms were interrelated and symptomatic of rape trauma syndrome.

The Chicken or the Egg: I was diagnosed with chronic post-traumatic stress disorder in the past, and at the time I found some relief having a name for my distress. Nevertheless, my addiction was already in control. So how does one address these kinds of issues when they inevitably trigger the return of substance abuse?

Today, I realize that it does not matter which came first, the chicken or the egg. The abuse and my addictions went hand and hand. I have since learned that for me to refrain from returning to substance abuse, I must address my past traumas.

My victimization began in early childhood when our non-Native grandfather molested my sister and me. His selfish violation of our childhood directly led to the loss of my virginity on a date rape at age 19. I know today that this past trauma kept me from developing appropriate boundaries, self-worth, and basic trust of my own instincts.

I drank so I would not feel or remember. And as my alcoholism progressed, I became more vulnerable to rape. At the time, I did not know why I drank the way I did. Today I know that booze, and later cocaine, became my only means of survival.

The Rapes: Thus, my victim cycle emerged. I was raped 13 times between the ages of 19 and 28. Four of those were gang rapes. One of the rapists was Native American, another Hawaiian mixed, four were African American, and the rest were young white men. I was always extremely intoxicated before the rapes, and could only remember bits and pieces prior to each one, but had very clear memories afterwards. Three of the rapes (one of them a gang rape) happened in Madras, Oregon, a small town just outside my reservation, and the place I made my first and last attempt to seek justice in 1981.

The rape occurred after I was offered a ride to Warm Springs by a non-Native local man, who was drinking in the same bar I was. He said that he was a friend of my ex-boyfriend, and I thought he was a nice guy. On the drive home he took a detour off the road before the grade goes down to Warm Springs. He pulled the car over and raped me.

After he was done, he acted like nothing was wrong and said that no one would believe me anyway. He actually had the audacity to drop me off where I was living. I called the Warm Springs police department only because my brother was a tribal policeman at the time. This incident was the first time that I had the courage to report it. My brother, who happened to be on duty, chased and apprehended him on the flats between Madras and Warm Springs. The rapist was no longer on tribal land, so the Jefferson County police took over and held him in custody overnight.

The next day, I went to the Jefferson County police station only to pick up the evidence: my beaded belt and torn bra the officers found in his car. I decided not to press charges because while I was being questioned, the officer told me it was my word against his, and the rapist had told him that the sex was consensual. The officer also stressed that the rapist had a wife and children to support. I left the police station with my head held down in shame, and walked to the nearest bar never to pursue justice again.

The Shame: It was not long before my whole essence became a warehouse of shame. I was on a road to self-destruction, and became so expert at drowning each incident with booze that I thought no one would ever suspect what had happened to me. Deep down inside I blamed myself and felt I deserved the abuse. During periods of recovery, I told only a few therapists, counselors, and close friends. I have only recently been able to disclose the number of times I've been raped to others.

Today, when I openly share the amount of times I've been raped, it not only takes away the rapists' power, but also alleviates some of the shame. I also know in my heart that no one deserves to be raped, regardless of the shape they are in.

The Addiction: After relapsing in April 1995, I went into treatment in April 1996. But I relapsed within a month after I returned to Warm Springs. My drug of choice was very accessible at the time, and sometimes all it took was one call or an unexpected visit from one of my using buddies. In addition, one of the former gang rapists worked at the Indian Health Service, and I did not realize that he was a constant trigger of my PTSD symptoms.

The Suicide Attempt: My family eventually intervened, and my daughters were taken away from me. I do not think that I ever experienced so much shame and utter hopelessness in my life. On the evening of February 28, 1997, I unsuspectingly came home while my daughters were packing some clothes to take to my family's house next door. I silently watched as they left—full of disgust for me. I was still coming down from alcohol and cocaine, and became overwhelmed with shame and all the pain that I caused in my life and in their lives.

I truly wanted to die. The pain was so unbearable that I impulsively took all my antidepressants and called my pastor. I was comatose and hospitalized for three or four days, and was sent directly from the hospital to Oregon Science Hospital (OSH) in Portland for evaluation. I later learned that I had taken more than a lethal dose of pills.

The Overdose: I was at OSH for a few days when I found out that I could be legally held for 72 hours. I persuaded them to let me out and left the hospital on March 6, 1997, only to return two days later. When I escaped from

OSH, I allowed a stranger to shoot me up with heroin, a drug that I had no resistance to. I had already consumed a combination of alcohol, cocaine, and crank, and the big hit of heroin was it all it took to overdose me. The stranger dragged my lifeless body down a few flights of stairs to the alley below and left me there to die. The paramedics later told me that someone probably saw me and called 911. I found out that I had been dead for five minutes, and by the time the ambulance arrived, my skin was blue and cold. I was injected with the drug Narcon to help neutralize the heroin, but it didn't work. The paramedics then used defibrillation to get my heart pumping. I remember how I reluctantly returned to my body. I believe my Creator sent me back to put an end to the cycle of abuse in my life, in my children's lives, and in their children's lives.

After my two-week stay at OSH, I was invited to stay in Oregon City with a loving family in long-term recovery. (This family is my oldest daughter's biological father's family, which I have since adopted.) I was able to stay clean and sober for several months. Unfortunately, as soon as I returned to my reservation, it was just a matter of days before I relapsed. I finally accepted the fact that I was not going to die using. My hell was living my addiction.

My Return: On August 18, 1997, my Creator intervened and my tribe allowed me to receive treatment at Sundown M Ranch in Selah, Washington. I was advised by my counselor to continue with treatment, and I agreed to go to a 60-day transitional treatment program at the St. Joseph Recovery House in Bellingham, Washington. I chose to leave everything, my home and the opportunity to be closer to my children, because I knew deep inside that I could not return to Warm Springs. I could not return because of all the triggers and my family's unfaltering animosity toward me, which was created by my relapse.

The guilt and shame from my relapse slowly lifted. I eventually fell in love with Bellingham—the beautiful scenery and all the new friends that I gained through treatment and support groups. After I completed the 60-day treatment program, my tribe helped me again by paying the rental deposit for the Towanda Oxford House, which is a clean and sober house for women. I then sought the services of the local Private Industry Council and was given the wonderful opportunity to work while being trained to teach art part time at the Northwest Indian College.

However, after I had made it through seven months of sobriety, the PTSD symptoms were so strong that I was again suicidal. This time the suicidal thoughts were more serious because I was not under the influence of alcohol or drugs. I found my way to the Whatcom Crisis Center and was very lucky to be the first and only recipient of a newly funded program that offered one-on-one counseling with a woman specially trained in these issues.

On the first visit, my counselor was so concerned about my obvious symptoms that she immediately contacted the Whatcom Counseling and Psychiatric Clinic to have me reevaluated. She scheduled a visit right away, and I was finally prescribed a medication that specifically helped to control many of the PTSD symptoms.

My true healing began in the one-on-one counseling. I learned that my mind was able to dissociate during my rapes as a form of protection, but my subconscious mind still remembered, causing severe flashbacks and nightmares. I learned that my closed body language was prevalent in people who have suffered from both incest and rapes. I also learned that some compulsive behaviors I had developed over the years, from my choice of abusive men to my self-destructive substance abuse, were related to my childhood and young adult rapes.

Internalized Oppression: That my Native American heritage played a significant role in the rapes was an extremely agonizing recognition. In America's history of the colonization of Native peoples, rape has been used as a weapon of warfare, ethnic cleansing, humiliation, and oppression against us. In turn, Native peoples have internalized this oppression and passed it down through the generations. My Native grandmother's shame and oppression was passed down to my mother, who passed it on to me to the point that I blamed myself entirely for everything that happened to me.

An example of how whites use rape as a colonial tool of domination against Native women is embedded in my memory as a severe flashback. I thank my Creator for allowing me to remember the details only when I am in a safe place.

The Drunken Savage: A few days after I was admitted to the first alcohol and drug treatment center since my relapse began in 1995, a kind nurse found me wandering the halls late at night in a catatonic-like state. I had just experienced one the worst rape flashbacks, and she held me and let me cry as I explained to her what I remembered. When I was living in Hawaii, I was abducted by a group of young Caucasian military men. They took me to a warehouse building on a military base and repeatedly raped me. After they were done, they were concerned about letting me go so they inserted a tall, full bottle of beer inside me to flush out their semen. Throughout the gang rape, they called me derogatory names. One of the rapists asked what might happen if they broke the bottle inside me. An apathetic voice responded, "Who cares? She's nothing but a drunken Indian whore."

In this incident and in the one in Madras in which the police office discouraged me from pressing charges against the white male that raped me, it is clear that rape continues to be a tool of domination against Native women.

It's Not My Fault: After several months of working with my counselor, I finally gained the courage to attend Whatcom Crisis Center's 12-week sexual assault program. This group was very empowering because, for the first time, I was able to share my story, in the absence of feeling judged or ashamed, with a group of women who were also survivors of traumatic sexual assaults. I also grew to understand that the lifetime of victimization was not my fault and, most of all, I learned that I do not have to be ashamed anymore. Then I moved into Dorothy Place, a transitional housing complex for women and children survivors of domestic violence, and was surrounded by brave women who were taking the steps needed to break their cycles of abuse and violence.

In 1999, I began the Master of Education in Art program at Western Washington University and graduated in December 2000, with a cumulative 3.8 GPA. Currently, I am the director of a nonprofit Art Marketing Program located at the Northwest Indian College.

I now know it was my Creator who sent me back to heal by sharing my story with other survivors and as a way to validate their pain. It was to let them know that they no longer have to feel the deep-rooted shame because they were drunk or high when they were raped. It was also to educate professionals in the alcohol and drug treatment field on how important it is to address these issues before the cycle escalates, as well as to be a consultant in the development of new programs that would help survivors heal through artistic expression.

The Revictimization: During this time I was also fighting to regain custody of my youngest daughter, who was placed with her father, the man I divorced in 1990 because of domestic violence. I decided to share this part of my struggle because, unfortunately, it is quite common for families to blame and re-victimize survivors. This often happens out of denial and the family's need for the survivor to maintain their social identity as the scapegoat. In addition, as the dually diagnosed family member, I constantly felt their frustration over the years.

My brother, who is a tribal judge, and his wife, who works for Children's Protective Services, had understandable contempt and anger toward me. Further, during my relapse I had exposed a past deception and, in retaliation, they used their influence to assure that my youngest daughter's father maintained custody of her, despite knowing his history of violence. I do not deny the effect my relapse had on my daughters or my family, and I take full responsibility for this. Nevertheless, professionals I contacted inform me that if I were living anywhere else when my relapse occurred, I would never have lost permanent custody of my girls.

I believe my brother's abuse of power in the tribal court system made it impossible for my voice to be heard by an objective ear. However, I did not give up. I made phone calls, sent hundreds of letters and e-mails to domestic violence, child abuse, rape, incest, civil liberties, and tribal and state law organizations nationwide. I received dozens of responses, referrals, validations, and kind words of support, but they basically referred me back to each other.

The Idaho Coalition Against Sexual and Domestic Violence asked me for permission to use part of my story when the National Organization for Women addressed Congress for the reauthorization of the Violence Against Women Act. Edna M. Frantela, from the National Coalition Against Domestic Violence, also asked permission to share my story at a Safe Child Summit, in hopes of affecting the judicial decision-making process regarding high-conflict custody disputes. I was happy that my story might be of some help to other survivors, yet time was running out as my daughter began sharing more about abuse she was experiencing from her father.

Just as I was about to give up all hope, my Creator sent my first angel. Her name is Terilynn Steele and she founded For the Children Advocacy in California. Having read one of my online messages on a tribal-law clearinghouse message board, she wrote me series of e-mail messages of care and support, which renewed my hope. Soon after, my second angel, Lynn Thompson, arrived. She, too, responded to my desperate cry for help after reading a message I had left on another tribal law message board. Miraculously, Lynn is not only a Native sister, but also a tribal legal advocate in Idaho. These two women became my angels on earth because they were the only people who were actually willing to do something beyond referring me to another agency. Lynn volunteered her services by preparing my second appeal, which was granted after the tribal court raised my child support in my absence. This allowed the Tribal Court of Appeals to finally hear my case, and these wise men and woman eventually validated me and recognized the injustice my daughters and I had endured because of my brother's influence.

Please understand that I do not blame my family for giving up on me; they witnessed my on-and-off self-destructive behaviors over the years. They were genuinely and understandably concerned for my children's safety. However, l believe their anger, lack of knowledge, and my brother's retaliation should never have taken precedence over what was in the best interest of my children.

Ending the Cycle of Violence: Though I am still estranged from my brother and his family, today I realize that for me to release victim consciousness, I must learn to embrace forgiveness. My oldest daughter, now 24, is living with me and working on her associates degree at the Northwest Indian College. She is determined to heal from the cycle of abuse and addiction that I passed down to her. No words can describe how proud I am of her courage to stop the cycles before they take over her life.

My 21-year-old daughter is now a senior at a university in Oregon. She is an honor roll student and their track team's number one pole-vaulter. I will always be grateful that my brother and his wife took care of her during her last year of high school. This decision resulted from the verbal sexual abuse she experienced from her father, whom the tribal court and Children's Protective Services earlier had recommended and granted permanent custody. Even though she was born and raised on my reservation, she is not an enrolled tribal member; unlike me, she has never received tribal financial aid for her higher education. She has worked hard to pay her own way and plans to attend nursing school after she graduates. Again, words cannot describe how proud I am of her courage and inner strength.

My youngest daughter is now 14 years old and has been with me for over two years. We are understandably very close and I am proud to say that she prefers staying at home creating art to hanging out at the mall with friends. She is my mainstay.

All my daughters are true inspirations and have endured the effects of my past cycle of violence, victimization, and substance abuse. They also bear witness to the changes I have made in my life toward my healing and recovery. I hope they will come to understand the priceless gift I have been given and how my healing will someday help them and their children.

Blaming the Victim: I ask not for sympathy, but for your willingness to understand. This understanding is not just for me, but also for the countless women and children who are sexually abused and raped. I know some people still think that women who drink and use drugs deserve to be raped. Yet the majority of the so-called hopeless alcoholics and addicts, both women and men found repeatedly in alcohol and drug treatment centers, psychiatric hospitals, and state and tribal courtrooms, are survivors of childhood traumas such as emotional and/or physical abuse, incest, and rape. It continues to horrify me about our society that rape is still tolerated and is an accepted consequence for drinking by women. A female cousin from my reservation laughed as she blamed a Native sister for being gang raped at a party, saying it was her own fault for getting so drunk.

My Healing Journey: By disclosing the many times I have been raped, I continue to erase any debris of shame left inside and pray my disclosure will help other women to break their silence. My continued recovery, the healing I have been able to accomplish with counseling and through my art, is all part of my journey toward resolution. Much work remains for me to do and I will always have remnants of these horrid traumas, but they will no longer have the power to control my life or define my being.

My Spirit Lives: Reaching this point in my life has taken me though years of self-destruction—up to 10 alcohol-induced suicide attempts, six inpatient treatment centers, four outpatient treatment centers, three psychiatric hospitals, and several relationships with abusive men. No one should ever have to suffer alone in silence and shame. My grandfather's rape of me as a child led to all the sexual assaults and abuse I experienced in my life. It all started with him, but it ends now. I am not at fault, yet I am responsible. I have returned from a living hell and have found a new purpose in life. Healing is where my spirit lives.

Pretty Ones

It's the pretty ones
that age so quickly,
sitting on the same barstool
day after day she tries not to remember.
At first her youth and beauty
captivate an admiring audience
but they too,
wonder what will happen
when her beauty begins to fade.
The jealous ones
try to cut her,
scar her pretty face,
but no one could imagine
the scars she already has.
It's the pretty ones,
they say are lucky,
because she has drinks all lined
up for her.
But there's no one there to protect her,
when she's drunk herself into a stupor,
blinded by all the booze.
Or when they dump her out on the highway,
after her use was put beyond human test.
She walks alone trying to forget
what just happened,
and the shame she feels from being
one of the pretty ones.
She goes back to her barstool.
(Written just before my relapse in 1995.)

ROXANNE CHINOOK (Wasco) B.F.A., M. Hd., is a tribal member of the Confederated Tribes of the Warm Springs Indian Reservation in Oregon (e-mail: Rjchinook@aol.com). She is the great, great granddaughter of Billy Chinook, her tribe's second treaty signer and an Indian scout for the legendary Kit Carson. Her grandmother, Jeanette Brunoe, was full-blooded Wasco, a gifted header, trick-rider, and rodeo princess in Indian rodeos. Roxanne is an accomplished artist, painter, and believes her art emulates a personal and cultural experience from the spirit of the trickster to help her heal from the traumas of her past. Her artwork and other Native American artists she represents can be viewed at www.ebuynativeart.com. Copyright © 2004 by Roxanne Chinook.

The Problem with Drinking

CHERYL HARRIS SHARMAN

Efraím was already drunk when he left the wedding at 2 A.M. It had been a "nice wedding," which in Costa Rica means only hard liquor was served. The 21-year-old headed to a local bar for a "sarpe," or nightcap, with some friends. At 5 A.M., one of them finally sent him home in a taxi. Shivering and wrapped in towels, he sat on the carpet near the toilet and threw up.

Hours passed before his father found him in the same spot around 6 in the evening and rushed him to the hospital. The nightmare finally ended after an emergency room doctor injected him with medication for alcohol poisoning.

Tadeo, a young Costa Rican, went to the beach with three friends for a few laughs and a lot of drinks. After eight beers each, they drove home on the dark highway. A truck sped by, its rear lights obscuring the curve ahead. Their car skidded off the road and into a tree. Pinned in the wreckage, Tadeo broke three ribs, fractured his skull, fell unconscious, and remained in a coma for a week.

In Costa Rica, as in most Latin American countries, social gatherings more often than not include alcohol. Weddings and funerals, births and baptisms rely at least in part on drinks to ease grieving or encourage celebration. Aside from special occasions, many homes keep well-stocked bars that facilitate impromptu gatherings.

The drive home, particularly in the half-year-long rainy season, can entail a mix of alcohol and slick, winding roads, with potentially catastrophic results. But no one abstains for this reason. Statistics reflect the outcome: 13 percent of emergency room consultations in 1987 and 33 percent of auto fatalities in 2003 were alcohol related. Yet only 5 percent of Costa Ricans are alcohol dependent.

"The biggest misconception people have is that the problem of alcohol is alcohol dependence, or alcoholism," says Maristela Monteiro, regional advisor on alcohol and substance abuse at the Pan American Health Organization (PAHO). "In terms of society, most public health problems come from acute intoxication."

Medical research shows that long-term alcohol abuse causes liver diseases such as cirrhosis and hepatitis, as well as memory loss, ulcers, anemia, impaired blood clotting, impaired sexual performance, malnutrition, depression, cancer and even brain damage. But from a public health perspective, alcohol's greatest impact comes from occasional high-risk drinking by normally light to moderate drinkers.

"Homicides, traffic accidents, suicides, violent behavior, domestic violence, child abuse or mistreatment, neglect—these are from heavy drinking occasions, but most of these people are not alcohol dependent," says Monteiro.

Studies in the United States show that alcohol is a factor in 25 percent of deaths among people aged 15 to 29. Its direct costs to the U.S. health care system add up to some $19 billion a year, and for the economy as a whole, some $148 billion. As a risk factor for the global burden of illness, alcohol rivals tobacco: It is ranked number five among risks to health worldwide (tobacco is number four), and number one in all but two countries—Canada and the United States—in the Americas.

The most effective policies prevent intoxication by reducing the amount of alcohol people drink.

Experts note that alcohol takes a disproportionate toll on the poor, despite the fact that alcohol consumption tends to increase with educational levels and development. Poor people spend a greater proportion of their income on alcohol, and when drinking problems occur, they have less access to services, may lose their jobs, and bring major hardship on their families.

For all these reasons, many public health experts believe that alcohol policy should be a top priority in every country of the Americas.

Costa Rica is one of many countries that have instituted programs to reduce the toll of alcohol using a variety of measures: taxes and licensing, restrictions on advertising, minimum-age laws, and controls on the hours of operation and location of outlets that sell alcohol.

In addition, Costa Rican law bans alcohol consumption in most public buildings, at sporting events, in the workplace, in parks or on the street, within 100 meters of churches, and on public transportation.

"It is important to use various measures to be effective," says Julio Bejarano, head of research at the Instituto sobre Alcoholismo y Farmacodependencia (IAFA) in San José.

Programs like Costa Rica's are the outcome of a 30-year trend toward viewing alcohol less as an individual malady and more as a problem of public health. The shift began with the 1975 publication of *Alcohol Control Policies in Public Health Perspective* by the Finnish Foundation for Alcohol Studies. Since then, new definitions of alcohol use and abuse have emerged, including classifications for levels of drinking according to their risks to health.

According to the emerging consensus, people with what the U.S. health sector calls "alcoholism" and what the World Health Organization (WHO) calls "alcohol dependence" need to seek treatment. But those engaged in occasional overuse that causes mental or physical health problems—"alcohol abuse" in the United States and "harmful use" disorder for WHO—should be made aware of its impact on their health and urged to reduce their consumption before they become alcohol dependent. A third WHO category, "hazardous use," implies high-risk consumption, or what is sometimes referred to as "binge drinking." "You never had a car accident," Monteiro explains, "but you drink too much and drive." This is a large group of people who also need to cut back.

But the bottom line, says Monteiro, is that good public health policies must aim at preventing intoxication. And the best way to do this is by reducing consumption.

"What has been proven over and over in developed countries and more and more in developing countries, is that we need to reduce the overall consumption of the population," she says.

Monteiro says that experience shows that the most effective way of reducing overall consumption is by increasing prices and taxes on alcohol and restricting availability—that is, where it can be sold, to whom, how much, at what times and on which days.

"Once you reduce the hours of sale, for example, you also control the amount of alcohol people can access and drink. You reduce homicides, accidents, violence—many of the acute consequences decrease significantly. There are several examples—for a long time in Europe, the U.S., and Canada, and now in Latin America and elsewhere—that show that closing bars earlier reduces both accidents and violence."

A 2003 book, *Alcohol: No Ordinary Commodity*, published by Oxford and WHO, reviewed three decades of research and concluded that reducing consumption is key. Their top-10 list of specific measures includes minimum-age laws, government monopolies, restrictions on outlets and hours of sale, taxes, drunk-driving counter-measures and brief interventions for hazardous drinkers.

Limiting Access

Raising the minimum age for purchasing alcohol has long been one of the most effective means of reducing access. Only a handful of countries have emulated the U.S. minimum age of 21, but this has proven to be an effective policy. When all 50 U.S. states raised their minimum age from 18 to 21, the country as a whole saw a 19 percent net decrease in fatalities among young drivers. The National Highway Traffic Safety Administration estimates that raising the minimum age has saved 17,359 lives since 1975.

Government monopolies on alcohol have also proven effective, but these are increasingly unpopular. Until 1968, Finland prohibited the sale of beer anywhere but in government-owned outlets. In 1968, the country began to allow grocery stores to sell beer, and alcohol consumption climbed by 46 percent overall (increasing particularly among 13- to 17-year-olds). Government monopolies today oversee production, sales or distribution (but not all three) in parts of the United States, Canada, Russia, India, southern Africa and Costa Rica. In Scandinavia, multinational companies have waged legal battles invoking international trade rules to break up longstanding government monopolies on alcohol, increasingly limiting their ability to restrict consumption.

Short of holding monopolies, governments can control where, when and to whom alcohol is sold, restricting the density of outlets through limited licensing and restricted hours of sale. They can also restrict the availability of high- and medium-strength alcoholic beverages. Before 1965, Swedish grocery stores could not sell beer with more than 3.5 percent alcohol. When 4.5 percent beer became legally available in grocery stores, total alcohol consumption increased nearly 15 percent. Twelve years later, Sweden returned to the 3.5 percent limit, and consumption dropped again by the same amount.

Hours of sales are equally important. When Norway closed bars on Saturdays, researchers noted that those most affected by the restricted access were also those deemed likely to engage in domestic violence or disruptive intoxication. An Australian Aboriginal community, Tennant Creek, closed bars on Thursdays and noted that fewer women required hospital attention for domestic injuries.

In Latin America and the Caribbean, Colombia provides one of the leading success stories of limiting alcohol consumption through restricted hours of operation. Rodrigo Guerrero, a physician and public health expert, served as mayor of the second-largest city, Calí, in the mid-1990s and dedicated much of his effort to tackling the city's surging violence problem. He commissioned surveys that found that 40 percent of violence victims and 26 percent of violent death victims in his city were intoxicated. In response, Calí passed a *ley semi seca* ("semi-dry law"), which closed bars and discotheques at 1 a.m. on weekdays and 2 a.m. on Fridays and Saturdays. These and other measures reduced homicides from 80 per 100,000 to 28 per 100,000 in eight years.

Costa Rica also limits hours and days of sale. The law prohibits selling or purchasing alcohol in public places after midnight, the day before and the day after a national election, and during Holy Week, "the period of highest alcohol consumption in Costa Rica," IAFA's Bejarano notes.

Probably the most effective policy to reduce consumption, however, is raising taxes on alcoholic beverages. Worldwide, raising the price of alcohol always reduces consumption. According to the recent WHO report *Global Status Report: Alcohol Policy*, the price of beer should always be more than the price of a soda. And because the harmful effects of alcohol use stem from alcohol content, higher-content beverages should be taxed at higher rates.

Drinking and Driving

After restricting access, the next most effective policies are those aimed at reducing drunk driving. WHO's *Global Status Report: Alcohol Policy* lists among the most effective countermeasures sobriety checkpoints, lowered blood-alcohol limits, license suspension and graduated licensing for novice drivers. Enforcement is key. Police intervention must be visible and frequent, and lawbreakers must be punished to the extent of the law.

Blood-alcohol limits are a critical part of these efforts. "Very little alcohol impairs motor coordination," explains Monteiro.

"If you drink just over a drink, you are at risk—actually, it's less than a drink."

Costa Rica sets the legal blood-alcohol limit for drivers at 0.05 percent, although many experts say that problems often begin at 0.04 percent. Belize, Guatemala, Mexico, Nicaragua, Paraguay, Canada and the United States set the limit at 0.08 percent. These limits are most effective when used with checkpoints and random breath testing, according to research.

Other effective measures include screening and "brief interventions," prevention tools that have become a cornerstone of WHO's alcohol policy recommendations. During routine visits to health facilities or the family doctor, patients are asked simple questions that screen them for behavioral risk factors—including alcohol, cigarettes, poor diet, physical inactivity and seatbelt use—and doctors provide brief counseling sessions based on the responses.

"This is the epitome of low-technology medicine," says Thomas Babor, one of the researchers who designed the Alcohol Use Disorders Identification Test, or AUDIT.

"It's not the kind of thing, like MRIs, that seem to capture the interest of clinicians. But it probably is of equal importance, because it provides a way to prevent problems before they occur and to minimize problems if they've already started to develop."

AUDIT has been tested in a variety of countries and has proven easy to use, inexpensive to implement, and effective in reducing alcohol consumption at all levels of the population. Translated into many languages (including a Spanish version available through PAHO), the test and booklet include everything a clinician needs to give the 10-question test, to score it for one of four levels of risk for alcohol use, and to talk to patients about cutting back (including scripts for doctors who are unsure of what to say).

Patients take the test in about one minute, a nurse or receptionist scores it in another minute, and the clinician takes a few minutes to talk to the patient. Those testing in the first risk level are cautioned and advised to avoid drinking at least two days a week. Clinicians tell second-level scorers to minimize the number of drinks per day or week and to cut back on heavy drinking. Those in the third level receive brief counseling with more tools and goal-setting. Only fourth-level scorers are referred to an alcohol specialist.

To reduce drunk driving, lawbreakers must be prosecuted and punished to the full extent of the law.

A 1999 study by Michael Fleming, at the University of Wisconsin–Madison Medical School, showed that, with a single counseling session, subjects cut back on their drinking in the first six months and kept it down for four years. The

study also found that every $10,000 invested in interventions saved $43,000 in health costs, with even greater savings when researchers factored in societal benefits, such as fewer auto accidents and crimes.

Other policies have been found to be somewhat less effective, but combined with the "top 10," they help minimize the burden of alcohol. These include having alcohol outlets refuse to serve intoxicated patrons; training their staff to prevent and manage aggression; promotion of alcohol-free events; community mobilization; and public service campaigns in schools and colleges, on television, and in print, including warning labels. Bans and restrictions on alcohol advertising and marketing can help reduce youth exposure to pro-alcohol messages. In Latin America, Costa Rica and Guatemala have completely banned alcohol companies from sponsoring youth and sporting events, and several other countries forbid alcohol advertising on Sundays and holidays.

The challenge ahead, says PAHO's Monteiro, is to build on the work of international alcohol policy experts, using the available scientific evidence to judge which mix of policies works best. But she offers a note of caution: "In Europe, there's almost a reversal of the gains they had before because of trade agreements. The trade agreements that opened the markets for equal opportunity for everyone mean that you cannot have higher taxes or higher prices. You have to allow advertising for everyone."

She notes that in Sweden, foreign companies have challenged laws forbidding alcohol advertising, arguing that they give local, better-known products an unfair advantage.

"That is a point that will be critical in the region," says Monteiro, "how to deal with the economic benefits of alcohol in certain countries while protecting public health and reducing its social costs."

Moving forward, Monteiro and researchers from 11 countries are embarking on a multicountry study that will show, with precision and hard data, the public health burden of alcohol in the Americas. The study will focus on alcohol use in Belize, Nicaragua, Paraguay and Peru. The results will be added to existing data from Argentina, Brazil, Costa Rica, Mexico, Uruguay, the United States and Canada.

Monteiro believes the new study is particularly timely, as several trends in the region point to a growing alcohol problem. For example, in most countries, women drink more as their educational levels rise. In Costa Rica, the percentage of children 13 to 15 who have tried alcohol rose from 16.3 percent in 1990 to 28.4 percent in 2000. In many countries, pressure from industry has been growing along with the spread of public health measures aimed at reducing alcohol sales.

All these developments call for more research and more action, says Monteiro, because "people not only die from drinking too much; they harm and kill those who don't drink, too."

CHERYL HARRIS SHARMAN is a freelance journalist based in New York City.

Reprinted from *Perspectives in Health*, the magazine of the Pan American Health Organization, published in English and Spanish, vol. 10, no. 1, 2005, pp. 19–23. Copyright © 2005 by Pan American Health Organization (PAHO). Reprinted by permission.

High on the Job

Drug dealers and users are more savvy in workplaces today. Businesses need policies and training to counter these trends.

MICHAEL A. GIPS

When he finally got the job he coveted with the food processing company, Jim (not his real name) was buoyant. The position offered the chance to make important contacts and earn a steady income. Jim and his girlfriend could finally begin to smell the flowers.

The problem was, the flowers came from cannabis plants, and he wasn't only smelling them, but also cutting, grinding, and selling them to his coworkers. In fact, Jim had applied for the job largely for the purpose of gaining access to the employees, to whom he could purvey marijuana, cocaine, methamphetamines, and other drugs. As one of the largest employers in the area, the food processor offered Jim a steady income and a large potential clientele.

Jim was entrepreneurial and successful. Not only did he sell to the younger crowd, but he had also cultivated many of the older workers as clients, men who had worked for the food processor for more than 25 years and had never regularly used drugs before. A convincing salesman, Jim got these workers to experiment with his wares, and he got many of them hooked.

No cash available until payday? No problem. Jim accepted credit and ATM cards, using a portable reader he borrowed from the beauty parlor operated by his girlfriend. The business thrived for more than three years, until the wife of an addicted worker placed an anonymous call to a company hotline.

The company brought in outside experts to conduct an investigation, but doing so was tricky, because of the multiple unions representing the workers and the work rules they enforced. Finally, a single investigator was approved to conduct a covert operation, systematically observing goings-on at the round-the-clock operation. When the investigator determined that he would have to buy drugs to obtain physical evidence, the company asked local law enforcement to get involved.

A four-month investigation revealed a web of drug dealing and use that startled upper management. Four dealers, including Jim, were identified, terminated, and prosecuted. Twenty other employees, who were discovered to have either used drugs at work or shared them with other workers, were also fired. Staff members who had bought and used drugs only off of company property were referred to the company's employee assistance program.

After the incident, the company realized how fortunate it had been that no drug-impaired worker had contaminated or otherwise negligently prepared food that would be distributed to the public. The company ended up completely revamping its substance abuse policy.

Not the First Time

Cases involving sophisticated dealers who insinuate themselves into the culture of an organization aren't anomalies, says George J. Ramos Jr., vice president of Diversified Risk Management, Inc. Ramos, whose company conducted the investigation at the food processing operation, notes that drug dealers in the workplace are becoming increasingly savvy and more difficult to identify.

Pro and Cons of Test Methods

They may be long-time workers, new hires—as in the case of Jim—or even temps. "A lot more planning goes into how they sell and how they get in to sell," Ramos says.

The growing sophistication of dealers and shifts in the types of drugs used are two trends in workplace substance abuse identified by experts in the field who provide consulting, training, policy development, testing, and investigative services. Yet many businesses—despite a rise in drug tests—lack effective policies and training to prevent workplace substance abuse.

Drugs of Choice

Dozens of illegal drugs can be found in the workplace, but a few in particular account for most of the abuse and attendant concern. Marijuana continues to be the most prevalent.

More than half of all the positive tests conducted in the first six months of 2005 by testing lab Quest Diagnostics revealed the use of marijuana. In second and third place in the Quest Index, respectively, were cocaine (15.2 percent of all positive tests conducted for the total U.S. work force) and amphetamines (10.6 percent), which includes methamphetamine, or "meth." Depending on location, company culture, and other factors, meth and cocaine jockey for second in popularity within the United States.

Marijuana. As has been the case for years, marijuana continues to be far and away the most popular drug used at work. It's relatively cheap and accessible.

Problems associated with marijuana use at work include distorted perceptions of time and space, dulled physical reflexes, and reduced capacity for learning, memory, or concentration—all of which hinders performance.

Crystal meth. Use of methamphetamines—also called "crystal meth" when it is in crystalline form—has been surging. Crystal meth is a stimulant used to increase alertness and reduce fatigue, traits that make some workers believe it will be beneficial at work.

But what goes up must come down: when they're not high, users of the various forms of meth become mentally exhausted. The result is mental and physical sloppiness. The drug can also produce anxiety, hallucinations, psychosis, and periods of depression.

Among the general U.S. population, meth use rose from less than two percent in 1994 to more than five percent in 2004, according to the National Survey on Drug Use and Health, which is sponsored by the U.S. Substance Abuse and Mental Health Services Administration and the Department of Health and Human Services. In a recent Drug Testing Index, Quest Diagnostics reported that between 2000 and 2004, yearly growth rates in the incidence of positive drug tests attributed to methamphetamines were 16 percent, 17 percent, 44 percent, and 6 percent, respectively. For safety-sensitive U.S. workers who are federally mandated to undergo drug testing, the incidence of positive drug tests attributed to amphetamines rose 13 percent in the first half of 2005, while the positivity rate for the general U.S. work force actually dipped by 4 percent.

Ramos, whose company conducts investigations in more than 40 states, Canada, and Mexico, says that crystal meth is "the number one drug we see. It has taken over across the board." A national summit on methamphetamine abuse, held in 2005, declared the problem a "national epidemic."

Others see the methamphetamine problem as more localized. In a recently released paper titled Methamphetamine Use: Lessons Learned, Dana Hunt, Ph.D., a substance abuse expert at the University of Maine, writes that meth use varies widely across the United States.

Abuse of crystal meth, as measured by the number of people who enter treatment, is highest in western states such as Oregon and California, Hunt writes, but is being rivaled by midwestern states like Iowa and southern states like Arkansas. Hunt also cites spiraling rates of emergency room visits for crystal meth in Minneapolis, Seattle, and St. Louis.

Gene Ferraro, CPP, PCI, whose firm, Business Controls, investigates workplace drug dealing and use, says that methamphetamine production and use have percolated across the United States, but generally thrive in rural areas. He points out, however, that every organization has a unique culture in

which different types of drugs may take root. His firm once did undercover investigations at companies right next door to one another. Marijuana was entrenched at one company, while coke ruled at the other.

Meth is also making headlines in Canada. Young men are flocking to Fort McMurray, a town in northern Alberta, where good money can be made in the oil extraction industry, says Barbara Butler, a Toronto-based management consultant with an expertise in workplace drug use. Anecdotal evidence and media reports suggest that meth use is spiraling there because the bored, overworked young men have money to buy drugs, like to party, and may need meth to stay awake on the job.

Cocaine. Despite the widespread attention received by crystal meth, cocaine use still remains strong. In fact, it registered a higher percentage of use than methamphetamine in the latest Quest index. The disparity between coke and crystal meth use is even greater when it comes to U.S. workers who are in safety-sensitive positions, and are thus federally mandated to undergo drug testing. Cocaine accounted for 23.5 percent of positive tests in the first half of 2005, compared to 14.7 percent for amphetamines.

Ferraro points out that cocaine use remains strong in African-American communities, though he thinks that it has ebbed since its heyday in the 1990s. In businesses with a high percentage of African-American workers, there is notably higher use of cocaine than other drugs among staff who test positive.

Other illegal drugs. Drugs producing hallucinogenic or other disabling mental or physical effects, such as heroin and LSD, tend not to be used heavily in the workplace, for a simple reason: "You can't use them consistently and still perform a job," says Ferraro.

Still, such disabling drugs do turn up in workplaces and in drug tests. Ferraro has seen some use of OxyContin at workplaces. PCP and opiates (generally, drugs derived from opium, such as heroin) appear as well. In 2004, according to the Quest index, 6.1 percent of all drugs uncovered in testing were opiates and about one-quarter of one percent was PCP. For the first half of 2005, those numbers had trended up, to 6.6 percent and four-tenths of one percent, respectively.

Substitute drugs. Debate has raged for decades in the United States about legalizing drugs such as marijuana. But the debate may be moot. "There are a number of substances that a committed drug user can use to substitute one high that's illegal and testable for a similar high that is legal and untestable," states Bruce R. Talbot, an instructor, trainer, and expert on substance abuse prevention and detection measures.

In some cases, a substance is legal if prescribed, but the user does not have a legitimate medical reason for obtaining a prescription, so the drug would have to be illegally obtained, and the use would be illegal. Users seek substitutes for these drugs as well. One example is kratom, a substitute for the prescription pain killer OxyContin, a popular drug with addicts seeking a high. Kratom's leaves can be smoked or put in a tea ball and brewed, and the resultant concoction drunk.

Kratom looks like marijuana and smells like sweet tea, but it produces the same effects as OxyContin: an opium-like high. "You can be actively high and still pass a drug test," Talbot says. Talbot says that most police officers aren't aware of it, and, in fact, none of the other experts interviewed for this story had heard of kratom or various other substitute drugs.

Drug users who favor marijuana and need to beat a drug test might substitute salvia divinorum, otherwise known as diviner's sage, says Talbot. Not only is it legal (and available on the Internet) and undetectable in urine, Talbot says, but it produces a more intense high than marijuana and is much cheaper. At a major state narcotics officer conference, recalls Talbot, one officer freely admitted that he smoked salvia and had done so for a long time.

The extent of use of these drugs is hard to determine because people don't get arrested for it and tests don't screen for it. The only evidence of use is anecdotal. The attractiveness of these drugs begs the question why they aren't more popular. "People are creatures of habit," replies Talbot, who adds that these drugs rarely make the front pages because "they typically don't kill people."

Testing

All workers in safety-sensitive positions are already subject to mandatory drug testing, but most other employees are currently not asked to take drug tests. That is slowly changing, however. Companies are reevaluating their testing programs, says one executive at a large testing laboratory.

"In particular, many companies that never tested before are trying to do it," he says, pointing to a growth in testing since 2000 and a particular spike in the last year. He says the trend is part of a resurgence in background checks, partly precipitated by the events of 9–11.

Another spur to increased testing is pressure brought to bear by insurance companies. They are encouraging, and in some cases mandating, that companies set up drug testing programs, says the lab executive. "I'm inundated with small and medium-sized companies needing drug testing," he says. "Insurers are threatening rates through the roof" if a testing program is not implemented.

> ## "Some companies collect specimens from all employees, then randomly select samples to test, perhaps one in every ten."

A few companies are becoming shrewder about maximizing deterrence while minimizing costs, notes Ferraro. These companies collect specimens from all employees, then randomly select samples to test, perhaps one in every ten. The money saved by not testing most of the samples is being invested in training managers in how they can better identify reasonable suspicion of drug use to determine whether there is just cause for ordering a drug test. The results have been encouraging, Ferraro says.

Nontraditional methods of drug testing have been increasing as well, for reasons ranging from efficacy to convenience. In fact, "There's been a revolution in alternative specimens," says Douglas J. Blaine, Sr., vice president of Penn Services, a Pennsylvania-based testing company.

Urine. "Urine is still the liquid gold standard" for testing, says Blaine. Urinalysis is the method sanctioned by the U.S. Department of Transportation for testing workers in safety-sensitive positions, "because it's easy to handle and collect, and all the work is done—the standard is there," he says.

According to the executive at the testing lab, urine tests account for more than 90 percent of the 30,000 tests the lab performs nightly.

But some companies are adding tests to accompany urinalysis or substituting for urinalysis altogether. One reason is that a whole industry of products to adulterate or substitute for urine specimens has been developed.

Other reasons are that urine doesn't show same-day drug use, which makes it less effective for detecting the presence of drugs in an employee's system when he or she is tested on reasonable suspicion of drug use or in the immediate aftermath of a workplace accident.

Hair. Drug testing labs report that they are doing more hair testing. One trend is the use of a combination of hair and urine testing for preemployment screening. That's proving to be a "very powerful" combination since the two complement each other well, says Blaine.

Unlike urine, hair can't be tampered with, as far as experts know. It also can detect the presence of drugs much farther back in time as compared with urine—90 days versus just a few days.

Employers, especially casino venues, want to find out, "Did he use drugs this weekend, and did he use [them] two months ago?" says Joseph Reilly, the president of Florida Drug Screening, Inc., and chairman of the Drug and Alcohol Testing Industry Association.

But it takes a hair two weeks to grow out, meaning that an analysis of hair can't be used to detect recent drug use. Also, hair testing is not an effective means of identifying marijuana, which shows up readily in urine.

Kraft Foods uses the dual-testing approach, says Ferraro. The result is a lower frequency of positive tests and fewer substance abuse issues at the company, he says.

One place where hair testing hasn't taken root is in Canada, says Butler. That country's human rights law stipulates that to conduct a drug test, employers need a bona fide reason directly related to an occupational requirement. "If your objective is to eliminate impairment, the test has to be able to do that," she says. Because hair testing doesn't identify current use, it cannot be said to be a means of testing for impairment; rather, it is only for detecting historic use.

Oral fluids. "Saliva testing is very exciting right now," says Talbot, though it's in its infancy. The Department of Justice (DOJ) is field-testing oral-fluid testing at police departments across the country, he says; the goal is to be able to perform a saliva test for drugs or alcohol on the roadside and have a result available in two minutes.

> **"One frequently cited trend was the use of a combination of hair and urine testing for preemployment screening."**

For the corporate world, it offers great potential for post-accident testing. Some companies are starting to use this method, because they can administer it themselves as long as they use a medical review officer.

A report funded by the DOJ, titled Evaluation of Saliva/Oral Fluid as an Alternate Drug Testing Specimen, concludes that "oral fluid is a promising specimen for drug testing and has several advantages over other testing specimens." These include simplicity of collection, the noninvasiveness of the procedure, and ease of processing. But more research is necessary on how to identify whether a sample has been diluted. And for instant tests, the technology has a long way to go, says the testing lab representative.

Pupillometry. Pupillometry is the measurement of the reaction of the pupil to stimuli. It is beginning to be used to test workers for drug impairment.

It works like this, according to Blaine: A person looks into a box, and a technician observes how the person's pupils react to a series of lights. Then a urinalysis is conducted. If the urine test is clean, the reaction of the pupils to the lights is established as a baseline performance of the subject when he or she isn't under the influence of drugs or alcohol. This "light test" then can be repeated at any time and checked against the baseline to determine impairment.

The method is promising, says Blaine, but the hurdles are obvious. For example, establishing a baseline depends on more factors than just the presence or absence of alcohol or drugs in a person's system. Also, legally prescribed drugs could affect the baseline pupil response. Moreover, a pupil response indicating impairment might reflect fatigue or some other factor, not necessarily the presence of drugs or alcohol.

Blood. As the most highly invasive measure, blood testing is still typically reserved for legal purposes or extreme cases. For example, it might be used to detect drugs in the body of a deceased worker whose family is filing a lawsuit or workers' compensation claim. It might also be used instead of urinalysis for workers who are on dialysis.

But as the basis of a regular testing program, it has too many disadvantages. For one, drugs leave the blood system quickly. In addition, the testing process is invasive and expensive, and it requires that the specimen taker employ certain precautions that are mandated for needle use. The resultant medical waste must be properly handled and incinerated, notes Blaine.

Subverting the Test

Countless products are available, especially over the Internet, to help workers beat drug tests. More than 400 on the market attempt to dilute or adulterate a specimen, according to the Department of Transportation (DOT). Others enable someone to substitute a different specimen. Their existence is no secret, but companies are often blasé about testing for adulterants either because they aren't familiar with them or because they don't want to incur the extra cost.

Another factor, says Reilly, is that government agencies "haven't been definitive on what labs have to do" to test for adulteration.

That's changing. In late 2004, the Department of Health and Human Services (HHS) adopted a rule requiring federal agencies to conduct so-called "specimen validity testing" to determine whether urine specimens collected under federal workplace drug testing programs had been adulterated or substituted. In an attempt to follow suit, DOT has issued a Notice of Proposed Rulemaking to make specimen validity testing mandatory.

Reluctance to screen for adulterants may also be a reaction to the statistics. Quest Diagnostics' Drug Testing Index for 2004 indicates that "oxidizing adulterants" accounted for an infinitesimal percentage—0.05 percent—of all tests of the general work force that turned up positive, and findings that a specimen was substituted accounted for only 0.49 percent. For safety-sensitive workers, those rates are 0.42 percent and 2.4 percent, respectively. The just-released figures for the first six months of 2005 show even lower rates—oxidizing adulterants turned up in less than 0.01 percent of the positive tests in the general work force and in 0.09 percent of the positive tests of safety-sensitive workers.

Asked why this should be, Quest's Dr. Barry Sample says one reason might be that the lab tests for "abnormal oxidizing activity," which is suggestive of adulteration but not a direct test for it. In other words, the tests are imperfect and may be missing occurences.

The company has seen an increase in cases where an oxidant has been found, but not in large enough quantities for the lab to conclude that a sample was adulterated. The result is an invalid specimen. Though Quest doesn't report the number of cases in which low levels of oxidants are identified, Sample says that the number of invalid specimens has risen. That could be a sign that attempts at adulteration are up. Getting an invalid specimen requires a retest, but it successfully buys time for workers.

Policies

A drug testing program is only as effective as its policies. Unfortunately, many corporations have let their workplace substance abuse policies stagnate, says the testing lab executive. He says that of his lab's large corporate clients hasn't rewritten its policy, which runs less than a page, in years. The reason? "Substance abuse, once a hot topic at the forefront of the minds of many organizations, has slipped in importance" as other security priorities—like terrorism—have grabbed attention, says Ferraro.

Revising policies is important, says Ramos, to keep pace with changing laws and developments. For example, he says, many companies have policies prohibiting use of drugs on company property, but don't say anything about use of drugs on company time. This could provide a loophole for a worker to get high at home during lunch, for example.

Also, Ramos says, some courts have ruled that policies that use the language "under the influence" are referring to alcohol, while "impaired" refers to drug use.

Some companies have no policies at all. When companies do have policies, observes Blaine, they often fail to address what will happen to an employee who is found guilty of adulteration.

Policies should specifically equate a verified adulterated test with a positive, he says, and prescribe consequences, such as requiring the user to work with the company's employee assistance program (EAP) or referring the person to law enforcement for prosecution.

There are some companies that are strengthening their drug abuse policies. For example, companies with which Ramos has worked have been moving toward harsher sanctions in their policies. When drug abuse is accompanied by theft, more businesses have been willing to prosecute.

"Typically an employer wanted to just eliminate the problem and get on with business," he says. "Now they want to send a message to existing employees and to prosecute theft by dealers; substance abuse is secondary."

Training. Corporate policies should also mandate that staff and supervisors undergo training so that they will be able to identify signs of substance abuse and will know how and where to report it. "Often an employer puts in a beautiful policy, but then they don't train people on it down through the levels" of the organization, says Blaine.

An insufficiently or untrained low-level supervisor who suspects a worker of drug abuse may run afoul of proper procedures in dealing with the user or conducting a drug test. If the user is terminated on the basis of such a test, an arbitrator will reinstate that person, Blaine says.

Management consultant Butler has seen this in Canada. She has had many companies come to her because they recognized that they had to ramp up training for their supervisors to comply with demands of new clients.

Ramos's firm also does this type of work. It performs three levels of training. At the first and second levels, executives and supervisors, respectively, learn to identify behavior and patterns emblematic of drug use or sales. The third level teaches employees about the impact of substance abuse on their work and family life, and it lays out the legal ramifications. This tiered training makes sure the message gets to the whole organization, he says.

For his part, Talbot says that he teaches managers and supervisors how to document the signs and symptoms of drug impairment so that they can write a convincing fitness-for-duty report. They can use that report to impel management to order a test on the user.

The ultimate question is whether all this activity has actually led to less drug abuse on the job. One indication of progress is that since Quest began reporting the percentage of drug tests that turned up positive, the number has declined markedly, from 13.6 percent in 1988 to 4.5 percent in 2004 to 4.3 percent for the first half of 2005. Ferraro isn't so sure, however. The numbers may simply indicate that employees have gotten very good at beating the tests.

Michael A. Gips is a senior editor at Security Management.

UNIT 6

Creating and Sustaining Effective Drug Control Policy

Unit Selections

40. **Reorienting U.S. Drug Policy,** Jonathan P. Caulkins and Peter Reuter
41. **Is Drug Testing of Athletes Necessary?,** Matthew J. Mitten
42. **Medical Marijuana, Compassionate Use, and Public Policy,** Peter J. Cohen
43. **Researchers Explore New Visions for Hallucinogens,** Susan Brown
44. **State's Evidence,** Will Baude
45. **Durbin, Grassley Introduce Bipartisan Bill to Combat Meth**
46. **How to Stand Up to Big Tobacco,** Noreena Hertz

Key Points to Consider

- How has the war in Iraq influenced current drug policy?

- How does drug policy shape public opinion of drug-related events?

- What role do the media play in shaping drug policy?

- Are the problems and issues surrounding the legal use of alcohol different from those surrounding the illegal use of heroin, cocaine, or methamphetamines? How?

- To what degree would you argue that the current problems with drug abuse exist because of current drug policies, or in spite of them?

Student Web Site
www.mhcls.com/online

Internet References
Further information regarding these websites may be found in this book's preface or online.

Drug Policy Alliance
   www.drugpolicy.org
DrugText
   http://www.drugtext.org
Effective Drug Policy: Why journey's end is legalisations
   http://www.drugscope.org.uk/wip/23/pdfs/journey.pdf
The Higher Education Center for Alcohol and Other Drug Prevention
   http://www.edc.org/hec/pubs/policy.htm
The National Organization on Fetal Alcohol Syndrome (NOFAS)
   http://www.nofas.org
National NORML Homepage
   http://www.norml.org/

Mikael Karlsson

The drug problem consistently competes with all major public policy issues, including the war in Iraq, the economy, education, and foreign policy. Drug abuse is a serious national medical issue with profound social and legal consequences. Formulating and implementing effective drug control policy is a troublesome task. Some would argue that the consequences of policy failures have been worse than the problems they were attempting to address. Others would argue that although the world of shaping drug policy is an imperfect one, the process has worked generally as well as could be expected. The majority of Americans believe that failures and breakdowns in the fight against drug abuse have occurred in spite of various drug policies, not because of them. Although the last few years have produced softening attitudes and alternatives for adjudicating cases of simple possession and use, the get-tough, stay-tough enforcement policies directed at illegal drug trafficking remain firmly in place and widely supported.

Policy formulation is not a process of aimless wandering. Various levels of government have responsibility for responding to problems of drug abuse. At the center of most policy debate is the premise that the manufacture, possession, use, and distribution of psychoactive drugs without government authorization is illegal. The federal posture of prohibition is an important emphasis on state and local policy making. Federal drug policy is, however, significantly linked to state-by-state data which suggests that illicit drug, alcohol, and tobacco use vary substantially among

states and regions. The current federal drug strategy began in 2001 and set the goals of reducing drug use by 25 percent over five years. Although these goals have not been met, President Bush advised Congress that the plan has been successful at impacting drug abuse citing the 19 percent reduction in drugs by young people. With a few exceptions, most of the goals of the current strategy are in sight. Core priorities of the overall plan continue to be to stop drug use before it starts, heal America's drug users, and disrupt the illegal market. These three core goals are re-enforced by objectives outlined in a policy statement produced by the White House Office of Drug Control Policy. All three goals reflect budget expenditures related to meeting goals of the overall policy. The current drug control policy in terms of budget allocations continues to provide for over $7 billion to reduce supply and almost $5 billion to reduce demand. Each year produces modifications to the plan as a result of analysis of trends and strategy impacts. For example, more federal funds have been allocated to local communities for treatment options, and new emphasis is being directed as the ecological impacts of illegal drug trafficking such as those caused by large marijuana growing operations on public lands.

One exception to prevailing views that generally support drug prohibition is the softening of attitudes regarding criminal sanctions that historically applied to cases of simple possession and use of drugs. There is much public sentiment that incarcerating persons for these offenses is unjustified unless they are related to other related criminal conduct consensus. The federal funding of drug court programs remains a priority with $70 million dedicated to state and local operation. Drug courts provide alternatives to incarceration by using the coercive power of the court to force abstinence and alter behavior through a process of escalating sanctions, mandatory drug testing, and out-patient programs. Successful rehabilitation accompanies the re-entry to society as a citizen, not a felon. The drug court program exists as one important example of policy directed at treating users and deterring them from further involvement in the criminal justice system. Drug courts are now in place in all 50 states.

The majority of Americans express the view that legalizing, and in some cases even decriminalizing, dangerous drugs is a bad idea. The fear of increased crime, increased drug use and the potential threat to children are the most often stated reasons. Citing the devastating consequences of alcohol and tobacco use, most Americans question society's ability to use any addictive, mind-altering drug responsibly. Currently, the public favors both supply reduction, demand reduction, and an increased emphasis on prevention, treatment, and rehabilitation as effective strategies in combating the drug problem. Shaping public policy is a critical function that greatly relies upon public input. The policy-making apparatus is influenced by public opinion, and public opinion is in turn influenced by public policy. When the president refers to drugs as threats to national security, the impact on public opinion is tremendous. Currently, record amounts of Opium are being produced in Afghanistan and the implications for it providing support for the Taliban and terrorism are clear. The resulting implications for sustaining enforcement oriented U.S. drug policy are also clear; and in the minds of most Americans, absolutely necessary.

Although the prevailing characteristic of most current drug policy still reflects a punitive, "get tough" approach to control, an added emphasis on treating and rehabilitating offenders is visible in policy changes occurring over the past 10 years. Correctional systems are reflecting with greater consistency the view that drug treatment made available to inmates is a critical component of rehabilitation. The California Department of Corrections, the largest in the nation, was recently renamed the California Department of Corrections and Rehabilitation. A prisoner with a history of drug abuse, who receives no drug treatment while in custody, is finally being recognized as a virtual guarantee to reoffend. In 2006, the National Institute of Drug Abuse published the first federal guidelines for administering drug treatment to criminal justice populations.

Another complicated aspect of creating national as well as local drug policy is consideration of the growing body of research on the subject. The past 20 years have produced numerous public and private investigations, surveys, and conclusions relative to the dynamics of drug use in American society. Although an historical assessment of the influence of research on policy produces indirect relationships, policy decisions of the last few years can be directly related to evidence based research findings and not just political views. One example is the consistently increasing commitment to treatment. This commitment comes as a direct result of research related to progress achieved in treating and rehabilitating users. Treatment, in terms of dollars spent, can compete with all other components of drug control policy. Over 35 percent of the current federal budget is dedicated to drug education, prevention, research, and treatment. Two current examples of dedicating treatment funds is NIDA's $47 million program, Developing New Ways to Treat Methamphetamine Addiction, and The Anti-Meth Campaign targeting meth abuse in eight western states.

One important issue affecting and sometimes complicating the research/policy making relationship is that the policy making community, at all levels of government, is largely composed of persons of diverse backgrounds, professional capacities, and political interests. Some are elected officials, others are civil servants, and many are private citizens from the medical, educational, and research communities. In some cases, such as with alcohol and tobacco, powerful industry players assert a tremendous influence on policy. As you read on, consider the new research-related applications for drug policy, such as those related to the rehabilitation of incarcerated drug offenders.

Reorienting U.S. Drug Policy

The nature and extent of the illegal drug problems in the United States have fundamentally changed during the past two decades; now policy needs to change as well.

JONATHAN P. CAULKINS AND PETER REUTER

The United States will soon surpass the half-million mark for drug prisoners, which is more than 10 times as many as in 1980. It is an extraordinary number, more than Western Europe locks up for all criminal offenses combined and more than the pre-Katrina population of New Orleans. How effective is this level of imprisonment in controlling drug problems? Could we get by with, say, just a quarter million locked up for drug violations?

Now is an opportune time to consider this issue. The illegal drug problem has fundamentally changed during the past two decades, in both its nature and its extent. With a few exceptions, the drug problem has stabilized and begun to improve in the United States during the past 15 years. Notably, the number of people dependent on expensive drugs such as cocaine has dropped significantly from its peak. The terrifying spike in drug-related homicides of the late 1980s has long ended. Today, we are dealing with an older, less violent, and more stable population of drug abusers. Despite these changes, the number of drug prisoners continues to increase.

Tough enforcement is supposed to drive up prices and make it more difficult to obtain drugs, and thus reduce overall drug use and the problems that it causes. Yet the evidence indicates that it has had quite limited success at reducing the supply of established mass-market drugs. Thus, even assuming that tough enforcement was an appropriate response at an earlier time, today's situation justifies considering different policy options.

Would the United States really be worse off if it contented itself with 250,000 rather than 500,000 drug prisoners? This would hardly be going soft on drugs. It would still be a lot tougher than the Reagan administration ever was.

In particular, there is little reason to believe that the United States would have a noticeably more serious drug problem if it kept 250,000 fewer drug dealers under lock and key. Given the social harms that result from imprisonment as well as the considerable taxpayer tab for incarceration, there is a case to be made for working out ways to reduce the number of people in jail and prison for drug offenses.

Among affluent nations, U.S. rates of drug use are not exceptionally high by contemporary international standards. About 1 in 15 Americans aged 12 and over currently uses drugs, a much smaller figure than in, for example, Great Britain. By a wide margin, prevalence is highest among older teenagers and those in their early 20s, peaking at around 40% using within the past 12 months for high-school seniors. Most Americans who try drugs use them only a few times. If there is a typical continuing user, it is an occasional marijuana smoker who will cease to use drugs at some point during his 20s. Marijuana use in the 15- to 26-year-old age group has been at high levels throughout the past three decades, but there have also been notable ups and downs. Usage rose through the 1970s, fell in the 1980s, and bounced back up in the early 1990s, but only among adolescents and very young adults.

What these data from general population surveys do not describe well are the trends in the behaviors that dominate drug-related social costs, which primarily involve drug-related crime, health consequences, premature mortality, and lost productivity. These problems are worse in the United States than they are in most other countries, and they are driven by the number of people dependent on cocaine (including crack), heroin, and methamphetamines, drugs that might collectively be called the expensive drugs to distinguish them from marijuana. Marijuana is by far the most widely used of the illicit drugs, but its use directly accounts for only about 10% of those adverse outcomes, in part because a year's supply of marijuana costs so little that its distribution and purchase engender relatively little crime or violence.

The compulsive use of expensive drugs in the United States is a legacy of four major drug epidemics. The notion of a drug epidemic captures the fact that drug use is a learned behavior, transmitted from one person to another. Contrary to the popular image of the entrepreneurial drug pusher who hooks new addicts through aggressive salesmanship, it is now clear that almost all first experiences are the result of being offered the drug by a friend or family member. Drug use thus spreads much like a communicable disease, a metaphor familiar from marketing and new-product-adoption models. Users are "contagious," and some of those with whom they come into contact become "infected." Initiation of heroin, cocaine, and crack use shows much more of a classic epidemic pattern than does marijuana use, although the growth of marijuana use in the 1960s may have had epidemic features.

In an epidemic, rates of initiation (infection) in a given area rise sharply as new and highly contagious users of a drug initiate friends and peers. At least with heroin, cocaine, and crack, long-term addicts are not particularly contagious. They are often socially isolated from new users. Moreover, they usually present an unappealing picture of the consequences of addiction. In the next stage of the epidemic, initiation declines rapidly as the susceptible population shrinks, because there are fewer nonusers and/or because the drug's reputation sours, as a result of better knowledge of the effects of a drug. The number of dependent users stabilizes and typically declines gradually.

The first modern U.S. drug epidemic involved heroin. It developed with rapid initiation in the late 1960s, primarily in a few big cities and most heavily in inner-city minority communities; the experiences of U.S. soldiers in Vietnam may have been a contributing factor. The annual number of new heroin initiates peaked in the early 1970s and then dropped by ~50% by the late 1970s and remained low until the mid 1990s. Heroin addiction (at least for those addicted in the United States rather than while in the military in Vietnam) has turned out to be a long-lived and lethal condition, as revealed in a remarkable 33-year followup of male heroin addicts admitted to the California Civil Addict Program during the years 1962–1964. Nearly half of the original addicts—284 of 581—had died by 1996–1997; of the 242 still living who were interviewed, 40% reported heroin use in the past year and 60% were unemployed.

Cocaine in powder form was the source of the second epidemic, which lasted longer and was more sharply peaked than the heroin epidemic. Initiation, which was broadly distributed across class and race, rose to a peak around 1980 and then fell sharply, by ~80% or more during the 1980s. Dependence always lags behind initiation, and cocaine use became more common in the mid-1980s as the pool of those who had experimented with the drug expanded. The number of dependent users peaked around 1988 and declined only moderately through the 1990s.

The third epidemic was of crack use. Although connected to the cocaine epidemic—crack developed as an easy-to-use form of freebase cocaine—the crack epidemic was more concentrated among minorities in inner-city communities. Its starting point varied across cities; for Los Angeles the beginning may have been 1982, whereas for Chicago it was as late as 1988. But in all cities initiation appears to have peaked within about two years and to have again left a population with a chronic and debilitating addiction.

The fourth important epidemic, of methamphetamine use, has gradually rolled two-thirds of the way across the country, from west to east, taking hold where cocaine use was less common. It had already stabilized on the West Coast by the time rapid spread began in the Mississippi and Ohio River valleys; it still has not reached most of the East Coast. There have been other epidemics (for example, ecstasy use), but heroin, cocaine (including crack), and methamphetamine probably account for close to 90% of the social costs associated with illicit drugs in the United States.

What is particularly interesting is that big declines in cocaine and heroin prices (discussed below) have not triggered new epidemics. Initiation goes up when prices go down, but once a drug has acquired a bad reputation, it does not seem prone to a renewed explosion or contagious spread in use. That is a great protective factor, though presumably not eternal.

U.S. Drug Policies

The United States spends a lot of money on drug control. The drug czar claims that federal expenditures are $12.5 billion, but that figure excludes big items that everyone else thinks should be included, notably federal prosecution and prison costs. Excluding these figures allows the federal government to claim to roughly balance supply reduction (mostly enforcement) and demand reduction (prevention and treatment). Putting in the full list of programs might take the federal figure to more than $17 billion. State and local governments, which provide most of the policing and prison funding, probably spend even more. So across all levels of government, drug control spending may exceed $40 billion annually.

How well do the different kinds of programs work? Everyone likes the idea of preventing kids from starting drug use, but drug prevention is nothing like immunizing kids against drug abuse. The most widely implemented programs have never been shown by rigorous evaluations to have any effect on drug use, and even cutting-edge model programs that fare better in evaluation studies produce reductions in use that mostly dissipate by the end of high school. Even recognizing the historical correlation between delayed onset and reduced lifetime use, projected reductions in lifetime consumption are in the single-digit percentages. Modest effects should not be surprising. It is hard to do anything within 30 contact hours that overrides the impact of the thousands of hours that typical young people spend with peers, listening to music, watching television, and so on. The good news is that the budgetary cost of school-based prevention is low, so prevention appears to still be modestly cost-effective unless one ascribes a particularly high value to the opportunity cost of diverting classroom hours from academic subjects or volunteers' hours from other causes.

Mass-media campaigns are notoriously difficult to evaluate because they are so diffuse; it is hard to find a control group so that one can distinguish the effects of the campaign from other factors affecting drug use. Still, it is sobering that evaluations by Westat and the Annenberg School of Communications of the federal government's high-profile media campaign suggest that it has had no effect on drug use

Treating those with drug problems is the one kind of intervention for which there is a fairly good empirical base to judge effectiveness. About 1.1 million individuals received some kind of treatment for drug dependence or abuse in 2004, plus another 340,000 for whom alcohol was the primary substance of abuse. Federal expenditures on that amounted to about $2.4 billion; the states may add about as much again. Heroin addicts mostly get methadone, a substitute opiate. Everyone else gets, in some form, counseling. Even though the majority of clients entering treatment drop out and of those who complete their treatment more than half will relapse within five years, it is easy to make the case that the intervention is cost-effective. This comes from the fact that many of those who enter treatment, certainly those with heroin or cocaine problems, are very high-rate criminal offenders. During treatment, their drug use goes down a lot and that cuts their crime rates comparably. These crime-reducing benefits from treatment help the community as well as the patient.

It is disappointing that the number in treatment at any one time (~850,000, including 500,000 who also abused alcohol) is only a modest fraction of the 3 to 4 million who are dependent on cocaine, methamphetamine, or heroin. There are a similar number who are dependent only on marijuana, which is the single most common primary substance of abuse for those treated; however, those dependent only on marijuana are less likely to be frequent offenders or to suffer acute health harms, so the social benefits of treating them are quite different and much smaller. (Most marijuana-only users who are compelled into treatment by an arrest are low- to medium-rate users.)

Most U.S. drug efforts go to enforcing drug laws, predominantly against sellers; oddly enough, that is also true for other less punitive nations, including the Netherlands. Although eradication and crop substitution programs overseas in the source countries, primarily in the Andes, get a lot of press coverage, they account for a small share of even the federal enforcement budget, about $1 billion. More money—about $2.5 billion in 2004—is spent on interdiction: trying to seize drugs and couriers on their way into the country.

Neither source-country programs nor interdiction has much promise as a way of producing more than a transitory reduction in drug consumption in the United States. They focus on the phases of the production and distribution system at which the drugs are still cheap and easily replaced because there is plenty of land, labor, and routes available to adapt to government interventions. In addition to creating occasional transitory disruptions, interdiction (in contrast to source-country interventions such as crop eradication) has long made drug smuggling surprisingly expensive, but it has not managed to raise smugglers' costs further in a long time.

The majority of all drug control expenditures go to the enforcement of drug laws within the United States. Between 1980 and 1990, dependent drug use and violent drug markets expanded rapidly, and the number of people locked up for drug law violations increased by 210,000. Between 1990 and 2000, drug problems began to ease, but drug incarcerations increased

by still another 200,000. Simply put, incarceration has risen steadily while drug use has both waxed and waned.

The great majority of those locked up are involved in drug distribution. Although a sizable minority were convicted of a drug possession charge, in confidential interviews most of them report playing some (perhaps minor) role in drug distribution; for example, they were couriers transporting (and hence possessing) large quantities or they pled down to a simple possession charge to avoid a trial.

Society locks up drug suppliers for multiple reasons. Drug sellers cause great harm because of the addiction they facilitate and the crime and disorder that their markets cause. Thus there is a retributive purpose for the imprisonment. Still, sentences can exceed what mere retribution might require. Perhaps the most infamous example is that in federal courts the possession of 5 grams of crack cocaine will generate a five-year mandatory minimum sentence, compared with a national average time served for homicide of about five years and four months, even though that $400 worth of crack is just one fifty-millionth of U.S. annual cocaine consumption, or about two weeks' supply for one regular user.

Does Tough Enforcement Work?

An important justification for aggressive punishment is the claim that high rates of incarceration will reduce drug use and related problems. The theory is that tough enforcement will raise the risk of drug selling. Some dealers will drop out of the business, and the remainder will require higher compensation for taking greater risks. Hence the price of drugs should rise. It should also make drug dealers more cautious and thus make it harder for customers to find them. So the central question is whether the huge increase in incarceration over the past 25 years has made drugs more expensive and/or less available.

The science of tracking trends in illicit drug prices is not for purists; there are no random samples of drug sellers or transactions. However, the broad trends apparent in the largest data sets (those stemming from law enforcement's undercover drug buys) are confirmed by other sources, including ethnographic studies, interviews with or wire taps of dealers, and forensic analysis of the quantity of pure drug contained in packages that sell for standardized retail amounts (for example, $10 "dime bags" of heroin). During the past 25 years, the general price trends have gone more or less in the opposite direction from what would be expected (see figure). Incarceration for drug law violations (primarily pertaining to cocaine and heroin) increased 11-fold between 1980 and 2002, yet purity-adjusted cocaine and heroin prices fell by 80%. Methamphetamine prices also fell by more than 50%, although the decline was interrupted by some notable spikes. Marijuana prices unadjusted for purity rose during the 1980s and 2000s but fell during the 1990s. Declining prices in the face of higher incarceration rates does not per se contradict the presumption that tougher enforcement can reduce use by driving up prices. Other factors may have driven the price declines. Drug distributors might have been making supernormal profits in the early 1980s that were driven out over time by competition, or "learning by doing" might have improved distribution efficiency

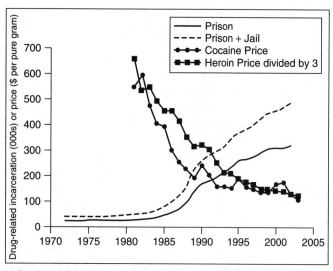

U.S. Drug-Related Incarceration and Retail Heroin and Cocaine Prices

by incarcerating the users would not have cost much more (40 person-years ¥ $30,000/cell-year = $1.2 million) and might also have yielded some deterrent effects; yet almost no one thinks long prison terms make sense for users who were not involved in drug distribution.

As another way to understand how meager this cost-effectiveness ratio of 5 kilograms per million dollars is, model-based estimates predicated on that same elasticity done by RAND's Drug Policy Research Center had projected a cost-effectiveness of 27.5 kilograms per million dollars even when including arrest and adjudication costs. Yet that much larger cost-effectiveness figure was still perceived as comparing unfavorably to other control options and as being a rather expensive way to suppress drug use.

Nor is there any evidence that tougher enforcement has made cocaine or other drugs harder to get. The fraction of high-school seniors reporting that cocaine is available or readily available has been about 50% for 25 years; for 85% of respondents, the same statement remains true for marijuana.

within the supply chain. Hence, it is possible that prices would have fallen still farther had it not been for the great expansion in drug law enforcement.

We should consider impossing shorter sentences on drug offenders and then employ the innovation of coerced abstinence as a means of keeping them reasonably clean while on parole.

Ilyana Kuziemko and Steven D. Levitt published a study of this question in the *Journal of Public Economics* in 2004. They found that cocaine prices in 1995 were 5 to 15% higher as a result of the increases in drug punishment since 1985. That result helps save the economic logic that supply control ought to drive retail prices up, not down, but the estimated slope of the price-versus-incarceration curve is so flat that expanded incarceration appears not to have been a cost-effective tool for controlling drug use.

During that 10-year period, incarceration for drug law violations increased from 82,000 to 376,000, about two-thirds of which were cocaine offenders. Thus, to achieve the modest increase in cocaine prices, it cost an extra $6 billion a year just for incarceration (assuming a cost of $30,000 per year to house an inmate). Annual cocaine consumption then was about 300 metric tons. So even assuming an elasticity of demand as large, in absolute value, as–1, a 10% increase in price would avert only about 30 metric tons of consumption, or less than 5 kilograms per million taxpayer dollars spent on incarceration.

To put this figure in perspective, 5 kilograms is about 40 person-years of use for a heavy user. Eliminating that use

Changing Times, Changing Policies

With a few exceptions (notably oxycontin and methamphetamine), the drug problem in the United States has been slowly improving during the past 15 years. The number of people dependent on expensive drugs (cocaine, heroin, and methamphetamine) has declined from roughly 5.1 million in 1988 to perhaps 3.8 million in 2000, the most recent year for which figures have been released. The residual drug-dependent populations are getting older; more than 50% of cocaine-related emergency department admissions are now of people over 35, compared to 20% 20 years ago. The share of those treated for heroin, cocaine, and amphetamine dependence who were over 40 rose from 13% in 1992 to 31% in 2004. Kids who started using marijuana in the late 1990s are less likely to go on to use hard drugs than were kids who started in the 1970s.

What we face now is not the problem of an explosive drug epidemic, the kind that scared the country in the 1980s when crack emerged and street markets proliferated, but rather "endemic" drug use, with stable numbers of new users each year. The substantial number of aging drug abusers cause great damage to society and to themselves, but the problem is not rapidly growing. Rather, it is slowly ebbing down to a steady state that, depending on the measure one prefers, may be on the order of half its peak.

Rising imprisonment probably made some contribution to these trends. Some of the most aggressive dealers are now behind bars; their replacements are no angels but may be both less violent and less skilled at the business. However, the discussion above raises doubts about whether incarceration accounts for much of the decline. If prices have not risen and if the drugs are just as available as before, then it is hard to see how tough enforcement against suppliers can be what explains the ends of the epidemics and the gradual but important declines in the number of people dependent on expensive drugs.

This provides an opportunity. Changed circumstances justify changed policies, but U.S. drug policies have changed only marginally as the problem has transformed. The inertia can be seen by examining why the number of prisoners keeps rising even as drug markets get smaller. Drug arrests have been flat at 1.6 million a year for 10 years, and more and more of them are for marijuana possession (almost half in 2003), which produces very few prison sentences.

Three factors drive the rise in incarceration. First, today's drug offenders are not just older; they also have longer criminal records, exposing them to harsher sentences. Second, legal changes have made it more likely that someone arrested for drug selling will get a jail or prison sentence. Third, the declining use of parole has meant longer stays in prison for a given sentence length. On average, drug offenders who received prison sentences in state courts in 2002 were given terms of four years, of which they served about half. Is it a good thing that those being convicted are now spending more time behind bars?

Any case for cutting drug imprisonment should not pretend that prisons are bulging with first-time, nonviolent drug offenders. Most were involved in distributing drugs, and few got into prison on their first conviction; they had to work their way in. The system mostly locks up people who have caused a good deal of harm to society. Most will, when released, revert to drug use and crime. They do not tug the heart strings as innocent victims of a repressive state.

Still, would the United States really be worse off if it contented itself with 250,000 rather than 500,000 drug prisoners? This would hardly be going soft on drugs. It would still be a lot tougher than the Reagan administration ever was. It would ensure that the United States still maintained a comfortable lead over any other Western nation in its toughness toward drug dealers. Furthermore, incarcerating fewer total prisoners need not mean that they all get out earlier. The minority who are very violent or unusually dangerous in other ways may be getting appropriate sentences, and with less pressure on prison space, they might serve more of their sentences. Deemphasizing sheer quantity of drug incarceration could usefully be complemented by greater efforts to target that incarceration more effectively.

There is no magic formula behind this suggestion to halve drug incarceration as opposed to cutting it by one-third or two-thirds. The point is simply that dramatic reductions in incarceration are possible without entering uncharted waters of permissiveness, and the expansion to today's unprecedented levels of incarceration seems to have made little contribution to the reduction in U.S. drug problems.

Drug treatment as an alternative to incarceration has become a standard response, more talked about than implemented. Drug courts that use judges to cajole and compel offenders to enter and remain in treatment are one tool, but they account for a modest fraction of drug-involved offenders because the screening criteria are restrictive, excluding those with long records. Proposition 36 in California, which ensured that most of those arrested for drug possession for the first time were not incarcerated, seems to have been reasonably successful in at least cutting the number jailed without raising crime rates or any other indicator one worries about. These, though, are interventions that deal with less serious offenders, most of whom will only go to local jail rather than to prison.

A more important change would be to impose shorter sentences and then use University of California at Los Angeles Professor Mark Kleiman's innovation of coerced abstinence as a way of keeping them reasonably clean while on parole. Coerced abstinence simply means that the criminal justice system does what the citizens assume it is doing already, namely detecting drug use early via frequent drug testing and providing short and immediate sanctions when the probationer or parolee tests positive. The small amount of research on this kind of program suggests that it works as designed, but it is hard to implement and needs to be tested in tougher populations, such as released parolees.

A democracy should be reluctant to deprive its citizens of liberty, a reluctance reinforced by the facts that imprisonment falls disproportionately on poor minority communities and that many U.S. prisons are nasty and brutalizing institutions. Further, there is growing evidence that the high incarceration rates have serious consequences for communities. A recent study suggests that differences in black and white incarceration rates may explain most of the sevenfold higher rate of HIV among black males as compared to white males. If locking up typical dealers for two years rather than one has minimal effect on the availability and use of dangerous drugs, then a freedom-loving society should be reluctant to do it.

Yet we are left with an enforcement system that runs on automatic, locking up increasing numbers on a faded rationale despite the high economic and social costs of incarceration and its apparently quite modest effects on drug use. Truly "solving" the nation's drug problem, with its multiple causes, is beyond the reach of any existing intervention or strategy. But that should not prevent decisionmakers from realizing that money can be saved and justice improved by simply cutting in half the number of people locked up for drug offenses.

JONATHAN P. CAULKINS (caulkins@andrew.cmu.edu) is a professor of public policy and operations research at Carnegie-Mellon University's Qatar Campus and Heinz School of Public Policy and Management. Peter Reuter (preuter@umd.edu) is a professor in the School of Public Policy and Department of Criminology, the University of Maryland, and codirector of RAND's Drug Policy Research Center.

Is Drug Testing of Athletes Necessary?

"Rather than imposing an external drug-testing program on sports organizations, the Federal government should focus on preventing access to performance-enhancing drugs that pose health risks and prosecuting persons who distribute these substances illegally."

MATTHEW J. MITTEN

In today's society, the economic and intangible rewards for extraordinary athletic achievements and winning performances are substantial. Therefore, there is a significant incentive for athletes to maximize their on-field performance, which is the paramount objective of sports competition. Virtually all athletes use various artificial means to enhance their body's natural performance while playing their respective sports.

Some substances and training techniques are not characterized as "unfair" competitive advantages, even if they are not universally available to all athletes because of their differing economic resources. It generally is permissible for athletes to ingest nonmuscle building dietary supplements that facilitate athletic performance such as carbohydrates, electrolyte drinks, energy bars, vitamins, and minerals—and they often are encouraged to do so. Even the use of creatine as a muscle-building substance currently is not considered to be "doping" or an improper means of athletic performance enhancement.

However, athletes' usage of federally controlled substances such as anabolic androgenic steroids, which include "designer steroids" such as THC (*i.e.*, tetrahydrogestrinone), and steroid precursors is characterized as doping by sports governing bodies and, if detected, punishable by sanctions. Anabolic androgenic steroids are synthetic variations of the male hormone testosterone that mimic its effects by having muscle-building (anabolic) and masculinizing (androgenic) characteristics with potentially harmful health consequences.

Steroids are a legitimate, therapeutic treatment for muscle-wasting conditions, but sports organizations prohibit their usage by athletes to enhance on-field performance. Also generally banned are steroid precursors such as androstenedione, which was admittedly used by former Major League Baseball player Mark McGwire. These substances function like steroids after being ingested and metabolized by the body. Sports organizations also ban and test for stimulants such as ephedrine and caffeine, which are contained in some over-the-counter products, because of their potential usage for "unfair" athletic performance enhancement.

Risking Severe Sanctions

Some athletes at all levels of sports competition are willing to use banned performance-enhancing drugs, even though doing so violates the rules of the game and exposes them to sanctions, could adversely affect their health, and may violate Federal or state laws. Several former Major League Baseball and National Football League players such as Jose Canseco, Ken Caminiti (deceased). Bill Romanowski, and Steve Courson have admitted using anabolic steroids to enhance their on-field performances. Prominent Olympic athletes (*e.g.,* Ben Johnson and Jerome Young) have tested positive for steroid use, and other Olympians are suspected or accused of using steroids. Approximately one percent of the 11,000 National Collegiate Athletic Association student-athletes who randomly are tested each year come up positive for usage of banned performance-enhancing substances. According to a 2003 Centers for Disease Control and Prevention survey of ninth to 12th graders, steroid use by high school students has more than doubled from 1991 to 2003—to more than six percent.

Anabolic steroids, when combined with vigorous physical training, do enhance athletic performance by making users bigger, stronger, and faster—while also speeding up their recovery time after strenuous exercise. If steroids effectively enhance performance, what is wrong with allowing athletes to take advantage of modem medicine and pharmacology? After all, athletes frequently are given painkillers and are fitted with artificial devices designed to enable continued participation in a sport despite an injury, and these generally are considered to be acceptable practices. Although there is concern about potential health risks, libertarians point to the current lack of compelling medical evidence that steroid usage by adult athletes causes serious health risks beyond those already inherent in competitive sports. Some commentators, including physicians, advocate allowing athletes to use steroids with medical supervision after full disclosure regarding their known health risks rather than banning and imposing sanctions for their usage.

Is there really an appropriate line that can be drawn between legitimate athletic performance enhancement through artificial means and unethical doping to achieve an unfair competitive advantage? For example, athletes' usage of artificially created low-oxygen living environments in low-altitude training areas currently is permitted, whereas their use of erythropoietin (EPO) to achieve similar effects are prohibited by sports governing bodies. Moreover, who is the appropriate entity to draw this line?

Perhaps it is easier to answer both questions by considering the second question first. Sports governing bodies have a legitimate interest in establishing uniform rules necessary to maintain the sport's integrity and image, ensure competitive balance, and protect athletes' health and safety. Although achieving maximum individual performance and winning is the objective of athletic competition, the essence of sports is that all participants play by the same rules. Antidoping regulations are an integral part of the "rules of the game," similar to those regulating playing equipment, scoring competition results, and penalizing infractions. Even if a sport's rules of play are arbitrary (and they often are), the sport's governing body has the inherent authority to promulgate clearly defined boundaries to ensure fair play and enforce them in a uniform, nondiscriminatory manner.

Moreover, anabolic steroids are a Federally controlled substance. Medical experts have identified several potential negative side effects of using them. Clinical experiments involving athletes' use of steroids solely to improve on-field performance would raise serious ethical issues. For example, East German athletes who were given steroids under medical supervision, which enabled them to win Olympic medals during the Cold War era, now are suffering serious adverse health effects.

Courts and arbitration panels have upheld the legal authority of sports governing bodies (and educational institutions) to use random urinalysis drug testing of high school, college, and Olympic athletes. These tribunals generally conclude that protecting the integrity of athletic competition and sports participants' health and safety outweigh athletes' legitimate privacy interests. An athlete who uses these banned substances is a "cheater" whose unethical conduct may be punished.

Athletes who use prohibited substances directly expose themselves to potential adverse health consequences and indirectly subject others to similar risks. By nature, many athletes are risk-takers who will adopt their counterparts' successful training methods—even dangerous ones—if doing so enhances their performance. Thus, other athletes' actual or perceived usage of steroids creates a strong incentive to "level the playing field," which may cause an individual who would not otherwise ingest or inject steroids to do so.

Pharmacological performance-enhancing substances are banned because of their adverse effects on both athletes' health and competitive integrity. For example, the World Anti-Doping Agency (WADA) Code only prohibits usage of a substance that satisfies at least two of the following criteria: it enhances or has the potential to enhance sports performance; it creates an actual or potential health risk; or it violates the spirit of sport. No single criteria is a sufficient reason for prohibiting usage. For example, the first criteria includes the use of creatine and artificial low-oxygen living environments, which are permitted because neither of the other criteria presently are deemed to be satisfied. Conversely, the use of anabolic steroids is prohibited because at least two, and arguably all three, of these criteria have been met.

The WADA Code governs Olympic sports competition. It generally provides for strict liability and mandatory minimum suspensions for athletes' usage of banned substances. Pursuant to a contract with the United States Olympic Committee, the United States Anti-Doping Agency (USADA), an independent entity, administers and oversees the drug-testing program for American Olympic athletes. An individual has the right to appeal USADA's finding of a doping violation to an arbitral tribunal and to seek a reduced sanction because of mitigating circumstances.

The NCAA has a random drug-testing protocol applicable to all student-athletes participating in its member institutions' intercollegiate athletics program. It provides for strict liability and a one-year suspension from participation in all NCAA sports (along with a loss of one year of eligibility) for testing positive for a banned substance, with the right to an administrative appeal before members of the NCAA's Competitive Safeguards and Medical Aspects of Sports' drug education and testing subcommittee. Effective Aug. 1, 2005, the NCAA's drug-testing protocol was modified to make it more consistent with the WADA Code by withholding an athlete from NCAA competition who is under a doping suspension by a national or international sports governing body that has adopted the WADA Code, and by allowing consideration of a reduced penalty for a positive test in extenuating circumstances.

Because of the large number of students participating in interscholastic athletics and the high cost of testing ($50–100 per test), no state high school athletics governing body presently requires testing for performance-enhancing drugs. For the same reasons, very few school districts test for anabolic steroids. The California Interscholastic Federation, which regulates the state's high school athletics, recently adopted a policy to curb steroid use. It requires a student and his or her parents to agree in writing that the athlete will not use steroids without a physician's prescription and that coaches complete a certification program having a significant component regarding steroids and performance-enhancing dietary supplements. It also prohibits school-related personnel and groups from selling, distributing, or advocating the use of muscle-building dietary supplements.

Professional team sport athletes such as Major League Baseball, National Basketball Association, National Football League, and National Hockey League players generally have chosen to unionize, and drug-testing programs are a mandatory subject of collective bargaining. Thus, unlike the USOC, NCAA, and the governing bodies for nonunionized professional sports, MLB and the NBA, NFL, and NHL cannot unilaterally impose drug-testing programs on their players. The NFL and NBA have had collectively bargained mandatory drug-testing programs for several years.

As part of the Bay Area Laboratory Co-Operative (BALCO) grand jury investigation into the illegal sale and distribution of THC, several prominent baseball players were called to testify in December, 2003, regarding whether they used anabolic steroids to enhance their athletic performance, to the wake of this scandal, Pres. Bush, in his 2004 State of the Union Address, urged professional sports leagues to adopt voluntarily more stringent drug policies that effectively will eliminate steroid use and set a better example for America's youth. In January, 2005, Major League Baseball and its players union established their first testing program for performance-enhancing drugs.

Current penalties for a first drug testing violation are unpaid suspensions of 10 days for MLB players, four games for NFL players, and 10 games for NBA players. Meanwhile, the NHL's new policy, negotiated through collective bargaining after last year's lockout (non)season, has yet to be made public.

To protect public health and safety, the Federal government recently has taken steps to restrict access to performance-enhancing drugs and prevent their usage by athletes (particularly youthful ones). Anabolic steroids have been federally regulated since 1990. However, many athletes used steroid precursors, which were sold as legal over-the-counter dietary supplements under the Dietary Supplement Health and Education Act of 1994. Except for dehydroepiandrosterone (DHEA), steroid precursors now are regulated by the Anabolic Steroid Control Act of 2004, which became effective Jan. 20, 2005. As reflected by the BALCO grand jury proceeding, the Federal government also is actively prosecuting those who illegally provide performance-enhancing drugs to athletes.

In addition to these measures, there have been several 2005 Congressional committee hearings regarding professional athletes' use of steroids and proposed Federal laws to reduce their demand for these substances. These bills would establish a uniform random drug testing policy for professional athletes, with substantial fines imposed on sports organizations for failing to implement and comply with this policy.

The Clean Sports Act of 2005—which by no means is guaranteed to become law—is intended "to protect the integrity of professional sports and the health and safety of athletes generally," with the objectives of eliminating performance-enhancing substances. This proposed legislation would apply only to the NFL, NBA, NHL, MLB, Major League Soccer, Arena Football, and the United States Boxing Commission, which must develop drug-testing policies and procedures as stringent as those of USADA. However, the proposed bill provides the sense of Congress that all professional sports leagues should comply with these standards. Each athlete would be tested five times annually. There would be a mandatory two-year suspension for a first offense and a lifetime ban for a second offense, with the possibility of a reduced penalty for unknown or unsuspected usage of a banned substance.

The Director of the Office of National Drug Control Policy would be empowered to include other professional sports leagues or NCAA colleges and athletes within the Act's coverage based on a determination that doing so would prevent the use of performance-enhancing substances by high school, college, or professional athletes. Noncompliance with the Act's substantive provisions would constitute unfair or deceptive acts or practices in violation of the Federal Trade Commission Act with a potential civil penalty of $1,000,000 per violation.

A $5,000,000 Fine

The Secretary of Commerce would be directed to promulgate regulations requiring testing for steroids and other performance-enhancing substances and may fine a professional sports league $5,000,000 for failing to adopt testing policies and procedures consistent with the regulations.

With some variations, similar bills titled the Professional Sports Integrity and Accountability Act and the Professional Sports Integrity Act of 2005 have been introduced in the Senate and House, respectively. Do not be surprised if more legislative proposals are on the way.

Congress clearly has jurisdiction to establish a drug-testing program for professional leagues based on its authority to regulate interstate commerce, and there are other potential bases for enacting such legislation. Nevertheless, professional athletes and their unions may assert that federally mandated drug testing violates their rights under the Constitution. Targeted drug testing of professional athletes, but not other private employees, is inconsistent treatment. However, the Federal equal protection clause requires only a rational basis to justify treating professional athletes differently, which is satisfied by their prominence in American society and imitation by youngsters.

A more interesting issue is whether mandatory drug testing of adult professional athletes without an individualized suspicion of illegal drug usage constitutes an unreasonable "search" in violation of the Fourth Amendment. In recent years, the Supreme Court has upheld mandatory random drug testing of high school athletes for recreational drugs by public educational institutions to protect their health and safety. Other courts have rejected college athletes' legal challenges to mandatory random drug testing for performance-enhancing and recreational drugs as a condition of participation in intercollegiate athletics. This judicial precedent, which holds that random drug testing is an appropriate means of maintaining the integrity of amateur athletic competition and protecting athletes' health, also may be applied to professional sports.

Although Congress may have valid regulatory authority, this proposed Federal legislation inappropriately would interfere with the internal governance of professional sports, which historically have not been subject to direct government regulation. Athletic governing bodies are in the best position to establish appropriate drug-testing programs in order to regulate the permissible bounds of competition and to protect athletes' health and safety. The primary harm that results from athletes' usage of banned performance-enhancing substances is to the sport's integrity. Thus, the sport's governing body should have the exclusive authority to establish sanctions that effectively reduce athletes' incentives to engage in doping. Market considerations, combined with political pressure, should provide a strong economic incentive for a professional sports league and its players union to establish an effective drug-testing program. For example, MLB recently adopted its first testing program for performance-enhancing substances in response to these factors. Its program appears to be reducing steroid usage by its players, although Baseball Commissioner Bud Selig has called for more severe penalties than befell the Baltimore Orioles' Rafael Palmiero, a first-time offender who tested positive for steroids after testifying under oath at a Congressional hearing in March that he does not used banned or illegal substances.

Rather than imposing an external drug-testing program on sports organizations, the Federal government should focus on preventing access to performance-enhancing drugs that pose health risks and prosecuting persons who distribute these substances illegally. The government potentially could fine and imprison athletes for violating controlled substances laws by knowingly using illegal performance-enhancing substances, which would penalize them for the indirect harm caused to American youths who view professional athletes as role models and emulate their conduct. (However, the International Olympic Committee is opposed to using criminal law to punish sports doping.) Both the Federal government and sports governing bodies have important roles to play in eradicating the use of banned performance-enhancing substances by athletes. However, their respective roles should be complementary rather than overlapping.

MATTHEW J. MITTEN is professor of law and director, National Sports Law Institute, Marquette University Law School, Milwaukee, Wisc., and chair of the National Collegiate Athletic Association's Competitive Safeguards and Medical Aspects of Sports Committee, which oversees the NCAA's drug education and testing program for student-athletes.

Medical Marijuana, Compassionate Use, and Public Policy

Expert Opinion or Vox Populi?

PETER J. COHEN

A recent article in the *Hastings Center Report* reviewed the Supreme Court's current (but undoubtedly not final) delineation of the boundaries of federal power as set forth by the Constitution's commerce clause.[1] The question before the Court was straightforward: Did federal authority asserted under the Controlled Substance Act of 1970 (CSA) trump California's legalization of "medical marijuana" when these plants were grown within the state and were not bought, sold, or transported into another state?[2] By a six to three vote, the *Raich* court held that the federal Drug Enforcement Administration could enforce the CSA against two individuals who were growing marijuana for their own medical use in full compliance with California's Compassionate Use Act (Proposition 215). At the same time, the Court's holding neither struck down Proposition 215 nor demanded that California bring criminal charges against its citizens who were using marijuana on the advice of their physicians.

Unfortunately, the far more significant policy question raised by Proposition 215 was never adjudicated. In effect, Proposition 215 declared that some compounds used to treat disease could be evaluated and approved by a vote of the people rather than "by experts qualified by scientific training and experience," as mandated by the Food, Drug, and Cosmetic Act.[3] But Proposition 215 was wrong as a matter of public policy. Anecdotes, Internet blogs, and advertisements do not provide a sound basis for assessing the safety and efficacy of pharmacologic agents.[4] "Medical marijuana" should be subjected to the same scientific scrutiny as any drug proposed for use in medical therapy, rather than made legal for medical use by popular will.

In *Raich* and other cases[5] involving Proposition 215, marijuana's advocates presented this compound to the courts as a drug, a pharmaceutical agent efficacious in the treatment of serious and even life-threatening illnesses:

Indeed, for Raich, 39, a mother of two teenagers who says she has been suffering from a litany of disabling ailments since she was a teenager herself, medical cannabis has worked where scores of other prescribed drugs have failed. . . . It relieves pain, she said, from progressive scoliosis, endometriosis and tumors in her uterus. Raich even believes it has something to do with arresting the growth of an inoperable brain tumor.

She is convinced that her use of medical marijuana, which began in 1997 after she had been using a wheelchair for two years, made her strong enough to stand up and learn to walk again. She said doctors could find no other explanation.[6]

These extravagant claims notwithstanding, marijuana has been used as a therapeutic agent throughout history, as Mathew W. Grey noted in a 1996 review of the use of medical marijuana:

Cannabis, more commonly referred to as marijuana, has a long history of medical use in this country and worldwide. Accounts dating back as far as 2700 B.C. describe the Chinese using marijuana for maladies ranging from rheumatism to constipation. There are similar reports of Indians, Africans, ancient Greeks and medieval Europeans using the substance to treat fevers, dysentery and malaria. In the United States, physicians documented the therapeutic properties of the drug as early as 1840, and the drug was included in the United States Pharmacopoeia, the official list of recognized medical drugs, from 1850 through 1942. During this period, lack of appetite was one of the indications for marijuana prescription.[7]

Such anecdotal reports have been used by marijuana's adherents to support their wish to exempt the drug from the same scrutiny required for any other compound that is used to treat, ameliorate, or prevent human disease. Specifically, they have never campaigned vigorously for medical marijuana's evaluation by the Food and Drug Administration. Had those who favored the use of smoked marijuana as a drug elected not to circumvent the Food, Drug, and Cosmetic Act, and had smoked marijuana successfully traversed the same FDA regulatory process required for any drug proposed for use in medical treatment, it would have attained the status of an approved pharmaceutical. It could then have been purchased legally and used for medical purposes when prescribed by a properly licensed physician.

Why should FDA approval have been sought? Why should "medical marijuana" have been classified as a drug rather than a botanical, an herbal medication, or a folk remedy? The answer is in the Food, Drug, and Cosmetic Act itself: "The term 'drug' means articles intended for use in the diagnosis, cure, mitigation, treatment, or prevention of disease in man . . . and articles (other than food) intended to affect the structure or any function of the body of man."[8] That smoked marijuana is both a "controlled substance" and a plant product is extraneous to this discussion. Controlled substances have widespread use in legitimate medical practice. As an anesthesiologist, I have legally administered more narcotics (in the course of providing medical care) than many low-level illegal drug dealers. Plants and their derivatives can be potent medications. During my internship, I used digitalis leaf (derived from the foxglove plant) to treat congestive heart failure. Botanicals are the active ingredients in tincture of opium[9] and belladonna suppositories,[10] both of which are legal and FDA approved when employed for legitimate therapeutic use. Smoked marijuana could achieve the same status were the FDA to find it safe and effective for medical use.

A Consensus Conference convened by the National Institutes of Health on February 19–20, 1997, to discuss the role of legitimate scientific research in evaluating the safety and efficacy of smoked marijuana reiterated the need for accurate and nonbiased scientific investigation of medical marijuana. The final report from the conference acknowledged that the FDA has approved a drug known as Marinol, which contains tetrahydrocannabinol (THC, the active psychotropic ingredient of *Cannabis sativa*, and a controlled substance), for oral use in treating both loss of appetite due to the AIDS-wasting syndrome and chemotherapy-induced nausea and vomiting, but then offered a caution:

> [This] does not fully satisfy the need to evaluate the potential medical utility of marijuana. The Expert Group noted that, although [THC] is the principal psychoactive component of the cannabis leaf, there may be other compounds in the leaf that have useful therapeutic properties. Furthermore, the bioavailability and pharmacokinetics of THC from smoked marijuana are substantially different than those of the oral dosage form.[11]

The Consensus Conference also observed that other pharmacologic agents had already been approved to treat many of the disorders for which marijuana's claims had not been scientifically substantiated. Yet, the report stated, "this does not mean, however, that the issue should be foreclosed. It simply means that in order to evaluate various hypotheses concerning the potential utility of marijuana in various therapeutic areas, more and better studies would be needed."[12]

Finally, the consultants felt that the evidence to date showed medical marijuana might have a significant role in the areas of appetite stimulation and cachexia (bodily wasting in the late stages of cancer), nausea and vomiting following anticancer therapy, neurological and movement disorders, analgesia,

and glaucoma. At the same time, they made it clear that these possibilities would never reach fruition in the absence of scientific data:

> Until studies are done using scientifically acceptable clinical trial design and subjected to appropriate statistical analysis, the questions concerning the therapeutic utility of marijuana will likely remain much as they have to date—largely unanswered. To the extent that the NIH can facilitate the development of a scientifically rigorous and relevant database, the NIH should do so.[13]

The Food, Drug, and Cosmetic Act requires that drugs may not be advertised and sold in the absence of "evidence consisting of adequate and well controlled investigations, including clinical investigations, by experts qualified by scientific training and experience to evaluate the effectiveness of the drug involved."[14] However, the road to approval is not easy, and many investigators attempting to carry out scientific studies of marijuana have encountered political obstacles. Consider, for example, the difficulties faced by Donald Abrams, Professor of Medicine at the University of California, San Francisco, and chair of the Bay Area's Community Consortium on HIV research, in his attempts to study the effects of smoked marijuana on AIDS wasting. Abrams, a clinical pharmacologist, had proposed a study to provide objective data on whether smoked marijuana could ease the symptoms of AIDS wasting and produce gains in body weight. His university's institutional review board had approved the study, the FDA had approved it, and the university planned to fund it. Nonetheless, his request to import marijuana from the Netherlands was rejected.

Since the National Institute on Drug Abuse (NIDA) grows marijuana that is supplied to appropriate scientific investigators, the professor requested their assistance. However, because his funding had originated at his university, and not the NIH, of which NIDA is a part, he was denied access to the product. The NIH stated that its policy was to make marijuana available only to investigators who had received a peer-reviewed NIH grant to conduct the proposed study.

> In May of 1996, Dr. Abrams resubmitted his study proposal to the National Institute of Health, believing that he had addressed NIDA's concerns. At that time, the study was still approved and funded at the university level. In October 1996, four years after he had initiated requests to obtain marijuana legally, he was again informed that NIH's Mississippi marijuana "farm" would not supply the needed cannabis. . . . The following month, the people of California voters passed Proposition 215 by a wide margin.[15]

Political barriers to the performance of scientifically valid studies of medical marijuana do not obviate the argument that marijuana should be assessed in the same way as other drugs proposed for therapy. The sick still need medically sound treatments. In the case of Angel Raich, unfortunately, scientific evidence of this drug's efficacy in curing her inoperable brain tumor is simply nonexistent.

> **Had *Cannabis sativa* not been prescribed by the Controlled Substances Act, every "medical marijuana" case would have been moot. As long as smoked marijuana was not advertised as an FDA-approved pharmaceutical, it would have become one of this century's premier herbal medications.**

Decades ago, the Supreme Court gave an ample argument for protecting people from the vain hope of unproven therapy:

> Since the turn of the century, resourceful entrepreneurs have advertised a wide variety of purportedly simple and painless cures for cancer, including liniments of turpentine, mustard, oil, eggs, and ammonia; peat moss; arrangements of colored floodlamps; pastes made from glycerine and limburger cheese. . . . In citing these examples, we do not, of course, intend to deprecate the sincerity of Laetrile's current proponents, or to imply any opinion on whether that drug may ultimately prove safe and effective for cancer treatment. But this historical experience does suggest why Congress could reasonably have determined to protect the terminally ill, no less than other patients, from the vast range of self-styled panaceas that inventive minds can devise.[16]

Smoked marijuana ought not to be allowed to take the easy path to drug approval. Marinol, containing pure THC, has already been approved in the United States. Sativex, another formulation of THC, has been approved in Canada and is under consideration in the United States. Smoked marijuana might also be approved and legally prescribed for appropriate therapeutic uses.

I cannot resist a final thought. Had *Cannabis sativa* not been prescribed by the Controlled Substances Act (and been taxed and regulated, as are alcohol and tobacco, two substances that cause far more "societal pathology"), every "medical marijuana" case would have been moot. And under this scenario, as long as smoked marijuana was not advertised as an FDA-approved pharmaceutical (which would hardly have been necessary), it would undoubtedly have become one of this century's premier herbal medications.

References

1. C.E. Schneider, "A Government of Limited Powers," *Hastings Center Report* 35, no. 4 (2005): 11–12.
2. *Ashcroft v. Raich*, 124 S. Ct. 2909 (2004). "Medical marijuana" refers to any form of *Cannabis sativa* used to treat a wide variety of pathologic states and diseases. Its adherents claim (with pharmacologic justification) that smoking allows easy titration and rapid onset of its pharmacologic effects.
3. Section 505(d) of the Federal Food, Drug, and Cosmetic Act, United States Code, Title 21, as amended, sec. 321 et. seq. (2000).
4. See P.J. Cohen, "Science, Politics, and the Regulation of Dietary Supplements: It's Time to Repeal DSHEA," *American Journal of Law & Medicine* 31, nos. 2 and 3 (2005): 175–214.
5. See *United States v. Oakland Cannabis Buyers' Cooperative*, 121 S. Ct. 1711 (2001).
6. E. Nieves, "User of Medical Marijuana Says She'll Continue to Fight," *The Washington Post*, June 7, 2005.
7. M.W. Grey, "Medical Use of Marijuana: Legal and Ethical Conflicts in the Patient/Physician Relationship," *University of Richmond Law Review* 30, no. 1 (1996): 249–74.
8. Food, Drug, and Cosmetic Act, United States Code, Title 21, as amended, sec. 201(g)(1)(B) and (C).
9. J.H. Jaffe and W.R. Martin, "Opioid Analgesics and Antagonists," in *The Pharmacological Basis of Therapeutics*, ed. A.G. Gilman, L.S. Goodman, and A. Gilman (New York: Macmillan, 1980), 494–534: Paregoric, U.S.P. (camphorated opium tincture) is a hydroalcoholic preparation in which there is also benzoic acid, camphor, and anise oil. The usual adult dose is 5 to 10 ml, which corresponds to 2 to 4 mg of morphine.
10. *Physicians' Desk Reference* (Montvale, N.J.: Thompson PDR, 2005), 2816.
11. National Institutes of Health, "Workshop on the Medical Utility of Marijuana," February 19–20, 1997, Executive Summary; available at http://www.nih.gov/news/medmarijuana/MedicalMarijuana.htm, p. 2.
12. Ibid., 4.
13. Ibid., 4.
14. Section 505(d) of the Federal Food, Drug, and Cosmetic Act.
15. P.J. Cohen, "The Politics of Marijuana," in *Drugs, Addiction, and the Law: Policy, Politics, and Public Health* (Durham, N.C.: Carolina Academic Press, 2004), 290–92.
16. *United States v. Rutherford*, 442 U.S. 544, 558 (1979).

PETER J. COHEN, "Medical Marijuana, Compassionate Use, and Public Policy: *Expert Opinion or* Vox Populi?" *Hastings Center Report* 36, no. 3 (2006): 19–22.

Acknowledgment—I wish to acknowledge Cynthia B. Cohen, senior research fellow at the Kennedy Institute of Ethics, Georgetown University, for her help, encouragement, and insightful comments and suggestions.

Researchers Explore New Visions for Hallucinogens

After a long hiatus, medical investigators return to studying the benefits of once-banned compounds.

Susan Brown

Recently, 36 people who had never taken hallucinogens before gave them a try. The pill they took launched a daylong psychedelic journey, sometimes fantastic, sometimes frightening. When it was over, a few who took the drug said it was the most meaningful experience of their lives, as momentous as the birth of a first child or the death of a parent. Others wished never to repeat it.

The drug they took was psilocybin, the hallucinogenic molecule found in "magic" mushrooms.

Their tales do not come from an all-night desert trance or a radical festival like Burning Man but from Baltimore, where they participated in an experiment at the Johns Hopkins University Bayview Medical Center.

The study, which began in 2001, explored the drug's ability to induce a mystical state. Published in the journal *Psychopharmacology* this summer, it was the first federally approved research on psilocybin in humans to be reported in four decades and leads a vanguard of studies that mark a quiet revival of research on psychedelic drugs.

When scientists in the United States and Europe first learned of the mushrooms' strange effects in the 1950s, along with those of related hallucinogens like LSD, research on the topic exploded. More than a hundred published reports cataloged the effects of the drugs, some rigorously, others not so.

Most notorious of the researchers was Timothy Leary, a psychologist at Harvard University who abandoned standard research conventions from the start and relied instead on testimonials, encouraging his subjects to record their experiences in whatever way they felt appropriate. He also took the drug along with his student subjects and conducted his "research" in his home, where participants listened to music and looked at art. Harvard took a dim view of this and, in 1963, declined to renew his contract.

By then, hallucinogens had escaped from the laboratory, and Mr. Leary and others began promoting their use as paths toward spiritual enlightenment. Legislators swiftly made the drugs illegal following alarming reports of bad trips and people arriving at emergency rooms convinced they had gone mad. Public opinion turned against the work, making psychedelic research a bad career move for scientists and a public-relations minefield for research institutions.

> **To eliminate hallucinogens "as research tools just doesn't make any sense to me from a scientific point of view, from understanding the nature of consciousness. . . ."**

"It was a crazy period where these compounds were irresponsibly promoted for recreational use, and their use was widespread," says Roland R. Griffiths, a psychiatrist who led the study at Hopkins. "We got into what appears to me to be a little bit of cultural hysteria about their risks. They were swept out of the research domain."

Dr. Griffiths agrees that the compounds should have been made illegal. "That was a wise and prudent thing to do, given what happened," he says. "But to eliminate them as research tools just doesn't make any sense to me from a scientific point of view, from understanding the nature of consciousness and cognitive and perceptual experience."

Now the inquiry is quietly resuming. Federal agencies have granted a handful of investigators the licenses they need to do the work. And ethics-review boards at universities are approving the studies, after careful (and sometimes lengthy) consideration. Four studies of psilocybin in humans are either in progress or have recently been completed.

The researchers want to learn how to safely induce transcendent states that could help patients make positive changes in their lives or, with lower doses, end intractable pain or halt intrusive thoughts. Advocates hope this is the beginning of a new era of carefully considered exploration of the possible benefits of psychedelic drugs.

Wall Street to Haight Ashbury

Nearly 50 years ago, a Wall Street banker and fungi enthusiast named R. Gordon Wasson first brought hallucinogenic mushrooms to widespread attention in the United States and Europe.

When he heard that traditional Mexican healers used mushrooms to summon their visions, he traveled to Oaxaca to try them himself and emerged from the experience awestruck. "I was seeing the archetypes, the Platonic ideas, that underlie the imperfect images of everyday life," Mr. Wasson later wrote. His article, published in *Life* in May 1957, gave the fungi their popular name: magic mushrooms.

Within a year, a Swiss chemist had isolated the active chemicals in the mushrooms by sampling the extracts himself to determine which altered his perceptions. He named the compounds psilocybin and psilocin, and his employer, Sandoz Pharmaceuticals, quickly patented the drugs.

In contrast to Mr. Wasson's vigil in a cave guided by a traditional healer, Mr. Leary's first experience with mushrooms was poolside at a Cuernavaca resort. He too was enchanted. Upon returning to Massachusetts, Mr. Leary joined a growing number of researchers who, intrigued by anecdotal accounts of the effects caused by the curious chemicals, began to study their mind-altering properties.

Some thought psychedelic drugs might help the troubled by making them more responsive to psychotherapy. Others hoped a spiritual experience might help alcoholics abstain from drink or convicts renounce crime. Still others thought psychedelics might open a window into the human mind, providing a telling glimpse of how our brains assemble the experience we call consciousness, or explaining how that shatters in mental illnesses like schizophrenia.

In one famous experiment, Walter Pahnke, a physician and minister working on a Ph.D. with Mr. Leary, assembled 20 theology graduate students in the basement of Marsh Chapel at Boston University for a worship service on Good Friday in 1962. The idea was simple: Would psilocybin enhance their spiritual experience, even induce a mystical state? Half were given psilocybin and half nothing at all.

The result was chaos. One participant had a psychotic reaction and needed to be restrained, and those who were disappointed not to receive the drug became bored and disruptive. Still, those who received psilocybin were reportedly transformed by the experience.

> ## "Their outcomes were best with people who had what they described as a mystical experience, or a full-on, spiritual, transpersonal epiphany."

But the promise of mind-opening experience also led to widespread misuse, and the researchers' hopes were dashed in 1970 when Congress outlawed hallucinogenic drugs. Federal money and support for the work vanished and commercial supplies were recalled, making further research, even responsible studies, nearly impossible.

As memories of the excesses of that time have faded, a more tolerant public climate has emerged. In 1989 the Food and Drug Administration reorganized its division in charge of drug testing, and the officials in charge of psychedelics signaled they would approve well-designed studies that met established criteria for good clinical research. That shift made it possible for researchers to once again consider studying hallucinogenic compounds.

Among the first to venture forward was Dr. Griffiths of Hopkins. He wanted to see if psilocybin could induce a mystical experience, like those reported by some participants in Dr. Pahnke's Good Friday experiment, but in a safe environment, with careful experimental controls. It took him two years to get the approval of the FDA, a license from the Drug Enforcement Administration, and the permission of the university committee that oversees human research.

The committee at Johns Hopkins reviewed Dr. Griffiths's proposal with unusual caution. "The concern that went into the approval process was unlike anything I've ever experienced in my 30-plus years of doing human research," he says.

The review board wondered if people given psilocybin during the study might go on to abuse the drug. But people have been taking psilocybin for decades, and that history has shown that it is not addictive. Reviewers also worried that a vulnerable subject could be tipped into psychosis by taking psilocybin. Dr. Griffiths and his colleagues ruled out potential participants who had previous mental troubles or even a family member with psychiatric illness.

That screening left them with 36 adult participants who had never used hallucinogens before. All the participants followed some sort of spiritual practice, whether it was participation in organized worship or individual meditation. Curiosity led them to join the experiment: They wished to try psilocybin in a context of self-reflection.

Transcendence and Fear

Each subject took the drug in one of two sessions. During the other, they were given methylphenidate, commonly known as Ritalin, which changed their physiology—their heart rate, for example—in a way similar to psilocybin but possessed no hallucinogenic properties.

Participants spent each daylong session in a room furnished with an Oriental carpet, pictures, and a sofa on which they were encouraged to lie down. Their monitors gave them eye masks and earphones with a playlist of classical music and encouraged them to focus inward. At the end of each session, after the drug wore off, they answered questionnaires designed to assess their spiritual and perceptual experiences.

After taking psilocybin, participants reported intense emotions—grief, joy, anxiety—and feelings of transcendence, a reprieve from the normal constraints of space and time. Colors brightened, and some people reported a confusion of senses called synesthesia—musical tones that take on hues, for example. In contrast, the methylphenidate improved self-control and concentration.

But nearly a third of the participants felt fearful after taking psilocybin, and four of the 36 spent their entire session in unpleasant psychological struggles. Two compared the experience to being in a war, and three said they would never wish to repeat the experience, the research team reports.

"It really underscores the risks of using these kinds of compounds in a nonsupervised, nonresearch setting," Dr. Griffiths says. "It's really not difficult at all to imagine that under uncontrolled conditions these kinds of things could escalate into panic and engaging in risk-taking behaviors."

Yet two months later, none of the subjects, not even those who reported an unpleasant encounter with the drug, said that the experience had decreased their sense of well-being or satisfaction with life.

Rachel Yehuda, a psychologist who specializes in post-traumatic stress at Mount Sinai School of Medicine and the Bronx Veterans Affairs Medical Center and who was not involved in the study, says she is not concerned by the anxiety experienced by some of the participants in the experiment. "What people don't realize about trauma is that it often ends up being a meaningful experience," she says. "It's a watershed event."

Other researchers hope Dr. Griffiths's article will stand as a benchmark for a new era of psychedelic research. "It sailed through the review process because it was a well-done study by a very recognized researcher," says Harriet de Wit, a behavioral pharmacologist at the University of Chicago who, as a principal editor of *Psychopharmacology*, shepherded the paper through review.

Dr. Griffiths hopes his work with healthy, well-functioning adults might eventually help those who struggle with addiction. The most effective interventions in use now are 12-step programs. But they rely heavily on a belief in a "higher power," and people who lack faith have trouble embracing them.

"It's possible that if you could occasion a single primary transcendent experience of the type that was seen in our study," he says, "that that single experience alone would allow somebody subsequently to engage in a 12-step process with renewed interest, vigor, and excitement in a way that they couldn't otherwise."

Charles S. Grob, a psychiatrist at Harbor-UCLA Medical Center, agrees that this line of inquiry is worth pursuing again. Some of the most impressive work in the 1960s was done with alcoholics, he says. More support comes from Dr. Grob's own work 10 years ago with a native church in Brazil. He found that former alcoholics who drank a hallucinogenic herbal brew twice a month as part of a religious ceremony stayed sober.

Dr. Grob is in the midst of a study that asks whether psilocybin might ease the anxiety of people who are dying. In an experiment similar in design to Dr. Griffiths's, he is giving the drug to patients with end-stage cancer. So far, seven patients have received psilocybin, and Dr. Grob has approval to treat five more.

The Harbor-UCLA study follows up on research done by Stanislav Grof and Dr. Pahnke, who worked at the Maryland Psychiatric Research Center, in Baltimore, in the late 1960s, the very end of the psychedelic era. They gave the more powerful hallucinogen LSD to patients with terminal cancer. About two-thirds of their subjects got by with less pain medication as a result. They feared death less or not at all, and their anxiety abated, which is known to help ease pain.

"Their outcomes were best with people who had what they described as a mystical experience, or a full-on, spiritual, transpersonal epiphany," Dr. Grob says.

Because the review board at his institution required a lower dose of psilocybin than he had wanted to use, about half of that used in the Hopkins experiment, his patients' experiences are not as intense. "We're hoping to get approval, when we're done with this group, for a higher dose," says Dr. Grob.

A Target in the Brain

Advances in neuroscience over the past four decades have helped pave the path toward acceptance of this revived line of research. "At one time, when people were just exploring consciousness, it was hard to justify," says John H. Krystal, a psychiatrist at Yale University School of Medicine who was an editor of *Psychopharmacology* when Dr. Griffiths's paper was submitted.

But once researchers had worked out the molecular basis of the drugs, he says, "then a whole new opportunity to study important aspects of the neurobiology of consciousness opened up."

David E. Nichols, a medicinal chemist at Purdue University who synthesized the psilocybin used in two of the recent studies, agrees. "We know quite a bit more about the brain now than we did then, and human experimental methods are certainly much better," he wrote in a commentary that appeared in the same issue of *Psychopharmacology* as Dr. Griffiths's paper.

Psilocybin closely resembles serotonin, a neural signaling molecule or neurotransmitter. Calm, happy states coincide with the release of serotonin in the brain. Psilocybin fits serotonin receptors that are especially abundant in a kind of cell in the cerebral cortex that gathers and sorts signals coming in from other parts of the brain.

Psilocybin's effect is to make these "computational" cells more likely to register an incoming signal, Mr. Nichols explains, "potentially amplifying processes that are normally running, but which are not generally apparent in everyday awareness."

Psilocybin could have medical uses if the way it latches onto brain cells remedies an imbalance or malfunction in the serotonin system. In fact, a few patients have found relief from their maladies in magic mushrooms, and those reports of self-medication have led to two recent clinical reports.

The first was spurred by an online discussion group on cluster headaches. The pain from such headaches repeats in regularly timed bouts that typically continue for two to four months, and it strikes quickly, without warning, and rapidly becomes excruciating. Some of the people posting on the site reported relief from LSD or magic mushrooms.

That those drugs would help is not particularly surprising: LSD was initially created as a potential treatment for migraine, and psilocybin is chemically related to sumatriptan, the most commonly prescribed drug for heading off cluster headaches.

One member of the group, a 34-year-old man, had suffered cluster headaches since he was 16, except for a period of two years in early adulthood when he was experimenting with LSD. Later he found he could prevent his attacks altogether if he drank mushroom tea every three months. When that patient contacted a group of psychiatrists at Harvard University's McLean Hospital, R. Andrew Sewell, then a postdoctoral fellow, and John H. Halpern, an assistant professor of psychiatry, decided to follow up.

The team found 53 people who had been treating their headaches with psilocybin or LSD and were willing to release their medical records. When they questioned their subjects by telephone or e-mail about their drug use, they found that for many, the drugs could end the paroxysms of pain in the midst of a headache and extend the pain-free period between attacks, something no other treatment could do.

"Research on the effects of psilocybin and LSD on cluster headache may be warranted," the researchers conclude in their case reports, which were published in the journal *Neurology* this summer.

No serious opposition to this new work has yet emerged. *The Chronicle* contacted more than a dozen psychiatrists and psychologists—including specialists on anxiety and post-traumatic stress—and none expressed concern about this round of research, in part because the experimenters closely supervised each subject.

Mindful of the past, though, all of the scientists said they did not advocate illegal or indiscriminate use of mushrooms or other hallucinogens. And most said further work should be pursued if the initial results of carefully designed studies showed promise, particularly if they helped patients for whom standard treatments failed.

Quieting Intrusive Thoughts

That is exactly the kind of patient that Francisco A. Moreno hoped to help. Last month Dr. Moreno, a psychiatrist at the University of Arizona, reported success in treating particularly difficult cases of obsessive-compulsive disorder with psilocybin.

Dr. Moreno was inspired to try the drug when a patient reported that the only time his symptoms had ever abated was when he was using magic mushrooms as a young adult. Prozac and similar drugs, which extend the working period of serotonin, sometimes help people with OCD. Others find no relief. Dr. Moreno thought psilocybin might help patients for whom approved drugs and psychotherapy had failed. He gave the drug to nine patients with OCD.

The patients he treats are seriously impaired. They have intrusive thoughts of harming themselves or others, he says, such as "the urge to pinch or bite little babies." But they are not suicidal or homicidal. "They are horrified by their thoughts," he says.

In this small and preliminary study, psilocybin ended the obsessive thoughts and compulsive actions—such as hand washing—of some patients completely, and for the first time in their adult lives, for at least the brief follow-up period of 24 hours. The symptoms of all nine subjects markedly improved.

That the drug worked so soon was surprising: Other medications can take weeks to kick in. "Nothing works as quickly and as drastically as these hallucinogens do," Dr. Moreno says.

Despite his promising results, Dr. Moreno is not an advocate for the drug. He published his report quietly in the *Journal of Clinical Psychiatry* last month. Neither the journal nor the university has alerted the media as they usually do when a promising new treatment is found.

Dr. Moreno hopes his work might lead to the discovery of a safer drug that treats OCD more effectively. He does plan,

A Trip Through Modem Research on Hallucinogens

1914: First scientific account of "mushroom intoxication" published in *Science.*

1938: LSD isolated from ergot fungus, synthesized by Albert Hofmann, a chemist at Sandoz Pharmaceutical.

1943: Hofmann takes the first dose of LSD.

1947: First scientific article on the mental effects of LSD published in the *Swiss Archives of Neurology.*

1953: Humphrey Osmond begins to treat alcoholics with LSD.

1954: Aldous Huxley publishes influential book, *The Doors of Perception,* based on his experimentation with mescaline.

1955: R. Gordon Wasson, a banker, tries his first mushroom, led by a Mexican traditional healer, Maria Sabina.

1957: Osmond coins the term "psychedelic."

1957: Wasson writes classic "trip lit" article, "Seeking the Magic Mushroom," for *Life.*

1958: Hofmann synthesizes psilocybin and psilocin, the active ingredients of hallucinogenic mushrooms.

1960: Timothy Leary establishes the Psychedelic Research Project at Harvard.

1963: Harvard declines to renew Leary's contract.

1966: LSD makes the March 25 cover of *Life* with an article titled "LSD: The Exploding Threat of the Mind Drug That Got Out of Control."

1966: Sandoz Pharmaceutical recalls LSD and withdraws sponsorship of research on LSD in April.

1966: Ken Kesey and the Merry Pranksters hold the "Acid Test Graduation" in San Francisco on Halloween.

1967: U.S. government bans LSD.

1970: Congress passes the Comprehensive Drug Abuse Prevention and Control Act. LSD, psilocybin, psilocin, mescaline, cannabis, and MDMA are classified as having no accepted medical use. Research on hallucinogens effectively ends.

1979: Hofmann publishes *LSD: My Problem Child.*

1986: Rick Doblin founds the Multidisciplinary Association for Psychedelic Studies, a nonprofit organization that helps scientists finance and obtain approval for research on psychedelics.

2006: Roland R. Griffiths, a psychiatrist at the Johns Hopkins U. Bayview Medical Center, and colleagues publish first double-blind, placebo-controlled study of psilocybin.

however, to continue his work with psilocybin, following his patients for longer periods next time, he says. "If this, if any drug, could help people with OCD, with mental illness," he says, "then we should explore it."

State's Evidence

WILL BAUDE

Yesterday the Supreme Court issued its long-awaited decision in *Gonzalez v. Raich*, upholding a federal ban on marijuana possession despite California's efforts to legalize medical marijuana. The plaintiffs, Angel Raich and Diane Monson, were two seriously ill women in California who used marijuana on the advice of their doctors, pursuant to a 1996 California law, the Compassionate Use Act. After officials decided that their conduct was legal under local law, they were targeted by federal agents for violating the nationwide Controlled Substances Act. Raich and Monson argued that the federal government had exceeded its constitutional authority under the Commerce Clause and therefore could not preempt California's medical marijuana law; but a majority of the Supreme Court ruled against them, while Justices O'Connor, Rehnquist, and Thomas dissented. The Court's decision exposes the major flaw in its recent Commerce Clause jurisprudence: an unwillingness to take states seriously and an unwillingness to admit that the constitutionality of a federal law sometimes depends on what laws states adopt.

Between 1937—when Roosevelt won Supreme Court support for the New Deal—and 1995, the Court was very reluctant to enforce general limits on congressional power. The recent line of Commerce Clause cases began in *United States v. Lopez,* when the conservative majority of the Court struck down a ban on handguns near schools because the ban threatened to obliterate "the distinction between what is truly national and what is truly local." In *United States v. Morrison* in 2000, the same five justices struck down the controversial Violence Against Women Act, which created a federal rape law, and held that once again Congress was exceeding its powers to reach areas traditionally governed by the states. Advocates of federalism and decentralization hoped that *Raich* would be the next case in that line. But yesterday six members of the Court voted to uphold the federal law.

All of the justices on the court agreed (or professed to agree) that Congress can only enact a law if it is "necessary and proper" to one of its other powers enumerated in the Constitution, like the power to "regulate commerce among the several states." They all also conceded that Congress can clearly regulate interstate marijuana trade. The argument in *Raich* therefore should have been over whether it really is "necessary and proper" for the federal government to preempt California's medical marijuana laws—in other words, is there some flaw in California's regulation that jeopardizes the federal prohibition of the

interstate drug trade? Whether the federal government has constitutional power to regulate herbs that are never bought, never sold, and never leave California, depends—has to depend—to some extent on what the regulatory scheme would look like without federal intervention. But the Court emphatically rejected this notion, suggesting that it "would turn the Supremacy Clause on its head" to let state laws have any effect on the scope of federal power; and the majority offered barely any analysis along these lines, writing instead that Congress was entitled to preempt California's scheme as a matter of "common sense."

As an empirical matter, it is far from common sense that California's laws would undermine the enforcement of drug laws elsewhere. The state regulatory scheme would have required all medical marijuana users to carry identification cards with security measures and the ability to be checked against a statewide database, required a doctor's approval to get marijuana, imposed sanctions on erroneous recommendations, and levied further criminal penalties on those who diverted their medical marijuana to the black market. This may explain why three strongly anti-marijuana states nonetheless wrote a brief to the Court arguing that the federal ban on intrastate medical marijuana was unnecessary and that "the States are ready, willing, and able to police and prosecute local drug crimes." There was no evidence or argument that California would enforce its regulations or restrictions in bad faith.

Indeed, the Court's invocation of the Supremacy Clause of the Constitution—which says that federal laws that are not unconstitutional are "the supreme law of the land"—is misleading. Nobody doubts that when a valid federal law and a valid state law conflict, the federal law prevails. But to determine whether the federal law is valid in the first place, state law is relevant. The federal law is valid only if it is necessary for the interstate drug laws to work, so one has to look at whether the interstate drug laws would work if California's scheme were in place. It is possible, of course, to imagine that having a haven to grow medical marijuana would make it much easier to smuggle marijuana into the interstate market. But given that California continues to police unlawful marijuana production (seizing *a record-setting* $2.5 billion worth of plants last year), and given the program's relatively modest scope, the state law should have been entitled to more than being summarily dismissed.

The Court is probably reluctant to give the presence of state laws any weight in its constitutional analysis at all because it is difficult to establish exactly when a state law has failed at keeping intrastate activity separate, and because different approaches in different states could make a lot more work for the Court and for Congress. It is far easier to leave Congress to be the judge of its own powers, an approach that is sometimes called "process federalism." But the Court's opinions shape that process, and help determine what concerns Congress must address when it wishes to regulate. As University of Texas law professor Ernest Young has pointed out, because the Controlled Substances Act was enacted years before California's medical marijuana initiative, Congress never passed judgment on California's regulation scheme one way or the other; only the lawyers in the Justice Department did. The Court could at least make sure that Congress preempts state regulations only when it actually examines them and decides they do not work. As it stands, the only democratic body to even make a judgment about California's regulations was California itself. The Court does not have to second-guess Congress in every case so long as it retains the possibility of meaningful judicial review.

This problem is not unique to the Court's decision in this case. Since 1995, the Court has struck down a few federal statutes that it saw as outliers but without serious investigation of whether the state had managed to create a class of activity with minimal interstate spillovers. This Congress-centered view has meant that the Court is unable to create a Commerce Clause jurisprudence that works—one that would spur a dialogue between state and federal governments.

To be sure, states sometimes fail to live up to their constitutional obligations, and sometimes lax enforcement or misguided regulation can cause one state's laws to jeopardize a federal regulatory scheme. But federal courts analyze constitutional and legal claims against state and local governments all the time, and by providing some meaningful review, they both give governments an incentive to behave well and help sustain the balance of power between local and national governments. When it is actually necessary for the federal government to take over local regulations to solve a national problem, nobody doubts that it can. But the fact that the federal government's power is supreme does not make it unlimited or unreviewable; and it should not mean that the states have no say in the matter either.

WILL BAUDE is a student at Yale Law School.

Durbin, Grassley Introduce Bipartisan Bill to Combat Meth

U.S. Senators Dick Durbin (D-IL) and Chuck Grassley (R-IA), both members of the Senate Anti-Meth Caucus, today introduced the Methamphetamine Production Prevention Act of 2007. This legislation will promote the use of electronic logbook systems by pharmacies to better track the sales of ingredients that could be used to make meth. Most of the chemicals necessary to produce methamphetamine are readily available in household products or over-the-counter cold or allergy medicines such as pseudoephedrine. Current law restricts the amount of these ingredients that can be purchased at one time by a single person. Some meth producers have been able to get around restrictions by "smurfing"—purchasing illegal amounts of meth precursor drugs by traveling to multiple pharmacies and buying small quantities at each.

"'Smurfing' now accounts for at least 90% of the pseudoephedrine used to make meth in Illinois," said Durbin. "Electronic logbook systems provide a more effective method of tracking the purchases of these drugs. With the proper resources, pharmacies can keep their logbook information electronically and share that information with law enforcement. The information can then be used to identify and prosecute meth manufacturers attempting to beat the system."

"The Midwest has been hit especially hard by meth and the ability to buy the ingredients over the counter," Grassley said. "Despite the positive impact the Combat Meth Act has had on lowering the production of home cooked meth, people are exploiting loopholes that allow one to smurf between different pharmacies. An electronic logbook will be a tremendous asset for local law enforcement and businesses as they work to end the devastating impact of meth on our communities."

Today's legislation revises the technical logbook requirements found in the Combat Methamphetamine Epidemic Act ("Combat Meth Act"). Enacted in 2006, the Combat Meth Act limits the amount of meth precursor drugs—drugs that can be used to make meth, such as pseudoephedrine—that a customer can buy and requires pharmacies to keep written or electronic logbooks recording each purchase of the drugs. This approach has led to a drop in the number of meth labs discovered in many states, however, meth producers are beginning to adapt to the current restrictions through the practice

of "smurfing". "For years, methamphetamine has been plaguing communities in Illinois and throughout the nation," said Durbin. "Law enforcement agencies are forced to devote a large percentage of their time to finding, busting and cleaning up meth labs—taking away precious resources that should be used for crime prevention. Law enforcement experts agree that electronic logbook systems are an important tool in our efforts to combat meth. We can, and should, do more to help make these logbook systems work."

Today's legislation

- Creates a federal grant program that would provide money to states to create or enhance electronic logbook systems;
- Assists law enforcement in combating the meth epidemic by improving the effectiveness of the electronic logbook systems;
- Awards federal grants on a priority basis to encourage states to design logbook systems that will be effective in stopping smurfing across state and county lines; and
- Preserves existing privacy safeguards that are currently found in federal and state law. This bill has been endorsed by numerous organizations, including the National Alliance of State Drug Enforcement Agencies, the National Narcotics Officers' Associations' Coalition, the National Criminal Justice Association, the National Sheriffs' Association, the Major County Sheriffs' Association, the National Troopers Coalition, the National District Attorneys Association, the National Association of Countries, and the Community Anti-Drug Coalitions of America.

On March 15, Durbin and Senator Norm Coleman (R-MN) introduced another meth-related bill, the Family-Based Meth Treatment Act of 2007 which seeks to improve comprehensive, family-based substance abuse treatment for methamphetamine addiction.

On April 25, Grassley and Senator Dianne Feinstein (D-CA) introduced legislation to increase federal penalties for drug dealers who entice children with candy flavored meth. Senator

Grassley was an original co-sponsor of the Drug Endangered Children Act of 2007 which was introduced in April. He was also an original cosponsor of the Combat Meth Act of 2005.

Here is a copy of Grassley's prepared statement for the record.

Mr. President, I am pleased to join my colleague, Senator Durbin, in introducing the Methamphetamine Production Prevention Act of 2007. Together we offer this important legislation in an effort to strengthen existing law by providing some necessary changes and updates.

During my time in the Senate, I've come to the floor many times to speak about methamphetamine (meth) and how it has destroyed individuals, families, and communities across the country. The Midwest was hit especially hard by meth and the impacts of this drug were devastating to rural areas. As opposed to other illegal drugs, meth is often times home cooked and made in rural areas using ingredients that are largely available over the counter. I am proud to say that Congress has taken action to attack this problem head on by working to cut off access to these over the counter products that form the basis of the drug.

Legislation such as the Combat Methamphetamine Act of 2005 (Combat Meth Act), which was included into the USA Patriot Act Reauthorization in 2005 immediately impacted the production of home cooked meth. Just a week ago when I joined with Senator Feinstein in introducing two other separate bills—the Saving Kids from Dangerous Drugs Act and the Drug Endangered Children Act—I noted that because of the efforts of Congress in passing the Combat Meth Act, the number of clandestine meth lab seizures has dropped across the country.

The Combat Meth Act was a tremendous step in the right direction limiting access to psuedoephedrine (PSE), the main ingredient in methamphetamine. The Combat Meth Act required this product to be removed from store shelves and placed behind the counter at pharmacies across the country. It also limited the number of products containing PSE a person could buy at once. Further, it required a logbook system be kept by pharmacies containing information regarding the individuals that purchased products containing PSE. Despite these successes, ever determined meth cooks and users have learned how to game this system and continue to produce home grown meth.

The preferred method of these meth cooks is to "smurf" between different pharmacies for PSE products. Smurfing, occurs when a person visits a number of different locations buying the legal maximum amount of PSE product at each site. The result is an amount of PSE sufficient to produce home cooked meth. Smurfing occurs because the Combat Meth Act only required that retailers keep a logbook which could be kept on paper or electronically. It did not require interoperability or electronic transmission of data. As a result, these unscrupulous individuals have learned that if they provide false information or visit multiple stores, tracking and arresting these individuals is more difficult and time consuming for law enforcement. This is especially true in metropolitan communities that share a common border, one such example is the Quad Cities on the Iowa/Illinois border.

Recently, the Quad City Times highlighted the successes of the Combat Meth Act in an article titled, The Next Step in Meth War. This article detailed the efforts of a Scott County Deputy and his dedication in fighting the meth war. One noteworthy portion of this article raised a question about the lengths that were required for this deputy to do his job in combating mom and pop meth labs. The article stated, "Now we're stuck with this image of a detective in each Iowa county sorting through thousands of paper forms." It read further, "He must call county to county to find out if those purchasing the limit in Scott County might be doing so elsewhere as well." This statement gets right to the heart of our bill. We can't effectively combat meth if we don't close the smurfing loophole.

To address this loophole, Senator Durbin and I have introduced the Methamphetamine Production Prevention Act of 2007. This legislation would revise the technical requirements of the Combat Meth Act to allow for electronic logbook systems. The bill would also create a federal grant program for states looking to create or enhance existing electronic logbook systems. Finally, this bill would prioritize these federal grants to states that design and implement the most effective systems for sharing information via an electronic logbook system.

This legislation will take a big step forward in closing this loophole that home grown meth cooks abuse. Additionally, it does so without creating burdensome mandates upon states to meet requirements. This bill facilitates innovation and growth by offering financial assistance to states looking to create an electronic logbook system. By avoiding mandates, this legislation seeks to promote innovation and growth of electronic logbook systems.

This bill has broad support from the law enforcement community and has been endorsed by the National Sheriffs' Association, the National Narcotics Officers' Associations' Coalition, National Alliance of State Drug Enforcement Agencies, the National Criminal Justice Association, the National Troopers Coalition, the National District Attorneys Association, the National Association of Counties, and the Community Anti-Drug Coalitions of America among others.

As you can see, this legislation has a broad base of support. Working together, state and local governments can use this legislation and grant program to create interoperable networks that will reduce the illegal smurfing of PSE products and lead us to the goal of ending domestic production of meth. I urge my colleagues join us in support of this important legislation and pass the Methamphetamine Production Prevention Act of 2007 and help wipe out domestic production of meth.

Capitol Hill Press Release, May 3, 2007.

How to Stand Up to Big Tobacco

Noreena Hertz

A satirical film, *Thank You for Smoking*, looking at the power of Big Tobacco, hits our cinema screens on 16 June. It's a sharp reminder of just how sinister tobacco companies are. Five hundred million people will die of smoking-related illnesses over the next 50 years, yet the tobacco lobby continues to do all it can to keep up its sales.

Despite the tobacco industry's zeal, however, its efforts in developed countries have been somewhat thwarted. In the developed world, smoking rates are on the decline, thanks in large part to the hike in tobacco taxes that has taken place–on average, in high-income countries, two-thirds of the price of a packet of cigarettes is now tax.

In low-income countries the story is very different. Tax rates on tobacco products are often as low as one-third: in a quarter of developing countries examined in a recent study, tobacco was actually becoming more affordable in 2000 than it was in 1990, owing to increased wages. The upshot is that by 2030, if nothing changes, 70 per cent of smoking-related deaths will stem from low- and middle-income countries.

Why are low- and middle-income countries so reluctant to raise taxes, given that it is a policy measure proven to save lives? The evidence is now clear that, for every 10 per cent increase in price, ten million lives would be saved. The spin of the tobacco lobby goes a long way in explaining this. "Increased taxes would mean less revenue" is the main line the lobbyists peddle. Their evidence is typically cobbled together from research published by economists and academics they have funded. Yet any economist worth her salt knows that when the demand for a product is as price-inelastic as it is for tobacco, increases in taxes will generate net gains in tax take, not losses.

Other objections to raising taxation favoured by the tobacco lobby are similarly false. Lobbyists claim that taxes "are the main cause of large-scale smuggling." But smuggling is a function of corruption. And anyway, smugglers don't seek out tax arbitrage opportunities: they try to avoid paying any taxes at all, a commercial benefit that has led some tobacco companies to support and participate in the illicit tobacco trade themselves.

As for the line that raising taxes is "inequitable" because the taxes hit the poor more, although it is true that smokers from lower-income groups are more likely to quit in response to price rises, that doesn't mean the policy is unfair. The poor spend disproportionate amounts of their income on tobacco. In Morocco, for example, poor households spend more on tobacco than on health and education combined. If this group of smokers stopped smoking, we would see a reduction in health and educational inequalities in that country.

Poor households in Morocco spend more on tobacco than on health and education combined.

But if the spin is so transparent, why aren't developing countries ignoring it and raising their taxes? Put yourself in the shoes of a cash-starved government faced with a big multinational company dangling billions of pounds'-worth of potential investment if only the terms of engagement are just "right." Wouldn't you, too, perhaps be swayed?

Which means that if hundreds of millions of lives are to be saved, governments in the developed world will have to help their developing-country counterparts to stand up better to Big Tobacco. This will involve helping them create alternative investment opportunities, doing something real to help them export their products and break the deadlock on trade, and also dangling their own carrot to developing countries—if you raise your tax on tobacco, we will increase your aid. A controversial one, that, as it implies an endorsement of the micromanagement of policies chosen be another state. But to hell with political correctness here. If additional resources could be raised, and especially if those additional resources would be earmarked for health, then everyone would be better off. Everyone except the tobacco companies, that is.

The earmarking of tobacco taxes for health is not an unrealistic goal. Earmarking is very much in vogue. Only this past week a group of 14 nations announced a new mechanism to provide greater access to drugs in Africa, funded by a tax on airline tickets. Nor is it unrealistic to believe that governments in the developed world might actively support such tax measures. Almost all developed countries have now ratified the World Health Organisation's Framework Convention on Tobacco Control. This requires them to support anti-smoking measures in developing countries. And active support for higher tobacco taxes would be a tangible way to make good that pledge.

So come on, Tony Blair, run with this one. It fits with your concern for developing countries. It fits with the mandate you chose for your G8 presidency, It is in keeping with Labour's great success in reducing the numbers dying of smoking-related diseases at home. Britain itself earmarked some of its tobacco taxes for the National Health Service, and is one of the 14 countries that is going to impose the airline tax.

With Kenneth Clarke the chairman of British American Tobacco, and the Tories having voted against the ban on smoking in public places, this is one of the few areas where Blair could still secure the moral high ground.

UNIT 7

Prevention, Treatment, and Education

Unit Selections

47. **Keeping Drug Prevention for Kids 'Real',** Michael L. Hecht and Amber Johnson
48. **An Update on Adolescent Drug Use,** Scott Hiromoto et al.
49. **Combination Treatment for One Year Doubles Smokers' Quit Rate,** Patrick Zickler
50. **Parent Power,** Joseph A. Califano, Jr.
51. **Nonconventional and Integrative Treatments of Alcohol and Substance Abuse,** James Lake
52. **Exercise and Drug Detoxification,** Simon Oddie
53. **Rehab Reality Check,** Jerry Adler
54. **No Longer Theory: Correctional Practices That Work,** Harvey Shrum

Key Points to Consider

- What three goals exist as the primary guidelines for federal drug policy?

- Can you impact the drug problem by targeting demand and not supply? Why?

- Explain the concept of 'denial' and explain why it is a critical obstacle to providing successful drug treatment.

- What is the association between drug abuse and mental illness?

- Should it be the job of correctional systems to be involved in treating drug dependency of prisoners? Why?

Student Web Site

www.mhcls.com/online

Internet References

Further information regarding these websites may be found in this book's preface or online.

American Council for Drug Education
www.acde.org

D.A.R.E.
http://www.dare-america.com

Drug Watch International
http://www.drugwatch.org

Join Together
www.jointogether.org

Marijuana Policy Project
http://www.mpp.org

National Institute on Drug Abuse
http://www.nida.nih.gov/Infofacts/TreatMeth.html

Office of National Drug Control Policy (ONDCP)
http://www.whitehousedrugpolicy.gov

Hazelden
http://www.hazelden.org

KCI (Koch Crime Institute) The Anit-Meth Site
http://www.kci.org/meth_info/faq_meth.htm

The Drug Reform Coordination Network (DRC)
http://www.drcnet.org

United Nations International Drug Control Program (UNDCP)
http://www.undcp.org

There are no magic bullets for preventing drug abuse and treating drug-dependent persons. Currently, 22.6 million American are classified as drug dependent on illicit drugs and/or alcohol. Of those, 15.6 million abuse alcohol, and 6.8 million were dependent on or abused illicit drugs. Of those who abused illicit drugs, 4.2 million were dependent on marijuana followed by those dependent on cocaine. Males continue to be twice as likely to be classified as drug dependent as females. Research continues to establish and strengthen the role of treatment as a critical component in the fight against drug abuse. Some drug treatment programs have been shown to dramatically reduce the costs associated with high-risk populations of users. For example, recidivism associated with drug related criminal justice populations has been shown to decrease 50 percent after treatment. Treatment is a critical component in the fight against drug abuse but it is not a panacea. Society cannot "treat" drug abuse away just as it cannot "arrest" it away. It is estimated that there are over 20 million persons in the United States today who are in need of drug treatment.

Drug prevention and treatment philosophies subscribe to a multitude of modalities. Everything seems to work a little and nothing seems to work completely. The articles in this unit illustrate the diversity of methods utilized in prevention and treatment programs. Special emphasis is given to treating the drug problems of those who are under the supervision of the criminal justice system. All education, prevention, and treatment programs compete for local, state, and federal resources.

Education: One critical component of drug education is the ability to rapidly translate research findings into practice, and today's drug policy continues to emphasize this in its overall budget allocations. Funding for educational research and grants is generally strong with the trend being toward administering funds to local communities and schools to fund local proposals. For example, in 2008 $52 million dollars were again made available to schools for research based assistance for drug prevention and school safety programs. Another example is the $120 million National Youth Media Campaign designed to help coach parents in processes of early recognition and intervention. Encouraging successful parenting is one primary emphasis in current federal drug policy. Other significant continuing research efforts support important education, prevention, and treatment programs such as The National Prevention Research Initiative; Interventions and Treatment for Current Drug Users Who Are Not Yet Addicted; the National Drug Abuse Treatment Clinical Trial Network; and Research Based Treatment Approaches for Drug Abusing Criminal Offenders. In 2007 and 2008 federal research related grants totaling almost $100 million were made available to local and state school jurisdictions.

Prevention: A primary strategy of drug prevention programs is to prevent and/or delay initial drug use. A secondary strategy is to discourage use by persons minimally involved with drugs. Both strategies include (1) educating users and potential users, (2) teaching adolescents how to resist peer pressure, (3) addressing problems associated with drug abuse such as teen pregnancy, failure in school, and lawbreaking, (4) creating community support and involvement for prevention activities, and (5) involving parents in deterring drug use by children.

Prevention and education programs are administered through a variety of mechanisms, typically amidst controversy relative to what works best. Schools have been an important delivery apparatus. In 2007, and again in 2008, the Substance Abuse and Mental Health Administration announced that drug use by youth was down 19 percent since 2002. Funding for school prevention programs is an important emphasis within the efforts to reduce the demand for drugs. Subsequently, an increase in federal money was dedicated to expanding the number of high school programs that implement student drug testing. Drug testing in high schools, authorized by the Supreme Court in a 2002 court decision, has produced a positive and measurable deterrent to drug use. Despite its controversy, school drug testing is expanding as a positive way to reinforce actions of parents to educate and deter their children from use. The testing program provides for subsequent assessment, referral, and intervention process in situations where parents and educators deem it necessary.

Additionally, in 2008 $90 million in grant funds were again dedicated to support the federal Drug-Free Communities Program which provides funds at the community level to anti-drug coalitions working to prevent substance abuse among young people and in local neighborhoods. There are currently more than 700 local community coalitions working under this program nationwide. Also, there are community-based drug prevention programs sponsored by civic organizations, church groups, and private corporations. All programs pursue funding through public grants and private endowments. Federal grants to local, state, and private programs are critical components to program solvency.

The multifaceted nature of prevention programs makes them difficult to assess categorically. School programs that emphasize the development of skills to resist social and peer pressure produce generally varying degrees of positive results. Research continues to make more evident the need to focus prevention programs with specific populations in mind.

Treatment: Like prevention programs, drug treatment programs enlist a variety of methods to treat persons dependent upon legal and illegal drugs. There is no single-pronged approach to treatment for drug abuse. Treatment modality may differ radically from one user to the next. The user's background, physical and mental health, personal motivation, and support structure all have serious implications for treatment type. Lumping together the diverse needs of chemically dependent persons for purposes of applying a generic treatment process does not work. In addition, most persons needing and seeking treatment have problems with more than one drug—polydrug use. Current research also correlates drug use with serious mental illness (SMI). Current research by the federal Substance Abuse and Mental Health Services Administration (SAMHSA) reports that adults with a drug problem are three times more likely to suffer from a serious mental illness. The existing harmful drug use and mental health nexus is exacerbated by the fact that using certain powerful drugs such as methamphetamine push otherwise functioning persons into the dysfunctional realm of mental illness. Subsequently in 2007, one new federally funded treatment program dedicated $41.6 million dollars to enhance research on methamphetamine addiction. In 2008, an additional federally funded anti-meth campaign was launched targeting the states of Alaska, Washington, Oregon, California, Ohio, Iowa, Indiana, Illinois, and Kentucky, Methamphetamine's mechanism of action, behavioral and physical effects, and prevention and intervention processes are being examined in research grants and contracts, and clinical trials in geographical areas where methamphetamine abuse is highest. In 2008, a federally funded anti-meth campaign was launched specifically targeting the states of Alaska, Washington, Oregon, California, Ohio, Iowa, Illinois, and Kentucky. This campaign, in collaboration with the National Synthetic Drug Action Plan, hopes to initiate state and local interventions related to the latest research and science.

Although treatment programs differ in methods, most provide a combination of key services. These include drug counseling, drug education, pharmacological therapy, psychotherapy, relapse prevention, and assistance with support structures. Treatment programs may be outpatient-oriented or residential in nature. Residential programs require patients to live at the facility for a prescribed period of time. These residential programs, often described as therapeutic communities, emphasize the development of social, vocational, and educational skills.

The current trend is to increase the availability of treatment programs. One key component of federal drug strategy is to continue to fund and expand the Access to Recovery treatment initiative which began in 2004. This program funds drug treatment for individuals otherwise unable to obtain it through a voucher system. This program, now operational in 14 states and one Native American community, allows dependent persons to personally choose care providers, including faith-based care providers. It is hoped that this program will encourage states to provide a wider array of treatment and recovery options. As one example, the State of Missouri has transformed all public drug treatment within the state to an 'Access to Recovery-Like' program in which involved persons choose their providers and pay with state vouchers. It is hoped that this and similar programs will allow a more flexible delivery of services that will target large populations of dependent persons not reached through other treatment efforts.

Keeeping Drug Prevention for Kids 'Real'

A culturally grounded substance abuse prevention curriculum makes kids and their input part of the program.

MICHAEL L. HECHT AND AMBER JOHNSON

O n any given day, young people in this country are presented with difficult choices. Simply saying no to offers of drugs and other risky behaviors can be an act of bravery and highly precarious. How can our youth turn away from these risks without being humiliated, losing friends, or possibly facing physical threats? How do we, as adults, enter that ever-changing world of adolescence and develop understandable, usable lessons?

This is the problem we face in school-based substance abuse prevention. We deal with kids who need help (even though they may not know it) and adults who want to help. Both groups speak very different "languages," including words, dress, and gestures. These differences are heightened when they include layers of cultural diversity arising from ethnicity, gender, economics, and geography.

This article is a synopsis of the Drug Resistance Strategies Project (DRS) and its *keepin' it REAL* (KIR) curriculum. It explains the ways in which the DRS Project uses communication and culture as starting points for school-based drug prevention.

Culture and Drugs

Ethnicity, race, and culture play significant roles in the type and frequency of substance use and abuse, as well as in the effectiveness of school-based prevention.[1] Although researchers recognize the importance of reflecting adolescents' culture in prevention programs, as well as their learning styles and the specific types of drugs and alcohol they are exposed to, few programs take these elements into consideration. This is the main focus of Penn State University's DRS Project, funded since 1989 by the National Institute on Drug Abuse. The project uses an ecologic resiliency model, which recognizes that indigenous cultural strengths can be capitalized, rather than trying to substitute an entirely new value and behavior system.

Curriculum

The DRS Project involves the design, implementation, and evaluation of the KIR curriculum, a culturally grounded, school-based, substance abuse prevention program that emphasizes participants' cultures. The program developed a model of social and life skills from preliminary, basic research. These models are taught through videotapes presenting scenarios in which adolescents are seen refusing drug offers. These videotapes reflect the students' cultures and values, including traditional, indigenous, and ethnic differences. Lessons help with the development of risk assessment, decision making, and resistance skills, and enhance antidrug norms and attitudes. The KIR curriculum was designed using an innovative approach to substance abuse prevention, customizing the curriculum and media messages in creating materials that speak to kids. The program's development was grounded in two basic premises. First, we used a communication approach centering on adolescent narratives or stories about refusing drug offers that capture their cultural norms and values. While we focused on ethnicity and gender, we were also concerned with general youth culture, as well. As a result, the program uses videotaped performances to teach these narratives.

Second, we adopted a "from kids through kids to kids" model. We started with the narratives we collected from middle-school students in the Phoenix area. Next, we employed high-school students to mold the narratives into the curriculum, which are ultimately presented to middle-school students.

These principles came together in videos that are the core of the middle-school curriculum. The KIR videos teach students how to say no through presenting practical drug-resistance strategies that are easy to remember and use. *REAL* stands for the four resistance strategies uncovered in our research: Refuse, Explain, Avoid, and Leave. Students learn how to think competently and critically in different situations so that they can recognize risk, value their perceptions and feelings, and make choices that support their values. These strategies are the program's central message and are based on research that was the first to study how adolescents resisted drugs and described ethnic and gender similarities and differences in these processes.[2] The videos incorporate this research, presenting narrative examples of the resistance strategies using quick cuts, music, and a lot of action.

While the videos are the curriculum's core, the ten lessons (table) include other activities such as role-playing, homework,

The Ten Lessons of the *Keepin' it REAL* Curriculum

1. Options and Choices
2. Risks
3. Communication and Conflict
4. Refuse
5. Explain
6. Avoid
7. Leave
8. Values
9. Feelings
10. Support Networks

and discussions to teach decision making, risk assessment, resistance, and other communication skills, as well as encouraging more conservative drug-related attitudes and norms.

Three culturally grounded versions of the curriculum were produced for the Phoenix middle schools.[3,4] The Latino version was targeted at Mexican-Americans and other Latinos, the largest ethnic group in the schools, while the non-Latino version targeted European-and African-American students, the next largest groups. The third version was multicultural, combining the other two's lessons. All three versions were created by using the narratives as the basis for many materials, infusing cultural values into the lessons, and instructing teachers about cultures during training. This approach allows the students to see themselves, their communities, and their ethnic cultures in the prevention messages.

The KIR curriculum's overall objective is to reduce substance abuse by providing students with communication and life skills. KIR is a ten-week, ten-lesson program during the seventh grade that is supplemented by TV and radio public service announcements, as well as a billboard campaign, and followed up with a booster program during eighth grade. Each session requires approximately 40 to 45 minutes and is highly interactive. Teachers are encouraged to use a discussion rather than lecture style, and the activities are designed to be fun, as well as educational. Five of the lessons, the introduction, and the lessons teaching the four resistance skills are video-based. The eighth-grade boosters, created by the school faculty and staff, project staff, and students, consist of activities such as assemblies, poster projects, murals, neighborhood night outs, and essay contests. Each school administers approximately one booster activity each month.

Implementation

The project was conducted over a three-year period, starting with program development during the 1997 to 1998 school year, a pretest during fall semester 1998, the two-and-a-half month implementation, and a series of posttests leading to the fourth and final one in spring 2000, 14 months after the end of the implementation. During year one, the research team developed the prevention program and research materials, with input from teachers and students; trained project personnel, including the teachers who implemented the program;[3,4] and obtained a sample by first categorizing 35 schools according to enrollment and ethnicity, then randomly assigning each school to one of the three KIR versions or a control group. The control schools continued to use their existing drug-resistance programs. During year two, the research team administered the preprogram questionnaire, implemented the curriculum, and administered follow-up questionnaires. During year three, booster activities were conducted, and the remaining follow-up questionnaires were administered, including the final one 14 months after the end of the curriculum.

The final sample consisted of 6,035 students: 3,318 Mexican or Mexican-American students; 1,141 students other than Latino or multiethnic-Latino origin; 1,049 non-Hispanic white students; and 527 African-American students. The seventh-grade classes in the 35 schools varied in size from 52 to 725 students.

Evaluation

The intervention showed exceptionally promising results, including substantial and significant effects on personal and descriptive norms, expectations of substance abuse, use of resistance strategies and, most importantly, on the use of the gateway drugs—alcohol, cigarettes, and marijuana.[1] The program's greatest impact was on alcohol use, the substance most widely used and that showed the most rapid growth (figure).

The cultural grounding also proved successful. Both the Mexican-American and multicultural versions were effective (the other version was not shown to have statistically significant results). In addition, we found that students who were matched with their version according to their ethnic/racial backgrounds (e.g., Mexican-American students receiving the Latino version) did not benefit more than those who were not matched (e.g., Mexican-American students receiving the multicultural or non-Latino versions) and, perhaps most significantly, the multicultural program had the broadest and longest-lasting effects. While precise ethnic matching did not prove necessary, culture grounding still influenced effectiveness. Thus, our findings indicate no need to narrowly tailor drug-prevention programs to individual ethnic groups for optimal effectiveness. Instead, creative programs are needed to allow students to see their own cultures represented. It is important to note that this does not mean starting with the predominantly white, middle-class culture and adding a few faces of members of other groups. Rather, we believe KIR worked because it was grounded in students' cultures, including their narratives and cultural values.

Conclusion

Overall, the DRS Project can create the momentum for drafting and implementing multicultural and culturally grounded substance abuse prevention programs in our schools. We believe that

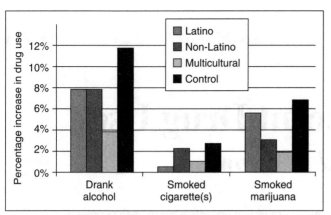

Figure The bar graph illustrates the percentage increase in the number of students using substances from the time of the pretest (T1) to the last posttest (T4) in the last 30 days of the program. Note how the results of the culturally grounded versions of the curriculum compare with controls. Interestingly, though, the findings indicate no need to narrowly tailor drug-prevention programs to individual ethnic groups for optimal effectiveness.

is especially important for schools that are ethnically diverse, where prevention programs should reflect all of the students' cultures and build on their indigenous cultural resiliencies. To achieve this goal, we recommend starting with adolescents' own experiences as expressed in narratives and examining their cultural values and strengths. While we found that it was not necessary for messages to match individual ethnic cultures, we believe that the multicultural nature of our program provides the greatest range of inclusion and impact and is an effective prevention strategy. Although our research indicates that specific cultures do not need to be targeted, the inclusion of all cultures within a school appears to provide cultural grounding and representation and, thus, a broader and more effective program.

Ours is not the only program that considers culture. Yet few programs are available that take this vital factor into consideration, and even fewer have achieved the status of an evidence-based, effective program in the Center for Substance Abuse Prevention's National Registry of Effective Programs and Practices. Still fewer have achieved "model program" status, a status achieved by the DRS program's KIR curriculum. No matter what the makeup of the community, a program like this can be effective because it comes from the community. It can reflect the subtle differences of ethnicity, race, gender, and even history and tradition. Such a program addresses these differences, and honors and reinforces the best aspects of our differences.

References

1. Hecht ML, Marsiglia FF, Elek E, et al. Culturally grounded substance use prevention: An evaluation of the keepin' it R.E.A.L. curriculum. *Prev Sci* 2003;4:233–48.

2. Miller MA, Alberts JK, Hecht ML, et al. *Adolescent Relationships and Drug Use.* New York: Erlbaum Publications, 2000.

3. Gosin M, Marsiglia FF, Hecht ML. Keepin' it R.E.A.L.: A drug resistance curriculum tailored to the strengths and needs of pre-adolescents of the southwest. *J Drug Educ* 2003;33:119–42.

4. Gosin MN, Dustman PA, Drapeau AE, Harthun ML. Participatory Action Research: Creating an effective prevention curriculum for adolescents in the Southwestern US. *Health Educ Res* 2003;18:363–79.

MICHAEL L. HECHT, PhD, is a Professor and Amber Johnson, MA, is a doctoral candidate in the Department of Communication Arts and Sciences at Penn State University. Dr. Hecht can be reached at (814) 863-3545 and Johnson at (814) 863-0127. For more information, visit http://cas.la.psu.edu/drsp/index.html.

To send comments to the authors and editors, e-mail hecht1105@behavioral.net. To order reprints in quantities of 100 or more, call (866) 377-6454.

An Update on Adolescent Drug Use
What School Counselors Need to Know

School counselors need to have accurate and age-appropriate prevention education information in order to counsel teens on drug use. This article presents developmentally specific prevention materials for the most important emerging substances of abuse: Ecstasy, methamphetamine, cough and cold medication, prescription opiates and stimulants, and the "date rape" drugs. Because developing appropriate materials requires understanding how adolescents develop, an expert panel approach was used, supplemented with a literature review and teen focus groups.

SCOTT HIROMOTO ET AL.

Substance use affects many areas of the brain and can cause adverse behavioral, psychological, and social consequences. This is particularly true during adolescence. Adolescence is a unique period of development marked by rapid changes in brain structure, behavior, and social functioning. Recent research strongly suggests that the brain continues to mature during adolescence and into young adulthood (Giedd et al., 1999). For example, millions of new synapses (connections between brain cells) in the frontal lobes are created and organized during adolescence. Nerve cells develop a fatty coating called myelin during adolescence, which allows the brain to function more efficiently. The adolescent brain also has a heightened biological vulnerability to the development of addiction (Chambers, Taylor, & Potenza, 2003); addictive disorders identified in adults usually begin in adolescence or young adulthood (Kandel, Yamaguchi, & Chen, 1992; Wagner & Anthony, 2002).

Because of these changes in the brain, adolescents may be particularly susceptible to the influence of external factors such as substance use (Dahl, 2004). Substance use can interrupt brain development. Some changes in the brain and in functioning may be reversible when drug use stops, but other changes appear to be either permanent or very long-lasting, leading to persistent deficits in memory and motor coordination (National Institute on Drug Abuse, 2001; Tapert & Schweinsburg, 2005). In addition, because each developmental period sets the stage for the next period, delayed development during adolescence may "reverberate" over the course of later development.

Recent information about the nonmedical use of prescription drugs, misuse of some over-the-counter drugs, and the use of club drugs (drugs such as Ecstasy and methamphetamine that are closely tied to the all-night dance club scene) heightens the need for school counselors to familiarize themselves with these substances, in addition to the more commonly abused substances such as alcohol, tobacco, and marijuana (Monitoring the Future, 2005). School counselors are uniquely positioned to inform and educate adolescents about the harmful effects of substance use, a role spelled out by the American School Counselor Association (2005). They can do so successfully if they have accurate, up-to-date prevention education materials designed for use with adolescents.

In this article we provide data on the most important harms associated with adolescent substance use for the following drugs: Ecstasy (MDMA), methamphetamine, cough and cold medication (dextromethorphan), prescription opiates and stimulants, and "date rape" drugs, including sedatives and gamma hydroxybutarate (GHB). We also include key prevention messages specific to each drug class, as well as more general prevention messages to use when communicating with adolescents. After alcohol, cigarettes, marijuana, and crack/cocaine, these drugs are the most commonly used and abused by adolescents (Monitoring the Future, 2005).

Data come from research conducted as part of a project to develop technical assistance materials (Ellickson, Watkins, Vaiana, & Hiromoto, 2005) for Project ALERT, a drug education and prevention curriculum that has been nationally recognized as an exemplary school-based drug education program (BEST Foundation for a Drug Free Tomorrow, 2005). Based on the social influence model of prevention, Project ALERT is designed for middle school adolescents and has been proven effective in curbing cigarette and marijuana use, mitigating alcohol misuse, and reducing pro-drug attitudes in two large-scale, multisite trials—one that included 3,800 students from 30 schools in two Western states (Ellickson & Bell, 1990; Ellickson, McCaffrey, Ghosh-Dastidar, & Longshore, 2003; Ghosh-Dastidar, Longshore, Ellickson, & McCaffrey, 2004). Developed by RAND and disseminated by the BEST Foundation, it currently reaches over a million students each year.

The research questions for the current project were as follows:

1. Excluding alcohol, tobacco, marijuana, and cocaine, for which drugs is it most important to develop supplementary prevention materials for seventh and eighth graders?
2. Which harms and prevention messages are the most important to emphasize, taking into account seventh and eighth graders' likely exposure to these drugs and their developmental stage?

Methods

Our approach to identifying the harms and prevention messages most relevant to adolescents involved three steps. First, we conducted a literature review to identify current estimates of prevalence and the adverse consequences associated with use of these drugs. We included physical and medical harms, psychological harms, and adverse social and developmental consequences. We also assessed differences by gender and ethnicity. We searched drug information Web sites produced under the auspices of the federal government (e.g., National Institute on Drug Abuse, the Drug Enforcement Administration, and the National Drug Intelligence Center, among others) and confirmed all statements with peer-reviewed scientific articles obtained by searching Medline and Ovid.

Second, we reviewed these findings with an expert panel to identify those harms most relevant and important to adolescents. We recruited 10 panelists with expertise in adolescent substance use to participate in three day-long workshops covering the different drugs. The panelists included physicians, a toxicologist, drug treatment and drug prevention specialists, undercover law enforcement officers, research communicators, and an ethnographer. Before the meeting, we provided panelists with summaries of our literature review, selected prevalence data, and sample Project ALERT materials. We asked the panelists to review the material and to consider the most important consequences or harms to which seventh and eighth graders would be exposed if they used these drugs. We also asked the experts to identify the consequences that would be most likely to deter teens from using the drugs, as well as particular harms that might occur because of polydrug use and/or the addition of other ingredients to specific drugs.

During the meeting, panelists identified the most important harms associated with each substance and then rated how relevant the harm was to seventh and eighth graders, taking into account their probable exposure to the substance and adolescent characteristics that affect their responsiveness to different types of information. For example, adolescents are likely to consider immediate harms such as losing one's friends or being taken to the emergency room to be more serious than harms such as liver disease that might occur in the distant future. During the third session, panelists synthesized the data on prevalence and harms to produce an overall rating of which drugs and which prevention messages were the most important to emphasize in prevention education efforts.

Our third step was to obtain a teen perspective on the results of the expert panel. This was done to ensure that no harms identified as critical by teens had been omitted from the list of most important harms developed by the expert panel and to guide the framing of prevention messages. We conducted four focus groups with a total of 34 teens between the ages of 14 and 21 who were recruited from area high schools and treatment programs. The teens came from diverse socioeconomic and ethnic backgrounds and all but one were in high school. Teens were asked to discuss which harms they perceived as most important and how they would package an avoidance message for middle-school adolescents. We also tapped user Web sites and teen magazines for illustrative material.

While the expert panelists and teens identified which emerging drugs to include and the most important harms for teens associated with each, the research team crafted the specific prevention messages. That effort was guided by Project ALERT's theoretical focus on the seriousness and salience of drug use consequences, as well as the relevance of those consequences to adolescents, their likely exposure to harm, and their developmental readiness to hear specific messages, as indicated by the focus groups and our drug prevention experience in more than 85 middle schools.

Based on the social influence model of prevention, the Project ALERT curriculum synthesizes three theories of behavioral change: (a) the health belief model, which focuses on cognitive factors such as seriousness of consequences that motivate healthy behavior (Becker, 1974; Rosenstock, Strecher, & Becker, 1988); (b) the social learning model, which emphasizes social norms and significant others as key determinants of behavior (Bandura, 1985); and (c) the self-efficacy theory of behavior change, which views the belief that one can accomplish a task as essential to effective action (Bandura, 1977). Project ALERT specifically seeks to change students' beliefs about the physical, social, and emotional consequences of using drugs and norms surrounding use; to help them identify and resist pro-drug pressures from peers, parents, the media, and others; and to build resistance self-efficacy, the belief that one can successfully resist pro-drug influences. The prevention messages are similar in style and content to those in the current curriculum on alcohol, tobacco, marijuana, and cocaine. All prevention messages were reviewed and approved by the expert panel.

Results

Much of the information about adverse consequences identified by both teens and our expert panelists was not drug specific. In fact, even older teens were unaware of the differences between drugs, and they often grouped disparate drugs together. This suggests that it may be difficult for adolescents to assimilate drug-specific information, and that the most important messages for school counselors to communicate are the same across these drugs.

Appendix A shows the general drug prevention messages identified as the most relevant for adolescents in the seventh and eighth grades. We group them by what teens say and by what science and the experts say.

As Appendix A indicates, the teens emphasized how drug use would affect the people they care about, especially family and friends. They were also quite clear that using drugs can negatively affect performance in school, as well as in sports and other activities, and increase the likelihood of getting in trouble, having an accident, or doing something else that one will regret. All of these consequences, which deal with how drug use can affect one's daily life and social relationships, strike a chord with teens and heighten their sense of personal susceptibility to the negative effects of using. They apply across drugs and should be included in the overall prevention message.

The experts, on the other hand, emphasized harms associated with how drug use affects the brain and body, noting that some drugs can change the brain and body permanently and even cause death. They also emphasized the uncertainty associated with drug use—that you never know exactly what you're getting, cannot predict how your body and mind will react, and cannot count on the notion that just trying something once is harmless. These messages are designed to help adolescents understand that drug use can have serious and permanent consequences and that teens are susceptible to these harms because no one can predict if and when they might happen. They are also key components of the Health Belief Model, a common approach to promoting healthy behavior that stresses the importance of recognizing the bad personal consequences of specific behaviors in motivating resistance to them (Rosenstock et al., 1988).

Because teens know so little about how specific drugs might affect them (and often have the wrong information), it is important that counselors be equipped with the knowledge they need to answer questions that arise and to correct misperceptions and myths that adolescents may have acquired. In the text below, we provide information about each of the drugs listed above and some of their most important harms. The appendixes provide specific prevention messages crafted from material drawn from our teen focus groups, user Web sites, and teen magazines.

Ecstasy

Ecstasy (MDMA) is an illicit, illegally produced stimulant with mild hallucinogenic properties. It is also known as E, X, XTC, Bean, or Roll. It elevates energy, heart rate, blood pressure, and body temperature, and it makes users feel emotionally open, sociable, and uninhibited. It is almost always taken in pill form. Ecstasy use is closely tied to the all-night dance club scene—hence its label as a "club drug." However, it is also used in small social settings, at home, and elsewhere.

Ecstasy is dangerous because it can cause overheating, which is particularly likely to happen when people take Ecstasy to increase their energy level when dancing. A body temperature of more than 105 degrees is a medical emergency and can quickly lead to death if not treated in time. Users often drink liquids to avoid dehydration, but drinking too much water can be harmful because it dilutes the salt in one's body to dangerous levels. Teens who use Ecstasy at dance clubs or all-night dance events are likely to mix it with alcohol or other drugs, a particularly dangerous form of use because Ecstasy pills are notoriously impure. The disinhibition associated with Ecstasy use can cause teens to behave in ways that make them vulnerable to sexual assault or other violence. Key prevention messages, summarized in Appendix B, stress problems with overheating, not knowing what's in the drug, and feeling overconfident.

Methamphetamine

Methamphetamine is a strong physical and mental stimulant, also known as meth, crystal meth, crank, ice, tweak, glass, and speed. Methamphetamine raises blood pressure and heart rate and makes the heart beat with greater force. It can permanently damage nerve cells that produce important brain chemicals. Methamphetamine can be snorted, smoked, injected, drunk, or taken as pills or powder. Methamphetamine is less of a party drug than Ecstasy, although teens at dance events may take it unknowingly when it has been added to the latter substance. Teens who use it to enhance performance or lose weight are likely to use it by themselves.

Methamphetamine can cause permanent psychosis, even with first use. It is highly addictive, and users may feel they are being very productive when, in fact, they are engaging in pointless, repetitive activities. Chronic use can cause permanent brain damage, paranoia, a weakened immune system, and heart problems. Regular methamphetamine users frequently become "tweakers," emaciated people with rotten teeth who neglect basic hygiene and pick at their skin, creating sores that often become infected. Appendix C highlights prevention messages that are particularly relevant for teens, including the possibility of harm after a single dose, the thin line between "just trying it" and getting hooked, and the effects of regular use on one's brain, outlook, and appearance.

Over-the-Counter Cough and Cold Medicines with DXM

Some cough and cold medicines are used as "recreational" drugs, often by young teens. The ingredient most commonly abused is DXM (Dextromethorphan), a cough suppressant found in many over-the-counter cough and cold medications. DXM is generally safe when used at recommended doses, but high doses of DXM can produce hallucinations and the sensation of having out-of-body experiences. When abused, DXM is used at up to 30 times the recommended dose.

Street names for DXM include dex, tussin, drex, robo, rojo, skittles, triple C, and velvet. DXM is available as a liquid and in powder, lozenge, tablet, capsule, and gel cap form. At lower doses, teenagers often use it in a social setting or at dance clubs and all-night dance parties. At higher doses, teens probably use by themselves, pursuing the drug's hallucinogenic effects.

Using DXM is particularly dangerous because almost all cough and cold remedies contain multiple ingredients, including acetaminophen, antihistamines, and pseudoephedrine. In order to get a recreational dose of DXM, teens take many times the recommended amount of the cough and cold medications. This greatly increases the amount they ingest of the other ingredients and raises their risk of organ damage. Ingesting large amounts of cough syrup also can lead to protracted vomiting.

DXM alters cognitive processes and judgment; high doses cause hallucinations and psychosis. People under the influence of DXM can exhibit bizarre, violent, uncontrolled behavior. Appendix D presents prevention messages designed to resonate with younger teens, who are particularly likely to abuse these medications.

Prescription Painkillers

Prescription painkillers (opiates) are used medically to relieve pain. The most commonly prescribed, and the most commonly abused by teens, are OxyContin, Darvon, Vicodin, Percocet, Percodan, and Tylenol with Codeine. Prescription painkillers work by changing how the brain perceives pain. They slow down the body's processes (breathing, heart rate, digestion) and produce a sense of well-being and calm drowsiness. Teens usually use prescription painkillers in pill form, but they also may crush the pills and snort the powder or mix it with water and inject it. Teens may use these drugs alone when self-medicating, or at school or parties to get high.

When not used as prescribed, prescription painkillers are very dangerous. Even one dose of prescription painkillers can suppress breathing and be lethal. Prescription painkillers are extremely addicting, and teens who self-medicate for relatively minor pain can become addicted quickly. Tolerance builds with drug use, so the more often teenagers use these drugs the larger the dose they need the next time. Abusing prescription painkillers can have permanent effects on the brain, including loss of interest in everything except the drug, inability to enjoy normal pleasures, and depressive symptoms. Prevention messages are listed in Appendix E.

Prescription Stimulants

Prescription stimulants (amphetamines) are drugs that speed up brain and physical activity by stimulating the central nervous system. They are used medically to treat depression, obesity, and attention deficit hyperactivity disorder. The prescription stimulants most commonly abused by teens are Dexedrine, Ritalin, and Adderall. Street names for these drugs include speed, dex, dexies, and jollies. Adderall is sometimes called "kiddie cocaine." Teens typically swallow these drugs in pill form, but they also can be snorted or injected.

Using prescription stimulants in a manner inconsistent with how they were prescribed can cause sleeplessness, dangerously high body temperature, and nervousness. Users may become hostile and paranoid; long-term abuse can lead to severe weight loss, mental illness, heart failure, seizures, and even death. When not used as prescribed, stimulants are very addicting and tolerance develops. Sudden withdrawal produces fatigue; long, disturbed periods of sleep; irritability; and intense hunger and overeating. The prevention messages in Appendix F stress how stimulant use leads to loss of control (sleeplessness, paranoia, hallucinations), as well as how easy it is to get addicted.

Sedatives

Sedatives (benzodiazepines and GHB) are central nervous system depressants—they slow normal brain function. Commonly prescribed and commonly abused by teens are Xanax (known as Zanies or Z bars), Valium, Ativan, and Klonopin. Candy, downers, sleeping pills, and tranks are other street names for these drugs. GHB is a sedative that became illegal in 2000. However, increasingly teens are turning to alternative forms of GHB that are easier to get. Sedatives are usually used in pill form; GHB can be produced in a white powder, clear liquid, or capsule form.

Misusing sedatives is dangerous because it is easy to overdose. Users who mix these drugs with other sedatives such as alcohol or opiates may go to sleep and never wake up. They also may lose the normal reflexes that protect their airway and choke to death on their own vomit. Sedatives can make teens feel uninhibited and result in undesired and/or high-risk sexual activity. GHB, an odorless, colorless liquid, is particularly dangerous because it is easily added to beverages without the teen noticing it and because the margin between a recreational dose of GHB and a lethal overdose is narrow. Appendix G highlights the lethal nature of sedatives, particularly when mixed with alcohol, and the importance of preventing anyone from adding anything to one's beverage glass at social gatherings.

Discussion

Among the most important emerging substances of abuse among teens are Ecstasy, methamphetamine, DXM, prescription painkillers and stimulants, and sedatives (Monitoring the Future, 2005). School counselors need to have accurate and age-appropriate prevention education information in order to respond to students' questions about these substances and to counsel all teens on why not to use drugs. This role is consistent with the ASCA National Model® (American School Counselor Association, 2005), which recommends that school counselors collaborate with teachers to provide guidance curriculum lessons.

This article presents accurate and developmentally specific material for the most important emerging substances of abuse. Because developing appropriate and effective materials requires understanding how adolescents develop, as well as how drugs affect young people and how adolescents respond to prevention messages (D'Amico et al., 2005), we used an expert panel approach supplemented with teen focus groups to develop age-appropriate prevention education information. Because all materials were developed within the theoretical context of Project ALERT, a program with demonstrated effectiveness, we expect these supplemental materials will be effective, too. Project ALERT materials are also in alignment with national and state health education standards (BEST Foundation for a Drug Free Tomorrow, 2005).

Teens are likely to have general notions that drug use can mess them up, get them in trouble at home or school, and make friends and family suffer. These are important prevention messages that resonate with young people. But adolescents are less likely to understand that using many of these substances amounts to playing Russian roulette with their health and, frequently, with their lives. Because certain kinds of drugs or ways of using them can result in permanent damage or even loss of life, prevention messages that accurately and credibly convey this information are important as well. School counselors are uniquely positioned to convey accurate and age-appropriate prevention messages to teens in a nonthreatening and nonjudgmental manner.

Many teens do not realize that a single dose of drugs like Ecstasy, methamphetamine, and some opiates can cause long-lasting harm to the brain or body and even death. Such severe and immediate consequences do deter adolescents from use, but only if they get the information and believe it (Masterman & Kelly, 2003). Counselors who have established trust and credibility with their students have a good chance of successfully conveying this information. Many teens also discount the likelihood of getting addicted and having the drug control everything they do. Counselors can motivate teens against experimenting with dangerous drugs like methamphetamine and prescription painkillers by helping them understand the link between addiction and loss of control, and the thin line between experimentation and addiction. Counselors also can help teens understand why all pills of a single substance aren't the same and how a given dose may interact with other substances such as alcohol.

A particularly problematic form of experimentation is "pharming," the practice of putting pills obtained from home or friends in a bowl, reaching in for a few, and swallowing them. Because many teens believe that drugs prescribed by doctors are "safe," they also tend to discount the risks associated with this form of Russian roulette (Falkowski, 2003). Vulnerability to group pressure makes refusing to join in particularly difficult. Counselors can help teens to understand the immediate harms that are associated with this practice and to realize that drugs may have idiosyncratic effects, particularly when mixed with other drugs.

Counseling adolescents about drug abuse prevention can be effective, but only if counselors convey credible and age-appropriate information (D'Amico et al., 2005). Because counselors are likely to come in contact with students at risk for alcohol and drug problems, they may be particularly effective at persuading them to adopt lower-risk behavior. Techniques that emphasize teens' responsibility for decisions about substance use fit well with adolescents' need for autonomy and individuation (Masterman & Kelly, 2003) and with the nonjudgmental style used by many school counselors.

This research was underwritten by the BEST Foundation for a Drug-Free Tomorrow. The authors thank Luke Bergmann, Carol J. Boyd, Edward W. Boyer, Carol Falkowski, Linn Goldberg, Sharon Levy, Karen Miotto, Jim Mock, Luanne Rohrbach, and Glen Stanley for their expert advice.

Appendix A
General Drug Abuse Prevention Messages
What teens say:

- You can permanently derail your future, wreck your family, and lose your friends.
- Your performance in sports and at school will suffer.
- You can get in trouble—at home, at school, and with the cops.

- You'll come to see yourself as a failure, and that's how others will see you, too, including the people you care about the most.
- You can lose physical coordination and good judgment, making yourself vulnerable to serious accidents or sexual abuse.

What science and experts say:

- Some drugs can change the brain and body permanently—even after just one dose. In cases such as OxyContin, Ecstasy, GHB, or methamphetamines, one dose can be lethal.
- You never know exactly what you are getting. Illegal drugs can contain anything, and teens abusing prescription drugs don't read labels.
- Even if you know what you are getting, you don't know how your body and mind will react. Everyone reacts differently—it's random chemistry.
- Teens think they can handle trying something just once, but the line between experimentation and addiction is very fuzzy.

Appendix B
Ecstasy: Most Important Prevention Messages

- What you don't know can—and will—hurt you. Ecstasy pills can contain anything from methamphetamine to DXM. Buying it from the same dealer or using the same brand makes no difference. So taking Ecstasy is a lot like flipping a chemical coin.
- Ecstasy makes you feel like you can dance forever, and dancing makes you overheat. Overheating can kill you, and once your body overheats, it's more likely to do it again—for the rest of your life—because you've damaged your body's ability to regulate temperature.
- Ecstasy makes you feel self-confident and on top of the world. But it also can blind you to a potentially bad situation, where you could be sexually attacked.

Appendix C
Methamphetamine: Most Important Prevention Messages

- Meth is a one-way ticket to disaster. The line between "just trying it" and being hooked is thin and blurry.
- Using meth just once can lead to psychotic episodes as well as to long-term psychosis—you see and hear things that aren't real.
- Using meth regularly fries your brain. It can cause permanent brain damage and change forever the way you view the world.
- Regular meth users become "tweakers," skeleton-like people with rotten teeth who pick at their skin, creating sores that often become infected.

Appendix D
Over-the-Counter Cough and Cold Medications with DXM: Most Important Prevention Messages

- Your friends may start avoiding you.
- You won't be able to stop throwing up.
- You will look so freaked out that your friends may take you to the emergency room and the doctors will call your parents.

Appendix E
Prescription Painkillers (Opiates): Most Important Prevention Messages

- Prescription painkillers can kill you—even one dose. You just stop breathing.
- What you don't know can hurt you. All prescription painkillers aren't the same, and you don't know the effect of one pill compared with another.
- It's very easy to get addicted—easy to go from experimenting to having the drug be the most important thing in your life.

Appendix F
Prescription Stimulants (Amphetamines): Most Important Prevention Messages

- It's easy to get hooked on these drugs; pretty soon the only thing that matters is getting more.
- You may start taking these drugs to keep awake, but you'll end up not being able to sleep when you want to.
- Your heart will pound, you'll wonder who's out to get you, you'll see things that aren't there.
- Experimenting with drugs prescribed for other people is a huge gamble. There are so many important things you can't control—what you actually took, how powerful the pill is, and how it will affect you.

Appendix G
Sedatives (Benzodiazepines and GHB): Most Important Prevention Messages

- Mixing sedatives with alcohol can be deadly.
- These drugs can put you into such a deep sleep that you can literally choke on your own vomit.
- You don't know how strong the pill is that you are taking or how you are going to react to it.
- Always watch your glass or bottle at a party—even if you are just drinking a soft drink.

References

American School Counselor Association. (2005). The ASCA national model: *A framework for school counseling programs* (2nd ed.). Alexandria, VA: Author.

Bandura, A. (1977). *Self-efficacy: Toward a unifying theory of behavioral change.* Psychological Review, 84, 191–215.

Bandura, A. (1985). *Social foundations of thought and action.* Englewod Cliffs, NJ: Prentice Hall.

Becker, M. H. (1974). *The health belief model and personal health behavior. Health Education Monographs,* 2, 324–473.

BEST Foundation for a Drug Free Tomorrow. (2005). Project ALERT. Retrieved February 2, 2006, from http://www.projectalert.best .org/Default.asp?bhcp = 1

Chambers, R. A., Taylor, J. R., & Potenza, M. N. (2003). *Developmental neurocircuitry of motivation in adolescence: A critical period of addiction vulnerability.* American Journal of Psychiatry, 160(6), 1041–1052.

D'Amico, E. J., Ellickson, P. L., Wagner, E. F., Turrisi, R., Fromme, K., Ghosh-Dastidar, B., et al. (2005). Developmental considerations for substance use interventions from middle school through college. *Alcoholism: Clinical and Experimental Research,* 29(3), 474–483.

Dahl, R. E. (2004). *Adolescent brain development: A period of vulnerabilities and opportunities.* Annals for the New York Academy of Sciences, 1021, 1–22.

Ellickson, R. L., & Bell, R. M. (1990). *Drug prevention in junior high: A multi-site longitudinal test. Science,* 247(4948), 1299–1305.

Ellickson, P. L., McCaffrey, D. F., Ghosh-Dastidar, B., & Longshore, D. L. (2003). *New inroads in preventing adolescent drug use*: Results from a large-scale trial of Project ALERT in middle schools. American Journal of Public Health, 93(11), 1830–1836.

Ellickson, P. L., Watkins, K. E., Vaiana, M. E., & Hiromoto, S. (2005). Project ALERT: *A supplemental resource manual.* In Project ALERT: A drug prevention program for middle schools. *Los Angeles:* BEST Foundation.

Falkowski, C. L. (2003). Dangerous drugs: An easy-to-use reference for parents and professionals (2nd ed.). Center City, *MN: Hazelden Publishing and Educational Services.*

Ghosh-Dastidar, B., Longshore, D., Ellickson, R. L., & McCaffrey, D. F. (2004). *Modifying pro-drug risk factors in adolescents:* Results from Project ALERT. Health Education and Behavior, 31(3), 318–334.

Giedd, J. N., Blumenthal, J., Jeffried, N. O., Castellanoes, F. X., Liu, H., Zijdenbos, A., et al. (1999). Brain development during childhood and adolescence: A longitudinal MRI study. Nature Neuroscience, 2(10), 861–863.

Kandel, D. B., Yamaguchi, K., & Chen, K. (1992). *Stages of progression in drug involvement from adolescence to adulthood: Further evidence for the gateway theory.* Journal of Studies on Alcohol, 53(5), 447–457.

Masterman, P. W., & Kelly, A. B. (2003). *Reaching adolescents who drink harmfully: Fitting intervention to developmental reality.* Journal of Substance Treatment, 24(4), 347–355.

Monitoring the Future. (2005, September 19). A continuing study of American youth. Retrieved September 20, 2005, from http:// www.monitoringthefuture.org/

National Institute on Drug Abuse. (2001). *Ecstasy: What we know and don't know about MDMA, a scientific review.* Retrieved September 20, 2005, from http://www.drugabuse.gov/Meetings/ MDMA/MDMAExSummary.html

Rosenstock, I. M., Strecher, V. J., & Becket, M. H. (1988). *Social learning theory and the health belief model.* Health Education Quarterly, 15(2), 175–183.

Tapert, S. F., & Schweinsburg, A. D. (2005). The human adolescent brain and alcohol use disorders. In M. Galanter (Ed.), *Recent developments in alcoholism: Vol. 17. Research on alcohol problems in adolescents and young adults* (pp. 177–197). New York: Springer.

Wagner, F. A., & Anthony, J. C. (2002). From first drug use to drug dependence: Developmental periods of risk for dependence upon marijuana, cocaine, and alcohol. Neuropsychopharmacology, 26(4), 479–488.

KATHERINE E. WATKINS, MD, **PHYLLIS L. ELLICKSON,** PhD, **MARY E. VAIANA,** PhD, and **SCOTT HIROMOTO,** MA, are with the RAND Corporation, Santa Monica, CA. E-mail: Katherine_Watkins@trand.org

Combination Treatment for One Year Doubles Smokers' Quit Rate

PATRICK ZICKLER

Most smokers understand the health risks associated with tobacco use and want to stop, but the addictive grip of nicotine makes quitting difficult; nearly 80 percent of smokers who try relapse within a year. Those poor odds can be improved, NIDA-supported investigators say, by extending the length of smoking cessation therapy to at least 1 year.

Among smokers who received medication and counseling for 12 months rather than the conventional 12 weeks, half were abstinent a year after quitting. This is more than double the success rate of other treatment programs, says Dr. Sharon Hall, who investigated the extended treatment approach at the University of California, San Francisco. "Smoking is not just a bad habit; it is a powerful and deadly addiction," Dr. Hall says. "It has to be treated with methods that are commensurate with its addictive properties, which are extensive and long term."

Dr. Hall and her colleagues assigned each of 160 trial participants who smoked 10 or more cigarettes daily to one of four

After an initial 12-week therapy regimen, patients who received monthly counseling for 40 more weeks maintained higher abstinence rates than patients who did not.
Concurrent nortriptyline therapy enhanced the advantage of extended counseling.

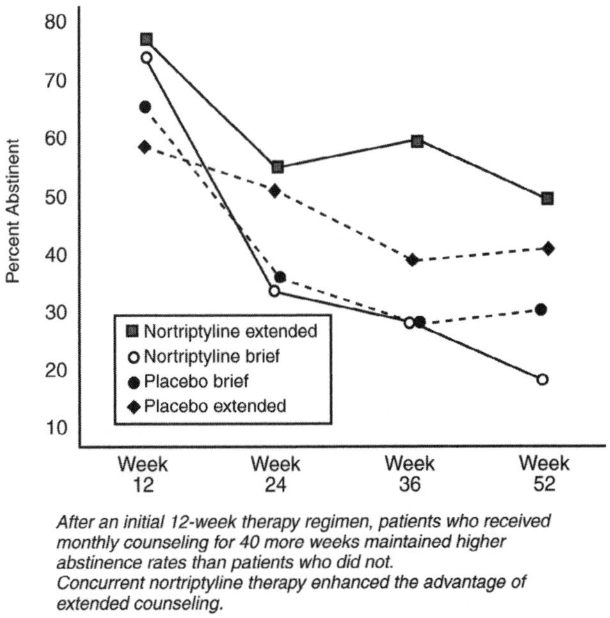

Figure 1 Smoking cessation rates improve with year-long treatment.

regimens. All the participants received nicotine replacement therapy (transdermal patch) and took part in five group counseling sessions during the first 12 weeks of the study. These 90-minute sessions concentrated on understanding health issues associated with smoking and quitting, developing personalized quit strategies, and avoiding relapse. The investigators gave half the participants a placebo and half nortriptyline, an antidepressant that Dr. Hall's research group had previously found helps smokers to quit. The researchers adjusted participants' medication doses to maintain blood concentrations of 50 to 150 ng/L.

At the end of 12 weeks, treatment ended for half of the participants. The rest continued their regimens of nortriptyline (40) or placebo (41) for 40 more weeks. During this time, they continued to participate in monthly 30-minute group counseling sessions and were contacted by phone 2 weeks after each session to reinforce counseling lessons.

At the end of weeks 24, 36, and 52, far fewer of the participants in extended treatment were smoking than were participants whose treatment ended after 12 weeks. At the end of 1 year, 50 percent of patients who had received nortriptyline and counseling throughout were abstinent, compared with 18 percent who got this treatment for only 12 weeks. Forty-two percent of patients who received extended counseling and placebo were abstinent at 1 year, compared with 30 percent of those who got them for 12 weeks.

"The highest success rate was with nortriptyline and counseling for 52 weeks," Dr. Hall says. "Extended treatment with placebo and counseling came in a very close second, suggesting that prolonged psychological support and counseling are important components in improved treatment outcomes." The mix of long-term combination treatment with both pharmacological and behavioral therapies reflects the complexity and power of smoking addiction, says Dr. Hall. "Smoking is more complex than just the physical addiction. There are psychological factors such as stress that can trigger a desire to smoke. There are social and environmental factors—a certain group of friends or a certain kind of meal or a certain type of gathering—that make a contribution, too," Dr. Hall says. "Simply treating the physical addiction doesn't address these psychological influences, which can trigger a relapse to smoking months or years after a person has quit."

"These findings are significant because they show that a combination treatment provided over an extended period has great potential to improve smoking cessation rates," says Ms. Debra Grossman of NIDA's Division of Neuroscience and Behavioral Research. "Dr. Hall has shown that providing smokers with a comprehensive extended treatment can achieve better abstinence rates than have ever previously been reported from a controlled trial."

Dr. Hall and her colleagues are continuing to test long-term treatments in two other studies. One involves smokers older than 50, a group with markedly poorer outcomes than younger smokers. The second will evaluate bupropion, a prescription medication specifically approved for smoking cessation treatment, in combination with counseling.

For some smokers, the prospect of a year-long course of treatment is daunting, Dr. Hall acknowledges. "But this may be what you need to do if you want to be successful. Smokers, as well as the practitioners who treat them, need to know that it is possible to achieve high rates of long-term abstinence. It is not a simple process because it's not a simple addiction. But it is worth it to stop doing something that can kill you."

From *NIDA Notes,* March 2006. Published by The National Institute on Drug Abuse.

Parent Power

The price young people pay for parental pessimism and nonchalance is high.

Joseph A. Califano Jr.

The 10th Annual Survey of 12- to 17-year-olds by the National Center on Addiction and Substance Abuse at Columbia University (CASA) has a loud and clear message: Parents, if you want to raise drug-free kids, you cannot outsource your responsibility to their schools or law enforcement.

The odds are that drugs will be used, kept or sold—or all of the above—at the school your daughter or son attends and that laws prohibiting teen use of tobacco, alcohol, marijuana and other illegal drugs will have little or no impact on your child's decision to smoke, drink or use marijuana.

What will motivate your kids to stay drug free is their perception of how Mom and Dad will react to their smoking, drinking or drug use, their sense of the immorality of such use for someone their age, and whether they consider such use harmful to their health. It is not much of an overstatement to say that reducing the risk of teen substance use is all in the family. Engaged and nourishing parents have the best shot at giving their children the will and skills to say no.

For any who doubt the frontline importance of the family in combating teen drug use and for parents who think they can outsource their responsibility, this year's CASA survey sends a grim message that a teen's world outside the family is infested with drugs.

The most disturbing finding is the extent to which our nation's schools are awash in alcohol, tobacco, and illegal and prescription drugs. Since 2002, the proportion of middle schoolers who say that drugs are used, kept or sold in their schools is up by a stunning 47 percent, and the proportion of high schoolers attending schools with drugs is up by 41 percent. This year, 10.6 million high schoolers, almost two-thirds, and 2.4 million middle schoolers, more than a quarter, are attending schools where drugs are used, kept or sold.

Sadly, many parents accept drug-infected schools as an inevitable part of their children's lives. Half of all parents surveyed report that drugs are used, kept or sold on the grounds of their teen's school, and a despairing 56 percent of these parents believe that the goal of making their child's school drug free is unrealistic. When asbestos is found in a school, most parents refuse to send their children there until it is removed; yet these same parents send their kids to drug infected schools day after day. When parents feel as strongly about drugs in schools as they do about asbestos, they will give our teens a chance to be educated in a drug free environment.

The price young people pay for parental pessimism and nonchalance is high. Teens who attend schools where drugs are used, kept or sold are three times likelier to try marijuana and get drunk in a typical month, compared with teens who attend drug-free schools. Students at high schools with drugs estimate that 44 percent of their schoolmates regularly use illegal drugs, compared with a 27 percent estimate by students at drug free schools.

This year's survey provides overwhelming additional evidence of the increasingly drug drenched world of American teens. In just one year, from 2004 to 2005, the percentage of 12- to 17-year-olds who know a friend or classmate who has abused prescription drugs jumped 86 percent; who has used the drug Ecstasy is up 28 percent; who has used illegal drugs, such as acid, cocaine or heroin, is up 20 percent.

Given the availability of substances throughout their lives—in their schools, among their friends—it is no wonder that teens continue to name drugs as their number one concern, as they have since CASA began conducting the survey in 1996. This year 29 percent of teens cite drugs as their top concern. (Remarkably, many parents don't understand this. Only 13 percent of those surveyed see drugs as their teens' biggest concern; almost 60 percent of parents consider social pressures their teens' biggest concern, a view only 22 percent of teens share.)

And little progress, if any, has been made in curtailing teens' ability to buy marijuana. Forty-two percent of 12- to 17-year-olds (11 million) can buy marijuana within a day; 21 percent (5.5 million) can buy it within an hour. This situation has remained unchanged over the past three years.

The abysmal failures of our schools to achieve and maintain a drug free status and of our government to reduce the availability of marijuana should by themselves be enough to alert parents to the critical significance of their role. But the clincher comes out of the mouths of teens themselves, who make it clear that morality and parental attitude trump illegality as deterrents to their smoking, drinking and drug use:

- Teens who believe smoking cigarettes or drinking alcohol by someone their age is "not morally wrong" are seven times likelier to smoke or drink than those who believe teen smoking is "seriously morally wrong."

- Teens whose parents would be "a little upset or not upset" if they smoked or drank are much likelier to smoke or drink than those whose parents would be "extremely upset."
- Teens who believe using marijuana is "not morally wrong" are 19 times likelier to use marijuana than teens who believe it is "seriously morally wrong."
- Teens who say their parents would be "a little upset" or "not upset at all" if they used marijuana are six times likelier to try marijuana than those whose parents would be "extremely upset."

At the same time, most teens say legal restrictions have no impact on their decision to smoke cigarettes (58 percent) or drink alcohol (54 percent). Nearly half of teens say illegality plays no role in their decision to use marijuana, LSD, cocaine or heroin.

The point is not that criminal laws are irrelevant; they serve an important purpose to protect society and as a formal consensus of society's judgment about seriously harmful conduct. The point is that a child's sense of morality, which most 12- to 17-year-olds acquire from parents, and a clear appreciation of parental disapproval are far more powerful incentives to stay drug free.

Parents also have an important responsibility to monitor their children's conduct and know their children's friends. Forty-three percent of 12- to 17-year-olds see three or more R-rated movies in a typical month. These teens are seven times likelier to smoke cigarettes, six times likelier to try marijuana and five times likelier to drink alcohol than those who do not watch R-rated movies. Teens who report that half or more of their friends are sexually active are at nearly six times the risk for substance abuse as those teens with no sexually active friends. Similarly, teens who report that most of their friends drink or use marijuana are at much higher risk of substance abuse.

The good news is that strong, positive family relationships are a powerful deterrent to teen smoking, drinking and drug use. Teens who would go to either or both their parents with

a serious problem are at half the risk of teens who would seek out another adult. The substance-abuse risk for teens living in households with frequent family dinners, low levels of tension and stress among family members, parents who are proud of their teen and a parent in whom the teen can confide is half that of the average teen.

Frequent family dinners are a simple yet powerful way to influence teen behavior. Compared to teens who have at least five family dinners a week, those who have family dinner less often than three times a week are much likelier to smoke, drink and use marijuana. Only 13 percent of teens who have frequent family dinners have tried marijuana, compared with 35 percent of teens who have dinner with their parents no more than twice a week.

Teens who attend weekly religious services—or who say that religion is an important part of their lives—are at half the risk of smoking, drinking or using drugs as those who do not attend such services. And it is unlikely in this nation that 12- to 17-year-olds go to church each week without their parents.

Parent power is the greatest weapon we have to curb substance abuse. When mothers and fathers realize how much power they have—and use it sensitively—we will turn back this scourge that has destroyed so many children and brought so much grief to so many families and friends.

This nation's drug problem is all about kids. CASA's research has consistently shown that a child who gets through age 21 without smoking, abusing alcohol or using drugs is virtually certain never to do so. The CASA survey and 12 years of my life devoted to understanding this problem have led me to this bottom line: America's drug problem is not going to be solved in courtrooms, legislative hearing rooms or schoolrooms—or by judges, politicians or teachers. It will be solved in living rooms and dining rooms and across kitchen tables—and by parents and families.

Joseph A. Califano Jr., chairman and president of the National Center on Addiction and Substance Abuse at Columbia University, was secretary of health, education and welfare from 1977 to 1979. His most recent book, *Inside: A Public and Private Life,* will be available in paperback.

Nonconventional and Integrative Treatments of Alcohol and Substance Abuse

JAMES LAKE

Exercise

Persons who chronically abuse alcohol frequently experience depressed mood, which may trigger increased drinking. Those who exercised daily while hospitalized for medical monitoring during acute detoxification of alcohol reported significant improvements in general emotional well-being.[1] Persons abstaining from alcohol use who were enrolled in outpatient recovery programs reported improved mood with regular strength training or aerobic exercise.[2,3] Because of its demonstrated mental health benefits, regular exercise should be encouraged in all patients who abuse alcohol and drugs (assuming that there are no medical problems that would be aggravated by physical activity).

Mindfulness Training

Mindfulness training is offered widely in drug and alcohol relapse prevention programs and may reduce the risk of relapse in persons with substance use disorders.[4] Two studies suggest that transcendental meditation may be especially effective in reducing the relapse rate in persons who abstain from alcohol.[5,6] One study found that 12-step programs that emphasize a particular religious or spiritual philosophy may be more effective than "spiritually neutral" programs.[7]

Virtual Reality Graded Exposure

VRGET is a rapidly emerging technological intervention with a wide range of promising clinical applications for psychiatric disorders, including posttraumatic stress disorder, phobias, eating disorders, cognitive rehabilitation following stroke, and substance abuse and dependence. Most virtual reality tools are in the early stages of development and are not commercially available. VRGET protocols have been created with the goal of stimulating drug or alcohol craving in patients followed by response prevention and desensitization.

Regular VRGET sessions result in diminished nicotine or illicit drug cravings in real-life situations that would be expected to trigger craving. In a small controlled trial, 20 nicotine-dependent adults who were not taking conventional anticraving medications were enrolled in a VRGET protocol.[8] The patients were exposed to virtual smoking cues that resulted in increased nicotine craving and physiological indicators of craving, including elevated pulse and respiration rates. Subjects exposed to neutral virtual reality stimuli in the sham arm did not report symptoms of increased nicotine craving.

Other virtual reality environments are being developed to stimulate alcohol or marijuana craving, and future virtual reality tools will be combined with cognitive therapy strategies aimed at response prevention and desensitization to real-life situations that would be expected to stimulate craving or drug-seeking behavior. Future VRGET tools will couple cognitive therapy with increasingly realistic virtual cues to achieve the goal of desensitizing persons who abuse alcohol or drugs to environments that would be expected to stimulate craving or drug-using behavior. A significant emerging virtual reality tool is the "virtual crack house," which is currently under development at the University of Georgia.

Cranio-electrotherapy

CES involves the application of weak electrical current to specific points on the scalp or ears. In a 7-year prospective study of CES in the treatment of alcohol, drug, and nicotine addiction, acute and chronic withdrawal symptoms were diminished, normal sleep patterns were restored more rapidly, and more patients remained addiction-free following regular CES treatments compared with conventional medication management. Patients addicted to alcohol, drugs, or nicotine who were treated using CES reported significantly fewer anxiety symptoms and higher quality-of-life measures than patients who underwent conventional drug treatments.[9]

Protocols that use daily CES treatments compare favorably with combined psychotherapy, relaxation training, and biofeedback for reducing anxiety in patients abusing any substance.[10] Preliminary findings suggest that daily 30-minute CES treatments significantly improve cognitive functioning and reduce measures of stress and anxiety in inpatient alcohol abusers or polysubstance abusers.[11]

In a 4-week, double-blind study, 20 patients who were depressed and abused alcohol were randomized to daily CES treatments (70 to 80 Hz, 4 to 7 mA), versus sham treatment. The patients treated with daily CES reported significantly reduced anxiety by the end of the study. These preliminary data suggest that CES may be a reasonable alternative treatment for anxiety in persons withdrawing from alcohol or other substances while avoiding the risk of cross-tolerance and dependence that is associated with the use of benzodiazepines in this population.[12]

EEG and Electromyogram Biofeedback

Limited data suggest that electromyogram and thermal biofeedback[13] as well as EEG biofeedback training may reduce relapse risk in abstinent alcoholics.[14,15] In EEG biofeedback training, the patient learns how to self-induce brain states that correspond with deep relaxation. Limited findings from case studies suggest that EEG biofeedback using an alpha-theta entrainment protocol reduces relapse risk in persons abstaining from alcohol,[16] but not in persons abstaining from cocaine.[17]

Dim Morning Light

Findings from a small controlled trial suggest that early morning exposure to dim light (ie, narrow-spectrum light with an intensity of 250 lux in contrast to full-spectrum white light with an intensity of 10,000 lux) improves depressed mood in persons abstaining from alcohol who have seasonal affective disorder.[18] Since depressed mood is an established risk factor for alcohol addiction relapse, the postulated mood enhancing effects of early morning dim light may provide a beneficial approach to relapse prevention in persons abstaining from alcohol who experience seasonal mood changes. More research is needed to confirm these preliminary findings.

Acupuncture

The effectiveness of acupuncture as a treatment for enhancing abstinence from alcohol, cocaine, and other drugs cannot be ascribed solely to a placebo effect.[19] Numerous early studies showed that regular acupuncture treatment increased brain levels of endogenous opioid peptides.[20–22] Stimulating specific acupuncture points on the ears, hands, and back of the neck may reduce alcohol craving and decrease withdrawal symptoms in persons who abuse alcohol; however, acupuncture probably does not reduce craving and relapse after treatment is discontinued.[23,24]

There are inconsistent findings for acupuncture in relapse prevention in persons abstaining from alcohol. Ambiguous findings may reflect the criteria used to select acupuncture points, the different treatment protocols (ie, conventional vs electroacupuncture), as well as differences in frequency or total duration of treatments, and the skill level or specialized training of individual practitioners. In 1 sham-controlled study, persons who abuse alcohol reported significant reductions in withdrawal symptoms within hours of initial treatment and no withdrawal symptoms within 72 hours of the second acupuncture treatment.[25] There is emerging evidence for correlations between specific acupuncture protocols and a significant reduction in alcohol craving and relapse rates in persons recovering from an alcohol addiction.[26,27] However, other findings do not support the hypothesis that acupuncture reduces craving and relapse risk among persons who abuse alcohol.[28]

In spite of the fact that findings of most controlled trials on smoking have been negative or equivocal, acupuncture is widely used in the United States and in Western Europe to facilitate smoking cessation and to lessen symptoms of nicotine withdrawal. Initial open trials of acupuncture for smoking cessation were very promising[29]; however, more recent sham-controlled trials have yielded equivocal results. Significant differences in the severity of withdrawal symptoms were not found in nicotine-dependent patients who were randomized to an accepted protocol of electroacupuncture versus a sham procedure.[30] Two hundred thirty-eight high school students who smoked cigarettes were randomized to weekly auricular acupuncture treatment based on a well-defined protocol for smoking reduction versus a nonspecific protocol. By the end of the 4-week study, only 1 student had stopped smoking and there were no significant differences between the 2 groups in terms of nicotine craving; however, students who completed the smoking cessation protocol smoked fewer cigarettes per day than students in the sham group.[31]

A Cochrane systematic review and meta-analysis of 22 sham-controlled studies and more than 2000 patients on the efficacy of acupuncture for smoking cessation found no evidence of therapeutic efficacy. Sham-controlled studies on conventional acupuncture, acupressure, electroacupuncture, and laser acupuncture were included in the meta-analysis.[32] Because most studies to date are relatively short and do not specify the acupuncture protocol used, longer sham-controlled studies are needed to determine whether optimizing the frequency, duration, and type of acupuncture treatment may be beneficial for smoking cessation.

Negative findings from a Cochrane systematic review and a separate independent review support the conclusion that both conventional acupuncture and electroacupuncture are ineffective in reducing symptoms of nicotine withdrawal and in controlling cocaine addiction.[33,34] Nevertheless, persons who use cocaine frequently report subjective calming and diminished craving after only 1 or 2 acupuncture treatments, and this effect is apparently sustained with repeated treatment.

A study comparing 3 auricular acupuncture protocols for relapse prevention in persons abusing cocaine and other narcotics concluded that auricular acupuncture reduced drug craving regardless of the protocol used.[35] In an 8-week controlled study comparing acupuncture with conventional drug therapies and placebo in persons using cocaine who were being treated with methadone (Dolophine, Methadose) maintenance therapy, half of the enrolled subjects dropped out, but almost 90% of those who completed the study achieved abstinence after 8 weeks of treatment.[36] Patients who successfully achieved abstinence reported diminished narcotics craving and improved mood.

Qigong

Findings of sham-controlled trials suggest that external qigong treatment-which must be provided by a qigong healer/master-reduces the severity of withdrawal symptoms in persons who are addicted to heroin.[37] Animal studies suggest that external qigong applied to morphine-dependent mice lessens the behavioral symptoms of withdrawal following pharmacological blockade of morphine at the level of brain receptors.[38] Regular qigong treatments may provide a useful adjunct to conventional pharmacological and behavioral management of detoxification and withdrawal from heroin and other opiates. The unskillful practice of qigong can potentially result in agitation or psychosis in patients. Persons with an addiction disorder who are interested in qigong should work with a skilled qigong instructor or medical qigong therapist.

Dr Lake is in private practice in Monterey, Calif, and is on clinical faculty in the department of psychiatry and behaviorial sciences at Stanford University Hospital. He co-chairs the American Psychiatric Association Caucus on Complementary, Alternative, and Integrative Care (www.APACAM.org) and is author of the Textbook of Integrative Mental Health Care (Thieme).

References

1. Palmer J, Vacc N, Epstein J. Adult inpatient alcoholics: physical exercise as a treatment intervention. *J Stud Alcohol.* 1988;49:418–421.

2. Palmer JA, Palmer LK, Michiels K, Thigpen B. Effects of type of exercise on depression in recovering substance abusers. *Percept Mot Skills.* 1995;80:523–530.

3. Skrede A, Munkvold H, Watne O, Martinsen EW. Exercise contacts in the treatment of substance dependence and mental disorders [in Norwegian]. *Tidsskr Nor Laegeforen.* 2006;126:1925–1927.

4. Breslin FC, Zack M, McMain S. An information-processing analysis of mindfulness: implications for relapse prevention in the treatment of substance abuse. *Clinical Psychology: Science and Practice.* 2002;9:275–299.

5. Alexander CP, Robinson P, Rainforth M. Treating and preventing alcohol, nicotine, and drug abuse through transcendental meditation: a review and statistical meta-analysis. *Alcohol Treat Q.* 1994;11:13–87.

6. Taub E, Steiner SS, Weingarten E, Walton KG. Effectiveness of broad spectrum approaches to relapse prevention in severe alcoholism: a long-term, randomized controlled trial of transcendental meditation, EMG biofeedback and electronic neurotherapy. *Alcohol Treat Q.* 1994;11:187–220.

7. Muffler J, Langrod J, Larson D. There is a balm in Gilead: religion and substance abuse treatment. In: Lowinson JH, Ruiz P, Millman RB, eds. *Substance Abuse: A Comprehensive Textbook.* 2nd ed. Baltimore: Williams & Wilkins; 1992.

8. Bordnick PS, Graap KM, Copp H, et al. Utilizing virtual reality to standardize nicotine craving research: a pilot study. *Addict Behav.* 2004;29:1889–1894.

9. Patterson MA, Firth J, Gardiner R. Treatment of drug, alcohol and nicotine addiction by neuroelectric therapy: analysis of results over 7 years. *Journal of Bioelectricity.* 1984;3:193–221.

10. Overcash S, Siebenthall A. The effects of cranial electrotherapy stimulation and multisensory cognitive therapy on the personality and anxiety levels of substance abuse patients. *Am J Electromed.* 1989;6:105–111.

11. Schmitt R, Capo T, Boyd E. Cranial electrotherapy stimulation as a treatment for anxiety in chemically dependent persons. *Alcohol Clin Exp Res.* 1986;10:158–160.

12. Krupitsky EM, Burakov AM, Karandashova GF, et al. The administration of transcranial electric treatment for affective disturbances therapy in alcoholic patients. *Drug Alcohol Depend.* 1991;27:1–6.

13. Sharp C, Hurford DP, Allison J, et al. Facilitation of internal locus of control in adolescent alcoholics through a brief biofeedback-assisted autogenic relaxation training procedure. *J Subst Abuse Treat.* 1997;14:55–60.

14. Peniston EG, Kulkosky PJ. Alpha-theta brainwave training and beta-endorphin levels in alcoholics. *Alcohol Clin Exp Res.* 1989;13:271–279.

15. Peniston EG, Kulkosky PJ. Alcoholic personality and alpha-theta brainwave training. *Med Psychother.* 1990;3:37–55.

16. Schneider F, Elbert T, Heimann H, et al. Self-regulation of slow cortical potentials in psychiatric patients: alcohol dependency. *Biofeedback Self Regul.* 1993;18:23–32.

17. Richard AJ, Montoya ID, Nelson R, Spence RT. *J Subst Abuse Treat.* 1995;12:401–413.

18. Avery DH, Bolte MA, Ries R. Dawn simulation treatment of abstinent alcoholics with winter depression. *J Clin Psychiatry.* 1998;59:36–42.

19. Brewington V, Smith M, Lipton D. Acupuncture as a detoxification treatment: an analysis of controlled research. *J Subst Abuse Treat.* 1994;11:289–307.

20. Cheng RS, Pomeranz B, Yu G. Electroacupuncture treatment of morphine-dependent mice reduces signs of withdrawal, without showing cross-tolerance. *Eur J Pharmacol.* 1980;68:477–481.

21. Clement-Jones V, McLoughlin L, Lowry PJ, et al. Acupuncture in heroin addicts; changes in Metenkephalin and beta-endorphin in blood and cerebrospinal fluid. *Lancet.* 1979;2:380–383.

22. Ng LK, Douthitt TC, Thoa NB, Albert CA. Modification of morphine-withdrawal syndrome in rats following transauricular electrostimulation: an experimental paradigm for auricular electroacupuncture. *Biol Psychiatry.* 1975;10:575–580.

23. Konefal J, Duncan R, Clemence C. The impact of the addition of an acupuncture treatment program to an existing metro-Dade County outpatient substance abuse treatment facility. *J Addict Dis.* 1994;13:71–99.

24. Richard AJ, Montoya ID, Nelson R, Spence RT. Effectiveness of adjunct therapies in crack cocaine treatment. *J Subst Abuse Treat.* 1995;12:401–413.

25. Yankovskis G, Beldava I, Livina B. Osteoreflectory treatment of alcohol abstinence syndrome and craving for alcohol in patients with alcoholism. *Acupunct Electrother Res.* 2000;25:9–16.

26. Bullock ML, Culliton PD, Olander RT. Controlled trial of acupuncture for severe recidivist alcoholism. *Lancet.* 1989;24:1435–1439.

27. Bullock ML, Umen AJ, Culliton PD, Olander RT. Acupuncture treatment of alcoholic recidivism: a pilot study. *Alcohol Clin Exp Res.* 1987;11:292–295.

28. Worner TM, Zeller B, Schwarz H, et al. Acupuncture fails to improve treatment outcome in alcoholics. *Drug Alcohol Depend.* 1992;30:169–173.

29. Fuller JA. Smoking withdrawal and acupuncture. *Med J Aust.* 1982;1:28–29.

30. White AR, Resch KL, Ernst E. Randomized trial of acupuncture for nicotine withdrawal symptoms. *Arch Intern Med.* 1998;158:2251–2255.

31. Kang HC, Shin KK, Kim KK, Youn BB. The effects of the acupuncture treatment for smoking cessation in high school student smokers. *Yonsei Med J.* 2005;46:206–212.

32. White AR, Rampes H, Ernst E. Acupuncture for smoking cessation. *Cochrane Database Syst Rev.* 2002;2: CD000009.

33. D'Alberto A. Auricular acupuncture in the treatment of cocaine/crack abuse: a review of efficacy, the use of the National Acupuncture Detoxification Association protocol, and the selection of sham points. *J Altern Complement Med.* 2004;10:985–1000.

34. White AR, Resch KL, Ernst E. A meta-analysis of acupuncture techniques for smoking cessation. *Tob Control.* 1999;8: 393–397.

35. Konefal J, Duncan R, Clemence C. Comparison of three levels of auricular acupuncture in an outpatient substance abuse treatment program. *Altern Med J.* 1995;2:8–17.

36. Margolin A, Avants SK, Chang P, Kosten TR. Acupuncture for the treatment of cocaine dependence in methadone-maintained patients. *Am J Addict.* 1993;2:194–201.

37. Li M, Chen K, Mo Z. Use of qigong therapy in the detoxification of heroin addicts. *Altern Ther Health Med.* 2002;8:56–59.

38. Mo Z, Chen KW, Ou W, Li M. Benefits of external qigong therapy on morphine-abstinent mice and rats. J Altern Complement Med. 2003;9:827–835.

Exercise and Drug Detoxification

SIMON ODDIE

Introduction

Leeds prison is a local category B male prison serving the communities of North, West and East Yorkshire. Its operational capacity is 1,254 and is regularly fully used. Over a number of years the prison had noted an increase in prisoner use of substances, particularly class A drugs. Many prisoners suffer withdrawal symptoms and medication was viewed as the main means of managing their recovery. It has long been recognised, within the physical education community, that physical exercise has a major role in therapeutic detoxification and rehabilitation. As a result a research project was instigated at Leeds to move beyond anecdotal observations and towards the formation of a first stage detoxification programme. The programme itself is broken down into three stages:

- identification of the user type and history;
- a short induction period that places the emphasis on detoxification; and,
- a detoxification treatment programme with continuous individual reviews.

Identification of Clients

When a prisoner arrives at Leeds prison they are processed through the reception centre. Important aspects of the reception process are individual interviews for medical assessment and CARAT assessment, these are the two methods used to identify substance misusers. The criteria for entry to the programme are that those referred should be identified as being:

- at risk of self-harm (F2052 SH);
- chaotic polydrug users;
- likely to be on a short sentence;
- having a history of mental health or suffers depression; a crack cocaine user; and,
- having not previously received drug treatment.

Spaces are limited to 12 per week. Programmes are voluntary and the initial contact is very important. The team have learnt the importance of the programme induction, particularly developing an environment of mutual respect and a genuine desire for the client to achieve success.

The Induction Process

The induction process is important not only to set standards but also as a motivational tool. Induction sessions are held in groups to enable the development of trust and mutual support. Individuals are informed about the programme, making it clear that it is not rehabilitation, but is purely about detoxification and improving well-being. Clients are helped to recognise that they are at the start of the process and are aware of the next stages. Many report that they simply 'want to feel better' and this is a powerful motivation.

Many prisoners are sceptical about the process particularly those who are experiencing depression, finding it difficult to comprehend that exercise at an intense level will make them feel better. The vast majority have not engaged in any form of physical exercise and find it hard to believe that they can exercise at all. During a one-to-one appraisal they complete a medical questionnaire covering a variety of physical conditions that may affect exercise, which is also used as our compact and consent form. This is a valuable time where we can address their fears.

Detoxification Programme and Individual Review

The programme is based on frequency and intensity. To promote improvement, the group exercises for one hour, starting at a low intensity, quickly rising as the sessions move on. The duration stays the same but the intensity increases, in most cases quite dramatically. From experience we aim to have a minimum heart rate of 130+ dependent on age and ability, it is at this level we have experienced greater feelings of euphoria when the individual has completed a session. This is due not only to the physical effects of exercise, but also the effects on the brain—the neurological effect. For the individual this gives them a feeling of well-being and in some cases a 'high' which we observe after each session. This feeling of well-being is most likely exaggerated due to the chemical suppression in the brain resulting from drug misuse.

It has been noted that, even on completion of the first session when the intensity is at the lowest level, individuals exhibit an improved sense of well-being. This is only short-lived but important as it can motivate the individual to continue. The sense of well-being develops during the detoxifying period and becomes self-perpetuating.

The exercise programme is as follows, changing every two days:

Week one

- Day one and two—six sets of ten minutes
- Day three and four—four sets of 15 minutes

Week two

- Day five and six—three sets of 20 minutes
- Day seven and eight—two sets of 30 minutes

This is not set in stone and often the group moves through the programme quicker than expeded, depending upon ability. There is just enough time between sets to have a drink and change machine. It is our experience that motivation is very important, as most of the clients have never used a structured exercise programme as a form of treatment.

The next step after the first two weeks detoxifying, is to encourage the individual to continue with a structured exercise regime on a regular basis. This can only have a positive effect towards drug abstinence.

The Detox Gymnasium

Our aims at HMP Leeds detox gymnasium are:

> To have a positive effect on those who attend the programme, to help them detox efficiently and safely, helping to speed up the body's natural processes and its ability to heal itself.

The detox gymnasium consists of cardio-vascular equipment, bikes, rower, steppers and cross-trainers. These machines were chosen for safety and ease of use. All the machines can monitor heart rate and all are programmable. We also have an Infra-red Heat Therapy Sauna which has therapeutic benefits too numerous to list, but is primarily used for individuals who have joint conditions which could be made worse by exercise, and it is used as an incentive or reward. Fitech software is used to assess well-being. Many drug users are dangerously under weight, lacking vital fat and muscle, and it is important that this is discussed with the individual.

Keeping groups small (up to 12) allows us to monitor individual progress and set individual targets during the sessions. This intervention has been proved to achieve our aim.

Building an Individual's Motivation to Achieve

Motivation is the key to success. Physical Education Officers are renowned for having good motivational skills. To deliver this kind of programme a basic understanding on addiction and how drugs affect the body is essential and understanding how exercise can be an effective treatment for withdrawal. This information plays a large part in the motivational aspect of delivering this programme. As already stated, the opportunity to get through the withdrawal quicker is a good start. Other techniques include setting individual goals, altering duration and intensity, using hill climbs, random and manual settings on a selected machine, creating a group atmosphere, and—would you believe it—singing! We have found that by putting the onus back to the individual (we are only there to guide them through the process, they are the ones who need to put the effort in), they gain control of their own therapy process. Peer motivation is also a very useful tool: for instance, when an individual is struggling, the group rally round and help. However, group competition is not encouraged, as we do not want to further reduce the self-esteem of the less capable. Individual goals are preferable.

Aches, pains, cramps and the general feelings of withdrawal should be expected, and being sick occasionally happens. These people are relatively ill and do not need to be encouraged to be ill, our aim is clear: positivity and understanding are more appropriate. This is why it is the combination of motivational techniques that get the best from a group or individual.

Physical Education Officers are renowned for having good motivational skills.

Recovering from Addiction with Exercise

A drug is a chemical or mixture of chemicals which when taken alters the body's biological function (the way the brain/body works) and possibly its structure (body organs, liver brain, muscles etc) WHO 1980. One of the reasons that drug misuse can exert such powerful control over behaviour is that it has neurological effects: through the brain drugs take over the role of controlling behaviour. What happens in the brain is that drugs alter the way the pleasure centre and other parts of the brain function. This includes neuro-chemicals such as Dopamine (pleasure/reward), Serotonin (well-being, regulating mood, aggression, sexual activity, sleep and sensitivity to pain) and Endorphins (pain control). Drugs affect these parts of the brain, this is what provides the pleasurable and addictive qualities. However, recent evidence shows that long-term use is likely to impair the brain's ability to return to normal function, hence the withdrawal effects.

Pharmacological interventions are readily used to combat addictions. Today, the right amount of medication used in combination with a behaviour modification plan yields the best results during recovery from addiction. In order for the brain to re-establish a state of equilibrium, the user must use again or be treated with a different synthetic intervention that decreases cravings for illicit drugs. Unfortunately, using drugs to combat drug addiction is not always the most desirable approach because treatment medication may actually be affecting the brain in a similar way. Some illicit drugs such as crack cocaine do not have a synthetic intervention. The reality however, is that drugs provide the most immediate response to recovery from drug abuse. One of the keys to effective recovery and prevention is making the process both tolerable and attainable. This can be a difficult task when a drug user is comparing his/her feelings during recovery with the euphoric feeling of being on a 'high'.

So, can exercise serve as an effective treatment for the prevention and recovery of drug misuse? Recent research shows that as well as causing cardio-vascular affects, exercise changes behaviour, brain chemistry and brain growth. This is central to dealing with the affects of drugs described above. In particular, exercise stimulates the production of neuro-chemicals such as endorphins, which control pain. In light of this, exercise should certainly be considered as a treatment option. Its dual approach can be effective in correcting chemical imbalances in the brain resulting from drug misuse as well as repairing some of the damage.

Physical activity plays a significant role in providing the brain with nourishment and stimulation. This is especially true when complex skills are integrated as part of activity. Exercise is one of the vehicles that can facilitate an increase in brain activity, but more importantly it increases the amount of blood flowing to the brain. Certain levels of cardio-intense exercise will facilitate changes in brain chemistry. As the chemical needs of the brain are met, instinctive motivation becomes less of a priority. The need for the body to be active subsides and a state of equilibrium becomes more constant, this state helps the body to think and act more appropriately. Evidence supports the negative role that depression, anxiety, stress and other debilitating moods play in recovery. If exercise can improve the subject's mood then its use in conjunction with other strategies is valuable. Helping individuals reduce the impact of depression alone may be significant enough to integrate exercise as a serious component of both recovery and prevention programmes.

Evaluation

The evaluation of our programme is based on information collected on PE evaluation forms, which are completed confidentially by the prisoners following the two-week programme. Some of the results are shown in the graph on next page.

The prisoners also made further comments about the course. Their answers can be put into four sub headings: Physical, Mental Health, Service and Personal Comments.

Physical issues

This evidence goes to show that after just two weeks we are getting a very positive response, individuals were 'feeling better and a lot fitter'. Comments like 'gets your detox done quicker' and 'it helps you get through your rattle (withdrawal) a lot easier' go to endorse our aim. We have found that individuals have gained a basic understanding about exercise and detoxification, 'it sweated a lot of shit out of my system', burns the rubbish out of your body' and 'because it does help sweat it out of you and improves your health'. Out of the 30 individuals questioned we did not receive any negative comments. 'I felt so good' is not the kind of comment you would usually expect from a withdrawing drug misuser, but was typical of the comments after the course.

Mental Health issues

Again there was a very positive reaction, the main benefits in the short term seem to be directed at keeping the body and mind occupied: 'taken my mind off wanting to use by giving me something more to do than just lying on my bed and counting away the days'. Most found the course very motivating and made them feel better about themselves. One individual said he would recommend this course 'for someone who wants a positive outlook on life, to achieve his aims of staying off drugs, feeling good and gaining knowledge in all drugs areas'. The programme also encourages team effort ready for group work this is highlighted by comments like this, 'the lads open up and say what they really think, and feel relaxed enough with each other to say what problems they have had with drugs and achieve new goals in other ways', and 'the groups pull together'. Another stated 'thought I'd be the same when I went out but I'm more aware now, it's a lot better when you've got help'.

Service issues

The course is generally thought of as 'an excellent course' where both PEOs and Officers are praised for making it 'a good experience'. One individual stated 'this is the first time I have been given any help in prison the staff were excellent caring and very patient'. Another said 'I've been to jail on several occasions and done many courses; this course is sensational and really serves its purpose well'. One of the main issues is the length of the course. Most of the groups wanted at least another week, as one individual said 'it's the best detox course I have done, needs to be twice as long you just get into it after two weeks'. All the above comments reflect the opinions of all the courses we have completed approximately 25 groups) not just the 30 individuals chosen.

Personal Comments

Most of the personal comments are of thanks, but now and again you get a comment like 'I feel that being a member of such a group as this helps people that may be feeling isolated and find it hard to talk to people they don't know'. This course is not the easy option, individuals push themselves further than they may ever have done. However, they also get a lot of rewards from it, 'what you put in is what you get out, you learn stuff about yourself'.

Exercise is proving to be a more beneficial therapeutic treatment to aid recovery than first thought.

Conclusion

Detox is a way of giving the individual an informed choice about the next step. Whether that next step is re-tox, maintenance or abstinence. Opiate based medical detox also suppresses the brains chemical activity in areas already covered and though assists in reducing the effects of withdrawal does not help to address the brains chemical balance. If this detox is not available then the

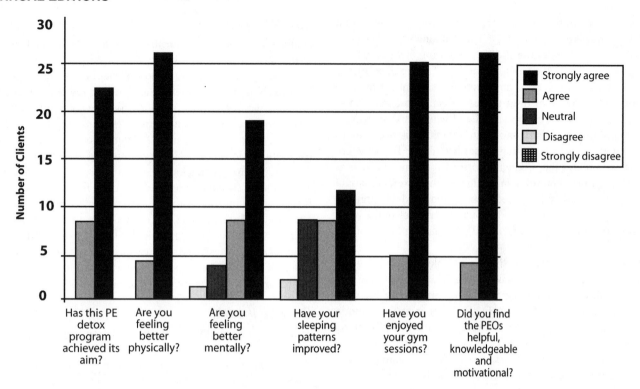

Figure 1   Detox Gymnasium

individual's choice is influenced by the depressive nature of the addiction: no choice.

This paper has demonstrated the importance of intense exercise for drug addiction prevention and recovery. Physical education within prison and community based programmes has a major role in detoxification and rehabilitation. A simple structured programme based on the foundations of exercise, frequency and intensity as outlined above, will improve the physiological and psychological well-being of recovering drug misusers. It also has a dramatic effect on reducing the length of the withdrawal process. It is well documented that physical exercise/training has an increased effect on physical fitness, self-confidence, self-discipline, personal responsibility etc. Research and experience show that exercise is proving to be a more beneficial therapeutic treatment to aid recovery than first thought. Intense exercise should now be recognized as a fundamental part of any detoxification and rehabilitation programme for recovering drug misusers.

References are available from the author.

Rehab Reality Check

As the traditional treatment centers do battle with glitzy newcomers, everyone is debating what works.

JERRY ADLER

The time is coming—perhaps even within the decade—when doctors will treat alcoholism with a pill. As they improve their understanding of the biochemistry of addiction, researchers will find new ways to interrupt the neurological sequence that begins with pulling the tab on a can of beer and ends with sobbing on the phone to someone you dated twice in 1987. It will be a paradigm shift as profound as the one wrought by Prozac in the treatment of depression, says Dr. Mark Willenbring of the National Institute on Alcohol Abuse and Alcoholism: people with drinking problems will get a modicum of counseling and prescriptions from their family doctors. This will be a great boon to most people except for athletes, congressmen and movie stars, who will lose one of the defining rites of passage of modern celebrity: the all-absolving, career-rejuvenating, Barbara Walters-placating ritual of *checking into rehab.*

It has been a fixture of our culture since as far back as 1983, when Elizabeth Taylor checked her aura of tragic, tawdry glamour into the Betty Ford Center, setting an example of courageous humility for future generations of troubled divas, wild-man comics and hard-partying rockers. Since that time, residential treatment programs for the middle and upper classes have proliferated across both the geographic and the therapeutic maps. Heated disputes have erupted between proponents of different treatment models. This is exacerbated by a growing rivalry between old-guard institutions like the Ford Center, with its comparatively austere campuslike ambience, and the new class of superluxury rehab centers in ocean-view mansions that supplement the traditional 12-step approach with acupuncture, massage, equine therapy and Native American Talking Circles. Charging from $40,000 to $100,000 for a 30-day stay, the deluxe centers approach rehab from the point of view that the dark night of the soul is a little less dreary if it's preceded by a sunset over the Pacific, viewed from the Malibu hills.

It's easy to mock the idea that these places rehabilitate anything other than the images of high-profile clients who appear to have chosen "addict" as a less embarrassing label than "sexual predator" or "bigot." But simple math suggests that, with as many as 26 residential treatment centers in Malibu, Calif., alone, there aren't enough celebrities to fill all the beds; the rest, presumably, are occupied by people—lawyers, executives, housewives—sincerely trying to overcome addiction, but who don't see themselves fitting in the "highly structured" environment of Phoenix House down the coast in Venice. (An exception appears to be San Francisco Mayor Gavin Newsom, who said he would do his rehab at his city's Delancey Street Foundation, where about 400 residents, many of them ex-convicts, spend up to two years learning "life skills" and staffing the foundation's restaurant and other businesses. How he would do that in practice was unclear last week.) "People feel more supported in an environment that mimics their real life," says Richard Rogg, founder and CEO of Promises Residential Center in Malibu. Rogg won't name clients, but among those who reportedly sought serenity on its lush grounds were Ben Affleck, Kelly Osbourne and Diana Ross. Daniel Gatlin, executive director of Renaissance Malibu, asserts that the ocean views aren't just an amenity, but serve a positive therapeutic function: "When you go out and overlook the ocean, you can take yourself out of yourself." At Sierra Tucson, in whose adobe casitas former congressman Mark Foley sought refuge, patients can work out their "relationship issues" by learning to bond with horses, animals that, unlike voters or studio executives, are considered nonjudgmental.

To John Schwarzlose, president and CEO of the Betty Ford Center in Rancho Mirage, Calif., the blurring of lines between "spa" and "treatment center" is disheartening. "They say, 'We have 500-count sheets.' It trivializes what we do." Schwarzlose may be sensitive in part because some of the Malibu places have been known to spread the rumor—which he denies—that Elizabeth Taylor had to clean the bathrooms when she was at Betty Ford. But Willenbring agrees that gourmet chefs and riding stables run counter to the spirit of treatment. "The best thing for you in rehab," he says, "is to sit next to a guy from skid row and realize, you're just as much an alcoholic as he is. Learning humility is part of the recovery process."

In fact, with a few exceptions most residential programs run along broadly similar lines. The typical stay is a month, which might not be optimal but is as much as most insurance plans covered back in the 1980s when the programs were designed. Now most plans barely pay for residential treatment at all. The reigning paradigm is the 12-step program pioneered by the Hazelden Foundation in the 1960s. Its advantage is that it provides a model and a ready-made, worldwide network for post-rehab support at Alcoholics Anonymous and its spinoffs. Most experts believe this is essential to recovery. "When people are released from their 28-day rehabs, relapse rates are pretty high without consistent after-care," says G. Alan Marlatt, director of the Addictive Behaviors Research Center at the University of Washington. "One of our expectations is that patients will go to AA and get a sponsor after they leave us," says Dr. Shari Corbitt, clinical director of Sierra Tucson. The disadvantage of the 12-step program, according to Chris Prentiss, cofounder of Passages Addiction Cure Center in Malibu, is that its emphasis on helplessness in the face of addiction makes people feel stupid and ashamed. Prentiss, whose background was in real estate before he got interested in rehab as a way to rescue his own son from addiction, is almost alone in rejecting the 12-step model, and in advertising his own program of intensive one-on-one therapy and personal empowerment as a "cure." "We don't send people to meetings," he boasts. "When they leave, they're cured"—which flies in the face of what virtually the entire drug-treatment community believes about the possibility of "curing" addiction.

Some programs supplant, or supplement, 12-step programs with newer therapies. Cognitive Behavioral Therapy focuses on overcoming poor self-esteem and defeatist thinking. ("I'll be an alcoholic all my life and I'll never amount to anything.") Motivational therapy aims to encourage and reinforce the desire for change. ("What don't you like about drinking? How much do you want to stop?") In a study involving alcoholics, according to Willenbring, these were each about equally successful, and no better nor worse than 12-step programs. The exact form of therapy, he says, is less important than just the fact of seeking treatment. A year after completing a rehab program, about a third of alcoholics are sober, an additional 40 percent are substantially improved but still drink heavily on occasion, and a quarter have completely relapsed.

There is an ongoing debate in the field between the hermetic model of places like Sierra Tucson, which bans cell phones and magazines as distractions from therapy, and the secular approach that attempts to integrate sober behavior into clients' ordinary lives. Wonderland Center, which has undertaken the Sisyphean challenge of treating Lindsay Lohan, sends its patients out into the world of temptation—it's located in West Hollywood, so they don't have to travel far for it—with a "Sober Companion" to utter for them the life-giving phrase, "mineral water with a twist." Individuals respond better to one program or another, but overall, the most important variable is simple motivation. Schwarzlose, whose facility has treated 76,000 people over the years, some more than once, points out that licensed health-care professionals and commercial pilots who go through rehab at Betty Ford usually stay clean afterward, because they know they'll be out of work for life if they fail another drug test. If movie studios treated actors the same way, he muses, gossip columns would have a lot less to write about.

But the real breakthrough, the paradigm shift, will come when safe, reliable drug treatments are available for addiction. Although they are no more likely to end addiction forever than Prozac ended depression, such drugs could make a big difference in the lives of people struggling with addiction. Their eventual likelihood got a big boost when researchers made the astonishing claim last month that people with injuries to a specific region of the brain instantly lost the desire to smoke. "There are probably 10 new drugs in development for alcoholism," says Willenbring, "and some are very exciting." Of course, people were very excited in the 1990s about using antidepressants to treat addiction, but that approach hasn't lived up to its promise. (Another disappointment was Antabuse, which reacts with alcohol to make you throw up; naltrexone, a more sophisticated drug, blocks the brain's opiate receptors—you can still drink, but it won't make you feel good. It can reduce relapse rates in the three months after treatment by 20 to 40 percent.)

'The best thing for you in rehab is to sit next to a skid-row guy and realize you're just as much a drunk as he is.'

But as researchers learn more about how addiction works, even more ingenious and effective drugs are possible. One, Topamax, an existing epilepsy drug (which means it has a leg up on safety testing), affects the balance between two brain chemicals, glutamate and GABA. Addicts have an excess of glutamate, which enhances the desire for drugs or alcohol; GABA inhibits it, so restoring the balance reduces cravings. You could call it willpower in a pill. A second class of drugs, nearing clinical trials, dampens the stress response, which researchers believe is crucial to preventing relapses after treatment. Willenbring cautions, though, that even the most effective drugs will undoubtedly have to be combined with some form of behavioral support.

But the paradigm shift goes deeper, because research will almost certainly also show that, under the $500 haircuts, celebrity brains are a lot like everyone else's. The advent of these drugs may also portend an end to that peculiar medical specialty, celebrity addiction, with its ego-soothing trappings and Pacific sunsets. One authority on this is William Moyers, 47, the son of TV journalist Bill Moyers, and himself a recovering alcoholic and crack addict. After four rounds of treatment he finally achieved sobriety in 1994. He is now vice president of external affairs of the Hazelden Foundation, which runs the highly respected treatment center in Minnesota. Hazelden, like Betty Ford, takes celebrities, but also many ordinary people struggling with addiction. "The best way to recover," he says, "is to level the playing field, so that people understand they're not alone. Whether they're actresses or waitresses."

With Anne Underwood, Raina Kelley, Karen Springen and Karen Breslau

No Longer Theory: Correctional Practices That Work

Criminologists and politicians have debated the effectiveness of correctional rehabilitation programs since the mid-1970s when criminal justice scholars and policy makers throughout the United States embraced Robert Martinson's credo of 'nothing works.' Programs based around punishment and surveillance grew. They are being embraced even stronger today despite the fact that Martinson later admitted that he was wrong. An ample amount of research exists that suggest that there are successful programs available to reduce future criminality of not only offenders but also of potential offenders. This article presents correctional practices that effectively reduce recidivism rates and recommends two additional programs, Logotherapy and the Intensive Journal, proven to be cost-effective in the fields of prevention and rehabilitation.

HARVEY SHRUM

L ife is difficult and seemingly unfair. When parents divorce, when one or both parents die, when we are bullied, or suffer a catastrophic illness or accident, when a friend is killed in an accident or war, we know that life is unfair and often very painful. But, Dr. Viktor Frankl (1997), survivor of the Holocaust, emphasized that the meaning of life is not what happens to us. It is what we do with that which happens to us.

When life appears to be unfair and painful many resort to self-medication. America comprises only five percent of the world's population, yet it consumes over 60 percent of the world's illicit drugs. Of those consuming illicit drugs, 77 percent are employed (Ferrell, 2003). Others attempt to divert pain and grief, usually onto those closest to them. Still others attempt to bury pain with their addiction to work, hobbies, or possessions. Often those who attempt to drug, divert, or bury their pain surround themselves with those of similar beliefs.

Sometimes laws are passed in the belief that they will make life fairer. Prisons are built at $100,000 per cell and $30–50,000 in annual costs per inmate are added to the tax burden. But, prisons and harsher laws tend to divert valuable funding away from public schools and other programs that tend to make our communities much safer. America has become so focused upon prisons as the answer to its social ills that today one in every 37 Americans is either in a state or federal prison or jail, or has been in the past (The Associated Press, August 18, 2003). The costs to American families are also enormous. The odds of a child of a recidivist father ending up in jail or prison at some point in his life are approximately 92 to one when compared to the general population. Increasing prison sentences do not reduce those odds.

Better ways do exist. Programs that lower recidivism rates result in less crime, lower costs for incarceration, fewer broken families, less welfare and social services, less prison overcrowding, less new prison construction, more funds for schools and alternatives to incarceration, and ultimately safer communities.

Recidivism and crime rates are readily reducible 16–62 percent and more by broader use of existing rehabilitation programs—substance abuse treatment, academic and vocational education, post-secondary education, intermediate sanctions, and alternatives to incarceration (Cypser, 1997). Some programs work so well that the rate of recidivism is as low as five to 15 percent (Manitonquat, 1996).

Addictions and "Will to Meaning"

Over 80 percent of those incarcerated committed their offense under the influence of drugs, committed their offense to get money for drugs, or committed their offense under the influence of alcohol (Bureau of Justice Statistics, 1993). The majority of inmates with drug and alcohol problems still do not receive sufficient treatment while in prison. And the number of drug/alcohol-using arrestees who are probably in need of treatment exceeds two million (Lipton, 1995). Dr. Frankl (1997) noted that there tended to be a significant inverse relationship between drug involvement and meaning in one's life. Ninety percent of students in high school and college who were addicted to alcohol and one hundred percent who were addicted to drugs reported that "meaning" was lacking in their lives. They may have purpose, but they do not have meaning. When men and women in prison are offered a drug and alcohol rehabilitation program, it is generally limited to a 12-step program, the only program generally acceptable to many parole boards, and 12-step programs do not address the lack of meaning in their lives.

Treatment for Addictions

The type of addiction treatment may not matter as much as whether sufficient treatment has been provided, usually a minimum of 12–24 months combined with education leading to a GED and/or vocational training. Addiction recovery begins with treatment inside prison. But, to be most effective, the addict must continue his treatment following his release to parole. The strongest predictors of outcome for substance abuse treatment, noted Condelli and Hubbard (1994), regardless of the type of treatment, are both time of duration and number of sessions in treatment. One program in Brooklyn (1996) placed second felony drug offenders into residential drug treatment usually for 18 to 24 months. After three years, the re-arrest rates for offenders who completed the program were 6.7–8.2 percent.

A study conducted for the state of California provided the most comprehensive cost-benefit examination on the effectiveness of substance abuse treatment. Looking at all treatment programs in the state, researchers concluded that every dollar spent on treatment resulted in seven dollars in savings on reduced crime and health care costs (Mauer & Huling, 1995). Caulkins et al (1997) demonstrated that treatment of heavy drug users is 15–17 times more effective in reducing crime than spending the same money on mandatory minimum sentences. In another study these same researchers noted that spending money on treatment reduces consumption of cocaine 3.7 times more than spending that same money on conventional enforcement, and 7.6 times more than spending it on mandatory minimum sentences for drug dealers.

Caulkins et al (1997) noted that spending money to treat heavy cocaine users was four times more effective in reducing total national consumption than spending it on conventional enforcement against drug dealers, and nearly eight times more effective than spending it on mandatory minimum sentences for the same dealers. Additionally, treatment reduces about ten times more serious crime than conventional enforcement and fifteen more than mandatory minimums.

In a joint study by the RAND Corporation, the U.S. Army, and the Office of National Drug Control Strategy, researchers Rydell and Everingham (1994) found that drug treatment programs are seven times more cost-effective in reducing cocaine consumption than other programs that aim at controlling the supply of drugs. Treatment is eleven times more effective than border interdiction and twenty-two times more effective than trying to control foreign production. This study further concluded that drug treatment could reduce cocaine consumption a third if extended to all heavy users.

Cognitive Approaches to Addictions Treatment

Rational Emotive Behavior Therapy, developed by Dr. Albert Ellis, is a cognitive-behavior therapy approach to addictions (Dryden, 2002). The major reasons for its popularity are its effectiveness, short-term nature, and low cost. It works best for individuals desiring a scientific, present-focused, and active treatment for coping with life's difficulties. It is based on a few simple principles having profound implications: 1) You are responsible for your own emotions and actions. 2) Your harmful emotions and dysfunctional behaviors are the product of your irrational thinking. 3) You can learn more realistic views and, with practice, make them a part of you. 4) You will experience a deeper acceptance of yourself and greater satisfactions in life by developing a reality-based perspective.

Another alternative to the 12-step program is Logotherapy, developed by Dr. Viktor Frankl (1997). In logotherapy, or "health through meaning" emphasis is given to the absence in the "will to meaning." When we lack a will to meaning, noted Frankl, we generally seek to fill the existential vacuum with a "will to pleasure" that often leads to addictions, or a "will to power" that often leads to violence. He also noted that "people are most likely to become aggressive when they are caught in this feeling of emptiness and meaninglessness" (Frankl, 1997). Robert Jay Lifton (1969) appeared to agree with Frankl when he stated that "men are most apt to kill when they feel overcome by meaninglessness."

Dr. Viktor Frankl (1984, 1997) noted that the predominant factor leading to incarceration is the lack of meaning in one's life and that a first-termer differs from those who have never been in prison with respect to purpose in life. Criminality and purpose in life, Frankl noted, are inversely related. The irony is that the more persistently one offends, the more likely he is to be sentenced to longer terms of imprisonment and the less likely he is to increase his sense of purpose in life, and so the more likely he is to continue offending when released. The spreading existential frustration lies at the root of this phenomenon.

Frankl (1997) repeatedly emphasized the importance of meaning, rather than pleasure and power, as essential for the health of the body, the mind, and the spirit. He believed that the key to a positive view of life is an awareness that life has meaning under all circumstances, and that we have the capacity to find meaning in our life "experientially, creatively, and attitudinally." We can rise above ill health and blows of fate if we see meaning in our existence. Logotherapy helps people say yes to life, whether the suffering they experience comes from difficult human relations, job dissatisfaction, life-altering illness, survivor's guilt, or death of a loved one, or from self-made problems such as hypochondria or an overwhelming hunger for pleasure and power.

Logotherapy was introduced to inmates at the California Rehabilitation Center in Norco about 40 years ago as a short-term project (Crumbaugh, 1972). The program aimed at giving inmates a purpose and direction in life, and at helping them acquire the knowledge needed to pursue a new direction during and after their prison experience. The inmates, who participated in the project learned to see that their very experiences as criminals gave them a unique opportunity to help other criminals, thus turning their liabilities into assets society could use. Only one group of inmates went through the program before it was terminated. The recidivism rate for those who completed the program prior to parole was only 5.5 percent. Furthermore, when utilized as an addictions treatment program, it was found to be four times as effective as any other program.

I re-introduced Logotherapy to inmates nearing parole at Folsom State Prison in 1990. In 1998 Drs. Viktor Frankl and Joseph Fabry were invited to conduct a workshop for men serving life sentences for violent crimes. Dr. Frankl was too ill and weak at the time, so Dr. Fabry agreed to conduct two workshops on the principles of Logotherapy. Nineteen men serving life sentences attended both workshops. I supplemented these with several followup workshops and correspondence study assignments. One of the men was assisted in putting together a fifteen-hour workshop that enabled him to present what he had learned to his fellow peers. Five of the original group of nineteen men paroled. Three of those discharged from parole. The rate of recidivism since 1998 is zero percent.

Drs. Viktor Frankl (1997) and his colleague and friend Joseph Fabry (1988, 1994, & 1995) attempted to introduce logotherapy to the inmates at San Quentin and Folsom State Prison. At San Quentin one group of inmates formed a support group based on the principles of logotherapy. The group maintained contact following each individual's release from prison. Only one inmate in the logo-group returned to prison. Dr. Louis S. Barber (Frankl, 1997) holds that logotherapy is particularly applicable to the treatment of juvenile delinquents, noting that "almost always the 'lack of meaning and purpose in their lives' appeared to be present, said Barber, 'We have one of the highest rehabilitation rates in the U.S. working with young people in a rehabilitation setting, a recidivism rate of less than 17 percent against an average of some 40 percent.'"

The value of writing in alcohol and drug recovery has long been noted in treatment and twelve-step circles. However, Dr. Ira Progoff (1992), creator of the Intensive Journal wrote that unguided journal writing results in decreasing effectiveness over time. He also noted that whereas unguided journal writing often declines into behavior analysis and circuitous thinking, the Intensive Journal process does not. Instead, through its non-judgmental, non-analytical nature, along with "Journal Feedback," it gives the writer a mirroring capability that increases the energy, power, and effectiveness of the process over time. This experience has an empowering effect upon the Intensive Journal writer.

First introduced in 1992 at Folsom State Prison, the Intensive Journal is a practical method of self-development that utilizes writing exercises through a unique journal writing system. It's based on depth psychology and helps people access and work with their life experiences, feelings about family relationships, job, health, and meaning in life. Through a two-day introductory workshop, inmates discover improvement in job retention (Sealy and Duffy, 1977), in dealing with the causes of substance abuse and relapse and in rehabilitation while incarcerated. The first workshop introduces inmates to the first half of the Intensive Journal process. A second two-day workshop introduces inmates to the second half of the Intensive Journal. In the ten years since its introduction at Folsom State Prison, not one inmate who had completed at least the introductory Intensive Journal workshop returned to prison. In 2003 the Federal Bureau of Prisons adopted the Intensive Journal into its comprehensive re-entry program for inmates nearing parole.

In a related study of the impact on inmates at Folsom State Prison, 308 men were asked to provide a list of eight to twelve significant emotional events—ups and downs—that appeared to help shape their lives. Specifically identified as "Steppingstones" this writing exercise is only one segment of the Intensive Journal process. The lists were provided anonymously over a six-month period. They included important events from childhood to the present education, relationships, family life, mental, physical and spiritual health, marriages and divorces, births and deaths, and significant conflicts. The men were asked not to make any judgment—criticism or praise—for the actions they took or for the circumstances that were forced upon them, only to list them in the order that they came to mind.

A pattern appeared to take place. Without positive intervention following significant emotional events, particularly when they were traumatic in nature, all resorted to self-medicating, diverting, and/or burying their childhood pain. Every individual had been, is, or will be a victim in some way or other to trauma that causes loss of meaning. One in every two men in this study experienced the death of a loved one as a significant emotional event. One in every three listed growing up in a single-parent home; in most cases the custodial parent was the mother. And one in every five listed experiencing some form of traumatic physical, emotional and/or sexual abuse in childhood. When questioned later, four in every five verbalized acceptance of childhood abuse as "normal" and therefore did not list it as significant in their list of Steppingstones. Many also accepted as normal parents self-medicating with illicit drugs in their presence. Without therapeutic intervention shortly after these events, they became at greater risk for antisocial behavior, low self-esteem, depression, low educational attainment, underemployment, substance abuse, mental illness, and suicidal ideation. The Intensive Journal enabled them to deal with their issues in a safe, supporting environment.

Education and Recidivism

Nearly 80 percent of state prison inmates have not completed high school (Bureau of Justice Statistics, 1993). Eighty percent of these may have learning disabilities (Ross, 1987). A RAND study by the Office of Correctional Education (1994) noted that the cost effectiveness of graduation incentives, in serious crimes averted per million dollars spent, was calculated to be five times better than that of the 3-strikes program. Recidivism of young parolees is also related to the amount of prior education. Recidivism did not increase despite the fact that, as an incentive, graduates were released to parole about 10.6 months prior to their court determined minimum period of incarceration according to a 1996 legislative report by the New York Department of Correctional Services. Many states are granting early release to non-violent prisoners, cutting sentences, sending drug offenders to treatment centers, and revising tough-on-crime laws in reverse of a 20-year trend as cost-saving measures (McMahon, 2003).

One study found that the recidivism rate for those who received both the GED certificate and completed a vocational trade was over 20 percent lower than for those who did not reach either milestone. The overall recidivism rate for college degree holders was a low 12 percent, and inversely differentiated by type of degree: Associate, 13.7%; Baccalaureate, 5.6%; and Masters, 0% (U.S. Department of Education, 1988–1994). The more educational programs successfully completed for each six months confined the lower the recidivism rate (Harer, 1994). In 1983 a study of the Folsom State Prison college program revealed a zero percent recidivism rate for inmates earning a bachelors degree, while the average recidivism rate for the state's parolees was 23.9 percent for the first year, increasing to 55 percent within three years (Taylor, 1992). College education does reduce the likelihood of recidivism principally through post-release employment (Batiuk, Moke, and Rounree, 1997). Employed ex-felons become taxpayers and reduce the odds of their children eventually ending up in prison.

Recommendations by Judges, Wardens and Police Chiefs

In 2003 Supreme Court Justice Anthony Kennedy suggested that "prison terms are too long and that he favors scrapping the practice of setting mandatory minimum sentences for some federal crimes" (Cearan, 2003). The American Society of Criminology recommended expanding drug courts, alternatives to incarceration for nonviolent offenders, and community-based sentencing and treatment for those arrested for drug crimes. Furthermore, in a survey of prison wardens across America over 90 percent supported greater use of alternatives to incarceration, drug treatment, vocational training, and literacy and other educational programs (Sullivan, 1995). In another nationwide survey nearly 60 percent of police chiefs said placing drug users in court-supervised treatment programs is more effective than sentencing them to jail or prison. Nearly half of them said that more resources are needed to improve education, prevention, and treatment (Law Enforcement News, 1996). Finally, the American Correctional Association President, Bobbie Huskey (Sullivan, 1995), emphasized promoting greater use of sentencing options for nonviolent crime.

Additional time served in prison has little impact on recidivism. How can sentencing a child to life in a federal prison for delivering a small package, containing a small quantity of crack cocaine, for her uncle make the public safer? This is a child who was doing well in school and had never been in trouble with the law. Policies such as "truth-in-sentencing" that lengthen prison terms may be ineffective in improving public safety. Longer prison terms may provide some additional incapacitation effects, but they do so at great cost to our social-economic system and at the expense of more effective alternatives that make our communities safer. It is time that correctional educators and the voters reverse the current trend, emphasizing rehabilitation rather than punishment. When we suspect that we are not being told the truth, we have a duty to do the research, educate policy makers and legislators, and take the positive steps that lead to programs that work, regardless of the prevailing trend.

Summary and Recommendations

The background of this paper is a long-term interest in the psycho-spiritual nature of proven rehabilitation programs for offenders. I have focused on "What works?" Some clear conclusions and cause for recommendations have emerged.

- Rehabilitation does have an impact in reducing recidivism.
- Rehabilitation programs that have a significant impact on reducing recidivism rates are those which are intense, of 18–24 months minimum in duration and continue following release to the community.

- Program success depends on the selection of offenders who have the potential of assuming responsibility. It also depends on the patience and understanding of the program director in dealing with prison authorities, prospective employers, and clients, who are often suspicious, easily discouraged, and respond to negative peer pressure from fellow inmates.

- Logotherapy holds great promise in restoring the "will to meaning" to those who have lost it, not only to those in jail, prison, or drug/alcohol rehabilitation programs, but also to those in grades K–16. Dr. Fabry's Guideposts to Meaning (1988) is an excellent resource for program development.

- The Intensive Journal also hold great promise in rehabilitating inmates as well as preventing young people from taking the path that often leads to addictions and incarceration. It is not only conducive in fostering self-improvement, but also in fostering/developing vocational interests, in increasing awareness and healing of health, addictions, and relationships. It also improves writing and communication skills, enhances relationships with family, and achieves breakthroughs in issues and decision-making.

Methods of prevention and rehabilitation do work, but correctional, educational, spiritual and psychiatric staff on both sides of the prison walls must support these goals if reduction in recidivism rates is to be achieved. When we embrace rehabilitation as a goal, we embrace hope. Hopefully, prevention and alternatives to incarceration will be emphasized to a much greater degree in the future. In the words of Nietzsche: "When we treat a man as he is, he only becomes worse. But, when we treat a man as he can be, he will be that which he can be."

References

Batiuk, Mary Ellen (June 1997). The State of Post-secondary Education in Ohio Journal of Correctional Education, 48 (2), 70–72.

Batiuk, M. E., P. Moke, and P. W. Rounree (March 1997). Crime and Rehabilitation: Correctional Education as an Agent of Change: A Research Note Justice Quarterly, 14, (1).

Caulkins, J. P., C. P. Rydell, W. Schwabe, and J. Chiesa (1997). Mandatory Minimum Drug Sentences: Throwing Away the Key or the Taxpayer's Money? RAND Corporation Study.

Condelli, W. S. & R. L Hubbard (1994). "Relationship between Time Spent in Treatment and Client Outcomes from Therapeutic Communities Journal of Substance Abuse Treatment, 77 (1), 25–33.

Crumbaugh, James C. (May 1972). "Changes in Frankl's Existential Vacuum as a Measure of Therapeutic Outcome" Newsletter for Research in Psychology, H (2).

Cypser, R. J. (October 1997). What Works in Reducing Recidivism and Thereby Reducing Crime and Cost. New York: CURE.

Dryden, Windy (2002). Handbook of Individual Therapy. Sage Publications, Fourth Edition.

Edelstein, M. R. and D. R. Steele (1997). Three-Minute Therapy: Change Your Thinking, Change Your Life. Clendbridge Publishing Company.

Fabry, Joseph B. (1988). Guideposts to Meaning: Discovering What Really Matters. Oakland, California: New Harbinger Publications, Inc.

Fabry, Joseph B. (1994). Pursuit of Meaning. Abilene, Texas: Institute of Logotherapy Press.

Fabry, Joseph B. (1995). Finding meaning in Life: Logotherapy. New York: Jason Aronson.

Ferrell, Vance (2003). Hard Drugs Can Ruin You. Altamont, Texas: Harvestime Books.

Frankl, Viktor (1984). Man's Search for Meaning. New York: Washington Square Press.

Frankl, Viktor (1997). Man's Search for Ultimate Meaning, New York & London: Plenum Press.

Gearan, Anne (April 9, 2003). Kennedy: Too Many People Are Behind Bars. The Associated Press.

Harer, Miles (1994). Recidivism Among Federal Prisoners Released in 1987. Federal Bureau of Prisons Office of Research & Evaluation.

Lifton, Robert Jay (1969). History and Human Survival. New York: Random House.

Lipton, Douglas S. (November 1995). The Effectiveness of Treatment for Drug Abusers Under Criminal Justice Supervision. National Institute of Justice Research Report.

Manitonquat (1996). Ending Violent Crime: A Vision of a Society Free of Violence. Publisher.

Mauer, Marc and Tracy Ruling (October 1995). Young Black Americans and the Criminal Justice System: Five Years Later. The Sentencing Project.

McMahon, Patrick (August 10, 2003). "States Revisit 'Get-Tough' Policies as Revenue Slows, Prisons Overflow." USA Today.

Progoff, Ira (1992). At a Journal Workshop. New York: Washington Square Press.

Ross, J. M. (1987). "Learning Disabled Adults: Who Are They and What Do We Do With Them?" Lifelong Learning 77, No. 3: 4–7, 11. (ERIC #EJ 361 993).

Rydell, Peter and Susan S. Everingham (1994). Controlling Cocaine: Supply vs. Demand Programs. A joint study by the RAND Corporation, the U. S. Army, and the Office of National Drug Control Strategy.

Sealy, S. A. and T. F. Duffy (1977). The New York State Department of Labor Job-Training Program: Applying the Progoff Intensive Journal Method. Abridged Report.

Sullivan, J. (1995). From Classrooms to Cellblocks: A National Perspective. Center on Juvenile and Criminal Justice.

Taylor, Jon M. (September 1992). "Post secondary Correctional Education: An Evaluation of Effectiveness and Efficiency" Journal of Correctional Education, 43 (3), 132–141.

Waldon Jr., Alton R. (April 1996). Unhealthy choice: Prisons Over Schools in New York State. State Senator, 10th District.

—— (March 1993). Survey of State Prison Inmates, 7997. Bureau of Justice Statistics, NCJ136949.

—— (1996). The Eighth Annual Shock Legislative Report 1996. New York Department of Correctional Services and the Division of Parole.

—— (1994). The Impact of Correctional Education on Recidivism, 1988–1994. Office of Correctional Education, U.S. Department of Education.

—— (1996). Brooklyn Treatment Alternatives to Street Crime (TASQ, 7997–7992.)

—— (April 30, 1996). Law Enforcement News.

—— (August 18, 2003). Study: 7 in 37 U.S. Adults Have "prison experience". The Associated Press.

—— (August 18, 2003). The Associated Press.

—— (September 30, 1996). U.S. News & World Report.

HARVEY SHRUM, Ed.D., is a Re-Entry teacher at Folsum State Prison. At the urging of the late Dr. Fabry, Institute of Logotherapy, Dr. Shrum is nearing completion of a self-help book entitled Seeking Meaning in a Cell.

Test-Your-Knowledge Form

We encourage you to photocopy and use this page as a tool to assess how the articles in *Annual Editions* expand on the information in your textbook. By reflecting on the articles you will gain enhanced text information. You can also access this useful form on a product's book support Web site at *http://www.mhcls.com/online/*.

NAME: DATE:
_____

TITLE AND NUMBER OF ARTICLE:
_____

BRIEFLY STATE THE MAIN IDEA OF THIS ARTICLE:

_____

LIST THREE IMPORTANT FACTS THAT THE AUTHOR USES TO SUPPORT THE MAIN IDEA:

_____

WHAT INFORMATION OR IDEAS DISCUSSED IN THIS ARTICLE ARE ALSO DISCUSSED IN YOUR TEXTBOOK OR OTHER READINGS THAT YOU HAVE DONE? LIST THE TEXTBOOK CHAPTERS AND PAGE NUMBERS:

_____

LIST ANY EXAMPLES OF BIAS OR FAULTY REASONING THAT YOU FOUND IN THE ARTICLE:

_____

LIST ANY NEW TERMS/CONCEPTS THAT WERE DISCUSSED IN THE ARTICLE, AND WRITE A SHORT DEFINITION:

We Want Your Advice

ANNUAL EDITIONS revisions depend on two major opinion sources: one is our Advisory Board, listed in the front of this volume, which works with us in scanning the thousands of articles published in the public press each year; the other is you—the person actually using the book. Please help us and the users of the next edition by completing the prepaid article rating form on this page and returning it to us. Thank you for your help!

ANNUAL EDITIONS: Drugs, Society, and Behavior 08/09

ARTICLE RATING FORM

Here is an opportunity for you to have direct input into the next revision of this volume.
We would like you to rate each of the articles listed below, using the following scale:

1. **Excellent: should definitely be retained**
2. **Above average: should probably be retained**
3. **Below average: should probably be deleted**
4. **Poor: should definitely be deleted**

Your ratings will play a vital part in the next revision.
Please mail this prepaid form to us as soon as possible.
Thanks for your help!

RATING	ARTICLE	RATING	ARTICLE
	1. Over the Limit		30. New Study Shows 1.8 Million Youth Use Inhalants
	2. Smoking, Drugs, Obesity Top Health Concerns for Kids		31. Teens and Prescription Drugs
	3. Living the High Life		32. Studies Identify Factors Surrounding Rise in Abuse of Prescription Drugs by College Students
	4. Methamphetamine Abuse: A Perfect Storm of Complications		33. The Role of Substance Abuse in U.S. Juvenile Justice Systems and Populations
	5. HIV Apathy		34. Sobering Thoughts
	6. Not Invented Here		35. Students with Fetal Alcohol Syndrome
	7. Did Prohibition Really Work?		36. Keep Your Older Patients Out of Medication Trouble
	8. Vice Vaccines		37. My Spirit Lives
	9. Pass the Weed, Dad		38. The Problem With Drinking
	10. Reducing the Risk of Addiction to Prescribed Medications		39. High on the Job
	11. Predicting Addiction		40. Reorienting U.S. Drug Policy
	12. Better Ways to Target Pain		41. Is Drug Testing of Athletes Necessary?
	13. The Effects of Alcohol on Physiological Processes and Biological Development		42. Medical Marijuana, Compassionate Use, and Public Policy
	14. A Small Part of the Brain, and Its Profound Effects		43. Researchers Explore New Visions for Hallucinogens
	15. The Changing Science of Pain		44. State's Evidence
	16. The Toxicity of Recreational Drugs		45. Durbin, Grassley Introduce Bipartisan Bill to Combat Meth
	17. Stress and Drug Abuse		46. How to Stand Up to Big Tobacco
	18. Does Cannabis Cause Psychosis or Schizophrenia?		47. Keeping Drug Prevention for Kids "Real"
	19. Methamphetamine Abuse		48. An Update on Adolescent Drug Use.
	20. Mexico Drug Cartels Reap Big Profits from Meth		49. Combination Treatment of One Year Doubles Smokers' Quit Rate
	21. The Taliban's Opium War		50. Parent Power
	22. The Opposite Result		51. Nonconventional and Integrative Treatments of Alcohol and Substance Abuse
	23. The Teen Drinking Dilemma		52. Exercise and Drug Detoxification
	24. An Update on the Effects of Marijuana and Its Potential Medical Use		53. Rehab Reality Check
	25. Fentanyl-Laced Street Drugs "Kill Hundreds"		54. No Longer Theory: Correctional Practices That Work
	26. A Nation Without Drunk Driving		
	27. Some Cold Medicines Move Behind the Counter		
	28. Drug Addiction		
	29. The Right to a Trial		

ABOUT YOU

Name   Date
_____

Are you a teacher? ❑ A student? ❑
Your school's name
_____

Department
_____

Address   City   State   Zip
_____

School telephone #
_____

YOUR COMMENTS ARE IMPORTANT TO US!

Please fill in the following information:
For which course did you use this book?
_____

Did you use a text with this ANNUAL EDITION? ❑ yes ❑ no
What was the title of the text?
_____

What are your general reactions to the Annual Editions concept?
_____

Have you read any pertinent articles recently that you think should be included in the next edition? Explain.
_____

Are there any articles that you feel should be replaced in the next edition? Why?
_____

Are there any World Wide Web sites that you feel should be included in the next edition? Please annotate.
_____

May we contact you for editorial input? ❑ yes ❑ no
May we quote your comments? ❑ yes ❑ no